SHAKESPEARE:
THE EVIDENCE

Also by Ian Wilson

The Turin Shroud
Mind Out Of Time
Jesus: The Evidence
The Exodus Enigma
The Evidence Of The Shroud
Worlds Beyond
Undiscovered
The After Death Experience
The Bleeding Mind
Superself
Holy Faces, Secret Places
The Columbus Myth

SHAKESPEARE: THE EVIDENCE

Unlocking the Mysteries of the Man and his Work

Ian Wilson

St. Martin's Press
New York

Library of Congress Cataloging-in-Publication Data

Wilson, Ian
Shakespeare, the evidence : unlocking the mysteries of the man
and his work / Ian Wilson.
p.   cm.
ISBN 0-312-11335-8
1. Shakespeare, William, 1564–1616. 2. Dramatists, English—
Early modern, 1500–1700—Biography. I. Title.
PR2894.W569 1994
822.3'3—dc20
[B] 94-32247 CIP

First published in Great Britain by Headline Book Publishing Ltd.

First U.S. Edition: December 1994
10 9 8 7 6 5 4 3 2 1

Contents

To the memory of
the late Sam Wanamaker
and in the hope that his lifetime ambition,
the recreation of Shakespeare's Globe on London's Bankside,
will achieve full realisation

Sam Wanamaker's pioneering reconstruction of Shakespeare's Globe, although well under way at the time of this book going to press, is still urgently in need of financial support. Those readers interested to help, or simply to be kept informed of progress, are invited to become 'Friends of Shakespeare's Globe' (current subscription £10 p.a.) by writing to Friends of Shakespeare's Globe, PO Box No. 70, London, SE1 9EN.

Author's Preface

Hugh Trevor-Roper, now Lord Dacre, once wrote that 'of all the immortal geniuses of literature, none is personally so elusive as William Shakespeare'. The pursuit of that elusiveness effectively forms the keynote of *Shakespeare: The Evidence*. A decade ago, with *Jesus: The Evidence*, I tried to penetrate through all the mysteries and mythologies of Christianity to the real man that was Jesus, and Shakespeare seemed to lend himself to the same approach. The book has also taken its cue from Sam Wanamaker's current pioneering reconstruction of Shakespeare's Globe theatre close to its original site on London's Bankside, and the whole new interest in the theatre of Shakespeare's time that richly demands to be aroused when this most commendable venture achieves its goal.

Precisely because of lacking formal academic grounding on the literary side of Shakespearean scholarship, I have tried instead to look dispassionately at all the diverse theories and approaches to the historical Shakespeare as advanced by others, then to steer a sensible middle course among these. Accordingly, I have not omitted to address the claims that Shakespeare's works might have been written by someone else. I have tackled, hopefully even-handedly, the often conflicting approaches and arguments of scholars such as Professor Samuel Schoenbaum, Professor Ernst Honigmann, Dr Leslie Hotson, and Dr A. L. Rowse. And where there has been an interesting but offbeat theory, such as the one claiming that Shakespeare's surviving will is in his own handwriting, I have sought independent specialist guidance in order to reach a fair evaluation.

Inevitably, with so many uncertainties surrounding its central subject, a book of this kind is prone to weaknesses, biases and omissions. In common with every other author on Shakespeare, I have had to confront the lack of any consensus on the dates when Shakespeare wrote his plays, and in the main have followed the broad framework set by the late Professor Peter Alexander, the editors of the Arden editions, and Dr A. L. Rowse, picking my own way where these differ from each other. I have fully discussed the great majority of Shakespeare's plays, and tried to set them in their likeliest historical context. However, in the case of a few, the inadequacy of my treatment has been due to the particular chronological difficulties they present, and the disproportionate diversion attention to these would cause in a book intended for the general reader.

In the course of the book I point to other writers who have moulded Shakespeare according to the way they would *like* him to have been, and I may well be accused of having fallen into the same trap. The reader will note a perhaps undue attention to Shakespeare's religious inclinations. This was not originally intended, but was undeniably sparked off by my own liberal Roman Catholicism, combined with the discovery, in the course of my researches, of pioneering and little-known studies by Fathers H. S. Bowden, Christopher Devlin, Peter Milward and Herbert Thurston. Among these, Fr. Peter Milward's *Shakespeare's Religious Background*, published back in 1973, proved especially helpful. Frustratingly, not until the first edition of this book was in press did I discover Hugh Ross Williamson's *The Day Shakespeare Died*, published in 1962, which takes a similar line.

The literary-minded will perhaps frown at my comparative neglect of Shakespeare's literary sources, but this has been quite intentional as this aspect has been exhaustively and expertly covered by others altogether more familiar with these sources. More easily excusable, perhaps, is my inattention to claims like the one that the John Rylands Library's so-called Grafton portrait is of Shakespeare at the age of twenty-four; also that Hand D of the British Library's playscript *The Booke of Sir Thomas Moore* is a specimen of Shakespeare's own handwriting. While intrigued by both arguments, in the event I felt that proper consideration of them interrupted the book's general flow and that they were therefore best omitted.

Overall, I have tried to aim the book mid-way between the overly scholarly and the overly popular, but this in turn has involved diffi-cult choices. Should quotations from Shakespeare's plays be from the authoritative Arden texts, or from Peter Alexander's likewise excellent and more generally available edition of the complete works as adopted by the BBC for their complete cycle of the plays? Since I have heavily used both, there are bound to be inconsistencies when quoting line references. Among the other difficulties: should documents be quoted in their original spellings and punctuations? Should the reader be reminded every time an Old-style calendar date has been adjusted to the new? And what about the lack of standardisation of the spellings of the names of many of Shakespeare's associates, for example: Heminges/Heminge/Hemmings; Burbage/ Burbadge; Brend/Brand; Persons/Parsons? Should these be given just as they appear in the original documents, or should some arbitrary standardisation be adopted? In the main, for easier readability, I have fully and uncompromisingly modernised spellings and punctuations in all texts where the meaning is not in dispute, and automatically adjusted all Old-style dates. For consistency, I made my own choices for the spelling of non-standardised names, again automatically adjusting all divergences from this. But in certain instances where there is textual controversy, a virtue in quaintness, or some historic purpose to be served, as for instance on the dedication page of the *Sonnets*, I have reproduced the original exactly or near exactly.

As main, essential reference I have been heavily indebted to Sir Edmund Chambers' two-volume *William Shakespeare: A Study of Facts and Problems* (1930); to the same author's four-volume *The Elizabethan Stage* (1923); also, as already noted, to the corpus of Arden texts of Shakespeare's plays, with their ever-helpful introductions. Also invaluable has been Dr A. L. Rowse's prodigious output of books on Shakespeare, in particular those dealing with his researches on the Earl of Southampton and Emilia Lanier. Deserving equal if not greater note, however, has been the contribution of American academics to Shakespearean scholarship during the present century: Professor Charles Wallace and his wife Hulda of the University of Nebraska, who discovered the vital documents identifying one of Shakespeare's London lodgings; Professor T. W. Baldwin of the University of Illinois, whose book *The Organisation and Personnel of the Shakespearean Company* has never been accorded the recognition it deserves; Professor Mark Eccles of the University of Wisconsin, who managed to make himself a foremost authority on Shakespeare's Warwickshire; and, by no means least, Professor Samuel Schoenbaum of the University of Maryland, whose recently re-issued *Shakespeare's Lives* is a classic, and whose monumental *William Shakespeare: A Documentary Life* has rarely been far from my side.

The list is a long one of the individuals to whom I owe special thanks for their direct help in the course of the writing of this book: Mike Abbott, Public Relations Manager of the International

Shakespeare Globe Centre, for keeping me in touch with developments regarding Sam Wanamaker's Globe reconstruction; Anne Baker, of the Jesuit periodical *The Month*, for copies of hard-to-obtain articles from back issues; Sylvia and Ras Bogdanescu, for sleuthing on the Brend family; Bob and Val Bootle, for hosting a visit to Shakespeare's Dark Lady's Cookham; Mrs Brenda Burgess, librarian to the Earl of Derby, for help well above the call of duty with my enquiries concerning Ferdinando, fifth Earl of Derby; Dr Michael Clift, for medical advice on the likely cause of Ferdinando's death; Dr Barry Coward, of Birkbeck College, London, for guidance relating to the history of the Stanley family; London photographer Andrew Fulgoni, for definitive photographs of the Rose and Globe archaeological excavations; Noel Currer-Briggs, for a wealth of genealogical information; R. J. Elvin, of the Public Record Office, for perseverance aiding my quest for good quality photographs of Shakespeare's will; Geoff and Mary Gilborson, for tracking down out-of-print reference works on Shakespeare; Brian Glover, of the Royal Shakespeare Company Collection, for information on the 'Flower' portrait of Shakespeare; the Reverend Maurus Green and Matthew Jordan, for sleuthing regarding Worden Hall; Michael Hare and Mrs Sally Wise, for information on the Southampton tomb at Titchfield; Dr Vernon Harrison, handwriting specialist, for rigorously evaluating the recently resurrected arguments that Shakespeare's will is in his own handwriting; C. Walter Hodges, for up-to-the-minute advice on reconstructions of the Shakespearean theatres; Professor Ernst Honigmann, retired Professor of English Literature at the University of Newcastle-upon-Tyne, for a memorable afternoon spent discussing Shakespeare's 'Lost Years'; Stephen Marvell, Under-Beadle at the Grocers' Hall, London, for information on John Heminges' membership of the Grocers' company; Mrs Mary A. Porter, for allowing me to study and photograph her portrait of Ferdinando Stanley, fifth Earl of Derby; Felix Pryor, for kindly sending me an advance copy of his book *The Mirror and the Globe*; Dr A. L. Rowse, for much general advice; David Smith, Gloucester County and Diocesan Archivist, for supplying copies of Shakespeare patron Sir George Carey's letter; Jeremy Smith, of the Guildhall Library, London, for help with copies of the 'Agas' map; Sir Roy Strong, for much helpful advice on the portrait of Ferdinando, fifth Earl of Derby; Dr Conrad Swan, Garter Principal King of Arms, for help with my enquiries concerning the John Shakespeare application for a coat of arms; Gerard Swarbrick for topographical information on Lathom, Lancashire, in Shakespeare's time; archivist Jan Piggett and librarian Mr. Hall of Dulwich College, London, for kindly allowing me access to the Henslowe Diary and other documents in the College archives; Michael Uphill, of the Southwark Cathedral Society of Bellringers, for kindly arranging for me to climb the tower of Southwark Cathedral; Professor John Vincent, of the School of Historical Studies, University of Bristol, for keeping me in touch with relevant Bristol University lectures; and Ms P. M. White, archives assistant at the Hampshire Record Office, for supplying copies of the eighteenth-century plans of Titchfield House. As usual in the writing of my books, I have also particularly benefited from the helpfulness of the staffs of the British Library, the Bristol University Library, the Bristol Central Library, and also, in this instance, the Bodleian Library, Oxford.

Working on Shakespeare has proved easily as demanding as any subject I have tackled, and even more than with any other book I have worked on, my wife Judith supported me heroically on every aspect. During the all-too-frantic final weeks, additional sterling help was given by our son Noel and our god-daughter Clare, currently a student at the Bristol Old Vic Theatre School. In a book of this scale there are bound to be mistakes, but assiduous copy-editor Janet Ravenscroft has saved me from many, together with Ian Marshall who patiently and expertly took charge of the day-to-day publishing progress. Special thanks are also due to my agent, Bill Hamilton, and my editor, Alan Brooke of Headline, both of whom enthusiastically supported the project from the outset, and gave me every encouragement throughout the long path from concept through to completion.

Bristol, April 1993
[updated March 1994]

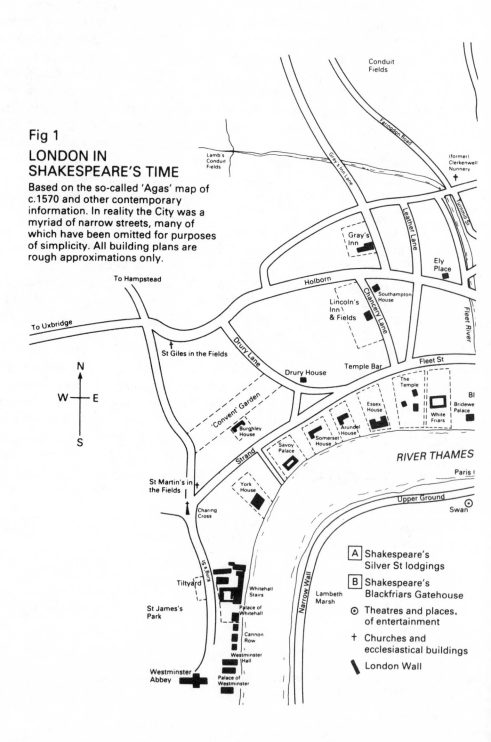

Fig 1

LONDON IN SHAKESPEARE'S TIME

Based on the so-called 'Agas' map of c.1570 and other contemporary information. In reality the City was a myriad of narrow streets, many of which have been omitted for purposes of simplicity. All building plans are rough approximations only.

Conduit Fields

Farringdon Road

Lamb's Conduit Fields

Gray's Inn Lane

(former) Clerkenwell Nunnery

Turnmill St

Gray's Inn

Leather Lane

Ely Place

To Hampstead

Holborn

Chancery Lane

Southampton House

Fleet River

Lincoln's Inn & Fields

To Uxbridge

St Giles in the Fields

Drury Lane

Temple Bar

Fleet St

Drury House

The Temple

Bl

N
W — E
S

'Convent' Garden

Essex House

White Friars

Bridewell Palace

Burghley House

Arundel House

Somerset House

Savoy Palace

Strand

RIVER THAMES

Paris (

St Martin's in the Fields

York House

Upper Ground

Swan

Charing Cross

A Shakespeare's Silver St lodgings

Bury St

B Shakespeare's Blackfriars Gatehouse

Tiltyard

Whitehall Stairs

Lambeth Marsh

Narrow Wall

⊙ Theatres and places. of entertainment

St James's Park

Palace of Whitehall

+ Churches and ecclesiastical buildings

Cannon Row

Westminster Hall

Westminster Abbey

Palace of Westminster

London Wall

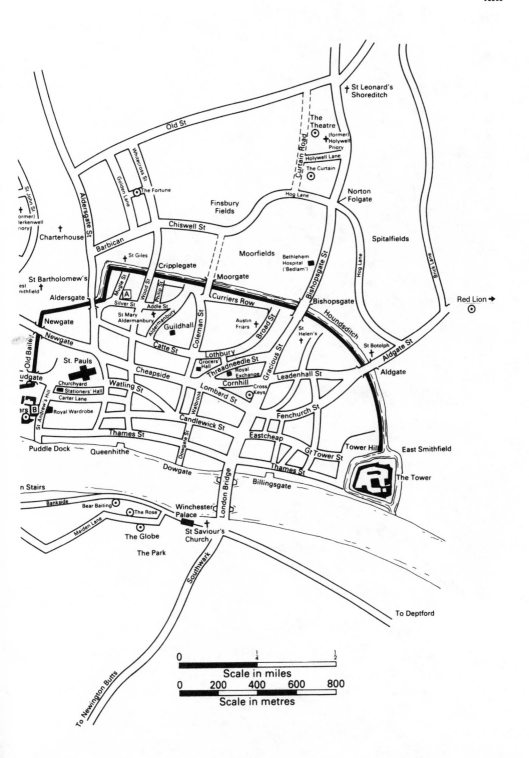

CHAPTER 1

Through a Glass Darkly

On a summery day late in King Charles I's ill-fated reign, the Bohemian artist Wenceslaus Hollar entered a small doorway at the base of the tower of St Saviour's Church, Southwark, close to the southern abutment of London Bridge. Ascending a dark, narrow and seemingly interminable spiral staircase, a hundred and thirty steps later he reached a narrow gallery, a dizzying height above the choir. Negotiating this and the spacious bell-ringers' room, he found himself in darkness again as more steps took him yet higher, past the loft with the church's peal of eight bells. Although Hollar would not have known it, on a freezing December day thirty years before, just about the year he had been born several hundred miles away in Prague, the largest of these bells had tolled at the funeral of obscure young actor Edmund Shakespeare, youngest brother of the famous William. Indeed, a sad and black-clad William himself must have stood on the very flagstones below as the order for the Burial of the Dead was intoned, and Edmund's shrouded body solemnly lowered into an unmarked grave.

For Hollar any such thoughts would have been very far from his mind as, inevitably a little breathless, he emerged into the bright daylight of St Saviour's lead-encased roof. What he had come for lay all around him: just about the finest view of London to be obtained from anywhere before the invention of the aeroplane. From St Saviour's northernmost parapet he had an uninterrupted panorama of the Thames traversing from horizon to horizon. In the immediate foreground, just beyond the great mediaeval palace of the bishops of Winchester, lay the infamous Clink prison and a district notorious for the prostitutes prominent among the bishop's tenants. A little further off, dozens of huge chained mastiffs strained at the leash awaiting the next bear-baiting. From the riverside moorings ferrymen noisily touted for fares with cries of 'Eastward Ho!', 'Westward Ho!'. Across the river sprawled the entire City of London, a myriad of wood-gabled houses punctuated by the spires of more than a hundred churches, crowned by the venerable bulk of Old St Paul's, majestic despite the steeple that it had lacked ever since a lightning strike in 1561. Just to the right, distantly watched over by the forbidding Tower, London Bridge straddled the Thames, seemingly top-heavy with shops and multi-storey dwellings. Down-river, over the tiled rooftops of eastern Southwark, thousands of shipwrights, sailors, clerks and carriers busied themselves in the royal shipyards and naval stores of Deptford. The royal palace of Greenwich could be glimpsed on the eastern horizon, while Charles I's imminently-doomed Whitehall, with its protective cluster of courtiers' river-front mansions, loomed mistily just over a mile to the west.

Hollar aimed to create from this and from related viewpoints one of the longest, most accurate and most comprehensive views of any great city ever made. He intended to etch this onto a set of seven plates from which commercially profitable prints could be made. But such a work could only be assembled from sketches of individual sections, and his target for this day was the west Southwark area immediately visible from the tower's north-western corner. Being as much a technician as an artist, in a well-practised manner he set up a special apparatus comprising fixed eyepiece and reticulated glass screen. On the latter he carefully marked in the main features and rooftop perspectives exactly as he saw them through his viewfinder. Then, probably back in his studio, he transferred this image to paper by a simple tracing procedure, holding glass and paper together against the light, pencilling in what he saw, then inking it over for permanence.

Remarkably, the original drawing that Hollar made that day has survived. After turning up at a Sotheby's auction in 1931,[1] today it forms part of the Paul Mellon collection at Yale University's Center for the Study of British Art in Connecticut, USA [see pl. 5]. It is approximately twelve by five and one eighth inches in size and because of the exact perspective methods Hollar used, it is a surprisingly accurate snapshot of London's Bankside as it appeared circa 1640. The sight-lines of precisely locatable landmarks, such as a water-tower and still extant churches, have all been checked and found accurate.[2]

But what makes this 'photograph' of special Shakespearean interest is the fact that clearly visible in the middle distance are two imposing amphitheatres. Although in his later master-engraving, published in Antwerp in 1647, Hollar would muddle the two, from a wealth of independent topographical data it is certain that the one nearest the river is a bear-baiting pit, the other, somewhat larger and set among trees, Shakespeare's Globe. Admittedly this is the second Globe, rebuilt two years before Shakespeare's death, after a fire had destroyed the first in 1613. But essentially we are provided with a contemporaneous image of the very setting in which many of Shakespeare's plays were first performed by him and his fellow actors. Drawn within the lifetimes of Londoners who had known Shakespeare, the world depicted is almost exactly as he would have recognised it. Due to the small size of Hollar's drawing and because he viewed the Globe from a distance of some 900 feet, we are not provided with fine detail. Nonetheless we can see that the stage was surmounted with a twin roof and lantern, that it faced north, that there were staircase turrets by which the wealthier patrons reached upper galleries, that one of these upper galleries was illuminated by a line of small windows, and that immediately adjoining the theatre, as if belonging to some caretaker, there was a small private house.

Driven overseas by the Civil War, Hollar left England no later than 1644, so he must have made his 'photograph' before this time. But what makes his sketch doubly, if not trebly, important is that within months of his tracing it onto his topographical glass the ostensibly so-tranquil vista began to change beyond recognition. First to go was, in fact, the Globe. As early as 2 September 1642 the Puritan-dominated Parliament ordered all public stage plays to cease on the grounds of the inappropriateness of such 'spectacles of pleasure' at a time when the priority was 'to appease and avert the wrath of God'. Because the Globe was no longer bringing in rent for its landlord, on 15 April 1644 it was, according to a note added to a 1631 edition of Stow's *Annales*, 'pulled down to the ground by Sir Matthew Brend [owner of the land on which the theatre was built] . . . to make tenements in the room of it.'[3]

A year later the same fate befell the royal Masque House at Whitehall where many of Shakespeare's plays had been performed before the royal Court. Then in 1655 it was the turn of Shakespeare's other great, more exclusive theatre, the Blackfriars, destroyed like the Globe to make way for tenements. Although the bear-baiting house lasted longest, it too went the way of the rest. On 9 February 1656 its last surviving seven bears were 'shot to death . . . by a company of soldiers', and six weeks later their former performing arena was 'pulled down to make tenements, by Thomas Walker, a petticoat maker in Cannon Street'.[4]

But these destructions were simply the most visible signs of a process that was eroding all too many of the memorials of Shakespeare's world, along with the people who had rubbed shoulders with him. Directly as a result of the Civil War the acting company to which Shakespeare had belonged, and which still included actors who Shakespeare had known as youngsters, was forced to break up. Most of the more able-bodied members of the company joined the Royalist side. Later its stock of 'apparel, hangings, books, and other goods' was sold off and dispersed without trace.[5] Since 'books' for an acting company meant in particular its prompt copies of play scripts, that is, original scripts edited and annotated for production purposes, these will almost certainly have included ones in Shakespeare's own hand. Many who had known Shakespeare died during the Civil War or through natural causes, and their memories died with them. As the old aristocracy fought gallant but ultimately futile last stands in their great houses, so their records often went to the torch in the ensuing frenzies of destruction. And although upon the monarchy's restoration in 1660 the theatre was reintroduced with astonishing swiftness, reviving Shakespeare's plays with it, the 1665 Great Plague took toll of yet more lives and memories. Worse, the Great Fire of a year later turned much of the London that Hollar had so painstakingly sketched into heaps of smoking rubble.

It is because of these circumstances that Hollar's deceptively ordinary-looking drawing needs to be regarded as one of the most priceless pieces of surviving evidence of the world Shakespeare knew. Today the church from which Hollar made his sketch has been renamed Southwark Cathedral, and it is still possible, with appropriate permission, to climb the very staircases Hollar climbed, and even to stand on the very spot on which he must have set up his apparatus those three hundred and fifty years ago – hence our introductory reconstruction.

Yet to look out over that parapet is to see a world otherwise so totally changed that with the exception of the occasional church spire, virtually every other man-made feature has been swept away and replaced: here a power station, there railway lines, everywhere drab, towering office blocks. Wren's St Paul's has long supplanted the spireless edifice Shakespeare knew. A mere black memorial plaque on a grimy side-street wall marks the spot where stood the Globe. The little that remains of the Clink prison has been turned into a dingy private museum. Of the bishop of Winchester's palace there stands just a forlorn, empty rose window and a few ruinous walls. Little more than some plaintive, quaint-sounding street names – Clink Street, Bear Gardens, Winchester Walk, Cardinal Cap Alley, Skin Market Place, Horseshoe Alley – survive to remind us of the world that has gone.

And if so much that was once solid brick and mortar, oak and stone has been swept away by the vagaries of time, to what extent have the frail records of Shakespeare's age disappeared likewise? Here we meet the essential problem confronted by this book: just how much is left from which to attempt to gain a meaningful glimpse of the man whose work, nearly four hundred years after his death, continues to draw enthusiastic audiences, and to keep actors around the world in gainful employment?

As is well known, during Shakespeare's lifetime some eighteen of his plays were published in cheap Quarto editions, several of these apparently produced 'pirate' fashion from covert shorthand writers, or from casual actors paid to try to remember the lines from their participation in performances. Seven years after his death there then appeared the monumental First Folio, the authorised complete canon of thirty-six of his 'Comedies, Histories & Tragedies', put together by Shakespeare's leading fellow-actors, and emphatically attested on its title page as 'published according to the True Originall Copies'. Of the original estimated one thousand First Folios printed in 1623, thankfully 238 survive, no less than 79 of these in the Folger Shakespeare Library, Washington, compared to no more than five in any one collection elsewhere.

In fact, just one copy would have sufficed, the main point being that since there survives not a single 'true originall' manuscript of any of Shakespeare's plays – nor have any been heard of since the prompt books were sold off during the Civil War – it is the First Folio, together with certain of the 'good' Quartos, that provides our closest link with what Shakespeare originally penned.

Now textually this is fair enough, it being well established by literary sleuths that John Heminges and Henry Condell, the duo of Shakespeare's fellow actors who provided the 'true originall copies' from which the First Folio was typeset, were generally punctilious in using only the most authoritative manuscripts for this purpose.

Mostly they chose either Shakespeare's original 'foul papers', that is, the original pre-production scripts in his own hand, or careful copies made from these, and/or prompt copies by a professional scribe, or, failing all else, the texts of good Quartos. With due allowance for inevitable minor infelicities of transcription, each play preserved in the First Folio is recognised as being very much as Shakespeare intended it, representing an outstanding piece of dramatic entertainment as well as being of enduring literary interest.

At the same time each play is also a historical document: a unique product of its author's mind at the particular point in his life when he committed it to paper. Here, however, the crucial question arises: to just which point in his life does each play belong? How much do we know or not know about the time when each was first written and performed, and about what was happening to the author that may have had a bearing upon his choice of subject, his mood, his use of particular effects, etc?

And here either Shakespeare and/or his compilers John Heminges and Henry Condell have failed us. Whereas Ben Jonson, in his pioneering Folio of his works published in the year of Shakespeare's death, methodically incorporated each play's first performance date, and even the names of the cast who acted in it at that time, the First Folio contains no such information. Nor can Heminges and Condell have arranged Shakespeare's plays in anything remotely resembling the chronological order in which they were written. For instance, although the First Folio begins with *The Tempest*, from a variety of independent clues this is generally agreed to have been one of the plays that Shakespeare wrote last. Apart from the very rough and often misleading clues provided by the publication dates of the Quarto editions – which in any case represent only half of Shakespeare's surviving output – Shakespeare's plays can be likened to beautiful, individually shaped beads dropped from a unique necklace of which the vital connecting thread has been lost. Even to this day there is no general consensus on the exact sequence in which they should be rethreaded, let alone the nearest year in which each was written.

If this is unfortunate in itself, it is compounded by other losses caused by the passage of time, to which Shakespeare has been particularly prone. Shakespeare's acting company must have kept books of its accounts – that is, records of its day-to-day income from the takings of each day's performance, public or private, and records of its outgoings for such expenses as performers' and backstage crew's wages, costume purchases, theatrical refurbishment costs, etc. It is quite definite that such books were kept, for John Heminges, the company's business manager, specifically mentions in his will of 1630 the company's 'good yearly profit, as by my books will in that behalf appear.'[6] Yet if Heminges' books have survived, their whereabouts, which could revolutionise our knowledge of Shakespeare's career as actor and dramatist, remain quite unknown.

Illustrating just the sort of material that we would like to have for Shakespeare's company is the notebook kept by Philip Henslowe, a London businessman and theatre owner who was chiefly associated with the acting company that was for many years Shakespeare's company's chief rival, the Admiral's Men. Handsomely rebound, and preserved under lock and key in the archives room of the library of Dulwich College, south London, Henslowe's 'Diary'[7], as it is called, comprises 242 folio pages that include records kept between 1592 and 1597 of Henslowe's theatres' daily productions, when and where each play was performed and the box office takings. Also listed are Henslowe's outgoings for his purchases of the 'books' of new plays, costumes, repairs, pawnshop loans to hard-up actors, etc. Henslowe also interspersed among these his occasional jotting of a medical recipe, or a slick card trick. Although we shall later see that the play titles include some rare early Shakespearean ones from a time when there was a brief association between Shakespeare's company and Henslowe's, frustratingly Shakespeare's name as such is nowhere to be found.

It is the same picture with regard to personal correspondence. Shakespeare includes the texts of several fictional letters in the corpus of his plays – for instance, one from Macbeth to his wife, Falstaff's two identical ones to Mistresses Ford and Page, and Maria's faked letter from Olivia to Malvolio. It is inconceivable that someone with such a literary output – particularly, as it would seem, working for much of his life away from his home in Stratford – should not have been the author of a considerable number of letters to a variety of friends and acquaintances. Yet there survives not a single example of any letter written or dictated by Shakespeare, and only one that was addressed by anyone to him – one that, in the event, would seem never to have been sent [see pages 235 and 476]. By way of illustration of the loss, from the same Dulwich College archives that preserves Henslowe's Diary there also survives a bound collection of theatrical life letters of which the following is but one example. It was sent by Henslowe's son-in-law Edward Alleyn (founder of Dulwich College, hence the preservation of this material there), to his newly-wed wife Joan, while he was away on tour at a time of plague:

> My good sweet Mouse, I commend me heartily to you, and to my father, my mother, and my sister Bess, hoping in God, though the sickness be round about you, yet by his mercy it may escape your house ... Therefore use this course: keep your house fair and clean, which I know you will, and every evening throw water before your door and in your back side, and have in your windows good store of rue and herb of grace ...
>
> And Jug, I pray you, let my orange tawny stockings of wool be dyed a very good black against I come home, to wear in the winter. You sent me not a word of my garden but next time you will. But remember this in any case, that all that bed which was parsley, in the month of September you sow with spinach, for then is the time. I would do it myself, but we shall not come home till All-Hallowstide. And so sweet Mouse, farewell – and brook our long journey with patience.[8]

Even from such a few lines, immediately obvious to anyone is the deep affection that existed between Edward and his then twenty-two-year-old Joan, a bond that we know from later correspondence to have continued to death. We can also determine that Edward and Joan were a literate and God-fearing couple, that they missed each other acutely when they were apart, that they enjoyed sharing news, that they valued cleanliness, and that Edward was both fussy about his clothes, and a keen and knowledgeable gardener. The existence of even a single letter of such a kind from Shakespeare to his wife Anne could resolve literally reams of scholarly disputes over the state of his marriage, his wife's literacy, his domestic interests, and much else. Although such letters normally form the core of any literary biography, in Shakespeare's case we have no option but to do without.

Since Shakespeare lived in the full spotlight of England's Renaissance, during which there were some highly prolific letter-writers, we might expect several of these to have mentioned meetings or conversations with him, or to have remarked on his presence on some public or private occasion. In the case of Ben Jonson, for instance, the Scottish literary enthusiast Drummond of Hawthornden took down detailed notes of conversations he had with Jonson when the latter came to visit him at his Scottish estate. This experience enabled Drummond to make some shrewd and none too favourable observations upon Jonson's character. But although Jonson's remarks as recorded by Drummond actually include brief mention of Shakespeare, these are mere criticisms of his work, rather than comments that tell us anything of the man. And while there are other mentions of Shakespeare from during his lifetime, these are almost invariably of literary or poetic nature and so raise more questions than they answer.

Now it is important not to seize on all this, as some have inevitably done, as evidence of a deliberate 'big secret' peculiar to Shakespeare. For instance, Shakespeare is by no means without background documentation, albeit mostly of a dry-as-dust legal variety. With occasional exceptions, the christenings, marriages and deaths of the close members of his family are all to be found in the still-extant registers of his home parish church, Holy Trinity, Stratford-upon-Avon. As record of his life as a successful working actor, his name appears high in Ben Jonson's First Folio's cast lists of the performances of some of Jonson's plays by Shakespeare's company. In the case of some, but by no means all, of Shakespeare's plays as published in his lifetime, his name is linked with them formally both on the title page and on the surviving official register of the Stationers' Company, the official trade union of the booksellers and printers of his time. London Public Record Office documents show him to have acted as witness in a court case, complete with his authenticated signature to this effect. Also in London's Public Record Office and elsewhere are to be found deeds of his property dealings (with two more of his signatures), the wills of his London fellow actors and Stratford friends, which include some kindly remembrances of him, and his own will, the latter of which bears the final three of the six signatures generally agreed as authentically his.

By way of contrast, for the fellow playwright of Shakespeare's early years, Christopher Marlowe, not a single signature was thought to have survived until comparatively recently, when one was found on a will that he had witnessed in 1583. Another near contemporary of Shakespeare's was the dramatist John Webster, creator of *The White Devil* and *The Duchess of Malfi*, yet no one has discovered even the precise years of Webster's birth and death. Even in the case of Ben Jonson – more popular than Shakespeare in Court circles, and in general better known at the time – no one has yet discovered when or where he was born, the names of his parents, or the number of his children. Neither, until comparatively recently, had anyone found the name of his wife, nor when or where the couple had married.[9] Of Tom Nashe, yet another of Shakespeare's fellow dramatists, just one single autograph letter has survived.[10] With regard to play manuscripts, only in rare instances have any sixteenth- or seventeenth-century examples come down to us, and almost invariably not from those authors from whom we would most like to have them. Among some genuinely well-regarded dramatists of Shakespeare's time, men such as Henry Chettle, thought to have authored or co-authored some thirty-five plays, and Tom Watson (of whom one contemporary described Shakespeare as his literary 'heir'), absolutely no texts of their plays have survived, either in manuscript or published form.

This said, there is nonetheless the most extraordinary gulf between the Shakespeare of Literature and the Shakespeare of History. The first was arguably the greatest dramatist of all time, filled with the most amazing insights into the innermost thoughts of kings and princes, prelates and politicians, counts and courtesans; the second is the obscure, provincial-born, grammar-school-educated London actor, who put all his theatrical earnings into Stratford property, and whom hardly anyone of real importance seems to have noticed in his own time. As recently remarked by the Oxford scholar Dr Blair Worden: 'The relationship between an artist's biography and his writing is always a difficult subject, but there can be no other important writer since the invention of printing for whom we are unable to demonstrate any relationship at all.'[11]

Particularly in the face of such a paucity of biographical information many have argued that Shakespeare's works are all that matter, and have affected supreme indifference towards the circumstances in which he created them. Samuel Beckett wrote 'The author is never interesting'. C. S. Lewis dubbed as the 'personal heresy' the idea that a writer's life might throw significant light on his or her work. The English Literature schools at both Oxford and Cambridge universities continue a now long-established trend of excluding biographical information from the consideration of an author's works. A television production executive discussing a proposal to make a series from this book commented: 'Isn't the great wonder of Shakespeare the work, not the teasing *lack* of evidence?'[12]

In these circumstances it is perhaps hardly surprising that among those who, like me, believe the author of Shakespeare's works *has* to have been interesting, some have very understandably felt that such masterly plays and poems simply could not have been written by any mere provincial-born actor. Surely there must have been some subterfuge? Surely the works must have been written by someone of university education, someone with the means to afford a substantial library, someone who genuinely mixed in the heady world of the Court, watched every royal mood-swing, knew every aristocratic gambit, had the experience of high-level deliberations over matters of domestic or foreign policy? Surely because of the lowly status accorded to the dramatic arts, this unknown someone simply arranged for Shakespeare's name to be used as a pseudonym in place of his (or her) own?

If for no other reason than to discount such a possibility, we will first turn to the case for precisely such a viewpoint.

CHAPTER 2

Was 'Shakespeare'
Really Shakespeare?

While we might reasonably suppose that those who lived within a century of Shakespeare's lifetime were better informed about him than we are today, this is hardly the case. So effectively had the Puritan Commonwealth snapped all continuity with the past that, when shortly after Charles II's accession a Third Folio of Shakespeare's Works was brought out (there had been a Second in 1632 that was almost identical to the First), the second printing of this new version proudly included 'seven new plays, never before printed in folio.' No matter that six of these were not Shakespeare's, this 1664 edition was regarded as such an improvement on the old that Oxford's Bodleian Library disposed of its First Folio as now redundant. Forty-five years later, lawyer-turned-dramatist Nicholas Rowe, upon bringing out a handsome new edition of Shakespeare's Works, was still accepting the six 'rogues' as genuine Shakespeare plays when he decided to attempt as part of this same magnum opus a first serious Shakespeare biography.

As close to Shakespeare's lifetime as the year 1709, Rowe became effectively the first to confront just how few memories or material records of Shakespeare had survived. To Rowe's credit he did his best to find out what he could, even advertising for information and using retired Shakespearean actor Thomas Betterton to scout Warwickshire on his behalf. But after imparting little more than that Shakespeare's father John had been a wool dealer (refuted by nearly every subsequent biographer), that the young William had once been a deer poacher, and that he had married while still very young 'the daughter of one Hathaway, said to have been a substantial yeoman in the neighbourhood of Stratford', Rowe rounded off: 'This is what I could learn of any note, either relating to himself or family. The character of the man is best seen in his writings.'[1] Likewise after some considerably more scientific researches conducted towards the end of the eighteenth century, the London scholar George Steevens could still only conclude:

> all that is known with any degree of certainty concerning Shakespeare is that he was born at Stratford-upon-Avon, married and had children there, went to London where he commenced actor, and wrote poems and plays, returned to Stratford, made his will, died and was buried. . . .[2]

It is hardly surprising, therefore, that around the very time Steevens wrote those words, some disturbing thoughts began to occur to the Reverend James Wilmot, recently retired from London's literary scene to become rector of Barton-on-the-Heath, a tiny Warwickshire village some fourteen miles to the south of Stratford-upon-Avon. In Wilmot's time the imposing Stratford house that Shakespeare had once owned had been pulled down by another clergyman, and all that was left was a nondescript butcher's shop where Shakespeare was said to have been born – as the then local tradition had it – to a butcher who could neither read nor write.

Coming from such a socially inferior background, pondered Wilmot, how could Shakespeare ever have acquired the so-confident, well-travelled literary and political expertise that he exhibited in the plays? How could he possibly have been 'received as a friend and equal by those of culture and breeding who alone could by their intercourse make up for the deficiencies of his youth'?[3] Wilmot found equally puzzling the fact that, despite the most diligent searches in private libraries throughout an area of some fifty miles around Stratford, he could find no book once owned by Shakespeare, nor any letter written by him, nor a single page of one of his play manuscripts, nor any mention by local gentry of their ever having met the playwright. So could it be that perhaps Shakespeare the Stratford-upon-Avon-born actor had never actually written the plays published in his name?

In his search for clues Wilmot noted that the plays exhibited a surprising amount of legal terminology and knowledge, as if their author had perhaps been trained in this profession. Even more intriguing, however, he observed that some of the French names used for the characters in *Love's Labour's Lost*'s Court of Navarre – Berowne, Dumain, Longaville – were with very slight variations the names of French ministers at the French King Henri IV's Court of

Navarre, at which Anthony Bacon had resided in Shakespeare's time. From this Court Anthony Bacon had sent back a series of letters to his famous brother Francis, later Sir Francis Bacon [see pl. 1]. And with his literary interests, legal training, and his Lord Chancellorship of England during King James I's reign, Francis Bacon was just the sort of man who could be believed to have written the plays accredited to Shakespeare.

The more Wilmot considered the matter, the more he felt he was on the right track. Sir Francis Bacon's father had been Elizabeth I's Lord Keeper, his mother was Elizabeth's first Minister's sister-in-law. This seemed a perfect nurturing ground for the 'Shakespeare' author's apparent familiarity with royal courts and foreign potentates. Furthermore Bacon's usage of the humble actor Shakespeare's name as a pseudonym would have been a perfectly logical ploy given the undesirability of someone of his high estate being seen dabbling in the lowly craft of writing plays. Even in our own time the late Poet Laureate C. Day Lewis, asked by a young author why he wrote detective stories under the name Nicholas Blake, loftily responded, 'Because, young man, a poet can't write detective stories'.[4]

In his old age Wilmot freely discussed his musings with those who called at his rectory. But he declined to publish them, not least because Stratford-upon-Avon just up the road was already developing its Shakespeare tourist industry, and he could not bear to upset those of his friends and neighbours already involved with this trade. Accordingly, shortly before his eightieth birthday he ordered all his papers to be burnt. Even so, there proved no shortage of others to take up his ideas, most formidable among them being Delia Bacon, born in 1811 in the backwoods of Ohio, whose assessment of the historical Shakespeare was even more down-grading than Wilmot's. As she summed him up in the more lucid prose of her six-hundred-and-seventy-five-page *The Philosophy of the Plays of Shakspere Unfolded*, he had been nothing more than a 'stupid, ignorant, third-rate play-actor', from a 'dirty, doggish group of players'. It was quite impossible that such a man should have written the plays that carry his name. Later in the century Delia was followed by her fellow American Ignatius Donnelly, already notable for his monumental *Atlantis: The Antediluvian World*. In 1888 in *The Great Cryptogram: Francis Bacon's Cipher in the So-Called Shakespeare Plays*, Donnelly announced his epoch-making finding that Bacon had hidden among 'Shakespeare''s works a cipher revealing his true authorship, to which, of course, he, Donnelly, had found the key. His enthusiasm for Baconian cryptography proved so infectious that it set off years of frantic but fruitless treasure-hunts throughout southern England in the quest for sixty-six buried iron boxes that purportedly would prove Bacon's authorship of 'Shakespeare'.

Donnelly and other 'Baconians' also found many literary parallels between Bacon and whoever had authored the 'Shakespeare' works. They noted that Bacon had been a poet, just like 'Shakespeare'. They observed that like 'Shakespeare''s, Bacon's writings exhibited a marked distaste for crowds. Like 'Shakespeare', Bacon delighted in nature, his essay on *Gardens* featuring no less than thirty-two out of the thirty-five flowers mentioned by 'Shakespeare'. Not least, in 1910, English aristocrat Sir Edwin Durning-Lawrence in his *Bacon is Shakespeare*, amazingly revealed that the longest word anywhere in 'Shakespeare' – Honorificabilitudinitatibus, a nonsense word used by Costard the clown in *Love's Labour's Lost* – was 'without possibility of doubt or question' an anagram of the Latin *Hi ludi F. Baconis nati tuiti orbi*, that is, 'These plays, F. Bacon's offspring, are preserved for the World.' Even Mark Twain and Sigmund Freud became sucked into such Baconian fervour, and arguably only the curse inscribed upon Shakespeare's grave saved it from being dug up in the continuing quest for the manuscripts supposed to prove Bacon's authorship.

Yet Bacon was merely the first of a whole succession of proposed 'alternative' authors of 'Shakespeare''s works. Another to be attracted by *Love's Labour's Lost*'s allusion to the French Court of Navarre was the Belgian M Demblon, lecturer in the history of French literature at the University of Brussels.[5] Demblon's attention became gripped by the discovery in 1908 of a most intriguing entry in an old accounts book kept by the stewards to the Earls of Rutland, whose family seat was at Belvoir Castle, Leicestershire. The entry showed that in the year 1613, shortly after the death of fifth Earl of Rutland Roger Manners, the Rutland estate's steward had paid 'Master Shakespeare' and his fellow actor Richard Burbage the sum of twenty-two shillings each for their making of a witty, painted shield carried by the new sixth Earl of Rutland at a jousting contest commemorating the tenth anniversary of King James I's accession. The discovery was undoubtedly valid and intriguing and we will return to it later in this book. But for Demblon its key revelation was that actor Shakespeare was working for the Earls of Rutland. According to literary experts the 'Shakespeare' plays mysteriously ceased to be written around 1613, just about the time of fifth Earl of Rutland Roger Manners' death (and three years before actor Shakespeare's). Could fifth Earl Roger have been their true author, concealing his hand by using Shakespeare's name as a pseudonym, as had been conjectured of Bacon?

When M Demblon researched the facts of Earl Roger's life, this idea began to gain more and more cogency. As a young man Rutland had been a particularly close friend of the Earl of Southampton, both being wards of Lord Burghley. And since it was to Southampton that in 1593 'Shakespeare' dedicated his *Venus and Adonis*, surely in reality the poem was the work of the then seventeen-year-old Rutland? This also made sense of 'Shakespeare''s *Sonnets*, whose male recipient was likewise thought to have been Southampton.

Demblon also found that in 1596 Rutland went on a European tour, visiting Venice, Verona and Padua. The first two locations clearly provided the background for *The Merchant of Venice* and *Othello, The Moor of Venice. The Two Gentlemen of Verona* and *Romeo and Juliet* were set chiefly in Verona. As for Padua, Demblon found in this University's registers the names of two Danes, Rosencrantz and Guildenstern, who had been among Rutland's fellow students there. Disregarding these names as being common among Danes of the time, Demblon understandably saw them as the inspiration for the two famous sycophants in *Hamlet*. Adding further fuel to his thesis was his discovery that in 1603 Rutland visited Denmark's Court to confer the Garter upon King Christian IV. This readily explained the otherwise puzzling differences of length and content between the Quarto versions of *Hamlet* as published before and after 1603. Rutland must have revised and improved the play after his visit, in the process making it the longest of all 'Shakespeare''s works. M Demblon's master-work, *Lord Rutland est Shakespeare*, duly appeared in 1913.

But compelling as the Baconian and the Rutlandian arguments might have appeared, to discerning Collège de France professor Abel Lefranc they seemed to suffer from at least one rather serious flaw. Not only was there no real evidence that either Bacon or Rutland had ever written plays, but whoever composed 'Shakespeare''s *Sonnet* 135 conveyed as explicitly as anything can be in the realm of poetry that his Christian name was neither Francis, nor Roger, but Will. So did this mean it was all back to Will Shakespeare after all? Not necessarily, according to Lefranc.

Lefranc's attention had been caught by the reputable scholar James Greenstreet's discovery in London's Public Record Office of a hitherto unknown letter written in 1599 by Catholic secret agent George Fenner. This letter included mention of William Stanley, sixth earl of Derby, and that he was 'busy in penning comedies for the common players'.[6] Greenstreet published a sober enough monograph *A hitherto unknown noble writer of Elizabethan comedies*,[7] and he might have developed it further had he not died soon after. But for Lefranc the discovery was a revelation. Here was a bluest-blood aristocrat from the very circles with which 'Shakespeare' seemed so familiar, specifically recorded as writing plays (and for the *common* players no less). And no record existed of any of those plays coming down to us under William Stanley's name. Moreover not only did William Stanley have the surely more than coincidental initials W.S., his surviving letters revealed him to have signed himself 'Will' – unlike the actor Shakespeare, who signed himself merely 'Wm' or 'Willm'. So was it William Stanley, sixth Earl of Derby who had been the real Will Shakespeare?

William Stanley's dandyish-looking portrait [see pl. 2] smiles amiably upon those privileged enough to view it at the present Earl of Derby's stately mansion at Knowsley, near Preston, Lancashire, and as Lefranc found, Derby was actually a far better candidate for 'Shakespeare' than either Bacon or Rutland. Thus whereas Bacon had merely received letters from his brother at the Court of Navarre, Derby's stately mansion at Knowsley, near Prescot, Lancashire, and 1587, positively rubbing shoulders with the Biron ('Berowne'), Mayenne ('Dumain') and de Longueville ('Longaville') featured among the play's main characters. He had been accompanied on this trip by his tutor Richard Lloyd, whose version of the Chester pageant the 'Nine Worthies' was cleverly parodied in this same play. As for the foreign travel arguments that had favoured the fifth Earl of Rutland, Derby had not only been to many of the same locations, thereby experiencing exactly the same sources of inspiration, he was actually far better travelled than Rutland. According to one ballad, he even went as far as Russia.

But even as copies of the first of Lefranc's four books on this theme lay fresh on the Paris bookstalls, in November 1918 an English Literature teacher from Gateshead lodged with the British Museum Library another and seemingly yet more convincing solution to the Shakespeare authorship enigma. My slight hesitancy in giving this teacher's name will become understandable when we reveal it as John Thomas Looney. Although apparently this good Manx surname should be pronounced 'Loney', there is something admirably quixotic in Looney's refusal of one publisher's offer to accept his book providing he adopt a pseudonym.

In any event Looney's *'Shakespeare' Identified*[8] was launched upon English bookstalls in 1920, and to his credit he was refreshingly honest in acknowledging his lack of professional expertise and was commendably more methodical than many of his predecessors in setting about his task. First, he set down lists of what he considered the identifying characteristics that 'Shakespeare' revealed in his works. Some of these – genius, literary tastes, and an enthusiasm for the world of drama – were rather obvious. But others were more specialised. For example, he listed Lancastrian connections; a love of music and things Italian; a penchant for sports, particularly falcony; probable Catholic sympathies; and not least, an aristocratic upbringing.

Looney then sought in the historical records the one individual who more than any other seemed to match up with all these characteristics, finding him in Edward de Vere, seventeenth Earl of Oxford [see pl. 3]. As in the case of William, Earl of Derby, high in the supportive evidence for Oxford was some historical attestation that he wrote plays. In 1598 the literary reviewer Francis Meres had set him first in a list of those 'best for Comedy'. And as no known examples of Oxford's plays have survived – exactly as in the case of William, Earl of Derby – surely these have to be the plays of William Shakespeare?

Among all the claims for authorship of Shakespeare's plays, this so-called 'Oxfordian' one has continued to attract the most ardent adherents to the present time. One inheritor of the Looney mantle has been New York lawyer Charlton Ogburn, author of two massive pro-Oxford tomes, the most recent of these his nine-hundred-page *The Mysterious William Shakespeare*,[9] published in 1984. Another, also an American lawyer, is David Kreeger, promoter of a spirited 'Stratfordians' versus Oxfordians debate, conducted in 1987 by two teams of high-powered lawyers at the American University, Washington D.C.,[10] and followed a year later by a similar exercise at the Middle Temple Hall, London. A third equally vociferous pro-Oxfordian is young, blue-blooded Charles Francis Topham de Vere Beauclerk, Lord Burford, apparently a collateral descendant of the seventeenth Earl of Oxford. In his mid-twenties and normally based in Devon, Burford has energetically toured the States preaching the rightness of his ancestor's cause.

Now, from the historical record at least, the Earl of Oxford hardly emerges as one of the Elizabethan era's more appealing characters. Early in his career he skewered to death an under-cook with his fencing sword. He was prone to the most vicious quarrels, including with his wife. And, reportedly on one occasion usually glossed over by the Oxfordians, 'making of his low obeisance to Queen Elizabeth, [he] happened to let a fart, at which he was so ashamed that he went to travel, seven years'.[11] Of course we should not let a small matter of his bowel control obstruct his identification with 'Shakespeare'. Far more serious a difficulty, however, is that he died in 1604, whereas whoever wrote Shakespeare's plays went on for at least another nine years turning out masterpieces of the calibre of *King Lear*, *Macbeth*, *The Winter's Tale*, and *The Tempest*.

No matter, those who seek an alternative author for 'Shakespeare' are rarely baulked by such small difficulties as raising the dead. In this vein yet another alternative authorship group, the 'Marlowians', necessarily deny an official report of 1593 that their Shakespeare candidate Christopher Marlowe died that year as a result of being stabbed through to the brain during a quarrel at Deptford. They contend instead that the Deptford killing was all a sham, that in reality Marlowe's patron Thomas Walsingham had him spirited away to France and Italy (obviously to absorb the local colour), and that he was then clandestinely brought back to Walsingham's Chislehurst mansion to write his heart out for another two decades under the name William Shakespeare.[12] So convinced was Long Island press agent Calvin Hoffman of this idea that in 1956 he gained permission for the opening up of Walsingham's monumental tomb at Chislehurst in anticipation that it would contain a vital tell-tale cache of 'Shakespeare' manuscripts. In the event, apart from Walsingham's lead coffin, all that Hoffman found was clean sand.

Another form of raising the dead has been resorted to. During the 1940s, Oxfordian Percy Allen decided that the best way to sort out all the authorship arguments had to be by contacting the sixteenth century directly. Accordingly, with the aid of spiritualist medium Mrs Hester Dowden (a Shakespeare scholar's daughter), and her guide 'Johannes', Allen established an 'automatic writing' link to Bacon, Shakespeare and the seventeenth Earl of Oxford.[13] Allen learned that 'Shakespeare''s plays were a collaborative effort by all three. Apparently Shakespeare, with his hands-on theatrical expertise, would work out the plots, while Oxford would flesh out the characters. The pair would then submit their joint effort to Bacon, whose role was to suggest revisions – not always acted upon apparently. Three schools of Shakespeare argument were satisfied in one, and Mrs Dowden's gifts of diplomacy have to be admired!

However, we have not yet exhausted the list of proposed 'Shakespeares', for a change of the author's sex has not been ruled out. Dr Lillian Schwartz, consultant to AT & T Laboratories of Murrayfield, New Jersey, contends not only that 'Shakespeare' was a woman, but that she was none other than Queen Elizabeth I. A specialist in the computer-matching of facial features, in 1986 Schwartz was approached by Oxfordian Dr Leslie Dressler of the Virginia Commonwealth University, Richmond, Virginia, in the hope that she might be able to demonstrate a computer match between the First Folio's famous 'Shakespeare' engraving and surviving portraits of the Earl of Oxford. Although Schwartz could not, a little later, on visiting London's National Portrait Gallery, she happened to find herself before George Gower's portrait of Queen Elizabeth I [see pl. 4], as painted in 1588. In Schwartz's own words: 'I saw the Queen's eyes staring out at me and I thought, my God, this is incredible. I had been working with the engraving for months, but I had not even really considered the Queen...'[14]

When she set photographs of the First Folio 'Shakespeare' and the Gower 'Elizabeth' into her computer-matching equipment, lo and behold her first impression was amazingly verified. In her words, 'You could take the two portraits, scale them down to the same size on a xerox machine, and lay them on top of each other and see for yourself'. Of course there were a few slight differences such as the 'Shakespeare' engraving's beard, and small variations to the jawline and forehead. But these were readily attributable to the engraver's attempt merely to change the sex of the portrait.

Easy as it is to be beguiled by, or make fun of, these alternative authorship claims, in fact they represent merely one of the hazards caused by the scarcity of documentation on Shakespeare the man. Another, all too predictably, has been the outright counterfeiting of those materials that history had been unable to provide. In the late eighteenth century, Stratford-upon-Avon's local wheelwright John

Jordan, in addition to acting as the town's self-appointed tourist guide, developed his own profitable little side-line of supplying the easiest of all forgeries, genuinely old books carefully inscribed 'William Shakespeare his Booke'. Examples of such handiwork by Jordan are now museum specimens in their own right.

More ambitious was Londoner William-Henry Ireland, who actually came up with his idea when accompanying his antiquarian father on a Jordan-conducted tour of Stratford. Ireland first tried writing a 'Shakespeare' mortgage deed in period script and spelling onto a piece of parchment cut off from a rent roll. He claimed to have found it in an old chest that a mysterious rich man had invited him to rummage through for anything that took his fancy. Finding his father and some serious scholars surprisingly easily deluded by this, during 1795 Ireland proceeded to a yet more ambitious invention: a promisory note in 'Shakespeare''s hand.

In quick succession there emerged a letter from 'Shakespeare' to the Earl of Southampton, and Southampton's reply; an earnest profession of faith by 'Shakespeare' attesting his Protestant orthodoxy; a love letter from 'Shakespeare' to Anne Hathaway ('Dearesste Anna ... Thyne everre, Wm Shakspeare'), together with a lock of 'Shakespeare''s hair; even an admiring letter from Queen Elizabeth to 'Master William Shakspeare atte the Globe bye Thames'. Successfully deceiving the great James Boswell and the Prince of Wales, Ireland smoothly proceeded to his greatest creations of all, 'Shakespeare''s original manuscript of the *Tragedye of Kynge Leare*, some equally original fragments from 'Shakespeare''s *Hamblette*, and a transcript of 'Shakespeare''s hitherto quite unknown play *Vortigern and Rowena*, (in this instance Ireland's mysterious source apparently declined to part with the original).

Such was the scale of Ireland's deception that Drury Lane theatre paid him a small fortune for the rights to *Vortigern and Rowena*, and the production was just two days from its grand opening night, with John Philip Kemble in the lead, when there landed upon London's bookstalls the most devastating exposé[15] of Ireland by Dublin-born lawyer turned Shakespearean scholar Edmond Malone. Malone, who had earlier exposed 'mediaeval' forgeries by the boy poet Chatterton, demonstrated with overwhelming conviction Ireland's historical mistakes and the amateurish nature of his 'olde Englishe' spellings. In like manner *Vortigern and Rowena* failed its live audience test on the opening night, the audience managing to contain their impatience until act five, only to fall about with helpless laughter at Kemble's most sepulchrally delivered lines 'And when this solemn mockery is o'er'. Ironically, Ireland survived his exposure surprisingly well, even, a decade later, writing a popular *Confessions* of the hoax he had perpetrated.

Nor did the failure of Ireland's hoax deter others, not least one man who should certainly have known better: John Payne Collier, a director of the Shakespeare Society of his time, and author of several genuinely scholarly studies of the lives of Shakespeare and his fellow actors. A readily likeable individual with, at the time, an unsullied reputation, Collier was allowed free access to the already mentioned Edward Alleyn papers preserved at Dulwich College, also to Lord Ellesmere's library at London's Bridgewater House. The latter contained sixteenth- and seventeenth-century manuscripts from Shakespeare's time. While working in these and similar collections Collier made some perfectly genuine and creditable finds, and it was his very freedom of access that seems to have tempted him irresistibly to improve upon these. Occasionally he would slip into a pile of genuine material a forged manuscript of his own creation. At other times he would simply add a 'Shakespeare' line or so to a document that was otherwise completely genuine. Unlike Ireland, he attempted nothing too spectacular, in the main preferring to make documents that simply proved a point he wanted to argue, such as that Shakespeare lived in Southwark in a particular year, or that his fellow actors had an early connection with the Blackfriars Theatre.

Like Ireland before him, however, Collier over-reached himself. In his case it was with an old copy of the Second Folio to which he added thousands of marginal and textual annotations in an old script. He then suggested in the *Athenaeum*[16] that these had most likely been made by someone holding 'purer manuscripts' than those used for the First Folio. If it had been true it would have been a revolutionary find, but suspicions began to surface when fellow scholars noticed partly erased pencil marks below the annotations. The doubts increased as chemical tests showed the 'ink' to be a watercolour, rather than any true ink, ancient or modern. Then in 1861 the scholar C. M. Ingleby brought out, Malone-style, *A Complete View of the Shakspere Controversy, Concerning the Authenticity and Genuineness of the Manuscript Matter Affecting the Works and Biography of Shakspere, Published by Mr. J. Payne Collier as the Fruits of His Researches*. Despite its ponderous title, it tore Collier's reputation to shreds, and although Collier lived on for another twenty-two years, his Diary, preserved in Washington's Folger Shakespeare Library, reveals his ultimate deep regret for the follies that ruined what otherwise would have been a worthy place in the field of Shakespearean scholarship. As he wrote on 14 May 1882, in his ninety-third year:

> I am bitterly and most sincerely grieved that in every way I am such a despicable offender. I am ashamed of almost every act of my life. J. Payne Collier. Nearly blind. My repentance is bitter and sincere.[17]

Cranks and hoaxers aside, even among the more orthodox of scholars there has been, and continues to be, no easy consensus on exactly what should or should not be accepted about Shakespeare. The safest way, of course, is to avoid all conjecture and stick to the documentary evidence that has survived for Shakespeare's life: the dull but factual materials such as wills, mortgage deeds, lists of payments, birth, marriage and death registrations, etc. In the late eighteenth century Edmond Malone and George Steevens pioneered this sort of approach. In the process they also tried – none too successfully – to set Shakespeare's plays in a proven chronological order and to eliminate those who in their opinion were of doubtful authenticity.

In the nineteenth century, they were followed by great Shakespearean scholars, such as James Orchard Halliwell-Phillipps and Sir Sidney Lee, an editor of the *Dictionary of National Biography*, solidly but unspectacularly making the occasional real find, as in 1864 when Halliwell-Phillipps came across an entry in a manuscript volume of Shakespeare and his fellows each being awarded four and a half yards of 'skarlet red cloth' for taking part in King James I's coronation procession through London. At the beginning of the twentieth century an American couple, Professor C. W. Wallace and his wife Hulda, hailing from the backwoods of Nebraska, stole an astonishing march on English scholars. They found, right under the latters' noses, hitherto unknown court-case documents from 1612 that revealed where Shakespeare had lodged in London during the early 1600s.

During the 1920s, although he added little in the form of documentary discoveries, Board of Education civil servant Edmund Chambers made a particularly monumental contribution to Shakespearean scholarship by assembling the work of others into a readily accessible form. Every morning once he had dealt with his office post, Chambers would retire to the Reading Room of the British Museum where he would spend most of the rest of the day, returning to his office in the late afternoon to sign the letters he had dictated earlier. Although his subsequent knighthood was for his services to the Board of Education it would have been more deserved for his work on Shakespeare. His two meticulously researched volumes *William Shakespeare: A Study of Facts and Problems*, and his four on *The Elizabethan Stage*, published in 1930 and 1923 respectively, represent to this day the most indispensable anthologies for anyone making a serious study of Shakespeare. They offer an encyclopaedic account of the facts relating to every known historical document with some bearing on Shakespeare's life, to every one of his plays and poems, canonical and non-canonical, to the theatrical companies of his time, to the theatres in which he played, and much more.

Today, Chambers' mantle has fallen with almost equal distinction upon American Samuel Schoenbaum, Professor of Renaissance Literature at the University of Maryland. Schoenbaum's *William Shakespeare: A Documentary Life* is undeniably the soundest study of the available documentation. Safe as houses, indeed so safe that Schoenbaum makes a virtue of not venturing an opinion on such issues as when and with whom Shakespeare began his career, when he began to write his first plays, the identity of the Fair Youth and the Dark Lady to whom Shakespeare addressed Sonnets, and much else.

And here, to wax Shakespearean, is the rub. Admirable as such an approach is, it fails just where the ordinary reader most seeks – it fails to give us the real feel of Shakespeare, the smell of his grease-paint, the taste of that cocktail of genetic and environmental chemistry that brought into being the fun of Falstaff, the heart-searching of *Hamlet*, the magic of *A Midsummer Night's Dream*. For the essence of Shakespeare lies neither in the legal phrases of wills and mortgage deeds, nor in the printed text of his plays and poems, but in emotion. Every time that a Shakespeare play is performed the actors and actresses reactivate, with varying degrees of success, those emotions that Shakespeare felt on behalf of each character as he set the part down on his manuscript page. Whether in the frothiest of comedy or the darkest of tragedy, the very power, the very genius of Shakespeare lies in the range and depth of those emotions. And the root question to be faced is where did these emotions come from?

What lay behind the life of the man who set down those words that he could scale such heights and plumb such depths of emotion?

Of course there has been no shortage of writers who have attempted to set down the answers to these questions, but invariably they have stepped into a literary and historical no-man's-land. In the case of Shakespeare more than anyone else those who write about him see him the way they want to see him, mould the sparse hard facts of his life into the sort of biography they would like him to have had. Thus homosexual Oscar Wilde saw him as one of his own kind, believing the male recipient of Shakespeare's *Sonnets* to have been a child actor and 'darling boy' called William Hughes,[18] for which there is not a shred of hard historical information. Libertine, turn-of-the-century American editor Frank Harris[19] saw him as the most ardent heterosexual, forced to abandon the love of his life Anne Whately for the shrewish Anne Hathaway, driven to London to escape Anne's nagging, there to fall helplessly in love with one of Queen Elizabeth's Maids of Honour. Effete Lytton Strachey saw him as 'bored with people and real life'.[20]

Equally as daunting is the problem of dating Shakespeare's work, there being hardly a play or poem whose date or composition by Shakespeare is beyond dispute. Exemplifying just how far apart even the professional academics can be on such issues is the single Shakespeare's *Sonnet* 107, carrying the deceptively simple line 'The mortal moon hath her eclipse endur'd'. As almost everyone agrees, this must embody a crucial clue to the sonnet's date. But the problem is, what date? According to the American historian Leslie Hotson[21] the 'mortal moon' refers to the Spanish Armada. He has pointed to contemporary engravings of the Spanish invasion fleet which show it ranged in a *falange*, 'a battle like a halfe Moone' and on the strength of this he set the date of the Sonnet at 1588, when Shakespeare was just twenty-four.

But this has been far too early for a galaxy of other scholars, from John Dover Wilson, a contemporary of Sir Edmund Chambers, to present-day Armada historian Garrett Mattingley.[22] These have insisted that the 'mortal moon' has to have been Queen Elizabeth I, who was often depicted with a crescent moon as her headdress. And if the 'mortal moon' was Elizabeth her 'eclipse' must have been her death in 1603.

This is nonsense according to the foremost historian of the Elizabethan period A. L. Rowse of All Souls, Oxford. Yes, the 'mortal moon' is Elizabeth. But the line says she has *endured* her eclipse, that is, that she has survived it. This points to the year 1594 when the French wars ended, and when Elizabeth escaped a serious poisoning attempt on her life by her double-agent, Portuguese physician, Dr Lopez.[23]

All this epitomises the evidential minefield through which somehow we must find our way on every page that follows. And here, however easy it has been to lampoon and denigrate those who would attribute Shakespeare's plays to someone other than Stratford-born William, they have had a point. The one theme that has more than any underscored all their arguments is the difficulty of understanding how anyone of William's humble origins could have attained his literary heights, without apparent benefit either of university or of the literary resources of some wealthy, aristocratic household. And it is a serious and valid difficulty, all too often glossed over by even the very best of Shakespeare scholars. Accordingly we will hold this at the forefront of our minds as, taking absolutely nothing for granted, we start with what exactly *is* known of how and when Shakespeare the actor began.

CHAPTER 3

Stratford-upon-Avon 'One of the Biggest Frauds in England'?

For the two million or so visitors who each year make their pilgrimage to Stratford-upon-Avon as Shakespeare's birthplace, the prevailing impression is of a bijou market town delightfully little touched by the ravages of time. Even on the town's approaches the thatched, timber-frame cottages, their frontages cascading with floral colour, immediately evoke the 'Merrie England' image. Traffic, though now four wheeled rather than four legged, still straggles over the same fourteen arched stone bridge built for the town more than sixty years before Shakespeare was born. The street names – Bridge Street, Sheep Street, High Street, Henley Street, Chapel Lane – still remain much as Shakespeare knew them. There still stands the school house he knew, and the Angel Inn of his time, though its then rivals, the Bear and the Swan, have gone. Swans still grace the same Avon river from which would have been drawn the water for the small beer Shakespeare drank. To the south of the town an avenue of ancient lime trees leads to the same Holy Trinity Church that saw the christenings and burials of both himself and many members of his family. Overall Stratford beguilingly exudes the air of an olde England of log-fires, spit-roasted beef, rosy-cheeked serving wenches and claypipe-smoking tipplers that everyone would like to believe was the actual world in which England's great Bard grew up, and from which he drew much of his inspiration.

In reality all was rather different, in particular earlier in the lifetimes of Shakespeare's parents and grandparents when their genuinely untouched-for-centuries world was rudely shattered by Henry VIII's Reformation. In a manner strikingly akin to the Chinese Communist takeover of Tibet within our own lifetime, from 1536 onwards some six hundred and fifty religious houses all over England had been declared redundant, everything of value in their contents stripped and confiscated, their inmates pensioned off, their lands and buildings adaptable for other purposes sold off to the highest bidder. In 1547 orders had gone out for the total destruction of all holy images, whether in churches or private houses, followed in 1550 by insistence upon the destruction of these even in books, followed in March 1551 by demands for the immediate surrender of all churches' gold or silver plate, vestments and church furniture. Church buildings that for centuries had positively glowed with colour, inside and out, had to be rendered drab and unostentatious.

On the receiving end like every other town in the country, for Stratford such orders spelled the termination of the centuries-old Guild of the Holy Cross, which had employed the town's four priests, cared for the poor, and provided almshouses for the aged. They meant for the Guild's Chapel, built by Sir Hugh Clopton, the pulling down of its rood loft and screen, the defacing and breaking up of its images, and the whitewashing over of its great wall-painting, the 'Dance of Death'. For Holy Trinity Church they meant the destruction of the great red- and gold-painted rood loft with its many carved images, and the obliteration of a local master's ceiling paintings depicting St George and the Dragon, the Last Judgment and the history of the Holy Cross.

Temporarily interrupted only by a return to Roman Catholicism under Mary Tudor between 1553 and 1558, such orders reached into every home, with a mixture of emotions all too little recorded, and all too easily forgotten after four hundred years of Anglicanism. Those of staunch Puritan persuasion understandably approved, and Puritans were particularly strong in London and the bigger cities. Those of traditional Catholic sympathies inevitably bitterly objected, their feelings being closer to the surface the further away from London one went, particularly towards the north. In between, equally inevitably, lay an indefinite but arguably very substantial number of middle-of-the-road individuals neither happy about the changes, nor happy about disregarding them. And few places in England were, by sheer fact of geography, more middle-England and middle-of-the-road than Stratford-upon-Avon, home, in the mid-sixteenth century, of those who brought into being William Shakespeare.

And here the sharpest realism is needed about the house into which Shakespeare was born, and the emotions that stirred within it, a need regarding which the Stratford of the tourist guide book entirely fails

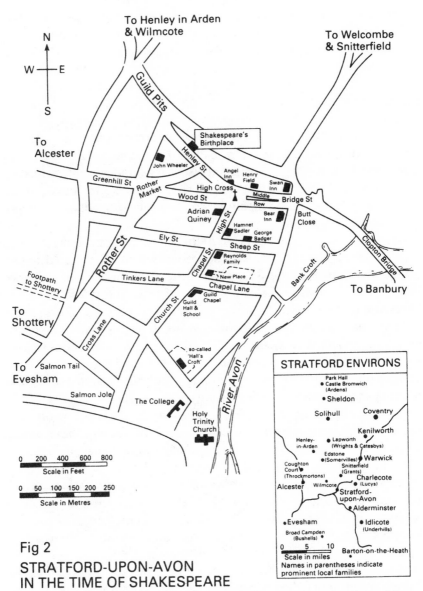

Fig 2
STRATFORD-UPON-AVON
IN THE TIME OF SHAKESPEARE

Based upon the researches of Edgar Fripp and others, it shows locations of the homes of the principal known associates of John and William Shakespeare, also (right), some of the Shakespeare-associated towns, villages and country houses in Stratford-upon-Avon's immediate vicinity.

us. There is a certain justice to a comment made back in February 1965 by the then *Daily Mail* literary critic Bernard Levin.

> Stratford permits – indeed encourages – one of the biggest frauds in England to rage unchecked ... I mean those two monumental frauds, 'Shakespeare''s Birthplace and Anne Hathaway's Cottage.

This so-called 'Birthplace' house [see pl. 6], which lies in Henley Street, just off the High Street, comprises a large tile-roofed, detached timber-framed property set behind railings, with a substantial garden behind. While the eastern part is fitted out as a modest museum, the western half, where the guide books say Shakespeare was born, is furnished just as if he had left but yesterday, even complete with a period cradle. The air conveyed is that of a mint piece of Elizabethan England which time essentially has left untouched.

In reality what appears today as a single house was in Shakespeare's time two quite separate properties, timber- not tile-roofed. Although both were owned by the Shakespeare family, not a jot of evidence tells in which young William was born. If it was either, it was more likely the eastern half, the notable Stratford authority Edgar Fripp arguing that the western portion was not purchased until 1575, by which time William was eleven. The tenuous local tradition that he was born in the western part probably derives from this being the section that members of the family continued to occupy after Shakespeare's father's death, leasing out the rest.

More serious, and partly because of the leasing, the properties went through several quite radical transformations, some within Shakespeare's lifetime. Possibly as early as 1603, but certainly before 1646 the eastern part's tenant transformed it into an inn called successively The Maidenhead and then the Swan and Maidenhead. Around 1762 Lichfield watercolourist Richard Greene made a watercolour sketch that is the earliest representation of the house known to exist [see pl. 7], and is now, along with so many other items relating to Shakespeare, in the Folger Shakespeare Library, Washington. Although this features two dormer windows and gable, a deep porch and a bay window, a second sketch made just thirty years later shows the property now without the dormer windows. The gable and the bay window were altered to an ordinary lattice, and the porch dismantled so that the frontage could serve as a butcher's shop.

Butchery was also the order inside, where visiting Shakespeare devotees were regularly sold lumps of wood from a chair said to have been Shakespeare's favourite.

About 1808 a new buyer, Thomas Court, took out a lot of old timber-framing and refaced the Swan and Maidenhead part in red brick. Only in 1847, after a scare that it all might be sold and shipped to America, was a proper Shakespeare Birthplace committee formed to secure effectively both western and eastern portions as an official Stratford tourist attraction. Once acquired, the Swan and Maidenhead brickwork was taken down, and the two adjoining properties that up to that time had formed a continuous frontage onto Henley Street were demolished, ostensibly to form a firebreak and create room for a truly impressive garden. Only then was the present semblance of a single detached house created, the whole structure then being stripped back to that which was supposed to be original and rebuilt to conform as closely as possible to the sketch of its appearance made back in the 1760s. As for the 'period' furniture, this has no known Shakespeare associations, having been collected from anywhere over the years simply to give an impression of the sort of furniture the Shakespeares might have had around them.

Ironically we know such details thanks to the generations of Shakespeare researchers such as Halliwell-Phillipps,[1] Fripp[2] and others who have fine-toothcombed the entire Stratford area's records for every conceivable crumb of relevant information. It is to their efforts that we likewise owe a surprising amount regarding the lives of Shakespeare's parents.

His mother Mary, for instance, was of a gentility too often shamefully down-played by Oxfordians and their ilk. She was the daughter of Robert Arden, of the Arden family that were one of the few in England who could trace their ancestry back to before William the Conqueror. The vast and ancient forest that once stretched from Tamworth to the Cotswolds carried their name, the same Forest of Arden that Shakespeare would use as his background for *As You Like It*. The family's main branch, the very Catholic Ardens of Park Hall, were based at Castle Bromwich, near Birmingham, and although Mary's father's exact relationship to these has never been established with certainty,[3] his will[4] as made out in November 1556 shows him to have been a gentleman – a specific and respected status in the sixteenth century's social order – and of taste and substance. Dying as he was during the reign of the Catholic Mary, the will readily discloses his devout Catholicism: 'First I bequest my soul to Almighty God and to Our Blessed Lady Saint Mary, and to all the holy company of heaven, and my body to be buried in the churchyard of Saint John the Baptist in Aston'.

The will also shows that Mary, Robert's eighth and youngest daughter by his first marriage, was quite a favourite of his. Earlier Robert had made settlements on other daughters who were already married, but in 1556 when he was clearly dying and Mary remained unmarried he left her all his copyhold tenure of the 'land in Wilmcote called Asbyes and the crop upon the ground sown and tilled as it is', together with ten marks (£6.13s.4d). He also made her one of his two executors – in pointed contrast to his surviving wife Agnes, to whom he simply left the Wilmcote roof over her head, plus another ten marks, conditional upon her living in harmony with Mary's remaining sister Alice.

Typifying the sham that is Stratford-upon-Avon tourism, there is today, still commanding the green at Wilmcote (a small village three miles to Stratford's northwest), a fine two-storied half-timbered sixteenth-century house that the Shakespeare Birthplace Trust labels 'Mary Arden's House'. This is one of the five star Shakespeare attractions for which visitors can buy sets of tickets. With its polished oak floors, ostensibly period farmyard, dovecote, cow byre, pig sty and barns containing historic farm implements, it seems genuinely to have been spared many of the depredations of the Birthplace, and it would be pleasant to believe that Shakespeare's mother once lived there.

The problem is that only the less-than-reliable word of John Jordan attests that the house ever belonged to any member of the Arden family. Such records that exist show that in Robert Arden's time it was actually owned by one Thomas Finderne of Nuneaton, and that in 1561 it was sold on to an Adam Palmer and George Gibbes.[5] Furthermore the location of the land Robert Arden described as 'called Asbyes' has never been satisfactorily identified.

Nonetheless, whether or not one and the same as the present-day Mary Arden's House, Robert Arden's Wilmcote residence must certainly have been substantial. A still-extant house contents inventory that accompanied Robert's will[6] includes solid oak furniture, beds and bedding, linen, copper pans, brass pots and candlesticks, quern and kneading trough, vessels for milking and brewing, bacon in the roof, wheat in the barn, wood in the yard, carts, ploughs, eight oxen, two bullocks, seven cows, four horses, three colts, fifty sheep, nine pigs, poultry and bees. In addition there are listed eleven painted cloths, two in the 'hall' or living-room, five in the adjoining 'chamber', and four in the bedrooms over. For the Tudor period, these were the more affordable but still pricey equivalent of tapestries, and were usually painted with Biblical or allegorical scenes. Shakespeare would refer to such tapestries in *The Rape of Lucrece* and *As You Like It*, and as remarked by Dr A. L. Rowse, they denote 'a standard of taste above that of the ordinary farmer'.

This then was the inheritance of Shakespeare's mother while she was still young and unmarried, and small wonder that within what could only have been a matter of months she was wooed and whisked to the altar by one John Shakespeare. Although the place of their marriage is not known, it was almost certainly Wilmcote's parish church, the charming St John the Baptist's at neighbouring Aston Cantlow. There the registers for the period have not survived, if they were ever kept, hence there is no record of the date. However it would definitely have been after the making of Robert Arden's will in November 1556, and necessarily before the baptism of John and Mary's first child Joan on 15 September 1558. We can therefore comfortably assume it to have been 1557, or early 1558 at the very latest.

But given that Arden heiress Mary was quite a catch for John Shakespeare, what of he for her? Certainly she married beneath her, John being the son of Richard Shakespeare from the neighbouring hilltop village of Snitterfield, where he farmed as a tenant on additional land that Robert Arden owned in that area. Richard lived on in Snitterfield until the winter of 1561, but sometime before 1552 John must have left to set up in his own right in Stratford, for in that year he somewhat ingloriously enters the historical record with a fine for amassing a dunghill, (in the Latin of officialdom, a *sterquinarium*), in the road outside his house. He was not alone in this misdemeanor, his fellow citizens Chambers, Reynolds and Quiney being also fined in this same crack-down. John had apparently been expected to use the common muck-hill more hygienically located up at the country end of Henley Street. For the sixteenth century his offence would have been about as serious as a modern parking ticket.

Now, Oxfordians and their ilk often like to make out that John Shakespeare's occupation was that of a common butcher. They quote non-contemporary traditions in support of this, inevitably fuelled by the fact already noted that one of the Shakespeares' Henley Street properties later did indeed see service as a butcher's shop. However, Shakespearean England's meat quality controls required butchers to have licences, and Stratford's only known licensed butcher in John's time was town Alderman Ralph Cawdrey of Bridge Street.

Further, the historical record is quite positive that certainly part of John Shakespeare's occupation was that of glover. In the Proceedings of Stratford's Court of Record, preserved in the Shakespeare Birthplace Trust's Record Office, 'Johannem Shakyspere de Stretforde' was specifically so described when in 1556 he was unsuccessfully sued for £8 by Thomas Siche, a husbandman from the village of Armscote, several miles to Stratford's south. Other official documents from the 1560s onwards show that he sometimes dextrously drew as his mark a pair of glover's compasses, the instrument he would have used for measuring and making the ornamental cuttings to glove-backs fashionable at the time. Elizabethan portraits and surviving examples of gloves of the period show the glover's trade to have been a sophisticated one[7] and John would have had to serve a seven year apprenticeship, which he had most likely already completed by the time he met Mary. Among many instances of the author of Shakespeare's plays having a homely familiarity with the glover's trade is Dame Quickly's remark about Slender in *The Merry Wives of Windsor*: 'Does he not wear a great round beard, like a glover's paring knife?'[8]

But there was clearly considerably more to John Shakespeare than just being a trained craftsman. From somewhere or other even before his marriage he found the money to buy property. Already a householder in Henley Street in 1552 (hence his dung-heap fine), in 1556 he purchased not only what would seem to have been the eastern portion of the Henley Street 'Birthplace' but also a *tenementum* with garden and croft in nearby Greenhill Street, on the road leading north to Alcester. Later in the 1570s he would buy more.

Unlike his son-to-be, John was also quite definitely a man eager to play his part in local affairs. As early as September 1556, during the reign of the Catholic Mary Tudor, he was appointed one of Stratford's two ale tasters. These were men chosen as 'able persons and discreet' to check on the quality of the local ale-brewing and bread-making, and to bring before the local manorial court any who failed to match up to the prescribed standards. Amusingly, John can be seen to have neglected this duty during his 'courting' year of 1557, for he was noted as missing three meetings. But he was clearly forgiven for this, for when newly married in the autumn of 1558, he was enrolled as one of the town's four constables, worthy part-time vigilante-cum-fire-officers of the kind that son William would later lampoon in the person of *Love's Labour's Lost*'s Constable Dull.

In November of 1558 the Roman Catholic Queen Mary died, to be succeeded by Anne Boleyn's daughter the twenty-five-year-old Elizabeth, who almost immediately summoned her first Parliament, reversing Mary's Catholic policies in favour of the harsh, anti-traditionalist Protestantism earlier enacted by her half-brother Edward VI. This included a new Act of Supremacy declaring Elizabeth supreme head of the Church of England, ratifying Henry VIII's break with Rome, imposing the English prayer book of 1552 in place of the Latin Missal, and requiring all churches once more to remove and destroy all their images and altar furniture and to board up their chancels so that the congregation could concentrate on the sermon. Attendance at the new services was made obligatory.

Inevitably, the effectiveness of such legislation was heavily dependent on the cooperation or otherwise of those locally empowered to carry it out, and so far as Stratford was concerned all we know is that very shortly after Elizabeth's accession – the exact date is unrecorded – John Shakespeare was elected to serve as one of the town's fourteen burgesses. These were the local worthies who replaced the Guild that had previously managed the town's affairs, and who made decisions on local matters once each month in the Guild Hall. One of the earliest deliberations in which John Shakespeare would have been involved was the case of curate Roger Dyos, the incumbent of Stratford-upon-Avon's Church of the Holy Trinity. Just three months before Queen Mary's death Dyos had christened John and Mary's first-born Joan according to the then-approved Latin rite. Dyos declined to switch to the new Protestant ways, and whatever John Shakespeare's vote on the matter, a majority of the burgesses voted to stop Dyos's salary, depriving him of his living, and opening the post to an incumbent more amenable to the new order, John Bretchgirdle.[9]

Whatever John's personal politics, here was power, local govern-mental power that was to be part and parcel of his life throughout at least the next decade and a half. From 1561 to 1566 he was the active chamberlain administering the borough's property and revenues, overseeing the accounts along with John Taylor, a shearman in Sheep

Street. Interestingly, it was only during this period (1564 to be precise), that after Stratford's burgesses had clearly 'overlooked' the matter, the 'idolatrous' religious images in the Guild Chapel were defaced and pulled down, probably at the insistence of the Bishop of Worcester who made his first visitation to his new diocese in this year. However, when also this same year vicar Bretchgirdle died of plague, somehow a Catholic sympathiser, William Butcher, formerly President of Corpus Christi College, Oxford, was installed in his place. The next year John Shakespeare was proudly donning the black-furred gown of an alderman, having been elected to replace William Bott, owner of the big house called New Place, who had been 'expulsed' the year before for insulting behaviour towards council officers. John would have worn this gown, together with the thumb-ring that marked the rank of an alderman, when processing to church each Sunday, and on all official occasions, and he could also expect to be respectfully addressed as 'Master Shakespeare', the status of a gentleman.

But yet higher honours were in store, for in September 1568 he was elected Bailiff, the town's equivalent of Mayor, and John Wheeler, his neighbour from across Henley Street, was elected alongside him as Deputy. His prescribed furred gown was now scarlet, and for all official functions he would have been escorted from his house by buff-uniformed, mace-bearing serjeants, the sixteenth century's equivalent of a police escort. Holy Trinity's front pew would have been reserved for him and his family, and he could likewise expect the front row seats for all entertainments.

Along with this new office inevitably also went heavier responsibilities. Not only did he automatically preside over Council meetings, but he assumed the powers and responsibilities of Justice of the Peace at the monthly Courts of Record, a Crown court. Although there is no evidence that he could read or write – clerks were available for this – he was responsible for issuing arrest warrants, for supervising poor relief, and fixing the weekly price of corn. He was also the recipient of instructions from Queen's Privy Council regarding matters of state affecting his jurisdiction.

Of this latter, most notable in his particular year was the rising of the Northern Earls, a serious pro-Catholic rebellion that threatened to overthrow Elizabeth and replace her with the Catholic Mary Queen of Scots, now Elizabeth's prisoner in England. The corporation's minutes convey the homespun preparations of the time: January 1569 'for dressing of three goones' [guns]; January 1570 'for dressing of harness, 11s.6d.; to the soldiers at their first muster, 4s.; to Robert Joiner for a gunstock, 2s.; to Simon Biddle for dressing of two pikes and a bow, 2s.4d.'. Stratford provided eight men to serve in the local Earl of Warwick's troops as part of the army sent northwards to put down the rebellion. Although the rebellion was successfully suppressed the government was badly winded by it, and almost certainly as part of the countermeasures in Stratford the recently introduced pro-Catholic vicar William Butcher was replaced by the more reliably Protestant Henry Heycroft, the latter's Protestantism attested by his award of a preacher's licence from the Bishop of Worcester in 1571. In the same year, John Shakespeare became Deputy in his turn to incoming Bailiff Adrian Quiney, the High Street wool draper who had been one of his fellow offenders back in the dunghill year of 1552. In January 1572 he and Quiney rode to London together on business to plead the town's case against the Earl of Warwick over a local grievance. While in London he successfully fought in the Court of Pleas the recovery of a debt of £50 owed to him by a fellow glover from Banbury – a large debt, easily the value of a comfortable house, indicative of a man used to dealing in substantial sums of money. He was also still dabbling in property, as in 1575 he paid £40 for two Stratford houses; the transaction by which the western part of the Henley Street 'Birthplace' was probably acquired. In about this same year he also exercised his right, as a man who had achieved the heights of civic office, to apply for a coat of arms, the effective rubber-stamp that he had made the coveted social leap from yeoman to gentleman.

Meantime there had of course taken place the event that Stratford's citizens of that time could never have dreamed would have such import and fascination for future generations: the birth of John and Mary's first-born son William in 1564. Although we do not know the exact day, we can date it near enough, for in the Stratford Birthplace Trust Records Office a seventeen and a half by seven and a half inches, three-hundred-and-thirty-five-page leather-bound volume lists the baptisms, marriages and burials performed in Holy Trinity Church from the year 1558 to the eighteenth century. And in folio five of the baptismal register, towards the bottom of the page, under the year 1564 and against the date 26 April can be read the Latin entry *Gulielmus filius Johannes Shakspere*, 'William, son of John Shakespeare'.

Although this provides only the christening date, high infant mortality meant that christenings were rarely left later than the first following Sunday or Holy Day, so William almost certainly entered the world no more than two or three days before the 26th, quite possibly on the birthday traditionally attributed to him, 23 April, St George's Day, which in 1564 fell on the Sunday. John and Mary would probably have avoided the ceremony being held on the Tuesday, 25 April, because this was St Mark's Day, inauspicious because traditionally it was the day the altars and crosses used to be swathed in black.

The font into which vicar Bretchgirdle would have dunked him still survives in Holy Trinity Church, on a new pedestal near Shakespeare's grave, somewhat the worse for wear for having been discarded during the seventeenth century and used as a water cistern by the parish clerk. But although it would be pleasant to think that the entry on the register was made the same day, the same Wednesday of the baptism, in Mary and John's presence, with the young William's lungs still protesting in the immediate vicinity, the facts dictate otherwise. The register's cover bears the date 1600, and all its entries up to that date, including not only William's but those of his various brothers and sisters, have clearly been copied from an earlier, no longer extant register. There is nothing suspicious in this, since we know it to have been made necessary by a change in regulations late in Elizabeth's reign requiring all records previously kept in paper registers to be transferred onto longer-lasting parchment. And since the Holy transcriptions have clearly been made with care, we have no reason to distrust their accuracy. They also provide markedly better information than we have for the births of Ben Jonson, John Marston, Thomas Dekker and many other of Shakespeare's playwright contemporaries.

This is also by no means the end of the register's interest, for if we turn back to its first page, against the date 15 September appears the christening of John and Mary's already mentioned first-born daughter Joan. On the third page, against the date 2 December 1562, it can be seen that the Shakespeares had a second daughter whom they named Margaret. On the seventh page, against the date 13 October 1566, can be found the christening of Gilbert, a younger brother for William, and on the ninth page, against the date 15 April 1569, that of another daughter named Joan.

Now of course no family gives two living offspring the same

Christian name, so clearly the other Joan had died, even though no entry recording her death appears. This probably happened around 1559 to 1560, when the register appears to have been kept only spasmodically. Joan was shortly followed by her younger sister Margaret, whose death we do find in the burials register against the date 30 April 1563. This is typical infant mortality for the time, though for the Shakespeares particularly distressing since it rendered them temporarily childless. There would therefore have been all the more delight at the birth of first son William within less than a year of Margaret's death, tinged with more than a little anxiety, in view of the fateful words *hic incepit pestis*, 'here began plague', in the burial part of the register three months later. Just how close this dread flea-borne disease was to the Shakespeares can be gauged from the fact that their Henley Street neighbour Roger Green lost four of his children and town clerk Richard Symons three. One estimate[10] suggests that the town lost around two hundred, or about fifteen per cent, of its population during this single outbreak. It is a sobering thought how much the world could have lost at this time by one ill-chanced flea-bite.

As the registers further show, the Shakespeares went on to have one more daughter, Anne, who would die at the age of eight and, in addition to the already mentioned Gilbert, two more brothers for William: Richard, christened 11 March 1574, and Edmund, christened 3 May 1580. Since we otherwise know so little about the people behind these names, it is worth noting that John and Mary Shakespeare, in a manner common for the time, seem always to have chosen their offspring's Christian names with care.[11] The two Joans were named after Mary's elder sister Joan, who had married Edmund Lambert of Barton-on-the-Heath; Margaret after another of Mary's sisters of this name, who had married Alexander Webbe, her stepmother's brother, from Bearley, just to the north of Wilmcote; Gilbert after John's fellow glover and Henley Street neighbour Gilbert Bradley; Edmund after the above mentioned Edmund Lambert. Who inspired young William's name is anyone's guess, but interestingly we will certainly see how William in adulthood would give the same careful thought to the naming of the characters in his plays.

Now if it may be felt that we have dwelt overlong on the Stratford register, this has not been without justification. That simple entry of the date of William's christening, not even an original, represents all the truly hard information we have on William for the next eighteen years of his life. Although Shakespeare biographers queue one behind the other to assume that he was educated at Stratford-upon-Avon's King's New School, in Church Street, behind the Guild Chapel, only John's entitlement as burgess to have his children educated free at the school justifies this assumption. The King's New School's registers perished long before anyone realised they might be of historical interest, and first biographer Rowe's 1709 information that John Shakespeare maintained William 'for some time at a Free-School' neither gives the location, nor breeds confidence.

We could spend a great deal of time considering the education the young William might have received at King's New School. The very room he probably sat in survives as the 'over hall', above the armoury in Stratford's Guild Hall, which had formerly belonged to the Guild of the Holy Cross until Henry VIII's Dissolution of the Monasteries. Today filled with old desks into which clearly umpteen generations of schoolchildren have carved their names, we should envisage it without these in Shakespeare's time. Contemporary engravings of Elizabethan schoolrooms show the pupils sitting on benches, books on their knees, the schoolmaster alone enjoying the privilege of a desk. It is also notable that in such engravings the pupils depicted are all boys. Except in the most aristocratic house-holds, where there would have been personal tutors, girls were expected to stay at home with their mothers to learn more womanly skills.

Most likely the surviving schoolroom was not where the young William learned the basic rudiments of reading and writing. From about the age of four to seven he would have been at the so-called 'petty school', a room often simply adjoining the main schoolroom, under the supervision of an usher or *abecedarius*. First there was the hornbook, a handled wooden tablet bearing a printed page of the letters of the alphabet, vowels and 'Our Father' protected by a sheet of transparent horn, the sixteenth century's equivalent of clear plastic. Then pupils tackled their first simple books, the *ABC with the Catechism* (remembered in Act II of *Two Gentlemen of Verona*: 'To sigh, like a schoolboy that has lost his ABC'), and the *Primer*. Here also he would have been taught handwriting before graduating to the care of the schoolmaster proper.

Since we know the names of the King's New School schoolmasters throughout Shakespeare's formative years, it is straightforward enough to determine that the first of these whom he encountered would have been Simon Hunt, a young man arriving in Stratford only three years after his graduation from Oxford in 1568. It would almost certainly have been Hunt who took the young Shakespeare through his first Latin predictably, given the uniformity of Elizabethan education, using fifteenth-century schoolmaster William Lily's *Shorte Introduction of Grammar*. Shakespeare's vivid memory of the grindingly dull but necessary delights of this are enshrined in the oft-quoted schoolroom scene in Act IV of *The Merry Wives of Windsor* in which the schoolboy William Page's lines are a direct quote from Lily:

> Articles are borrowed of the pronoun, and be thus declined: Singulariter, nominativo; hic, hæc, hoc.

But Hunt stayed at Stratford only four years, his successor being fellow Oxford graduate Thomas Jenkins, who lasted from 1575 to 1579. And since these years corresponded with Shakespeare being from ten to fifteen – his sixth form or high school years by the Elizabethan age's intensive standards – arguably Jenkins is to be seen as the man of potentially the profoundest influence on Shakespeare's education.

Here, if we are looking for calibre, the little that is known of Jenkins indicates that he was far from wanting in this direction. A. L. Rowse and others have supposed him to be Welsh,[12] fondly imagining him as a model for *The Merry Wives of Windsor*'s schoolmaster parson who made 'fritters of English'. In fact he was a Londoner,[13] the son of an old servant of Sir Thomas White, the founder of the Catholic-tinged St John's College, Oxford. Through this connection, and what would seem to have been sheer ability, he took his B.A. at St John's in 1566, thereupon becoming one of its fellows, and proceeding to M.A. in 1570. He would seem to have been a dedicated teacher, because in his graduation year he pleaded for a two-year leave of absence 'that he may give himself to teach children'. And he was married; the Stratford register shows the burial of his daughter Joan in 1576 and the christening of his son, given the same name as his father, in 1578.

This was the man who, so far as can be determined, introduced Shakespeare and his fellow pupils to the virtues of rhetoric, as enshrined in Cicero and Quintilian, and who took them through practice orations and declamations. It would have been Jenkins who

sparked off Shakespeare's undoubted subsequent life-long enthusiasm for the poetry of Ovid, particularly the *Metamorphoses*, the
mythical tales he would deploy in one form or another in everything
from *Titus Andronicus* to *The Tempest*. It would have been Jenkins
who gave Shakespeare a taste for history as set down in Caesar
and Sallust.

We can be confident of such reading at least, not simply because
Shakespeare shows his familiarity with these works, but because they
were staple fare for the senior level of most well-run Elizabethan
schoolrooms. It simply needed the right sort of schoolmaster to make
them live for his pupils, and in this respect Shakespeare does not
seem to have been alone in being thus inspired by Jenkins. Stratford
mercer's son William Smith, shown in the Stratford register as one of
the twenty-seven other boys born in the town in the same year as
Shakespeare, went on to Winchester College, then to Oxford, and
subsequently became a schoolmaster. And Bridge Street tanner's son
Richard Field, just over two years older than Shakespeare, but
arguably of the same Jenkins generation, went off to London to
devote himself to the printing of books.

Now while it is well recorded that Field departed Stratford to begin
his long apprenticeship in 1579 – the same year that Jenkins finished
his term at Stratford – when Shakespeare left (and when he began) is
unknown. It is therefore important to turn back to what had been
happening to his father, the hitherto upwardly thrusting Alderman
John, whereupon we find something immediately intriguing and to
this very day unexplained.

From having been utterly conscientious about attending the
council's meetings, in about 1576 John Shakespeare suddenly ceased
to attend completely, with the exception of one isolated instance. It is
a measure of the esteem in which he had been held that for years his
fellow aldermen kept his name on their register, clearly hoping he
would rejoin them, but each time they regretfully recorded his
absence. There has to have been some financial problem, for the levy
he should have paid as an alderman was thoughtfully halved in his
case, yet he proved either unable or unwilling to pay even this
reduced amount. He was also absolved any penalty for non-
attendance of the 1578 election meeting, even though his fellow
absentee John Wheeler was fined twenty shillings. Eventually, when
in September 1586 two new aldermen were elected in his and
Wheeler's stead, the Council minutes explained 'for that Master

Wheeler doth desire to be put out of the Company and Master Shakespeare doth not come to the Halls when they be warned nor hath not done of long time'.[14]

John's property dealings also reveal the same picture. Whereas up to and including 1575 the pattern had been one of consistent acquisition, in 1578 he can be seen raising £40 cash from Mary's Barton-on-the-Heath brother-in-law Edmund Lambert by mortgaging to him part of Mary's Wilmcote inheritance. And he already owed Lambert money. In this same year he can be found raising money with Mary's stepmother's family, the Webbes, using another eighty-six acres of the Wilmcote inheritance, and in the event letting this go for a paltry amount. When in 1580 John's agreement with Lambert required that he either repay the £40, or lose his title to the property, he proved unable to repay not only then, but throughout the seven years that remained before Lambert died. He defaulted on sureties. In 1582 he was pleading for protection against four men 'for fear of death and mutilation of his limbs'.[15]

Clearly something had drastically affected John's life, and at just the time when his eldest, William, had reached the age to go out into the world. But was the problem simply financial – or did it lie deeper? Here we are about to consider a most unusual and tantalising clue.

CHAPTER 4

A Curious Testament

It was in the year 1757, when the Shakespeare Birthplace house was being occupied by Thomas Hart (William's great-great-great-nephew by his sister Joan), that the house's complete retiling became necessary. Hart called in the local building firm of Joseph Mosely and by 29 April the work was well apace when suddenly Mosely came across a small, handwritten booklet carefully wedged between the tiling and the rafters.

At first sight it seemed nothing special, just five sheets of paper stitched together on which were written a series of paragraphs in old-fashioned handwriting. The revelation, however, was that most paragraphs began with the words 'I John Shakespeare'. And they were then followed by some profound religious statements, for example:

> I John Shakespeare . . . will patiently endure and suffer all kind of infirmity . . . ; I John Shakespeare . . . do pardon all the injuries and offences that any one hath ever done to me; I John Shakespeare beseech . . . all my dear friends, parents and kinsfolk . . . to assist and succour me with their holy prayers . . . especially with the holy sacrifice of the Mass; I John Shakespeare . . . bequeath my soul . . . to be entombed in the sweet and amorous coffin of the side of Christ.[1]

Not least:

> I John Shakespeare have made this present writing . . . in presence of the blessed Virgin Mary, my Angel guardian, and all the Celestial Court . . . for the better declaration hereof, my will and intention is that it be finally buried with me after my death.

The Catholic nature of the document was all too apparent, and despite the fact that enthusiasm for Shakespeare was already well advanced, few were to learn of its existence for many years. Thomas

Hart showed little interest, allowing Mosely not only to hold on to it, but to pass it on to Stratford alderman Mr Payton of Shottery. Probably the earliest man to see the document's potential significance was our old friend Stratford wheelwright and tour guide John Jordan who, seeing that it appeared to lack a first page, made up an appropriate-sounding one of his own. Jordan then sent a transcript of his finished product to the *Gentleman's Magazine*, the eighteenth century's equivalent of *Reader's Digest*. The editor, although he declined to publish it, indirectly imparted its contents to Edmond Malone, at that time yet to make his exposé of the William-Henry Ireland forgeries. Upon Malone contacting Stratford's vicar James Davenport, Alderman Payton duly sent him the original five pages as first discovered by builder Mosely.[2]

Malone found the document profoundly puzzling. Clearly it seemed to be a sort of spiritual will as made by William's father John Shakespeare, presumably from some Catholic formulary. But, as he was aware, there was no known evidence that John Shakespeare could write. Also, could the father of England's greatest Bard really have been a Catholic?

Nonetheless, when Malone published the original five pages in 1790 as part of the historical section of his *The Plays and Poems of William Shakespeare*, he declared himself 'perfectly satisfied' that it was genuine. From his enquiries made directly with Hart and with Mosely's daughter (Mosely having died in the interim), he verified the basic circumstances of Mosely's discovery, also that Mosely had been 'very honest, sober, [and] industrious'. Malone was altogether more suspicious of what he learned from his questioning of the ever-shifty Jordan. Consequently, although he went on to publish Jordan's front page as an addendum to *Plays and Poems* six years later in the course of his exposure of William-Henry Ireland, he declared he had changed his mind about the 'Spiritual Will':

> In my conjecture concerning the writer of that paper, I certainly was mistaken, for I have since obtained documents that clearly prove it could not have been the composition of any one of our poet's family; as will be fully shewn in his Life.[3]

Unfortunately, Malone did not live to write the Shakespeare 'Life' in which he clearly intended to explain this statement. Even more regrettably, not only were the documents to which he referred untraceable among his papers after his death, also missing were the five pages originally found by Mosely. These have never reappeared.

As a result of Malone's statement and the original's disappearance, serious interest in the will understandably died for well over a century. The great nineteenth-century Shakespearean scholars Halliwell-Phillipps and Sir Sidney Lee both assumed that wheelwright John Jordan must have concocted the whole thing, Lee even going so far as to remark that Jordan's 'greatest achievement was the forgery of the will of Shakespeare's father'.[4] Because John Shakespeare served on Stratford's corporation at the time of the whitewashing over of the frescoes in the Guild Chapel, some scholars even supposed him to have been Puritan. Nor has there survived a secular will that might have suggested that he had any alternative religious persuasion.

But around 1923 the Jesuit scholar Reverend Herbert Thurston,[5] in the course of non-Shakespearean researches in the British Museum Library, happened to come across a Spanish language devotional publication entitled *Testamento O Ultima Voluntad del Alma. Hecho en Salud para Asegurarse el Christiano de las tentaciones del Demonio, en la hora de la muerte*, 'Last Will of the Soul, made in health for the Christian to secure himself from the temptation of the Devil at the hour of death'. Although this had been printed in Mexico City in 1661, its original author had been St Charles Borromeo, a Catholic archbishop who lived between 1538 and 1584, and who was canonised in 1610 for his exceptional selflessness caring for the sick during the great Milan plague of 1576. Borromeo and John Shakespeare were thus direct contemporaries. And since John Shakespeare's five pages corresponded so closely to Borromeo's wording they must have been made from some English language version of Borromeo's text.

Further light was shed only as recently as 1966 when a single English language copy, *The Testament of the Soule*, 'made by S. Charles Borrom. Card. & Arch. of Millan' and published in 1638, turned up [see pl. 8]. Now yet another acquisition of the Folger Shakespeare Library, Washington,[6] this comprises twenty-four of the tiniest pages, each measuring a mere one and three-quarters by three inches. The earliest part does not correspond to Jordan's first page of text, and thereby confirms his fraudulence. But the rest shows an essentially word-for-word correspondence with the five pages as found by builder Mosely, strongly indicating that Mosely's find was indeed a genuine one.

But what is the explanation for such an indubitably Catholic 'spiritual will', devised by a Catholic archbishop, being found in John Shakespeare's name, and secreted in the rafters of the house in which he lived out his days? Here the great pity is that the original has not survived. Malone was a worthy and conscientious scholar whose word we can trust on the document he made his transcription from. Unfortunately he told us nothing about the paper on which it was written, which might have revealed its country of origin. Nor did he make clear whether the name 'John Shakespeare' appeared in the document in a different hand from the rest. Nor whether the signature, denoted by the concluding paragraph 'signed with mine own hand', was an actual signature, rather than the mark John Shakespeare normally used for his corporation business.

Even so, it is not too difficult to deduce how and when a copy of the will might have travelled from Borromeo to John Shakespeare's Warwickshire; also why John would have been at considerable pains to conceal the document's existence. The Folger Library 1636 English language edition reveals the *Testament* as a publication of the Jesuits. These were the Roman Catholic Church's most militant arm, founded in 1534 to counter the tide of Protestantism, and specifically favoured by Borromeo. Young Englishmen who wanted their country to return to the Catholic fold journeyed to the Continent to be trained at seminaries in Rome and Douai, and later in Rheims, in order to supply the urgent demand for priests among England's secret Catholics. Although from the mid-1570s some hundred priests returned to England to make a mission of this kind, the first major Jesuit mission was that which set off from Rome in 1580 under the leadership of Fathers Edmund Campion and Robert Persons, both former Oxford graduates.

Importantly, Borromeo's connection with Campion and Persons' mission is quite definite. His archdiocese of Milan lay squarely on the route they would have taken overland from Rome to England, and they are known to have called on him in the spring of 1580. Almost certainly they had already brought with them from Rome copies of his *Testament*, for just over a year later the head of the English College in France was writing to his opposite number in Rome:

Father Robert [Persons] wants three or four thousand or more of the *Testaments*, for many persons desire to have them.[7]

Equally definite is that Campion and Persons visited Shakespeare country. Persons was certainly in Warwickshire, for later in life he described being entertained by Mary Shakespeare's relatives (whether close or distant), the Ardens of Park Hall.[8] At Park Hall his host would have been Edward Arden, the county's High Sheriff in 1575, who was subsequently displaced and revealed and executed as a Catholic plotter in 1584. Persons also very likely stayed with Arden's cousins, the staunchly Catholic Throckmortons, at their still-extant mansion Coughton Court, a few miles to Stratford's north-west.[9] Campion, for his part, was put up by the again Catholic Sir William Catesby, father of Gunpowder-plotter Robert (then an eight-year-old), at his house Bushwood, or Lapworth Hall, part of the parish and manor of Stratford-upon-Avon, though twelve miles to the north. For refusing to admit to this piece of hospitality, Catesby was subsequently hauled before the Court of Star Chamber and thrown into the Fleet prison.

Why Warwickshire was so favoured by the Campion–Persons Jesuit mission is because Shakespearean Stratford was ringed not only by Ardens, Throckmortons and Catesbys, but several more Catholic families of similar prominence. Among these were the Grants of Northbrooke, Snitterfield (John Shakespeare's birthplace), the Somervilles of Edstone (related through marriage with the Ardens), the Underhills of Idlicote, nine miles to Stratford's south (William would later purchase New Place from William Underhill), and the Smiths, lords of the manor of Shottery, the village associated with William Shakespeare's future wife, Anne Hathaway. Yet closer to Stratford were the Reynolds family, owners of Stratford's largest household of some twenty-two persons, and the Cloptons of Clopton House, descendants of the Sir Hugh Clopton who had built Stratford's fine stone bridge.

It is important to recognise that such families were not wilful malcontents pitching themselves Canute-like against the tide of an inevitable English Protestantism. From the perspective of many living in the latter half of the sixteenth century, Protestantism's Blitz-like ruin of so much of the old fabric of religious life, both buildings and customs, had been totally disproportionate to the Catholic ills it had been meant to rectify. The labels Catholic and Protestant had not yet developed the historical distinctions they have for us today, but under Mary Tudor everything had swung back to Catholicism, and given that the Catholic Mary Queen of Scots, though Elizabeth's prisoner, was her most logical successor, there was every hope that Protestantism in time would go away. Nor was the great silent majority of English Catholics anti-Elizabeth. Of the greatest disservice to them had been Pope Pius v's excommunication of Elizabeth as a heretic in 1570, declaring her monarchy illegitimate and thereby sanctioning any Catholic attempt to overthrow her. It meant all English Catholics could be regarded as, and treated as, traitors, whatever their true feelings on the matter.

As with Communism in eastern Europe in the present century, the situation created a self-supporting Catholic underground movement that paid lip service to the existing order while preserving its own conscience. In John Shakespeare's case a typical instance would have been his taking up office as Stratford's Bailiff, for which he would have been obliged to swear the anti-papist Supremacy oath acknowledging Elizabeth as supreme governor of the Church of England. Since the man at the time responsible for tendering this oath, Warwickshire's Sheriff Robert Middlemore, was himself a Catholic, any Catholic conscience on John's part need not have been too greatly stretched.[10]

Even so, when wanted men like Edmund Campion and Robert Persons turned up in Warwickshire it would inevitably have been a nail-biting time for Catholic sympathisers like the Shakespeares, if that is indeed what they were. For John Shakespeare to have acquired his *Testament* – probably already written out, with just his name to be filled in – we have no need to envisage Campion and Persons ever having ventured under his roof. In a small town like Stratford any stranger, even in disguise, would stand out too much. Altogether safer were the big out-of-town manor houses owned by the wealthier Catholic families, where priests could be smuggled into pre-prepared hiding-holes in the event of a government raid. Probably John would have gone to Sir William Catesby's for the Mass in which he received his *Testament*, sixteen-year-old William perhaps with him, since as we shall see later there would be some strong influences of Persons in his plays.

Despite all precautions, Campion was caught in a hiding-hole as a result of a raid at Lyford Grange, Berkshire, following a tip-off. When he was brought before Elizabeth, he assured her that his only mission was to save souls, and that he acknowledged her as his queen. However, she sent him off to be tortured to try to persuade him to divulge the names of those who had helped him. He was then tried with seventeen others and condemned to death, gently admonishing his judges:

> If our religion do make us traitors, we are worthy to be condemned; but otherwise are, and have been, as good subjects as ever the queen had. In condemning us you condemn all your own ancestors – all the ancient priests, bishops and kings – all that was once the glory of England, the island of saints, and the most devoted child of the see of Peter.[11]

At Tyburn on 1 December 1581 Campion and two fellow priests were despatched by being publicly hanged, cut down while still alive, then having their genitals cut off and their bowels drawn out before their eyes. Slightly earlier Persons, after wrestling with his conscience, had quietly slipped back over the Channel, never to return.

The Campion–Persons mission, and indeed Campion's very martyrdom, did much to stiffen the resolve of England's secret Catholics. In direct response Elizabeth's government brought in a new Act making it high treason for anyone to try to convert another to the Catholic faith, while even to be found present at a Mass meant a fine and a year's imprisonment. Conversely, anyone over sixteen who did not attend Anglican services was liable to a fine of £20 per month, a sum equivalent to a year's wages for those of middle income, and therefore quite impossible to pay except for the very rich. To facilitate the Act's effectiveness, rewards were offered to informers, promoting yet further a spy system around the country, where, in the words of one nineteenth-century historian 'no one with any conscience or religious scruples could hold himself safe for an hour'.[12]

The use of such informers was nothing new. Campion's betrayal had been by a rapist and murderer who had got out of difficulties by offering his services to the government to hunt down priests. Informers were also encouraged to watch for other infringements of laws passed by the Tudor parliaments, their 'perks' being a half share in the penalties imposed. In the last few years evidence has come to light that John Shakespeare was one of their victims – initially, at least, not for his religion, but for his money-lending activities. In 1552 money-lending at interest had been forbidden as 'a vice most odious and detestable', and an Exchequer Memoranda Roll studied by London Public Record Office staff members D. L. Thomas and N. E. Evans[13] records two separate instances of John 'Shakespeare' of 'Stratford upon Haven', glover, being informed against for loaning sums of between £80 and £100 at £20 interest to a certain John Musshem of Walton D'Eiville, a small village a few miles to Stratford's east. Musshem was an individual with whom John Shakespeare seems to have been frequently in business; they were sued together in 1573 by a Henry Higford of Solihull for a debt of £30. Both informers were from just outside Warwickshire, the first, Anthony Harrison, of Evesham, Worcestershire; the second James Langrake of Whittlebury, Northamptonshire.

The first accusation was dropped without explanation, probably because Harrison and John Shakespeare, in a manner typical of the time, came to an out-of-court settlement. Shakespeare no doubt paid off his accuser with an amount greater than the latter expected to gain from any government reward. In the second instance John Shakespeare, while denying guilt, offered to pay the court a reasonable fine rather than face trial by jury, and was duly fined forty shillings.

But Langrake, an unpleasant individual accused in 1570 of raping one of his servant girls, seems to have really had his knife into John Shakespeare, for in 1572 he was after him again, accusing him of acting as a middle-man in wool-dealing, a practice that a statute of 1552 restricted to manufacturers and properly accredited merchants of the Staple. Langrake made two specific claims. The first was that on or after 26 February, in Westminster, John Shakespeare and John Lockeley (also of Stratford-upon-Avon) had illegally purchased from Walter Newsam and others 5,600lbs of wool (two hundred 'tods') at fourteen shillings per tod. The second was that on or after 1 September 1571, at his parental village of Snitterfield, John Shakespeare purchased from the local landowners Edward and Richard Grant, and various others of unknown name, 2,800lbs of wool (a hundred tods) at the same price.

The first interesting feature of this information, unavailable to virtually all previous Shakespeare biographers, is that it now gives proper cohesion to other previous hints that as a major adjunct to his glover's trade, John Shakespeare had been a dealer in wool. Back in 1709 William's first biographer Nicholas Rowe reported a Stratford tradition that John had been 'a considerable Dealer in Wool'.[14] The western part of John's Henley Street premises was long known as 'The Woolshop'.[15] Early in the nineteenth century London publisher Sir Richard Phillips was told by the Swan and Maidenhead's then landlord that 'when he re-laid the floors of the parlour, the remnants of wool, and the refuse of wool-combing, were found under the old flooring, imbedded with the earth of the foundation'.[16] All this also ties in with Shakespeare scholar Leslie Hotson's discovery, back in the 1940s, that in 1599 John Shakespeare sued in the Court of Common Pleas John Walford, clothier and three times mayor of Marlborough, for non-payment of £21 for 588lbs (twenty-one tods) of wool that had been supplied to him thirty years before.[17]

Notable here is the considerable scale of John's money-making sidelines, both in money-lending and wool-dealing. The loans the informers reported him to have made in 1568 totalled £180 – nine times the annual salary of a schoolmaster or parson of the time, or approximately £90,000 at today's values. And the amount of wool the informers knew John to have been dealing in in 1571 was valued at £210, or (again at a rough approximation), £105,000 at today's prices. At the very least the standard biographers' picture of John as little more than a simple, civic-minded glover needs serious revision. Equally notable is the considerable curiosity of John waiting thirty years to sue John Walford, a thirty years during which all the evidence seems to show John to have been in serious need of that money.

And in this regard a further feature of interest is the light shed by the newly discovered Exchequer documents on those with whom John Shakespeare associated in his shadier dealings. While some are obscure, certainly not obscure are the Grants of the manor house called Northbrook, near John's home village of Snitterfield. As already mentioned, they were one of the most actively Catholic of Warwickshire's leading families. In October 1583 Edward Grant's wife's Catholic nephew John Somerville, who was married to Margaret, a daughter of the Catholic Ardens of Park Hall, set out from his house Edstone, six miles north of Stratford, with the avowed intention: 'I will go up to the Court and shoot the Queen through with a pistol'. Such was the efficiency of the Elizabethan informer network that Somerville got little further south than Banbury before being arrested and hauled to the Tower, ultimately to be found mysteriously strangled in his cell at Newgate just one day before he was due for execution.[18]

But the matter did not end there. With the aid of the Puritanical local magistrate and squire Sir Thomas Lucy of Charlecote (the man whom, according to local tradition, the young William Shakespeare annoyed by poaching his deer), government raids were carried out on all those suspected of having some complicity with Somerville. The Ardens' Park Hall was raided, and Edward Arden and his wife Mary (John's wife's namesake) taken prisoner. Edward was subsequently executed and his head, along with that of John Somerville, set up on London Bridge. The Grants' Northbrook House was also raided, along with the Underhills' Idlicote.

At the height of such searches those with tell-tale Catholic objects would inevitably have had to hide or dispose of them. This was, therefore, a likely time for John Shakespeare to have secreted the *Testament of the Soule* in his loft. Indeed, local council clerk Thomas Wilkes reported precisely this activity to government chief-spymaster Sir Francis Walsingham in the immediate aftermath of the Somerville and Arden arrests:

> the papists in this country [i.e. Warwickshire] do greatly work upon the advantage of clearing their houses of all shows of suspicion.[19]

The government's difficulties in enforcing anti-Catholic legislation is quite clear from a report of 1586 complaining how some Catholics:

> escape indicting through the corruptness of juries; some ... winked at by judges in respect of kindred or friendship; some go untouched through the fault of the custos rotulorum [keeper of the rolls] clerk of the assizes and sheriff.[20]

In these circumstances there has to be a serious possibility that John Shakespeare's apparent debt problems after 1575 were an example of a common subterfuge that Catholics employed to avoid the penalties for not attending church. One indication that he still had wealth derives from the fact that in 1586–7 he stood surety for friends for the considerable amounts of £22 and £10, hardly likely if his debts had been genuine ones. Catholics of Elizabeth's reign, well represented in the legal profession, became increasingly clever at organising their properties in such a way that these could hardly be confiscated from the real owners. It is even possible that William's unusually extensive legal knowledge, as would later appear in his plays, may have been deliberately cultivated early to help his father keep clear of the government's clutches.

Again having a bearing on John's *Testament* are further indications of just how deeply entrenched Catholicism was within Stratford-upon-Avon education during William's formative years. As we noted in the last chapter, probably the schoolmaster whom the young Shakespeare knew best was Thomas Jenkins. His religious affiliations are not known, only that he was a Fellow of the same Oxford College, St John's, of which Edmund Campion had been a Fellow, the College being a particularly tolerant one towards Catholics.

But the Catholic tinge deepens when we learn of Jenkins' predecessor Simon Hunt, who was at Stratford from 1571–5 when William was between the ages of seven and eleven. In the same year as Hunt's departure from Stratford a Simon Hunt, thought to be the Stratford schoolmaster, joined the University of Douai in France. This had been founded only a few years before for English Catholics, and was rapidly developing as a centre for missionary priests. Quite definite is that with Simon Hunt there ventured on this same overseas journey one of young William's fellow pupils, Robert Debdale, whose parents lived in Shottery, just outside Stratford, as neighbours of William's future wife's parents, the Hathaways.[21]

The Douai Hunt and young Debdale were certainly in Rome around 1577–8. Hunt was admitted to the Society of Jesus there on 20 April 1578, and in 1580 he succeeded Robert Persons as English Penitentiary at St Peter's, thus freeing Persons and Campion to make the journey during which they brought *Testaments* of the kind subsequently discovered in John Shakespeare's roof rafters.

Meanwhile Debdale of Shottery travelled to Rheims to which the Douai seminary had just been transferred, and where there was another man with a Stratford connection, Thomas Cottom. A fully ordained Catholic priest, Cottom was the younger brother of John Cottom,[22] who succeeded Thomas Jenkins as Stratford's school-master in September 1579 – probably too late to have instructed the fifteen-year-old Shakespeare. On 5 June 1580 Thomas Cottom left Rheims for England carrying a letter and religious gifts for Debdale's family in Shottery, but before he could reach them he was arrested and cast into the Tower, the Debdale letter thereby being intercepted and preserved.

Thomas Cottom was executed on 30 May 1582 at Tyburn, following hard upon the similar martyrdom of his fellow Jesuit Campion the previous December. Debdale, who had unwittingly crossed to England just a fortnight after Cottom, was likewise arrested and imprisoned in the Gatehouse at Westminster. His Shottery family did not even learn of his whereabouts until more than a year later, when they sent him a letter and food parcel via Stratford's regular carrier, William Greenaway. Although later temporarily released, Debdale was soon rearrested during a later crackdown and tried and executed in 1586. As for Stratford schoolmaster John Cottom, clearly his brother's execution as 'a traitor' was incompatible with his continuance at his post. Sometime after September 1581 he either resigned or was asked to resign, subsequently inheriting his father's lands in Lancashire and there, on safer ground, overtly declaring his Catholicism.

There is one element in John Shakespeare's *Testament* that deserves mention, not least because it seems previously to have been overlooked by other writers. As evident from the text of the Folger Library's copy a space was left for the testator to indicate the name of his patron saint. In Malone's transcript of John Shakespeare's lost original [see Appendix C: Miscellaneous Documents, page 469] we are able to see that John or someone acting on his behalf inserted 'Saint Winefride' as John's patron saint. The interesting point is that Saint Winifred is patron saint of North Wales, her shrine at Holywell, Flintshire, having a reputedly miraculous healing spring that was a most popular place of pilgrimage for Catholics both before and after the Reformation. Did John and family perhaps visit this on occasion? Curiously, William will later exhibit some otherwise unexplained links with this part of North Wales. His 'The Phoenix and the Turtle', for instance, was dedicated to Sir John Salisbury of nearby Lleweni and one of the tributes to Shakespeare in the First Folio is by an obscure Hugh Holland from Denbighshire.

Now nothing that we have revealed up to this point can be said to have proved John Shakespeare's religious affiliations, still less those of his eldest son. In fact, in William's case, he must have attended many Protestant services for his subsequent plays are full of allusions to Protestant homilies and the words of the Protestant Prayerbook –

though this proves nothing as he would simply have been fulfilling what everyone was required to do to comply with the law. And equally too insubstantial to support certain Catholicism is a tradition that William received his early religious training from an old Benedictine monk, Dom Thomas Combe, who was apparently related to the wealthy Combe family of Stratford.

But hopefully at the very least we have succeeded in establishing that the atmosphere in which William grew up was far more subtle and politically charged than that normally to be expected of a simple glover's (or butcher's) shop as conveyed by too many biographers. Arguably, John Shakespeare was not the insignificant man as usually portrayed, and there was a lot more behind his seeming 'fall' than might be apparent from the historical record.

Ironically, if John's fall was only a semblance, so too may have been the altogether more Biblical 'fall' that occurred to William at this point. Again the documentary evidence as to exactly what happened is predictably incomplete, but sufficient information survives to form a reasonably cogent picture.

The first piece of evidence consists of an entry for 27 November 1582 in the register of the Bishop of Worcester for the granting of a special marriage licence, one whereby a couple could be married without the usual triple calling of the banns. According to the entry, the licence was to be 'inter Willelmum Shaxpere et Annam Whateley de Temple Grafton', that is, between William Shakespeare and Anne Whateley of Temple Grafton. The second document, only discovered in 1836 by book collector Sir Thomas Phillips, is dated a day later than the first, and consists of a bond for £40 lodged by two worthy Stratford farmers, Fulke Sandells and John Richardson, indemnifying the Bishop against any impediment that 'William Shagspere' on the one part, and 'Anne Hathwey of Stratford in the Diocese of Worcester, maiden' might 'lawfully solemnise matrimony together and in the same afterwards remain and continue like man and wife'. Sandells and Richardson are known to have been associates of the Shottery farmer Richard Hathaway who had died that very July, leaving a will stipulating that in the event of his daughter Anne getting married she was to receive ten marks, or £6.13s.4d. on her wedding day.

Now the first curiosity is that the woman's name linked with William's on 27 November was Anne Whateley, whereas a day later it was Anne Hathaway. All sorts of skulduggery has been suggested to account for this. Was William's true beloved the mysterious Anne Whateley, only for him to be forced into marrying Anne Hathaway?

In fact, the explanation seems to be the simple one of clerical incompetence. Worthy of a place in Shakespeare's comedies, the Worcester registry office clerk can be seen elsewhere to have written Baker for Barbar, Darby for Bradeley, and Edgcock for Elcock. Since on the same day a William Whateley of Crowle was involved in a long-standing tithe dispute, it was probably this name on the clerk's mind that caused him absent-mindedly to write it in place of Hathaway.

More interesting is the clerk's attribution of Anne Whateley/ Hathaway to Temple Grafton. Although this may simply have been a slip of his pen, Shottery residents were part of Stratford-upon-Avon parish but the tiny church at Temple Grafton was closer. As no entry for William and Anne's marriage appears in the Stratford register, they may well have married at Temple Grafton, where no records survive for the period. From a highly Puritan-minded report about Warwickshire's clergy made in 1586,[23] we know something about the incumbent at Temple Grafton. His name was John Frith and according to the report's compiler, he was 'an old priest and unsound in religion; he can neither preach nor read well, his chiefest trade is to cure birds that are either hurt or diseased, for which purpose many do usually repair to him'. In other words, he was a Catholic, but too old and in too small and unimportant a parish for it to be worth turning him out of his living. The possibility must therefore be allowed for that Temple Grafton was chosen for Shakespeare's marriage specifically because of Frith's Catholicism, and that the marriage missed the official record for the very same reason.

Whatever the circumstances, the need for a special licence alerts us to one thing: that in November 1582 there was some compelling reason for Anne and William's official marriage – whatever and wherever the religious ceremony had been celebrated – to be conducted in haste. And we do not have to look far for that reason. In the baptismal section of the register of Stratford's Holy Trinity Church, under the date 26 May 1583 we find 'Susanna, daughter to William Shakspeare'. Working backwards from this, it is apparent that young Shakespeare, unmarried and three years before the age of his majority, must have bedded Anne the previous September, just two months after Anne's father's death. By November, when that special licence was being sought in Worcester, Anne's condition was clearly already known and the pressures for a 'shotgun' official wedding were inevitably at their most intense.

A glance at the wording on Anne Hathaway Shakespeare's gravestone, to the left of her husband's in Holy Trinity Church, reveals something else. It tells us that Anne 'departed this life the 6th day of August 1623, being of the age of 67 years'. Assuming that this is accurate, if Anne was 67 in 1623 she must have been born in 1556, eight years before William, making her eight years his senior. Of the exact dynamics of this relationship – the extent to which an 'on-the-shelf' Anne may even have lured the young William into her bed – again we can only conjecture. But unlike others of the time in the same situation, even ones of far more exalted station, William certainly did the honourable thing.

That he and Anne agreed to the name Susanna for their first-born is worthy of at least passing mention, for it was not a common one in Elizabethan times. Originating in the Old Testament, it carries a hint of Puritanism, possibly attributable to the Hathaways from the little that can be deduced from Anne's father's will. Despite their impetuous parenthood, that the couple settled down into some sort of married life is evident from the fact that just two years later, on 2 February 1585, the Stratford parish register had another christening to record: 'Hamnet & Judeth, sonne and daughter to William Shakspere'.

Twins! With still two months to run before his twenty-first birthday William had become the father of three. The Christian names chosen in this instance were those of a local couple, Hamnet and Judith Sadler in High Street, who must have been chosen as godparents. It is perhaps significant that, although the vicar who would have conducted the baptism at Holy Trinity was a newly appointed Puritan, Richard Barton, Hamnet and Judith Sadler would later appear on the lists of Stratford's known Catholics.

Difficult though it has been to be certain of anything throughout this early phase of William's life, at least we can be sure of one thing. Fatherhood of three could only concentrate wonderfully even the most impetuous young man's mind on what he should do to support his new family. And it is in trying to determine precisely what William did next that we approach yet another of the mysteries with which his life is so consistently shrouded.

CHAPTER 5

'As an Unperfect Actor on the Stage'

The details of Shakespeare's life continue to be elusive. Between the christening of twins Hamnet and Judith and the first clear reference to William working as an actor in London in 1592, there yawn seven so-called lost years. Arguably among the most formative years of his life, any direct contemporary reference to where and with whom he was working during this time is entirely lacking.

Nor, when we fall back upon anecdotal stories from the decades immediately following Shakespeare's death do these shed much light. From as late as 1681, but earlier than Rowe's first biography, is a modicum of information in the manuscript of late seventeenth-century gossip John Aubrey's *Brief Lives*. Now separated from the main manuscript and preserved in the Bodleian Library as a specially mounted page, it tells us:

> Mr William Shakespear was born at Stratford upon Avon in the County of Warwick. His father was a butcher, and I have been told heretofore by some of the neighbours that when he was a boy he exercised his father's trade, but when he killed a calf he would do it in high style and make a speech.... This William being inclined naturally to poetry and acting, came to London I guess about eighteen, and was an actor at one of the play-houses and did act exceedingly well.... He began early to make essays at dramatic poetry, which at that time was very low, and his plays took well....[1]

Aubrey concluded with a morsel which he attributed, in a margin note, to 'Mr Beeston', identifiable as William Beeston, son of Christopher Beeston, who was one of the lesser members of the acting company for which Shakespeare worked in maturity:

> Though as Ben Jonson says of him that he had but little Latin and

less Greek, he understood Latin pretty well, for he had been in his younger years a schoolmaster in the country.

Now the problem is to what extent Aubrey can be believed. He went around assiduously gathering information about people of note from anyone and everyone who might have known something about them. But he was none too discriminating: even one of his former friends described him as 'exceedingly credulous', 'shiftless . . . roving and maggoty-headed, and sometimes little better than crazed'. As we have already seen, he was quite wrong in his information that Shakespeare's father was a butcher. So how accurate is the rest?

In fact, his idea that the young Shakespeare might at some stage have worked as a 'schoolmaster in the country' – perhaps as an usher in a grammar school, or a private tutor to a wealthy family – is one that Shakespearean scholars have warmed to. They have noted his apparent familiarity with the profession as exhibited by characters in his plays such as the pedant Holofernes in *Love's Labour's Lost*, the Latin tutor Sir Hugh Evans in *The Merry Wives of Windsor*, and the fact of Lucentio disguising himself as a tutor in *The Taming of the Shrew*. They have also noted that while he panned the Protestant Hugh Evans, he was altogether more sympathetic to Lucentio as 'one that have long been studying at Rheims, so cunning in Greek, Latin and other languages'. Since Rheims was a training centre for most of England's covert Catholic priests, twentieth-century scholars Frances A. Yates[2] and John Dover Wilson[3] have both suggested that Shakespeare may have been tutor to a Catholic family.

Almost equally favoured has been the already mentioned suggestion that Shakespeare somehow familiarised himself with law, perhaps by working as a lawyer's clerk. From the most casual perusal of his plays it is obvious how many feature vivid trial scenes, the one in *The Merchant of Venice* being merely the most famous. He would frequently use legal and particularly conveyancing terms, even in the most inappropriate circumstances, as in Romeo's talk of 'engrossing Death', and having the Greeks and Trojans in *Troilus and Cressida* speak of fee farm and fee simple. Former barrister Malone surmised as early as 1790 that Shakespeare had most likely been 'employed, while he yet remained at Stratford, in the office of some country attorney, who was at the same time a petty conveyancer, and perhaps also the Seneschal of some manor-court'.[4] Present-day lawyers, particularly American ones, have almost queued up to agree with him.

But this sort of clue-searching from the plays has more than a few dangers. For instance, reviewing the realistic war scenes in *Henry V* and elsewhere, Duff Cooper drew on his experience of World War I trenches to argue that Shakespeare enlisted with the Earl of Leicester to fight in his expedition to the Low Countries in the mid-1580s. On the grounds that 'a man of his intelligence was not likely to remain for long a private soldier', Duff Cooper even promoted him to sergeant during this expedition.[5] Other authors have had Shakespeare conscripted into the civil guard when the Armada threatened in 1588.[6] According to canoeing expert William Bliss he ran away from home in 1577 when he was just thirteen to sail around the world on Sir Francis Drake's famous voyage on the *Golden Hind*. This is apparently proved by a reference in *As You Like It* to 'remainder biscuit', a variety purportedly carried only on very long voyages.[7] On the grounds of Shakespeare's plays' extraordinary political insights, former government minister Enoch Powell has insisted that Shakespeare must either have been very close to politics or been a politician himself. Overall, civil servant Sir Edmund Chambers' advice is safest: 'it's no use guessing'.

The one universally agreed fact about Shakespeare, even among the Oxfordians and their ilk, is that Shakespeare was an actor. The only area of uncertainty is when he developed his interest in this calling. And here, for all John Aubrey's faults, he provided a highly important snippet, the significance of which he did not realise, because he did not understand it. This is his remark, following on from his misinformation about John Shakespeare having been a butcher, that when William, following his father's trade 'killed a calf, he would do it in a high style, and make a speech'. The picture that Shakespeare biographers generally evoke from this is the rosy, Merrie England one of the humble Stratford-upon-Avon butcher's/glover's shop, and embryonic prodigy William, in the act of slaughtering a calf for its skin, amazing his parents by declaiming a poetic funeral oration on the poor creature. And indeed some very erudite scholars have accepted it at face value.

In fact, as Aubrey was clearly unaware, 'Killing the Calf' was a piece of sixteenth-century popular travelling theatre, akin to Punch and Judy. A clown–ventriloquist would have a comic argument with the dummy head of a calf pushed through a curtain. When the calf's answers had provoked him beyond endurance, the clown would seize a wooden sword and strike off its head, which would then tumble onto the stage, to inevitable squeals from the audience. The 1521 Court accounts for Mary Tudor, when she was a five-year-old princess, show that during the Christmas entertainments put on for her at Windsor an entertainer was paid 'for Killing of a Calf before my Lady's grace behind a cloth'.[8] That Shakespeare, in adult life, was certainly familiar with this piece of illusion is quite evident from the *Hamlet* Act III scene with Polonius:

> *Hamlet*: My lord, you play'd once i' th' university, you say?
> *Polonius*: That did I, my lord, and was accounted a good actor.
> *Hamlet*: What did you enact?
> *Polonius*: I did enact Julius Caesar. I was kill'd i' th' Capitol. Brutus kill'd me.
> *Hamlet*: It was a brute part of him to kill so capital a calf there.[9]

In his usual muddled way, then, Aubrey may well have retailed someone's genuine memory of the young Shakespeare performing such an entertainment for his family and friends, much along the lines of the impromptu play-acting he would have Falstaff and Prince Hal indulge in together, impersonating Henry IV in *Henry IV Part I*. And here we arrive at something central to our understanding of Shakespeare: his apparent discovery at an early age of the thrill an actor gets from so suspending an audience's disbelief that they believe in the dramatic illusion he is creating, simple or sophisticated, laughing, crying, holding their breath or gasping with horror, just as if what they were watching was real.

As we will discover, everything that has come down to us from Shakespeare's plays suggests their author was a man who enjoyed just such a process, a man well-grounded in the business of being an actor. Hence however fragile Aubrey's anecdote might seem, it has the backing of the whole ethos of Shakespeare's works to suggest that Shakespeare's love of creating dramatic illusion began at an early age.

Now if this is so, what was the state of the English theatre as the young Shakespeare first encountered it? People from even the best of Church of England education backgrounds often fondly suppose that there had been virtually nothing in the way of English popular theatre before Shakespeare. Mention Catholic Mystery plays and Morality plays and they may conjure up an image of Bible stories performed by people on painted carts dressed up as devils with fireworks exploding out of their bottoms. Only those who have witnessed modern revivals of such Mystery plays take a different view, as, for instance, attested by Bristol drama lecturer, Professor Glynne Wickham:

> Confronted with one of the most moving dramatic experiences of their lives, audiences have paused to ask how it came about that they should never have been told what they might expect of these mediaeval plays, or why it was that they had been so seriously misled by historians and critics.[10]

The fact is that English drama had been flourishing for several hundred years before Shakespeare – initially under the auspices of the Roman Catholic Church. It began with re-enactments in Latin of the Passion and other stories as part of church services. These developed into productions on holy days by members of the mediaeval Craft Guilds, performed in English in great cities such as Coventry, York and Chester. Although performed on high carts, the stage-craft of these was often highly sophisticated: systems of weights and pulleys were used to resurrect Jesus from the tomb, or to enable gilded winged angels to float from aloft, and John the Baptist's beheading was often re-enacted by deftly switching a false severed head and headless cadaver for the actor playing John.

Even impeccable authorities like the *Oxford Dictionary of the Christian Church* like to suggest that Mystery plays simply 'decayed' after the Reformation, but this is not so. As shown by Father H. C. Gardiner in *Mysteries' End: An Investigation of the Last Days of the Medieval Religious Stage* they had to be forcibly suppressed during Elizabeth's reign on exactly the same grounds that the abbeys had been destroyed and the churches despoiled of all their belongings: that they were 'idolatrous' and 'papistical'. Against considerable local opposition, Chester lost its right to perform its Mystery plays in 1574, York in 1575, Wakefield in 1576 and Coventry in 1581 (when Shakespeare was seventeen). As Coventry is only twenty miles from Stratford it is most likely that Shakespeare saw the Coventry Cycle before it was suppressed, particularly since in *Hamlet* he has Hamlet advise his actors not to 'out-Herod Herod' – a reference to the

Biblical Herod at his most tyrannical in one of the Mystery plays. And the *Macbeth* Porter scene is widely regarded as being derived from the Mystery plays' Harrowing of Hell.

No better illustration can be provided of the sort of popular theatre that began to fill the vacuum left by the Mystery plays than a lively painting[11] by Pieter Brueghel the Younger (born the same year as Shakespeare), now in the City Gallery of Auckland, New Zealand [see pl. 13]. Entitled 'A Village Fair', although the painting's setting is Brueghel's native Flanders, it shows a small town arguably not dissimilar to the Stratford of Shakespeare's day, in which, amidst festivities, apparently in honour of St Hubert and St Anthony, can be seen the open air performance of a play, on a makeshift stage, just in front of a ramshackle inn.

In typical Brueghel fashion, it is all rumbustious stuff. Except for a few people perched on the roof of the inn, the members of the audience can be seen standing around a stage that is surfaced with what seem to be boards or planks. The level of the stage is only just lower than the audience's heads and although for us this might seem surprisingly high, it would have suited a standing audience. In a similar painting by Brueghel's father, dated 1559, a rear view of a street-play performance reveals that the stage boards are set on beer barrels. That the same method was used in England is evident from a passage in Ben Jonson's *The Poetaster*. Here a down-at-heel actor is told that, if he wants to improve his luck he should go to a certain successful playwright so that he will no longer need to travel with a clapped-out horse, with his shoes full of grit 'and stalk upon boards and barrel heads to an old crack'd trumpet'.[12] Suddenly the theatrical expression 'treading the boards' takes on a whole new meaning.

Inns were chosen as venues for performances because their galleried yards could be quickly adapted. Also, receipts could be shared with the landlords who inevitably welcomed thirsty captive custom. Both the Brueghel paintings show a curtained room behind the actors from which a prompter appears, and which was clearly the actors' makeshift dressing-room, referred to in sixteenth-century parlance as the tiring house.

This is the image we should hold in our minds when trying to visualise the arrival in Stratford of the sort of company that might first have sparked off Shakespeare's idea to become an actor. As part of their advance publicity the performers would have noisily heralded their approach with drums and trumpets played by the musicians among them. They often wore gaudy suits that made them stand out from normal citizens, and their first obligation was to call upon the town's chief citizen – in Stratford's case the Bailiff. This was in order to declare under which great Lord's name they travelled, and to give the most senior citizen and his colleagues a sample performance. They would have given this in Stratford's Guild Hall, and only afterwards could the players gain approval for their money-making public shows of the kind depicted by the Brueghels.

Thanks to Stratford Corporation records, we know that when John Shakespeare was the town's Bailiff in 1568–9 he hosted the first two companies of this kind to be recorded in the town. To the company who called themselves the Queen's (not to be confused with the 1580s company of that name), John approved a munificent gratuity of nine shillings. To the other, the Earl of Worcester's Men, he awarded a miserly one shilling, the lowest on record in Stratford's accounts.[13] This is a delightful indication that John had some strong views on the varying qualities of working actors, and we might be forgiven for envisaging the five-year-old William sitting on his father's knee while watching these performances, or John certainly talking about them to his young son when he returned home.

But if William did become attracted to joining a professional theatre company which did he choose, and when? One suggestion has been that as early as 1581, even before he was married, he joined a company of players owned by Alexander Hoghton, a Catholic gentleman of Lea Hall near Preston. Hoghton, in his will of 1581,[14] commends a certain William Shakeshafte whom he says 'now dwelleth with me' and who seems to have been a young actor, to the special care and protection of Sir Thomas Hesketh of nearby Rufford Hall, who, like Hoghton, maintained a small company of players and musicians. One school of thought identifies William Shakeshafte as our William Shakespeare but although, as we shall show later, our Shakespeare exhibits some definite connection with Lancashire, and indeed with Rufford, Shakeshafte has been found to be too common a Lancashire name for the identification to carry conviction.

Of the companies who came to Stratford during the 1570s there were various visits of ones travelling under the names of the Earls of Leicester, Warwick and Worcester. In the years 1583 and 1584, when William and Anne's young Susanna would have been teething, there arrived the companies of the Earls of Oxford, Essex, and again of

Worcester. In the pre-Armada year of December 1586 to December 1587, while Hamnet and Judith were still very young, five companies passed through: the Queen's, the Earl of Essex's, the Earl of Leicester's, Lord Stafford's and another unnamed, and it is among these that we might endeavour to identify the one that Shakespeare joined.

In this regard, the premier acting troupe of the 1580s was undoubtedly the Queen's Men, formed in 1583 by Elizabeth's Master of the Revels, Edmund Tilney, around the time of the demise of the former Lord Chamberlain, the Earl of Sussex. According to an insert in the 1615 edition of Stow's *Annales* relating to Elizabeth's reign:

> Comedians and stage-players of former time were very poor and ignorant . . . but being now grown very skilful and exquisite actors . . . they were entertained into the service of divers great lords: out of which companies there were twelve of the best chosen. . . . Among these twelve players were two rare men, viz. Thomas Wilson, for a quick, delicate, refined, extemporal wit, and Richard Tarlton, for a wondrous plentiful pleasant extemporal wit. . . . He was so beloved that men use his picture for their signs. . . .[15]

Richard Tarlton, besides being a qualified master of fencing and writer of plays such as *The Seven Deadly Sins*, was the sort of comedian who made people laugh the moment he peeked out from behind a curtain. A contemporary drawing [see pl. 14][16] shows him as a short man with a broad face, curly hair, comically attired in a russet suit and buttoned cap, playing on a drum and pipe. It has been suggested that he was the fellow 'of infinite jest' whom Shakespeare had in mind for the Yorick of *Hamlet*'s famous graveyard scene.

In 1587 when Tarlton and his Queen's Men were performing in Abingdon they proved so popular that the crowd, in their eagerness, broke the windows of the town's Guild Hall. But during this same tour the company also suffered a serious set-back when at Thame, Oxfordshire, actor John Towne killed fellow actor William Knell, robbing the Queen's Men of one of its leading lights (Towne was acquitted for acting in self-defence). The incident has given rise to speculation that, since the company visited Stratford during this same tour, Shakespeare might have been recruited as Knell's replacement.[17] But there is a total lack of evidence that Shakespeare ever belonged to the Queen's Men. Nor is he likely to have been one of the

Admiral's Men, the company for which Philip Henslowe acted as business manager, because his name doesn't appear anywhere in Henslowe's well-preserved accounts.

However, even though it has to be emphasised that there is no evidence that Shakespeare belonged to any company before 1592, one document is too often neglected for its historical value. This is the list of 'principal actors' in Shakespeare's plays, as published as part of the introduction to the 1623 First Folio of his works [see fig 3 overleaf]. At first sight this appears to be a haphazard collection of names, with only a few readily recognisable, such as Richard Burbage, John Heminges and Henry Condell; more careful scrutiny reveals that it has an order. The names following Shakespeare's own at the head of the first column are all of actors associated with him from his earliest documented emergence onto the London acting scene, some of whom died in the 1590s while others outlived him. Those at the bottom of the second column are all relative newcomers who joined his acting company when, as the King's Men, it was better documented towards the end of his career. In a very rough-and-ready way, therefore, the list represents a mini-chronology of Shakespeare's principal actor associates, at least from the time he began writing plays. Adding to its authority is that it was compiled by two of those very associates – Heminges and Condell – who trod the boards with him throughout the entire known period of his acting and writing career.

Now crude as this is, if we are prepared to accept it as at least a pointer to the acting company with which Shakespeare might have been first associated, we find in fact that it is surprisingly revelatory. Of immediate significance are the omissions. Had Shakespeare worked with the Queen's Men, it is hardly likely that that company's 'greats', such as Richard Tarlton and Robert Wilson would have been omitted. Yet these do not appear.

Equally important are the inclusions. Looking at the First Folio first column, and setting aside Shakespeare himself and his two editors, Heminges and Condell (who would naturally want themselves somewhere to the fore), there appear the names Richard Burbage, Augustine Phillips, William Kemp, Thomas Pope and George Bryan. Of these, considerably the youngest, though ultimately the greatest, was Richard Burbage, who became an actor following in the steps of his father, James Burbage.

James Burbage was recorded as one of the five founding players of

The Workes of William Shakespeare,

containing all his Comedies, Histories, and
Tragedies: Truely set forth, according to their first
O R J G J N A L L.

The Names of the Principall Actors
in all these Playes.

Illiam Shakespeare.

Richard Burbadge.

John Hemmings.

Augustine Phillips.

William Kempt.

Thomas Poope.

George Bryan.

Henry Condell.

William Slye.

Richard Cowly.

John Lowine.

Samuell Crosse.

Alexander Cooke.

Samuel Gilburne.

Robert Armin.

William Ostler.

Nathan Field.

John Underwood.

Nicholas Tooley.

William Ecclestone.

Joseph Taylor.

Robert Benfield.

Robert Goughe.

Richard Robinson.

Iohn Shancke.

Iohn Rice.

Fig 3
List of the principal actors in Shakespeare's plays, as published in
the First Folio of Shakespeare's works, 1623.

the Earl of Leicester's Men in 1574. In 1586 we find the names of Thomas Pope, George Bryan and William Kemp likewise among a troupe of Leicester's Men who gave performances in the Low Countries as part of the part-military, part-diplomatic expedition led by Leicester on which Duff Cooper supposed Shakespeare to have served as a sergeant. In a letter during this expedition, Sir Philip Sidney spoke of 'Will my Lord of Leicester's jesting player'[18] which Cooper took to have been an allusion to Shakespeare, but which almost certainly refers to William Kemp, subsequently noted for his comedy roles. But, intriguingly, one of company's venues was the recently built Danish castle of Helsingør, better known to us as Hamlet's 'Elsinore'. Another of their appearances was before King Christian I of Saxony, who personally recorded how they entertained him with instrumental music and acrobatic performances.

James Burbage does not seem to have gone overseas on this occasion and, almost certainly, at least part of the company continued to tour England, for they are recorded as doing this while the rest were away. On Pope, Bryan and Kemp's return in spring 1587 the members all seem to have reassembled, and the company's summer tour took in not only Stratford, as earlier mentioned, but also Coventry and Bath to the west. They even got as far north as Lancashire where, in July, they were giving performances for Henry, fourth Earl of Derby and his family at their magnificent castle, Lathom.

These performances must have impressed, because upon the Earl of Leicester's death in 1588 Burbage's company was transferred to the patronage of Henry Earl of Derby's son and heir, Ferdinando Lord Strange, thereupon becoming known as Lord Strange's Men. It was under this company's name that the Burbages, Pope, Bryan, and Kemp performed during the next years – a period during which even the most conservative scholars recognise that Shakespeare wrote his first plays. It is therefore most likely that the first company Shakespeare would have joined is the one that began as the Earl of Leicester's Men and became Lord Strange's Men. And given that Shakespeare would necessarily have joined in a junior apprentice-like capacity, there would be no reason for his name to appear in documentary sources during these earliest years.

So what do we know of the Earl of Leicester's/Lord Strange's Men? First to be stressed is that its effective founder and leader, James Burbage, was a real pioneer in developing what may be best termed the popular theatre. As part and parcel of the same Puritanical attitudes that had outlawed the Mystery plays, during much of Elizabeth's reign acting on the public stage lacked the social respectability it is often supposed to have had by those unfamiliar with the Elizabethan period.

At the universities, well-born young men might take part in elegant classical comedies and tragedies, but these were mostly performed in respectable Greek and Latin, were held in university halls, and were enormously costly productions, performed for visiting dignitaries that might include the Queen. Even so, it was only the less Puritanically-minded colleges – such as St John's and Christ Church at Oxford, and St John's and Trinity at Cambridge – that were prepared to put on such spectacles. Likewise at Court and in aristocratic private houses companies of boy actors might be commissioned to perform dramatic entertainments of a suitably elevated nature.

But attitudes towards public theatre of the kind depicted by Brueghel were quite different. Both Oxford and Cambridge university authorities paid acting companies not to bring productions into their towns. The substantial Puritan element in the country, which was particularly strong among London's civic authorities where shopkeepers resented their employees and customers going off to the theatres, wanted them banned altogether on the grounds of popery, idolatory, whoredom and immorality. Thus in 1574 one Geoffrey Fenton fulminated:

> players ... corrupt good moralities by wanton shows and plays. They ought not to be suffered to profane the Sabbath day in such sports, and much less to lose time on the days of travail [work]. ...[19]

In 1582 Stephen Gosson stressed the rootless background of those that took up play-acting:

> Most of the players have been either men of occupations which they have foresaken to live by playing, or common minstrels, or trained up from their childhood to this abominable exercise and have now no other way to get their living.[20]

Earlier, in 1572 Elizabeth's Parliament passed an Act demanding that all 'common players . . . and minstrels not belonging to any baron of this realm, or to any other honourable personage of greater degree . . . shall be . . . deemed rogues, vagabonds and sturdy beggars.' The prescribed penalties for such vagabondage were severe:

> when one shall be taken, he shall be stripped naked from his middle upwards and shall be openly whipped until his or her body be bloody, and forthwith be sent from parish to parish the next, straightway to the parish where he was born. . . .[21]

It was precisely because of such legislation that the acting companies visiting Stratford and elsewhere all carried the names of elevated individuals in Elizabeth's Court, for without such noble patronage they were indeed, in the eyes of the time, no better than vagabonds.

So in what way can James Burbage, as head of the company that Shakespeare is likeliest to have joined, be said to have been a pioneer? It is quite clear that Burbage, perhaps more than any other individual of his time, aimed to elevate the theatre from its popular boards-on-barrels ethos and into something rather more respectable. He had begun modestly enough. From an isolated document in the court books of the Carpenters' Company[22] it would seem that as early as 1567 he formed a partnership with his grocer brother-in-law John Brayne, to create what was almost certainly England's first permanent playhouse 'at the house called the Red Lion' in Stepney, beyond Whitechapel to London's east.

Of this venture only the meagrest of details are known.[23] Indeed Burbage's name does not appear in the Carpenters' Company document, and all we do know is that the theatre had a five-foot-high 'scaffold' or stage with a trapdoor (it is the only Elizabethan theatre for which we actually know the height of the stage), and a 'turret' or tower which seems to have incorporated the actor's tiring house or dressing-room.

But, two years after the passing of the 1572 Vagabonds Act, Burbage successfully sought and obtained the Earl of Leicester's protective patronage for his players, the patent for this being the first such known. And in 1576, again in partnership with grocer John Brayne, he negotiated with landowner Giles Allen a twenty-one-year lease on an undeveloped site in Shoreditch, a little to the north of the Bishopsgate entrance to the City of London. On this he built what became called, simply, the Theatre.

Now, thanks to a variety of sources usefully brought together by the scholar Herbert Berry,[24] we know a reasonable amount about James Burbage's Shoreditch Theatre. We know, for instance, that it was of a timber-framed construction, such that could be taken apart and reassembled on another site – and this is just what happened to it. On the expiry of Allen's twenty-one-year lease Burbage and his company took the Theatre to Southwark to be rebuilt as the famous Globe. An engraving preserved in the University Library at Utrecht, Holland, [see pl. 15] shows the Theatre in its Shoreditch setting towering above the roofs of the surrounding houses, a flag flying from the tower that protects its unseen stage.[25] From court cases relating to it, we know that it had a yard for those members of the audience who stood, an 'attiring house or place where the players make them ready', and 'galleries' from which richer patrons, for an extra payment, could sit and watch the performance protected from the weather.

The location is also interesting. It was built among the ruins of Holywell Priory, home to a community of nuns up to the time of Henry VIII's Dissolution of the Monasteries, whereupon even the priory's original holy well became reduced to feeding a horse pond. The proximity of this priory was one of the reasons for Burbage's choice of location since, in common with other such monastic sites, the priory's environs still carried the status of a 'Liberty', a status that once gave the Catholic Church legal immunity from interference. Although with the Reformation and the selling-off of the Church's lands this Liberty theoretically passed to the Crown, those within a Liberty were still free of the jurisdiction of London's ever Puritanical civic authorities. The site of the Theatre can still be identified today [see fig 4 opposite]. Although the landmarks that Shakespeare would have known have long been obliterated by unsightly later developments (not least, the railway line from Liverpool Street), the priory lives on in the place name, Holywell Lane, and the site of the Theatre itself lies somewhere below the premises of old-established hardware factors A. Oakden & Sons on the corner of Curtain Road and New Inn Yard. Indeed, a somewhat dingy plaque remarks this fact.[26]

If then we have been right that it was with Burbage's company that Shakespeare began as an actor, then it may well have been on the stage of the Shoreditch Theatre that he began to learn what was expected of him. Scholars disagree as to whether he would

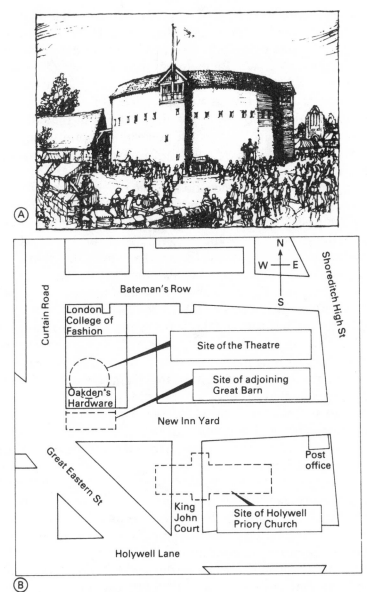

Fig 4
THE THEATRE, SHOREDITCH
As built by James Burbage and John Brayne in 1576.

Ⓐ Reconstruction of its original appearance, by C. Walter Hodges.

Ⓑ Location in relation to present-day London, after London County Council survey of London 1922.

All sites are approximations only.

have had to serve any sort of apprenticeship as an actor, too many of them fondly imagining that an actor's skills can be picked up by anyone overnight. The much under-valued American scholar Professor T. W. Baldwin, author of *The Organisation and Personnel of the Shakespearean Company*,[27] felt sure that Shakespeare must have served an apprenticeship. Civil servant and critic Sir Edmund Chambers disagreed, pointing out that acting was not a profession specified in the acts governing apprenticeship, and that actors would have been unlikely to have bothered with such formalities.

Despite Chambers' eminence, on balance the evidence is in favour of Baldwin's view that Shakespeare's company did indeed operate an apprenticeship system, and that Shakespeare would have had to serve something along these lines regardless of the age at which he joined. Almost every craft at the time had an apprenticeship system, and Burbage would have wanted his company to earn the same professional respect. The Chambers view also ignores the fact that Augustine Phillips, a member of Burbage's company, actually left forty shillings in his will of 1605 to 'Samuel Gilborne, my late apprentice'.[28] Also, the Henslowe papers at Dulwich College reveal a clear hierarchy within Philip Henslowe's Admiral's Men, a carefully graded structure that ranged from young beginners to hired men, to veterans who expected to be addressed as Master.

There also survives in Henslowe's papers a contract for an actor named Robert Dawes that enables us to see some of the rules that even experienced actors were expected to subject themselves to upon joining an acting company:

> the said Robert Dawes shall play with such company for three years and shall at all times attend all such rehearsals which shall the night before the rehearsal be given publicly out. And if at any time he shall fail to come at the hour appointed, then he shall pay twelve pence. And if he come not before the said rehearsal is ended two shillings. If [he] shall not every day whereon any play is to be played be ready apparelled to begin the play at the hour of three o'clock he shall pay three shillings. And if that he happen to be overcome with drink at the time when he ought to play, by the judgement of four of the said company, he shall pay ten shillings. And if he shall fail to come during any play, having no license or just excuse of sickness, he is to pay twenty shillings. And if he shall

at any time after the play is ended go out with any playhouse apparel on his body he shall forfeit the sum of £40 of lawful money.[29]

The need for such severe disciplines (the lowest fine, twelve pence, represents two days of an ordinary man's wage), becomes all too apparent when, as the Henslowe Diary reveals, it was commonplace for a London-based theatrical company to put on six different plays during a working week of six afternoons, and over a period of six months to stage some thirty different plays, about half of these new titles. Many would contain complicated action, sword fights, fits of madness, rapid changes of costume, mood and tempo, etc. As any present-day professional actor will instantly recognise, the pressures of such a programme would have been intense, demanding the strongest concentration, physical agility, personal self-discipline, and closest interdependence between performers, particularly since doubling-up of parts was commonplace.

Added to such demands upon the actor were the peculiar physical ones of the Elizabethan popular theatre. Whether performers were playing in an inn-yard or in a purpose-built Theatre such as Burbage's at Shoreditch, the actor had his audience ranged around him on three sides, with many standing. Not only did he have to project himself to all three sides, he was extremely close to those he was entertaining and as performances were continuous, with no intervals, he had no respite from the pressure of constantly keeping their attention. Adding to the difficulty was the distraction of vendors plying the audience with drinks and snacks.

One possibly surprising feature from the Dawes contract is the huge fine that an actor was expected to pay should he misappropriate any of the costumes. In fact the reason for this is evident enough when we consider the immense importance attached to dress as an indication of status in Shakespeare's time. In order to impersonate a king or a member of the aristocracy, an actor had to wear suitably magnificent – and expensive – clothing to carry conviction. Although one source tells us of actors buying their costumes cheaply from gentleman's servants who had been bequeathed hand-me-downs, the Dulwich College papers show Henslowe's son-in-law Edward Alleyn spending £16 for 'one cloak of velvet with a cape embroidered with gold, pearls and red stones, and one robe of cloth of gold'; and £20 and ten shillings for 'a black velvet cloak with sleeves embroidered all with silver and gold, lined with black satin striped with gold'.[30] The latter cost represented a year's salary for an Elizabethan vicar or schoolmaster.

Of the audiences before whom the actor, experienced or otherwise, had to perform, snippets of information survive from which some picture can be built up. They had to be people who were able to take some leisure time in the afternoon since that is when, in an age before electricity and when candle lighting was an expensive luxury, public theatre performances were ordinarily held. This is why the Dawes contract, for one, demands of its actor employee 'be ready apparelled to begin the play at the hour of three o'clock'. Women were able to attend plays, but the social norms of the age expected these, whatever their social rank, to be accompanied, since a woman on her own was automatically thought to be a prostitute. A penny, one sixth of an ordinary man's daily wage, bought a standing space in the yard around the stage. A further penny, handed to a collector at the bottom of the stairs to the galleries, purchased a gallery seat, which provided protection from the elements, though it removed the spectator a little further from the action. Another penny secured a cushion.

We have no idea what, as an apprentice actor, Shakespeare might have been paid, but for regular actors the system, at least at Burbage's Theatre, seems to have been that the profits were divided between the company so that the players received a share of the money from those who stayed in the yard, while proprietor Burbage and his partner Brayne (later to be succeeded by Brayne's widow), received the moneys from those who went up into the galleries. Before sharing, all monies were put into a locked 'common box', hence our term, box office.

Even though we cannot be absolutely sure Shakespeare was with Burbage's company, this at least gives us a taste of the stresses and strains of the profession to which he had decided to devote himself. He must have wanted very badly to be an actor to be prepared to spend what must have been long months away from his family, if, as we can only assume, these stayed behind in Stratford. John Aubrey wrote that Shakespeare 'did act exceeding well' and we have every reason to believe that this was so. But at some point something must have prompted Shakespeare to extend his talents beyond merely acting out words that someone else's pen had provided for him. And so, in a move whose long-term implications he could hardly ever have dreamed of, in some long-forgotten room four hundred years ago, he began to write.

CHAPTER 6

Trials of a Writer

Where was the room in which Shakespeare stayed while working in London, and in which he arguably first set quill to paper to write his earliest plays? So much of Elizabethan London has been erased by time that we can be virtually certain that the room and the house have long been reduced to dust, just like his manuscripts. Nonetheless, if we have been right to associate Shakespeare's earliest acting years with James Burbage's company, then he probably lived quite close to Burbage's Shoreditch Theatre. And here, ironically, it is once again to John Aubrey that we owe the glimmer of a clue.

On a leaf inserted into the third part of the manuscript of Aubrey's *Brief Lives* are rough notes that Aubrey seems to have made around 1681 when he talked to William Beeston, son of the Christopher Beeston who had worked with Shakespeare. According to one portion of these notes, Beeston was living 'in Shoreditch ... at Hog Lane, within six doors Norton Folgate [a district just south of Shoreditch]'. Then just above this note Aubrey jotted 'W. Shakespeare', then: 'he was not a company keeper ... lived in Shoreditch, wouldn't be debauched ...'[1]

Although this provides no indication of when Shakespeare might have been living in Shoreditch, inevitably this would most likely have been as and when he worked at the Shoreditch Theatre. This immediately sets a time limit of not later than 1598. Shoreditch is equally logical for his lodgings because it was a theatrical community. Its parish church, St Leonard's, whose vicar was notorious for melting down its memorial brasses,[2] became known as the Old Players' Church on account of the substantial community of actors who lived in its environs. St Leonard's surviving registers show that James Burbage lived in Holywell Street, almost certainly one and the same as present-day Shoreditch's surviving Holywell Lane. And lawsuits of the time[3] indicate that the house that Burbage seems to have built himself was in the Holywell priory's old inner cloister yard, a little to the Lane's north. The great Queen's company actor Richard

Tarlton, who we have already mentioned, likewise lived in Holywell Street, dying there in the late summer of 1588, nursed by 'one Em Ball' a Shoreditch woman 'of very bad reputation'.[4] (If Tarlton was Shakespeare's Yorick, this may well have been how Shakespeare 'knew him'). Richard Cowley, another man listed in the First Folio as a 'principal actor' with Shakespeare, and who had certainly joined Burbage's company by 1592, also lived in Holywell. Like Tarlton and the Burbages, he was buried at St Leonard's.

From the chronicler Stow and from Privy Council memoranda, the picture evoked of late-sixteenth-century Shoreditch and its immediate environs is one of rapidly developing 'small and base tenements', 'alleys backward', 'stables, inns, alehouses, taverns, garden houses converted into dwellings ... dicing houses, bowling alleys and brothel houses'.[5] Inevitably Shakespeare would have had to familiarise himself with this district, and he would later reflect some of its colour in Falstaff's haunts in *Henry iv*, *Parts i* and *ii*. But with his need for writing materials and particularly for books, Shakespeare would have had to stroll towards the south, past marshy Moorfields, past the harrowing sounds of the Bedlam hospital for the insane, and through Bishopsgate into the City of London proper.

For us to try to capture an image of the London that Shakespeare would have known, there can be no finer source than a six feet long by two feet four inches high woodcut view, of which just three impressions survive, one in the Guildhall Library, one in the Public Record Office, and one in the Pepysian Library at Magdalene College, Cambridge.[6] Although often wrongly attributed to Elizabethan surveyor Ralph Agas, who died in 1621, the map's actual originator is unknown. The main indication of its date is an obvious alteration to one of the engraving blocks to show the Royal Exchange, which was completed in 1570. This, therefore, indicates that it was made within less than two decades of Shakespeare's arrival in London. The so-called 'Agas' map is known to have been copied from a lost larger and more detailed copperplate version of which two sections survive, one specifically featuring the area south of Shoreditch and depicting on Bishopsgate, through which Shakespeare must have passed many times, the spikes on which, in common with other of London's gates, were regularly displayed the decapitated heads of those executed as traitors. These were usually Catholics, like Shakespeare's relative Edward Arden whose head had been impaled upon the entrance way to London Bridge back in 1583.

When Shakespeare first arrived in London it is likely that his accent and even his clothes would have made him stand out as a countryman, thereby making him a target for the 'cony-catchers', the cheats who preyed upon those unused to the ways of the city. But arguably now familiar with it, pressing on he would have contemplated the towers and spires of the hundred or so churches with which the city was dotted, even though inside each had suffered its own share of depredations from the Reformation. He would also have seen how Henry VIII's Dissolution of the Monasteries had turned over to commercial and residential redevelopment the once tranquil precincts of the Carmelite Whitefriars, the Franciscan Greyfriars, and the Dominican Blackfriars. In the latter of these Shakespeare's fellow Stratfordian Richard Field was serving out the last years of his apprenticeship in a printing shop.

To the east of the city he would have seen the huge bulk of the Tower of London and to the south a single bridge, London Bridge, that provided the only way to cross the river on foot. Leaving the city at one of its western gates, he might have strolled along the long road, known as the Strand, that ran parallel to the River Thames. He probably looked admiringly at the large and splendid houses of some of the country's greatest nobles, buildings that guarded the approaches to the Palace of Whitehall, seat of Elizabeth I's government – the only one he had ever known. He might have seen the Queen as the 'Agas' map shows her: in her royal barge, heading along the river, towed by rowers in a tugboat surrounded by protective pikemen, clearly identifiable as such by her great Tudor coat of arms.

Shakespeare may also have come across scaffolds erected for public punishments and executions which, like his own trade, were always a source of popular amusement. The occasion was sometimes the execution of a Catholic priest or a mutilation. For example, in 1579 writer John Stubbes had his writing hand cut off for daring to criticise the idea then being mooted of the Queen marrying the Duc d'Alençon.

Shakespeare would also have seen the notorious prisons, Newgate, the Marshalsea, the Fleet, the Clink and not least the Tower itself, where people he knew would spend varying uncomfortable terms of incarceration. But the premier place that, as a writer, he would inevitably have sought out must have been St Paul's Cathedral. Thanks to the Reformation this had not only been allowed to decay, but to become something between Grand Central Station and an Eastern kasbah. As we know from contemporary reports, 'men of all professions, not merely mechanick [i.e. manual workers]' used it as a meeting place.[7] As a result of deals struck with the clergy, trunk makers, bookbinders, carpenters, teachers and glaziers were among a variety of tradesmen allowed to set up under its roof. Hauliers used the aisles as a short cut, sometimes even bringing through their horses and carts and loads of anything from coal to carcasses.[8]

The steeple, struck by lightning in 1571, had never been repaired and, in what remained of it, two of the Cathedral's bell-ringers acted as pimps for their attractive wives, apparently stationing themselves 'openly in the south aisle of [the] Church daily to take every man's money for going up into the steeple, by reason whereof there is great occasion of suspicion . . . also a scandal to the Church'.[9] Scarcely surprisingly, the Cathedral often stank of a 'very ill savour greatly prejudicial to men's health' particularly due to the drunks and down-and-outs who would 'lie and sleep upon the forms and about the choir doors . . . where they do very often times leave all that is within them, very loathsome to behold'.[10] Small boys were another hazard, apparently in the habit of 'pissing upon stones' in order to make these slippery for any unwary visitor.

Perhaps fortunately for Shakespeare, his goal would not have been the Cathedral building itself, but its twelve-acre yard. Here, as one of the clergy's further money-making ventures, every available square inch of space had been rented out to stall holders who plied all manner of trade, but in particular to stationers and booksellers. Book after book from the Elizabethan period proclaims its origin as this particular churchyard on its title page: 'to be sold . . . in St Paul's Churchyard, at the sign of the Fox'; 'to be sold in Paul's Churchyard, over against the Cross'; or 'to be sold in Paul's Churchyard, at the sign of the Green Dragon'. Here, in one central mart, were to be found the works of historians, travel writers, popular science writers, medical experts, gardening experts, translators of classical texts, poets, pamphleteers (in the days before daily newspapers, the newsmongers of their time), and of course dramatists. From one contemporary writer, John Eliot, we can even hear something of the booksellers' cries: 'Honest man, what book lack you?' and 'Buy some new book, sir! There are the last news from France. What books buy you?'[11]

Everything about Shakespeare's subsequent work shows that he read widely, magpie-like, and injected into his plays all sorts of snippets that he had gathered from books, suggesting therefore that he had become quite a habitué of St Paul's churchyard. Nonetheless, this is by no means necessarily where he picked up ideas from his fellow playwrights. The last thing that a dramatist wanted in the days before proper copyright regulations was to be published, for this meant that anyone could go off and perform their works without the author making any money from it. Besides, Shakespeare inevitably came across these individuals' works when performing them on stage. Equally inevitably he would have seen the writers in person as, like present-day sales representatives, they called at Burbage's Theatre to tout their latest 'book' hoping to persuade the company to choose this for its next production.

In this regard the 'common stage' dramatists must have appeared to Shakespeare a motley crew. In the case of productions performed at Court and at universities there were aristocrats and some highly respected academics who wrote plays, often in Latin or Greek. One such was William Gager, whose comedy *Rivales* and tragedy *Dido*, were performed in June 1583 in the Great Hall of Christ Church, Oxford, for the entertainment of the Count Palatine of Siradia. In 1553 Nicholas Udall, who was headmaster of Eton and Westminster during his career, pioneered one of the earliest English language comedies, *Ralph Roister Doister*. In 1561 Thomas Sackville, later to become Lord Buckhurst, Lord Treasurer, and one of Elizabeth's most trusted ministers, co-authored possibly the earliest English tragedy *Gorboduc*, which was performed by Inner Temple students for the entertainment of the Queen.

John Lyly, according to contemporary descriptions, a small, dapper, dandified individual who was variously secretary to the Earl of Oxford, and Member of Parliament for Wiltshire, wrote a series of witty, fanciful comedies for performance by the boy actors of St Paul's School. These pieces all revelled in the affected dialogue he had pioneered with his prose romance *Euphues*, which had become a fashion for those in courtly circles. Likewise, the Earl of Oxford had undoubtedly written plays for these same Court circles, and although these works have not survived, there is no reason to believe that Oxford would have been ashamed to have been known as their author, despite the theories of the Oxfordians.

But those who provided plays for popular stages, such as Burbage's Shoreditch Theatre, were of an altogether lower order. In the main they were university men who tended to resent their talents being prostituted in this way, but who needed the money to support their often dissolute life-styles. Typical of this breed was Robert Greene, a saddler's son six years Shakespeare's senior, who became an Oxford M.A. and who authored some half a dozen plays and forty pamphlets during the late 1580s and early 1590s. Sometimes able to command more than £6 for a play, Greene was the ultimate Bohemian, with a long beard peaked like the spire of a steeple, which 'he cherished continually without cutting, what man might hang a jewel . . . it was so sharp and pendant'.[12] His contemporary Gabriel Harvey wrote of him: 'Who in London hath not heard of his dissolute and licentious living', his 'unseemly apparel and more unseemly company', and his 'scandalous and blasphemous raving'?[13]

Also Oxford-educated was Thomas Watson, a translator of works from French, Italian, Latin and Greek, who seems to have been a Catholic and who, during the 1570s, spent time at least twice at the Catholic seminary at Douai. Reportedly Watson had had many plays performed on London's Bankside, though none have survived, and one of his employers, the wealthy London Catholic William Cornwallis, for whom he worked as a tutor, said of him that he 'could devise twenty fictions and knaveries in a play, which was his daily practice and his living'.[14]

Representing Cambridge among the dramatists was Christopher Marlowe. Born to a Canterbury cobbler within a few weeks of Shakespeare's birth, besides winning a scholarship to Corpus Christi College, Cambridge, he was recruited by Elizabeth's chief spymaster Sir Francis Walsingham to pose as a Catholic student at the Rheims seminary, in order to report on its trainees. When Corpus Christi, hearing of his apparent plan, were about to withhold his degree, it needed an express command of the Privy Council pleading that Marlowe had been working 'for the benefit of his country' in certain secret 'affairs' for this to be granted to him. Notoriously quarrelsome, in 1589 he and Watson became involved in a fight with an innkeeper's son in Shoreditch's Hog Lane in which the latter died, resulting in both playwrights spending a time in Newgate prison before successfully pleading their innocence. Marlowe's *Tamburlaine*, performed at least as early as 1587 when its author was just twenty-three years old, became one of the most popular works of the time. It was renowned for the scene in which Tamburlaine yokes to his chariot four defeated kings, the famous 'pampered jades of Asia', and then horse-whips them into hauling him across the stage.

Another spy (being mobile, educated, ever-impecunious individuals, many writers easily drifted into spying), was London draper's son Anthony Munday who enrolled in the late 1570s at the English College in Rome to find out who was staying there. He then returned to England to act as an anti-Catholic informer on behalf of the government. Munday was at the scene of Edmund Campion's execution at Tyburn, notebook in hand, to record every detail for a book.

One of the few non-university men among the leading lights was Thomas Kyd, author of the box-office record-breaker *The Spanish Tragedy* – subtitled *Hieronimo's Mad Again!* – who, rather better than many, had a feeling for what would work theatrically. With its opening ghost scene through to its distraught lovers, its murders, its discovery of dead bodies, scenes of madness and self-mutilations and the gripping play-within-a-play climax, *The Spanish Tragedy* proved such a crowd-puller that it ran and ran.

If the savagery typifying many of the popular plays was part of their success, this merely reflected what was happening on the national political stage. Inevitably a major cause of controversy at the beginning of 1587 was the execution of Mary Queen of Scots, the Catholics' great hope as Elizabeth's successor. The pretext for this was her alleged involvement in the Babington plot, one so shot through with government 'plants' that it is virtually impossible that the true guilty parties will ever be known. Epitomising the feelings of England's Catholics, upon Mary's subsequent interment in a vault in Peterborough Cathedral, a loyal follower travelled secretly to Peterborough and put up on the wall above where she was laid a long epitaph in Latin, carrying as its central message:

> with the sacred ashes of this blessed Mary, know that the Majesty of all kings and princes lieth here, violated and prostrate.[15]

Inevitably it was quickly removed.

Ironically, it was only upon Mary's execution that Philip II of Spain seems to have been spurred into at last launching the Armada that Mary had long hoped might come to her rescue. In the event, this suffered its well-known and all too desultory defeat. And this in its turn again made life worse for England's Catholics. One of these was Derbyshire-born priest Father William Hartley, who had been educated at the Rheims seminary, and who suffered public execution on the doorstep of Shakespeare's theatre-land in Shoreditch. Possibly Shakespeare witnessed this public hanging, drawing and quartering, if he could bear to watch.

Although there have long been differences of opinion on exactly when Shakespeare began to write his first plays, it was probably against this historical background. Frustratingly, despite centuries of the most intense literary investigation, there is still no consensus as to which was his first play. There is a list of six plays – *Titus Andronicus*, *The Comedy of Errors*, *King John*, and *Henry VI, Parts I, II,* and *III* – that some, by no means all scholars accept as belonging to Shakespeare's first period, although individually they would add other choices of their own.

Of this six, our first concern is *Titus Andronicus*, a rarely performed play which, despite its clear attribution to Shakespeare in the First Folio, was so lowly regarded by John Aubrey's contemporary Edward Ravenscroft that he insisted it should not be attributed to Shakespeare at all, remarking ''tis the most incorrect and indigested piece in all his Works; it seems rather a heap of rubbish than a structure'.[16] Yet, after a long vogue in which not only this but several other of Shakespeare's weaker plays were ascribed to co-authorship between him and other dramatists, this phase has passed. Certainly in the case of *Titus* the modern literary trend is confidently to ascribe the play to Shakespeare in as near entirety as makes no difference.

Dr A. L. Rowse calls *Titus* Shakespeare's 'prentice piece'[17], and undeniably its most notable feature is a certain primitive horror. Its tone is obvious from the very first scene, set in an imperial Rome of an indeterminate date, in which the warlord Titus Andronicus is about to bury the twenty-first of his sons slain in the wars against the Goths. For the expiation of their dead brother's soul at this funeral, Titus' four surviving sons urge the sacrifice of Alarbus, the eldest of the three surviving sons of the recently defeated queen of the Goths Tamora, upon which Tamora makes an emotional appeal for Alarbus' life: 'Thrice-noble Titus, spare my first-born son'.

Titus rejects this answer, and moments later his sons return with bloodied swords, declaring:

> Alarbus' limbs are lopped,
> And entrails feed the sacrificing fire. . . .

Thus, an ear deaf to mercy, that may or may not hark back to Elizabeth's treatment of Mary and the Catholic martyrs, sets off the most appalling series of misfortunes for Titus Andronicus and his family. Tamora, whose name evokes blackness,[18] along with her physically and spiritually black henchman Aaron the Moor, begins to work her revenge.

Titus' daughter Lavinia is raped, has her tongue cut out and her hands lopped off. His sons are sentenced to be executed for a murder they did not commit. Titus is tricked into believing that they can be reprieved if he allows his hand to be cut off, but upon surrendering this – on stage – it is returned moments later with the heads of his sons. At this point Titus reacts in a way that provides one of the most powerful moments in the play. With the frank admission 'I have not another tear to shed' he bursts into a fit of helpless sardonic laughter. His only way forward now being to revenge Tamora's revenge, he ultimately succeeds by luring Tamora to a banquet in which she unwittingly eats from a pie baked with the flesh of her two guilty sons.

It is more than apparent from the play that Shakespeare was already familiar with all the theatrical illusions inherited from the days of the Mystery Plays, and that he expected his performers to deploy them with all the simulated goriness to which popular theatre audiences were already accustomed. For on-stage stabbings and amputations actors of the time used concealed bladders filled with pigs' blood for extra effect, and no doubt they were given a lot of practice during their performances of *Titus Andronicus*, which undoubtedly became extremely popular, and continued to be performed well into the 1590s.

Equally important, however, is that for all *Titus Andronicus'* undisguisable goriness, those who have witnessed modern productions of it insist that it is also a work of brilliantly engineered dramatic force. This is particularly evident in scenes such as that revealing the tongueless Lavinia and leading up to Titus' so seemingly inappropriate fit of laughter. Already evident is a Shakespeare so well versed in the acting craft that he knew, as only an experienced actor could, just how what he created with words would work when acted out with human emotions upon the stage.

Given the all too obvious grimness of Shakespeare's first (?) chosen subject matter, thankfully we have no need to believe that he conjured up *Titus* purely out of his imagination. While a contemporary copy of his source has not come to light, a mid-eighteenth-century chapbook preserved in the Folger Shakespeare Library, Washington, which carries on its title page 'Newly Translated from the Italian Copy printed at Rome', has a Titus Andronicus story sufficiently close to Shakespeare's to suggest that its original pre-dated his play, and that Shakespeare simply subjected it to certain key adaptations. Although we do not know in what form Shakespeare came upon this source, or whether it was in Italian, or translated for him, the murders, the mutilations and the cannibalism are all there. What Shakespeare can be seen to have done for dramatic purposes is to heighten Aaron's villainy and tighten the tension with certain changes of order, thus providing what modern-day scholar Emrys Jones has dubbed the 'scenic form'[19] that is one of Shakespeare's distinctive hallmarks. Shakespeare also notably introduced certain elements, such as the tussle for succession in the Court of Rome; this was a subject of enormous topicality for his own England, due to the uncertainty surrounding Elizabeth's succession, and one on which courtiers were forbidden to speak. Here we see how Shakespeare, even in what was possibly his earliest play, although adroitly setting this in the distant past, was clearly addressing his own time.

By a happy accident of history *Titus Andronicus* is the only play of Shakespeare's for which we have a drawing, from within Shakespeare's own lifetime, of how it was costumed [see pl. 10]. The drawing is to be found on a single folded sheet in the library of the Marquess of Bath at Longleat House, Wiltshire,[20] and, as corroborated by an accompanying extract from the text of *Titus Andronicus*, it portrays the play's opening scene with Tamora pleading with Titus for her son's life. In the centre of the composition we see Titus holding an impressive-looking ceremonial staff, confronting the crowned Tamora who is on her knees, her hands clasped in supplication; behind Titus stand two figures with pikes and behind Tamora two of her sons, both bound, and at far right Aaron the Moor, menacingly brandishes a sword.

Because the drawing carries a supplementary inscription 'Henry Peacham's hand, 1595', this is often regarded as the date of the drawing, even though the inscription has long been suspected as a piece of meddling by the fraudster John Payne Collier. But unquestionably the drawing was made in Shakespeare's time, and it is of priceless interest in indicating what Shakespeare and his fellow actors would have worn when performing it. Thus Titus can be seen wearing a 'Roman'-looking cuirass, robe and buskins. And although there's an unmistakeably Elizabethan look to the rest, Aaron is in a 'period' tunic, his legs, face and hands have been blacked up in some form of body make-up (demanded in the text by references to 'his body's hue'),[21] and his head is covered with a tight-curled black wig, probably made of sheepskin since it is referred to in the play as 'my fleece of woolly hair'.[22]

But if dating the costume drawing is difficult, far more so is that of trying to determine exactly when Shakespeare may have set his pen to *Titus*. As we will learn in Chapter 11, the play was first published in a pirate edition of 1594, a single copy of which survives and is held by the Folger Shakespeare Library, Washington. But given, as already mentioned, that it was totally against the interests of dramatists for their plays to be published, 1594 simply provides a 'not later than' date to the play's composition. Of the true date there is just one highly important clue deriving from a remark made by Shakespeare's fellow dramatist Ben Jonson in his Induction to *Bartholomew Fayre* as written in 1614:

> He that will swear *Jeronimo* [an alternative name for Kyd's *The Spanish Tragedy*] or *Andronicus* are the best plays . . . [is] a man whose judgment has stood still these five and twenty, or thirty, years.

Loose though Jonson's remark might seem, we will see later how he was a man who prided himself as greatly superior to Shakespeare regarding attention to historical and geographical accuracy. From his words, five and twenty, or thirty years' back from 1614 would date *Tragedy* and *Titus* to between 1584 and 1589. A further indication of roughly this same date for *The Spanish Tragedy* is provided by another work of Jonson's, dated 1600, *Cynthia's Revels*, in which he wrote of *The Spanish Tragedy* as 'departed a dozen years since', this effectively setting it to around 1588. On this basis, although a generation or so ago such an early date would have been rubbished by great authorities such as Sir Edmund Chambers, today a dating of *Titus Andronicus* to around 1589 is much more acceptable.[23]

In *Titus* the young Shakespeare may be adjudged to have written an almost copybook classical tragedy in the mould of the Roman Seneca, who was a tutor to Nero. Equally, *The Comedy of Errors* may be regarded as Titus' copybook counterpart in the style of the celebrated Plautus, a Roman comedy writer of the third century BC. Arguably indicative of it being an early work is the fact that, almost unique among Shakespeare's plays,[24] it preserves the classical ideal of unity of place and time; its entire action takes place at one location, and within the space of a day. One of Plautus's most popular comedies was his *Menaechmi*, based on the story of twins, and it is surely not unreasonable to suppose that this made Shakespeare, as the father of twins Hamnet and Judith, particularly attracted to this theme.

In the vein of its inspirer, Plautus, the play has its fair share of bawdiness, as in one of its sub-plots in which the servant Dromio of Syracuse, mistaken just like his master for his twin by the latter's wife – fat cook Nell whom we never see – describes her to his master:

> *Dromio of Syracuse*: ... she is spherical, like a globe; I could find out countries in her.
> *Antipholus of Syracuse*: In what part of her body stands Ireland?
> *Dromio of Syracuse*: Marry, sir, in her buttocks; I found it out by the bogs.
>
> ...
>
> *Antipholus of Syracuse*: Where stood Belgia, the Netherlands?
> *Dromio of Syracuse*: O sir, I did not look so low.[25]

From the considerable number of ways in which *The Comedy of Errors* follows the same plot as *Menaechmi*, there can be no doubt that this was the base upon which Shakespeare built. It would have been easy enough for him to do so, since printed editions of Plautus' Latin text were plentiful, and his Latin would have been good enough for this.

But in a manner we will find crucial to Shakespeare, far more revealing than his sources are the ways he chose to depart from them. For instance, while he successfully sustains the comedy by devices such as doubling up the number of twins (Plautus having no equivalents to the twin servants Dromio), instead of Plautus' dwelling on a husband's relations with a prostitute, Shakespeare sets

Biblically-inspired passages into the mouth of Antipholus of Ephesus' wife Adriana, extolling the ideal relationship between a husband and wife.[26]

Given that St Paul's letter to the Ephesians lies behind one of these remarks, it is of similar interest that instead of following Plautus in locating *Comedy*'s action in Epidamnum, Shakespeare chooses Ephesus. This is seemingly for another Biblical reason, that in the Acts of the Apostles, 19, Ephesus features as a place of magic, spells and spirits: precisely the impression of the city that Shakespeare wants to put into the minds of Syracusans Antipholus and Dromio:

> *Antipholus of Syracuse*: They say this town is full of
> . . . nimble jugglers that deceive the eye,
> Dark working sorcerers that change the mind,
> Soul-killing witches that deform the body,
> Disguised cheaters, prating mountebanks.[27]

With his audience always aware that the real cause of the sorcery is the confusion between the identically dressed, identically named twins, Shakespeare develops the theme of Ephesus being bewitched to the point where exorcism of Antipholus of Ephesus becomes necessary by the comic person of Pinch the schoolmaster. And here there may be an important historical allusion, for in the mid-1580s Shakespeare's fellow Stratfordian the martyred priest Robert Debdale had been involved in exorcisms. These had been a cause of widespread pro-Catholic interest, but in 1590, when Puritans became involved, they were sternly condemned as 'popish jugglings' by the anti-Catholic R. Phinch. In his *The Knowledge and Appearance of the Church* Phinch wrote of the 'false miracles, lying powers and wonders' of the Papists. So was Shakespeare, in his schoolmaster Pinch, turning the tables on R. Phinch – and does this give us a clue to the early date when *Comedy* was written?[28]

The American scholar T. W. Baldwin[29] noted yet another of Shakespeare's departures from Plautus – his introduction into Plautus' story of the old merchant Aegeon being under threat of execution. This is coupled with the location – all the more notable for *Comedy*'s pagan Classical setting – of Aegeon's intended place of execution close to an abbey being used as a convent. Indeed, Shakespeare goes out of his way to describe this precisely as:

the melancholy vale
The place of death and sorry execution
Behind the ditches of the abbey here.[30]

Now as noted by Baldwin, and as we have already seen, James Burbage's Theatre at Shoreditch, to which we have suggested Shakespeare became attached, was hard by the old Shoreditch priory that had formerly been a convent for nuns. Furthermore, again as Baldwin spotted, and we have mentioned, right by the Theatre, there took place in October 1588, just after the Armada, the typically gruesome public execution of Catholic priest William Hartley, who was put to death specifically for conducting exorcisms within the Puritan Starchie family. So was Shakespeare making a very topical allusion, although for safety setting his play into times well past?

A further notable feature, from precisely this same scene, relates to the part of the Abbess Emilia. Although her role is a small one, nonetheless it provides the crux of the whole play. For like a *deus ex machina* or fairy godmother, it is only when she comes into the action at the very last moment that the accumulation of pain and confusion suddenly dissolves, and order and harmony are restored. The important element is that as his vehicle Shakespeare had moved far from Plautus to make her a nun, indeed an abbess, one of that breed whom Henry VIII and his bully boys had sought to remove from the scene, and whom other writers of Shakespeare's time continued to vilify. Emilia conveys real spiritual authority, and her sympathetic approach to an apparent case of possession is in great contrast to Pinch/Phinch's.

So far, then, we have seen just two plays of Shakespeare's, both difficult to date, but carrying some signs that they were written around 1589–90, that is, about the time that Burbage's company came under Ferdinando Lord Strange's patronage. While we cannot be sure that they were Shakespeare's earliest, with whatever plays Shakespeare began we are faced with the question: why did he? That is, why did he begin to write at all? However odd the question may seem, the point behind it is that unlike Christopher Marlowe, Thomas Kyd, Robert Greene, and all the others writing for the common stage, Shakespeare did not have to write to earn a living. His job – the only chosen career on which the historical record is in agreement about him – was as an actor, presumably beginning in the late 1580s and steadily working his way up the ladder of this profession. Without a university background, he even lacked the attributes normally to be expected of anyone writing plays.

So did he decide to write simply of his own volition, perhaps because he felt he could do better than his contemporaries? Or did he do so as a means of supplementing whatever financial reward he received from his company, the better to provide for his growing young family back in Stratford? Although these are possibilities, indeed probabilities, they may only represent part of the picture. For the third alternative is that both *Titus* and *Comedy* were really 'prentice pieces' in which Shakespeare was trying to show someone what he could do, and not necessarily just James Burbage. One would hardly expect Shakespeare to have been so politically daring in his deft, necessarily subtle pro-Catholic touches for purely commercial purposes.

There is also the interest in the supernatural, which will recur in the next plays from his early period. And perhaps even more strikingly is the inclusion in *Titus* and other early plays of an interest in deer-hunting.[31] While most authors, including Dr A. L. Rowse, have assumed this simply to have been an enthusiasm from Shakespeare's youth in the Forest of Arden (particularly given the apocryphal Stratford legend of Shakespeare poaching the Puritan Sir Thomas Lucy's deer at Charlecote), it may not have been this at all. This is not only because Sir Thomas Lucy did not have a deer park at Charlecote, but because, as observed by Caroline Spurgeon in her specialist study of Shakespeare's imagery, in Shakespeare's references to deer-hunting and like blood sports, his sympathies lie 'scarcely ever with the hunters, but consistently and obviously on the side of the hunted or stricken animal'.[32]

Here the alternative to be considered on the subjects of deer-hunting, the supernatural and Catholicism is that Shakespeare may have been tailoring his work to please someone else who had these inclinations. If at present there may appear but the merest glimmerings of a 'someone' behind the scenes, a figure altogether more illustrious than James Burbage directing Shakespeare's earliest dramatic endeavours, all is about to come into fascinating sharper focus.

CHAPTER 7

Found – the Mystery Patron?

Although we cannot tell which play Shakespeare wrote after *Titus Andronicus* and *The Comedy of Errors* (if indeed these were his first), there is one that, so far as scholars' attempts to date it are concerned, rolls around like a loose cannon between the years 1589 and 1596. The play is *King John*, and the loose cannon simile has a certain appropriateness because Shakespeare has his King John speak of 'the thunder of my cannon', when in the real King John's time (he ruled 1199–1216) the use of gunpowder weapons in England lay some two hundred years ahead, though it was encountered on Crusades. Such occasional anachronisms seem not to have troubled Shakespeare, as later and famously, for instance, he will have a clock in *Julius Caesar*.

But where *King John* is of particular interest is how Shakespeare's stance towards this king markedly differs from that of the unequivocally Protestant writers of his time. In the wake of Henry VIII's Reformation, the Protestant bishop John Bale had written a primitive play *King John*. In this he crudely combined historical figures, such as King John, Stephen Langton, etc, with traditional morality and symbolic figures, such as Widow England, in order to present King John as an early prototype for Henry VIII: steadfastly and patriotically taking his stand against papal supremacy. Protestant martyrologist John Foxe, in his *Actes and Monuments*, likewise portrayed John as heroically opposing the Pope of his day, and being poisoned by evil monks for his pains. In this same vein in 1591 there appeared on London's bookstalls a play called *The Troublesome Raigne of John King of England* which, although typically it did not carry the author's name, he was clearly a die-hard Protestant. Whoever the author was – possibly the spy Anthony Munday – he most favourably portrayed King John as an early Protestant hero, made the Papal Legate, Pandulph, appear an obsequious trickster, and gave free rein to scenes of lechery between monks and nuns.

Frustratingly, the publication of this anonymous author's *Troublesome Raigne* in 1591 is the one firm peg around which must somehow be hung the writing of Shakespeare's *King John*; in common with half of Shakespeare's entire œuvre, *King John* would not see publication until the First Folio of 1623. The scholarly view used to be that Shakespeare wrote it in *Troublesome Raigne*'s wake, possibly just after 1591 or as late as 1596. Indeed Dr A. L. Rowse, for one, still holds to this latter date. Professor Ernst Honigmann, on the other hand, in editing the authoritative Arden edition of *King John* has argued for Shakespeare writing the play before the appearance of *Troublesome Raigne*. He would date it to around the winter of 1590 or spring of 1591, making the Protestant version a deliberate riposte to Shakespeare's.

Now thankfully there is no overwhelming need for us to choose which preceded which. Far more important for us to be clear about is the difference between Shakespeare's and the Protestant attitude towards the historical King John. Unmistakeably, Shakespeare's John is not a hero, but a bad king, a clever but short-sighted tyrant who degenerates into feverish madness. Shakespeare's Papal Legate Pandulph is a dignified, far-seeing international statesman who gives sound advice that saves England from invasion. And Shakespeare does not have any unsavoury scenes with monks and nuns. Accordingly, whether the Protestant *Troublesome Raigne* author was responding to Shakespeare, or Shakespeare was responding to him, Shakespeare's affiliations, though set safely in a period several centuries back from his time, may be said to be leaning far more towards Catholicism than Protestantism.

Further indications of this trend emerge in the surprisingly explicit way Shakespeare can be seen to have manipulated his sources so that, although he seems to be recounting the reign of John, in reality he is presenting a mirror of the reign of Elizabeth. For instance, he presents John's right to rule as mere 'strong possession'[1], a view quite unjustified from the sources Shakespeare would have consulted for John, but just the way Elizabeth was regarded by those who accepted to the letter her papal excommunication of 1570. He presents the barons' rebellion against John in a manner strikingly reminiscent of the Catholic Northern Earls' rebellion against Elizabeth when his father had been Stratford's Bailiff. He has King John repudiate Papal Legate Pandulph with precisely the sentiments of Article 37 of the Protestant Thirty Nine articles which Elizabeth had approved in 1563:

Tell him [the Pope] this tale, and from the mouth of England
And thus much more, that no Italian priest

Shall tithe or toll in our dominions,
But as we, under heaven, are supreme head
So under Him that great supremacy
Where we do reign, we will alone uphold . . .[2]

He can be seen to have modelled Papal Legate Pandulph's resultant excommunication of John upon the same Papal Bull by which Elizabeth was so rashly excommunicated by Pope Pius v in 1570, a document requiring of her subjects that 'they shall not once dare obey her, or any of her directions, laws or commandments, binding under the same curse those who do anything to the contrary'. Also, Shakespeare's description of the French 'armada of . . . sail' against John, 'scattered and disjoined from fellowship' by 'a roaring tempest on the flood' seems an obvious allusion to the Spanish Armada of 1588, though A. L. Rowse has suggested Shakespeare meant another altogether lesser known one also sent by Philip ii in 1596.

Perhaps most interesting of all, however, is how Shakespeare, having equated John with Elizabeth, identifies John's hapless royal victim – Prince Arthur – with Elizabeth's equally ill-fated royal victim: Mary Queen of Scots. Thus when Shakespeare alludes to a will barring Arthur from the English throne,[3] this seems to have little to do with the historical King John and rather more with Elizabeth's father Henry viii's will barring Mary Queen of Scots from the same. And when in *King John* Shakespeare has John order Hubert secretly to murder Arthur, then go into a pantomime of pretended rage when he thinks (wrongly) that the deed has been carried out, this seems to pertain not to John, but to the way Elizabeth notoriously put the blame upon her secretary William Davison for implementing Mary Queen of Scots' execution (even to the extent of having him put on trial and fined), when it was undoubtedly she who had signed Mary's death warrant. If these were not pointers enough to the Arthur/Mary equation, Shakespeare surely makes them unmistakeable when, in the words he has said over Prince Arthur's dead body:

From forth this morsel of dead royalty
The life, the right and truth of all this realm
Is fled to heaven[4]

he echoes the sentiments of the all-too-short-lived epitaph that, as we noted in the last chapter, Catholics had illicitly set up over Mary's Peterborough grave [see page 84].

Now importantly, this association of Elizabeth and John, Mary and Prince Arthur, is not one that has been arrived at merely by twentieth-century critics. Even in Shakespeare's time, and indeed long before Mary's execution, John Leslie, Bishop of Ross and Mary's most loyal supporter, had made the Arthur analogy in urging Mary's right to the English succession.[5] But in *King John* it is all the more apparent for the very considerable violations of historical fact that Shakespeare has perpetrated in order to make the parallels between John's and Elizabeth's reigns. Indeed, *King John* has been called his most unhistorical play. Although later in his work Shakespeare would make many historical violations for dramatic purposes, this is not what we are witnessing in *John*. Its action has been described as 'wandering and uncertain' by one literary critic, and an 'incoherent patchwork' by another.

This highly political aspect to *John* therefore makes it particularly frustrating that we have no clear record of when Shakespeare wrote the play, nor when or where it was first performed during his lifetime – if indeed it was. The earliest documented performance was at Covent Garden in 1737,[6] and although the play is named as Shakespeare's in a list assembled in 1598, there were no 'pirate' Quarto editions. During King James I's reign it was editions of *Troublesome Raigne* that were published under Shakespeare's name in a clear pretence that they were his version. The genuine Shakespeare play, as published in the 1623 First Folio, seems to have been derived from Shakespeare's author copy, or 'foul papers', and one possibility that cannot be ruled out is that *King John* was yet another 'prentice piece', this time in the genre of history, for Shakespeare's mystery man in the wings, and only performed privately. It is certainly to be noted that like *The Comedy of Errors*, it demands very little in the way of special staging.

No such difficulties, however, apply to the three parts of *King Henry VI*, a group of historical plays that, as will become clear, we can be sure were performed, and specifically on the common stage, during the very early 1590s. This is not to say that in these we have yet reached Shakespeare by any means at his best. 'That drum-and-trumpet thing' was how one eighteenth-century critic commented upon *Henry VI, Part I*,[7] and as with *Titus*, from Edmond Malone right up to the scholars of a generation or so ago, all three parts of *Henry VI* were largely dismissed as works to which Shakespeare had at best merely contributed as a 'playpatcher'. It was not until as recently as 1963, with the productions by John Barton and Peter Hall, that the plays were revealed as works truly worthy of the early Shakespeare.

And indeed it is quite apparent that those audiences who first viewed the *Henry VI* plays during the early 1590s were treated to a presentation of comparatively recent English history of a very special kind, spectacle hitherto absolutely unknown upon the English common stage, and only touched upon by the rarest of Court or university productions. Typical is *Henry VI, Part I*'s opening scene, the funeral of Henry V, in which we are immediately confronted with a galaxy of great lords – the Dukes of Bedford, Gloucester, and Exeter, the Earl of Warwick and the Bishop of Winchester – all in full mourning gear of great black cloaks, as evident from Bedford's ensuing words: 'Away with these disgraceful wailing robes!'

Although this might be thought simple enough costuming, the complications set in when we realise that these great lords are mostly unidentified by the dialogue, and that Shakespeare seems to have expected his audiences to recognise who they were chiefly by their accompanying coats of arms, something to which the sixteenth-century audience was much more attuned than we are. We then also notice that Shakespeare included heralds in the scene, and these must likewise have been in full heraldic gear with the royal coat of arms (which incorporated the French fleur-de-lys), since the Messenger, announcing the disastrous loss of French territories in the wake of Henry V's death, pointedly exclaims:

> Cropp'd are the flower-de-luces in your arms:
> Of England's coat one half is cut away.[8]

Very helpful to our understanding of the original costuming of this single scene is a surviving drawing [see pl. 11] in Thomas Lant's *Sequitur Celebritas et Pompa Funebris*, published in 1587, which in depicting the magnificent state funeral of Sir Philip Sidney, shows great mourning cloaks, accompanying coats of arms, and heralds' tabards unmistakeably as Shakespeare must have envisaged the opening of *Henry VI, Part I*. And this is but one instance of the feast of costuming spectacle with which the *Henry VI* plays abound: others include scenes in the Courts of England and France; the hero Talbot in the colour and heat of battle; the plucking of the Wars of the Roses' red and white blooms in the Temple Garden; Joan la Pucelle (better known to us as Joan of Arc) with her devilish fiends; the coronation ceremony of Henry VI's queen, Margaret of Anjou, and much more. Such would seem to have been the attention to detail that those actors playing great nobles belonging to the Order of the Garter clearly had to wear replicas of this insignia, as is evident from the scene in which Sir John Fastolfe has the garter plucked from his leg for cowardice.[9] Likewise in *Henry VI, Part II* the actor playing Warwick must have worn a helmet displaying the earl's family crest since this is specifically demanded by his vow:

> Now, by my father's badge, old Nevil's crest,
> The rampant bear chain'd to the ragged staff,
> This day I'll wear aloft my burgonet....[10]

Now the interesting feature here is that while for Court and university productions those in high places could apply to the royal Great Wardrobe on St Andrew's Hill, near Blackfriars for loans from the vast collection of expensive ceremonial costumes this carried, such a privilege was certainly not normally extended to any common stage company. Given the expense of costumes that we noted earlier, before embarking on a venture such as the *Henry VI* plays, whichever company was staging them had to be very sure that they could either procure or make such lavish clothes. And they also had to be sure they had the means and expertise to make the necessary heraldry.

Another feature of the *Henry VI* plays is their necessarily expansive use of what must have been a large stage. Although an army featured in *Titus*, the action, for all its goriness, remained relatively staid and, with the single exception of the throwing of a body into a pit, all at one level. But in the three *Henry VI* plays, the stage directions involve lively action at some level higher than the stage itself. In *Part I*, for instance, Talbot and Salisbury fight 'on the turrets' at Orléans and Salisbury falls from this height after being shot.[11] Joan la Pucelle appears 'on the top, thrusting out torch burning',[12] and in the final act Reignier of Naples exits 'from the walls'.[13] Likewise in *Part II* Eleanor Duchess of Gloucester enters 'aloft' during the raising of spirits scene;[14] in the Killingworth Castle scene the King, Queen and Somerset are 'on the terrace',[15] and in *Part III* Warwick and others appear 'on the walls' of Coventry;[16] and Henry VI dies 'on the walls' of the Tower of London.[17] There must also have been a below-stage trap for the entrances and exits of Joan la Pucelle's hellish fiends, also for the spirit which 'riseth' during Duchess Eleanor's séance. While there is room for much debate on just how much the sets of the first *Henry VI* plays featured, for example, convincing-looking ramparts, or mere painted cloths, clearly Shakespeare wrote these plays confident that they would be performed on the sort of substantial and well-equipped stage to be expected of a major London playhouse.

Of further note is that in the *Henry VI* plays Shakespeare continues to toy with some of those elements that, as we earlier suggested, may have been possible enthusiasms of his mystery patron. With regard to the supernatural, for instance, not only do we have in *Part I* Joan la Pucelle with her fiends, in *Part II* there is a raising of spirits scene that goes substantially beyond Shakespeare's sources. While in Halle's *Chronicle*, which Shakespeare is known to have consulted, Duchess Eleanor and a group of occultists simply make, in black-magic style, 'an image of wax, representing the king, which by their sorcery, a little and little consumed, intending ... to waste and destroy the king's person', in *Henry VI, Part II* Shakespeare goes in for nothing less than a full-blooded spiritualist séance. At dead of night:

> The time when screech-owls cry, and ban-dogs howl,
> And spirits walk and ghosts break up their graves—[18]

the Duchess's medium-like cronies perform appropriate rites, make a circle, and utter a magic formula. With this, amidst thunder and lightning a 'spirit riseth' from below stage, and with all the ambiguity of a Greek oracle proceeds to answer three fortune-telling questions put to it, answers that in fact hold the whole play together, since each comes true after its fashion.

Shakespeare brings a scene with falconers into *Part II*, a pursuit in which he is accredited with being quite an expert.[19] He also introduces a deer-hunting scene into *Part III*.[20] Now of course the hawking and occultish elements may mean nothing. Deer-hunting and falconry were highly popular activities with the Elizabethan aristocracy, including with the Queen herself, and Shakespeare may simply have been making his appeal to this. Likewise the Elizabethan age had easily as great a thirst for astrology and its like as today's tabloid-newspaper reader. Even the Queen had her own pet astrologer, Dr John Dee, who had cast the horoscope for the most propitious day for her coronation. And Dee can hardly be said to have done badly, since there can have been few, back in 1558, who would have expected her to be still on the throne in the 1590s.

Even so, and largely because the *Henry VI* plays have long been unfashionable, too little attention has been paid to just how remarkable the appearance of this sudden clutch of English history plays was for the 1590s. That they were staged is quite definite, for as we will see in the next chapter, Henslowe's Diary noted some performances at his Bankside theatre during 1592, and we can be virtually certain that they were being performed earlier at Burbage's Shoreditch Theatre. Yet no plays dealing with what was at that time quite recent history had been known ever to have been performed on the English common stage. The only true precedent was university don Thomas Legge's *Richardus Tertius* (*Richard III*) staged at St John's College, Cambridge in 1580, and this was a university production, acted by students, and written and performed in Latin.

Nor, at this stage could Shakespeare be considered an expert in the history he was writing about. Classical history was on the syllabus of Elizabethan schools, but English history was not, so whichever school Shakespeare attended he is unlikely to have studied it. Corroborating this, Dr A. L. Rowse has pointed out how in the *Henry VI* plays Shakespeare clearly reveals his ignorance of English history outside the particular chronicle he is following, for if the chronicle makes a mistake, so does he.[21] Furthermore, the chronicles that from his mistakes he can be proven to have consulted, are principally the updated 1587 version of Raphael Holinshed's *Chronicles of England, Scotland and Ireland*, and Edward Halle's much older *The Union of the two noble and illustre famelies of Lancastre and Yorke*. These were large, expensive volumes, and it is hard to imagine them being speculatively purchased by an actor with a young family of four to support and a father who was theoretically on the breadline.

Perhaps most astonishing of all, according to the increasingly accepted thinking recently advanced by Oxford scholar Emrys Jones,[22] not only did Shakespeare write the three *Henry VI* plays as a quite deliberate sequence, he added *Richard III* so that the four plays would comprise a tetralogy. One indication of this lies in the way

Suffolk gives the closing speech in *Henry VI, Part I* and the opening one in *Part II*; then Warwick has the closing speech in *Part II* and the opening one in *Part III*; then in *Part III* the closing words clearly anticipate *Richard III*. A further indication occurs in *Richard III*, Act IV, scene iv in which the old Queen Margaret, Henry VI's widow, and the Duchess of York, mother of Edward IV, commiserate together over what has befallen in a passage that really only makes sense in the context of the four plays performed in sequence:

> *Queen Margaret:* I had an Edward, till a Richard kill'd him
> I had a husband, till a Richard kill'd him;
> Thou hadst an Edward, till a Richard kill'd him.
> *Duchess of York:* I had a Richard too, and thou didst kill him;
> I had a Rutland too, thou hop'st to kill him.
> *Queen Margaret:* ...Thy Edward he is dead, that kill'd my
>   Edward;
> Thy other Edward dead, to quit my Edward....
> Thy Clarence he is dead that stabb'd my Edward.[23]

Those of the present-day who have had the privilege and stamina to see the plays staged as a series of four attest to their extraordinary power when presented in this way. Predictably, Shakespeare can be virtually seen to rise in stature as a writer as the tetralogy proceeds. Although *Henry VI, Part I* is rather too full of drums and trumpet, background sound-effects that with greater maturity he will use more sparingly, by *Part II* he pioneeringly breaks classical convention by mixing elements of comedy with tragedy. Here, poking fun at the world of learning, he has rebel Jack Cade tell his prisoner:

> Thou has most traitorously corrupted the youth of the realm in erecting a grammar school; and whereas, before, our forefathers had no other books but the score and the tally, thou hast caus'd printing to be used; and contrary to the King, his crown and dignity, thou hast built a paper-mill. It will be proved to thy face that thou hast men about thee that usually talk of a noun and a verb, and such abominable words as no Christian ear can endure to hear.[24]

With *Richard III*, which again has occultish elements such as prophecy and dreams, Shakespeare of course reaches the tour de force in villainy that everyone knows. But when the *Henry VI* plays and *Richard III* are understood as a tetralogy, what an ambitious venture it appears! In the words of *Richard III* Arden editor Antony Hammond, it is 'as if Wagner had begun his career with the Ring cycle'. And given an undertaking of this scale, the historical implications are considerable. For can we really believe that Shakespeare, with neither apparent Court experience, nor thorough grounding in history, could have possibly dreamed up such an ambitious venture entirely without someone guiding and encouraging him? Likewise can we really believe that the Burbage company, or whichever one Shakespeare was with, would have dared commit itself to such a lavishly staged and costumed series of productions without there being someone in the wings willing and able to offer them some resources to call upon along the way?

But who, if anyone, could that someone in the wings have been? The answer lies in the way that in the *Henry VI* plays and *Richard III* Shakespeare subtly but unmistakeably enhances the roles of two great families: the Stanleys and the Cliffords. First, in the case of the Cliffords, in *Henry VI*, *Parts II* and *III*, Shakespeare gives unusual prominence to the deaths of Lord Clifford and his son,[25] and develops them as characters considerably beyond anything in Halle's *Union*, which simply has the young Clifford killing York's second son Rutland on the grounds 'thy father slew mine, and so will I do thee and all thy kin'.[26]

Far greater, however, albeit belatedly, is the emphasis Shakespeare gives the Stanleys. Thus although the Stanleys historically hardly figure in the reign of Henry VI, Shakespeare has Sir John Stanley act as a gaoler to the Duchess of Gloucester on the Isle of Man (one of the Stanley domains), and he again gives special feature to this in *Henry VI*, *Part II*, Act II scene iv. Likewise in *Henry VI*, *Part III* he has King Edward IV promising a reward to Sir William Stanley.[27]

But it is in *Richard III* that Shakespeare's pro-Stanley emphasis becomes unmistakeable as concentrated upon the person of Thomas Stanley, first Earl of Derby, who helps Henry Tudor defeat the evil Richard III and become King. Early in the play Shakespeare represents Thomas as the only Yorkist nobleman not deceived by Richard III, and the only great noble pointedly not cursed by Henry VI's widow, Queen Margaret, among those on-stage in Act I scene iii. Then in a scene for which there is no known historical source he has Thomas conduct a brilliant battle of wits versus Richard, culminating in the increasingly insecure Richard deciding to hold Thomas's son George Stanley as a hostage, prompting Thomas's double-edged response: 'So deal with him as I prove true to you'.[28]

But it is in the circumstances of the battle of Bosworth Field that Shakespeare makes his most blatant reworking of history. Whereas historically before the battle it was Henry Tudor who sought out Thomas Stanley's allegiance, in *Richard III* Shakespeare has Thomas much more riskily approach Henry. Whereas before the real battle Thomas Stanley hesitated from tendering King Henry his full support, saying he 'would come to him in time convenient', Shakespeare carefully omits this piece of ambivalence. Whereas during the actual battle it was Thomas' brother William Stanley who at the crucial eleventh hour directed his forces to fight for Henry, Shakespeare ignores this William and gives Thomas all the credit.

Not least, whereas according to the historical chronicles it was a Sir Richard Bray who found Richard's crown in a hawthorn bush, thereupon passing this to Thomas Stanley, Shakespeare attributes to Thomas not only the finding of the crown, but the plucking of it 'from the dead temples of this bloody wretch'.[29] Finally, as literally the crowning moment of the whole tetralogy, Shakespeare, at last following history, has Thomas set Richard's crown upon Henry Tudor's head, making him King Henry VII, and thus founding the Tudor dynasty of which Elizabeth represented the third generation. In a moment of the most blatant emphasis of the Tudor debt to the Stanleys, Shakespeare then has the new Henry VII ask, as his first question as crowned king: 'But tell me, is young George Stanley living?'[30]

Now if we are to ask who in Elizabeth's Court, with Clifford connections, would have gained the greatest public relations value from that scene of a Stanley crowning Henry King of England, there can be only one answer. This was Ferdinando Stanley, Lord Strange, son of Margaret Clifford, and great-great-great grandson of the Thomas Stanley, first Earl of Derby, who crowned Henry VII. And if we try to recall the legally required patron under whose aegis James Burbage and his company of actors performed, the company that all along we have *thought* to have employed Shakespeare – what name do we find? Ferdinando Stanley, Lord Strange.

Immediately, of course, the tempting question arises: could this Ferdinando have been interested in hunting and hawking? The answer is yes. A vast deer park lay just opposite Lathom,[31] the great

Lancashire palace-fortress that was the family seat of Ferdinando's father Henry, fourth Earl of Derby, and Ferdinando's enthusiasm for hunting and hawking is quite evident from entries in the still-extant Derby Household Books for the late 1580s, for example: '1587 . . . 23 December . . . My Lord Strange went abroad to kill venison';[32] 'New Park, 11 October . . . My Lord Strange abroad to hunt and hawk';[33] 1590 'Lathom . . . March 14 . . . My Lord Strange and Mr. William [his brother, later the sixth earl] went to hawk'.[34] Likewise a little-known poem about Ferdinando in Richard Robinson's *A Golden Mirror* carries the lines:

> Not marks and pounds but hawks and hounds
> Is ever his desire.[35]

And Ferdinando's cousin and close friend Gilbert Talbot, to whom Robinson's *A Golden Mirror* is dedicated, shared Ferdinando's enthusiasm for hawks, even to the extent of having one named after him, and was notably a descendant of the Talbot who features so heroically in *Henry vi, Part i*.

What about occult interests on Ferdinando's part? Again, these are quite evident. Around 1588, in the style of *The Comedy of Errors*, Ferdinando personally investigated the case of 'Richard Mainy, gentleman', who described himself as having been 'possessed with certain wicked spirits, and of them dispossessed by some priests of the Roman Catholic Church'.[36] Directly reminiscent of *Henry vi, Part ii*'s séance scene, in 1579 Ferdinando's mother, Margaret Clifford, was detected by government secret agents trying 'to discover by means of witchcraft . . . whether the Queen would live long',[37] and was temporarily imprisoned for these activities. Lathom's great hall featured a magnificent and sadly now lost wooden screen elaborately decorated with zodiacal devices that former Chester actor and poet Thomas Chaloner had painted in honour of the family's astrological interests.[38] As we will learn later, Ferdinando's death was surrounded by some extraordinary occult goings-on.

But these are mere peripherals. For just who was Ferdinando, and why, if we have been right in our thinking, should he have wanted something as elaborate as the *Henry vi/Richard iii* tetralogy to be staged? It is extraordinary, particularly given that Ferdinando has long been known as patron of Burbage's company, that he has been so undervalued and little known by Shakespeare scholars. Art expert

Sir Roy Strong spotted that even the portrait usually reproduced of Ferdinando, which is preserved at the present Lord Derby's home, Knowsley, cannot have been painted in his lifetime. It took the most determined sleuthing on my part eventually to track down the only truly authentic surviving portrait [see pl. 12], which turned out to be in private ownership not far from my home.

From this portrait Ferdinando looks out enigmatically, lightly bearded, a prominent mole on his forehead, in high hat, finest lace collar, silver-white satin doublet, and with jewelled sword-strap, and accoutrements of jousting, of which more later. He was born around 1559, the eldest son of Henry, fourth Earl of Derby, and elder brother of the William, sixth Earl of Derby, to whom the 'Derbyians' have accredited Shakespeare's works. Ferdinando was heir to one of England's vastest estates, which was still largely feudal, and controlled from the great moated seven-turreted palace-fortress of Lathom, Lancashire, of which today, thanks to the Civil War, hardly a trace remains. The Derby Household Books, which were kept by Comptroller William Farington, show a permanent retinue of some one hundred and forty manservants, including Grooms of the Bedchamber, Clerks of the Kitchen, a Master of the Horse, a Falconer, a Herald/Trumpeter, and a company of minstrels. Royal-style, the Derbys regularly moved house between Lathom and their other two Lancashire strongholds, Knowsley and New Park, while in London they had a great Thames-side mansion in fashionable Cannon Row, close to the Palace of Whitehall.

In 1579 Ferdinando married Alice Spencer, youngest of several daughters of wool magnate Sir John Spencer of Althorp (one of England's wealthiest men, and ancestor of the present Princess Diana of Wales), and the couple thereupon quickly became generous and much sought-after patrons of poets and writers, and of course actors. Ferdinando's father had supported the Chester Mystery plays right up until these were banned as 'popish' and the Derby Household Books for the years these survive, 1587–90, show regular visits by acting companies. It was in these years, of course, following the death of the Earl of Leicester, Ferdinando took over patronage of the Burbage company of actors, though whether William Shakespeare was with them at that time is undetermined.

In 1589 Shakespeare's fellow playwright Robert Greene dedicated his poem *Ciceronis Amor* to Ferdinando, hoping to be 'shrouded under the protection of so honourable a Maecenas' and thereby likening Ferdinando to the wealthy Roman literary patron of that name. Ferdinando wrote poetry himself, a few scraps of which have survived, and these are of surprising quality.[39] Indeed *Faerie Queene* poet Edmund Spenser, who (more obscurely) dubbed Ferdinando 'Amyntas', spoke of him as 'the noblest swain that ever piped' that is, wrote poetry. And in 1590 Spenser dedicated his poem 'Tears of the Muses' to Alice (whom he called 'Amaryllis'), and other of his works to the two of Alice's sisters with whom she was closest: Anne ('Phyllis'), about to marry the son of *Gorboduc* author Thomas Sackville, and Elizabeth ('Charyllis'), wife of George Carey, the son of Elizabeth's Lord Chamberlain and kinsman, Henry Carey, Lord Hunsdon.

Despite all this patronage of the arts, however, in the harsh world of politics of the late 1580s and early 1590s Ferdinando's head hung under the blackest of clouds. As powerful subjects with sway over vast tracts of land that lay uncomfortably far from the Court, the Stanley family's loyalty had always been a questionable matter for any holder of England's crown, as King Richard III had indeed learned to his cost. Ferdinando's father Henry Stanley, fourth Earl of Derby, had married as a Catholic in Queen Mary's reign, in a brilliant Whitehall Palace ceremony attended by Mary and her husband King Philip of Spain. Although during Elizabeth I's reign Henry appeared dutifully to follow the standard government instructions to crack down on Catholics, Elizabeth's eagle-eyed first minister Lord Burghley was aware that many known Catholics regularly frequented Lathom. Among these were: Sir Edward Stanley, whose suburban London home was under surveillance for harbouring priests; 'Baron' Langton, who would later be indicted on the same charge, and members of closely related local families such as the Heskeths, the Hoghtons, and Savages, the Halsalls, and the Gerards. The martyred Edmund Campion had been sheltered by such families. And in 1590 alone over seven hundred Lancastrians had been charged with recusancy (the failure to attend Church of England services) as Catholics.

Far worse, however, was what had happened at the time of the Earl of Leicester's 1586 expedition to the Low Countries (in which, of course, some of Shakespeare's fellow actors had been among the entertainers). Taking part in this as an already noted veteran of Irish campaigns was Ferdinando's cousin Sir William Stanley. He distinguished himself with the most commendable bravery against the Spanish at Zutphen (the siege in which Sir Philip Sidney was killed), also at Deventer, where he was described by the Earl of Leicester as 'worth his weight in pearl'. But then, with Leicester back in England, suddenly and without warning on 29 January 1587, William Stanley and his aide Sir Rowland Yorke simply handed Deventer back to the Spanish. Of Stanley's troop of nine hundred, three hundred who wanted to stay loyal to the Queen were allowed to leave. The remaining six hundred stayed on with Stanley, now on the side of Spain and the Catholics.

If this most flagrant example of Stanley perfidy was not cause enough for the deepest suspicion to fall on those members of the family still in England, far worse was the knock-on political effect of the event that took place just nine days after Sir William Stanley's defection: Mary Queen of Scots' execution. With this all too irremediable removal of the Catholics' prime candidate to succeed Elizabeth on the English throne, who else was there, with the necessary blood royal, to turn to? And herein, by quirk of genetics, lay one cause of considerable discomfort for Ferdinando. Through his mother Margaret Clifford, daughter of Eleanor Brandon, a granddaughter of Henry VII, Ferdinando was actually a great-great-great grandson of Henry VII and, with the failure of the male Tudor line, a more than possible candidate to succeed Elizabeth on the English throne.

Now discussion of anything to do with Elizabeth's succession was firmly forbidden in the English Court, and since any Stanley papers and correspondence from Ferdinando's time was destroyed along with Lathom during the Civil War, we have no way of knowing Ferdinando's private feelings on the matter. Nor, any more than in the case of Ferdinando's father, can we be sure of his personal religious affiliations. Nonetheless, of one thing there can be no doubt: for the sizeable number of English Catholics who had fled abroad to escape government persecution, not to mention any unspoken feelings of those back home, Ferdinando was a distinctly credible hope as Elizabeth's successor. Equally definite is that Elizabeth's first minister Lord Burghley and his cohorts of spies and secret agents held Ferdinando in the deepest distrust. Proof of this comes in the form of a surviving letter among Burghley's papers, apparently found in the possession of two priests, Father John Cecil and Father John Fixer, when these were arrested on their way to England. Dated 3 April 1591, the letter was from none other than

Father Robert Persons, the Jesuit who just over a decade before may have brought over John Shakespeare's *Testament*. It instructs Cecil and Fixer, highly cryptically, to sound out what they can find 'in the man my *cousin*', and goes on:

> The form in the which you may advertise me may be this, and I pray you note it: 'Your *cousin the baker* is well-inclined and glad to hear of you, and meaneth not to give over his pretence to the *old bakehouse* you know of, but rather to put the same in suit when his ability shall serve. . . .

> I request you that *my cousin's* matter be dealt in secrecy, lest it may turn the poor man to hurt, but great desire have I to hear truly and particularly of his estate.[40]

In the letter's margin the words I have italicised above are decoded, apparently from the information Burghley's agents had managed to extract from Cecil and Fixer: 'By his *cousin* is meant my Lord Strange', and 'by *baker* and *bakehouse* is understood my Lord Strange and the title they would have him pretend when Her Majesty dieth'.

This letter was followed in early July by another note found among the papers of Burghley and his son Sir Robert Cecil:

> The drift of his letter is charging us by means of John Garrat [Gerard], a priest, to make trial of my L. Strange, and see how he was affected to that pretence of the Crown after Her Majesty's death. The matter he would not communicate to any but Garnet and Southwell, who are Jesuits at liberty in England. I brought this letter that my Lord [i.e. Burghley] might not think that what I told him of Lord Strange was a chimera.[41]

Now such was the Machiavellian nature of the age, and in particular of Burghley and his son Robert Cecil, that there is some uncertainty as to whether the 'cousin the baker' letter was genuinely from Persons. The other possibility is that it was concocted by government agents to incriminate Ferdinando, much as Mary Queen of Scots was implicated by agents in the Babington Plot. But of one thing we can be certain. In the early 1590s Ferdinando's loyalty to Elizabeth was under the deepest suspicion, and whether or not Ferdinando *was* secretly Catholic, and whether or not he entertained any serious hopes as Elizabeth's successor, somehow he needed to demonstrate that a Stanley could be a true and loyal subject.

One way he could be seen positively to have done this was by adopting a personal motto: *Sans changer ma vérité*, or 'Without changing my truth', that is, without breaking faith. This seems to have had no ancestral precedent, but it can be seen below his coat of arms in his already mentioned portrait. Another was by his participation in the Accession Day Tilts, the colourfully presented celebrations of the anniversary of the Queen's accession held each year at Whitehall, on roughly the site of the present-day Horseguards Parade. On these occasions the more youthful and noble of Elizabeth's courtiers would enter with retainers dressed according to a topical theme. They would then present the Queen with an *impresa* shield (one painted with a wittily conceived 'device' or motto), then mount their horses and indulge in a friendly joust. Ferdinando, who is featured with jousting accoutrements in his portrait, took part in these tilts between 1589 and 1592, and here is how George Peele (thought by some to have been a collaborator of Shakespeare's), poetically described him making his entrance for the 1590 event:

> The Earl of Derby's valiant son and heir,
> Brave Ferdinand Lord Strange, strangely embarked
> Under Jove's kingly bird, the golden Eagle,
> Stanley's old crest and honourable badge,
> As veering 'fore the wind, in costly ship,
> And armour white and watchet [pale blue] buckled fast,
> Presents himself, his horses and his men,
> Suited in satin to their master's colours,
> Well-near twice-twenty squires that went him by
> And having by his trounch man pardon crav'd
> Veiling his Eagle to his sovereign's eyes
> As who should say, stoop Eagle to this Sun,
> Dismounts him from his pageant, and at once,
> Taking his choice of lusty tilting horse,
> Covered with sumptuous rich caparisons,
> He mounts him bravely for his friendly foe . . .[42]

Albeit whimsically, it is tempting to imagine Burbage and his men among the 'twice-twenty squires', perhaps even having prepared

Ferdinando's ship-like pageant cart. We might even go further and envisage Shakespeare as the pardon-craving 'trounch man', or spokesman, or at least as having written the script. Actors certainly did help out lordly patrons on these occasions;[43] and Shakespeare and Richard Burbage's later making of an *impresa* for the Earl of Rutland, readily enough indicates their sometime involvement in such spectacles (see page 371).

But could yet another way of Ferdinando's showing his loyalty to Elizabeth – whatever its sincerity – have been by commissioning from Shakespeare and his crew the spectacle of *Henry vi/Richard iii*? By presenting in dramatised form the events of the Wars of the Roses, with all its horrors of great lords struggling over royal succession, could Ferdinando have been demonstrating his distaste for such *lèse-majesté*? By revivifying Richard iii and his murder of the princes, could Ferdinando have been presenting a subtle warning to Elizabeth of the fate of tyrants who shed the blood royal? By re-enacting that moment of all moments, when none other than Ferdinando's own great-great-great grandfather had set the crown of England upon the head of Henry Tudor, might Ferdinando not have wanted to remind Elizabeth that it was to a *loyal* Stanley that she owed her crown?

Ferdinando was the one man who could have wanted to see just such a spectacle of English history performed, and he possessed the resources – an acting company with its own promising new dramatist – to put it into effect. Inevitably Ferdinando would have intended the tetralogy for a Court showing before allowing it to go on to the common stage, and it so happens that for the winter of 1591/2 the still-preserved Court accounts, although they do not show the titles of the plays presented before the Queen, record Lord Strange's Men performing for her the unprecedented number of six productions at Whitehall between 27 December and 8 February.[44] Furthermore this neatly coincides with the 1591 date for Shakespeare's writing of the last of the tetralogy, *Richard iii*, as advanced by Arden editor Antony Hammond.

While we cannot claim to have proved that this is what happened, we can be sure that there are any number of routes by which Stratford-born Shakespeare might have come to Ferdinando's attention. This may have been simply and straightforwardly as a member of Burbage's company who had shown he had a way with scene-setting and blank verse. But there are a variety of other possibilities that could have led Shakespeare to Lancashire and Ferdinando.

As a major Warwickshire wool-dealer, Shakespeare's father would have had connection with Ferdinando's wife Alice's family, the Spencers, for the Spencers had built themselves up into one of England's wealthiest families by purchasing Warwickshire and Northamptonshire sheep pastures, intensively breeding sheep, and then selling direct to wool merchants and to London butchers.[45]

Old John Spencer, the founder of the dynasty, had begun the family enterprise in the same tiny village of Snitterfield in which John Shakespeare had grown up. Shakespeare's schoolmaster, Thomas Jenkins, was a fellow of the Oxford College, St John's, where Ferdinando and his brothers received their university education. Another of Shakespeare's possible schoolmasters, the Catholic John Cottom, hailed from Tarnacre, Lancashire, which was on Ferdinando's own doorstep. And wealthy Thomas Combe of Stratford, with whose family Shakespeare would later exhibit many connections, had married a relation of the Stanleys in 1586.

While we cannot be sure which of these routes led Shakespeare to Ferdinando, patronage by him now makes sense for the first time of how Shakespeare could – while still remaining Shakespeare – have acquired so many of those insights into Courtly political intrigues that have so led astray all the Oxfordians, Baconians, Rutlandians, not to mention the Derbyians. For as we have already indicated, as crown prince of the Stanley empire, Ferdinando had such elevated status that the world in which he moved was a Court in itself. His family's Lathom fortress was so palatial that Henry VII was said to have modelled his own specially commissioned Richmond Palace [see pl. 40], also sadly lost, upon it.

Great officials, messengers, even (undoubtedly) spies made real-life entrances and exits upon the stage surrounding Ferdinando. Not least of the lessons Shakespeare would have learned more readily from him than from anyone else would have been the value of political and religious ambivalence, that trait of which generations of Stanleys had been past masters, and which Shakespeare would so brilliantly inject into his own work. Patronage by Ferdinando would also have provided, possibly at Lathom, but far more likely at the Cannon Row house in London, a suitably well-stocked library into which Shakespeare could freely dip and borrow without the huge financial burden of acquiring one of his own.

For most previous writers on Shakespeare, Ferdinando has existed as little more than a cipher: simply the name under which Burbage's acting company, if Shakespeare even belonged to it, plied their craft in order to avoid arrest for vagrancy. In the case of the lordly patrons of other acting companies, such minimal association may well have been true. All that a theatrical company normally expected of its patron was a few liveries, and licence to trade in his name. But was Ferdinando different, very different? Where our hypothesis breaks new ground is in suggesting not only such strong patronage by Ferdinando, but also one necessarily involving a substantial degree of trust between him and Shakespeare, albeit at an earl-to-subject level. As yet our hypothesis has little hard evidence to back it up, but it nonetheless behoves us to be on the watch for further Stanley/ Lancastrian connections as our investigation of Shakespeare proceeds. For as we reach the year 1592, Shakespeare at last begins to emerge more firmly onto the pages of history.

CHAPTER 8

Entry into History

If there is one piece of evidence that may reasonably be said to be the first proper record of a Shakespeare play being performed on a London stage, indeed any stage anywhere, this is a single-line entry in Philip Henslowe's Diary, as preserved at Dulwich College, London. This reads:

> ne – Rd at harey the vj the 3 of marche 1591 . . .iij^{li} xvj^s 8d[1]

Temporarily setting aside the first word 'ne', the meaning of the rest is straightforward enough: 'Received at *Henry VI* 3rd March 1591 £3.16s.8d.'.

We should be aware that 3 March 1591 actually means 1592 by our modern reckoning, as the Elizabethans, like modern-day tax inspectors, often did not set their new year until late March, or even April. (Elsewhere in this book, this adjustment has usually been made automatically.) It is highly important that Henslowe wrote at the beginning of his page listing the productions among which the *Henry VI* entry appears, that these were by 'my Lord Strange's Men'.

Crucially, then, here in Shakespeare's *Henry VI*'s first emergence onto the pages of history (and no one has seriously suggested this play, as listed, to have been other than Shakespeare's), we see Shakespeare's clearest link with the company that we have all along suggested he was first associated with. But there is also a curiosity. Not only is it surprising to find Lord Strange's Men being linked with Philip Henslowe, whose main dealings were with his son-in-law Edward Alleyn's Admiral's Men, also evident from the Diary is that the performances in question were being staged, not at Lord Strange's Men's normal north of London Shoreditch Theatre, but across the Thames at Henslowe's Rose.

Original contract[2] and related documents at Dulwich College show that Henslowe built his Rose theatre in 1587, in partnership with grocer John Cholmley, in an area of Bankside, Southwark, long noted for its bull- and bear-baiting, and its 'stews' or brothels. Effectively it was in a southern Liberty that was equivalent to Burbage's Holywell Liberty north of the river. What Henslowe's Diary also reveals, however, is that in late 1591 or early in 1592, just before the Lord Strange's Men's performances in which *Henry VI* appears, he commissioned some substantial alterations to be made. Clearly listed in his Diary are, in his own words, 'such charges as I have laid out about my playhouse',[3] including workmen's wages, purchases of deal boarding and other timber, lath, thatching, rafters, sand, lime and no less than 54,000 nails, the whole contract totalling some £105 – very roughly equivalent to about £50,000 at today's prices.

Fascinatingly, and quite uniquely for our understanding of the Elizabethan theatre, in recent years physical evidence of the work Henslowe had carried out at this time has come to light. The Rose's original location on the Bankside has never been lost, thanks partly to being preserved in the name Rose Alley, which can still be found on a London street map. The 1950 Survey of London pinpointed the site exactly from old tenement leases.[4] Yet extraordinarily, when in 1957 it was decided to build a new office block – Southbridge House – on the Rose's site, no one attempted an archaeological investigation, and huge concrete foundation piles were allowed to be driven straight through whatever lay beneath. Only in 1989, when Southbridge House was in turn demolished, were the foundations of Henslowe's Rose unmistakeably revealed – together with the havoc that building Southbridge House had caused. No less than nine sets of piles had smashed through the fragile outlines of the theatre like huge concrete bullets. Two had destroyed substantial parts of the original stage – as yet the only known example of an original Elizabethan popular theatre stage, and one certainly trodden by Shakespeare's fellow actors if not by Shakespeare himself.

Despite such modern philistinism, which might have been compounded with another office block had it not been for leading actors' well-publicised protests,[5] such rescue archaeology that has so far been possible has furnished priceless information, both about Henslowe's original 1587 Rose and the alterations he made for the coming of Lord Strange's Men.[6] The original Rose, instead of being circular as had previously been imagined, was a slightly irregular polygon of thirteen or fourteen sides, about seventy-two feet across. From photographs and archaeological plans [see pl. 16] it is

1

2

3

4

Some alternative 'Shakespeares'

1. Sir Francis Bacon (1561–1623). The 'Baconian' authorship claim has had advocates from as early as the eighteenth century.

2. William Stanley, sixth Earl of Derby (1561?–1642). 'Derbyians' have pointed to his initials 'W.S.', and historical mention that he was 'penning comedies for the common players' in 1599.

3. Edward de Vere, seventeenth Earl of Oxford (1550–1604). The 'Oxfordian' case has some particularly forceful present-day proponents. (*By courtesy of Christies, London*)

4. Queen Elizabeth I (1533–1603). Computer matching has apparently shown unusual similarities between her portrait and the Droeshout engraving of Shakespeare (pl. 52). (*National Portrait Gallery, London*)

The London Shakespeare knew

5. Within a generation of Shakespeare's death, Czech-born engraver
Wenceslaus Hollar drew from Southwark Cathedral's tower this 'photographic'
view of the 'West part o[f] Southwarke toward Westminster'. At top left can be
seen the Globe, with the bear-baiting pit to its right. Within another generation
these and much else of Shakespeare's London had been swept away. (*Yale
Center for British Art*)

6

7

Shakespeare's 'Birthplace' House

6. The house in Henley Street, Stratford-upon-Avon, in which Shakespeare is said to have been born. In 1815, Washington Irving described it as 'a small mean-looking edifice of wood and plaster'. It was 'restored' in the mid-nineteenth century. (*Shakespeare Birthplace Trust*)

7. Watercolour of the house made circa 1762 by Richard Greene. An engraving made from this formed the basis of the mid-nineteenth-century restoration. (*Folger Shakespeare Library, Washington*)

8

9

Evidence of Shakespeare's father's Catholicism?

8. Published version of an incontrovertibly Catholic 'Testament of the Soule', a form of spiritual will, a copy of which, made out in John Shakespeare's name, was found hidden in the rafters of the Birthplace House in 1757. (*Folger Shakespeare Library, Washington*)

9. Punishment of Catholics in Shakespeare's time. Increasingly severe government penalties made life all but intolerable for practising Catholics. Hunted down with the aid of paid informers, priests were publicly executed by hanging, drawing and quartering.

10

11

Lord Strange's Men perform . . .

10. Although we cannot be sure that Shakespeare was a member of Ferdinando, Lord Strange's Men, the company certainly performed his *Titus Andronicus*. The above drawing of a scene from this, preserved at Longleat, is the only known contemporary depiction of a Shakespearean play. (*By kind permission of the Marquess of Bath*)

11. 'Away with these disgraceful wailing robes. . . .' How the opening scene of *Henry vi, Part i* was probably costumed, from a contemporary depiction of the funeral of Sir Philip Sidney. (*Photograph: Folger Shakespeare Library, Washington*)

Shakespeare's first patron?

12.   Ferdinando Stanley, Lord Strange (1559–94), a unique contemporary portrait showing him dressed in the Queen's colours for the Accession Day tilts. Closely watched by government spies due to suspicions of his Catholicism, Ferdinando was undoubtedly the patron of many of the actors who became Shakespeare's 'fellows'. (*By kind permission of Mary A. Porter*)

The world of 'common players'

13.   As depicted by Pieter Brueghel the Younger (1564–1637/8), a company of common players performs in the inn-yard of a small town. Such a performance in Stratford-upon-Avon may well have been the young Shakespeare's first experience of the theatre of his time. (*Auckland City Art Gallery, New Zealand*)

14.   Richard Tarlton (?–1588), a hugely popular clown and playwright of Shakespeare's early years. It was said 'the people began exceedingly to laugh, when Tarlton first peeped out his head.' (*British Library*)

15.   The theatre in which Shakespeare served his apprenticeship? A view of what some have identified as the Burbage-built Theatre, Shoreditch, from a unique engraving, 'The View of the Cittye of London from the North towards the Sowth'. (*The University Library, Utrecht*)

14

15

16a

A stage that Shakespeare trod?

16. As revealed by excavations in 1989, the remains of Philip Henslowe's Rose theatre, where Lord Strange's Men performed Shakespeare's *Henry VI* in 1592. The foundations clearly reveal two different building phases (see plan right). The first phase came in 1587, but it is the second, 1592, stage that appears uppermost. (*Photograph: Andrew Fulgoni and (plan) the Museum of London*)

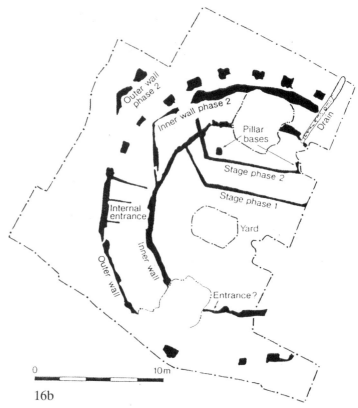

16b

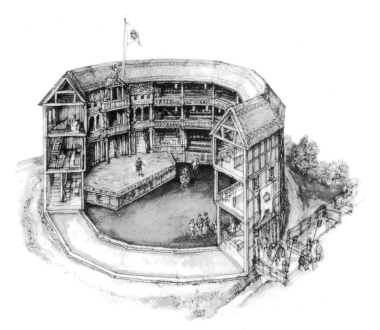

17A   The 1587 Rose

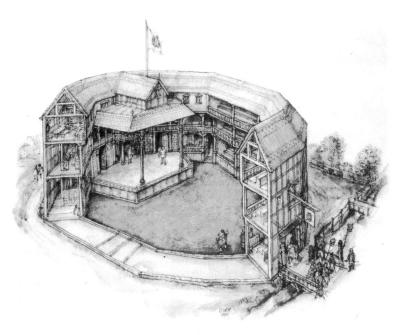

17 B   The 1592 Rose

The Rose reconstructed . . .

17.   Based on the archaeological findings, theatre historian C. Walter Hodges'
reconstructions [A] of the Rose's original appearance when first built in 1587,
and [B] when altered in 1592, just prior to its programme of the productions by
Lord Strange's Men that included *Henry VI*. (*By kind permission of C. Walter
Hodges and the Museum of London*)

An aide-memoire from the Rose?

18.   A 'Plot', or running-order, for one of Lord Strange's Men's productions, *The Second Part of the Seven Deadly Sins*, as performed at the Rose during their 1592 season. From the square hole cut in the middle of the sheet, this seems to have been hung on a peg in the actors' dressing-room as an aide-memoire to the play's running-order. The text includes the names of several of Shakespeare's fellow-actors. (*By kind permission of the Governors of Dulwich College*)

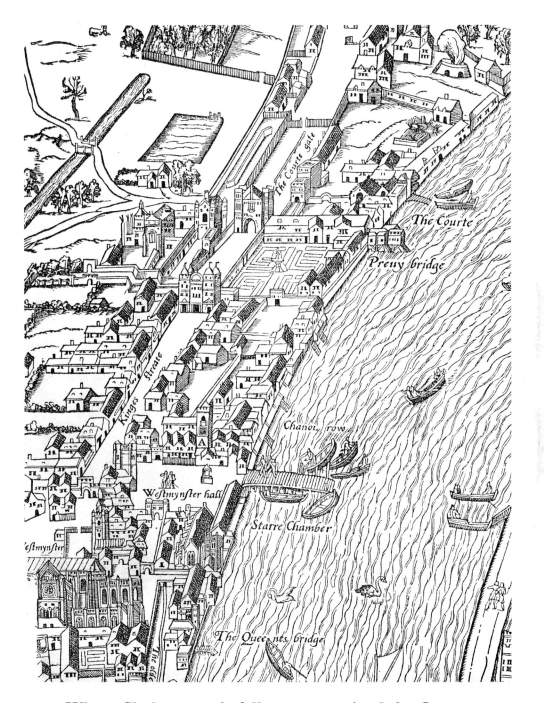

The Courte gate

The Courte

Preuy bridge

Kinges Streate

Chanoi row

Westmynster hall

Westmynster

Starre Chamber

The Queenes bridge

Where Shakespeare's fellows entertained the Queen

19.   The Palace of Whitehall and its environs in Shakespeare's time, a detail
from the so-called 'Agas' map of London. Lord Strange's Men gave six
Christmastime performances before the Queen here shortly before their 1592
appearances at the Rose. Just above the Court Gate can be seen the tiltyard
where Ferdinando, Lord Strange, and Shakespeare's undoubted later patron
the Earl of Southampton, took part in the annual Accession Day tilts.
(*Guildhall Library, Aldermanbury, London*)

20

The love I dedicate to your lordship . . .

20. What remains of Titchfield House, country seat of the third Earl of Southampton. Shakespeare dedicated his poems *Venus and Adonis* (1593), and *The Rape of Lucrece* (1594) to the young Earl who, like Ferdinando, was strongly tinged with Catholicism. Redesigned in an Italian manner, Titchfield's principal rooms were on the upper storey.

21. Dedication page of *The Rape of Lucrece*. This shows an increased familiarity with the Earl in the wake of *Venus and Adonis*, similarly dedicated to the Earl the previous year. (*Bodleian Library, Oxford*)

TO THE RIGHT
HONOVRABLE, HENRY
VVriothefley, Earle of Southhampton,
and Baron of Titchfield.

HE loue I dedicate to your Lordſhip is without end:wherof this Pamphlet without beginning is but a ſuperfluous Moity. The warrant I haue of your Honourable diſpoſition, not the worth of my vntutord Lines makes it aſſured of acceptance. VVhat I haue done is yours, what I haue to doe is yours, being part in all I haue, deuoted yours. VVere my worth greater, my duety would ſhew greater, meane time, as it is, it is bound to your Lordſhip; To whom I wiſh long life ſtill lengthned with all happineſſe.

Your Lordſhips in all duety,

William Shakeſpeare.

A 2

**'A woman's face, with Nature's own
hand painted . . .'** (*Sonnet* 20)

22.   Henry Wriothesley, third Earl of Southampton (1573–1624), as portrayed
in a miniature by Nicholas Hilliard, 1594. According to Dr A. L. Rowse and
others, Southampton was the 'lovely boy' of Shakespeare's *Sonnets*. Rowse
dates the *Sonnets* to about the time that Hilliard painted his miniature.
(*Fitzwilliam Museum, Cambridge*)

23

24

25

The Italian connection?

23.   John Florio (1553–1625), Italian tutor to the third Earl of Southampton. Shakespeare's *Love's Labour's Lost* seems to owe its title to a phrase from Florio. (*National Portrait Gallery, London*)

24.   Astrological chart of Emilia Bassano/Lanier (1569–1645), whom Dr A. L. Rowse identifies as the musically inclined 'Dark Lady' with whom Shakespeare and his aristocratic young patron (arguably Southampton) both had adulterous affairs. Emilia's half-Venetian, half-Jewish father Baptista was a royal musician, and Emilia was undoubtedly paramour to Lord Chamberlain Henry Hunsdon under whose patronage Shakespeare worked from 1594–6. (*Bodleian Library, Oxford*)

25.   Simon Forman (1552–1611), the astrologer and quack medical practitioner whose notebooks provided the crucial clues to identifying Emilia Lanier as Shakespeare's 'Dark Lady'.

possible to distinguish the outer and inner walls that supported galleries for seated spectators, also the mortar-floored pit or yard for the standing audience, purposefully sloped stagewards, so that those at the rear still had a reasonable view. The stage was of the shallow apron variety, trapezoidal in shape, eighteen feet from front to back, in width ranging from twenty-eight to nearly thirty-eight feet, and facing southeast to catch maximum daylight.

Also readily identifiable are the traces of the alterations that Henslowe's Diary shows he commissioned late in 1591 or early in 1592. His workmen can be seen to have demolished the outer wall behind the stage, rebuilt this some nine feet further north, then moved the stage back further north likewise. They also relaid the yard with compacted earth, cinder and cracked hazelnut shells in a mixture that seems to have been harder-wearing than before. It is particularly notable that, whereas the Rose's 1587 stage shows no sign of having had a roof, the remains of the 1592 version show traces of two front pillars, as if these once supported a roof [see reconstructions pl. 17]. It also has signs of where the rain ran off onto the floor, precisely outlining the area that a roof over the stage would have protected. Part of Henslowe's alterations, then, seem to have provided that extra protection from the weather that expensively-costumed productions such as the *Henry VI* plays would have particularly needed. In order to recoup his investment, Henslowe also clearly decided to enlarge the Rose, increasing its audience capacity by some twenty per cent, to hold, according to the latest calculations, between 2,000 and 2,400 people.[7] Yet fascinatingly, even thus expanded the theatre would seem to have remained intimate enough for most members of the audience, standing and seated, to appreciate nuances of voice, and subtleties of facial expression.

The Rose excavations also uncovered the occasional item from the Shakespearean age that had escaped instant pulverisation beneath Southbridge House's piles. Now being conserved in the Museum of London are a leather shoe (left foot), that someone once valued sufficiently to have it remodelled before discarding; a shingle from the stage roof, a baluster, a scabbard, and a quantity of unused nails, possibly left-overs from Henslowe's original 54,000.

More important than any of these, however, is a quite independently preserved document that seems once to have hung backstage at the Rose, and to have been used specifically by Lord Strange's Men during their 1592 season at the theatre [see pl. 18]. A much-prized item in the Dulwich College collection, the document in question is headed in bold letters 'The Platt of the Secound parte of the Seven Deadlie Sinns', and is a very rare example of the 'plot' or synopsis of a play's running order that Elizabethan theatrical companies used backstage as their *aide-mémoire* for which actors, props, sound effects, etc, were needed next. [For full text, see Appendix C, Miscellaneous Documents, page 472] It even sports a rectangular hole in its upper half, almost certainly cut so that it could hang upon a hook in the actors' tiring house, or dressing-room.

While no script of *The Seven Deadly Sins* has survived, it seems to have been a Morality play with elements from *Gorboduc* and dramatisations of the seven mortal sins, featuring both Henry vi and a monk called Lidgate as the 'chorus'. The comic actor Richard Tarlton (whom we suggested might have been Shakespeare's Yorick) is thought to have authored it. More importantly, as argued by the highly-regarded Victorian scholar Frederick Fleay, it seems to have been one and the same as a production listed in Henslowe's Diary as 'iiij playes in one', or *Four Plays in One*, which was performed by Lord Strange's Men at the Rose on 6 March of our 1592, that is to say, in the very same week that they performed Shakespeare's *Henry vi*.

Of paramount interest here is that while the 'Platt' sometimes refers to the play's actors by the characters they play (for example, 'King Gorbuduk', 'Ferrex & Porrex'), in other instances it often gives their own names, for example:

Enter King Gorbuduk . . . R. Burbadge, Mr Brian, Th. Goodale.
The Queen with Ferrex & Porrex and some attendants. . . .'

Immediately we are able to recognise Richard Burbage and George Bryan (the latter formerly one of Leicester's Men). Both of these later appeared in the 1623 First Folio as 'principal actors' with Shakespeare. Likewise, as we peruse further we come across 'Mr Pope' in a leading part, clearly Thomas Pope of the Leicester's Men and another First Folio 'principal actor'. We also find 'Mr Phillipps', with little doubt the Augustine Phillips of the same background. Where an actor appears as 'Mr' this seems clearly to denote his senior status.

Continuing among the 'Platt's' lesser actors we find without any accompanying 'Mr' the names Richard Cowley, John Duke, Robert Pallant, John Sincler, Thomas Goodale, William Sly, and J. Holland. Of these Richard Cowley and William Sly again appear in the First Folio's list of 'principal actors', and John Duke is included as a fellow actor with Shakespeare in a cast list of 1598. Holland and Sincler are particularly interesting, for although they don't appear to have merited a mention in the First Folio as 'principal actors', their association with Shakespeare at around the time he wrote the *Henry VI* plays is demonstrable from their featuring under their own names in early stage directions of these plays. When writing minor parts, Shakespeare seems to have not bothered to create names for them. He simply has John Holland appear under his own name in the First Folio text of *Henry VI, Part II*, while John Sincler features as 'Sinklo' in the Quarto of *Henry VI, Part III*.

Following the hierarchical system postulated earlier, the more junior actors appear in the 'Platt' under Christian names only. Though more guesswork is needed here, 'Harry' has been thought to be the First Folio's Henry Condell (years later, Condell will sign himself as 'Harry' during his churchwarden duties for St Mary Aldermanbury); 'Kit' is Christopher Beeston, father of the William Beeston who would later give Shakespearean information to John Aubrey, and 'Saunder', logically, is Alexander Cooke, another of the First Folio's 'principal actors'. Likewise 'Nick' may well be the Folio's Nicholas Tooley and 'Ro', or 'Ro. Go' its Robert Gough. Besides their Christian name status it is evident from their having been assigned female parts that the latter three were young men.

It deserves mention that one name in the 'Platt' not yet accounted for is a 'Will', but it is probably best to avoid the temptation to identify this person with Shakespeare. The part in question was a young female one, a somewhat unlikely piece of casting for a Shakespeare who would have been approaching twenty-eight years old in early 1592. If he was acting with the company in this production of *The Seven Deadly Sins*, the more likely explanation for his name not appearing could well be that he was among those identified only by the characters they were playing, such as the two 'Chorus' figures, Henry VI and Lidgate. These were parts that, as suggested by dramatic-companies' expert J. T. Murray, could well have been played by Shakespeare and by Folio editor John Heminges respectively.[8]

Inevitably, however, this is but one of a variety of loose ends. We do not know exactly how or why Burbage's Lord Strange's Men, with *Henry VI* on the repertoire, came to be acting at Henslowe's Rose for a four-month season from 19 February 1592. It may have been while some refurbishments equivalent to the Rose's were going on at the Theatre, or that doubling up was needed between Lord Strange's and the Admiral's Men in order to mount such major productions as *Henry VI*. The cooperation is certainly surprising given that the previous May there had been a fierce argument between James Burbage and the Admiral's Men (with which Henslowe was later principally associated), on how the takings should be divided between them, Burbage reportedly declaring 'by a great oath' that he cared neither for the Lord Admiral, nor 'for three of the best lords of them all'.[9]

Another mystery is the already noted 'ne' before Henslowe's logging of *Henry VI*. On the authority of the great Sir Edmund Chambers, many scholars have assumed it meant simply 'new', and that Henslowe meant it was being staged for the first time on 3 March 1592. Certainly 'ne' generally occurs in Henslowe's accounts when a play is making its first appearance in these, but it is important to recognise that this does not necessarily mean a first performance on stage. For instance, Henslowe often has plenty of room to write 'new' in full, yet when in several dozen instances elsewhere in his accounts he records actors pawning new clothes with him, invariably he notes these as 'new(e)', never 'ne'.[10] 'Ne', therefore, has to be interpreted cautiously. In like vein, as has been pointed out by Arden editor A. R. Humphreys, a 'harey the vj' entry in Henslowe's Diary does not necessarily denote the first part of *Henry VI*. The Elizabethans often neglected such niceties of distinction, even when making official registrations[11] and, as we will see shortly, the last part of *Henry VI* must have been performed before or during the early 1592 season at the Rose.

Arguably indicative of the *Henry VI* plays' popular success is that whenever the name appears in Henslowe's Diary, the receipts generated were highly impressive by comparison to works by certain other writers. The Diary's daily entries for the plays the Lord Strange's Men performed at the Rose between February and May of 1592 represent a punishing schedule for any company, with productions every day except Sundays and Good Friday, with never the same play repeated two days running. For the opening play on 19 February Henslowe listed 'fryer bacune', readily identifiable as writer Robert Greene's *Friar Bacon and Friar Bungay*, which was all about two friars who enlist the help of the devil to try to make a head made of brass speak. Attendance was clearly poor, Henslowe's share, whatever proportion it represented of the overall takings, being just seventeen shillings and three pence (86p). Two days later Henslowe listed 'Orlando', identifiable as another Greene play, *Orlando Furioso*. The takings from this were sixteen shillings and six pence (82½p). After some unidentifiable plays, the 26 February production 'the Jewe of malltuse', unmistakeably Marlowe's *The Jew of Malta*, brought in fifty shillings (£2.50).

But then, on 3 March we reach the *Henry VI* performance (whether Part I, II or III is indeterminable), that we can reasonably confidently identify as the first surviving record of the staging of a Shakespeare play. Henslowe's income from that performance suddenly shoots up to three pounds sixteen shillings and eight pence (£3.83, or approaching £2,000 at today's value), considerably the highest takings of productions mounted thus far. Three days later, another *Henry VI* performance (again we cannot be sure of which part) brought in three pounds, whereas a third Greene play *A Looking Glass for London and England* brought in a derisory seven shillings. In the course of the following three months the entry *Henry VI* occurs fourteen times, bringing in for Henslowe some thirty pounds overall.

It is already clear, therefore, that even at such an early stage of his career Shakespeare was achieving an audience popularity that rivalled Marlowe's, and was heavily out-gunning old reprobate Robert Greene, with repercussions that we will hear more about later.

But meanwhile, whatever the rapturous applause Lord Strange's Men were receiving from the London theatre-going public, some highly adverse Puritan attitudes were being aroused, particularly in London, and particularly among the civic authorities. On 25 February, less than a week after Lord Strange's Men's first performance at the Rose, the City of London's Lord Mayor complained to the Archbishop of Canterbury (John Whitgift, the former Bishop of Worcester who, coincidentally, had approved Shakespeare's special marriage licence), that:

    . . . by the daily and disorderly exercise of a number of players and playing houses erected within this City, the youth thereof is greatly corrupted and their manners infected with many evil and ungodly qualities, by reason of the wanton and profane devices represented on the stages by the said players, the apprentices and servants withdrawn from their works, and all sorts in general from the daily resort unto sermons and other Christian exercises, to the great hindrance of the trades and traders of this City and profanation of the good and godly religion established among us. To which places also do usually resort great numbers of light and lewd disposed persons, as harlots, cutpurses, cozeners [cheats], pilferers and suchlike, and there, under the colour of resort to those places to hear the plays, devise divers evil and ungodly matches, confederacies and conspiracies which by means of the opportunity of the place cannot be prevented nor discovered, as otherwise they might be.[12]

The moderate Whitgift's reply, if there was one, has been lost, but on 6 March (notably the day of *The Seven Deadly Sins* performance) the Lord Mayor followed up with another letter advising him that he had appointed aldermen to confer with Edmund Tilney, Master of the Queen's Revels 'for the better . . . restraint of the said plays in and about this City'.[13] Just over two weeks later London's Guild of Merchant Taylors minuted receiving from the Lord Mayor a precept 'showing to the Company the great enormity that this City sustaineth by the practice and profane exercise of players and playing houses in this City'.

Whether or not Shakespeare was acting with Lord Strange's Men at this time, just what a difficult path they trod in the face of these attitudes is more than evident from a riot that took place at Southwark, in the Rose's environs, on 11 June. It was a protest by London apprentices at the arrest of one of their number, after they had apparently gathered under the 'pretence of their meeting at a play'.[14] The civic authorities were always nervous of any large gatherings and that such social disorder should happen in the environs of a playhouse was just the sort of excuse they needed to have the theatres closed down. Accordingly, immediately following the riot, the Privy Council lost no time in granting them the necessary authority, and Henslowe's Diary tells its own story with an abrupt termination of entries after 22 June, just four days after Lord Strange's Men had mounted yet another showing of a *Henry VI*. Overnight, Lord Strange's Men had been turned out of business.

The company seems almost immediately to have taken the only course available to them, that of a provincial tour, though the income from such a venture was always uncertain because of the inevitably higher expenditure for usually poorer return. An entry for 13 July in the Canterbury civic records shows payment of thirty shillings (£1.50) to 'the Lord Strange his players' for their performance of an unspecified entertainment 'in the court hall before Mr Lawes, Mayor and other his brethren'[15] although as with many such entries, it is impossible to be absolutely sure this belongs to 1592. Likewise in the 1592 accounts for Gloucester and Coventry there appear similar entries, though without information on the exact date.

Meanwhile back in London the diminutive and waspish young pamphleteer Tom Nashe (the 1590s equivalent of a satirical-magazine editor), was doing his best to plead on the players' behalf. With the memory of a performance of *Henry VI, Part I* clearly vivid in his mind he penned a 'Defence of Plays' remarking how, despite the claims of 'some petitioners of the Council' that plays 'corrupt the youth of the City', there was a great deal both good and patriotic about the revivification of the history of a hundred or so years ago. This was particularly so with English forces in action on French soil at around the very time:

> How it would have joyed brave Talbot (the terror of the French) to think that after he had lain two hundred years in his tomb, he should triumph again on the stage, and have his bones new embalmed with the tears of ten thousand spectators at least (at several time) who, in the tragedian that represents his person, imagine they behold him fresh bleeding.[16]

Nashe may also have had in mind the new lavishness of productions such as *Henry VI* when he wrote, having obviously heard of the unseemly continental use of real women to play women's parts:

> Our players are not as the players beyond the sea ... bawdy comedians that have whores and common citizens to play women's parts ... our scene is ... stately furnished ... our representations honourable ... not consisting, like theirs, of a pantaloon, a whore and a zany, but of emperors, kings and princes ...[17]

Nashe's mention of *Henry VI*, appearing as it does in part of his *Pierce*

Penilesse, which was published no later than 8 September 1592,[18] represents the earliest known mention of a Shakespeare play. It is also Shakespeare's first favourable review, though swiftly to be followed by an unfavourable one as we shall see.

Meanwhile, barely had the notices gone out shutting London's theatres, than a rather more insidious force began to manifest itself, impelling anyone who could to leave the city for the rather healthier air of the country. In the summer of 1592 plague made one of its severer visitations. For Shakespeare's time no disease was more feared, not least because of its repulsive symptoms. First came swellings of the lymphatic glands, usually in the groin, then the bursting from these of an evil-smelling pus, the victim thereupon suffering a high temperature, delirium, coma and, in between forty and eighty per cent of cases, death.

At the time no one knew that the disease was transmitted by fleas from the black rat, still less did they have any idea how it could be cured. But during this summer one man, subsequently to have a rather unusual link with Shakespeare, came remarkably close. Up-and-coming London astrologer Simon Forman, having been unlucky enough to catch the disease, coolly decided his only recourse lay in trying to find his own cure, for which he resorted, with admirable resolve, to a distillation of his own pus. Astonishingly, it worked, and he not only lived to tell the tale, but to make a moderate living passing on the recipe to others.

Of Forman more later, for meanwhile a plague of quite another kind was wreaking havoc. In an exceptionally severe government crackdown on Catholicism, raids were taking place all over the country on respectable families who wanted nothing more than to be allowed to worship in their old traditional way without fear of extortionate fine or imprisonment. By 1592 Richard Topcliffe had become head of the Elizabethan secret police. He was controller of a huge network of informers, a gaoler, master inquisitor and torturer of those Catholics (predominantly priests), whom he netted, and chief executioner's assistant of those he successfully delivered to the gallows. Topcliffe had a readiness of access to the Queen envied by many a Court nobleman – he even boasted to his captives that he was allowed to fondle her breasts. One of his greatest coups in late June 1592, when Shakespeare's Lord Strange's Men were on their enforced provincial tour, was his capture of the poetic Father Robert Southwell, one of the Jesuits who the previous year had been reported 'at liberty in England' in the intercepted correspondence that implicated Ferdinando, Lord Strange.

Shakespeare was distantly related to Robert Southwell through the Arden connection.[19] Far closer to home, however, back in the March while *Henry VI* had been playing to packed houses, Shakespeare's father John had for the first time been listed among those reported to the government for not making their legal minimum once-a-month attendance at their local parish church – in the Shakespeares' case, Stratford's Holy Trinity. Almost certainly drawn up by church wardens, this listing was specially intended to flush out all those suspected of being undeclared Catholics, and of giving sanctuary to priests. John Shakespeare's name appeared third in a set of nine, headed by John Wheeler (who had been his Deputy when he had been Bailiff back in 1568–9), followed by Wheeler's son, of the same name. Against these an unidentified someone set the words 'We suspect these nine persons next ensuing absent themselves for fear of processes' [i.e. legal proceedings]. On 25 September the puritanical local squire Sir Thomas Lucy and his fellow commissioners then furnished to the government a list of those local Catholics who had agreed to conform, following this again with the list of nine, this time with the accompanying words 'It is said that these last come not to church for fear of process for debt'.[20]

Despite our earlier intimations of John Shakespeare's Catholicism, the list poses more questions than it answers, not least, for instance, because Stratford wool draper George Badger, unlisted among the nine, though totally open about his Catholicism, managed to retain his wealth, and also to hold on to his office as alderman for far longer than John Shakespeare. Are we seeing here evidence that John Shakespeare was genuinely in debt through failed business activities? Or that he was genuinely a Catholic merely pretending to be in debt, with friends among local officials to help him in this guise? Or perhaps a combination of both, that he was a Catholic who had been bled dry by blackmailing informers? Not least of the list's many enigmas is that among its remaining six names appear Fluellen, Bardolph and Court, names Shakespeare would later use – and hardly accidentally, surely? – for characters in *Henry V*.

Whatever the answer, we return to the play-less and plague-ridden London of August 1592 where, in a squalid hovel in Dowgate to the east of St Paul's, there lay dying the Bohemian playwright Robert

Greene, whose plays had fared so badly at the Rose compared to *Henry VI*. In the event, Greene's rapidly failing health was not due to plague, but to one excess too many: a feast of pickled herrings and Rhenish wine with Tom Nashe and other cronies. Already destitute, he might have expired in the gutter but for the kindness of a shoemaker and his wife, Mr and Mrs Isam, who took him, his prostitute mistress, and illegitimate son Fortunatus, into their lowly and lice-ridden home. During the month or so that it took him to die Greene wrote a form of last confession, *Greene's Groats-worth of Witte, bought with a million of Repentance* that was swiftly gathered up after his death on 2 September and, in the words of its title page 'published at his dying request'.

There are only two surviving copies of Greene's *Groats-worth*, one in the British Library, the other in the Folger Shakespeare Library, Washington. Yet it is one of the most crucial and oft-quoted documents concerning Shakespeare, for it makes quite clear that Greene in his dying moments had Shakespeare very much on his mind – and none too charitably. Greene's purpose seems to have been to warn other writers, his 'fellow scholars about this City', who, whatever their humble origins, had been university-educated like himself, that they needed to be wary of appalling ingratitude on the part of the common stage actors for whom they wrote. In particular, Greene cited the example of one of these actors who had had the nerve to try his own hand at writing plays:

> ... an upstart Crow, beautified with our feathers, that with his *Tiger's heart wrapped in a Player's hide*, supposes he is as well able to bombast out a blank verse as the best of you: and being an absolute *Iohannes fac totum* [Jack-of-all-trades], is in his own conceit the only Shake-scene in the country.[21]

Appearing not later than the end of September 1592, this passage provides the very first published quotation from a Shakespeare play, albeit a parodied one. The line 'Oh, tiger's heart wrapp'd in a woman's hide!' comes from a powerful moment in Act I of *Henry VI, Part III*,[22] in which Henry VI's wife Queen Margaret, with the Duke of York her helpless prisoner, heartlessly mocks him with a handkerchief soaked in the blood of his dead son – prompting him to liken her to a tiger merely in the semblance of a woman.

Although Greene, in typical Elizabethan literary manner, does not directly name Shakespeare, the pun 'Shake-scene', in combination with such a readily memorable line from *Henry VI, Part III* leaves the identification in absolutely no doubt. Outside parish and diocesan registers, it is the first clear mention of Shakespeare as an individual, and the most unfavourable review he would ever receive. To the discomfiture of Oxfordians and their ilk who insist that Shakespeare was never more than an actor, it clearly establishes Shakespeare as an actor who had impertinently stepped way out of line to become a writer, this the very source of Robert Greene's chagrin. It totally endorses our otherwise potentially weak assumption, from earlier in this chapter, that the *Henry VI* being performed at the Rose *was* Shakespeare's. Not least, in view of the fact that the quotation is from *Henry VI, Part III*, it demonstrates that whether at the Rose or at Shoreditch, or some other public theatre, all three parts of *Henry VI* must have been staged before the London theatres' enforced closure in mid-June 1592. Although it might be argued that Greene could have seen the play in manuscript, he would hardly have used the quotation unless he was confident that it and its source would be recognised.

While many writers have thought it sufficient to quote only the 'upstart Crow' passage from Greene's *Groats-worth* there are further passages from this same work that may have still more to tell us about Shakespeare at this, his so intriguing entrance upon the stage of history – though it is important to treat these others with more caution. Greene has the impoverished scholar 'Roberto', clearly a thin disguise for Greene himself, come upon a well-dressed countryman who tells him there is an easy way out of his financial difficulties 'for men of my profession get by scholars their whole living'.

'What is your profession?' said Roberto. 'Truly sir,' said he, 'I am a player.' 'A player!', quoth Roberto, 'I took you rather for a gentleman of great living; for ... by outward habit ... you would be taken for a substantial man.' 'So am I, where I dwell', quoth the player, 'reputed able at my proper cost to build a windmill. What though the world once went hard with me ... it is otherwise now, for my very share in playing apparel will not be sold for £200.' 'Truly', said Roberto, 'it is strange that you should so prosper in that vain practice, for that it seems to me your voice is nothing gracious.' 'Nay' ... quoth the player, 'I can serve to make a pretty speech, for I was a country author, passing at a moral, for it was I that penned the Moral of man's wit, the Dialogue of Dives, and for seven years space was absolute interpreter of the puppets.'[23]

On this passage, as well as on much else that we will come upon later, the two great present-day authorities on Shakespeare, Oxford University's Dr A. L. Rowse and University of Maryland Professor Samuel Schoenbaum, vehemently disagree. For Dr Rowse the well-dressed player is clearly Shakespeare, the 'seven years ... absolute interpreter of the puppets' an important reference to his seven-year apprenticeship as an actor. At the time of Greene's attack in 1592 it would have been 'precisely seven years since Shakespeare's recorded appearance in Stratford in 1585 [i.e. when he fathered his twins] ... and we do know that the expensive attire of actors, their rich costumes, were a valuable part of their possessions, from their wills.'[24] Although unmentioned by Rowse, Greene's phrase 'it is strange', mirrored further on by 'Is it not strange ... ?' just before the 'upstart Crow' passage, may also subtly allude to Shakespeare's belonging to Lord Strange's company. Rowse goes on: 'Most important, this actor is a provincial, a countryman, neither a university man nor a Londoner, like almost all the leading figures in the theatre world. And he has a provincial accent'.[25] Schoenbaum counters that the Morality play 'Dialogue of Dives' was pre-Shakespearean, and that Greene 'clearly represented as junior, was actually six years older than Shakespeare'.[26] Yet these may be nothing more than flashes of Greene wit that are lost upon us today.

Nonetheless, Rowse, Schoenbaum and indeed a general consensus of scholarship agree that Greene had hurled 'a desperate shaft' (Schoenbaum's phrase) at Shakespeare. Clearly Greene had been piqued that a mere uneducated actor should have entered the province of university-trained writers and (which went unsaid), should already have made a success of it. As usual we have next to no information on where Shakespeare was at this particular time, but there is one important document from which we may gauge at least something of his reaction. The man who had actually taken charge of Greene's manuscripts after his death was London printer, stationer and future playwright Henry Chettle. In the immediate aftermath Chettle appears to have received complaints from both Marlowe (whom Greene had advised to abandon his atheism), and from Shakespeare, for in his first book *Kind-Hart's Dream* entered on the

Stationers' Register 8 December 1592, Chettle wrote in its introductory 'Epistle':

> About three months since died M Robert Greene, leaving many papers in sundry booksellers' hands, among them his *Groats-worth of wit*, in which a letter written to divers play-makers is offensively by one or two of them taken. . . . With neither of them that take offence was I acquainted, and with one of them I care not if I never be [this is presumed to be Marlowe]. . . . The other, whom at that time I did not so much spare, as since I wish I had, for that as I have moderated the heat of living writers, and might have used my own discretion (especially in such a case), the author being dead, that I did not, I am as sorry as if the original fault had been my fault, because myself have seen his demeanor no less civil than he excellent in the quality he professes. Besides, divers of worship have reported his uprightness of dealing, which argues his honest, and his facetious grace in writing, that approves his Art.[27]

Once again Shakespeare is not named as the individual, even indirectly, yet there is a general consensus that it is he to whom Chettle referred, not least because of the description of his civil demeanor and 'uprightness of dealing' in his complaint about being libelled, which tallies with later, similar references to his courteous, ever-gentlemanly manner. 'Quality' in Elizabethan English meant profession, particularly a performing profession such as herald or actor, and Chettle may therefore be construed as also attesting to Shakespeare's excellence as an actor, the first to do so, and thereby corroborating John Aubrey's already quoted remarks, from ninety years later, that Shakespeare 'did act exceedingly well'.[28] From as early as 1592, then, we are provided with a tantalising glimpse of Shakespeare as he appeared to his contemporaries: gentlemanly, surprisingly well dressed, at least on the evidence of Greene's 'beautified with our feathers', a man of great integrity (Chettle's 'honesty' and 'uprightness of dealing') and courtesy (his 'demeanour no less civil').

Now, according to Chettle, that 'divers of worship' should vouch for Shakespeare is likewise interesting, for in Elizabethan English 'worship' pertained to individuals of high standing, just surviving today in archaisms such as 'His worship the Mayor'. It seems clearly to mean that Shakespeare had some friends in high places. So who could Chettle have had in mind? Ferdinando, Lord Strange? Possibly. But not necessarily, for just at this particular point there are disturbing signs that whatever the closeness of any relationship that Shakespeare had built up with Ferdinando during the *Henry VI* venture, this very favouritism had attracted to the same door other writers of arguably rather less savoury reputations.

First of these was Thomas Nashe, whose *Pierce Penilesse* with its already mentioned insert 'Defence of Plays', appeared on London's bookstalls no later than 8 September 1592. This not only carried the sub-title, *His Supplication to the Divell* (denoting its content as a satirical complaint to the Devil), its specific targeting of Ferdinando is quite clear from its glowing tribute to him, extolling him as 'the matchless image of honour and magnificent rewarder of virtue . . . . Eagle-born . . . thrice noble Amyntas'. Furthermore Nashe's present-day biographer Charles Nicholl has pointed out that in *Pierce* Nashe likewise speaks of his 'private experience' of Strange's generosity, saying how 'thankful' he is for 'benefits received' from Ferdinando, and also including a sonnet described as 'wholly intended to the reverence of this renowned Lord, to whom I owe the utmost powers of my love and duty'. Nicholl then goes on:

> Later in the year, warning against too precise an identification between 'Pierce' and himself, Nashe asserts: 'Neither was I pinched with any ungentleman-like want when I invented *Pierce Penilesse*', and he adds 'Pauper non est cui rerum suppetit usus'. . . . Nashe clearly implies he was being 'kept' while he wrote *Pierce*: his benefactor was doubtless that 'magnificent rewarder of virtue', Lord Strange. The bulk of *Pierce* was composed in May–July 1592. . . . During these months, at least, Nashe received hospitality, casual 'doles' and occasional errands from a courtier on the highest rung of the Elizabethan ladder.[29]

From this, and in the light of the previous chapter, we may perhaps find reflected something of the similar comforts that Shakespeare had arguably received from Ferdinando, hence his air of the 'substantial man' that had so offended Greene. In fact, Nashe need not necessarily have represented any great challenge, since he joined Archbishop Whitgift's service in 1592. Altogether different, however, may have been Shakespeare's attitude towards the second writer visibly courting Ferdinando, Lord Strange's patronage during the summer of 1592: dramatist and spy Christopher Marlowe. Some earlier link between Marlowe and Strange may well be indicated by the fact that Marlowe's *The Jew of Malta* had been part of Lord Strange's Men's repertory at the Rose between February and June of 1592, where it was performed nearly as many times as *Henry VI*, and with similar success.

But, as also pointed out by Charles Nicholl, at about this time Marlowe seems to have written for Ferdinando arguably his most famous play *Doctor Faustus*, all about a man rashly making a pact with the devil. Inspired by the source book *The Historie of the Damnable Life and Deserved Death of Doctor John Faustus* published only in the May of 1592,[30] *Faustus* must have been written between that date and before Marlowe's death less than a year later. So not only was Ferdinando being courted by yet another writer pandering to his taste for the occult (two works on supplications to the devil, and within so few months, can hardly be coincidence), this writer, as Shakespeare may well have been aware, was also that most insidious of individuals, a government spy.

Whatever therefore, may have been Shakespeare's association with Ferdinando, it seems more than likely that sometime during the second half of 1592 he stepped aside to allow this muscling in, and began to open himself to patronage by others 'of worship'. Whether this was an active or passive decision, it was to prove a shrewd move, for a whole new, altogether different phase of his life was about to dawn.

CHAPTER 9

'Unto Southampton do we Shift our Scene.'

The closure of the Rose and other theatres due to plague clearly caused considerable hardship to Lord Strange's Men. Among the Henslowe papers at Dulwich College is a plaintive petition from them 'To the right honourable our very good Lords, the Lords of her Majesty's most honourable Privy Council', reading:

> Our duties in all humbleness remembered to your honours. Forasmuch (right honourable) our Company is great, and thereby our charge intolerable, in travelling the country, and the continuance thereof will be a means to bring us to division and separation, whereby we shall not only be undone, but also unready to serve her Majesty when it shall please her highness to command us, and for that the use of our playhouse on the Bankside, by reason of the passage to and from the same by water, is a great relief to the poor watermen there, and our dismission thence, now in this long vacation, is to those poor men a great hindrance . . . both our and their humble petition . . . to your good honours is that you will be pleased . . . permit us the use of the said playhouse again. And not only ourselves but also a great number of poor men shall be especially bounden to pray for your honours.
>
> Your honours' humble suppliants
The right honourable the Lord Strange
his servants and players[1]

Accompanying this, which frustratingly carries none of the players' names, are two closely related documents. The first is a like petition from the Thames watermen[2] whose 'Eastward-Ho, Westward-Ho' water-taxi service between the north and south banks of the Thames had apparently been as badly affected as the actors' livelihoods by the theatre's closure. They appended no less than seventeen of their own signatures or marks. The second document, clearly in response to the two petitions, is a warrant from the Privy Council now specifically allowing Lord Strange's Men once again to perform at the Rose 'so long as it shall be free from infection of sickness'.[3] The latter document also seems to indicate that at some time during the interim the company had been allowed 'to play three days at Newington Butts', a theatre built in the late 1570s about a mile south of the Rose in what is today the district of the Elephant and Castle. But this had apparently never been a popular venue, 'by reason of the tediousness of the way'.[4]

Frustratingly all three documents are undated, but probably derive from the autumn of 1592 when the plague, always worse in warm weather, would have abated, and when the Queen and her Court would certainly have been anxious for companies of players to be ready and able to provide Christmas entertainments. From the Lord Strange's petition itself, clearly two prime concerns were the impracticability of so large a company going on tour, and the dangers of their break-up from any prolonged loss of livelihood. The Court Accounts show that Lord Strange's Men and a company called 'the servants of the Earl of Pembroke' gave performances at Court over the Christmas period, and it has been suggested that Marlowe's *Edward II* may have been included in this programme.

From 29 December Henslowe's Diary shows a renewed programme very similar to that before the closure. Marlowe seems to have been the dominant playwright, with performances of *The Jew of Malta* and of the now five-year-old *Tamburlaine the Great*, pulling in particularly good audiences. Curiously an entry previously called *Titus and Vespasian*, and therefore not thought to be anything to do with Shakespeare, now disappears to be replaced by one simply called *Titus*, which was performed three times, and with nearly as much draw as Marlowe's. Possibly this was Shakespeare's *Titus Andronicus*, which we would certainly expect to appear on Lord Strange's Men's repertory, even if there were perhaps special reasons for omission of *The Comedy of Errors* and *Richard III*. *Henry VI* as Henslowe's 'harey the 6' is certainly again listed, going through another two airings, and still attracting good audiences. But plague appears to have surfaced very early again in 1593. On 28 January a Minute of the Privy Council advised London's Lord Mayor and his aldermen that 'as by the certificate of last week it appeareth the infection doth increase . . . we think it fit that all manner of concourse and public meetings of the people at plays, bear-baitings, bowling and other like assemblies for sports be forbidden'.[5] Three days later, with a final, and still well-attended performance of Marlowe's *The Jew of Malta*, Henslowe's Diary comes to another abrupt break.

This particular plague outbreak was to prove one of the most serious for several decades past and to come. The chronicler John Stow would record 10,575 plague deaths between 29 December 1592 and 20 December 1593, probably a conservative figure, yet still one in fifty of London's entire population. The city's players seem to have held off going on tour in the hope of respite, but on 29 April the Earl of Sussex's Men were granted a licence 'to exercise their quality of playing comedies and tragedies in any county, city, town, or corporation not being within seven miles of London, where the infection is not'.[6] A week later a similar licence was granted to 'Edward Alleyn, servant to the right honourable the Lord High Admiral, William Kemp, Thomas Pope, John Heminges, Augustine Phillips and George Bryan, being all one company, servants to our very good Lord the Lord Strange'.[7]

This tour list is interesting for a variety of reasons. First, it shows that Edward Alleyn and Lord Strange's Men were still working together in partnership, despite Alleyn having married Philip Henslowe's step-daughter Joan the previous October, thus permanently cementing his alliance with Henslowe. Indeed it was while Alleyn was travelling with Lord Strange's Men during this same tour, which appears to have visited Bristol, Shrewsbury, York and West Chester (clearly heading towards Ferdinando), that he wrote his so affectionate 'good sweet Mouse' letter to Joan, reminding her of the precautions she needed to take against plague, and asking her to dye his socks [see page 8]. Other of Alleyn's remarks in this same letter endorse his friendly relations with the members of Lord Strange's Men, as for instance his telling Joan that he had received her letter 'at Bristowe [Bristol] by Richard Cowley', and that his own letter's bearer was 'Thomas Pope's kinsman', both Pope and Cowley being First Folio 'principal actors'.

Second, the tour list shows for the first time as a member of Lord Strange's Men John Heminges, whose subsequent association with Shakespeare would be of the closest. After Queen's company actor William Knell had been killed in a duel in 1587, the next year John

Heminges married Knell's widow Rebecca in a long, happy union that would produce some fourteen children. Seemingly originally to have hailed from Droitwich, not far from Shakespeare's Stratford,[8] Heminges' marriage licence shows him as 'of St Michael, Cornhill, gent'. But he apparently chose to live in what had been the Knell family home in St Mary Aldermanbury, his subsequent association with this parish spanning several decades. Although we cannot be certain he was with Lord Strange's Men before 1593, we have already suggested he played Lidgate in *The Seven Deadly Sins*, and the very fact that he emerges in a senior capacity certainly suggests that he had been with the company some while. It also seems quite possible that his eldest daughter Alice, baptised at St Mary Aldermanbury 10 November 1590, was so named in honour of Ferdinando's wife the Lady Alice.

Third, and most important, the tour list does not include Shakespeare, who we must recall has still not yet appeared in any list, despite Lord Strange's Men certainly performing his *Henry VI*. This may have been simply because even up to this time, and despite all the arguments we have advanced, Shakespeare never had been a member of Lord Strange's Men. Alternatively, as suggested by the American scholar T. W. Baldwin, it may have been because, despite his playwrighting prowess, he was still not yet of sufficient seniority in the company. A further and most likely alternative, however, is that he simply chose not to go on this tour because he had other irons in the fire. And in this regard, a fact of considerable relevance is the appearance on the bookstalls during this same plague-bitten spring of his first published work, the 1194-line poem *Venus and Adonis*.

Now, at least on this work some hard dates are possible. Without giving the name of the author, the Stationers' Register as preserved at Stationers' Hall, London, shows 'a booke intituled Venus and Adonis' entered under the name of printer Richard Field, and publisher/bookseller John Harrison, on 28 April 1593. Since the Stationers' Register simply recorded publishing intentions, this is not to be taken as when the book appeared on the bookstalls, yet it could not have been long after, for on 12 June elderly Richard Stonley of Aldersgate, one of the tellers of the Exchequer, methodically entered in his diary that he had purchased a copy, along with a work entitled the *Survey of France*. In three volumes, Stonley's diary was only rediscovered as recently as 1972, whereupon, with characteristic eagerness, it became acquired by the Folger Shakespeare Library, Washington. During a routine inspection of the new acquisition, an astonished and delighted Folger curator Laetitia Yeandle spotted the lines:

12th of June, 1593. For the Survey of Fraunce, with the Venus and Adhonay pr Shakspere, xii.d[9]

She had found the first known original record of any purchase of one of Shakespeare's published works, and the earliest known notice of Shakespeare as a published author.

Stonley's actual copy of that first edition of *Venus and Adonis* has not come down to us. Indeed, despite the poem proving extremely popular, going through nine editions in Shakespeare's lifetime, only one first edition survives, preserved in the Bodleian Library, Oxford. There is often surprise that the title page does not give the author's name, but this was by no means uncommon in Shakespeare's time. After the title 'Venus and Adonis', a Latin inscription, and printer's emblem, there follows simply the words: 'London. Imprinted by Richard Field, and are to be sold at the signe of the white Greyhound in Paules Church-yard'.

Yet even the fact that the printer was Richard Field is of considerable interest and relevance, for Richard Field, it may be recalled, was Shakespeare's fellow Stratfordian who, three years older than Shakespeare, had left Stratford in 1579 to serve an apprenticeship in London as a printer. His father, Stratford tanner Henry Field, of Middle Row, just across the High Street from the Shakespeares' Henley Street premises, was demonstrably well known to the Shakespeares. For, despite John's already mentioned failure to attend church during 1592 'for fear of processes', one duty John certainly did play some part in during this same year was the drawing up, upon Henry Field's death, of an inventory of all his worldly goods, a modest assemblage of some old bedsteads, painted cloths and other household stuff, valued at '£14.14s'.

By contrast to his father, Richard Field had in fact done rather well for himself. Although in 1579 he had been signed up for a normal seven-year apprenticeship with London printer John Bishop, the terms of his agreement were that he should work his first six years at French-born Thomas Vautrollier's flourishing printing business within the precinct of the old Blackfriars monastery, which lay between St Paul's and the Thames. Here, Richard undoubtedly developed his craft to his employer's high standards for, when in 1588 Vautrollier died, Field, in a manner not uncommon for the time, not only took over Vautrollier's business, but also married his widow, Jacqueline. We may therefore legitimately envisage Shakespeare about late April or early May of 1593, while his fellow actors fretted for the abatement of the plague, visiting his fellow Stratfordian's Blackfriars shop to check his proofs, an indication at the very least that he was in London at about this time.

Far more important for our understanding of Shakespeare, however, is the wording of *Venus and Adonis*'s dedication page:

To the Right Honourable
Henry Wriothesley, Earl of Southampton
and Baron of Titchfield

Right Honourable, I know not how I shall offend in dedicating my unpolished lines to your Lordship, nor how the world will censure me for choosing so strong a prop to support so weak a burden. Only if your Honour seem but pleased, [will] I account myself highly praised, and vow to take advantage of all idle hours, till I have honoured you with some graver labour. But if the first heir of my invention prove deformed, I shall be sorry it had so noble a god-father: and never after ear [i.e. till] so barren a land, for fear it yield me still so bad a harvest. I leave it to your Honourable survey, and your Honour to your heart's content which I wish may always answer your own wish, and the world's hopeful expectation.

Your Honour's in all duty,
William Shakespeare

Firstly, here we have the earliest historical appearance of the full name William Shakespeare in any printed form, for Greene, it will be recalled, had referred to Shakespeare only as 'Shake-scene'. Even the spelling is of interest. As is well-known, spelling was very much a matter of individual whim during the Elizabethan era, Shakespeare's father's name, for instance, where this appears in Stratford's civic records, being spelled some seventeen different ways, mostly as 'Shakspere'. One individual who tried to impose a standardised spelling for his name was Ben Jonson who, where he had control over printers' activities, chose to drop the 'h' deliberately to distinguish himself from other Johnsons, only to have this blithely ignored.[10] Shakespeare appears to have been less bothered, his name and signature on his will, for instance, taking the 'Shak' form. But if 'Shake' had been his preference for literary purposes, this was certainly not an affectation of his own devising. The 'Shake' form was used in respect of John Shakespeare as early as 1569, in the information accusing him of usury [see page 51].

Secondly, because there survives no known letter written by Shakespeare, these dedicating lines provide an exceptionally rare instance of Shakespeare speaking directly and personally, as distinct from in poetry, or in official documents. Unfortunately, even in this instance we are by no means necessarily hearing his true sentiments. It was the Elizabethan fashion for writers to couch dedications to their would-be patrons in language of the utmost servility, and although Shakespeare's is by no means an extreme example, the heavy accent on honour needs to be measured against the rather more sceptical sentiments that Shakespeare would set into the mouth of Falstaff less than five years later in *Henry vi*, *Part i*.[11]

Thirdly, if we ask the purpose of the lines, the standard thinking behind such dedications in Elizabethan times was the seeking of a gratuity. Depending on the illustriousness of the patron, and his or her satisfaction with the work offered, this would commonly be between thirty shillings (£1.50) and £3.[12] Much more rarely it could be a very substantial annuity. Given Shakespeare's apparent circumstances in 1592 – his father cited as the subject of 'processes for debt'; his original patron fickle in his support; his livelihood as a player cut off until further notice – it seems fair to regard him as fairly badly in need of financial support.

But why the Earl of Southampton? Who was he, and when exactly might Shakespeare have made his first approach to him? Here an immediately intriguing feature is that, like Ferdinando, Southampton was heavily tinged with Catholicism and, again like Ferdinando, just as ambivalently. Henry Wriothesley (pronounced 'Risley'), third Earl of Southampton, was only nineteen when the first copies of the poem that Shakespeare had dedicated to him emerged fresh from Richard Field's press, yet he had already been an earl for eleven years. His father, the second Earl of Southampton, who had been heavily implicated in the 1569 Catholic Rebellion of the Northern Earls (and spent spells in prison for his pains), had died in 1581, leaving some unseemly generous bequests to a manservant Thomas Dymoke, one of several indications that the Earl was homosexual. Such behaviour had understandably been a cause of serious friction between him and his strong-willed wife Mary, daughter of Anthony Browne, Viscount Montagu, another staunch Catholic who had similarly backed the 1569 Rebellion.

On succeeding to his earldom at just eight years old Henry had become a royal ward, under the tutelage of Elizabeth's first Minister, Lord Burghley. Among much else, Burghley supervised the youngster's education, sending him at the age of twelve to his own Cambridge college, St John's, and in the Armada year of 1588 likewise to his old law school, Gray's Inn. Two years later, when Southampton was still only seventeen Burghley set his sights firmly on Southampton marrying his grand-daughter, Lady Elizabeth Vere, the fifteen-year-old daughter of Burghley's recently deceased favourite daughter Anne, and the wayward Edward de Vere, seventeenth Earl of Oxford (whom, of course, we have already met as one of the candidates for the Shakespeare authorship).

Now at this point the historical record shows quite clearly that Southampton baulked at his guardian's plans. We do not know his exact reasons; he may simply not have found Elizabeth Vere attractive. He certainly seems to have wanted to avoid becoming tied to a marriage too early in his life. More pertinently still, however, he may well have detected in Burghley's enthusiasm to cement him to such a marriage alliance, one further means, along with the Burghley-style education that had been arranged for him, of checking any lingering hereditary leanings towards Catholicism. Almost certainly this was indeed Burghley's intention – it was characteristic of him – but even so Southampton's mother, the Dowager Countess Mary, herself still very staunchly Catholic, and well known for her hiding of priests, approved the match. In pursuing it, she assured Burghley 'no want shall be found on my behalf'. She may well have felt her son's future prospects to be rather better served if he were maritally enmeshed within, rather than outside, the established order.

So, if this was indeed what Countess Mary wanted for her petulant nineteen-year-old son, who could persuade him that he should marry? Someone who had already cut his teeth with some adroit public relations for the Stanleys? This is the moment for us to focus our attention on that most contentious, yet potentially most revelatory, of all Shakespeare's works, his *Sonnets*, which we need to see as partly synchronous with the publication of *Venus and Adonis*.

In the early 1590s, writing sonnets had sprung into high fashion in Court circles as a result of the publication, in 1591, of a set of classic fourteen-line sonnets that had been written several years before by the heroic Sir Philip Sidney to the love of his life Penelope Devereux, sister of the second Earl of Essex. Although early on betrothed to Philip, Penelope had been forced against her will to marry Robert, second Lord Rich, and was never happy in this marriage. Philip, despite having subsequently married, wrote the poems as a token of his undying love for Penelope. Under the title *Astrophel and Stella* the Sidney sonnets were first brought out in a crude pirate edition (with help from Tom Nashe) in 1591. In April 1592 Sidney's sister tried to do her best for her brother's memory by arranging a much superior, authorised version, which became exceedingly popular in the immediate months and years that followed.

Part of the enigma surrounding Shakespeare's *Sonnets* is that they were not printed until 1609, in what would seem to have been a similarly unauthorised edition, baldly entitled 'SHAKE-SPEARE'S SONNETS Never before Imprinted', and with, instead of a dedication page in the style of *Venus and Adonis*, a much cruder version beginning 'To the onlie begetter of these insuing Sonnets, Mr. W. H. . . . .', signed 'T.T.'. Although generations of enthusiasts have spent happy hours hunting for suitable 'Mr. W.H.'s among Shakespeare's contemporaries, scholars such as A. L. Rowse have argued that whoever Mr. W.H. was, he was the dedicatee of pirate publisher Thomas Thorpe ('T.T.'), not the original unnamed male in-dividual to whom Shakespeare addressed the majority of his poems. This latter Rowse has firmly argued to be the Earl of Southampton, whom, according to Rowse, Shakespeare first plied with sonnets towards the end of 1592, a little before his bringing out of *Venus and Adonis*. With a grandiose 'This writer takes satisfaction in having no theories of his own to offer', American Professor Samuel Schoen-baum, author of the definitive *William Shakespeare: A Documentary Life* has declined even to enter the fray, but such conscientious sticking to truly hard facts does not necessarily do Schoenbaum credit. It is an equally hard fact that the *Sonnets*, if their poetic language can be properly penetrated, represent the only pieces of truly personal and meaningful autobiography that Shakespeare has left for us.

While, as often with Elizabethan poetry, trying to elicit true facts from the fine phrases is fraught with difficulties and uncertainties, few can dispute that in his first twenty-six sonnets, all couched in the classic Sidneyan fourteen-line form, Shakespeare exhorts a very good-looking young man to marry. Flattering him in the first that he is 'the world's fresh ornament', Shakespeare reminds him in the second, that:

> When forty winters shall besiege your brow
> . . . Thy youth's proud livery, so gaz'd on now,
> Will be a tatter'd weed of small worth held.

This leads naturally to his urging in the third *Sonnet* that the young man should beget children:

> Look in thy glass, and tell the face thou viewest
> Now is the time that face should form another;
> . . . Die single, and thine image dies with thee.

As clues to his identity, the same *Sonnet* discloses that the young man's mother is still living:

> Thou art thy mother's glass, and she in thee
> Calls back the lovely April of her prime . . .

In the thirteenth *Sonnet* Shakespeare imparts that this is not the case with his father:

> You had a father: let your son say so.

All this, the deceased father, the still attractive mother, the exceptionally handsome son needing encouragement to marry, combined with Shakespeare's fully identifying dedication page in *Venus and Adonis*, all so exactly point to the young Earl of Southampton of the early 1590s that Rowse has reasonable but by no means overwhelming scholarly support that Southampton is by far the most likely individual to whom were directed those of Shakespeare's *Sonnets* addressed to a male recipient.

Proceeding on this assumption, therefore, just who was this intriguing young man who became target of Shakespeare's word-spinning at this moment in history? In a darkened basement room in Cambridge's Fitzwilliam Museum is displayed an exquisite miniature of Southampton [see pl. 22] painted by Elizabethan Court painter Nicholas Hilliard, and carrying the date 1594, the year immediately following the publication of *Venus and Adonis*.

Most importantly however, it is an image to be held clearly in the mind when reading any of the earlier *Sonnets*. When in his twentieth *Sonnet* Shakespeare describes the young man he is addressing as having 'A woman's face, with Nature's own hand painted' this is precisely what we see. Unusually for an age in which grown men quickly sprouted full beards, Southampton's face appears totally beardless and indeed feminine, the features soft, framed by golden hair of a length – for Elizabethan times as now – again more befitting a woman than a man.

Clearly the precise nature of the relationship between the twenty-nine-year-old Shakespeare and this nineteen-year-old youth raises all sorts of questions. First, how could Shakespeare, still, for all we have established with any certainty, merely a jumped-up actor, have been able to approach so refined a young aristocrat? Curiously, if there is validity to our earlier Ferdinando hypotheses, there was an occasion in late September 1592 when the paths of Southampton and Ferdinando are known to have crossed. In company with many other members of the Court, they both attended a visit of the Queen to Oxford University, Southampton being described on this occasion as 'no one more comely, no young man more outstanding in learning, although his mouth scarcely yet blooms with tender down'.[13] That Shakespeare might also have been present has been suggested from his soon-to-be-written lines in *A Midsummer Night's Dream* recalling the specially orchestrated speeches with which Oxford's academics customarily greeted their Queen:

> Where I have come, great clerks have purposèd
> To greet me with premeditated welcomes
> Where I have seen them shiver and look pale,
> Make periods in the midst of sentences,
> Throttle their practised accent in their fears,
> And in conclusion dumbly have broke off.[14]

More likely, however, given the pleas to a young man to marry that occupy so many of the first *Sonnets*, is our earlier suggestion that through some mutual, possibly Catholic , acquaintance Shakespeare was directly or indirectly approached by Southampton's mother, the

Dowager Countess Mary. That Shakespeare both knew her and admired her from as early as the third *Sonnet* is more than evident from the *Sonnet*'s otherwise almost impertinently personal words: 'Thou art thy mother's glass, and she in thee . . .'.

So assuming that Shakespeare did receive some such approach, and that it was with Southampton that Shakespeare formed the intensely personal relationship that the *Sonnets* reveal, against what sort of domestic background should we envisage this? Like so many other of the wealthier aristocrats of the time, Southampton had of course more than one residence. During his early years, when not at university, he was expected to stay under the roof of his guardian Lord Burghley, but he seems to have moved from this at the time of the rift over Elizabeth Vere, almost inevitably transferring to his mother's London residence, Southampton House. Although this is no longer extant, the name is still preserved in the present Southampton Buildings, at the angle of Chancery Lane with Holborn, and the so-called 'Agas' map shows its environs in one of London's leafier, less congested districts. We should envisage it as a typical late mediaeval house, with a series of chambers and galleries around an open court.

More important, however, is for us to be aware that it was a house constantly under surveillance for the comings and goings of Catholics. The already-mentioned government secret police chief Richard Topcliffe knew of the Dowager Countess Mary's activities in sheltering Catholic fugitives,[15] and had already claimed a victory. In 1590, the Southamptons' original Catholic tutor Swithin Wells,[16] having been relieved of his post by Lord Burghley upon Southampton's father's death, was caught at a mass in Holborn and in December 1591 hung, drawn and quartered at Gray's Inn Fields, a mere stone's throw from Southampton House.[17] Extraordinarily then once again Shakespeare, whatever his persuasion, came into the shadow of a Catholic household.

During the months around *Venus and Adonis*'s publication, however, with London's death toll at up to 1600 victims a week,[18] almost anyone able to leave London was bound to do so. As Shakespeare is unlisted among those of Lord Strange's Men who went on tour, and as he clearly had to have some time in which to develop the close relationship indicated in the *Sonnets*, it is at least reasonable to believe that he travelled to Hampshire to stay as a house guest with Southampton and his mother at their main country seat, Titchfield House, between Portsmouth and Southampton.

In a manner all too rare among the places Shakespeare may have known, something of Titchfield House just survives. It had formerly been an abbey, but in the wake of the Dissolution of the Monasteries Southampton's grandfather transformed the former monastic buildings into a grand mansion for himself, making a grand gateway from the nave, and a courtyard from the cloisters. Although today sadly all that remains is a partial and poorly attended shell [see pl. 20], architectural drawings made in 1737, preserved in Hampshire's Record Office[19] convey at least the broad plan of the house's appearance in Shakespeare's time [see fig 5 opposite]. The principal rooms, that is, the hall, the drawing-room, the great dining-room, the gallery, etc, can be seen to have been on the first floor, approached by a staircase from the courtyard. And this is highly important, for such a design would have been intentionally very much along the lines of Florentine and northern Italian palaces. These were likewise mostly built around a square, with the principal rooms on the first floor, or *piano nobile*, approached by an ornate staircase. Given the contemporary fashion for things Italian, Shakespeare's host no doubt felt very proud of this aspect of his home. At Titchfield, therefore, Shakespeare would have felt he was walking into a mini-Italy.

Nor was this the only touch of Italy Shakespeare would have found while familiarising himself with this new world of the Southamptons. To replace the executed Swithin Wells, Lord Burghley seems to have introduced as the Earl's Italian tutor John Florio [see pl. 23], in the government's service around the time of the Babington plot and thought to have been deliberately brought into the Southampton household to spy upon them. Born in England of an Italian father, Florio had been raised bilingual, and was therefore well-suited to teach Italian (and also French) to Englishmen. After the success of his conversation manual *First Fruites*, published back in 1578 and full of overly wordy expressions typical of its author, Florio followed this up with *Second Fruites* in 1591, a work notably prefaced by a beautiful, anonymous introductory sonnet 'Phaeton to his friend Florio'. Indeed, some have attributed this to Shakespeare,[20] in which light it is even possible that it was through Florio that Southampton and/or Southampton's mother were introduced to Shakespeare.

While opinions differ on *when* Shakespeare wrote his first sonnets for Southampton – if he wrote them for Southampton – parallels in

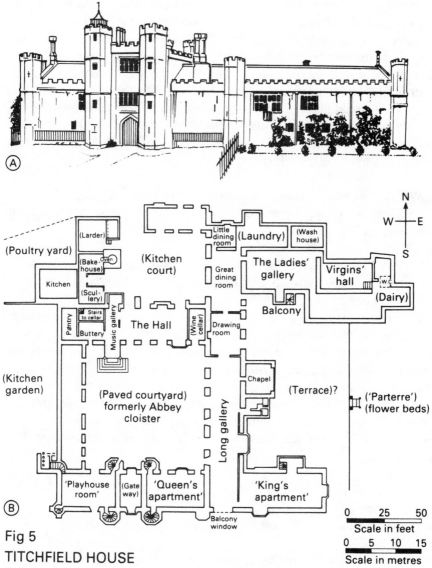

Fig 5

TITCHFIELD HOUSE

Formerly Titchfield Abbey, seat of the Earl of Southampton.

(A) Exterior aspect, after an engraving of 1733.

(B) Plan of the upper floor, after drawings made by John Acland in 1737, and
showing the house probably little changed since Shakespeare's time. A
highly unusual and intriguing feature is the 'Playhouse room' shown in the
south-western corner, to the left of the main entrance. Ground floor features
are indicated with parentheses.

imagery strongly suggest he wrote the earliest ones around the time of publication of *Venus and Adonis*. Dating considerations aside, however, upon any reading of the *Sonnets*, one of their most surprising features is the high degree of intimacy they reveal between Shakespeare and the unmistakeably elevated young aristocrat he is addressing. In Shakespeare's time, and well into the present century, the widest social gulf existed between anyone of the exalted status of an earl, and those of the status of actor, the latter barely above rogues and vagabonds. In 'A Description of England' Shakespeare's contemporary William Harrison wrote:

> We in England divide our people commonly into four sorts, as gentlemen; citizens or burgesses; yeomen; and artificers or labourers.

Harrison divided gentlemen into 'lords and noblemen' – princes, dukes, earls, etc – then 'knights and esquires', and lastly 'all they that are simply called gentlemen'.

In fact at the time of *Venus and Adonis* and the *Sonnets*, Shakespeare did not even qualify as a gentleman, a rank he would only achieve later by special application. Technically therefore he deserved relegation to 'below the salt', that is, below the salt-cellar that divided the lord and his guests from the rabble. Yet the *Sonnets* also reveal that Shakespeare in no way tried to hide his low degree, as early as *Sonnet* 23 which begins: 'As an unperfect actor on the stage'. In *Sonnet* 110 freely he acknowledges his life as an actor with the words:

> Alas, 'tis true I have gone here and there
> And made myself a motley to the view,
> Gor'd mine own thoughts, sold cheap what is most dear . . .

So for Shakespeare to have been able to develop any sort of relationship at such a high level argues for a very considerable degree of social grace and poise on his part, something he must have acquired from earlier upbringing, but yet more surprising still is the very openness of the relationship that the *Sonnets* reveal. In a climate in which anyone with even slight Catholic leanings to hide had to be ever vigilant for spies and informers, Shakespeare has clearly found a like-minded individual who was prepared to honour him as a most trusted companion. Despite the fact that Titchfield House was itself a despoiled abbey (the similarly ruined Beaulieu abbey was likewise a part of Southampton's estates), Shakespeare undisguisedly bewailed the Reformation's ravages, speaking in *Sonnet* 73 of the:

Bare, ruin'd choirs where late the sweet birds sang

and in *Sonnet* 64 of his sadness:

When sometime lofty towers I see down-razed,
And brass [i.e. church memorial brasses] eternal slave to mortal rage...

In *Sonnet* 66 Shakespeare specifically rails against the wrongs of his less than Merrie England, an age of 'purest faith unhappily foresworn' (of individuals being forced to attest against their true beliefs); of 'art made tongue-tied by authority' (of crushing censorship of the arts in general), and of 'simple truth miscalled simplicity' (of honesty being misconstrued as naivety).

All these and much more are instances of a deep 'marriage of true minds', to use Shakespeare's own phrase (*Sonnet* 116) between Shakespeare and this attractive young man whom we have assumed to be the Earl of Southampton. As we have already intimated, however, the suggestion of an intense relationship between Shakespeare and a young man with a womanly face – whom in the *Sonnets* he on occasion addresses as 'love', 'loving boy', and 'Lord of my love' – understandably causes a little eyebrow-raising among readers. Was England's greatest Bard gay? Can we actually believe that for Shakespeare to have written poems often praising the beauty of a very feminine-looking young aristocrat, that he can have been other than homosexually inclined? There can be no doubt that well before our own time some came to just such an interpretation and were shocked by it. Editing his fifteen-volume edition of Shakespeare's works in 1793 Edmond Malone's contemporary George Steevens wrote forcefully:

We have not reprinted the Sonnets & c. of Shakespeare because the strongest act of Parliament that could be framed would fail to compel readers into their service.... Had Shakespeare produced no other works than these, his name would have reached us with as little celebrity as time has conferred on that of Thomas Watson, an older and much more elegant sonneteer.

Closer to our own time others, such as (notoriously) Oscar Wilde, have reached the same conclusion and derived a certain self-mirroring satisfaction from it. Yet to do so is to misunderstand and arguably seriously misrepresent Shakespeare and Southampton. For this is not to say that there was no homosexuality in Shakespeare's time. Marlowe, for instance, of whom it was said 'almost into every company he cometh he persuades men to atheism',[21] was famously quoted as remarking that 'all they that love not tobacco and boys were fools'. Marlowe went unmarried throughout his thirty years of life, and in virtually every one of his works, from *The Tragedy of Dido* to *Edward II*, the theme of homosexuality either appears directly or is at least touched upon.

Shakespeare, however, was quite different. Everything about his work, even to his very gravestone, conveys that he was genuinely God-fearing, at a time when sodomy was a capital offence and religious people of all persuasions regarded it as an instant passport to hell. As we have already seen, he bedded and wedded an older woman while still in his teens, quickly having three children by her. His fellow actors were likewise mostly God-fearing married men with large families, who from the very fact that it was a serious part of their business to train their younger recruits to dress up as and impersonate women, are most unlikely to have tolerated an active homosexual in their midst. Quite unlike a work by Marlowe, *Venus and Adonis*, the poem that Shakespeare undoubtedly wrote for Southampton, is no work for sharing between gays. Light, racy, amusing, full of unashamedly erotic country images, it is the full-blooded story of a highly sexed older woman's seduction of a handsome young man. In line with the *Sonnets'* exhortation of their young man to marry, it is a poetic equivalent of a Titian painting, positively provoking man–woman desire as Venus tells Adonis:

> I'll be a park, and thou shalt be my deer,
> Feed where thou wilt, on mountain or in dale;
> Graze on my lips; and if those hills be dry,
> Stray lower, where the pleasant fountains lie.[22]

As has been stressed by A. L. Rowse, in *Sonnet* 20 Shakespeare, while acknowledging Southampton's beauty, specifically repudiates any homosexual interest in him, bluntly telling him that Nature:

> . . . by addition me of thee defeated
> By adding one thing to my purpose nothing.

that is, by adding one attribute of no use to Shakespeare, had:

> prick'd thee out for women's pleasure . . .

All too seldom realised is that in Shakespeare's time the word 'love' had not taken on its heavily sexual connotations of our own era. From the same decade as the *Sonnets*, Thomas Arundel wrote asking for a favour from Lord Burghley's son Robert Cecil, assuring him in the course of this

> I do truly love you and therefore wish that every man should love you, which love in these troublesome discontented times is sooner won by clemency . . . I am wholly yours. . . .[23]

No one would seriously suggest that Arundel meant those words in the way they would be taken today, and innumerable similar examples can be quoted, not least family-man Ben Jonson addressing Shakespeare as 'my beloved' in the First Folio.

In any case, such arguments are hardly necessary. For if we want direct evidence of Shakespeare's self-avowed heterosexuality at the time of the *Sonnets*, we need only look at those *Sonnets* that are clearly addressed, not to a man, but to a very mysterious 'Dark Lady'.

CHAPTER 10
'My Mistress' Brows are Raven Black'

Shakespeare's well-known lines 'Shall I compare thee to a summer's day' occur as early as his eighteenth *Sonnet* to his aristocratic young friend. Fifteen sonnets later, however, he speaks of the relationship now having fallen under a dark cloud, followed by his first similarly figurative words of reproof:

> Why didst thou promise such a beauteous day,
> And make me travel forth without my cloak . . . ?[1]

This same *Sonnet* reveals that Southampton, if indeed the young man was he, was now shedding tears over some 'grief' that he had caused Shakespeare. By *Sonnet* 40 we explicitly learn that he had apparently stolen Shakespeare's other love. Shakespeare tells him grimly:

> Take all my loves, my love, yea, take them all,
> What hast thou then more than thou hadst before?
> . . .
> All mine was thine before thou hadst this more.

Not until two sonnets later, however, does it finally become clear, and only then thanks to a feminine pronoun, that this other love was a woman:

> That thou hast her, it is not all my grief,
> And yet it may be said I lov'd her dearly . . .

Suddenly we are confronted with a mystery woman who seems to have had *both* Shakespeare and his aristocratic young friend as her lovers. So who was she? All becomes yet more intriguing when, after *Sonnet* 126 in the 1609 published edition of the *Sonnets*, it can be seen that the printer left an unusually large space and two sets of empty parentheses. There then follows *Sonnet* 127 commencing a set of sonnets that Shakespeare clearly addresses to his other love and which seem to belong to the same period as *Sonnets* 33 to 42:

> In the old age black was not counted fair,
> Or if it were, it bore not beauty's name
>
> . . .
>
> Therefore, my mistress' brows are raven black,
> Her eyes so suited, and they mourners seem . . .

'My mistress' – not only by line three does Shakespeare coolly tell us he had a mistress (perhaps not too surprising, given his necessary long periods spent away from home), he also provides a physical description of her. And it is an instantly arresting one. While the portraits from Shakespeare's time readily convey that the fair-haired Anglo-Saxon type was both the norm, and the accepted paragon of beauty, this woman was unfashionably black-haired, black-browed and black-eyed – so much so that Shakespeare felt bound repeatedly to allude to these characteristics.

In all we find Shakespeare addressing twenty-four *Sonnets* directly to this woman who was, as is quite obvious, not his wife, and they leave absolutely no doubt of the intensity of his love for her. As he tells her:

> For well thou know'st to my dear doting heart
> Thou art the fairest and most precious jewel.[2]

Whereas throughout the previous one hundred and twenty-six deeply emotional sonnets that Shakespeare addressed to the young man, there had been no suggestion of the love being on any physical level, in the case of the Dark Lady he makes no secret of having 'enjoy'd' full sexual intercourse with her. Nor does he hide his immediate shame and indeed revulsion at himself at having done so:

> Th'expense of spirit in a waste of shame
> Is lust in action
>
> . . .
>
> Enjoy'd no sooner, but despised straight;

> Past reason hunted, and, no sooner had,
> Past reason hated, as a swallowed bait,
> On purpose laid to make the taker mad—
> . . .
> Before, a joy propos'd; behind, a dream.
> All this the world well knows; yet none knows well
> To shun the heaven that leads men to this hell.[3]

Here to be noted is nothing of the casual, predatory attitude to sex with any willing female that for certain males could be as commonplace in Elizabethan England as in our own time. Instead we meet a married man with a conscience who 'past reason' has found himself committing adultery, and who is suffering the greatest conflict of emotions for having done so.

Here we also find the object of these emotions to be a most intriguing and unusual woman. Like Shakespeare, she is married, for the poet, in his very last sonnet to her, reminds her plainly: 'In act thy bed-vow broke'.[4] She is also musical. *Sonnet* 128 paints a vivid picture of Shakespeare listening to her performing on that precursor of the piano, the virginals:

> How oft, when thou, my music, music play'st
> Upon that blessed wood whose motion sounds
> With thy sweet fingers, when thou gently sway'st
> The wiry concord that mine ear confounds,
> Do I envy those jacks [keys] that nimble leap
> To kiss the tender inward of thy hand . . .

Without this being spelled out as such, we may also infer that she must have been a most witty and alluring woman to have attracted both Shakespeare, and a high-minded young aristocrat to fall for her charms.

Yet Shakespeare also does not mince matters about her less endearing attributes. Clearly she could be overbearing and cruel:

> Thou art as tyrannous, so as thou art,
> As those whose beauties proudly make them cruel . . .[5]

She could lie with impunity:

> When my love swears that she is made of truth,
> I do believe her, though I know she lies . . .[6]

She was habitually amoral

> . . . those lips of thine
> That have profan'd their scarlet ornaments,
> And seal'd false bonds of love as oft as mine;
> Robbed others' beds' revenues of their rents.[7]

Shakespeare's dilemma, one that would stay with him, was that he could clearly see these faults:

> In faith, I do not love thee with mine eyes,
> For they in thee a thousand errors note . . .[8]

Yet somehow, as if even by some witchcraft, she had him in thrall:

> O, from what pow'r hast thou this pow'rful might
> . . .
> To make me give the lie to my true sight?
> . . .
> Who taught thee how to make me love thee more,
> The more I hear and see just cause of hate?[9]

By far the greatest cause of his anguish over her, however, is clearly the new liaison between her and his aristocratic young friend. Whereas Shakespeare was merely reproachful yet forgiving towards the young aristocrat, he outrightly rails at her for having so wilfully captivated this young man's heart as well as his own:

> Is't not enough to torture me alone,
> But slave to slavery my sweet'st friend must be?
> . . .
> Of him, my self, and thee, I am forsaken;
> A torment thrice three-fold thus to be crossed.[10]

In the event the attitude Shakespeare adopts, one that from later instances we may interpret as characteristic of him, is of resignation, a

surrendering of his own will in favour of whatever the other two may
want in this so intriguing triangle:

> So now I have confess'd that he is thine,
> And I myself am mortgag'd to thy will;
> My self I'll forfeit . . .[11]

Yet even so he remains concerned for the physical and spiritual
welfare of his young friend in the Dark Lady's questionably
beneficent clutches:

> Two loves I have
> . . .
> The better angel is a man right fair,
> The worser spirit a woman colour'd ill.
> To win me soon to hell, my female evil
> Tempteth my better angel from my side,
> And would corrupt my saint to be a devil,
> Wooing his purity with her foul pride.[12]

The imagery here is fascinating for its contrasts. Most historians see
the Earl of Southampton as having been a rather vain, silly and
spoiled young aristocrat, very different to Shakespeare's image
of him as a pure and saintly 'angel', if Southampton was indeed
the *Sonnets'* male recipient. In the Dark Lady, on the other
hand, Shakespeare characterises her, in mediaeval fashion, as a
creature of hell. Yet she continues to haunt him, like an unremitting
malaria:

> My love is as a fever, longing still
> For that which no longer nurseth the disease
> . . .
> Past cure I am, now reason is past care,
> And frantic mad with evermore unrest
> . . .
> For I have sworn thee fair, and thought thee bright,
> Who art black as hell, as dark as night.[13]

Now this story, though represented by a mere sixth of the overall
number of *Sonnets*, vastly eclipses the rest for its power, fascination,

subtlety, and ability to convince. This is not least because of the self-evident war within Shakespeare himself. His reason readily told him that this woman was black in nature as well as in looks. Yet something else within him felt compelled to love her, come what may.

And immediately we confront the literature-versus-history debate. Literary scholars commonly remain content to regard the Dark Lady story as just that. Some have even elected to look upon it merely as a literary exercise on Shakespeare's part, with little or no bearing on anything he may have actually experienced. Historians, on the other hand, sense flesh-and-blood people behind all the poetic language. They have a cub-reporter's eagerness to find out places, dates. Most importantly, they want to know just who was the real-life Dark Lady that was so capricious towards England's greatest Bard.

Once again, as in the case of the search for 'Mr. W.H.', we are obliged to pick our way through a minefield of speculative theories. For Frank Harris, the American libertine of a century ago who cast Shakespeare in his own image, the Dark Lady was unmistakeably Mary Fitton, maid of honour to the Queen, historically known to have been made pregnant by the young William Herbert, Earl of Pembroke, whose initials nearly match those of the 'Mr. W.H.' to whom the 1609 edition of the *Sonnets* was dedicated. Mary Fitton was unmarried at the time of her association with Pembroke. Two portraits and surviving descriptions indicate Mary to have been fair-haired. Moreover, whereas William Herbert's affair with Mary Fitton took place in 1599, the imagery of the *Sonnets* suggests them to have been written around the same time as *Venus and Adonis*, that is in 1593, when Pembroke was a mere thirteen years old.

A more modern scholar, the late Professor G. B. Harrison identified the Dark Lady as a notorious London prostitute, 'Lucy Negro, abbess de Clerkenwell', also known as Lucy Morgan, Lucy Parker and 'Black Luce', madame of an off-limits London brothel frequented by students of Southampton's Gray's Inn law school. However, this again hardly has the right ring. Shakespeare's guilt was at having committed adultery with a married woman, not at having consorted with a prostitute. Printer Richard Field's French-born wife Jacqueline has been suggested, on the paper-thin grounds that, being French, she may have been dark-haired. Another equally tenuous suggestion has been Jane D'Avenant, wife of the inn keeper at the Crown Tavern, Oxford, where Shakespeare is thought to have stayed on his journeys between London to Stratford. According to gossip John Aubrey, Jane D'Avenant's son William intimated that Shakespeare might have been his father. But history is entirely silent on whether Mistress D'Avenant was even dark, let alone could play the virginals.

Professor Schoenbaum has predictably contented himself with criticising the theories of others rather than offering anything constructive of his own, thus leaving as by far the most convincing Dark Lady one discovered by chance by Dr A. L. Rowse.[14] During the early 1970s, in Oxford's Bodleian Library, browsing through the notebooks of London astrologer Simon Forman [see pl. 25] (whom we met earlier concocting his pioneering plague-cure recipe), Rowse's attention became drawn to Forman's jottings on a married couple who consulted him independently, but within four days of each other, in mid-May 1597. The husband was the royal musician Alphonse Lanier, born of a musical family that hailed originally from Rouen, France. His wife was Emilia, daughter of another royal musician Battista Bassano, who had died back in 1576, and who likewise was of a very musical family that hailed originally from Venice.

As noted by Forman for the dossier he built up for astrological purposes [see pl. 24], Emilia told him that 'She was paramour to my old Lord Hunsdon that was Lord Chamberlain and was maintained in great pride'. This Lord Hunsdon was elderly Henry Carey, a first cousin of the Queen, and Elizabeth's Lord Chamberlain from 1583 until his death in 1596. According to Emilia, Hunsdon had set her up 'with great pomp' but then in 1592 she became 'with child' by him, whereupon 'for colour' it was arranged for her to be married off to the 'minstrel' Alphonse Lanier.

As observed by Rowse, Emilia's dismissive description of her husband as 'a minstrel', is but one of many indications that having apparently 'been favoured much of her Majesty and of many noblemen' she felt she had married beneath her. Even the birth of her healthy son, Henry, named after his natural father, gave her little comfort. But what further fascinated Rowse about her was her amorality. In the September of 1597, while her husband was away she invited Forman to her house in Westminster where he 'went and supped with her, and stayed all night'. But she teased Forman, sometimes being 'familiar and friendly to him in all things', whereby 'he felt all parts of her body willingly and kissed her often', at other times repudiating him, causing him to comment 'She was a whore, and dealt evil with him after'. She was also a dabbler in the occult, one of Forman's later notes being a reminder to himself 'to put the question what happens concerning her tales as to the invocation of spirits, whether or not an incuba'.[15]

From all this we can put together that Emilia was married, musical, adulterous, high-handed, tyrannical and inclined to the occult – a tantalisingly close socio-psychological profile to the Dark Lady of Shakespeare's *Sonnets*. As the wife of a musician her home would have been the very sort to have possessed so expensive an instrument as a spinet, or virginals. And her Bassano genes, so powerful that her son became a musician to Charles I, would have readily given her the proficiency to play this as Shakespeare describes in *Sonnet* 128. There is even a Southampton connection, the Earl being recorded as having procured for Emilia's husband a monopoly on the weighing of hay into Westminster (on the site of the present Haymarket), a perquisite that would have provided a useful supplement to his musician's income.

Indeed, the only missing piece of information about Emilia is anything regarding her physical appearance: whether or not she had the black hair and eyebrows so vividly described in *Sonnet* 127. Rowse thought he had found this in Forman's words 'She was very brown in youth', but was swiftly corrected by critics spotting that Forman's actual word was 'brave', which in Elizabethan times could mean 'good-looking' or 'showy'.[16] However, since Emilia's father, Battista Bassano, had both Italian and Jewish ancestry there has to be a reasonable likelihood that she herself was indeed black haired. If she was indeed the Dark Lady, Shakespeare and Southampton's involvement with her would seem to have been within a few months of her marriage, on 18 October 1592, her pregnancy at this time denoted, according to Rowse, by Shakespeare's *Sonnet* 150:

> If thy unworthiness raised love in me,
> More worthy I to be belov'd of thee.

Accordingly, while Emilia Lanier's identification with Shakespeare's Dark Lady cannot be considered proven, she certainly comes close to the sort of woman who *might* have snared both Shakespeare and Southampton.

But if an adulterous triangle and at least strong hints of homosexuality are not enough to find in Shakespeare's *Sonnets*, *Sonnets* 79 to 85 signal yet another morsel of autobiography – a situation in which a rival poet seems to have been vying with Shakespeare for his aristocratic young friend's favour. Shakespeare writes how while formerly 'I alone did call upon thy aid' now another had come upon the scene:

> O how I faint when I of you do write,
> Knowing a better spirit doth use your name
> And in the praise thereof spends all his might
> To make me tongue-tied . . .[17]

This rival Shakespeare describes as one with 'polished' and 'well-refinèd' pen, to whom his own talents are 'inferior far to his'. While as usual there is no scholarly consensus on the identity of this rival poet, Marlowe [see pl. 26] is strongly suspected, not least because in 1593 he would readily have been considered the better writer. That Shakespeare certainly regarded him as such is evident from clear echoes of his style in the *Henry vi/Richard iii* tetralogy. Furthermore, when Shakespeare was writing *Venus and Adonis* for the Earl of Southampton, Marlowe seems to have been working on his unfinished *Hero and Leander*, very much in the same genre, and this may well have been intended for the same dedicatee.

But if Marlowe was dogging Shakespeare's footsteps with Southampton just as (arguably) he had been with Ferdinando, Lord Strange, fate was beginning to stack against him. Around the time of publication of *Venus and Adonis* the plague was still rife, there were economic difficulties and new, harsher measures against Catholics were passed through Parliament. In such a period it was not surprising that inflammatory notices began to appear in London threatening violence against London's large immigrant population, mostly skilled Dutch, Belgian and French Protestants who had fled to England to escape Catholic persecution in their own countries. On the night of 5 May a particularly vicious notice appeared, in the form of a doggerel poem pasted on the wall of the Dutch church in Broad Street.[18] Signed 'Tamburlaine', this instantly evoked Marlowe's bloodthirsty war-lord of the same name, while another line 'like the Jews you eat us up as bread' recalled *The Jew of Malta*. Yet another line:

We'll cut your throats, in your temples praying
Not Paris massacre so much blood did spill

was reminiscent of Marlowe's *The Massacre at Paris*. All these plays had notably been among Lord Strange's Men's productions just before the theatres had been forced to close. *Massacre*, according to Henslowe's Diary's box-office receipts, had been particularly well attended.

On the pretext that some aficionado of the theatre was behind the notices, the government began to question dramatists. The first of these, probably because he was immediately available, was Thomas Kyd, author of *The Spanish Tragedy*. Kyd was ruthlessly tortured and his belongings searched, and when among these there was found an old, atheistically tinged thesis which Kyd insisted belonged to Marlowe, Marlowe was summoned next for interrogation.

Now just as we have surmised Shakespeare to have been weathering out the plague with Southampton at Titchfield at this time, so Marlowe was quite definitely staying at the Chislehurst home of Thomas Walsingham, son and successor of Elizabeth's chief spymaster. Here he was almost certainly working on *Hero and Leander* as the manuscript of this would later turn up in Walsingham's hands.[19] Brought before the Privy Council on 20 May, for reasons that are by no means clear, Marlowe was bound 'to give his daily attendance on their Lordships'. Ten days later, again for unknown reasons, Marlowe and three other men – Ingram Frizer, Nicholas Skeres and Robert Poley – met in a room of a Deptford guesthouse that Frizer had hired from its owner, widow Mrs Eleanor Bull. That evening, after this quartet had been provided with a meal, there was purportedly an argument over the bill. During this Marlowe allegedly lunged at Frizer with his dagger, whereupon Frizer, acting in self-defence, somehow deflected this so that it went straight through Marlowe's right eye and into his brain, killing him instantly.

As modern investigators such as Leslie Hotson, and Charles Nicholl, have discovered, all four men in that Deptford room were in the upper echelons of the murky world of the spy, the *agent provocateur*, and the dirty trickster. Frizer was a racketeer in the pay of spymaster Walsingham. Skeres, Frizer's favourite accomplice in extortion rackets, was an informer for the Earl of Essex's intelligence service, and had been a minor government plant in the Babington plot that had given Elizabeth's government its excuse to execute Mary Queen of Scots. Poley, who had played a more major role in the Babington plot, had achieved a notoriety among Catholics as an international double-dealer, informer and *agent provocateur*.

Now, whatever score these men might have had to settle with Marlowe that day, Frizer's dagger ended, at just twenty-nine, the career of the man who was certainly Shakespeare's number one pacesetter, and whose subsequent potential we can never know. Strongly indicative that Marlowe was the rival poet referred to in Shakespeare's *Sonnets* 79 to 85 is the fact that in *Sonnet* 86 Shakespeare suddenly speaks of this rival in the past tense:

> Was it the proud full sail of his great verse,
> Bound for the prize of all-too-precious you [i.e. Southampton],
> That did my ripe thoughts in my brain inhearse,
> Making their tomb the womb wherein they grew?

As Dr Rowse has pointed out, the description strongly fits Marlowe, and the rival poet thereafter completely disappears from the *Sonnets*.

In fact, besides Marlowe, Thomas Kyd proved another victim of the strange affair of the Dutch House libel, never properly recovering from his rough handling by the government torturers, and dying within a year. Meanwhile, perhaps linked with all this cloak-and-dagger activity there arrived in England some particularly unwelcome news for Elizabeth and her ministers. During the past years Elizabeth had been sending men and money to help the Protestant Henri of Navarre against the Spanish-backed Catholics who were preventing him entering Paris and other key French cities to secure his right to the French throne. These struggles in France, with English troops involved, had been highly topical in England – adding to the patriotism with which *Henry vi, Part i* was received. The Stratfordian Richard Field (whose wife was a French Protestant), printed pamphlets detailing the latest French affairs, with names of major participants, the Duc de Longueville, the Duc de Mayenne and Biron, names that as we have seen [see pages 13 and 17] most certainly came to Shakespeare's attention. Despite the English help, however, in the early part of 1593 Henri saw little prospect of achieving his goal by remaining a Protestant and so on the famously cynical grounds that 'Paris is worth a mass' he announced his switch to Catholicism. At one fell stroke he defused much of his opposition and was able, within a year, to be crowned as Henri IV and to enter Paris.

For Elizabeth and her chief ministers this was a bitter piece of perfidy, any alliance between Catholic Spain and a now Catholic France threatening to leave Protestant England seriously isolated. In this very same month of July the spies circulating among the many English Catholics exiled abroad brought news of renewed interest in the succession prospects of Ferdinando, Lord Strange.[20] Apparently Father Persons and other prominent English Catholics had been holding a conference in Antwerp on the succession issue, a matter forbidden for discussion in England. Elizabeth was now sixty, and it is almost impossible to appreciate from our perspective quite how vulnerable she and her ministers would have felt at the time. Despite Elizabeth's apparent popularity and her victories against the Spanish, English Catholicism was now firmly on the increase once again, while the quality and morale of Protestant clergy remained depressingly low. It was acutely evident that recusancy rolls such as that on which Shakespeare's father's name had appeared represented but a small fraction of the true number of England's Catholics, most of whom outwardly conformed, but were ready at any time to welcome a credible Catholic or pro-Catholic successor.

We have already seen that Ferdinando, Lord Strange, still patron of those actors touring under his name, was under the deepest suspicion in this regard, even though, by every means possible, he tried to display his loyalty. On 25 September 1593 the matter was intensified when his father, the fourth Earl, died at Lathom, and Ferdinando succeeded as fifth Earl of Derby, thus assuming mastery of strongly Catholic Lancashire. Mysteriously, on the day of Derby's death there arrived at Lathom Richard Hesketh, a member of one of Lancashire's most noted families. He brought with him from London a letter he had apparently been handed to deliver to Lathom, upon his passing through the capital on his return from overseas. Ferdinando being preoccupied with his father's death, Hesketh handed the letter to Ferdinando's close relative and confidant, Sir Edward Stanley (an overt Catholic then staying at Lathom). Hesketh was then about to return to his Lancashire wife when Sir Edward, having apparently now shown the letter to Ferdinando, detained him in conversation, seemingly trying to pry how much he knew of its contents. With further blandishments Hesketh was then persuaded to accompany Ferdinando on a journey south to the royal Court where Ferdinando and Sir Edward's true concerns became readily apparent.

For the letter Hesketh had brought was nothing less than an invitation for Ferdinando to become figurehead candidate for the Catholics overseas as Elizabeth's successor. But Ferdinando could not be sure whether this had genuinely come from the Catholics overseas, or whether it had been concocted by Elizabeth's government secret agents, using Hesketh as a dupe, in very much the way Mary Queen of Scots had been trapped. Very likely suspecting the latter, Ferdinando rode with Hesketh straight to Elizabeth to show her what had been put to him. If the letter was, as he suspected, a government trap, their bluff would have been called. While politically it was a brilliant piece of gamesmanship it had a most unhappy outcome for Hesketh, who never managed to return to his wife, and who was swiftly executed at St Albans[21] on 29 November.

For those who had previously been acting under the name Lord Strange's Men the immediate effect of these events was their elevation to the title of the Earl of Derby's Men. But with the disruption caused by the plague, exactly what was happening among them and the other theatrical companies at this time is extremely obscure. There were few if any profits to be made from touring, and this seems to have taken a considerable toll upon the companies that had existed pre-plague, for on 28 September Henslowe wrote to the then still-touring Edward Alleyn:

> As for my Lord Pembroke's [Men], which you desire to know where they be, they are all at home, and have been this five or six weeks, for they cannot save their charges with travel, as I hear, and were fain to pawn their apparel for their charge.[22]

Shakespeare, for his part, may well have stayed with the Southamptons at Titchfield and arranged work for his own fellow actors there, for there is much to suggest that his likeliest piece of playwriting at this time was *Love's Labour's Lost*, arguably written not for the commercial theatre, but for a select circle such as at Titchfield. Although the first time that *Love's Labour's Lost* is positively heard of is in 1598, when a Quarto edition, one seemingly made from an original manuscript of Shakespeare's, was published after a Court performance, there are many signs that it was written several years earlier than that, and specifically during a plague year. As particularly noted by Dr A. L. Rowse, in the last Act the character Berowne says,

Write, 'Lord have mercy on us', on those three;
They are infected, in their hearts it lies;
They have the plague, and caught it of your eyes.
These lords are visited; you are not free,
For the Lord's tokens on you do I see.

As Dr Rowse points out, 'tokens' are plague-spots, the dreaded first signs of the disease,[23] and among the signs of *Love's Labour's Lost*'s having been written in the plague year of 1593 are the ways its imagery and themes closely parallel those of *Venus and Adonis* and the *Sonnets*, as if written at around the same period.

But there are also much deeper indications of its authorship at this time. For instance, the play's main storyline, a rare example of an apparently original theme by Shakespeare, is that of a King of Navarre and his courtiers who swear a solemn oath that, during the progress of the play, they are obliged to break. If this inclusion of a King of Navarre into the story is not pointer enough, Shakespeare underlines it by giving the King's courtiers names straight from the real life Henri of Navarre's most notable contemporaries: Berowne, Longaville, Dumain, clearly recalling the true-life Biron, the Duc de Longueville, and the Duc de Mayenne. In fact the vow that the King of Navarre and his compatriots take is that of abstaining from women for three years, one inevitably strained to breaking point when the attractive Princess of France and her ladies arrive. But given the names of the real Henri's courtiers, it is hard to avoid the conclusion that Shakespeare had in mind the break of faith that had taken place in France that very year.

But there is also another seeming allusion highly relevant to 1593. Although in the dialogue of *Love's Labour's Lost* the King of Navarre is never named, in stage directions and speech prefixes from the Quarto of 1598 the king is named as 'Ferdinand'. Ferdinando's personal motto, as it appears on his portrait, was *Sans changer ma vérité*, 'without changing my truth', or 'without breaking faith', and this is precisely what *Love's Labour's Lost* is all about. So in giving the King of Navarre the name 'Ferdinand', an alternative rendering of Ferdinando, was Shakespeare also gently alluding to Ferdinando's seeming break of faith over the Hesketh affair? Intriguingly, Shakespeare seems in no way censorious over this breaking of faith, Navarre being described as 'matchless Navarre', exactly paralleling the adjective used of Ferdinando in Nashe's *Pierce Penilesse*. Indeed, if the Princess of France may be taken to represent Catholicism, then the play's central message is simply that the king and his courtiers were foolish ever to have taken their abstinence vow in the first place.

Love's Labour's Lost's problem for many critics is that it is full of witty, topical allusions that are lost upon a twentieth-century audience. Nonetheless many are still recognisable, such as the identification of the 'fantastical Spaniard', Don Adriano de Armado, early described by 'Ferdinand' with the words:

> Our Court, you know, is haunted
> With a refined traveller of Spain,
> A man in all the world's new fashion planted,
> That hath a mint of phrases in his brain;
> One who the music of his own vain tongue
> Doth ravish like enchanting harmony . . .[24]

Dr A. L. Rowse has very plausibly identified Armado with the obnoxious Antonio Pérez, formerly King Philip of Spain's secretary of state, but now in exile as guest of Southampton's chief role model at Elizabeth's Court, the Earl of Essex. Another is the 'imp' Moth, Don Armado's page. *Love's Labour's Lost*'s descriptions of him as 'tender Juvenal'[25] and 'acute Juvenal'[26] have led many to identify him with the diminutive satirist Tom Nashe, whom Robert Greene in his *Greene's Groats-worth of Wit* had dubbed 'young Juvenal, that biting satirist'. *Love's Labour's Lost*'s many puns on 'pierce', 'purse', 'penny', etc, all cropping up around Moth have likewise been thought to allude to Nashe's *Pierce Penilesse* published in July 1592.

But what is the evidence for Shakespeare having written *Love's Labour's Lost* for Southampton's circle? One substantial indication is the fact that the play's very title derives from lines in the conversation manual *First Fruites*, written by the Earl of Southampton's Italian tutor John Florio, whom we have already suggested was planted in the Southampton household as a government spy. In *First Fruites* Florio wrote:

We need not speak so much of love, all books are full of love, with so many authors, that it were labour lost to speak of love.[27]

Florio's 'Venetia' proverb:

Venetia, Venetia,
Chi non ti vede, non ti pretia

quoted both in *First Fruites* and *Second Fruites* is also to be found in *Love's Labour's Lost*.[28]

Many have also suggested that *Love's Labour's Lost*'s pedant character Holofernes, like the braggart Armado, a figure straight out of the stock types in the Italian *commedia dell'arte*, may well have been based on John Florio. In the masque 'Nine Worthies' that Shakespeare included in the last act of *Love's Labour's Lost* Holofernes is cast as Judas Maccabaeus, his part requiring him three times to repeat the lines 'Judas I am' as a result of the masque's 'audience' mistaking him for Judas Iscariot. So was this a piece of fun-poking at Florio for his all too well-known 'secret' role as a government spy?

Yet another indication of the play having been written for Southampton and his circle is the appealing character Rosaline, a lady-in-waiting to the Princess of France. In Berowne's speech about her in Act IV she is described in almost exactly the same words that Shakespeare in the *Sonnets* uses for the Dark Lady:

> No face is fair that is not full so black.
>
> . . .
>
> O, if in black my lady's brows be decked,
> It mourns that painting and usurping hair
> Should ravish doters with a false aspect;
> And therefore is she born to make black fair.[29]

All the indications are, then, that *Love's Labour's Lost* was written for the private enjoyment of the Southampton circle sometime around the winter of 1593. But, if so, who would there have been to perform it? As it happens, the Christmas of 1593 was one occasion when the company we should now call the Earl of Derby's Men could have been at Titchfield, since they had already toured in the north, and would have returned south in the hope of making a Court appearance.

However, events there seem to have been against them. Their patron Ferdinando's turning in of the unfortunate Hesketh had not won him any favour with Elizabeth and her ministers. Rather the reverse, it seems to have increased their suspicions of him, for he found his appointment as Chamberlain of Chester inexplicably blocked. This was broadly the position of Lord Chief Justice for the Lancastrian north, which normally was vested in each Earl of Derby by hereditary right. Although when he returned from the Court to Lathom, Ferdinando wrote to Lord Burghley's son, Secretary Cecil, as though the Queen had verbally promised him this office, Ferdinando's entreaties on this and similar issues were ignored, and the Chester office eventually went to the Burghley/Cecil lackey Lord Egerton. Additionally, as a clear shot across the bows to Ferdinando, Cecil ordered the arrest of one of his key henchmen, Thomas Langton, on the pretext, which Ferdinando insistently refuted, that he had been implicated in the Hesketh plot.

When, because of the continuing plague, an Accession Day Tilts was held outside London at Windsor on 17 November 1593, for the first time in years Ferdinando did not take part, having returned to Lathom. And when at Christmas the Queen had her customary entertainments at Hampton Court, Ferdinando's company, now of course the Earl of Derby's Men, does not appear among those paid to perform, nor is there any other indication of their whereabouts at this time.

So the Christmas of 1593 was not only a time when Burbage and his band, at Shakespeare's possible behest, *could* have performed at Titchfield, there is also, from what is known of the original Titchfield House, at least the ghost of a clue that they may indeed have done so. The 1737 plan of Titchfield House, as preserved in the Hampshire Record Office, shows on the first floor, approached from below by a spiral staircase, a large chamber labelled the 'Playhouse room' [see fig 5, page 143]. Today only the outside walls of this remain [see pl. 29], with not even a notice pointing out the room's one-time function. But could this have been the very room in which Shakespeare and his fellow actors rehearsed their lines and worked out their moves for *Love's Labour's Lost*, perhaps then giving their performances in Titchfield House's courtyard?

Wherever, and indeed whenever, we should set the play's creation, it seems to have marked the commencement of a new mood in Shakespeare's work, one of lightness, a wittiness with words and a toying with manners that would herald a whole new phase of Shakespeare creations, and which it is difficult to attribute other than to the influence of the aristocratic young friend in Shakespeare's *Sonnets* whom we have identified as the Earl of Southampton.

Arguably as a result of this same inspiration Shakespeare was also scaling new heights in theatricality. In the very last scene of *Love's Labour's Lost* everyone is in their most colourful finery for the 'Nine Worthies' masque when there quietly enters a figure dressed all in black, Marcade, whose task, in a part of no more than twenty-eight words, is to tell the Princess of France her father is dead:

> *Marcade*: God save you, madam!
> *Princess*: Welcome, Marcade,
>   But that thou interruptest our merriment.
> *Marcade*: I am sorry, madam, for the news I bring
>   Is heavy on my tongue. The King your father—
> *Princess*: Dead, for my life!
> *Marcade*: Even so, my tale is told.

Properly directed, it is a jewel of a theatrical moment. It also perhaps serves as a fitting curtain-raiser for that final act we are about to witness in the life of Ferdinando Stanley, so lately created fifth Earl of Derby.

CHAPTER 11

'Murder Most Foul'

A hitherto unmentioned interest of Shakespeare's appears to have been funerary monuments – for his time rare among ancient church features to have escaped Reformation destruction. A particularly notable example of Shakespeare's fascination for these is to be found in *Henry VI, Part I* in which, when old Talbot dies with the dead body of his son in his arms (father and son thereupon seemingly frozen together in death in the manner of a funerary sculpture), Shakespeare has his fellow Warwickshireman Sir William Lucy declaim:

> Valiant Lord Talbot, Earl of Shrewsbury,
> Created for his rare success in arms
> Great Earl of Washford, Waterford and Valence,
> Lord Talbot of Goodrig and Urchinfield,
> Lord Strange of Blackmere, Lord Verdun of Alton,
> Lord Cromwell of Wingfield, Lord Furnival of Sheffield,
> The thrice victorious Lord of Falconbridge,
> Knight of the noble order of Saint George,
> Worthy Saint Michael and the Golden Fleece,
> Great Marshal to Henry the Sixth
> Of all his wars within the realm of France?[1]

Not only does this sound like a funerary epitaph, almost certainly it was old Talbot's authentic epitaph, as set up some years after his death at Falaise, in northern France.[2] Shakespeare happens to have been the first to record it, and he may well have gleaned the wording from someone who had copied it down while over in France supporting the cause of Henri of Navarre, perhaps then bringing it to Talbot's descendant Gilbert Talbot, Earl of Shrewsbury, already mentioned as a great companion of Ferdinando's.

But this is but one example. *Love's Labour's Lost* opens with the King of Navarre's lines:

Let fame, that all hunt after in their lives,
Live register'd upon our brazen tombs . . .

In *Sonnet* 55 Shakespeare tells his aristocratic young friend:

Not marble nor the gilded monuments
Of princes shall outlive this powerful rhyme . . .

followed by number 81:

Or I shall live your epitaph to make,
Or you survive when I in earth am rotten . . .

Most interesting of all in this regard is *Sonnet* 123:

No, Time, thou shalt not boast that I do change.
Thy pyramids built up with newer might
To me are nothing novel, nothing strange;
They are but dressings of a former sight.

Ostensibly, 'pyramids' of 'newer might' does not look too meaning-ful. After all, who in Shakespeare's age was building any replicas of the ancient Egyptian pyramids? Important to be realised, however, is that when in Shakespeare's time the traveller Edward Webbe wrote of the Pyramids he did not use the word pyramid, referring to them instead as 'mountains builded on the outside like unto the point of a diamond'.[3] This is because in Shakespeare's age 'pyramid' meant the spire shape of obelisks such as Cleopatra's Needle and the Washington Memorial. This is quite evident, for instance, from Shakespeare's contemporary George Puttenham's *The Art of English Poesie* in which Puttenham has a section 'Of the Spire or Taper called Pyramis' specifically describing obelisk shapes as pyramids. But even so, why should Shakespeare have alluded to obelisks 'of newer might' in a sonnet addressed to the Earl of Southampton?

The crucial clue lies in St Peter's Church, Titchfield, where in a small side chapel can still be seen the magnificent funerary monument [see pl. 27] belatedly erected for Southampton's staunchly Catholic father, the second Earl. This is flanked by four obelisks (or what Shakespeare would have called pyramids) in the exact semblance of the massive Egyptian obelisk that, in 1586, was re-erected by Italian engineer Domenico Fontana's herculean 'newer might' in the centrepiece of Roman Catholicism, the piazza of St Peter's in Rome. In 1589 Fontana wrote a book of his feat, *Del Modo tenuto del trasportare l'obelisco Vaticano*, and comparison of an engraving from this [see pl. 28] with the Titchfield obelisks reveals that the latter have unquestionably been modelled exactly upon Fontana's engraving, even to the little balls at the four bottom corners.

From a surviving bond in the Hampshire Record Office[4] we know that the monument was commissioned on 6 May 1594, and therefore that the designs must have been under discussion shortly before that, directly within the *Sonnets'* period. Indeed, even the master mason chosen is of interest, for he was the Fleming Gerard (or Gheerart) Johnson (or Janssen), whose workshop lay in Southwark and was therefore one that Shakespeare must have known from passing to and from the Rose. As we will go on to discover this same Johnson workshop will later be used for funeral monuments for friends and relations of Southampton, for Shakespeare's Stratford friend John Combe, and ultimately for Shakespeare himself.

But if then from this interpretation of *Sonnet* 123 we glimpse a project in which Shakespeare and Southampton shared a common interest, what was happening to Shakespeare's fellow actors in the early part of 1594? If they did perform for Southampton at Titchfield, they could hardly have lingered indefinitely, and in fact from Henslowe's Diary we know that the plague must have lifted sufficiently for the theatres to reopen. The Diary shows from the end of December a company calling itself the Earl of Sussex's Men put on a new programme, presumably at the Rose. One of the plays listed is Marlowe's old favourite *The Jew of Malta*. Another, 'titus & ondronicous', given a 'ne' by Henslowe on 24 January, produced the season's highest returns. This must now quite unquestionably have been Shakespeare's *Titus Andronicus*, whether or not those acting in it were of Shakespeare's company. Another play, listed by Henslowe simply as 'buckingham', has been suggested as Shakespeare's *Richard iii*, in which the Duke of Buckingham is a leading character. But it is all too vague, whatever was happening to Burbage and his company is unrecorded, and there are far too many missing pieces to the jigsaw. In any case, on 3 February Elizabeth's Privy Council once again closed the theatres due to renewed plague.

Only adding further to the complications are what happens to the published work, since suddenly Quarto editions of plays either definitely Shakespeare's or closely related to them begin to appear. Thus for 6 February 1594 the Stationers' Register shows the entry of 'a booke entitled a Noble Roman History of Titus Andronicus'. Thanks to the survival of a single published copy of this (acquired, as earlier mentioned by the Folger Shakespeare Library, Washington), we know it to be essentially Shakespeare's text (and a good one, seemingly derived from an autograph manuscript), even though the Quarto nowhere bears Shakespeare's name. The title page describes the play 'As it was played by the Right Honourable the Earl of Derby, Earl of Pembroke and Earl of Sussex their servants'. This we have no reason to doubt, since as Henslowe's Diary shows, the Earl of Sussex's Men were the last to perform the play, performing it 'ne' for Henslowe on 24 January, and on two further occasions before the theatres' renewed closure. The altogether obscure Earl of Pembroke's Men, it may be recalled, were the company who the previous autumn had been reported by Henslowe to be so impoverished from their touring that they had been obliged to sell their costumes, and it would appear that they had had to sell their play 'books', or scripts as well.[5] As for the Earl of Derby's Men, the fact that the title page names them first suggests they were the play's first owners in what can only have been their incarnation as Lord Strange's Men – taking us back by yet another route to the argument that they were the company who first employed Shakespeare.

But although *Titus Andronicus* was the only good text of Shakespeare's to appear in print in 1594, ranking as his first published play (albeit without his name), it was not the only play with Shakespeare affinities to be printed in this year. On 12 March the stationer Thomas Creed entered on the Stationers' Register *The First Part of the Contention betwixt the Two Houses of York and Lancaster*. The text of this duly appeared, and is now usually regarded as a poor piratical attempt to reconstruct Shakespeare's *Henry VI, Part II*.

For 2 May the Stationers' Register shows 'A plesant Conceyted historie called the Tayminge of a Shrowe', and for this again there survive copies, claiming to be 'As . . . sundry times acted by the Right honourable the Earl of Pembroke', and thus again indicating a Pembroke acquisition. This is the first indication of the existence of *The Taming of a Shrew* or *the Shrew* and while the Quarto version is not attributed to Shakespeare, it shows sufficient similarities to Shakespeare's subsequent First Folio text of 1623 to be troublesome. Scholars have been in a quandary whether *The Taming of a Shrew* was an original work by some other writer that Shakespeare improved, or whether it represents a bad Quarto of a work that Shakespeare had written earlier (1592 is one guess), and which someone subsequently pirated, the latter view being the one currently holding most scholarly favour.

The Taming of the Shrew must be another play that can be attributed to the time of Ferdinando's patronage when he was Lord Strange, and its virago-like Kate character may well have had some appeal at Lathom, where the marriage of Ferdinando's father, the fourth Earl, with the spendthrift and occult-obsessed Margaret Clifford had been highly stormy. In fact, the couple separated, Henry taking on a semi-official mistress, Jane Halsall, to whom he was devoted, and who bore him at least four children.[6] One notable feature of *The Taming of the Shrew* is the colour of his own local environs with which Shakespeare injects it, with references, for instance, to 'old Sly's son of Burton-heath', almost certainly Barton-on-the-Heath, Warwickshire, where Shakespeare had relatives; also 'Marian Hacket', the fat ale-wife of Wincot, who appears to have been a real-life individual from the hamlet of Wincot (where there were certainly Hackets in the area), just four miles south of Stratford-upon-Avon. But historically particularly interesting is the 'induction' scene in which a lord tricks the helplessly drunken tinker Christopher Sly by making a great pretence as the tinker begins to recover from his stupor, that Sly himself is a great lord who has been asleep for fifteen years. As a possible hint that Shakespeare might have written this for Lathom is the manner in which the awakening Sly deferentially greeted by a page pretending to be his lady wife bemusedly asks the real lord what he should call her:

Lord: Madam.
Sly: Alice, madam, or Joan madam?
Lord: Madam and nothing else, so lords call ladies . . .[7]

While there is no apparent significance to these names, which occur nowhere else in the story, 'Alice' instantly evokes Ferdinando's wife Alice Spencer, Lathom's first Lady, due to the old Earl Henry's prolonged separation from his wife. As for 'Joan', names in the Shakespearean era being ever imprecise, could this be Earl Henry's mistress Jane Halsall?

The page's reference a few lines later to 'Thrice noble lord', may again evoke an honorific specifically ascribed to Ferdinando, as in Tom Nashe's earlier quoted *Pierce Penilesse* tribute 'Thrice noble Amyntas'. When as in this case applied to a drunken tinker who has just invited 'Madam' to get into bed with him as his wife, that would no doubt have been hugely enjoyed by an audience in the Great Hall at Lathom.

But whatever Shakespearean comedy Ferdinando may have thus enjoyed in his northern haunt, the scene was about to change abruptly to real-life tragedy. Not least because of his ostensibly adept handling of the Hesketh letter affair, Ferdinando was a marked man. If the Hesketh-borne letter had been genuinely sent by European Catholics – and this is the view of most Protestant historians – then they are hardly likely to have taken kindly to Hesketh's fatal betrayal. If on the other hand the letter had been a government plant, then those who perpetrated this might well have thought Ferdinando too clever by half.

With the plague still raging the Queen stayed at Hampton Court during the first quarter of 1594, where fears of a secret plot to assassinate her suddenly erupted. At the end of January, the Earl of Essex, increasingly trying to take the place of the Earl of Leicester as the Queen's favourite, accused royal physician, Portuguese Jew Dr Roderigo Lopez, of plotting in league with the Spanish to poison the Queen. The already tight security around Elizabeth was doubled, and although Essex's accusations against Lopez were initially doubted, in late February a commission decided there was sufficient evidence against Lopez for him to stand trial.

Meanwhile Ferdinando up at Lathom, still being steadfastly rebuffed by Burghley and Cecil, might have felt some lift to his spirits upon the news that his wife Alice Spencer, who had so far produced only three girls, and the last of these seven years before, was unexpectedly pregnant again. Could her next be a son, thus securing his line of succession? In the middle of Lent any such hopes were rudely dashed when Alice miscarried, the foetus ironically proving to have been a boy.[8] To attend his wife Ferdinando summoned the Catholic sympathiser Dr Case, from his own St John's College, Oxford, and as a check upon his own health he asked Case to examine his urine. Case pronounced this 'a show of the most sound, perfect, able body that he had seen'. But on 4 April, while at the Stanleys' Knowsley mansion, suddenly Ferdinando fell sick, vomiting three times. Although he recovered sufficiently to ride to Lathom the next day, soon he was vomiting again, now almost uncontrollably, with blood in both this and his urine, and despite frantic purges, intestinal injections, and even doses of rhinoceros horn, his kidneys failed and he became seriously jaundiced.

By 11 April, just a week after the symptoms had begun, Ferdinando clearly realised he was dying, and appears to have had extremely strong reasons not to want his sole surviving brother William to succeed to his inheritance. Summoning his legal advisers to his bedside Ferdinando rearranged his estates to take the form of a 2,000-year trust to be administered by Gilbert Talbot, Earl of Shrewsbury (heavily suspected of Catholic sympathies); by Thomas Sackville, Lord Buckhurst (the *Gorboduc* author, believed to have been a crypto-Catholic);[9] by his brother-in-law Thomas Leigh of Stoneleigh, Warwickshire, and by local worthy Edward Savage, with whose family, as we shall learn later, Shakespeare will have an important subsequent connection.

On the same day, Ferdinando made his will, a contemporary transcript of which survives in the Public Record Office, London.[10] In this, Ferdinando stipulated that he did not want his estates 'divided and dismembered into many parts and partitions', but that instead his great houses such as Lathom, Knowsley, etc, and much else should pass intact to his wife the Countess Alice 'in augmentation of her dower' for the rest of her life, and after to his eldest daughter Anne. The clear intention was to deprive his brother of the Derby estates, and he had some precedent for his action in similar inheritance exclusions that Henry VIII had ordered in his will.

Five days later, at only thirty-five, Ferdinando died, staying lucid and fully conscious until moments before the end came, there surviving a particularly lurid account of his last hours compiled by his secretary John Golborne.[11] This and related descriptions are, however, sufficiently clinical to enable at least a reasonable twentieth-century assessment of Ferdinando's likely cause of death, and upon circulating the details to two physicians their confident diagnosis was poisoning by an inorganic substance, probably arsenic, administered in a single, highly lethal dose.[12]

Colourless, tasteless, odourless, and with no known test to detect its presence, arsenic was a favourite poison for the sixteenth century, and was certainly suspected at the time. Ferdinando's chief trustee Gilbert Talbot, who was also under government surveillance, immediately feared he might become another victim and even challenged his brother Edward to a duel in the belief he might be plotting this.[13] In the Gloucestershire Record Office there survives a hitherto unpublished letter of how the news was received in London by George Carey, eldest son of the Lord Chamberlain Henry Carey Lord Hunsdon who made Dark Lady Emilia his paramour.[14] Carey was married to Elizabeth Spencer, sister of Ferdinando's wife Alice, and since Elizabeth was then at their country home, Carisbrooke on the Isle of Wight, Carey urgently penned in his own hand:

My sweet life.... On Friday night I came to town, where I rencontred within an hour after the most unpleasing news . . . of the Earl of Derby's late and hateful death, whom . . . I find much more lamented after his death than to the world known in his life . . . his days [shortened] . . . by villainous poisoning, witchcraft and enchantment, whereof the bottom not yet found, the poisoning made manifest by the judgment of Doctor Case and three other physicans all affirming that his disease could be no other but flat poisoning.

Carey went on to tell his wife how, the Court now being back at Greenwich after an abatement of the plague, he had managed to gather the Queen's reaction upon talking with her during her 'walking abroad':

with tears . . . she professed she thought not that any man in the world loved her better than he [Ferdinando] did, that he was the most honourable, worthiest and absolutely honest man that she had in her life ever known . . .

While in classic Renaissance manner Elizabeth Tudor's affectations of sorrow were not always to be trusted, another certainly more genuinely distraught was the poet Edmund Spenser who upon revising the manuscript of his *Colin Clout's Come Home Again* inserted in this a touching epitaph to Ferdinando, characteristically addressing him by his poetic name Amyntas:

There also is (ah no, he is not now!)
But since I said he is, he quite is gone,
Amyntas quite is gone, and lies full low,
Having his Amaryllis [i.e. Alice] left to moan
Help, O ye shepherds [i.e. fellow poets], help ye all in this,
Help Amaryllis this her loss to mourn:
Her loss is yours, your loss Amyntas is,
Amyntas, flower of shepherds' pride forlorn . . .

Curiously, Spenser then went on to remark upon a fellow poet apparently also a beneficiary of Ferdinando's patronage:

And there, though last not least, is Aetion,
A gentler shepherd may nowhere be found
Whose Muse, full of high thought's invention
Doth like himself heroically sound.

The eighteenth-century scholar Edmond Malone, without any of our present insights, believed 'Aetion', which means 'of the eagle' (i.e. of the Stanley household), to have been a reference to Shakespeare, mainly on the grounds that the line 'Doth like himself heroically sound' is strikingly evocative of a name just like Shakespeare.[15]

But whatever the validity of any such identification, if Shakespeare was a member of the acting company that performed in Ferdinando's name, inevitably with Ferdinando's death the company was faced with a patronage problem. First, however, we can at this period see at least something of what Shakespeare was doing. On 9 May 1594 his poem *The Rape of Lucrece* was entered on the Stationers' Register, again with Richard Field as printer, and as in the case of *Venus and Adonis*, there is a first edition copy in the Bodleian Library, Oxford.

It is a dark work, the story of the chaste Roman wife Lucrece being secretly raped by her husband's friend Tarquin, whereupon after telling all to her father and husband, and securing their promise of revenge, she stabs herself to death. Derived from a story popular among Shakespeare's favourite authors, Ovid, Chaucer and Gower, it is a work of a tortured pessimism that one could almost believe he might have dashed off in the wake of Ferdinando's death. The one positive fact about the work is that, as in the case of *Venus and Adonis*, once again it has a dedicatory message to the Earl of

Southampton, this time clearly revealing the strong bond that, the Dark Lady affair notwithstanding, had grown between these two:

> To the Right Honourable Henry Wriothesley, Earl of Southampton and Baron of Titchfield:
> The love I dedicate to your Lordship is without end: whereof this pamphlet without beginning is but a superfluous moiety. The warrant I have of your Honourable disposition, not the worth of my untutored lines, makes it assured of acceptance. What I have done is yours, what I have to do is yours, being part in all I have, devoted yours. Were my worth greater, my duty would show greater; meantime, as it is, it is bound to your Lordship, to whom I wish long life still lengthened with all happiness.
>
> Your Lordship's in all duty,
William Shakespeare

If we may infer from the date of *Lucrece*'s registration that Shakespeare must have been in London about this time checking his proofs in Richard Field's shop, also definite is that Southampton was in London, at Court, at about this same period. This we can be quite sure of from George Carey's already quoted letter, for as part of his gossip about the Court he told his wife that Bess Bridges (one of the Queen's maids of honour, and later to be courted by the Earl of Essex), 'has forsaken the Earl of Bedford and taken the Earl of Southfil [Southampton]'. In the teeth of any theories of Southampton's homosexuality, this is indicative of his having a healthily heterosexual interest in Elizabeth's ever-attractive maids of honour, one that as we shall see later, he would pursue further.

But there remains as yet unresolved the mystery of Ferdinando's death. If he was poisoned, by whom? And why should he have been so anxious to disinherit his brother? George Carey, who seems to have shared some of Ferdinando's occult inclinations, pointed out some bizarre witchcraft and black magic elements accompanying reports of Ferdinando's death, among these the finding of Ferdinando's picture 'formed in wax with one of his own hairs pricked directly in the heart thereof'. While these serve to confirm the occult elements in which Ferdinando seems to have become enmeshed (a theme which

Shakespeare notably dropped immediately upon coming under Southampton's influence), it was no spirit who had slipped arsenic into Ferdinando's food or drink. George Carey was clearly aware of the desperate legal expedients to which Ferdinando had resorted to block his brother's inheritance, and indeed seems to have had some sympathy for these, telling his wife:

> in the time of his [Ferdinando's] sickness, finding himself at the first stricken with death he hath by good advice in law given Lathom, Knowsley, Colham, the Isle of Man and whatsoever he hath in England (besides what Henry VII gave to his ancestors) from the *nidicock* his brother, to your sister and her daughters . . . [italics mine]

The 'nidicock his brother'. The expression, though rare, is roughly equivalent to the present-day 'ninny', and reminds us that the brother in question was William, now sixth Earl, the very William Stanley to whom the Derbyians have subsequently accredited the works of Shakespeare. But what, as at April 1595, did Ferdinando know about William that he should have been so convinced, on his deathbed, that he needed to pull out all stops to deprive him of his otherwise rightful inheritance?

Protestant historians have almost invariably dismissed Ferdinando's poisoning as straightforward Catholic vengeance for Hesketh's execution, but this was certainly not how Ferdinando's continental-based cousin Sir William Stanley and his fellow English Catholic exiles saw it in 1594:

> Yorke [Stanley's co-defector] spake, being at dinner with [Sir William] Stanley, Williams being present and myself, about the death of the young Earl of Derby; they musing how he came by his end, Yorke said, 'It is no marvel, when Machiavellian policies govern England. I durst pawn my life that the Lord Treasurer [i.e. Lord Burghley] caused him to be poisoned that he [Ferdinando] being dead he [Burghley] *might marry the young Lady Vere unto the brother of the said Earl of Derby*.[16] [italics mine]

The 'young Lady Vere' is the same daughter of the Earl of Oxford whom Shakespeare, on behalf of the Dowager Countess of Southampton (and de Vere's grandfather Burghley), had earlier so unsuccessfully tried to persuade the young Earl of Southampton to marry! Suddenly all falls into place. While the married Ferdinando remained alive, Burghley had everything to fear from a convincingly kingly great lord who at any time of weakness, such as upon Elizabeth's death, might well be swept to the throne by Catholics as a perfectly legitimate successor to Elizabeth, thus ruining all the Protestant policies Burghley had so long pursued as Elizabeth's first minister. With Ferdinando dead, on the other hand, and the unmarried and easily manipulable 'nidicock' William in his place, a marriage of Burghley's granddaughter with this William would propel her straight into the power seat of the Stanley–Derby empire, thus enabling the sort of defusion of opposition that all his life Burghley had built his reputation upon.

That this was indeed Burghley's plan, and that it had arguably been hatched *before* Ferdinando's death, is evident from the fact that on 9 May, within just three weeks of Ferdinando's death, Ferdinando's widow Alice wrote bluntly to Burghley's son Secretary Cecil that she had already heard 'of a motion of marriage between the Earl my brother [i.e. William, now almost sixth Earl] and my Lady Vere your niece', adding with characteristic tartness: 'I wish her a better husband'.[17]

Alice even tried a stratagem of pretending that there had been no miscarriage (this news was known only to a few), and that she was still pregnant, in an apparent attempt to stall matters, for according to an imprecisely dated letter written by the priest Father Garnet:

> The marriage of the Lady Vere to the new Earl of Derby is deferred, by reason that he [William] standeth in hazard to be unearled again, his brother's wife being with child, until it is seen whether it be a boy or no.[18]

In the event, although Alice would fight long and hard legal battles to try to have Ferdinando's dying wishes honoured, at Greenwich on 26 January 1595 Earl William married Elizabeth de Vere in the presence of the Queen and her Court, nine months after the last moment that Alice might have conceived by Ferdinando. This is a wedding of no little relevance to Shakespeare because some scholars, unaware of its background history, have fondly supposed it to have been the occasion for which Shakespeare wrote *A Midsummer Night's Dream*. In fact, from the perspectives we have gained, this has to be extremely unlikely. Alice Spencer, as we shall shortly learn, made careful efforts to ensure that Ferdinando's acting company, whether or not Shakespeare was with them, did not pass to William. Also, Shakespeare makes some disparaging remarks about the state of virginity in the opening scene of *A Midsummer Night's Dream* which make it most unlikely that it was written for any occasion at which the Queen was present.

So given that the nuptials being celebrated in the opening and closing scenes do seem to suggest it was written to celebrate *some* aristocratic wedding, what other suitable such occasion was there at around this time? The answer lies in fact in the very same letter of George Carey that imparted the news of Ferdinando's death, which carried as another small ancillary piece of gossip:

the Vice-Chamberlain is thought shall marry the Lady Southfil . . .

The Vice Chamberlain in question was the highly trusted but now elderly Sir Thomas Heneage, who officiated in the investigations into the Lopez conspiracy and who was appointed to do the same in respect of Ferdinando. The 'Lady Southfil', translated from the curious linguistic mix that Carey affected, was none other than the Earl of Southampton's mother, the Dowager Countess Mary, who was still an attractive woman.

If we would like to think of a work that Shakespeare, idling out the plague in Titchfield, might have dreamed up for Southampton in anticipation of Heneage and the Dowager Countess needing a wedding celebration, there can be no finer candidate than *A Midsummer Night's Dream*. The bridal pair in it, Theseus and Hippolyta, are clearly of an older, wiser generation than the young lovers around whom the story otherwise revolves, thus readily suiting Heneage and the Countess.[19] But very revealing of the sort of atmosphere the young Southampton generated, and which arguably rubbed off on Shakespeare at this period, are remarks from a waiting woman of the Countess of Rutland, who asked by the Countess whether she thought the Earl of Bedford or the Earl of Southampton might make suitable suitors for her daughter, tartly responded: 'If they were in her choice . . . she would choose my lord Wharton [a widower with several children] before them, for they be so young and fantastical and would be so carried away that . . . she doubteth their carriage of themselves'.[20]

'Young and fantastical' is the very spirit of *A Midsummer Night's Dream* in which, in a manner unprecedented in his work, Shakespeare has given full rein to his imagination, filling it with delightful other-worldly characters: Oberon, king of the fairies, his queen Titania, the magical Puck, poor Bottom growing an ass's head. And it all happens in the lovers' month of May, the very time when Heneage and Countess Southampton plighted their troths. The play is a paean to the imagination, Shakespeare's realisation of this never more unforgettably expressed than in Theseus's ostensibly so dismissive lines in Act v:

> . . . I never may believe
> These antique fables, nor these fairy toys.
> Lovers and madmen have such seething brains,
> Such shaping fantasies, that apprehend
> More than cool reason ever comprehends.
> . . .
> The poet's eye, in a fine frenzy rolling,
> Doth glance from heaven to earth, from earth to heaven;
> And as imagination bodies forth
> The form of things unknown, the poet' pen
> Turns them to shapes, and gives to airy nothing
> A local habitation and a name.
> Such tricks hath strong imagination
> . . .
> How easy is a bush suppos'd a bear![21]

Giving extra edge to the fantastical, Shakespeare pokes gentle fun at his own world of down-to-earth actors, reminding us yet again that this was *his* world, as in his portrayal of the long-suffering book keeper Peter Quince giving out the parts, and the actors complaining about the roles given to them, in particular, Flute objecting to playing Thisbe:

Nay, faith, let me not play a woman; I have a beard coming.[22]

Likewise we hear Quince imploring his actors to 'con', or learn, their parts in time for rehearsal the next night, and promising that in the meantime he will 'draw a bill of properties, such as our play wants'. We hear Bottom urging:

> Get your apparel together; good strings to your beards, new
> ribbons to your pumps [light shoes]. . . . And, most dear actors, eat
> no onions nor garlic. . . .[23]

We seem to be hearing the banter, albeit caricatured, of Shakespeare's
acting world. But with the mastery of balance at which he was
becoming increasingly more adept, Shakespeare also pokes fun at the
actors' masters: members of the aristocratic world who paid the actors'
wages. Thus he has Theseus languidly musing:

> what masques, what dances shall we have,
> To wear away this long age of three hours
> Between our after-supper and bed-time?[24]

followed by his calling for his Master of the Revels:

> Where is our usual manager of mirth?
> What revels are in hand? Is there no play
> To ease the anguish of a torturing hour?
> Call Philostrate.

How much the Queen's real-life Master of the Revels Edmund Tilney
may have been mimicked here by the actor playing Philostrate, his
Midsummer Night's Dream equivalent, is anyone's guess. But it is
notable how even into this small part Shakespeare injected the most
delightful touches in the form of Philostrate's snobbish dismissal of
the tragedy the actors are intending to perform:

> A play, there is my lord, some ten words long,
> Which is as brief as I have known a play;
> But by ten words, my lord, it is too long
> . . .
> There is not one word apt, one player fitted.
> And tragical, my noble lord it is
> . . .
> Which when I saw rehears'd, I must confess,
> Made mine eyes water, but more *merry* tears . . .

However, most fascinating of all, perhaps, is *A Midsummer Night's
Dream*'s Peter Quince, since in this part Shakespeare seems to be

guying himself. This is indicated not only by Quince's capacity as general book keeper–producer to the play-within-a-play, but even by the opening words with which Quince addresses the Duke in his prologue:

> If we offend, it is with our good will.
> That you should think, we come not to offend,
> But with good will.[25]

Not only does the repetition of 'good will' seem to be a deliberate pun on Shakespeare's Christian name (a poem of 1610 addressed to Shakespeare will use this term for him),[26] in corroboration of the play having been written for the Southampton circle it is highly tempting to see in the words 'If we offend' as a deliberate allusion to the opening lines of his *Venus and Adonis* dedication to Southampton: 'I know not how I shall offend in dedicating my unpolished lines to your Lordship', an allusion further reinforced by Puck's concluding words:

> If we shadows have offended,
> Think but this, and all is mended...[27]

No hard evidence survives of where the Heneage–Southampton marriage was celebrated, if indeed it was the occasion for *A Midsummer Night's Dream*'s first-ever performance. Nonetheless the play, for all its classical setting, carries a subtle suggestion of an original staging in a Catholic household in Oberon king of the fairies' enchanting closing pronouncement of a Catholic blessing upon the bridal bed and upon the house in which the play is performed:

> To the best bride-bed will we,
> Which by us shall blessed be
> . . .
> With this field-dew consecrate,
> Every fairy take his gait,
> And each several chamber bless,
> Through this palace, with sweet peace;
> And the owner of it blest
> Ever shall in safety rest.[28]

Not only does the 'field-dew' evoke popish holy water, as has been observed by the Catholic scholar Father Joseph Crehan, Oberon's blessing reads almost like a paraphrase of the *Benedictio Thalami* in the Catholic Church's old Sarum rite.[29] While this might be difficult to envisage being appreciated by Heneage, who had been a persecutor of Catholics, fascinatingly his marriage to the overtly Catholic Countess suggests a change of faith in his old age. This is further suggested both by the mystery surrounding where such a high-ranking marriage should have been celebrated, and by a cryptic remark of George Carey's immediately after reporting the marriage plans to his wife: 'and no infection to grow to the one from the other, both being poisoned with the pox alike', the 'pox' arguably being Carey's disparaging reference to the Catholic faith.

Indeed the one hard fact of the Heneage–Southampton wedding is that it took place on 2 May 1594.[30] If *A Midsummer Night's Dream* was performed for it, then this would have been just a fortnight after Ferdinando's death. That, with or without Shakespeare, Burbage and his company were in the environs of Titchfield at this time, is attested by the fact that during this same month of May 'the players of the Countess of Derby' are recorded giving a performance in the nearby town of Winchester.[31] This is the company's only recorded mention under this name, and is a highly important indication that the news of Ferdinando's death had reached his players, and that Countess Alice, despite her many other concerns, wanted to ensure that her husband's players came under her temporary protection (and not her brother-in-law William's), until a more permanent arrangement could be made for them. Notably, it is the only instance up to 1611 of a woman other than the Queen having patronage of a theatrical company.

From Henslowe's Diary come the slightest glimpses of what happened next. Although for the time that the 'players of the Countess of Derby' were performing at Winchester, Henslowe shows 'my Lord Admiral's Men' staging three plays nothing to do with Shakespeare, from 3 June the Diary shows 'beginning at Newington my Lord Admiral's Men and my Lord Chamberlain's Men as followeth'. It then lists ten poorly attended performances over the next two weeks of which two are Marlowe's *The Jew of Malta*, two are *Andronicus*, and one *The Taming of A Shrew* (there is also a *Hamlet*, though certainly not the one we now know).

As we have earlier noted, Newington Butts was an out-of-town theatre of last resort, and whatever the reason for using it in June

1594, the takings were derisory, Henslowe recording a total of four pounds eleven shillings (£4.55) from the ten performances, little more than might be made in a single good night at the Rose. Far more important are that its repertoire now again quite definitely included works by Shakespeare, and that Henslowe described the company now jointly performing these as 'my Lord Chamberlain's Men'. This mention of the Lord Chamberlain's Men is the first record under this name of the company to which we can be absolutely sure Shakespeare belonged for the rest of his life. As already mentioned, the Lord Chamberlain in 1594 was of course elderly Henry Carey, Lord Hunsdon, lover of Dark Lady Emilia, and father of the George Carey whose letter to his wife, Ferdinando's widow's sister, we quoted earlier. For 8 October 1594 there survives a letter from Hunsdon to London's Lord Mayor, Sir Richard Martin, asking now that 'thanks be to God, there is . . . no danger of sickness', his 'now company of players' be allowed to perform as they 'have been accustomed . . . this wintertime within the City at the Cross Keys in Gracious Street'.[32] The words 'have been accustomed' tell us that this is an established company under Hunsdon's tutelage, also, interestingly, that when circumstances allowed they were wont to use a central London inn for their winter season.

But the really riveting information comes from the Court Accounts of the Treasurer of the Queen's Chamber, as prepared 15 March 1595, but relating to performances given by the Lord Chamberlain's Men before the Queen at Greenwich on 26 and 28 December:

> To William Kemp, William Shakespeare and Richard Burbage servants to the Lord Chamberlain . . . for two several comedies or Interludes showed by them before her Majesty in Christmastime last past, viz. upon St. Stephen's Day and Innocents' Day £13.6s.8d and by way of Her Majesty's reward £6.13s.4d.[33]

Discovered by the nineteenth-century Shakespearean scholar Halliwell-Phillipps on a pipe roll preserved in the Public Record Office, London, the highly important feature of this is that it represents the first solid, official piece of evidence to connect Shakespeare with any acting company. And from the fact that Shakespeare's name appears alongside those of William Kemp and Richard Burbage, known members of the old Lord Strange's/Earl of Derby's company, if Shakespeare did not belong to this company before, he did now. Indeed, from the fact that he appears in the responsible position of receiving payment on behalf of the company, it is reasonable to infer that he now held a senior position within it, further grounds for believing him to have been already with it for some years.

Having now, at long last, reached solid ground, it is perhaps worth making a reasonable guess at how Ferdinando's company had passed to Hunsdon. It is perfectly possible it was at Hunsdon's own initiative, since in his earlier years he had similarly patronised a company of players. But in practice, in his old age, many of his responsibilities were handled by his eldest son George Carey, Ferdinando's wife's sister's husband. It seems reasonable therefore to infer that it was through those very Spencer sisters, Alice, wife of Ferdinando, and Elizabeth, wife of George, that the company passed to Carey patronage. Whatever the answer, at last we can place Shakespeare in an acting company with absolute certainty. Equally thankfully, it is one we know he will stay with for the rest of his working life. From the theatrical point of view at least, throughout the next two decades Shakespeare's story, and that of the actors now calling themselves the Lord Chamberlain's Men, can be regarded as one.

CHAPTER 12

Lord Chamberlain's Man

If we have been right up to now in associating Shakespeare's early years as a dramatist with patronage by Ferdinando and by Southampton, there dissolves much of the mystery – so played upon by the Oxfordians and their ilk – behind how the low-born Shakespeare could have acquired his unerring dramatic feel for the ways of the high and the mighty. In the northern court of Ferdinando (among his Derby titles was King of the Isle of Man), Shakespeare would have automatically observed 'royal' style, accompanied by every shade of dynastic intrigue among the Catholics clustered around Lathom. The classic Renaissance murkiness surrounding Ferdinando's death would have been all too readily embryonic of a later *Hamlet*. In Southampton's southern court at Titchfield, by contrast, Shakespeare would have been the intimate of a 'fantastical' young aristocrat, full of all the witty *joie-de-vivre* of a wealthy undergraduate idealistically in love with love, and wanting to do anything but graduate into the harsh outside world. Arguably both schools of influence made their own distinctive and indelible impressions upon what the world now knows as 'Shakespeare'.

Whatever had gone before, Shakespeare had acquired his first certain patron in Henry Carey, Lord Hunsdon, Lord Chamberlain and first cousin to the Queen through his mother, Anne Boleyn's sister. From a portrait painted in 1591 [see pl. 30], the year before he sired a healthy son by Emilia Lanier, the then sixty-six-year-old Carey looks out vigorously, fingering the George of the Garter that he had now held for thirty years, and proudly grasping his wand of office as Chamberlain. A bluff, no-nonsense military man, noted for 'blasphemous oaths and threatenings', Carey played a key part in the crushing of the 1569 Rebellion of the Northern Earls and, despite a tolerance towards Catholicism, had always served his kinswoman the Queen with the utmost loyalty.

Seventy years old upon taking over patronage of what we can now confidently call Shakespeare's company, Carey had few if any of the literary leanings of a Ferdinando or a Southampton. But the prestige of being one of his entourage would have been considerable. The spectacle that went with the Chamberlain's role during the Queen's 'royal walkabout' would be most vividly described two years later by French diplomat Monsieur de Maisse:

> When the Queen goes abroad in public the Lord Chamberlain walks first, being followed by all the nobility who are in court, and the Knights of the Order that are present walk after, near the Queen's person, such as the Earl of Essex, the Admiral and others. After her march fifty gentlemen of the Guard, each carrying a halberd, and sumptuously attired and after that the Maids and Ladies who accompany them, very well attired.[1]

Whereas as one of Ferdinando's men Shakespeare would previously have worn the Stanley eagle on any livery he was granted, now, along with the other senior members of his company of actors, he would have worn the Carey swan.

In line with our suggestion that Spencer sisters, Alice and Elizabeth, were probably the prime movers, through George Carey, Henry's son, in securing the Lord Chamberlain's patronage, Henry appears to have taken little interest in his company's productions or day-to-day affairs, thereby leaving them very much to their own devices to decide what productions might next best suit the public mood. It put Shakespeare, a man who as a working actor did not *have* to earn his living as a writer, in the strongest of positions, his overriding purpose being to give his company better material than was otherwise available. Accentuating this was the fact that those who had been his greatest rivals, Greene, Marlowe, and Kyd were all dead, while Jonson, who would become a rival, had not yet surfaced.

Even so, Shakespeare had by no means the freedom enjoyed by today's dramatists. As pointed out by the American scholar T. W. Baldwin, who made a pioneering study of the working practices of Shakespeare's company:

> at every stage of his work the dramatist was forced to bear his company in mind. . . . However much or little the company actually detracted from or contributed to the plotting and writing of his play, the dramatist had still to fit his ideas to the actors who were to

perform that play.... His story must contain, or be capable of having inserted, a major part for each major actor in the company; and this part must be in the 'line of that major actor'.[2]

Here, therefore, is perhaps an appropriate cue for us to remind ourselves of those actors with whom Shakespeare found himself in 1595 (if he had not already been working with them for some years before), and for whom he would tailor acting roles for the rest of their and his working lives.

William Kemp is a name we have already noted to have preceded Shakespeare's and Burbage's in the Court Accounts. *The Seven Deadly Sins* 'Platt' shows him to have worked for Lord Strange's Men; other evidence indicates that before then he belonged to the Earl of Leicester's Company. He was therefore a leading, senior figure in the company, and it is also quite clear that he specialised as a comedian or clown. The anonymous *A Knack to Know a Knave*, which Henslowe's Diary recorded Lord Strange's Men to have performed seven times between June 1592 and January 1593, when published in 1594 was inscribed on its title page 'with Kemp's applauded Merriments of the Men of Goteham'. Kemp had only the tiniest of parts in this as a cobbler who has to deliver a speech to the king. So he must have improvised considerably upon his script for it to be worthy of special mention, and this was almost certainly his métier. In any play for the Lord Chamberlain's Men Shakespeare clearly, therefore, needed to include a part to suit Kemp's special characteristics.

Thomas Pope, as we have earlier seen, was of the same Leicester's/Lord Strange's Men pedigree as Kemp, and later documents make clear he too made the transition to the Lord Chamberlain's. The 'Platt''s reference to him as 'Mr' Pope again indicates his seniority. One source of 1600 speaks of him as 'Pope the clown',[3] suggesting that he could join or swap comic roles with Kemp. But since in *The Seven Deadly Sins* 'Platt' he appears as playing Arbactus, a gruff general who overthrows a king,[4] he clearly had versatility. Pope appears listed in the records of the parish of St Saviour's, Southwark, at least from 1593, and although he is not known to have been married, his will of 1605 shows him to have had a housekeeper, Goodwife Willingson, also to have adopted at least three children, one of whom was a mere eleven months old at the time of his death.

Augustine Phillips is known to have lived in Horseshoe Court, Bankside, Southwark, close to Pope, and would seem to have been a good friend of his. Although he played the part of the effeminate, cross-dressing Sardanapalus in *The Seven Deadly Sins*, he was married, and brought up four daughters. It has been suggested that he specialised in some of the more sinister roles, and he also clearly had musical talents, for in his will, in which Shakespeare would be a named benefactor, he bequeathed his cittern (an early form of guitar), his bandore (another type of cittern), and his lute to his apprentice of that time, James Sands.

George Bryan was another of the old Leicester's/Lord Strange's Men stable, although little of him is known, apart from the fact that he went on the Denmark and Germany trip of 1586, played some undistinguished parts in *The Seven Deadly Sins* and must have joined the Lord Chamberlain's Men, since he is recorded as receiving payment on their behalf in December 1596. He is known to have had a son in 1601, and the fact that *The Seven Deadly Sins* 'Platt' describes him as 'Mr' Bryan, also that he appears among the First Folio's list of 'principal actors', suggests him likewise to have been one of the company's senior figures.

John Heminges we find as very much the family man, already mentioned as having married Rebecca, widow of the Queen's company actor William Knell, back in 1588. By 1596 father of four (three living) of the fourteen children he would have by his beloved Rebecca, he seems to have been already senior with Lord Strange's Men at least as early as 1593, since, as previously noted, his name appeared among the company's principals who were granted a touring licence in that year. Although the actor lists for several of Ben Jonson's plays also include his name, it is impossible to determine from these the type of parts he would have played.

Richard Burbage, listed after Shakespeare in the Court Accounts, was of course the son of Shoreditch Theatre builder and proprietor James Burbage (still on the scene as the company's grand old man), and although the year of his birth has long been thought unknown, the American scholar William Ingram has very recently traced his christening, cloaked under the spelling 'Richard Briggys', to 7 July 1568.[5] This would make him twenty-seven in 1595, and thus perfectly poised for the command he would shortly assume of many of the lead roles in Shakespeare's finest works.

Working alongside these, much more dimly discernible because their names rarely figure in any record, would have been the principal actors of the future: beardless young men learning their 'quality', as acting skills were dubbed, by playing female roles. It was perhaps easier for them to accept such roles than it would be for young men today because it was then inconceivable that real women should perform on stage. There was also a long tradition, going back to the days of the Mystery plays, of young men playing women's parts. Among these youngsters T. W. Baldwin has suggested Alexander Cooke, Robert Gough and Nicholas Tooley of the First Folio list for the parts.

Also not to be forgotten is that acting is but one of the faces of any acting company, modern or Shakespearean, and that other equally vital roles – directing, prompting, carpentry, painting and decoration, providing background music and special effects, manning the box office, supplying front-of-house refreshments, etc, etc – all had to be filled by people with whom Shakespeare would have rubbed shoulders on a day-to-day basis. Here the Elizabethan world seems to have been less restrictive than the present, and considerable doubling-up was expected.

As a trained joiner and carpenter, elderly James Burbage may well have turned his hand to those tasks that demanded expert carpentry, while a variety of later sources mention that his son Richard, besides his acting skills, was a talented painter. For instance, in *Microcosmos*, a poem of 1603 by John Davies of Hereford are the lines:

> Players, I love ye, and your quality,
> As ye are men, that pass time not abus'd
> And some I love for painting, poesie . . .[6]

In the margin are the initials W.S. and R.B., generally thought to indicate that Davies was thinking of Shakespeare and Burbage. In Dulwich Picture Gallery there is even a competently executed self-portrait attributed to Burbage [see pl. 38] while, as earlier noted, it is quite definite that in 1613, again with Shakespeare, he would paint a tournament device for the Earl of Rutland.

Augustine Phillips, as we have noted, had a gift for playing stringed instruments, and he may well also have been in charge of scheduling which plays would be performed on any one day. Later, at the time of the Earl of Essex fiasco (see chapter 17), he would be pulled in for questioning over a specially commissioned performance. Phillips' later will shows he had an apprentice, James Sands at that time, and we may anticipate that most of the seniors devoted part of their time to training the company's youngsters.

However, perhaps one unexpected and certainly hitherto un-recognised example of such doubling-up, indeed trebling-up, concerns John Heminges. It has long been known that Heminges from 1596 became Shakespeare's company business manager, as evident not least from the Court Accounts from this date showing his name as recipient on the company's behalf of payments for performances at Court. Rather less well known, however, is that in his will of 1630,[7] as well as in a will in which he was a beneficiary in 1611,[8] Heminges is described as a grocer. Curiosity over this information led me to enquire with the still-surviving Worshipful Company of Grocers whether Heminges might by any chance have been one of their members, and if so, in what capacity. I discovered that Heminges had become a full member of the Company in 1595, the very year in which the newly created Lord Chamberlain's company was getting into gear again after the disruption caused by the plague. Nor was Heminges' subsequent part in the Grocers' Company a minor one. In 1621 he was admitted to the honour of its Livery, subsequently superintending special banquets for distin-guished guests. An initial surmise was that perhaps Heminges' wife Rebecca looked after the grocer's business in her husband's name, though this would hardly have been an easy task for her while rearing those fourteen children. But new significance became apparent upon studying the original partnership agreement which Philip Henslowe drew up with grocer John Cholmley for the build-ing of the Rose theatre. Towards the bottom of the page was the clause:

> And further the said Philip Henslowe doth . . . grant . . . that he will not permit or suffer any person or persons other than the said John Cholmley . . . to put to sale in or about the said parcel of ground [i.e. the environs of the Rose] . . . any bread or drink . . .[9]

Had not James Burbage's Red Lion and Shoreditch Theatre projects both been in partnership with grocer John Brayne? And was it not normal practice for Elizabethan audiences to be plied with apples, nuts, gingerbread, bottled beer and other tempting refreshments during theatrical performances?[10] The scale of business from the young 'nutcrackers' who went around the audience selling nuts is quite evident from the archaeological findings at the Rose site, revealing the second Rose's floor to have been literally paved with hazelnut shells that can only have been from the discards. Confectionery was another item that came under the province of grocers in the sixteenth century, as indeed was tobacco.[11] Clearly, for a theatrical company of Shakespeare's time, as for our own time, the sale of front-of-house foods and beverages would have been a valuable extra source of income, and this small empire would clearly seem to have been Heminges' special area of responsibility.

In this light Shakespeare's dual role as actor–writer, though undoubtedly rare for the time, begins to seem slightly less out of kilter with the burdens borne by his companions. In fact, even a trebling of responsibilities may be inferred in Shakespeare's case, for someone must have performed at least some of the duties of producer–director. And here it is noteworthy that whereas the stage directions for Shakespeare's earlier plays, indeed for the majority of his work, are relatively scanty, certain later ones, such as *Coriolanus* and *Henry VIII*, have unusually extensive stage directions. The normal and reasonable inference is that in the earlier productions Shakespeare would have been around in person to explain and direct his intentions. He would only have bothered to write fuller stage directions when he began increasingly to spend more time in Stratford.

Frustratingly it is all too dimly that we can glimpse such background to the Lord Chamberlain's Men's day-to-day activities, or establish what productions they were performing at any one time. This is for the reason that before the first hard evidence for Shakespeare's membership of the Lord Chamberlain's company, even the one fragile link we had with at least some of the Lord Chamberlain's Men's activities, Henslowe's Diary, was snapped. After the Lord Chamberlain's Men's apparently final joint performance (of Marlowe's *The Jew of Malta*), with the Lord Admiral's Men at Newington Butts on 13 June, 1594, Henslowe drew a line across the page, and from this time on the two companies seem to have gone their separate ways. No Shakespeare or Shakespeare-associated plays ever again appeared in Henslowe's listings, an indication in itself that Shakespeare had been with the Burbage-founded company all along. Because there has survived no equivalent to Henslowe's Diary for the Lord Chamberlain's Men, throughout Shakespeare's peak period as a writer we are left with mere glimpses from the accounts of those productions performed at Court (which usually fail to mention the plays by name), and the occasional ancillary instance when we may find a play mentioned, but lack other details.

One example of this latter occurs for 28 December 1594 (confusingly, the same day as a performance before the Queen at Greenwich), when we find record in the annals of Gray's Inn (the law school which the Earl of Southampton attended), of the staging in the Inn's hall of the first known performance of *The Comedy of Errors*. The occasion was the Inn's Yuletide revels, apparently so riotous that the special guest, unable to take his seat of honour upon the stage, retired in disgust, whereupon, according to a wry contemporary description published nearly a century later:

> it was thought good not to offer anything of account, saving dancing and revelling with gentlewomen, and after such sports, a *Comedy of Errors* (like to Plautus his Menaechmus) was played by the players. So that night was begun, and continued to the end, in nothing but confusion and errors, whereupon it was ever afterwards called 'The Night of Errors'. [12]

Now it is generally agreed that *The Comedy of Errors* was not being performed new at this time, an example of the important distinction between first record of a play's performance, and likely date of its composition (for the latter, see pp. 90–91). So if, as we must, we look for a play that Shakespeare is likeliest to have written next after *A Midsummer Night's Dream*, and sometime during 1595, then this was very probably that most immortal of all love stories, *Romeo and Juliet*.

Among the many indications that, unlike *Love's Labour's Lost* and *A Midsummer Night's Dream*, *Romeo and Juliet* was written for public performance in a large common theatre is its immediate scale. In the opening scene comic banter between two Capulet serving men escalates with the fierce intervention of Montague serving men. This is followed successively by sword-clashing between the young bloods Benvolio and Tybalt; by attempts at restraint by officers and citizens; by abuse being hurled between 'old Capulet' and 'old Montague' (held back only by their wives), and finally by calm being restored only by the entry of Verona's Prince Escalus 'with his train'. In perhaps three minutes of theatre time Shakespeare has filled all available stage capacity with colour and excitement for the unfurling of what has been called 'Shakespeare's first perfectly told story'.

That Shakespeare intended the play to be staged at a theatre with an upper level, as in the case of the *Henry VI* plays, is readily evident from two scenes, one of these, of course, the famous balcony scene, in which the stage directions specifically require action 'aloft'. In addition the action requires an inner chamber (usually called the 'discovery space'), for the scenes in Juliet's bedroom and, in the final act, for the Capulet burial vault, features not required in *Love's Labour's Lost* or *A Midsummer Night's Dream*, and which may be taken as signs that Shakespeare was now again writing for Burbage's Shoreditch Theatre. We may also include in Shakespeare's thinking the Cross Keys in Gracious Street, which Lord Hunsdon had mentioned in his letter of 8 October 1593 as the Lord Chamberlain's Men's winter theatre. Gracious Street is present-day London's Gracechurch Street, though any more exact location for the inn is unknown.

Nonetheless, why as at 1595, generally agreed by most scholars as the likeliest when *Romeo and Juliet* was written, did Shakespeare alight upon this particular story? As suggested by Dr A. L. Rowse, one possible source of inspiration may have been events associated with the Earl of Southampton that had happened only the previous year. For many years Southampton retainers the Danvers family had been locked in a bitter feud with the Long family of Wiltshire due to an incident in which one of the Longs had murdered a member of the Danvers clan and wounded another. This led, on 4 October 1594, to Sir Charles and Sir Henry Danvers and two of their henchmen murdering Henry Long at his Wiltshire home in revenge, then fleeing, saddles 'all bloody' to Titchfield to seek protection from Southampton, who was that very weekend celebrating his twenty-first birthday with family and friends. Fending off the hue and cry that followed the Danvers' trail to Titchfield, Southampton successfully smuggled the brothers over to France, where they stayed some years in exile until eventually reprieved by the Queen.[13]

This aside, however, far more definite are literary sources which Shakespeare undoubtedly turned to for his story, for although the basic Romeo and Juliet story originated as a late fifteenth-century Italian romance,[14] literary scholars are quite definite that Shakespeare took his version from Arthur Brooke's *The Tragical History of*

Romeus and Juliet, a translation from an Italian version published in 1562.

While we can only guess where Shakespeare might have come across this work, perhaps in Southampton's collection, unmistakeably what had been unremarkable under Brooke's pen, Shakespeare translated into the stuff of immortality. First and foremost, of course, *Romeo and Juliet* took the theme (an altogether more emotive one in the sixteenth century than it is now), of the virtues – as well as the hazards – of marrying for love, rather than in accordance with parental matchmaking. In this regard the play is a complete volte-face from Shakespeare's original sonneteering to Southampton urging the cause of Southampton's marrying Lord Burghley's granddaughter. Just how close to Southampton's heart was the theme of marrying for love is quite evident from the first reports that emanated in September 1595 from the Court gossip Rowland Whyte, that 'My Lord of Southampton doth with too much familiarity court the fair Mistress Vernon'.[15] Although it was always playing with fire to court a maid of honour of the Queen, and Elizabeth Vernon had no dowry to offer, and at about this time Burghley fined Southampton £5,000 for not marrying his granddaughter, it was love of the doll-like Elizabeth Vernon that Southampton would pursue, with consequences we will later discover.

In *Romeo and Juliet* as in his history plays we are able to learn a great deal about Shakespeare from the subtleties with which he has diverged from his sources, for typically (and this is one of the bigger arguments against him ever having visited Italy), his background flavour is English, as in the Capulets' servants' clearing of the banquet to make way for the masked dancing:

First Servant: Away with the joint-stools, remove the court-cupboard, look to the plate. Good thou, save me a piece of marchpane [marzipan], and as thou loves me, let the porter let in Susan Grindstone and Nell—Antony and Potpan![16]

Equally typically, every name counts. In the original Italian version Tybalt's equivalent is Thebaldo. By rendering this as Tybalt Shakespeare deftly introduced into his audience's mind the familiar nursery fable character Tibert the Cat, reinforcing the *Romeo* Tybalt's panther-like viciousness. In the Italian the warring families are the Montecchi and Capelletti, and while Montagu might seem a legitimate enough piece of anglicisation of the former, it also happens to have been the title borne by Southampton's mother's family. From a minor character called Marcuccio in one of the Italian sources Shakespeare coined the name Mercutio, suggesting the winged god Mercury, this character thereupon being bestowed with a seemingly superhuman speed of wit. Not least, although in Brooke's poem the character equivalent to Benvolio is un-named, Benvolio in Italian just happens to mean 'good will'. At one level this actually conveys Benvolio's chief attribute in the play. But at another, could it denote the part that Shakespeare perhaps took in the play, another pun on his name, such as we inferred from Quince's prologue in *A Midsummer Night's Dream*?

Of which members of Shakespeare's company played which parts in *Romeo and Juliet*, there is at least one we know with absolute certainty. For the part of Peter, servant to Juliet's Nurse, the 1599 Quarto version of the play (thought to have been made from a Shakespeare manuscript actually used for the production), has as its Act IV stage directions 'Enter Will Kemp' where the ultimate Folio version reads 'Enter Peter'. Although this very minor role may well not have been Kemp's only part in the production, it provides one of the all too rare instances of being able to name a particular actor for a particular part in the earliest Shakespeare productions.

In this same regard, whoever was the youngster cast as Juliet in the first-ever performances of *Romeo and Juliet* Shakespeare placed a great deal of trust in him to give him lines of the emotion:

> Give me my Romeo; and when he shall die
> Take him and cut him out in little stars,
> And he will make the face of heaven so fine
> That all the world will be in love with night,
> And pay no worship to the garish sun.[17]

While we cannot put a name to him (though T. W. Baldwin suggested Robert Gough), we may well know his age for Shakespeare gives a very curious emphasis to Juliet's age – first in old Capulet's:

My child . . . hath not seen the change of fourteen years.[18]

then in the Nurse's repeated:

> She's not fourteen. . . .
> Come Lammas Eve at night shall she be fourteen.[19]

Given that even for Shakespeare's time fourteen was unusually young for serious romance, could it be that Shakespeare was telling his audience that this was actually the fine young actor's age? Literary scholars see alternative explanations for Shakespeare's emphasis on Juliet's extreme youth, but these considerations aside, in the plays immediately following *Romeo and Juliet* Shakespeare notably again places heavy demands upon those playing the female roles, as if there were indeed one or more exceptionally talented youngsters upon whom he could absolutely rely to play their parts convincingly.

Romeo and Juliet is also interesting from the point of view of Shakespeare's religion. For aside from the out of context abbess Emilia, and the lordly prelates of the early history plays (with whom we have no reason to believe Shakespeare had any sympathy), *Romeo and Juliet* is the first in which we meet Catholic priests – and this at a time when, even after Ferdinando's death (at whoever's hands), the Catholic–Protestant tensions had by no means eased. For it was in the late February of 1595, after unspeakable tortures and long imprisonment, that the captured Jesuit Father Robert Southwell was brought out for trial, then executed at Tyburn two days later, throughout affirming his loyalty to the Queen as steadfastly as his faith in the Catholic Church. Such was the impact of his bearing on the scaffold that for fear of the crowd the executioners dared not carry out the usual disembowelling while Southwell was alive, and one nobleman present, Christopher Blount, Lord Mountjoy (later to be a noted enthusiast of Shakespeare's plays), remarked: 'I cannot judge of his religion, but pray God, whensoever I die, that my soul may be in no worse case than his'.[20] Four years later Mountjoy would indeed become a Catholic.

While we have no idea whether Shakespeare was present at this execution, what we do see in *Romeo and Juliet* are parts for two Franciscan friars, Friar Lawrence and Friar John, and it is important to note how Shakespeare deals with these by comparison to the attitudes exhibited by other playwrights of his time. Thus whereas Christopher Marlowe in his *Jew of Malta* joked about priests and monks, and in his *Massacre at Paris* spoke of 'five hundred fat Franciscan friars and priests', and while Robert Greene was likewise quite undisguised in his anti-Catholic stance, Shakespeare portrays his Friar Lawrence almost entirely sympathetically. While it can be argued that his stratagem for helping Romeo and Juliet involved deceiving Juliet's mother and father into believing their daughter dead, and ultimately causing both young lovers' deaths, the Catholic scholar Father H. S. Bowden has pointed out:

> the Friar's advice is always in accordance with the purest morality. He agrees to Romeo's marriage with Juliet, not as an intriguing match-maker, but as one who knows what human nature is. . . . He also hopes their alliance might heal the deadly enmity existing between the Montagus and the Capulets.[21]

Likewise, although Friar Lawrence's plan for Romeo and Juliet goes fatally wrong because Friar John has not delivered Juliet's letter, Shakespeare presents this as not through any incompetence on Friar John's part, as he might easily have done if he had wanted to present Catholic clergy in an unfavourable light, but for what to any Catholic would have been the most laudable and understandable of reasons:

> Going to find a barefoot brother out,
> One of our order, to associate me,
> Here in this city visiting the sick,
> And finding him, the searchers of the town,
> Suspecting that we both were in a house
> Where the infectious pestilence did reign,
> Seal'd up the doors, and would not let us forth. . . .[22]

It is worth noting that Archbishop Charles Borromeo, author of the *Testament* hidden in John Shakespeare's loft, was at the very time when Shakespeare was writing *Romeo and Juliet* being put forward for canonisation precisely for his visitations of the sick during Milan's great plague. And the practice of sealing up the doors of plague-smitten houses would have been all too familiar and understandable to Shakespeare's audience from their memories of London's plague of little more than a year before.

In *Romeo and Juliet*'s so dramatic final act Juliet is described as being laid in a vault 'where all the kindred of the Capulets lie',[23] and the terror of this place has been vividly evoked by Juliet's remarks of its 'foul mouth [that] no healthsome air breathes in' and its 'loathsome smells'; not least 'bloody Tybalt yet but green in earth/ Lies festering in his shroud'. Perhaps it may be no more than coincidence, but when the year before Ferdinando was laid to rest, quite possibly with representatives of his acting company among those present, it was in just such a family vault, that of the Earls of Derby in the church of St Peter and Paul, Ormskirk, where indeed, so far as can be determined, his remains rest to this day.

Although we have no Henslowe Diary to impart how many performances the Lord Chamberlain's Men staged of *Romeo and Juliet*, or the size of its audiences (the first recorded programme was not until 1662, attended by Samuel Pepys),[24] we have every reason to believe the play was hugely popular. Printer John Danter would pirate the script as early as 1597 – always a sign of popularity – prompting the Lord Chamberlain's Men to at least limit his profits by the issuing of their own official version, this latter being published in 1599, and carrying the subtitle 'as it hath been sundry times publicly acted by the Right Honourable the Lord Chamberlain his servants'. When Robert Allot in 1600 put together a collection of extracts from contemporary poets under the title *England's Parnassus* he included more lines from *Romeo and Juliet* than from any other play by Shakespeare.

If Shakespeare when devising a new play had to be always mindful of the talents and livelihoods of the actors within his company, he equally had to be alive to the current issues gripping public and Court attention, even if, as a matter of policy, he most assiduously avoided setting his plays in his own time and place. An ever-more pressing issue in 1595 was that of who should succeed the sixty-two-year-old Queen. The latest highlighting of this (after Member of Parliament Peter Wentworth had been imprisoned for raising it in Parliament in 1593), had been a two-part tract published in Antwerp late in 1594 entitled:

A Conference about the next Succession to the Crown of England, divided into two parts, whereunto is added a new and perfect . . . genealogy of all the kings and princes of England from the conquest unto this day, whereby each man's pretence is made more plain.

Apparently based on a conference of the English Catholics that had taken place in Antwerp during the April and May of 1593, the tract's author was given as R. Doleman. This was known at the time and today as merely an alias of Robert Persons, the priest who, with the ill-fated Edmund Campion, first brought copies of John Shakespeare's *Testament* to England some fifteen years before. Although couched in the most reasonable of language, the real 'hot potato' of Persons' tract was his consideration of whether 'princes may for good cause be deposed'. He reviewed how the evil John was followed by the good Henry III, the evil Edward II by the good Edward III; the evil Richard II by the good Henry IV, etc, and giving particular attention to the case of the latter, 'whether Richard II were justly deposed or no', concluded:

> First, for that it was done by the choice and invitation of all the realm or greater and better part thereof. . . . Secondly for that it was done without slaughter, and thirdly, for that the king was deposed by act of parliament . . . and brought to confess that he was worthily deprived . . . neither can there be any more circumstances required . . . for any lawful deposition of a prince.[25]

All in all the tract devoted some twenty-five pages to arguing with considerable force that Richard II had been justly deposed, the pertinent feature here being that, as Elizabeth and her ministers were aware, earlier in her reign those critical of her rule, among these her kinsman Sir Francis Knollys,[26] had particularly likened her to Richard II, especially on account of her tendency to be over-swayed by favourites such as the Earl of Leicester. Equally highly charged was the fact that as published, and distributed throughout England during 1595, the tract was dedicated on its title page to the man with whom the Earl of Southampton was being increasingly linked: the colourful and petulant Robert Devereux, second Earl of Essex. As stated in the tract as reason for directly addressing this to Essex:

> for that no man is in more high and eminent place or dignity at this day in our realm than yourself, whether we respect your nobility, or calling, or favour with your prince, or high liking of the people, and consequently no man like to have greater part or sway in deciding of this great affair (when time shall come for that determination) than your honour.[27]

Small wonder then that in the autumn of 1595, when the news of the Persons tract began to percolate through the Court, the work was immediately regarded as treasonable, and Essex, even though he may have had no part whatsoever in the publication, came under the blackest cloud. On 5 November the Court 'spy' Rowland Whyte wrote in his special code to Sir Robert Sidney:

> Upon Monday last 1500 [the Queen] showed 1000 [Essex] a printed book of t---t title [in a postscript he identifies this as the Persons tract] At his [Essex's] coming from Court he was observed to look wan and pale, being exceedingly troubled at this great piece of villainy done unto him: he is sick and continues very ill.[28]

It is against this background that Shakespeare's writing of his play *Richard II* at this time must be set. It is not of the greatest quality, not least because unlike in his previous histories, he seems at the expense of dramatic licence to have tried very hard to stay reasonably close to the historical facts – arguably because of the thin political ice upon which he was skating.

Again important to be emphasised is that with his innate sense of balance Shakespeare in no way made *Richard II* a seditious play. Into the mouth of his Richard II he sets seemingly powerful arguments in favour of unhesitating obedience to God's anointed rulers, and he has both the impressive old John of Gaunt and the Duke of York independently support these. John of Gaunt's famous speech of Act II enshrines arguably the most patriotic sentiments ever uttered by an Englishman in a play:

> This royal throne of kings, this sceptr'd isle,
> This earth of majesty, this seat of Mars
> . . .
> This happy breed of men, this little world,
> This precious stone set in the silver sea
> . . .
> This blessed plot, this earth, this realm, this England . . .[29]

But there are some unmistakeable hints that in presenting Richard II's Court, Shakespeare has in mind that of Elizabeth, as for instance in the otherwise largely anachronistic lines:

> Report of fashions in proud Italy,
> Whose manners still our tardy apish nation
> Limps after in base imitation.[30]

In the circumstances precipitating Richard's demise, in his surreptitiously engineered murder of his kinsman Thomas of Woodstock, Duke of Gloucester there are unmistakeable echoes of those surrounding Ferdinando's death the year before. Just as Ferdinando left behind his countess Alice to speak for his cause after his death, so we see Gloucester's Duchess in the same role on behalf of her royally murdered husband.

In the case of old John of Gaunt Shakespeare goes out of his way to make him represent all that was good of the traditional old England before Richard came on the scene, a notable departure from the self-seeking magnate that he actually was. As remarked by Arden editor Peter Ure, this is 'one of the most marked departures from Holinshed, and is one of the greatest things in the play'.[31] Upon his death Richard orders the seizure of 'his plate, his goods, his money and his lands'[32] to pay for the Irish wars. Is it not possible to see in Richard's behaviour to Gaunt what Henry VIII and Elizabeth had done to old Catholic England?

Almost all authorities, and most notably Dr A. L. Rowse, agree that in Shakespeare's description of Bolingbroke, the man who will usurp Richard II and become Henry IV, Shakespeare is painting a portrait of his own high-profile contemporary the Earl of Essex, the very man to whom the Persons tract was addressed, and particularly noted for his courting of the London crowds:

> You would have thought the very windows spake,
> So many greedy looks of young and old
> Through casements darted their desiring eyes
> Upon his visage
>
> . . .
>
> Whilst he, from the one side to the other turning,
> Bareheaded, lower than his proud steed's neck,
> Bespake them thus, 'I thank you, countrymen.[33]

But Shakespeare's most crucial scene is the deposition one that occupies all of Act IV, and which he sets as a great state occasion 'as to the Parliament' in Westminster Hall, the stage filled with all the colour of an assemblage of great lords, herald, officers, and so on, in a manner that must have made the most gripping spectacle at the Shoreditch Theatre.

Attesting to the popular success of *Richard II* is the fact that there were five Quarto editions before the First Folio, one in 1597, two in 1598, and one each in 1608 and 1615. Of the first edition just three copies survive, one in the British Library, one at Trinity College, Cambridge, and one in the Huntington Library, California, and fascinatingly in these and the two others from Elizabeth's reign the Act IV scene I deposition scene is omitted, clearly because it was regarded as too seditious to be put into print. Yet that it was there from the outset is quite evident from the Abbot's published words – 'A woeful pageant have we here beheld'[34] – which are quite meaningless unless the deposition scene has been performed before them.

Among powerful indications of Shakespeare's awareness of the contents of Robert Persons' tract, not least is the high drama he puts into Northumberland's attempt to persuade Richard to accede to one of the tract's most important principles – that the monarch should accept the worthiness of his deposition. Northumberland specifically commands Richard to read:

> These accusations, and these grievous crimes
> Committed by your person and your followers
> Against the state and profit of this land:
> That, by confessing them, the souls of men
> May deem that you are worthily depos'd.[35]

Here, then, we are able to gauge something of the real-life drama that Shakespeare was touching upon in 1595, even while setting his plays in the apparent safety of the distant past. Later, in a context we will come to, Elizabeth would remark bitterly that *Richard II* was played forty times in open streets and houses within London, which suggests that at least some of those performances were at the already mentioned Cross Keys Inn at Gracious Street.

All we do have, however, is the record of an invitation to Sir Robert Cecil, Lord Burghley's son, to a private showing of the play in 1595 at the house of Sir Edward Hoby in Cannon Row, Westminster (Ferdinando's residence was in the same road). In the words of Hoby's letter, still preserved in Robert Cecil's papers:

Sir, Finding that you were not conveniently to be at London tomorrow night I am bold to send to know whether Tuesday may be any more in your grace to visit poor Cannon Row where as late as it shall please you a gate for your supper shall be open and King Richard present himself to your view. . . .

> At your command. Edward Hoby[36]

The letter was endorsed '7 Dec. 1595' by Cecil's secretary, and a second addendum 'Readily' strongly indicates Cecil's acceptance. Although from so vague a reference the Hoby performance might have been of *Richard III* rather than *Richard II*, scholars of the authority of Sir Edmund Chambers and others have accepted this as indeed record of a private performance of *Richard II* by Shakespeare's company on this date, the words 'as late as it shall please you' acutely conveying the extent to which actors' working hours lay utterly at the whim of those who hired them.

Of whatever Robert Cecil thought of the production there survives no record, though within a very few years the matters the play touched on would flare up into one of the biggest political upheavals of Elizabeth's reign. But meanwhile, for all the signs of their burgeoning success, the careers of both Shakespeare and his Lord Chamberlain's Men faced some highly daunting and more immediate hazards.

CHAPTER 13

'To Show the World
I am a Gentleman'

If we have been right that during the 'depression' time of the plague Shakespeare's company had spent some time at Titchfield working on new Southampton-inspired plays from Shakespeare's pen, we may reasonably expect Shakespeare and the company to have been suitably rewarded. Lacking, of course, the company's account books we have absolutely no hard evidence of this, but one anecdotal snippet is worth mentioning. When in 1709 the lawyer–drama enthusiast Nicholas Rowe was putting together the first Shakespeare mini-biography he included the following:

> There is one instance so singular in the magnificence of this patron of Shakespeare's that if I had not been assured that the story was handed down by Sir William D'Avenant, who was probably very well acquainted with his affairs, I should not have ventured to have inserted: that my Lord Southampton, at one time, gave him a thousand pounds to enable him to go through with a purchase which he heard he had a mind to. A bounty very great, and very rare at any time. . . .[1]

Usually modern commentators have linked this anecdote with Shakespeare's dedication to Southampton of *Venus and Adonis* and *Lucrece*, and on hard evidential grounds they can claim every justification for doing so, for historically the two poems remain the only truly firm link between Southampton and Shakespeare. Yet for Southampton to have paid so much just for those poems strains credulity. Three or four pounds was regarded as a perfectly benevolent bounty for even the most illustrious patron to bestow upon a writer dedicating a work to him.[2] Shakespeare's personal financial affairs rank among the best documented aspects of his life, and they exhibit no evidence of anything so exorbitant.

If the story of the gift has any validity, it can be placed within a comparatively narrow band of time. This would have been between 6 October 1594, Southampton's twenty-first birthday, when he achieved proper control over his financial affairs, and 1596 when serious over-reaching of himself, exacerbated not least by Lord Burghley's fining him £5,000 for not marrying Elizabeth de Vere, necessitated a serious drawing in of his horns. And within this period, particularly if we recognise a certain musketeer-like 'all for one, one for all' attitude prevailing within Shakespeare's company, there is one company venture that would indeed fit Southampton's gift in terms of scale, timing and cost.

Three miles southwest of Guildford in Surrey lies Loseley House, in Elizabeth's reign the country seat of Member of Parliament Sir William More, and in Loseley's Muniment Room can be studied a little-known deed of purchase[3] dated 4 February 1596, between More as vendor and the grand old man of Shakespeare's company, James Burbage, as purchaser. By way of background, Burbage, it may be remembered, took out a twenty-one-year lease on the land upon which he built his common stage Shoreditch Theatre. In the very same year in which he did this, rival theatrical entrepreneur Richard Farrant took out a lease with Sir William More for some grand rooms which More owned in what had been part of the old Blackfriars Priory, and which Farrant wanted for the staging of up-market private theatre productions performed by the company of child actors he controlled. In 1596, while Farrant's company had been effectively put out of business by the popular success of the Burbage adult productions, Burbage, with a company much in demand, was faced with the imminent expiry of his lease at Shoreditch, and apparently little inclination from the elderly lessor, Giles Allen, to renew it. Furthermore the Cross Keys in Gracious Street, which was not in a Liberty, was under threat of closure at any time by London's ever-hostile Lord Mayor.

Burbage's plan, therefore, no doubt worked out in liaison with his company's senior partners, seems to have been to take over Farrant's grand rooms at Blackfriars, and to turn these into a new, considerably up-market, all-weather theatre ideal for the now more sophisticated plays that Shakespeare was writing, arguably as a result of Southampton's influence. The Blackfriars would be the first proper purpose-built adult playhouse within the City Walls, and with the right ambience could command suitably high entrance fees to exclude the rabble. More's deed at Loseley quotes £600 as the price paid by Burbage which, with the considerable amount of alterations needed (at hand-over the property was divided into seven rooms), neatly suits a possible estimate of £1,000 for the overall project. Indeed, given such a scale of capital investment, very approximately £500,000 at today's prices, it is difficult to envisage other than a gift of the munificence attributed to Southampton having made this possible.

The choice of Blackfriars [see pl. 46] is fascinating for a variety of reasons. As earlier mentioned, the great Blackfriars Priory had been one of the victims of Henry VIII's Dissolution of the Monasteries, but even before this there existed an arrangement for part of the premises to be made available for Crown use, on occasion as a luxury hotel, as in 1522 on the Holy Roman Emperor Charles V's visit to London, or as when in the following year the Upper Frater, the part purchased by Burbage, saw use as a Parliament Chamber. This same Upper Frater was also where, in 1529, Queen Katherine of Aragon suffered the humiliation of her divorce proceedings being argued between Henry VIII and cardinals representing the Pope. When Henry VIII fully took over the premises he passed the Upper Frater over to his Master of the Revels Sir Thomas Cawarden and it was from Cawarden that Burbage's vendor Sir William More inherited it in 1560. During Elizabeth's reign a number of prominent individuals took up residency within the Blackfriars environs, among these Lord Chamberlain Hunsdon, his son George, the Dowager Elizabeth Russell, and others, making it one of London's most fashionable districts. A theatre in the Upper Frater would therefore be ideal to Burbage and his company for attracting the very best clientele, one prepared to pay several times more than the Shoreditch groundlings for seats in England's first purpose-built indoor playhouse for adult actors. And since Blackfriars was a Liberty, this made it exempt from the jurisdiction of the civic authorities.

The actors' patron, old Chamberlain Hunsdon, then living at Somerset House, unquestionably knew of the Burbage plan, since just under a month before the signing of the contract he wrote to the vendor, William More, mentioning that he had heard that 'you [i.e. More] have already parted with part of your house to some that means to make a playhouse of it'.[4] Probably the players themselves had told him of their intentions, and certainly he would seem to have had no objection for he asked More if he might himself purchase

More's 'other house, which once I had also', which he had heard More was likewise intending to sell. Henry's son George would also inevitably have been aware of the plan, since he lived in the same precinct.

While alterations at the Blackfriars were taking place there is hardly the whisper of a record of Shakespeare and his fellow actors' productions at the Cross Keys Inn and at the Shoreditch Theatre. We can only guess that the schedule included perhaps *Romeo and Juliet*, *Richard II*, together with old favourites such as *Titus Andronicus* and the *Henry VI* plays. On the political front the Queen became seriously ill during the spring; in the April Calais fell to the Spanish, pressing Henri IV to conclude a truce with them, and the summer was notable for its excessive rains, the latter of which can only have strengthened the actors' desire for the Blackfriars project to be realised.

But if a damp summer can hardly have helped attendances at the Shoreditch Theatre, in July things began to go even more seriously wrong. First, given that any summer outbreak of plague was always a good excuse to close the theatres, sure enough, on 22 July the Privy Council sent out letters:

> to restrain the players from showing or using any plays or interludes in the places usual about the city of London, for that by drawing of much people together increase of sickness is feared.[5]

Just twenty-four hours later, whether plague-related or no, Lord Chamberlain Hunsdon breathed his last at Somerset House over-looking the Thames. In a classically Elizabethan death-bed scene he reportedly told his son George, who kept vigil, that he was 'to possess all and whatsoever I shall leave behind me, so I do think you worthy of it, and much more, for I have always found you a kind and loving son'.[6] Three weeks later Hunsdon was buried in Westminster Abbey, at royal expense, with an elaborate monument to his memory.

Predictably, Shakespeare's acting company was instantly taken over by Hunsdon's eldest son George Carey, who, as we have already suspected, may well have been the true patron ever since the handover from Ferdinando's widow, Countess Alice. This much is in fact inferred by a consolatory letter sent to Carey by Secretary Cecil three days after his father's death, conveying the Queen's grief and remarking:

> I shall think it strange if your Lordship should fail of succession in divers of those places all which, although your noble father worthily enjoyed, yet ... the world must needs attribute much more to yourself.[7]

Accordingly there would have been little reason for Shakespeare's company to have felt any crucial change of regime in acquiring George Carey as their patron. In the picture collection of Berkeley Castle, Gloucestershire, is displayed an exquisite, though unfinished portrait miniature of Carey by Isaac Olivier [see pl. 31],[8] painted in 1601. Forty-nine years old in 1596, like Ferdinando he seems to have had flamboyance. The Oliver portrait shows him simply with a badge of the Carey swan on his left shoulder, but among the jewellery he is described as having worn we hear of a 'topaz oriental set about with diamonds' and a 'great agate wherein is enclosed the portraiture of Perseus and Andromache'.[9] At their country seat, Carisbrooke Castle on the Isle of Wight, Carey and his wife Elizabeth entertained lavishly, according to the island's Deputy Lieutenant Sir John Oglander, with 'the best hospitality at the Castle as ever was or will be'.[10]

Tragically, however, the same bout of plague that closed the theatres and possibly took Henry, Lord Hunsdon may also have taken someone of far more immediate moment to Shakespeare. If, shortly after the theatres' closure, Shakespeare returned to Stratford to be with his family his stay can hardly have been for more than a few days before it was punctuated by the most personal of tragedies. Up until this time Shakespeare's family life, with the single exception of his father's apparent debts, would seem to have been remarkably trauma free by the standards of the age. Other actors had seen their entire families wiped out by the plague. By comparison Shakespeare had both his parents living, and although we do not know their birth dates, they were almost certainly into their early sixties. Along with his two daughters and a son, Shakespeare also had three brothers and a sister. He had not even known that all too common event of the Elizabethan age: the death of a child in early infancy. The last death of a really close member of his family had been that of his six-year-old sister Anne in 1579, when he had been just five. But for 11 August 1596 the Stratford-upon-Avon burial register solemnly records on folio 29: 'Hamnet, filius William Shakspere.'

At just eleven and a half years old we find all too sparsely recorded the death of young Hamnet, Judith's twin, and William and Anne's only son, a son whom, in the event, they would never replace. Since we have no way of being sure Shakespeare even attended the funeral, gauging his emotions is even more impossible. Dr A. L. Rowse has suggested Shakespeare wrote Hamnet's epitaph in the words of Arthur's mother Constance in *King John*:

> Grief fills the room up of my absent child,
> Lies in his bed, walks up and down with me,
> Puts on his pretty looks, repeats his words,
> Remembers me of all his gracious parts,
> Stuffs out his vacant garments with his form...[11]

But although the sentiments certainly evoke every reality of grief for a lost child, Dr Rowse's attribution of *King John* to the 1596-7 period somehow fails to satisfy, the play as a whole lacking the quality that Shakespeare was producing at this time. Since the words are possibly the most haunting in the play, one explanation may simply be that on his return to London after the funeral Shakespeare went to his old script in the Lord Chamberlain's Men's play book collection and interpolated the lines as an expression of his feelings.

Yet if it was indeed thus that Shakespeare set his emotions down, the signs that he let his grief interfere with his art, or indeed other family affairs, are scarce. To attend any funeral is to be reminded of one's own mortality, but it would also have been a reminder, when his own name came to be set down in the Stratford register as young Hamnet's father, that as yet it could not carry the highly prized prefix 'Mr' or suffix 'gent'. Rightly or wrongly, today the word gentleman may carry little if any worth or meaning, yet in Shakespeare's time class counted for almost everything. When in writing *Richard II* only the previous year Shakespeare had written of what provoked Bolingbroke into insurrection, it was in the ripping away of the signs of his class that he had Bolingbroke complain particularly emotively:

> From my own windows torn my household coat
> Razed out my imprese, leaving me no sign,
> Save men's opinions and my living blood
> To show the world I am a gentleman.[12]

And here yet again we come to a piece of evidence about Shakespeare and his life that is as ambivalent as anything that has gone heretofore. Preserved to this day at the College of Arms, London, are two rough draft applications for a coat of arms [see pl. 32] dated 20 October 1596, that is, just over two months after young Hamnet's death.[13] Prepared under the declared auspices of Garter King-of-Arms William Dethick, they are made out in the name of Shakespeare's father John, and claim his entitlement to a coat of arms by which he and his offspring could style themselves gentlemen. The grounds stated are that John's 'parents and late antecessors' had been 'for their valiant and faithful service advanced and rewarded by the most prudent . . . King Henry VII of famous memory' and that to his further social elevation John had 'married Mary, daughter and one of the heirs of Robert Arden of Wilmcote in the said County, gent.'

Although more damaged than the first and therefore lacking some of its text, the second draft appends that John had earlier presented 'a patierne [pattern] hereof under Clarent Cook's hand' on 'paper . . . twenty years past'. This 'Clarent Cook' may be identified as Robert Cook, Clarencieux King-of-Arms, the paper 'patierne' apparently being his proposed design for the arms set down for approval purposes prior to being committed to parchment. The second draft further adds that John Shakespeare had been 'Justice of the Peace . . . Bailiff officer and chief of the town of Stratford upon Avon fifteen or sixteen years past' (written in Roman numerals, this seems to have been a mistake for twenty-six) also 'that he hath land and tenements, of good wealth and substance, £500.' Both applications carry in their top left-hand corner neat if somewhat amateurly executed sketches of the coat of arms applied for, heraldically described in the accompanying text as:

Gold, on a Bend Sable, a spear of the first steeled argent. And for his crest or cognisance a falcon his wings displaying argent standing on a wreath of his colours: suppo[rting] a spear gold steeled as aforesaid set upon a helmet with mantles and tassels.[14]

In close proximity to the sketches of the arms is written their apparent intended motto accompaniment *Non Sanz Droict*, 'Not without Right'. The applications further set out the benefits the granting of such arms bestowed:

it shall be lawful for the said John Shakespeare gentleman and for his children issue and posterity (at all times and places convenient)

to bear ... the same blazon ... upon their shields ... seals, rings
... buildings, utensils, liveries, tombs or monuments.[15]

Although there is no record of when the grant of arms was approved –
as at January 1597 John Shakespeare was still described as a yeoman
in his sale of a strip of land to neighbour George Badger – there can be
no doubt that they were. John was also undoubtedly entitled to such
elevation. While a certain haziness shrouds his ancestors' services
back in the time of Henry VII, his role as Stratford's Bailiff
undoubtedly qualified him for the rank of gentleman, the greater
mystery being why his application had not been proceeded with
before. Probably this was for the very same reason that his approach
to the Clarencieux King-of-Arms Robert Cook had been abandoned:
the drying-up of his funds. Grants of arms by the College of Arms
almost always involved the applicants suitably greasing the palms of
the College's officers. Therefore, we may legitimately infer that it was
precisely some new financial liquidity in the Shakespeare camp
around 1596–7 that enabled this now successful application.

Here a key question concerns exactly who lay behind the
application: who most coveted the title 'gentleman'? Since we have
no reason to believe that John in his old age had markedly improved
his financial affairs, arguably the cash would have been provided by
son William. Again, since John is unlikely to have been overly
inclined or able to journey to London to progress the application,
most historians have reasonably inferred that it must have been
William who personally took the application to the College of Arms
on his behalf.

If this is valid we may therefore see William, perhaps still in
mourning black from the so-recent death of his son, walking into the
College of Arms office one autumn day in 1596. This was Derby
Place, a mansion entered from St Benet's Hill, a street leading south
from St Paul's Cathedral to Paul's Wharf, which, until the 1550s had
been London home of the Earls of Derby. Destroyed in 1666 in the
Great Fire of London, its successor the present College, although
built on roughly the same site, retains virtually nothing of the building
which Shakespeare visited. Nonetheless a eulogistic poem of 1572
recaptures something of its colour in this time:

About the walls (more wondrous work, than framed by mortal hand)
Each Herald's lively counterfeit, in seemly sort doth stand

Within these severed rooms ... each thing that [be]longs to
  Herald's art, doth perfectly appear.
There ledger books of ancient gestes [deeds],
... there pedigrees do stand.[16]

One of the reasons why we can be sure the arms were granted
is the fact that Sir William Dethick, the Garter King-of-Arms named
in the original application, was later to be accused by his colleague
York Herald of elevating unworthy individuals, and in these
accusations John Shakespeare's name appears fourth in a list of
twenty-three examples cited. Dethick had a reputation as a bad-
tempered, violent individual who, his enemies alleged, took
applicants' money, then delayed actually granting the arms until their
deaths.[17]

One American handwriting specialist, Charles Hamilton, has
recently made a vigorous and ostensibly convincing case for the
draft applications being penned in Shakespeare's own handwriting,[18]
but closer scrutiny in fact reveals it as unlikely. A later, ancillary
arms application of 1599, which according to Hamilton, is also
in the same hand, twice gives Shakespeare's grandfather's village
as Willingcote or Wellingcote, whereas the first draft of 1596
correctly has this as Wilmcote. Even allowing for the notorious
Elizabethan inconsistencies of spelling, such a discrepancy is difficult to attribute to the hand of Shakespeare, who would have
known the name of the village well because of the strong family
connections.

But the more interesting question is whether it was really
Shakespeare's father behind the application? Was John, in his old
age, perhaps determined to die with at least something of the high
social dignity he had so mysteriously lost during the previous quarter
century? In the applications for arms made in his name it is impossible
not to detect a certain massaging of the facts. There are the ten years
shaved from when he had been Stratford's Bailiff. And his 'good
wealth and substance, £500' (the truth or otherwise of this in 1596 we
have no way of determining), rings strangely at variance with the fact
that only four years before, in 1592, his presence in the recusant lists
had been pleaded as due to his inability to attend church 'for fear of
process for debt'.

The alternative is of course that it was son William who was the real
mover behind the application. In his *Sonnets* he repeatedly harped

upon the lowness of his social state. The phrase 'As I am a gentleman' equally repeatedly recurs in his writings. He had married into yeoman stock; his occupation neither as an actor nor as a writer qualified him as a gentleman. Surely therefore the real impetus for his father's gaining of status as a gentleman was that this passed straight to him?

Whichever of these alternatives is true, what is plain, given that any purchase of the status of gentleman in Elizabethan times cost between £40 and £50 (the price of a substantial house), is that by this stage the Shakespeare fortunes must have turned round, arguably by William's financial success, a success that could only have been possible if his company had likewise profited. Even without Henslowe-type accounts, it is possible to infer that the *Romeo and Juliet / Richard II* season must have been an extremely lucrative one.

But if Shakespeare during the later part of the 1596 spent at least some of his spare time trying to improve his social standing at the College of Arms, at the very same time there was an unexpected lowering of his company's standing. To the surprise and no doubt chagrin of George Carey, although he automatically became second Lord Hunsdon, he did not succeed to his father's post as Lord Chamberlain – as Secretary Cecil had led him to expect. On 8 August of 1596, on or about the day that young Hamnet had died in Stratford, the post went to William Brooke, Lord Cobham, Secretary Cecil's brother-in-law. This meant that instead of being able to continue to call themselves the Lord Chamberlain's Men, Shakespeare and his colleagues now became Lord Hunsdon's Men – in turn a shock for them, since this lost them the dignity of 'royal household' protection that their former title carried. To add to their inevitable problems caused by the theatres having been closed during the summer on account of plague, this meant that London's Puritan Lord Mayor had greater power to prohibit them from using the Cross Keys Inn in Gracious Street as their over-winter theatre.

Among the few scraps by which something can be glimpsed of how this affected Shakespeare and his fellow actors is the only surviving autograph letter by the satirist Tom Nashe, whom Shakespeare had lampooned as Moth in *Love's Labour's Lost*. Preserved in the British Library,[19] this was written to George Carey's aide William Cotton around the September of 1596. After complaining of the 'tedious dead vacation' that he found himself in, and of his frustrated hopes of writing 'for the stage and for the press', Nashe went on:

now the players . . . are piteously persecuted by the L[ord] Mayor and the aldermen, and however in their old Lord's time [i.e. Lord Chamberlain Hunsdon's] they thought their state settled, it is now so uncertain they cannot build upon it.[20]

Clearly all the security that Shakespeare had enjoyed while under old Hunsdon's patronage had disappeared.

If we are looking to a play that Shakespeare wrote during this time, arguably in direct anticipation of his company performing it at the new Blackfriars theatre, the most likely candidate is *The Merchant of Venice*. With settings in Venice giving every opportunity to display Italian fashions, and with scenes of the arrival of ostentatious foreign potentates in Portia's Belmont home, it has all the ingredients for what might have been a Blackfriars launch spectacular.

The Merchant of Venice is also a play that in fact can be dated to this period with a reasonable degree of precision. Like *Romeo and Juliet*, it is partly based on an old Italian tale, in this instance of Ansaldo, a rich merchant of Venice who lent money to his godson Giannetto to help him win a worthy wife, only, through Giannetto's dilatoriness, to fall victim of a pound-of-flesh-demanding Jew. This was published in 1558 as part of a collection entitled *Il Pecorone*, and in parallel to *Merchant* has elements such as Giannetto's new wife disguising herself as a lawyer to plead Ansaldo's case, though nothing about the illustrious suitors choosing from caskets. Since certain features of this latter scene can be clearly attributed to the 1595 edition of Elizabethan writer Richard Robinson's *Gesta Romanorum*, this automatically sets a post-1595 date for *Merchant*.

Narrowing the time-scale still further, however, is the fact that in the wake of the Spanish capture of Calais, during the summer of 1596 Southampton's mentor the Earl of Essex sailed on a punitive expedition to Spain, returning in the August with some ships he had captured from the Spanish. The most prominent among these were the *Andrew* and the *Matthew*, both loaded with merchandise, and the former so large that it nearly ran aground among the sands and flats off Chatham. The news of this certainly reached Shakespeare – indeed it may possibly have sparked off his idea of a foreign merchant being financially ruined by such loss of his ships – since *The Merchant of Venice* specifically alludes to the beaching of the *Andrew* in merchant Solario's early lines:

> I should not see the sandy hour-glass run
> But I should think of shallows and of flats,
> And see my wealthy *Andrew* dock'd in sand,
> Vailing her high top lower than her ribs . . .[21]

Only in the autumn of 1596 would an allusion of this kind have had the sort of topicality to make it instantly recognisable to its audience.

Now if *Romeo and Juliet* was all about love, and *Richard II* about the rights and wrongs of deposing an unworthy king, *The Merchant of Venice*, with its famous trial scene, hinges on the theme of the law, and may well have been designed particularly to appeal to the many upper-class Elizabethans who had been educated at London's law schools, and who were just the sort of clientele that Shakespeare's company hoped to attract to the Blackfriars. Also a key theme to the play is the Christian virtue of mercy versus the 'eye for an eye' values of the Jewish Old Testament, and in this regard Shakespeare may have had in mind the mercy needed in his own age towards unfortunates (such as the recently executed Father Southwell), who became victims of the dreaded Richard Topcliffe. The play specifically flashes at least once to Topcliffe's torture-chamber world when Bassanio, in his very first words to Portia, figuratively describes himself as living 'upon the rack', prompting Portia's witty rejoinder that she feared this was 'Where men enforced do speak anything'.[22]

Mention of *The Merchant of Venice*, of course, instantly evokes the character Shylock. Indeed so closely is he identified with the play that many suppose him to have been one and the same as the title character, though in fact this is Antonio, who puts himself into Shylock's clutches by the help he gives his friend Bassanio. Shakespeare's artistry shows even with his coining of the name Shylock. Such is its familiarity that we need to be aware that it neither occurs in any of Shakespeare's known sources, nor in any other known historical or literary work. Possibly he derived it from the Hebrew word *shalakh*, generally translated as cormorant, a particularly apposite choice for *The Merchant of Venice*'s voracious Jew, though from whom Shakespeare might have learnt this particular piece of Hebrew is one of his many mysteries.

With the character of Shylock, Shakespeare pandered to the same Elizabethan anti-Semitism that Marlowe had exploited with *The Jew of Malta*, and which the Lopez conspiracy had further fuelled.

Shakespeare also provided the meatiest of character parts for whichever of Lord Hunsdon's Men he envisaged as the first performer. Likewise, very likely for the same aspiring young actor who had played Juliet, Shakespeare created an even bigger and more demanding part as Portia. For Kemp and another of the company's comics he provided a suitable vehicle for their talents with the parts of Old Gobbo and his son Launcelot, these latter possibly being thinly disguised send-ups of the elderly new Lord Chamberlain, Lord Cobham, and his son, a touch that would surely have delighted new patron George Carey. For the company's musicians Shakespeare gave an opportunity for playing proper music to herald Portia's return, rather than simple trumpet calls and drum rolls. For those responsible for the play's settings the trial scene offered the opportunity to recreate something of the grandeur of the Venetian Court of Justice. For whoever made the company's costumes Shakespeare's scenes of the arrivals of Portia's suitors, the exotic Princes of Morocco and Aragon and their trains, gave many opportunities for filling the stage with particularly brilliant colour. There are also indications that Shakespeare intended the play to include a masque.

But while clearly Shakespeare and his company would have had every hope of such a play making a most spectacular launch production for the new Blackfriars theatre, during the closing months of 1596 the company's problems, already serious enough, became markedly worse. The first sign of something going seriously wrong involved Shakespeare himself, and his closest brush with the law to that date. In London's Public Record Office is a 'writ of attachment', basically the modern equivalent of a summons, directed to the Sheriff of the county of Surrey, and demanding:

> Be it known that William Wayte seeks sureties of the peace against William Shakspere, Francis Langley, Dorothy Soer wife of John Soer and Anna Lee for fear of death and so forth.[23]

The William Wayte who brought the charge according to a legal action of 1592 was 'A certain loose person of no reckoning or value', a bully-boy of Southwark's loathed local judge, William Gardiner. Almost certainly his grievance was that he had met resistance from Shakespeare and his three accomplices when trying to enforce a theatre closure notice. Frustratingly, Dorothy Soer and Anna Lee are not known.

But Shakespeare's most interesting associate in this writ is Francis Langley. He was builder and owner of the Swan Theatre which in 1596 was a new rival to Henslowe's Rose and the very latest addition to Southwark's entertainment scene. It was located, according to a 1627 plan, in the manor of Paris Garden at the western end of Bankside. Of this there survives in the University of Utrecht an important description written in Latin by a Dutch traveller Johan de Witt, who visited London about the year 1596. According to de Witt:

> Of all the theatres ... the largest and most magnificent is that one of which the sign is a swan, called in the vernacular the Swan Theatre; for it accommodates in its seats three thousand persons, and is built of a mass of flint stones ... and supported by wooden columns painted in such excellent imitation of marble that it is able to deceive even the most cunning. Since its form resembles that of a Roman work, I have made a sketch of it above.[24]

De Witt helpfully accompanied his description with a drawing of the Swan's interior [see fig 6 overleaf], which happens to be the only surviving depiction of any theatre interior of Shakespeare's time. But inevitably the crucial point of interest is what was Shakespeare doing associating with the owner of a rival theatre when his and his company's future interests surely lay with the new Blackfriars?

Dim though our information is, the answer lies in the fact that everything was going seriously wrong with the Blackfriars venture. From Henslowe's Diary it is apparent that there was a rescinding of the closure of the theatres, around the end of October; Henslowe's first renewed performance by the Admiral's Men was recorded as 27 October. We may therefore infer that Shakespeare's company would have been able to perform again – if they had the premises. And here, despite their massive £1,000 investment, lay the difficulty. Among the State Papers for Elizabeth's reign is a petition to the Privy Council from the inhabitants of the Blackfriars precinct advising that:

> one Burbage hath lately bought certain rooms in the same precinct near adjoining unto the dwelling houses of the right honourable the Lord Chamberlain and the Lord of Hunsdon, which the said Burbage is now altering and meaneth very shortly to convert and turn ... into a common playhouse.[25]

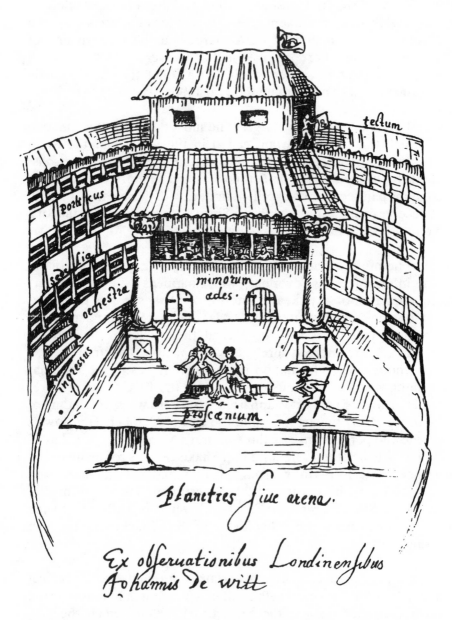

Fig 6
The Swan theatre. A sketch of the interior by Johannes de Witt, as copied by Arend van Bichell, c.1596. (University Library, Utrecht, shelfmark MS.842, f.132)

In this petition the Blackfriars inhabitants who were its signatories make clear they knew exactly what Burbage had in mind:

> now all players being banished by the Lord Mayor from playing within the City of London by reason of the great inconvenience and ill rule that followeth them, they think to plant themselves in liberties.

So far as the petitioners were concerned, however, this was most certainly not what they wanted for their nicely-ordered and genteel community. If allowed it would:

> grow to be a very great annoyance and trouble ... to all the inhabitants of the same precinct, both by reason of the great resort and gathering together of all manner of vagrant and lewd persons that, under colour of resorting to the plays, will come thither and work all kind of mischief.

As they pointed out, another problem was that 'the same playhouse is so near the church that the noise of the drums and trumpets will greatly disturb and hinder both the ministers and parishioners in time of divine service and sermons'. Accordingly the petitioners urged 'that the same rooms may be converted to some other use, and that no playhouse may be used or kept there'.

The petition carried an overwhelmingly impressive list of signatories. Heading it was the formidable Dowager Elizabeth Russell, in her late sixties, and none other than the mother-in-law of Lord Burghley, the Privy Council's chairman. Second was George Carey, the players' own patron; third was Henry Bowes (of the family of the present Queen Mother); fourth Stephen Egerton, of the powerful Ellesmere family. Among a variety of lesser known names there even occurs printer Richard Field, Shakespeare's fellow Stratfordian. Although the petition is undated and known only from a copy of around 1631, an extract from a document of 1619 informs us that it was in the November of 1596 that 'their Honours [i.e. the Privy Council] then forbade the use of the said house for plays'.

For the time being, therefore, Shakespeare's company's so-expensive Blackfriars theatre venture was holed below the waterline and, in the event, would not be allowed to surface again for another thirteen years. But meanwhile, with even their patron ranged against them, could Shakespeare and his fellow actors survive?

CHAPTER 14

Hand of the Censor

The shock and frustration at the high-powered blocking of his ambitious Blackfriars venture may well have been too much for old James Burbage to bear. Quite definite is that within just a few weeks of the Privy Council's upholding of the Blackfriars residents' objections to his theatre James was dead. His funeral is recorded in the register of St Leonard's Church Shoreditch as taking place on 2 February 1597, following a January in which torrential rain had turned many roads into quagmires. Almost certainly many if not all of James's company of actors would have been present to pay their last respects to the former joiner who had brought them together, and who had fought so hard to make theirs an honourable profession with proper purpose-built theatres for their workplace. In his last resting place James was laid not far from the comic actor Richard Tarlton.

Although Shakespeare, as a senior member of the company, would almost certainly have been among the mourners, there are indications that he may no longer have been lodging close to the Burbages in Shoreditch. When in 1795 the pioneering scholar Edmond Malone was sifting through his collection of Shakespearean documents he noted that:

> from a paper now before me which formerly belonged to Edward Alleyn the player, our poet appears to have been living in Southwark, near the Bear Garden, in 1596.[1]

Whatever document Malone was referring to subsequently disappeared along with Shakespeare's father's *Testament*. However, there is a list dating from November 1597 in London's Public Record Office in which Shakespeare's name appears among those of St Helen's parish, Bishopsgate (just south of Shoreditch), who had not paid their local taxes, apparently on account of all being 'either dead, departed and gone out of the said ward ... whereby the several sums ... neither might nor could ... be levied of them'.[2]

Also in the London Public Record Office is a later Exchequer entry likewise relating to Shakespeare's unpaid tax, and carrying the annotation 'Ep[iscop]o Winton[ensi]' (to the Bishop of Winchester).[3] This indicates that the county Sheriff apparently referred the matter to this bishop because Shakespeare was believed to be living in one of his Liberties. Since this bishop's only relevant Liberty was Southwark's theatre and red-light district – the Liberty of the Clink – there is a strong likelihood that Shakespeare had moved to Southwark, even though his name does not appear in the churchwardens' annual lists of those residents registered as having attended compulsory Easter Communion.[4] In all of this one cannot escape the feeling that Shakespeare's whole residency in London had a will o' the wisp quality to it that may well not have been entirely accidental.

Be that as it may, wherever Shakespeare lodged in London, there are signs that even before James Burbage's death, and despite the company's major setback relating to the Blackfriars, he and his fellow actors managed to turn their fortunes around. No surviving documentary evidence shows what public performances they managed to stage, or where, during the winter months, although Langley and his Swan Theatre in Southwark are serious candidates. Certainly there was no general closure of theatres, since Henslowe's Diary shows the Admiral's Men from 27 October giving continuous performances at the Rose with just the briefest break between 27 November and 2 December.

But particularly significantly, and a fact which must have cut very deep with Henslowe and his Admiral's Men, is that whereas the previous year the Admiral's Men had given five performances for the Queen's Christmas-to-Shrovetide entertainment at Court compared with Shakespeare's company's four, for the 1596-7 season the Chamber Accounts show Shakespeare's company giving no less than six performances between 26 December 1596 and 8 February 1597, whereas the Admiral's Men gave none.

We know Elizabeth's Court to have been at Whitehall this Christmas and, thanks to French ambassador de Maisse who later in 1597 would set down a particularly detailed report of his first encounter with the Queen, we can glimpse at least something of the impression that their now elderly but still sharp-witted royal observer would have made upon Shakespeare and his fellow actors. According to de Maisse, the Queen:

was strangely attired in a dress of silver cloth, white and crimson, or silver 'gauze' as they call it. This dress had slashed sleeves lined with red taffeta, and was girt about with other little sleeves that hung down to the around, which she was for ever twisting and untwisting. She kept the front of her dress open, and one could see the whole of her bosom, and passing low, and often she would open the front of this robe with her hands as if she was too hot.... On her head she wore a garland ... and beneath it a reddish-coloured wig, with a great number of spangles of gold and silver, and hanging over her forehead some pearls, but of no great worth.... Her bosom is somewhat wrinkled as well as one can see for the collar [ruff?] that she wears round her neck, but lower down her flesh is exceedingly white and delicate, so far as one could see.

As for her face it is and appears to be very aged. It is long and thin, and her teeth are very yellow and unequal ... on the left side less than on the right. Many of them are missing, so that one cannot understand her easily when she speaks quickly. Her figure is fair and tall and graceful in whatever she does; so far as may be she keeps her dignity....[5]

Although the Chamber Accounts as usual do not give the names of any of the six productions that Shakespeare's company performed before Elizabeth at this time, background circumstances shortly to be explained make it virtually certain that two of these were new plays by Shakespeare, ranking easily among his finest yet: the first and second parts of *Henry IV*. And assuming the correctness of this dating – and Arden editor A. R. Humphreys and others have favoured it – this would have meant they were Elizabeth and her Court's very first introduction to one of Shakespeare's most immortal figures, that Colossus of mirth, girth and duplicity, Falstaff. Except – and this much is certain – that for those thus privileged to see the play the name borne by the character we now know as Falstaff was Sir John Oldcastle. And while to us this may seem but a trifle, in fact it offers some further fascinating insights into Shakespeare at that time, heightened by the fact that he had now reached the maturest phase of his history plays.

In tackling the *Henry IV* plays, Shakespeare once more decided to deploy his company's comedians to the full. His clear plan was to offset the main historical events (in both parts rebellions against Henry IV's rule), with comedy – and comedy centring on the dramatically and physically huge character of Sir John Oldcastle. This raises the inevitable question of who was Sir John Oldcastle? According to fifteenth-century chroniclers such as Polydore Vergil and Thomas Walsingham he was an early friend of Prince Hal (the future Henry v); became Lord Cobham by marriage to Joan, Lady Cobham; held Lollard, that is, anti-Catholic beliefs, which he refused to recant; became an outlaw and was executed in St Giles's Fields in 1417.

With the Protestant Reformation, however, because Oldcastle seemed to have been an early apostle of Protestantism, English Protestants began to speak of him as a 'blessed martyr', as in Bale's *Brief Chronicle* of 1544. In 1563 the Protestant martyrologist John Foxe, tutor to Stratford-upon-Avon's Puritanical local magistrate Sir Thomas Lucy of Charlecote (who pursued John Shakespeare's apparent recusancy, and whose deer Shakespeare was said to have poached), elevated Oldcastle to the Protestant calendar of saints in his *Actes and Monuments of matters happening in the Church* (better known as Foxe's 'Book of Martyrs'). Giving him the appellation 'Syr John Ould Castell, Lord Cobham, Martyr', Foxe even accorded him a Protestant feast day, 6 February, which happens to have been one of the days of Shakespeare's company's Court performances in 1597. For Catholics such revering of Oldcastle seemed absurd, as argued for instance by Nicholas Harpfield in his *Dialogi Sex* of 1566, and by Stow in his reissue in 1574 of Walsingham's fifteenth-century chronicle. Effectively, therefore, while Catholics saw Oldcastle as a worthless renegade, Protestants saw him as a martyr, the truth lying somewhere in between.

Here, then, the position taken by Shakespeare is of immense fascination, for in the two *Henry iv* plays Oldcastle/Falstaff is most emphatically not the stuff of which martyrs are made. Taking his cue from information that appears in Foxe's 'Book of Martyrs' (undoubtedly used by Shakespeare), that Oldcastle at his trial acknowledged having in youth 'offended . . . most grievously in pride, wrath and gluttony, in covetousness and lechery',[6] Shakespeare made Oldcastle into a sack-swilling, self-indulgent braggart, the sort to lie and cheat his way out of any situation to preserve his skin. To emphasise the original Oldcastle's Protestantism Shakespeare has him quote the Geneva Bible almost every second line, yet in the same vein he immediately shows Falstaff's hypocrisy and his unrepentant awareness of his hypocrisy. While under any other pen he might seem utterly reprehensible, such is the magic of Shakespeare that even though theoretically Falstaff belongs to a sub-plot, he emerges head, shoulders and fat stomach as the play's most memorable character; his outrageousness winning every audience's affection through sheer gales of helpless laughter.

And despite the thinnest of religio-political ice upon which Shakespeare was treading, what is clear is that the character generated just as much helpless laughter back in Elizabeth I's Whitehall Court of 1597 as he continues to do today. The clue to the Queen's feelings on this is the strong tradition that she commanded Shakespeare, at the shortest notice, to write another play around the same character. According to Shakespeare's first biographer, Rowe, writing in 1709, Elizabeth:

> was so well pleased with that admirable character of Falstaff, in the two parts of Henry the Fourth, that she commanded him to continue it for one play more, and to show him in love. This is said to be the occasion of his writing *The Merry Wives of Windsor*.[7]

Two other writers of the eighteenth century's first decade, John Dennis[8] and Charles Gildon[9] attest to Shakespeare having written *Merry Wives* in a fortnight. Such haste is in fact intrinsically apparent from Shakespeare clearly not having had time to set this play into blank verse. And since *Merry Wives* was apparently written for one of the annual Knights of the Garter ceremonies (internal evidence suggesting this to have been the one that took place on 24 May 1597), this effectively forces the deduction that the likeliest time for the Queen to have seen both the *Henry IV* plays was during the Whitehall Court's Christmas–Shrovetide entertainments, the dates of which we already know.

Tradition and internal evidence alike, however, make it equally clear that there was one powerful Court figure less than amused by Shakespeare's newest character creation. This was seventy-year-old William Brooke, Lord Cobham, none other than the man who, much to Shakespeare company patron George Carey's chagrin, had succeeded Henry Hunsdon as Lord Chamberlain. As the eleventh to carry his title[10] Lord Cobham was a descendant of the original Oldcastle, and a variety of clues indicate that he took such offence at the caricaturing of his ancestor that he made the strongest representations to persuade Shakespeare to change the name. Thus writing about 1625, the librarian Dr Richard James, for instance, imparted that:

> the person with which he [Shakespeare] undertook to play a buffoon was not Falstaff, but Sir John Oldcastle, and that offence being worthily taken by personages descended from his title . . . the poet was put to make an ignorant shift of abusing Sir John Fastolf.[11]

In a letter that the Queen's Master of the Revels, Edmund Tilney, wrote about 1599 to Sir William More (from whom James Burbage purchased the Blackfriars premises), Tilney reminisced of having 'received divers brave letters from the last Lord Chamberlain when he and I were at odds', which seems specifically to refer to Cobham's complaint over the matter.[12] There survives the occasional tell-tale indication of the change of name from texts such as Hal's remark 'my old lad of the castle', an errant Quarto speech heading with the abbreviation 'Old' instead of 'Fal', also the apparently deliberately clumsy disclaimer in *Part II*'s Epilogue:

> Falstaff shall die of a sweat, unless 'a be killed already with your hard opinions, for Oldcastle died a martyr, and this is not the man . . .

That Shakespeare must have changed the name from Oldcastle to Falstaff during 1597 is evident from the fact that in the entry of the first Quarto edition of *Henry IV, Part I* on the Stationers' Register on 25 February 1598, the play is described as 'with the conceipted mirthe of Sir John Ffalstoff'.[13]

Here then we have a fascinating example of Shakespeare quite definitely having 'offended' – the fault the players in *A Midsummer Night's Dream* protested that they were being so conscientious to avoid – although to what extent this was deliberately anti-Cobham rather than just anti-Protestant on Shakespeare's part, is difficult to determine. Scholars often represent old Chamberlain Cobham as a humourless Puritan, yet during the 1560s and 1570s he notably had his own acting company, the Lord Warden's Men (after his post as Lord Warden of the Cinque Ports). Also, as a resident of the Blackfriars, he would have been affected by Shakespeare's company's plans for their Blackfriars theatre, but his name does not appear among the petitioners opposing the scheme.

Nonetheless, it was precisely during Cobham's regime as Chamberlain that, on Tom Nashe's earlier quoted evidence, the acting profession fell so badly prey to persecution by London's Lord Mayor and aldermen, and there is even sign that as a result of Cobham pressure Master of the Revels Tilney went over Shakespeare's script with a fine toothcomb, and forced not only a substitution for Oldcastle but also a change of certain other characters' names as well. Whereas in certain editions we find the names Harvey and Rossill (Russell), these became Bardolph and Peto. Perhaps Harvey was thought to be an allusion to Sir William Harvey, who in the wake of old Sir Thomas Heneage's demise (he died a little over a year after marrying the Earl of Southampton's mother), was now actively courting the Dowager Countess. An indication of Shakespeare's feelings over the whole matter may well have been his choosing of the deliberately anachronistic name Falstaff in place of Oldcastle. The true Sir John Falstaff had previously featured where he genuinely belonged: in Henry VI's reign, as the cowardly knight of *Henry VI, Part I*.

Despite all this behind-the-scenes flak, the powerful impression that Shakespeare's Oldcastle/Falstaff character made upon the consciousness of the time is quite apparent from the fact that in 1600, long after the name had quite definitely been changed to Falstaff, Sir Robert Sidney's spy Rowland Whyte would write of a feast at which 'Sir John Oldcastle' had been performed by the Lord Chamberlain's Men.[14]

Predictably, both the Earl of Southampton and his mentor the Earl of Essex enormously enjoyed the anti-Cobham propaganda, for early in 1598 Essex sent word to Secretary Cecil to tell Sir Alexander Radcliffe that his sister, one of the Queen's ladies-in-waiting, 'is married to Sir John Falstaff'. Although the exact purport of this might seem lost on us, the next year in what is the only surviving letter from Southampton's wife to her husband we read:

all the news I can send you that I think will make you merry is that I read in a letter from London that Sir John Falstaff is by his mistress Dame Pintpot made father of a goodly miller's thumb, a boy that's all head and very little body; but this is a secret.[15]

Since a 'miller's thumb' is a small freshwater fish also known as a 'cob',[16] the inference would seem that the Lord Cobham of the time (son of old Lord Chamberlain Cobham), had secretly made Margaret Radcliffe pregnant, though he certainly did not marry her, and she died the next year.[17] Robert Persons, the exiled Catholic priest responsible for bringing Shakespeare's father's *Testament*, seems also to have approved of Shakespeare's recreation of the character, even though he can only have heard of the performances of the *Henry IV* plays from his contacts in England. In 1603, writing a critical commentary on Foxe's 'Book of Martyrs', he commented.

> Sir John Oldcastle, a ruffian-knight as all England knoweth, and commonly brought in by comedians on their stages . . . was put to death for robberies and rebellion under the aforesaid K. Henry the fifth.[18]

Just how pro-Catholic and anti-Protestant Shakespeare's portrayal of Oldcastle/Falstaff was perceived to be is evident from the fact that the next year government spy Anthony Munday wrote the undisguisedly Protestant *Sir John Oldcastle* for the Admiral's Men. (It was Munday who had gloated over Edmund Campion's death and who may have written *The Troublesome Raigne*.) In Munday's play Oldcastle was now represented as the saintly victim of immoral priests and monks. In 1611 the antiquary Speed even outrightly accused Shakespeare of being in league with the Catholic priest Persons. After complaining of Persons representing Oldcastle as 'a ruffian, a robber and a rebel', Speed went on to say:

> And his [Persons'] authority, taken from the stage-players, is more befitting the pen of his slanderous report than the credit of the judicious, being only grounded from this Papist [Persons] and his poet [Shakespeare], of like conscience for lies, the one ever feigning and the other ever falsifying the truth.[19]

Quite aside from all the Oldcastle/Falstaff brouhaha, the *Henry IV* plays are also fascinating for innumerable other illuminating touches of Shakespeare's now ever more assured artistry. In the Boar's Head tavern scene at the end of *Henry IV, Part I* Act II, Falstaff and Prince Hal indulge in some impromptu play-acting during which Falstaff impersonates Henry IV's likely reproval of Hal for his part in the Gadshill robbery. Hal then takes over to act out what the king will say of Falstaff. Irresistibly evoked are scenes of Shakespeare and his fellows doing something of the same when working out ideas for a play.

Earlier in the same act the pre-dawn banter of the carriers in the Rochester Inn yard has a Brueghel-like peasant realism. The carriers moan about their flea-bitten overnight accommodation: 'the most villainous house in all London road for fleas; I am stung like a tench [a multi-spotted fish]'. They deplore the Inn's worm-inducing horsefeed, the 'way to give poor jades the bots'.[20] They blame inflated oat prices for the demise of honest Ostler Robin – 'Poor fellow never joyed since the price of oats rose, it was the death of him'[21] – thereby providing another indication of *Henry IV, Part I*'s date, since poor summers caused the price of oats to treble between 1593 and 1596, and subsequently to fall back.[22] This is the stuff of overheard conversations and Shakespeare even provides the clue to how he heard them, as when the Second Carrier tells his companion:

> Come, neighbour Mugs, we'll call up the gentlemen; they will along with company, for they have great charge.[23]

Here Shakespeare seems to be alluding to Elizabethan gentlemen often opting to travel with professional carriers for mutual protection from armed robbers. This is a custom that he may well have followed, since Stratford-upon-Avon's main carrier William Greenaway was a neighbour of John Shakespeare's in Henley Street, and Greenaway specialised in the London route.[24]

Another notable feature, albeit a negative one, is the way in which, throughout the plays that have followed Shakespeare's acquaintance with Southampton, Shakespeare has virtually ceased to introduce elements of the supernatural. In *Henry IV, Part I* the closest he gets to this is with a joke, as when the fey Welsh Glendower, solemnly assuring Hotspur 'I can call spirits from the vasty deep', gets the dry response 'Why, so can I, or so can any man, but will they come when you call for them?'[25]

The Elizabethans were emotional people, the men perhaps more obviously so than the women, and if we can only guess at the extent to which frustration over the Blackfriars theatre project may have hastened James Burbage's death, we are on surer ground with regard to another death that followed little more than a month after his: that of old Chamberlain Cobham. On 24 January of 1597, before

Shakespeare's company had even completed their programme of Whitehall entertainments, Cobham's daughter Elizabeth, who was married to Lord Burghley's son Sir Robert Cecil, unexpectedly died while giving birth to her third child. According to court gossip Rowland Whyte, the evidently grief-stricken Cobham retired ill to his Blackfriars house on 18 February, and made out his will on 24 February. Around midnight on 5 March he died,[26] thereupon automatically succeeded to the Cobham title by his son Henry Brooke, a friend of Sir Walter Raleigh.

Immediately, of course, the question arose of whether Henry Brooke would succeed his father as Lord Chamberlain. In the event, to what can hardly have been other than the delight of Shakespeare's company, the post went to their own patron George Carey, who had so frustratingly been baulked of it upon his father's death the previous year. This automatically meant that the players were restored to their comparatively recently lost status as Lord Chamberlain's Men, and two months later, for the Garter celebrations held on 24 May, the Queen further honoured Carey by bestowing upon him the Order of the Garter.

As earlier remarked, there is general agreement among scholars that it was for Garter ceremony celebrations, and almost certainly for the 1597 ceremony, that Shakespeare was commanded to write the new Falstaff play that became *The Merry Wives of Windsor*.[27] Several of the play's scenes take place at the Garter Inn at Windsor, and it is filled with Windsor lore and topography: 'Go about the fields with me through Frogmore',[28] 'Take this basket ... and carry it among the whitsters in Datchet Mead',[29] 'Marry, sir, the Pittie Ward, the Park Ward, every way; Old Windsor Way, and every way but the town way';[30] Mistress Anne Page marries her lover Master Fenton at Eton Church, within sight of Windsor Castle. Not least, the final scene includes a dénouement in which a Fairy Queen conveys in one of the play's few moments of verse, a vivid image of the Garter:

> Like to the Garter's compass, in a ring;
> Th'expressure that it bears, green let it be,
> More fertile-fresh than all the field to see,
> And 'Honi soit qui mal y pense' write
> In emerald tufts, flowers purple, blue and white;
> Like sapphire, pearl and rich embroidery,
> Buckled below fair knighthood's bending knee.[31]

As a mark of Shakespeare's unrepentance over Cobham, and showing that the controversy did not end with Chamberlain William Brooke's death, in *Merry Wives* there is further evidence of Shakespeare sailing very close to the wind with regard to the same family. In the *Merry Wives* Master Ford, enraged at Falstaff's clumsy attempts to seduce his wife, dons a disguise and a pseudonym. The pseudonym is Brooke, the Cobham family name. Shakespeare also includes a joke about 'brooks ... that oerflow with such liquor', as Henry Brooke, the new twelfth Lord Cobham, enjoyed a reputation as a bon viveur. Shakespeare seems to have been persuaded to make a deft change of the name to the safer one of Broome.

A notable feature of *Merry Wives* is that it is the first play in which Shakespeare ventures into writing regional and foreign accents for comic effect, rather than let the actors simply improvise their own. In Sir Hugh Evans he creates his second caricature of an Elizabethan parson, the first having been *Love's Labour's Lost*'s Sir Nathaniel, and by giving him a Welsh accent Shakespeare makes him yet more comic. With his own recently acquired gentleman's coat of arms clearly in mind, in the opening scene he has Sir Hugh hopelessly misunderstand Slender's mention of 'the dozen white luces in their coat' (an allusion to the luces, or pikefish, in the arms of Shakespeare's disliked local lord Sir Thomas Lucy of Charlecote), Sir Hugh supposing that Slender meant a coat that had become verminous:

The dozen white louses do become an old coat well; it agrees well, passant; it is a familiar beast to man, and signifies love.[32]

Hardly flattering to the image of a Protestant clergyman were the Welsh accented expletives he gives Sir Hugh in virtually every line:

Pless my soul! How full of chollors I am, and trempling of mind! I shall be glad if he have deceived me. How melancholies I am! I will knog his urinals about his knave's costard when I have goot opportunities for the ork. Pless my soul![33]

Exemplifying the danger of the extremely precarious politico-religious tightrope that Shakespeare walked with his humour was what happened at this time to the satirist Tom Nashe and his hitherto unknown co-dramatist, former bricklayer's apprentice Ben Jonson. Although exactly how these two came together is unknown, in the late July of 1597 their satirical comedy *The Isle of Dogs* was staged at 'one of the playhouses on the Bankside', almost certainly Francis Langley's Swan, and performed by a new company under the patronage of the Earl of Pembroke including actors Gabriel Spenser and Robert Shaa, formerly with Henslowe's Admiral's Men.

Although frustratingly, no copy of any kind has survived of *The Isle of Dogs*, nor even any clear description of its theme, on 28 July, London's Lord Mayor and aldermen professed themselves outraged at the 'profane fables, lascivious matters, cozening [cheating] devices and scurrilous behaviours,' which *The Isle of Dogs* appears to have contained, and urged nothing less than the 'final suppressing of the said stage plays, as well at the Theatre, Curtain, and Bankside'.[34] The Privy Council, clearly having their own independent information about the outrage, immediately ordered the Middlesex justices:

> that not only no plays shall be used within London or about the city or in any public place during this time of summer, but also those playhouses that are erected and built only for such purposes shall be plucked down, namely the Curtain and the Theatre near to Shoreditch.[35]

Likewise Surrey's justices, among them the loathed William Gardiner, whose bully-boy, William Wayte, Shakespeare had crossed only a few months previously (see page 216) were required:

> to take the like order for the playhouses in the Bankside, in Southwark or elsewhere in the said county within three miles of London.[36]

At a stroke, London's entire 'common stage' theatre land and the livelihoods of its employees lay under threat of imminent destruction. Although Nashe managed to escape into East Anglia, Jonson together with actors Gabriel Spenser and Robert Shaa found themselves in the Marshalsea prison under the less than gentle charge of Richard Topcliffe, who planted informers in with them ('two damned villains', as Jonson later remembered them), in an attempt to gather further evidence of their guilt. Henslowe in his Diary duly noted the cause of yet another interruption to his schedule of productions as 'by the means of playing "The Isle of Dogs".'

As was their now standard policy in the event of any closure, whether due to plague or any other reason, Shakespeare's company immediately went on tour to the provinces. Whether Shakespeare accompanied them, or returned to Stratford, we have no way of knowing, but during August the Lord Chamberlain's Men can certainly be traced heading eastwards from London – performing in Rye, Dover and Faversham – then during September heading westwards appearing in Marlborough, Bath and Bristol.[37]

However, the interesting feature about Shakespeare's life at this time is that everything that we know of his Stratford-upon-Avon affairs suggests that he was riding a wave of success, indicating that at least up to the time of the 'Isle of Dogs' débâcle the Lord Chamberlain's Men's business affairs had somehow managed to get back to a very healthy state. The prime evidence for this, derived from deeds both in the Stratford Birthplace Trust and in the Public Record Office, is Shakespeare's purchase on 4 May 1597 (shortly after Hunsdon had succeeded Cobham as Lord Chamberlain), of the second largest house in Stratford. This was New Place, which although demolished in the eighteenth century we know to have been located in Chapel Street, at the corner of Chapel Lane, and opposite the Guild Chapel.

New Place had been built at the end of the fifteenth century by the wealthy bachelor Sir Hugh Clopton, who gave Stratford its stone bridge and much embellished its Guild Chapel. Back in Henry VIII's reign the antiquary Leland described it as 'a pretty house of brick and timber' – the first Stratford house known to have been built of brick. In 1567 it had been purchased by William Underhill, an Inner Temple lawyer, upon whose death three years later it fell to Underhill's son of the same name, a staunchly Catholic recusant who was imprisoned for his faith in 1579, and who with his wife Mary divided his time between New Place and his manor at Idlicote to Stratford-upon-Avon's south.

Interestingly then, it was a Catholic house that Shakespeare acquired from Underhill in May 1597, officially paying £60 for it, though we cannot be sure of this since Elizabethan tax evasion practices often meant that a lesser figure appeared on deeds than had actually changed hands between the two parties.[38] With a frontage of over sixty feet on Chapel Street, and a depth of at least seventy feet southwards along Chapel Lane, the house was undoubtedly substantial, and thanks to a 1737 sketch made by engraver and antiquary George Vertue from the memories of a local of the time[39] [see pl. 33], today preserved in the British Library, we are even provided with an idea of its former·appearance. Coincidentally, Vertue made his sketch in exactly the same year as the only surviving plans of the Earl of Southampton's great mansion in Titchfield, and in a manner not unreminiscent of Titchfield, beyond the frontage with central gateway there lay, 'a little courtyard, grass growing there, before the real dwelling house, this outside being only a long gallery & c., and for servants'.[40]

What is important is that in May 1597, despite Shakespeare's company's recent chequered fortunes, Shakespeare himself had acquired sufficient cash to make a substantial property purchase. Significantly he chose to make this not in his place of work, London, but in his home town of Stratford-upon-Avon. He would even seem to have had spare cash for improvements, as the Stratford Chamberlain's Accounts for 1598 show him having sold the corporation a load of stone – interpreted by most historians as left over material from his repair work. This the corporation used, fittingly enough, for remedial work on Clopton Bridge. The records also suggest that Shakespeare moved his family into the new house during 1597, for a Stratford survey of household grain and malt supplies records him on 4 February 1598 as already a householder in Chapel ward, the ward in which New Place, as distinct from Henley Street, was situated.

At the same time that Shakespeare was exhibiting such clear signs of the profitability of his London theatrical activities, his Stratford neighbours, who had been finding things very hard from two disastrous fires in the town, combined with a run of poor summers and soaring food prices, clearly began to notice this. One indication derives from a letter of 28 January 1598 from Abraham Sturley, who had been Stratford's Bailiff in 1596, to his brother-in-law Alderman Richard Quiney who was the son of John Shakespeare's old neighbour and fellow tradesman Adrian Quiney:

This is one special remembrance from your father [i.e Adrian Quiney].... It seemeth by him that our countryman, Mr Shakespeare is willing to disburse some money upon some old yardland or other at Shottery or near about us. He thinketh it a fit pattern to move him to deal in the matter of our tithes. By the instructions you can give him thereof, and by the friends he can make therefore, we think it a fair mark for him to shoot at, and not unpossible to hit.[41]

Worthy of note is how Shakespeare's new status of gentleman is reflected in the use of 'Mr'. While Shakespeare does not appear to have immediately followed up this interest in tithes (though he would some years later), another indication of Stratfordian notice of his prosperity occurs in October 1598 when Richard Quiney, upon travelling to London to petition the Privy Council for some relief from the government's latest tax burden, seems to have had a mind to call upon Shakespeare for some temporary financial assistance. Dated 25 October 1598, and written from the Bell in London's Carter Lane, just south of St Paul's, there survives in Quiney's hand the only extant letter addressed to Shakespeare. It was discovered in 1793 among the Stratford records by the scholar Edmond Malone, and is preserved in the Birthplace Trust Records Office in Stratford.[42] The outside bears Quiney's instructions to the courier, reading:

H[aste] To my loving good friend and countryman, Mr W^{m}. Shackspere, deliver these.

The inside text is as follows:

Loving countryman, I am bold of you as of a friend, craving your help with £30 upon Mr Bushell's and my security, or Mr Mytton's with me. Mr Rosswell is not come to London yet, and I have especial cause. You shall friend me much in helping me out of all the debts I owe in London, I thank God, and much quiet my mind, which would not be indebted. I am now toward the Court in hope of answer for the despatch of my business. You shall neither lose credit nor money by me, the Lord willing. . . . My time bids me hasten to an end and so I commit this to your care and hope of your help. I fear I shall not be back this night from the Court. Haste. The Lord be with you and with us all, Amen. From the Bell in Carter Lane the 25 October 1598. Yours in all kindness,

Ryc. Quyney

In this letter, the very survival of which is almost certainly owed to the fact that it was never delivered, the names of the individuals who were apparently known to both Shakespeare and Quiney are of obvious interest. Mytton and Rosswell are straightforward enough, being gentlemen in the service of Stratford's local lord of the manor Sir Edward Greville, whom Quiney was hoping would help him in his petition. More intriguing is Bushell, a name ignored by both Samuel Schoenbaum and Dr A. L. Rowse, yet of interest because Edward Bushell, whose sister would marry Quiney's son Adrian, was recorded in 1591 as 'servant to the Lady Strange', that is Ferdinando Stanley's wife Alice. This was at the same time that, as we have argued, Shakespeare was in the Stanley employ. Intriguingly, Bushell would seem to have been a double-agent in the mould of the shady characters who hung around Marlowe, and he will appear later in a similar connection with the Earl of Essex (see page 275).

What is certain is that Shakespeare had come a long way since his father had been listed as in fear of process for debt five years earlier. Now he was giving every appearance to his Stratford neighbours of being one of his town's most successful residents. But had he overstretched himself? Could his company, even with their renewed patronage by a Lord Chamberlain, survive their latest, seemingly yet more alarming setback: the threatened destruction of all the common stage theatres in the wake of the *Isle of Dogs* affair?

CHAPTER 15

'Most Excellent . . .
for the Stage'

In the autumn of 1597, the popular theatre's hold upon all levels of Elizabethan society proved such that neither London's Lord Mayor and his aldermen, nor those of Elizabeth's Privy Council most opposed to the business of acting, were able to carry out all they had threatened in the summer. While there survive no details of the political manoeuvring that went on behind the scenes, the fact that the Lord Chamberlain's Men's patron George Carey and the Admiral's Men's patron Lord Howard of Effingham were both members of the Privy Council, together with the Queen's known enjoyment of the theatre, must have counted for something.

Certainly on 3 October Ben Jonson and the actors Gabriel Spenser and Robert Shaa were able to walk free from the Marshalsea prison, and at one and the same time at least some of the theatres were allowed to re-open. Henslowe's Diary entry for 11 October shows the Admiral's Men and the new Pembroke's company appearing at the Rose with that old but politically safe favourite, *The Spanish Tragedy*, a play that one suspects many of the cast would have been able to perform blindfold. Henslowe also signed up Ben Jonson with a twenty-shilling advance to write a new play, this time with an approved plot, in time for Christmas. Of the theatres south of the Thames, principal victim of the *Isle of Dogs* crackdown appears to have been Francis Langley's Swan theatre, which had staged the ill-fated production, and which seems never again to have been used by a major theatrical company.

North of the river the Lord Chamberlain's Men seem now to have abandoned their Shoreditch Theatre, their lease on the land on which it was built still not having been renewed by the elderly and recalcitrant landowner Giles Allen. Likewise there is no information on the company yet having found any use for its so costly Blackfriars investment. Though information is extremely sparse, the venue they appear to have adopted at this time is a little-recorded playhouse, nearly as old as the Shoreditch Theatre, and only just to the south of it, known as the Curtain. Its name still survives on the London street map as Curtain Road, just north of Liverpool Street Station [see fig 4, page 73]. Our main clue to Shakespeare's company using this playhouse derives from up-and-coming writer John Marston's *The Scourge of Villainy*, entered on the Stationers' Register 8 September 1598, which alluded in the same passage to the acting of *Romeo and Juliet* and to 'Curtain plaudeties'. Likewise minor satirist Edward Guilpin in his *Skialetheia*, entered just one week later, wrote of:

> how the unfrequented Theatre
> Walks in dark silence, and vast solitude.[1]

Once again, however, our chief guide to Shakespeare's company's still considerable popularity with the highest in the land comes from the Chamber Accounts for the Christmas and Shrovetide of 1597–8 which again show the Lord Chamberlain's Men getting the lion's share of royal command performances; between 26 December and 26 February they appeared four times to the Admiral's Men's once. Although as normal the accounts do not record the titles of the plays staged, again it is possible to be reasonably sure of at least one of these: Shakespeare's *Love's Labour's Lost*, written, as we have earlier argued, for private performance before the Southampton circle four years before, but now seemingly performed for the first time before the royal Court. Prime evidence for this particular Court showing comes from the publication during 1598 of a Quarto edition of *Love's Labour's Lost* specifically worded on its title page 'as it was presented before her Highness [that is Queen Elizabeth I] this last Christmas'. This edition, of which copies survive at the British Library, the Bodleian Library, Oxford, and Trinity College, Cambridge, declares itself as printed by 'W.W.' (William Whyte) for the publisher Cuthbert Burby, and also carries the words 'Newly corrected and augmented By W. Shakspere'. It thus qualifies as the first known book to appear with Shakespeare's name on the title page, and the first printed version of one of his plays to feature his name at all.

The previous year printer John Danter had brought out the first Quarto of *Romeo and Juliet*, without any accompanying entry in the Stationers' Register, without Shakespeare's name anywhere associated with it, and simply carrying on its title page 'As it hath been often (with great applause) plaid publiquely, by the right Honourable the L. of Hunsdon his Servants'. Unmistakeably this had been a pirate publication, textually corrupt and atrociously printed, in the opinion of the scholar G. B. Harrison 'the work of a reporter' who 'must have been helped either by someone who knew the play intimately or else had been a playhouse copy of the script'.[2] By contrast, Cuthbert Burby's 1598 Quarto of *Love's Labour's Lost* is quite different. From the most exhaustive textual analysis by J. Dover Wilson, this seems to have been prepared from an actual manuscript of Shakespeare's. Since in 1599 Burby would produce a similarly good Quarto edition of *Romeo and Juliet* to supplant Danter's pirate version, the reasonable inference is that Burby's *Love's Labour's Lost* was produced with Shakespeare's company's full cooperation in order to quash a bad Quarto of which no copy has survived. Even if this is not the case, in the published *Love's Labour's Lost* we seem to have at the very least the first author-approved printed book of Shakespeare's since *Venus and Adonis* and *Lucrece*. And as a mark of the extent to which Shakespeare had established himself by 1598, three other printed versions of his plays, also carrying his name, appeared during the same year: a second Quarto edition of *Richard III*, and second and third Quarto editions of *Richard II*, these latter still lacking the controversial deposition scene.

If as we earlier suggested, *Love's Labour's Lost* was written for Southampton, almost certainly his permission would have been needed for the play's performance before the Queen. This may even have been at his behest, as late in 1597 to early 1598 happens to have been a rare period of Southampton being in apparent favour with the Queen. While previously, and chiefly because of the suspicions of his Catholicism, the Queen had persistently blocked his venturing abroad, during the summer of 1597, when Shakespeare was getting used to his ownership of New Place, Southampton had been allowed his first real taste of overseas adventure. Under the command of his adopted mentor the Earl of Essex, and in a company that included his mother's third husband-to-be Sir William Harvey, Dark Lady Emilia's musician husband Alphonse Lanier and the young crypto-Catholic poet John Donne, he took part in July in an anti-Spanish expedition to the Azores, during which he managed to acquit himself rather better than his commander. While Southampton's vessel fought and successfully sank a Spanish man-of-war, Essex returned in some disgrace after allowing the main Spanish fleet to escape without a fight.

It was probably, therefore, still in the glow of this particular moment of glory that in the January of 1598, at the time that Shakespeare's company was making its appearances at Court, Southampton was tipped to accompany Secretary Cecil on an important diplomatic mission to France to persuade the now Catholic Henri IV not to make peace with Spain. For Southampton the intention was for this to be the first leg of a Grand Tour such as his friend Rutland had successfully made two years before.

One person whom we learn to have been desperately unhappy at Southampton's impending departure was the royal maid of honour Elizabeth Vernon whom three years before Court 'spy' Rowland Whyte had reported Southampton to have been courting 'with too much familiarity'. Of her Whyte again reported in the mid-January of 1598:

> I hear my Lord Southampton goes with Mr Secretary to France, and so onward on his travels; which course of his doth extremely grieve his mistress, that passes her time in weeping and lamenting.[3]

At about this time there was a full-blooded scuffle between Southampton and another courtier, Ambrose Willoughby, over some remarks the latter had made about this liaison, causing Southampton's temporary banishment from Court. But this blew over, and in the run-up to Southampton's going overseas Whyte records him and other aristocrats (among them Cobham) entertaining Cecil to 'plays and banquets' that must have been privately commissioned performances along the lines of the earlier mentioned 'King Richard' (see page 203). After Southampton departed leaving behind him, according to Whyte, 'a very desolate gentlewoman, that hath almost wept out her fairest eyes',[4] further privately commissioned plays were staged for those of Southampton's friends who stayed behind. On 15 February, just three days after Southampton had left, Whyte reported:

> Sir Gelly Meyrick [steward to the Earl of Essex] made at Essex House yesternight a very great supper. There were at it my Ladies Leicester, Northumberland, Bedford, Essex, Rich [Philip Sidney's

'Stella'], and my Lords of Essex, Rutland, Mountjoy and others. They had two plays which kept them up till 1 o'clock after midnight.[5]

Because we lack the Lord Chamberlain's Men's account books we cannot be sure it was they who were performing these plays, though this particular group of people would certainly commission them in a couple of years time. But here we glimpse another side to the company's business: genteel private performances in great houses of the kind that, to save all the problems transporting costumes and gear, they had so valiantly tried to bring under one roof with their Blackfriars theatre venture. While the performance of two plays in a single sitting is rare, and would have been quite a feat for both actors and their audience, Elizabethan theatrical companies could of course manage such private evening engagements because their normal common stage performances were held early afternoon so as to catch the daylight. And no doubt the bargain struck with a Gelly Meyrick, or any other commissioning host, would have included the cost of sufficient candle-power to light an evening private house production to proper advantage.

Meanwhile Southampton reached France safely, duly making his ambassadorial overtures with Cecil in Paris, and there meeting up with his old friends the Danverses, Henry Long's murderers, who had been working their safe admission back to England by a little adroit spying. In the event, Cecil's and Southampton's mission failed to dissuade Henri IV's Court from making peace with Spain. Cecil thereupon returned to England where, back in the Privy Council, his report provoked heated argument, Essex urging war against the perfidious French, fiercely opposed by the frail but ever-pragmatic Lord Burghley, who warned Essex 'Bloody and deceitful men shall live out half their days'.

For the seventy-eight-year-old Burghley this emotion seems to have proved too much, for it was to be his last official appearance. Taken ill soon after, by 4 August he was dead, the reins of power passing smoothly to his son Robert Cecil. Meanwhile in Paris, almost certainly via the same messenger who brought news of the Danverses conditional pardon, Southampton learned that in the heat of his passionate goodbyes he had made Elizabeth Vernon pregnant. For her accouchement she was apparently staying quietly at Leez Priory, Essex, the home of Essex's sister Lady Rich. Fully aware of the

Queen's invariable anger at any such unmaidening of her maids of honour, Southampton therefore secretly made his way back to England, equally secretly married his Elizabeth (to this day, no one knows the exact date or place), then slipped back to Paris to avoid the storm that he knew would erupt the moment the news broke. The Queen immediately summoned the now heavily pregnant Elizabeth to London for corrective custody in the Fleet prison, likewise sending to Paris for Southampton's instant recall. Slow to respond, when he did so it was immediately to suffer his own taste of Fleet. Southampton was eventually released at the Earl of Essex's instigation at the end of the November, a fortnight after his new wife's safe delivery of a baby daughter.

For Shakespeare, ironically on the same day that Elizabeth Vernon had been arrested, there was entered on the Stationers' Register a work that would break new ground in the contemporary recognition of his contribution to literature. The work in question, *Palladis Tamia*, *Wit's Treasury*, by Cambridge graduate and literary gadfly Francis Meres, comprised a near seven-hundred-page collection of quotations and maxims from various writers, a copy of which is preserved in Oxford's Bodleian Library. Its greatest interest to us, however, is Meres' roll of honour of all English literary effort from Chaucer right up to the year of publication. Despite the occasional lapse of judgment, he left no doubt of his high estimation of Shakespeare:

> The English tongue is mightily enriched and gorgeously invested in rare ornaments and resplendent abiliments by Sir Philip Sidney, Spenser, Daniel, Drayton, Warner, Shakespeare, Marlowe and Chapman.

Meres went on, in a passage that has been of greater value to generations of literary scholars than he could ever have realised:

> As Plautus and Seneca are accounted the best for comedy and tragedy among the Latins, so Shakespeare among the English is the most excellent in both kinds for the stage. For comedy, witness his *Gentlemen of Verona*, his *Errors*, his *Love's Labour's Lost*, his *Love's Labour's Won*, his *Midsummer Night's Dream*, and his *Merchant of Venice*; for tragedy his *Richard II*, *Richard III*, *Henry IV*, *King John*, *Titus Andronicus*, and his *Romeo and Juliet*.[6]

ANNO DÑI ÆTATIS SVÆ 21
1585

QVOD ME NVTRIT
ME DESTRVIT

The rival poet?

26.   Portrait at Corpus Christi College, Cambridge, thought to be of
Christopher Marlowe (1564–93), who seems to have rivalled Shakespeare for
patronage by both Ferdinando, Lord Strange, and by the Earl of Southampton.
Marlowe's untimely end in April 1593, at the hand of shady government agents,
left Shakespeare without peer as a leading dramatist of his time. (*By kind
permission of the Master and Fellows of Corpus Christi College, Cambridge*)

'Thy pyramids built up with newer might' (*Sonnet* 123)

27.   At St Peter's Church, Titchfield, the tomb of the very Catholic second
Earl of Southampton, commissioned in 1594 from Southwark-based
monumental mason Gheerart Janssen/Gerard Johnson apparently on the
orders of Shakespeare's young patron Henry Wriothesley, the third Earl.
Particularly notable are the four flanking obelisks, readily referred to as
'pyramids' in Elizabethan parlance. The same masonry workshop would go on
to make Shakespeare's memorial bust in Holy Trinity Church, Stratford-upon-
Avon. (*Charles Woolf*)

28. Inspiration for the Southampton tomb's obelisks? The massive ancient Egyptian obelisk erected (with internationally acclaimed engineering skill) just seven years before in the piazza in front of St Peter's, Rome. Engraving from an Italian work of 1589, describing the different lifting techniques suggested.

The mysterious 'playhouse room' . . .

29. Behind Titchfield House's entrance facade are the remains, on an upper storey, of what is identified in an eighteenth-century plan as the 'Playhouse Room'. Was this where Shakespeare's company prepared productions for the Earl of Southampton's private entertainments?

Henry Carey
Lord Hunsdon

BY MARK GERARDS

ÆTATIS SVÆ 6
AN 1591

Lord Chamberlain's man . . .

30.   Lord Chamberlain Henry Carey, first Lord Hunsdon (1524?–96), who, on
Ferdinando's death in 1594, became the first certain patron of Shakespeare as
an actor. The company at this time became known as the Lord Chamberlain's
Men. A cousin to Queen Elizabeth (his mother was Anne Boleyn's sister),
Carey set up Emilia Bassano as his paramour, and conceived a child by her.
(*By kind permission of the Trustees of the Will of the eighth Earl of Berkeley.
Photograph: Courtauld Institute of Art*)

31.   George Carey, second Lord Hunsdon (1547–1603), who was married to Ferdinando Stanley's wife's sister, and took over patronage of Shakespeare's company of actors upon his father Henry's death in 1596. George did not, however, succeed his father as Lord Chamberlain until Lord Cobham's death the following year. At this point, Shakespeare's company again became the Lord Chamberlain's Men. (*By kind permission of the Trustees of the Will of the eighth Earl of Berkeley*)

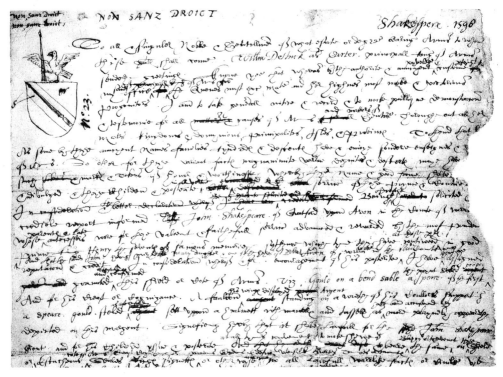

32

33

'And when thou feelest thy purse well lined'

32.   Draft of a grant of arms and crest to Shakespeare's father John, dated 20 October 1596, and preserved at the College of Arms, London. Upon the implementation of this grant (the 'fees' for which were usually equivalent to the cost of a house), Shakespeare and his heirs became elevated to the status of gentlemen. (*By kind permission of the Chapter of the College of Arms, London*)

33.   New Place, one of the largest houses in Stratford-upon-Avon, which Shakespeare purchased in 1597. It was heavily altered in 1702, and razed to the ground in 1759. This drawing of 1737 was made from living memories of the building's pre-1702 appearance. (*British Library*)

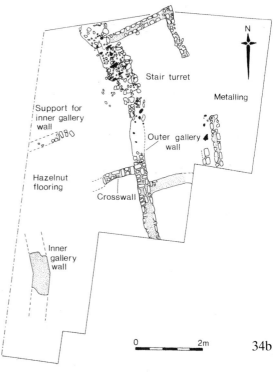

'This wooden "O" . . .'

34.   Archaeological remains of a small section of Shakespeare's Globe theatre, as revealed from excavations in October 1989. These comprise a length of the outer gallery wall, a very short stretch of the inner wall of the second, post-1613, Globe, and possibly a stair turret (see plan). Most of what remains of the Globe lies inaccessible beneath the Grade II listed Anchor Terrace building, erected between 1834 and 1837. (*Andrew Fulgoni and (plan) the Museum of London*)

34a

N

Stair turret

Metalling

Support for
inner gallery
wall

Outer gallery
wall

Hazelnut
flooring

Crosswall

Inner
gallery
wall

0   2m

34b

35a

Key

AA Main entrance
B The Yard
CC Entrances to lowest gallery
D Entrances to staircase and upper galleries
E Corridor serving the different sections of the middle gallery
F Middle gallery ('Twopenny Rooms')
G 'Gentlemen's Rooms' or 'Lords' Rooms'
H The stage
J The hanging being put up round the stage
K The 'Hell' under the stage
L The stage trap, leading down to the Hell
MM Stage doors
N Curtained 'place behind the stage'
O Gallery above the stage, used as required sometimes by musicians, sometimes by spectators, and often as part of the play
P Back-stage area (the tiring-house)
Q Tiring-house door
R Dressing-rooms
S Wardrobe and storage
T The hut housing the machine for lowering enthroned gods, etc., to the stage
U The 'Heavens'
W Hoisting the playhouse flag

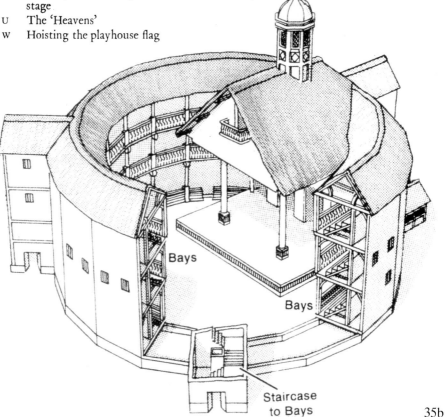

Bays

Bays

Staircase
to Bays

35b

35a

The Globe reconstructed?

35.   Because of the very limited documentary and archaeological information, all reconstructions of the 1599 Globe rely to a greater or lesser extent on conjecture. Note how C. Walter Hodges' reconstruction (above), made in 1968, differs from plans for the Sam Wanamaker Globe currently under construction on London's Bankside (left). Hodges remarks that, if he redrew his sketch today, he would remove the middle gallery's partition wall (marked E), and make the Globe's circumference wider. But he would not go to the width of the Wanamaker version, in his opinion 'over-enlarged to a proportion not in the character of such timber-framed buildings and which the archaeological finds on the Rose and Globe sites do not at present seem to justify' (personal communication to the author, May 1993). Note also the substantially different conceptions of the 'hut' over the stage. (*C. Walter Hodges and* The Times)

36

Ill-fated rebels

36.   Robert Devereux, second
Earl of Essex (1566–1601). By
special request, Shakespeare's
company performed
Shakespeare's *Richard ii*,
complete with its controversial
deposition scene, on the eve of
Essex's rebellion in February
1601. The rebellion failed and
Essex was beheaded on 25
February. (*National Portrait
Gallery, London*)

37.   The Earl of Southampton
in prison. A fellow-rebel of the
Earl of Essex, Southampton was
likewise sentenced to death, but
at the pleading of his wife and
mother his sentence was
commuted to life imprisonment
in the Tower. (*By kind
permission of the Duke of
Buccleuch, K.T., Boughton
House, Northamptonshire*)

Pioneer of many of Shakespeare's leading roles . . .

38.   Richard Burbage (c.1573–1619), from a supposed self-portrait in the
Dulwich Picture Gallery. One of the sons of James Burbage, founder of the
acting company that Shakespeare joined, Burbage played many of the lead
roles in Shakespeare's plays, and was accredited with a second talent as a
painter. (*Dulwich Picture Gallery, London*)

Queen Elizabeth in procession

39.   Created shortly after the Earl of Essex's execution, this fine painting at Sherborne Castle depicts the aged Queen under a canopy, escorted by her Knights of the Garter and followed by her Ladies in Waiting, just as Shakespeare must often have seen her. The long-bearded figure striding in front of the Queen, and grasping his sword hilt, is positively identifiable as Shakespeare's patron, Lord Chamberlain George Carey, who would die in the same year as the Queen. (*Private collection*)

End of an era

40. Richmond Palace, where Shakespeare's company entertained the Queen for the last time on 2 February 1603, possibly with a performance of *All's Well that Ends Well*. A group of strolling entertainers can be seen performing in the foreground. (*Fitzwilliam Museum, Cambridge*)

At the head of the Tombe are these verses

Not Monumentall Stone preserues our fame
nor sky aspireing piramides our name
The memorye of him for whom this stands
Shall out-liue marble, and defacers hands.
when all to times consumption shall be given
Standley for whome this stands shall stand in Heaven.

a little lower on the verge.

Beati mortui qui in Domino moriantur.

At the foote of the Monument

Aske who lies here, but doe not weepe,
He is not dead, he doth but sleepe.
This stonye Register is for his bones
His fame is more perpetuall then these stones
And his owne goodnes with himselfe being gone
Shall liue, when earthly monument is none.

41.   The Stanley monument at Tong, Shropshire, created for Sir Edward Stanley circa 1603, with verses purportedly written by Shakespeare. Notable are the four obelisks, as on the Earl of Southampton's monument at Titchfield. (*By kind permission of the Chapter of the College of Arms*)

Shakespeare's last patron

42.   King James VI of Scotland and I of England (1566–1625). By James'
enthusiastic patronage from his accession to the English throne in 1603,
Shakespeare's company became appointed the King's Men, a title they carried
throughout the rest of Shakespeare's life. (*National Maritime Museum,
London*)

43

Entertaining foreign dignitaries

43. After all the long years of war with Spain, in 1604 peace was negotiated at a high-powered conference held at Somerset House, with Shakespeare's company deputed to be in attendance upon the Spanish envoys. The principal negotiators for the two sides are depicted here, with Secretary Cecil, the only one taking notes, at foreground right. (*National Portrait Gallery, London*)

44. Ben Jonson (1572–1637), whose hugely expensive masques became a highly popular feature of James I's Court, devised particularly to impress foreign ambassadors. (*National Portrait Gallery, London*)

The particular value of this passage is that Meres' mentions of *The Two Gentlemen of Verona*, *A Midsummer Night's Dream*, *The Merchant of Venice* and *King John* in each case represent our first *documentary* notice of the existence of these plays. Meres thus enables us to be quite sure that Shakespeare wrote them before September 1598. Conversely, the omission of a known Shakespeare play from Meres' list implies that it was written after 1598, though this has to be treated more cautiously in view of the possibility that Meres may simply not have mentioned it through ignorance of its existence.

Of the plays thus named, only two have not so far been encountered in the course of this book, the first of these being *The Two Gentlemen of Verona*. There is no known text of this – authorised or pirated – dating before the First Folio in 1623. Equally the play was unmentioned, apart from by Meres, throughout Shakespeare's entire lifetime. Even the text of *The Two Gentlemen of Verona*, as it appears in the First Folio, has been incompletely thought out, Milan, Verona and Padua being hopelessly confused, and it also lacks many stage directions, as if it may not have been performed. Its story is of the rivalry of two male friends for the same woman, Silvia, culminating in one friend graciously forgiving the other for his act of betrayal, then meekly surrendering Silvia to him. This prompted Dr A. L. Rowse to note that it is effectively the story of Shakespeare, Southampton and the Dark Lady.[7] That *Two Gentlemen* was semi-autobiographical may well therefore explain the mystery shrouding any known public performances. As suggested by the play's Italian background, Shakespeare probably wrote it when riding out the 1593 plague at Southampton's Titchfield. Its performance most likely would have been limited to the sort of private evening entertainment mentioned earlier in this chapter.

Representing a far bigger puzzle than *The Two Gentlemen of Verona*, however, is Meres' mention of *Love's Labour's Won*. Since there is no play of this title in the canon of Shakespeare's work as enshrined in the First Folio, the options are: that this was a mistake on Meres' part; that it was a 'lost' play of Shakespeare's, or that it has come down to us under a different name. The first possibility was eliminated only as recently as 1953 when a piece of discarded manuscript used as a bookbinding hinge for a volume of sermons was revealed as a stationer's stocklist of the books that he had available for sale as at August 1603. Just as in Meres' *Palladis Tamia*, the stationer listed *Love's Labour's Won* immediately following on from *Love's Labour's Lost*.

Effectively proved, therefore, is that a Shakespeare play of the title *Love's Labour's Won* did exist, and must have been written before or during 1598, leaving us to conclude either that it is a genuinely 'lost' Shakespeare play, or (and this is today the most favoured), that it is one we know nowadays under a different title. One possible candidate for this, not least because, although definitely early, it is curiously omitted from Meres' list, is *The Taming of the Shrew*, which could easily be construed as a play in which love's labour is won. The main objection to this, however, is Henslowe's Diary's already mentioned recording of a *Taming of A Shrew*, whether of not one and the same as Shakespeare's version, at least as far back as 1594. An alternative particularly favoured by Professor T. W. Baldwin,[8] is *All's Well that Ends Well*, which could again be interpreted as a play in which love's labour is won. The objection to this, however, is that both literary scholars and the historian A. L. Rowse have assigned it on internal grounds to around 1602–03. Overall, therefore, it is perhaps safest to conclude with Professor Schoenbaum that *Love's Labour's Won* remains 'a minor Shakespearean enigma'[9] to which so far at least, there is no easy solution.

Meres is also invaluable for a further intriguing paragraph in *Palladis Tamia*, appearing on the very same spread on which he listed Shakespeare's plays, and now referring to Shakespeare's *Sonnets*:

> As the soul of Euphorbus was thought to live in Pythagoras, so the sweet, witty soul of Ovid lives in mellifluous and honey-tongued Shakespeare, witness his *Venus and Adonis*, his *Lucrece*, his sugared Sonnets among his private friends. . . .

Even though we must avoid assuming that the sonnets mentioned are necessarily the same, wholly or in part, as those that have come down to us as Shakespeare's, this is highly important as the first historical reference to the existence of any sonnets written by Shakespeare, and therefore a very helpful independent guide to their dates. Also whichever of the sonnets Meres refers to, he imparts that Shakespeare had a particular circle of 'private friends' with whom he shared them – yet another of those tantalising insights into the man, about which we would ideally wish to know so much more.

Meres also spoke of Christopher Marlowe in *Palladis Tamia*, remarking of his death:

> As the poet Lycophon was shot to death by a certain rival of his, so Christopher Marlowe was stabbed to death by a bawdy serving-man, a rival of his in his lewd love.[10]

In fact this is only the second literary reference of any kind to Marlowe's death, the circumstances of which were not widely known, and Meres himself seems to have heard only a garbled version, since there is no evidence of Marlowe's killer Frizer having been either a 'bawdy serving man' or a homosexual. As it happens, 1598 also saw the publication – like a ghost from the past – of Marlowe's unfinished *Hero and Leander*, the poem he is thought to have been working on for Southampton when he met his untimely end.

All the more intriguing, therefore, is that in *As You Like It*, which seems to have been written within a year of *Palladis Tamia* and *Hero and Leander*'s publication, Shakespeare reveals some signs of having had Marlowe and his fate more than a little on his mind. On the face of it, *As You Like It* is a light and airy play, a delightful pastoral love story based on Thomas Lodge's romance *Rosalynde*, which was published in 1590 and reissued in 1598. It is a ready vehicle for comedy centred on the 'wise fool' Touchstone, and in it Shakespeare makes yet another of his jibes at Anglican clergy in the person of parson Sir Oliver Martext, whose incompetence prompts Jacques to urge Touchstone:

> Get you to church, and have a good priest that can tell you what marriage is; this fellow will but join you together as they join wainscot.[11]

With Shakespeare's own Forest of Arden (alias the Ardennes) as its background, the play is full of music, dance and songs, among them 'It was a lover and his lass', and it ends in a wedding masque that has prompted at least one theory, probably misguided, that it was written for the private wedding of the Earl of Southampton and Elizabeth Vernon. But behind the lyricism there are darker undertones relating to Marlowe as when towards the play's end

Shakespeare has Rosalind musingly allude to the Hero and Leander legend:

> Leander, he would have lived many a fair year . . . if it had not been for a hot midsummer night.[12]

While on its own this might seem merely an allusion to the classical story of Leander drowning when trying to swim the Hellespont to Hero, earlier in the play Shakespeare has Touchstone go out of his way to quote from Marlowe:

> Dead shepherd, now I find thy saw of might
> 'Whoever loved that loved not at first sight'.[13]

As we noted earlier, 'shepherd' was a poetic Elizabethan term for another poet, while 'saw' simply means 'saying', but it is the saying itself that is important. It is a particularly famous line from *Hero and Leander* and this is the only instance in Shakespeare's entire output in which he directly quotes and effectively acknowledges – as distinct from quietly borrowing – a line from one of his contemporaries. This leads back to Rosalind's first Leander allusion, which happens to be from her elaborate claim that no one has ever died for love, ending

> But these are all lies: men have died from time to time, and worms have eaten them, but not for love.[14]

As has recently been argued by Marlowe author Charles Nicholl,[15] could Shakespeare have been trying to impart that whatever Marlowe's sexual inclinations, his death had nothing to do with 'lewd love' as stated by Meres, but rather more to do with government skulduggery? Rather neatly suggesting this is Shakespeare's inclusion, in the very middle of *As You Like It*, and again on the lips of Touchstone, the lines:

> When a man's verses cannot be understood . . . it strikes a man more dead than a great reckoning in a little room.[16]

At the inquest on Marlowe's death 'reckoning' was the word used for the 'sum of pence owed' that Marlowe and his companions had purportedly quarrelled over. Here we again detect, at best imperfectly, something of Shakespeare's ineffable subtlety. However much his work is enjoyable on a literary level, Shakespeare was also using his art to convey contemporary messages, many of which we can probably never hope to grasp, but some of which, as in this particular example, we can – just.

Ironically, it is in the year of this valediction to his old rival that we find Shakespeare behaving with arguably characteristic similar generosity towards the man who would increasingly become his new rival: Ben Jonson. Despite Jonson, on his release from the Fleet prison, certainly having been signed up to write a play for Henslowe and the Admiral's Men, it was the Lord Chamberlain's Men who performed his *Every Man in his Humour* less than a year later. A snippet from Rowe's 1709 biography of Shakespeare possibly conveys something of how this occurred:

His [Shakespeare's] acquaintance with Ben Jonson began with a remarkable piece of humanity and good nature. Mr Jonson, who was at that time altogether unknown to the world, had offered one of his plays to the players in order to have it acted, and the persons into whose hands it was put, after having turned it carelessly and superciliously over, were just returning it to him with an ill-natured answer that it would be of no service to their company when Shakespeare luckily cast his eye upon it, and found something so well in it as to engage him first to read it through, and afterwards to recommend Mr Jonson and his writings to the public. After this they were professed friends. . . .[17]

Whatever the truth of this, Shakespeare and his fellow actors certainly staged Jonson's *Every Man in his Humour* in 1598, less than a year after Jonson's release from the Fleet. The opening night seems to have been 16 September at the Curtain, and thanks to Jonson's commendable habit of keeping a list of the chief actors in each of his plays, we are able to read in the 1616 Folio edition of Jonson's works:

This comedy was first acted in the year 1598. . . .
The principal comedians were:
    Will. Shakespeare   Ric. Burbadge
    Aug. Philips   Joh. Hemings

Hen. Condel	Tho. Pope
Will. Slye	Chr. Beeston
Will. Kempe	Joh. Duke

Here the particularly fascinating feature is that we see Shakespeare, now thirty-four years old, actually heading this list, not as an already famous dramatist, but arguably in his own right as a talented and seasoned working actor – corroborating Henry Chettle's comment on his 'excellent' quality from back in 1592–3. The American writer Marchette Chute has made the point that while to a modern reader it might seem demeaning for Shakespeare to have acted other writers' characters on the stage, for Shakespeare and his fellow actors:

> such a notion apparently never occurred. . . . The stage was not a bondage to them. It was a persistent and stimulating challenge, and each new play was undertaken by the same group of close personal friends and experienced, intelligent craftsmen.[18]

Jonson's list is also of considerable importance in providing an updated roll-call of those who comprised the Lord Chamberlain's Men in 1598, a useful mid-point between *The Seven Deadly Sins* 'Platt' of around 1592 and the First Folio's list of 'principal actors' of 1623. Although we earlier suggested that Henry Condell was the 'Harry' of *The Seven Deadly Sins*' list, it is thanks to Jonson's *Every Man in his Humour* list that we can be absolutely sure Condell belonged to the Lord Chamberlain's Men by September of 1598. Besides Condell's St Mary Aldermanbury co-parishioner John Heminges, we see those grand old veterans of the Leicester's Men days Phillips, Pope and Kemp all still listed. Only Bryan seems to have dropped out about the previous year, apparently having retired from the acting life to take up a post as Groom of the royal Chamber, which he is recorded holding both at the time of Elizabeth I's funeral in 1603, and as late as 1611–13.[19]

Ben Jonson, it is to be noted, does not appear in *Every Man in his Humour*'s cast list, nor does the actor Gabriel Spenser with whom he had been imprisoned for his part in *The Isle of Dogs*. But at this stage of his life, and rather like Marlowe before him, Jonson seems to have been temperamentally incapable of staying out of trouble, for within two days of *Every Man in his Humour*'s opening night we hear of Jonson fighting a duel with Spenser in which the latter (notorious for his vicious temper) was fatally injured. On 26 September Henslowe wrote to his son-in-law Edward Alleyn:

> Since you were with me I have lost one of my company, which hurteth me greatly. This is Gabriel, for he is slain in Hogsden Fields by the hands of Benjamin Jonson.

Because Hogsden, or Hoxton, Fields were in the environs of Shoreditch, Jonson and Spenser had almost certainly attended an early performance of *Every Man in his Humour* at the nearby Curtain theatre. But whatever the cause of the quarrel, Jonson once again found himself in prison, this time the infamous Newgate, and facing a charge of murder.

In an age when a man could be hanged for stealing anything worth more than seven pence, this might have seemed to herald the end of Ben Jonson. In fact he was saved by an ancient legal loop-hole – 'benefit of clergy' – whereby any cleric, liberally interpreted as any man who could read and write, could once and once only plead exemption from even so serious an offence as murder, so long as he could prove he could read. Accordingly after a period of cooling his temper in Newgate Jonson managed to gain release simply with the forfeiture of his goods and the branding of the base of his left thumb with the letter 'T' for Tyburn, the mark that would spell his certain execution if he murdered again.

In fact Jonson's term in Newgate marked him in a different way also, for due to the powerful impression created by a Catholic priest who reportedly 'visited him in prison'[20] (this was quite probably one on the inside with him, facing death), Jonson added to his already complicated psychology by accepting the Catholic faith, which he would retain for the next twelve years.

For Shakespeare and his fellows, meanwhile, the problem of the lapsed lease for the Shoreditch Theatre still remained unresolved, the Curtain being apparently no better than a stop-gap substitute. In the wake of James Burbage's death, Richard Burbage's non-acting brother Cuthbert took principal charge of the negotiations with site owner Giles Allen. But although the company expressed their willingness to take a lease for another twenty-one years at a higher rent, and with a cash payment of £30 which Allen said Burbage had owed him, Allen continued to prove difficult. He demanded another £100 for repairs that were nothing to do with the Theatre, and also insisted that Shakespeare's company would only be permitted to use the Theatre for another five years, after which they would be obliged to turn it over to some more respectable usage than acting.[21]

Whatever the Lord Chamberlain's Men may have felt about this slur on their vocation, the continued uncertainty of any permanance for the Shoreditch site appears to have been the sticking point. Accordingly, with all the bargaining exhausted, they now resorted to direct action, inspired by a particularly useful covenant in their original lease which permitted them to pull down the Theatre and remove it should the lease not be renewed. As they were aware, the Theatre's main skeleton had been constructed according to the traditional timberframe method by which large pieces of high-quality timber were carefully cut into complex, individually unique mortise and tenon joints, then fitted together so that they held each other in place for maximum strength. Thanks to the special identifying marks which joiners used to show which mortise belonged to which tenon, much in the manner that present-day campers are helped to assemble their tent poles, the Theatre could be dismantled from Shoreditch and rebuilt on a new site – if only a suitable new location could be found.

In the event Shakespeare's company found what seemed to be the right spot in the increasingly popular entertainment land of Southwark among the Bankside properties of thirty-seven-year-old Surrey land-owner Nicholas Brend, who had just inherited the site upon his father Thomas's death back in the September.[22] Brend is known to have been in need of ready cash, and seems therefore to have been more than willing for the Lord Chamberlain's Men to set the Theatre's materials on the agreed site even before contracts had been exchanged. Accordingly, with all London under a thick blanket of snow, and Giles Allen usefully away 'in the country', at dead of night on or about Saturday 28 December 1598 a posse of sixteen men arrived at the Shoreditch Theatre and set to work.[23] Thanks to the legal proceedings subsequently instituted by Allen, we know that they were Cuthbert and Richard Burbage, their long-standing friend William Smyth, their appointed carpenter–builder Peter Street, and twelve workmen, while looking on was James Burbage's widow Ellen. This tells us that when it came to matters relating to the physical fabric of the Theatre it was the Burbages who were firmly in charge.

Allen, almost certainly at his country house at Hazeleigh, Essex, appears to have been caught totally off-guard. Those involved in the dismantling gained valuable time by telling two of Allen's friends who came to investigate that they were simply taking the structure down because of 'decays', and that once these had been rectified they would put it up again in the same place 'in another form'. But almost before he knew it Allen, who had thought his empire included a playhouse, suddenly found himself left with an empty plot while over the other side of the river Peter Street and his workmen were busy reassembling the old Theatre's timbers on the Lord Chamberlain's Men's new site.

The evidence of exactly where the new site was on Southwark's Bankside has long been somewhat contradictory. Generally supposed to have been south of present-day Park Street, which in Shakespeare's time was called Maiden Lane, confusion arose when early this century document sleuth American Professor Charles W. Wallace of Nebraska found papers from a lawsuit between Shakespeare's company's business manager John Heminges and his daughter Thomasine explicitly stating the location as 'all that place of ground . . . lying and adjoining upon a way or lane there on one side and abutting up on a piece of land called the Park up on the north . . . and also all that parcel of land . . . abutting upon a lane there called Maiden Lane towards the south'.[24]

Although this clearly states the site to have lain north not south of Maiden Lane, it provides a classic instance of the need for caution even over documents drawn up by lawyers, for thankfully the matter has been resolved by archaeological excavation. Early in 1989, probing close to Southwark's Grade II listed late Regency building known as Anchor Terrace, Museum of London archaeologists found what seem to have been part of the original chalk and timber foundations for the outer gallery wall [see pl. 34] as laid by the Lord Chamberlain's Men's builder Peter Street during the early months of 1599.[25] On a mundane level the discovery proves that despite the document found by Professor Wallace, the new site lay south, not north of present-day Park Street [see fig 7, page 255]. What is far more important, however, is that the new theatre that Street and his men put together using the old Shoreditch Theatre timber frame was the one the world knows today as Shakespeare's Globe. For Shakespeare and his fellow actors, as much as for the history of the English stage, a whole new era was about to begin.

CHAPTER 16

'This Wooden "O"'

Ironically we owe to the same Charles Wallace, who found the documents that mislocated the Globe, the far more rewarding discovery of papers revealing Shakespeare's close financial involvement in the Globe venture from its inception.[1] Preserved in London's Public Record Office, where Wallace and his redoubtable wife Hulda discovered them in 1909, the papers in question comprise a lawsuit of 1619, 'Witter v. Heminges and Condell',[2] providing precise details of an otherwise lost lease agreement which lawyers for the Burbages and five leading members of the Lord Chamberlain's Men drew up with Southwark landowner Nicholas Brend early in 1599. Backdated to 25 December 1598, when the Theatre's timber frame was snatched from Shoreditch, and granting a lease on the land for thirty-one years, the agreement was apparently signed on 21 February 1599, and was far more complex than the original Shoreditch one between James Burbage, his grocer partner and brother-in-law John Brayne, and Giles Allen.

Thus we learn that the playhouse that had been brought to Bankside and called the Globe became apportioned between the principals of the Lord Chamberlain's Men so that Cuthbert and Richard Burbage owned one half, while the other was held by a syndicate comprising Shakespeare, Augustine Phillips, Thomas Pope, John Heminges and William Kemp. It was a straightforward 'tenancy in common' arrangement intended probably to try to prevent the scattering of the shares and their falling into unsympathetic hands through inheritance (though if so, it failed).[3] Effectively it meant that Shakespeare and his four colleagues owned one tenth of the Globe each, and were obliged collectively to pay landlord Brend an annual ground rent of seven pounds five shillings (£7.25), with the Burbages to pay a similar sum for their half. All those involved in this arrangement also, of course, received their proportionate share of the profits from the venture. Accordingly, whatever rank Shakespeare had held with the Lord Chamberlain's Men before, from 21 February 1599 he became a fully fledged 'sharer' in the company, with a serious stake in its financial success.

The names of two non-theatrical individuals associated with Shakespeare and his four co-sharers in this same arrangement are also of considerable interest. According to the same set of 'Witter v. Heminges and Condell' legal papers, Shakespeare, Phillips, Pope, Heminges and Kemp all apparently made over their half share of the Globe to:

> William Leveson and Thomas Savage who regranted and re-assigned to every of them severally a fifth part of the said moiety.[4]

This seems to have been a form of trust arrangement, and both Leveson and Savage can be reasonably readily identified. Leveson's name, for instance, crops up with Heminges and Condell's in the latter's local St Mary Aldermanbury Church records as doing his spot of duty as churchwarden of the parish for the years 1597 and 1598.[5] Clearly a neighbour of Shakespeare's two colleagues, Leveson's known main occupation was as a high-flying merchant and merchant banker, precarious enough to have spent a short time in prison, rich enough to have lent the Queen several hundred pounds in 1597 to help pay the English troops serving in Picardy.

Yet more interesting is Thomas Savage whose will made out in October 1611[6] reveals him to have been a 'citizen and goldsmith of London' who owned property in and around the parish of St Mary Aldermanbury, specifically including a house in Addle Street 'wherein Mr John Heminges, grocer, now dwelleth'. Savage's will also discloses that he originated in Rufford, Lancashire, close to Ferdinando, fifth Earl of Derby's Lathom, so he was very likely the same Thomas Savage who acted as an executor of Ferdinando's estates along with Alice's sister Katherine's husband Sir Thomas Leigh.[7] His connection with Phillips, Pope, Heminges, and Kemp, and arguably with Shakespeare, may well, therefore, date back to the days when their company was under Ferdinando's patronage. The fact that he was continuing to associate with them, and was clearly highly trusted by them, indicates their link with Ferdinando's memory remained very much alive.

Now although we cannot be absolutely sure how long it took for builder Peter Street and his men to re-erect the Theatre's timbers as the new Globe, an inventory drawn up on 16 May 1599 of the exact assets left by Nicholas Brend's recently deceased father Thomas, includes, in Latin, the entry:

> One house, newly built, with a garden pertaining to the same in the parish of St Saviour's aforesaid . . . in the occupation of William Shakespeare and others.[8]

There is general scholarly agreement that this was the Globe, and not only does the inventory establish this as 'newly built' by 16 May 1599 (Peter Street and his workmen presumably already having completed their task), it is also the earliest surviving document positively to link Shakespeare with the new theatre on Bankside.

So what, then, did Shakespeare's Globe, as we may legitimately call it, actually look like? Frustratingly, because most of the remains lie beneath Anchor Terrace, the Museum of London archaeologists' probings of the pre-1614 foundations have so far revealed precious little, and there survive neither detailed drawing, nor adequate groundplan nor any full contemporary description. Probably the most reliable drawing, made within a few months of the Globe's erection, is to be found in a four-plate panorama of London, *Civitas Londoni*, prepared in 1600 by the professional surveyor and map-maker John Norden, a copy of which is preserved in the Royal Library, Stockholm. In the main a naturalistic vista of the whole city, drawn from the tower of St Saviour's (from where Wenceslaus Hollar would make his drawing forty years later), and with the Globe's roof just visible above tree tops, Norden's most helpful inclusion is an inset map [see fig 7, opposite], updated from one he had published in 1593. The purpose of the inset was to help identify key features, and whereas in the 1593 version Norden showed only the bear-baiting ring (the 'Beare howse') and a single 'play howse' (the Rose), he now added the Swan (the 'Swone') in its correct location then the Bearegard [en], then relatively close to this the Rose (misnamed 'The Stare'), then 'The Globe', clearly south of Maiden Lane / Park Street, just as so recently confirmed by the archaeologists.

Because the Globe appears as the very tiniest detail in Norden's overall picture, only a very limited interpretation is possible. The theatre looks as if it were circular, corresponding to a 'wooden O', as Shakespeare would describe it, though more likely it was polygonal, since this would have been a far more practical design for Elizabethan carpentry methods. Just as we earlier noted from the sketch of it as

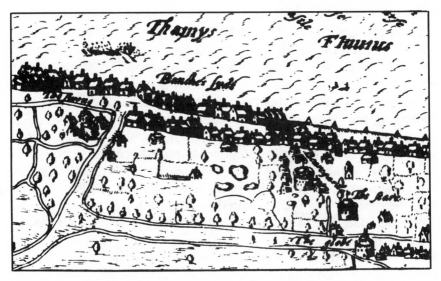

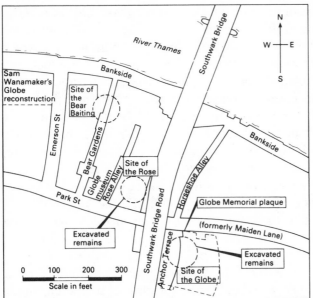

Fig 7

THE LOCATION OF THE GLOBE

(Above) Norden's map of Bankside, 1600, showing relative locations of the Swan ('The Swone') the Bearbaiting pit, the Rose (mis-named 'The Stare'), and the Globe. (Below) The locations of the Bearbaiting, the Rose and the Globe in relation to present-day London, as determined by recent archaeological excavations, topographical information and early maps.

the Shoreditch Theatre, it was clearly taller than surrounding houses, thereby probably having been at least three storeys high. As has again been indicated in the Shoreditch sketch, it seems to have featured some form of tower, presumably as a protection for, and extension of, the stage, as at the Rose. A flag, known signal that a play was in progress, can be seen flying from the roof, independent information indicating the design of this, in keeping with the theatre's chosen name, as Hercules carrying the world on his shoulders. The roof appears thatched, historically known to have been the case, since it would have some serious future consequences. Sparse though such data might seem, modern-day specialists such as C. Walter Hodges and the designers of the Wanamaker venture have built up impressively detailed, if still partially conjectural, Globe reconstructions, from them [see pl. 35].

In addition there is one piece of information that would be most valuable, but which is unascertainable from Norden's sketch, nor has it yet been determined by archaeologists. This is whether Peter Street laid the 1599 stage so that it faced towards the south, that is, so that it could catch all available daylight, or towards the north, so as to avoid it. While it has long been assumed that it must have been towards the south, as was certainly established by archaeology in the case of Henslowe's Rose, careful calculations made from Hollar's drawing of the post-1613 Globe showed this in fact to have faced about 48 degrees east of north, that is, with about the same relation to midsummer sunrise as Stonehenge.[9] As experiments with a model have incontrovertibly revealed, the intention, certainly upon the Globe's rebuilding in 1613, must have been for everything that happened on the covered stage to remain 'invariably and totally shaded', even on a midsummer afternoon.[10] With little doubt this would have been in order to have greater control over scenes that were theoretically set at night though performed on a bright summer's afternoon. As yet we cannot be sure whether Shakespeare had any such facility available to him in the 1599 Globe, though as we shall see, there are intriguing signs of this from the plays he wrote for this theatre.

Of these plays one of the first – if not indeed *the* very first – which he wrote specifically with the Globe in mind would seem to have been *Henry v*, by which Shakespeare completed the tetralogy he had begun, intentionally or otherwise, with *Richard ii*. One of the most distinctive features of this play's opening is a Prologue and a Chorus, or commentator, who steps out of the time-frame of the play; some present-day productions actually cast this part as if played by Shakespeare himself. This is for the very good reason that nowhere else in Shakespeare's plays do we find the author speaking more directly to his audience, nor do we find him exhibiting such self-consciousness over the physical fabric within which his play is being performed. As if a magician, in *Henry v*'s opening lines, the Chorus/Shakespeare invokes unearthly powers:

> O for a Muse of fire, that would ascend
> The brightest heaven of invention,
> A kingdom for a stage, princes to act,
> And monarchs to behold the swelling scene!
> Then should the warlike Harry, like himself,
> Assume the port of Mars . . .

Then, characteristically, he pleads his own and his theatre's unworthiness. With something of the same obsequiousness that he put into the mouth of *A Midsummer Night's Dream*'s Peter Quince when delivering his Prologue, and which he had affected himself for the dedications of *Venus and Adonis* and *Rape of Lucrece*, so in *Henry v* he craves

> But pardon, gentles all,
> The flat unraised spirits that hath dar'd
> On this unworthy scaffold to bring forth
> So great an object. Can this cockpit hold
> The vasty fields of France? Or may we cram
> Within this wooden O the very casques
> That did affright the air at Agincourt?
> O pardon!

This 'unworthy scaffold', 'this cockpit', 'this wooden O': spoken on the actors' behalf, these seem tongue-in-cheek depreciatory references to Peter Street's arguably highly impressive work of transforming the old Shoreditch Theatre's timbers into a pristine acting vehicle outshining its long-established neighbour the Rose. But then, speaking perhaps from the Globe's highest available location, Shakespeare assumes once again the role of hypnotist–magician:

> let us . . .
> On your imaginary forces work.
> Suppose within the girdle of these walls
> Are now confin'd two mighty monarchies . . .
> Piece out our imperfections with your thoughts:
> Into a thousand parts divide one man . . .
> Think, when we talk of horses, that you see them
> Printing their proud hoofs i' th' receiving earth . . .

In *Henry v* we see Shakespeare at the height of his powers as a dramatist of English history, and however much he might have urged his audiences to use their imaginations, by the very nature of the play, the earliest Globe productions must have been visual feasts. With scenes in which the most illustrious members of the English and French Courts appear in all their splendour, and lively action scaling ramparts and engaging in battle – attired with the full heraldry that Elizabethans would have expected – Shakespeare's script must have had every member of the Lord Chamberlain's Men, down to the lowliest backstage seamstress, giving of their utmost. Exactly as in modern productions, every sword thrust, every parry would have been carefully worked out and rehearsed for maximum effect and the maximum safety of audience and players alike.

With so much stirring action a strong comic sub-plot, as in the *Henry IV* plays, was hardly necessary. For *Henry v* Shakespeare notably killed off Falstaff, without him even making an appearance, via an appropriately poignant speech by tavern hostess Mrs Pistol (the former Mistress Quickly). Even so, the Welsh accent of whoever played Sir Hugh Evans in *The Merry Wives of Windsor* must have proved popular, for we find Shakespeare using this for the *Henry v* character Fluellen, arguably with the same actor. Possibly to increase his company's repertoire of regional accents he also introduced among Henry v's soldiery Jamy, a Scotsman, and Macmorris, an Irishman.

We also see him playing up to a necessarily sophisticated audience in the delightful scene of the princess of France trying to learn English from her maid, every English word that she discovers sounding like a more than dubious French one, a ploy then brilliantly reversed in Pistol's encounter with a French soldier. Such scenes may well have been specially written for inclusion in Court performances rather than necessarily for the generality, but even so they would have needed at least two young members of the Lord Chamberlain's Men to speak the lines convincingly in French, and one to coach them in this.

Particularly powerful in *Henry v* is the scene in Act IV, carefully introduced by the Chorus, of the king moving incognito among his troops at dead of night before the battle of Agincourt, an episode recounted in none of the chronicle sources. Shakespeare may have introduced it, not just for its dramatic effectiveness, but deliberately to try out the facility for convincing night scenes that, as we have suggested, the Globe may now have provided. Under the totally shadowed canopy, torches used during otherwise bright daylight could well have conveyed the feel of night. But however this was staged, Shakespeare's *Henry v* would have given the Globe audiences their money's worth.

Quite aside from the self-consciousness with which Shakespeare speaks of his 'wooden O', there is another indication that *Henry v* was written very early in the Lord Chamberlain's Men's Globe occupancy – in the Chorus' lines in the Prologue to Act V which liken London's citizens' welcome for the victorious Henry v to that to be expected in Shakespeare's own time:

> Were now the General of our gracious Empress—
> As in good time he may— from Ireland coming,
> Bringing rebellion broached on his sword. . . .[11]

As scholars are readily agreed, the 'General of our gracious Empress' (throughout Shakespeare's surviving work this is probably the kindest remark he ever makes about Elizabeth), can refer to none other than the Earl of Essex [see pl. 36]. Only a few days after Shakespeare and his fellows signed their contract with Brend, Essex, along with Southampton and other members of the cream of England's nobility, crossed the Irish Sea to quell a serious rebellion in Ireland, where the previous August more than two thousand English troops had been cut to pieces in a surprise swoop led by the English-educated Irish chieftain O'Neill. Throughout this expedition Elizabeth behaved towards Essex like a hopelessly interfering back-seat driver, becoming furious with him when against her express orders he appointed Southampton – who acquitted himself with bravery and distinction as a cavalry officer – as his

General of Horse. When Essex eventually returned from Ireland on 28 September, this was very much without the rebellion 'broached on his sword'. The strong inference, therefore, has to be that *Henry v* was written and performed between the March of Essex's departure and the September of his return: the exact time that Shakespeare and his company were becoming familiar with the new Globe.

If then Shakespeare's *Henry v* is one play that with reasonable confidence we can assign to the Lord Chamberlain's Men's first year at the Globe, another is *Julius Caesar*. During the autumn of 1599 young Thomas Platter from Basle, Switzerland, paid a month's educational visit to England and made a careful record of the entertainments he saw. He provided posterity not only with the earliest-known account of any production at the Globe, but also, specifically, with the earliest-known record of a performance of *Julius Caesar*. According to Platter, as translated from his original German:

> On September 21st after lunch, about two o'clock, I and my party crossed the water, and there in the house with the thatched roof witnessed an excellent performance of the tragedy of the first Emperor Julius Caesar with a cast of some fifteen people; when the play was over they danced marvellously and gracefully together as is their wont, two dressed as men and two as women.[12]

The combination of the date, the mention of 'the house with the thatched roof', and *Julius Caesar* as the production effectively make it signatory that this was Shakespeare's play of that name being performed at the Globe. Indeed that *Julius Caesar* was already in Shakespeare's mind when writing *Henry v* is evident from the Prologue to the latter's final Act (the same passage that refers to the Earl of Essex), in which Shakespeare remarks that London's mayor and chief citizens:

> Like to the senators of th'antique Rome,
> With the plebeians swarming at their heels—
> Go forth and fetch their conqu'ring Caesar in. . . .[13]

Besides its relevance to *Julius Caesar*, Platter's description is in fact particularly valuable for the detail it provides of the Elizabethan theatre. By stating when he attended the Globe he usefully confirms that afternoon performances were indeed the norm for the common theatre. Given that *Julius Caesar* has parts for some thirty-five named characters, not counting crowds of citizens, attendants, guards, etc, his information that the cast comprised 'about fifteen people' indicates that there must have been extensive doubling- and trebling-up on parts. Every one of the personnel, therefore, was repeatedly deployed, with accompanying changes of costume throughout the play. Also revelatory is that performances concluded with dances, independently confirmed in Ben Jonson's *Every Man in his Humour* which similarly mentions 'a jig after a play', but still somewhat unexpected.

A few lines following on from his description of *Julius Caesar* Platter provided further background, which is useful recapitulation and reinforcement of what we have earlier deduced:

Daily London has two, sometimes three plays running in different places, competing with each other, and those which play best obtain most spectators. The playhouses are so constructed that they play on a raised platform, so that everyone has a good view. There are different galleries, and places, however, where the seating is better and more comfortable and therefore more expensive. For whoever cares to stand below pays only one English penny, but if he wishes to sit he enters by another door and pays another penny, while if he desires to sit in the most comfortable seats which are cushioned, where he not only sees everything well, but can also be seen, then he pays yet another English penny at another door. And during the performance food and drink are carried round the audience, so that for what one cares to pay one may also have refreshment. The actors are most expensively and elaborately costumed.

Particularly notable is Platter's mention that those theatres 'which play best obtain most spectators'. Although we lack the vital box office returns, highly revelatory of the Globe's immediate and huge popularity during its opening year is clear evidence that, before the end of 1599, Philip Henslowe and his son-in-law Edward Alleyn of the Admiral's Men took the painful decision to abandon their Rose and move back across the river from whence the Lord Chamberlain's Men had come. Included in the Henslowe papers at Dulwich College, and dated 8 January 1600 (actually 1599, due to the Elizabethan New year being in the March), is a contract drawn up by Henslowe and Alleyn with the same Peter Street who had worked on the Globe, commissioning him to build them a new theatre close to Whitecross Street beyond Cripplegate.[14] This would become the Fortune, and the contract's repeated specification that the staircases, access passages, gallery divisions, stage, etc, should 'be contrived and fashioned like unto the ... said playhouse called the Globe' is indicative of the admirable work Street had done on the Globe.

There survive other pointers to *Henry v* and *Julius Caesar*'s powerful contributions to the Globe venture's rapid success in the notices they attracted. In the case of *Julius Caesar*, dating from the very same year of its first performance at the Globe,[15] though not published until 1601, are Cambridge graduate John Weever's lines in his *Mirror of Martyrs*:

> The many-headed multitude were drawn
> By Brutus' speech, that Caesar was ambitious
> When eloquent Mark Antony had shown
> His virtues, who but Brutus then was vicious?[16]

In his mid-twenties at this time, Weever is of some interest because he grew up in Ferdinando's domains under the care of Thomas Langton (so-called Baron of Walton), whom Ferdinando had tried to protect from Secretary Cecil's clutches at the time of the Hesketh plot (see page 164). At some time Weever must have viewed Shakespeare's early *Henry vi, Part ii*, since in a late work, *Funeral Monuments*, he mentioned its Jack Cade rebellion scene and the decapitated heads of Lord Say and his son-in-law 'upon high poles ... carried by the villains through the city of London, who caused their trunkless faces ... to kiss one another at every street corner'.[17] Far more pertinently, however, in the same year of *Julius Caesar*'s apparent first performance Weever brought out his *Epigrammes in the oldest cut and newest fashion*, a work comprising some hundred and fifty pithy poems, many devoted to Lancashire and Cheshire worthies such as Ferdinando and his tilting companion Thomas Gerard. Also included is one specifically addressed to Shakespeare:

> Honey-tongued Shakespeare when I saw thine issue
> I swore Apollo got them and none other.
> Their rosy-tinted features cloth'd in tissue,

Some heaven-born goddess said to be their mother:
Rosy-cheek'd Adonis with his amber tresses,
Fair fire-hot Venus charming him to love her,
Chaste Lucrece, virgin-like her dresses,
Proud, lust-stung Tarquin seeking still to prove her:
Romeo, Richard, more whose names I know not,
Their sugared tongues and power attractive beauty
Say they are saints although that saints they show not
For thousands vow to them subjective duty:
They burn in love thy children Shakespeare het [heated] them,
Go, woo thy Muse more nymphish brood beget them.[18]

Whatever we may feel about the quality of Weever's poetry, most notable here, as has been pointed out by Professor Ernst Honigmann, is that while the epigrams mostly vary in length from four to twenty lines this one to Shakespeare, uniquely in Weever's collection, is exactly fourteen lines long: the same length as Shakespeare's 154 sonnets.[19] Only our second signal of the existence of Shakespeare's *Sonnets*, this tantalisingly suggests that Lancashire-born Weever may somehow have been among that circle of 'private friends' privileged to share them, as mentioned by Francis Meres only the previous year.

But if Shakespeare and his fellows had seen off the competition from the Admiral's Men, before 1599 was out other rivals, of an altogether different nature, manifested themselves. These were the boys of St Paul's Cathedral school, better known as the Children of Paul's. As far back as the Middle Ages the pupils of St Paul's school had performed plays for Court and private entertainment under the tutelage of an unrepentantly Catholic songmaster, Sebastian Westcott, who established a long run of such productions between his appointment in 1560 and his death in 1582. Westcott had then been briefly succeeded by Thomas Gyles who had the boys perform some of John Lyly's plays. These had ceased after 1590, partly as a result of the competition from adult productions.

But in 1599 there emerged into the dramatic field the satirist John Marston, a red-haired Oxford graduate in his mid-twenties who had already achieved notoriety for his erotic poem *The Metamorphosis of Pygmalion's Image*, and his tract *The Scourge of Villainy*, which only the year before had been publicly burnt on the orders of the

Archbishop of Canterbury and the Bishop of London as part of a new ban on satiric writing. It was probably this ban, and Shakespeare's evident success, that caused Marston to turn to writing for the theatre. Not being an actor himself, he appears to have alighted upon the idea of having his plays performed by the Children of Paul's. Not least of the advantages was that the boys did not need to be paid in the manner of adults, and they already had an impromptu theatre of their own in an area of the Cathedral cloisters, one which needed comparatively little adjustment to turn it into a thoroughly serviceable private playhouse along the lines that old James Burbage had intended for the Blackfriars before the residents blocked his plans.

Even so, Marston needed a partner and financial backer, and the historical record is quite clear that this was William Stanley, sixth Earl of Derby, none other than the brother whose succession Ferdinando had tried so hard to block, and the 'nidicock' so despised by Shakespeare's company's current patron, George Carey. Included in the collection of gossipy letters by Rowland Whyte that reported Southampton's dalliances with Elizabeth Vernon, is one of 13 November 1599 imparting that 'My Lord Derby hath put up the plays of the children in Pauls to his great pains and charge'.[20] To this same time would seem to belong Catholic secret agent George Fenner's clearly related news that William Stanley was 'busy in penning comedies for the common players',[21] the comment we earlier quoted (page 17) as having caused the Derbyians to believe this William to have written the works of Shakespeare.

Marston's opening shot for his new venture, thought to have been written as a special 'taster' of what was intended, seems to have been his first-ever play, the *History of Antonio and Mellida*. This was performed by the Children of Paul's in their 'private' playhouse in the October of 1599 at the start of the winter season for which the Lord Chamberlain's Men, with their open-air Globe, were still poorly equipped. As evident from the play's surviving text, published in 1602, this began with an introductory scene in which the young actors made their first entrance as if still in rehearsal 'with parts in their hands', one, for instance, expressing concern at his ability to play the part of the Amazon Florizel on account of his voice having almost broken. In the main body of the play Marston showed off his verbal virtuosity by introducing into the English language words of his own devising; among these were 'strenuous', 'impregnably', and 'abstruse'.[22] In the final act a painter enters with two portraits, one, described as 'of a good settled age', seeming to have been of thirty-eight-year-old William, sixth Earl of Derby, the other, referred to as bearing the Latin inscription *Aetatis suae 24* ('at his age 24'), seeming to have been of Marston, since this was certainly his age at that time.

So what was the Lord Chamberlain's Men's response to this new competition? Fascinatingly, the overwhelming literary consensus is that *Hamlet* was the play with which Shakespeare followed *Julius Caesar*, signalled not least by Shakespeare's specific echoing of the latter in *Hamlet*'s opening scene's lines:

> A little ere the mighty Julius fell
> The graves stood tenantless . . .[23]

Also Shakespeare had Polonius remark to Hamlet that once at university:

> I did enact Julius Caesar. I was killed i' th' Capitol. Brutus killed me.[24]

According to one interpretation, this was a company joke because the actor playing Polonius in *Hamlet* had probably played Julius Caesar in the previous production.

But one of the many fascinations of *Hamlet*, by far Shakespeare's longest play, and full of references to actors and acting is that it conveys Shakespeare's considerable irritation at the time he was writing it with a company of child actors. Thus he has Rosencrantz tell Hamlet:

> there is, sir, an eyrie of children, little eyases [baby hawks], that cry out on the top of question, and are most tyannically clapped for't. These are now the fashion, and so berattle the common stages—so they call them—that many wearing rapiers [i.e. gentlemen] are afraid of goose-quills and dare scarce come thither.[25]

Hamlet then responds:

> What, are they children? Who maintains 'em? How are they escoted [provided for]? Will they pursue the quality no longer than they can sing? Will they not say afterwards, if they should

grow themselves to common players—as it is most like, if their means are no better—their writers do them wrong to make them exclaim against their own succession?[26]

Clearly these children and their writers represented serious competition for the adult actors, for on Hamlet's asking whether the boys 'carry it away' (that is, get the better of their elders), he is told by Rosencrantz: 'Ay, that they do, my lord, Hercules and his load too'.[27] At this point the actor playing Rosencrantz may well have gesticulated towards the Globe's flag on which Hercules carried the globe of the world, as if to acknowledge that even the Globe was being adversely affected.

Most literary scholars have generally understood Shakespeare in these passages to have been referring to competition from the boys of the Chapel Royal, commonly called the 'Children of the Chapel', who were formed at the end of September 1600 to perform private plays in the Blackfriars theatre (which had hitherto remained redundant), with Ben Jonson as one of their chief writers. Yet this has never made sense because it goes against certain indications that *Hamlet*, in the form we now have it, was written before this date, also the fact that since the Children of the Chapel were tenants of the Blackfriars theatre (which the Burbages still owned), the Lord Chamberlain's Men could easily have evicted them from this for causing any offence. It should certainly not have been necessary for Shakespeare's company to resort to the altogether lamer device of condemning them from the public stage.

Accordingly, it is thanks to some intriguing recent deductions by writer Felix Pryor[28] that an altogether more convincing case has been made for the Children of Paul's and their writers Marston and Earl William having been the objects of Shakespeare's ire, rather than the Children of the Chapel. According to Pryor, while reading a biography of Shakespeare in the London Library, and casually looking at the drawing of Shakespeare's coat of arms, his eye happened to alight on its falcon crest, at which point realisation dawned that since baby hawks, or 'eyases', are fledgling falcons, Shakespeare was referring to the troublesome young actors as fledgling Shakespeares. From the same heraldic thinking further light was cast on what Shakespeare intended when, during his apparent fit of madness, Hamlet remarks:

I am but mad north-north-west. When the wind is southerly, I know a hawk from a handsaw.[29]

Since Marston's family coat of arms has a saw-like serrated edge known as Fess Dencetty, Hamlet was effectively saying he knew Shakespeare's work from Marston's, there also being a possible secondary meaning in Hamlet's association of the handsaw with particularly poor acting technique, as in 'Nor do not saw the air too much with your hand, thus'. As for the phrase 'but mad north-north-west', Pryor noted that if a compass bearing was taken from the Globe site to the site of old St Paul's, the latter could be seen to lie exactly to the north-north-west. It was the Children of Paul's who sometime between late 1599 and early 1600 had made Shakespeare mad.

Now all this is of course but incidental to what Shakespeare was really aiming to do with *Hamlet*, and arguments over the play's many nuances will continue till doomsday.[30] On any level, *Hamlet* is a masterpiece of brilliant scenes, from its teeth-chattering opening on Elsinore's battlements in the dead of night (note how this would have had to be staged convincingly in afternoon light), to its second scene of the black-clad Hamlet as the odd man out in Claudius's otherwise so colourful court (a reprise of the device used with Marcade in *Love's Labour's Lost*'s closing scene); from Hamlet's unwitting murder of the eavesdropping Polonius, hidden behind a curtain or 'arras' to its breath-takingly bloody dénouement. With characters as varied as the infinitely interpretable Hamlet, the Lord Burghley-like Polonius and the foppish Osric, the play is a treasure house of masterly characterisations. For all Marston's word-coining in *Antonio and Mellida*, *Hamlet* gave us such phrases as: 'Frailty thy name is woman!'; 'More in sorrow than in anger'; 'The primrose path of dalliance'; 'The time is out of joint'; 'Brevity is the soul of wit'; 'More matter with less art'; 'Though this be madness, yet there is method in it'; 'I must be cruel only to be kind'; 'Alas, poor Yorick' and not least, of course, the much-quoted 'To be or not to be'.

Not least, *Hamlet* is one of the most cracking ghost stories of all time and Shakespeare's first significant return to the supernatural theme since the start of the Southampton period, tradition having it that he himself played the Ghost. If he did so, he certainly gave himself, in a part textually prescribed as costumed in full armour, some suitably bloodchilling lines with which to regale his Globe audience:

> I am thy father's spirit,
> Doom'd for a certain term to walk the night,
> And for the day confin'd to fast in fires,
> Till the foul crimes done in my days of nature
> Are burnt and purg'd away. But that I am forbid
> To tell the secrets of my prison-house,
> I could a tale unfold whose lightest word
> Would harrow up thy soul, freeze thy young blood,
> Make thy two eyes like stars start from their spheres,
> Thy knotted and combined locks, to part,
> And each particular hair to stand on end
> Like quills upon the fretful porpentine.[31]

Although the Ghost has but ninety-five lines to Hamlet's 1575 (the latter the biggest speaking part in Shakespeare's entire corpus), one interesting interpretation sees the Ghost as the *deus ex machina* of the whole play. As a result of the instantaneously acting poison administered by his villainous brother Claudius, Hamlet's father's has been despatched 'Unhousel'd, disappointed, unanel'd'[32] (i.e. deprived of the last rites) into the hereafter, and the whole state of Denmark infected with a 'something rotten' that needs cleansing. Hamlet thereby unhappily finds himself the unlucky chosen agent in the land of the living to carry out the physical cleansing – 'O cursed spite that I was ever born to set it right'.[33]

But the 'something rotten' also demands a spiritual cleansing by prayer and fasting – as suggested in Hamlet's lines 'and for my own poor part, I will go pray'[34] – in order for the Ghost to receive at least some relief from the 'certain term' he is otherwise obliged to spend in the fires of Purgatory. And here, as has been noted both by literary scholar J. Dover Wilson and by Catholic priests H. S. Bowden, Christopher Devlin and Peter Milward, Shakespeare reveals a very Catholic attitude: in the concept of Purgatory, one expressly denied by the Protestant church; in the idea of the efficacy of sacraments for the shriving of the dying; not least, in the idea of the efficacy of the prayers of the living on behalf of the dead. It can be rightly argued, of course, that Shakespeare hardly demanded belief in such offices, any more than today's writers of horror films either believe in their vampire creations, or expect their audiences to do so for any longer than the time they remain in the cinema. This is how *Hamlet* would have been perfectly acceptable to audiences of all persuasions in Shakespeare's time, as indeed he would have intended it to be, and as it continues to be.

But tantalisingly suggesting something more than this, however, are elements such as Horatio's famous epitaph upon the dead Hamlet: 'And flights of angels sing thee to thy rest.'[35] As pointed out by Arden *Hamlet* editor Harold Jenkins, the only logical inspiration has to be 'the antiphon of the old Latin burial service "In paradisum deducant te angeli ... Chorus angelorum te suscipiat ... aeternam habeas requiem",' that is, 'may the angels waft you to paradise ... choirs of angels sustain you ... [and] grant you eternal rest'.

So whose requiem did Shakespeare *really* have in mind? What was *Hamlet* really about? Are we seeing in Claudius' perfectly-observed, spy-packed Renaissance court more than a few reminiscences of the Court of Elizabeth? Are we glimpsing in the story of Hamlet's father's secret poisoning, and his succession by an unworthy brother, just the faintest of echoes of poisoning in another northern Court just a little closer to Elizabeth's than Elsinore? Is the whole play a hall of mirrors reflecting the real world in which Shakespeare moved? The play is an extraordinary one to find pitched against Ferdinando's brother at this time, and if it was indeed Marston and his 'nidicock' William who provoked Shakespeare into writing *Hamlet*, literature has more need to be grateful to them than they could ever know.

Whatever the answers – and first and foremost *Hamlet* was written to be, and remains, a work of the finest entertainment – the play's success in its own time is more than readily apparent. In 1603 it would receive the inevitable compliment of a bad Quarto pirate edition, though due to the cachet the author's name had acquired, readily accredited as 'By William Shake-speare'. One principal value of this is that it tells us that besides London the play was performed 'in the two Universities of Cambridge and Oxford and else-where'. This indicates, arguably precisely thanks to Shakespeare, the company's greater social acceptability at these universities where only a few years before they had been paid to stay away.

But if Shakespeare rode on a wave of creative virtuosity and success in the second half of 1599, there were ever those (like the man deputed to remind Caesar of his mortality), eager to put him down. Thanks to Ben Jonson's 1616 First Folio we know that one of the non-Shakespeare plays performed by the Lord Chamberlain's Men at the Globe in 1599 was his *Every Man Out of his Humour*. In this, in a manner that would almost certainly have been taken good humouredly by Shakespeare, Jonson seems to have aimed a typically waspish shaft at Shakespeare's proud new gentleman's coat of arms, with its carefully restrained motto *Non sanz droict* (not without right). In *Every Man Out of his Humour* Jonson has his rustic clown Sogliardo, fresh from spending £30 purchasing *his* coat of arms, adopt the motto 'Not without mustard'. At Henslowe's Rose, even though this was fading in popularity, the opportunity was taken for a Parthian shot by staging Protestantism's deliberate counterpart to Shakespeare's popular Falstaff–Sir John Oldcastle creation, the so-called 'true' *Sir John Oldcastle*, written by spy Anthony Munday and his cronies Dekker, Hathway and Wilson and proclaiming in its Prologue:

> It is no pamper'd glutton we present
> Nor aged Counsellor to youthful sin.

A year later the published version's title page would equally pointedly declare the play as: 'The True and Honorable Historie of the Life of Sir John Oldcastle, the Good Lord Cobham'.

Most pointed of all however, and often omitted by biographers, is Shakespeare's guying at precisely this same time by an unknown university dramatist (or dramatists) responsible for three short plays *Pilgrimage to Parnassus* and *Return from Parnassus* that have survived, partly preserved in a manuscript in the Bodleian Library, Oxford, Rawlinson MS.D.398. In them, one Ingenioso takes service with ultra-courtly Gullio, who seeks to shine as a poet and literary critic, his model apparently being Shakespeare as author of *Venus and Adonis*. Waxing lyrical about his hero, Gullio exclaims: 'O sweet Mr Shakespeare! I'll have his picture in my study at the court'. Spurning Ingenioso's writings in the style of Chaucer and Spenser, Gullio expresses himself satisfied only by those 'in Mr Shakespeare's vein' declaring:

> Marry, sir, these have some life in them! Let this duncified world esteem of Spenser and Chaucer, I'll worship sweet Mr Shakespeare, and to honour him will lay his Venus and Adonis under my pillow.

Clearly the ghost of Robert Greene was living on in the universities, for there can be no doubt that Shakespeare was being mocked by a university man seemingly as averse to him as Greene had been. Gullio's deliberate repetition of 'Mr Shakespeare' was a jibe at Shakespeare's recently won gentility, while the author's general despising of professional players is clear from the way he has characters called Burbage and Kempe ignorantly refer to 'that writer Ovid and that writer Metamorphosis'. Also he makes Kempe crow about the money that could be made from acting:

> Be merry lads, you have happened upon the most excellent vocation in the world for [making] money. They come North and South to bring it to our playhouse.

Most pointed and revealing of all is the way the *Parnassus* author contrasts the actors' luxury living with that of their intellectual betters, the scholars:

> Vile world, that lifts them up to high degree
> And treads us down in grovelling misery.
> England affords those glorious vagabonds
> That once carried their packs on their backs
> Fine horses to ride through the gazing streets
> Sooping [souping?] it in their glaring satin suits
> And pages to attend their masterships:
> With mouthing words that better wits have framed
> They purchase lands, and now Esquires are named.[36]

Although few of Shakespeare's biographers quote this passage, it paints the most vivid picture of the sheer spite felt in certain quarters about Shakespeare and his fellows in their heyday, and also represents one of the best arguments against those who cannot accept that Shakespeare could have been a mere low-born player who achieved dramatic success through his and his fellows' own efforts.

By now Shakespeare was sufficiently successful to shrug off such antipathies as mere pin-pricks. Waiting in the wings, however, partly to affect Shakespeare and his fellows, but more particularly to affect the now twenty-six-year-old young man to whom he had addressed his *Sonnets*, lay a high-profile drama in which real-life blood was about to be shed.

CHAPTER 17

'Like Favourites Made Proud'

Exactly one week after Thomas Platter had sat watching Shakespeare and his fellows play *Julius Caesar* at the Globe, a posse of well-armed and richly clad horsemen, inevitably weary from crossing the Irish Sea and three days' hard riding, clattered through London's outskirts. Head of the party rode the Earl of Essex, at his side Shakespeare's friend the Earl of Southampton. Taking a ferry across the Thames at Lambeth, on the Surrey bank they commandeered fresh horses and sped on to the Queen who was then at her Surrey palace of Nonsuch, near Cheam.

Essex's return to England was no triumphant celebration of the broaching of the Irish rebellion upon his sword, as Shakespeare's *Henry v* had led much of London's populace to expect. His purpose was simply to explain to the Queen the rather more pragmatic truce that he and the adroit Irish chieftain O'Neill had reached after parleying alone together at a border ford while their respective armies stayed out of earshot on either bank.

Elizabeth and her Council's suspicions of Essex were however already intense as a result of a book published about the time of his departure for Ireland: young lawyer John Hayward's *The First Part of the Life and Reign of King Henry iv*, which was dedicated to Essex. Rekindling as this did the story of Richard ii's deposition, it was immediately seized upon as being written with 'application' to current events, as a result of which Hayward was sent to the Tower, and in the June total censorship imposed on any writing of English history without government permission. Notably from this time on Shakespeare abandoned any more plays on English history until his very last, *Henry viii*.

Similar repression was applied to Essex even with regard to his day-to-day conduct of affairs in Ireland. On being apprised of the truce he had arranged with O'Neill, which was viewed back in London government circles with very much the same distaste as any treating with terrorists of today, Elizabeth sent a furious countermanding letter, just as she had earlier to the news that Essex had appointed

Southampton as his General of Horse. She behaved similarly petulantly upon hearing that Southampton's friend the Earl of Rutland had disobeyed her express orders by slipping over to Ireland to join Essex. Her scarcely abated anger at Southampton for his love-match with Elizabeth Vernon was fuelled further by the vindictive Lord Grey of Wilton, whom Southampton had rightly disciplined for disobedience during an Irish engagement, and who now bore the most massive grudge against him. Despite the fact that Essex and Southampton were fighting for their country on hostile terrain, and needing to make their own day-to-day decisions, in Elizabeth's eyes they could do no right.

Accordingly, at the end of his tether on the morning of 28 September, in a scene worthy of Shakespeare, Essex strode still mud-spattered from his break-neck journey straight into the Queen's private chamber at Nonsuch, finding her with her hair still down and far from completely prepared by her ladies. Throughout that day, during what was to be her last face-to-face meeting with Essex, Elizabeth kept the mood cordial, but as events proved, she was merely playing for time. By the evening the warrants were out, setting off an inexorable slide towards disaster that would come dangerously close to dragging even Shakespeare and his company into its train.

After careful deliberation by both Queen and Council, on 1 October 1599 Essex was sentenced to close house arrest at York House, a grand Thamesside mansion just east of where today stands Charing Cross station. Here he came under the charge of the house's then resident, Lord Keeper Sir Thomas Egerton, who was shortly to marry Ferdinando Stanley's widow Alice, dowager Countess of Derby. On the Queen's personal instructions Essex was expressly forbidden either to walk in the garden, or even to write to his wife after her giving birth to a daughter. Being thus unable to conduct his personal affairs, these were taken over for him by Southampton and Lord Mountjoy, the first of whom, together with his wife Elizabeth even took up temporary residence in Essex House for this purpose.

Essex had attracted considerable loyalty among the knights, captains, officers and soldiers who served with him in his Irish campaign, and many of these drifted back to England, inevitably keeping Cecil's spy service busy listening to the anti-government views they expressed in taverns. Ever with eyes and ears sharply tuned for what was going on, Rowland Whyte reported that Southampton and his friend Rutland 'pass away the time in London merely in going to plays every day'[1] – an important indication of the draw the theatrical world still held for Southampton and his circle. Although eventually Southampton and Mountjoy returned to Ireland, even then this was only to have the Queen reject out of hand Mountjoy's recommendation that Southampton be appointed to the then vacant governorship of Connaught. When Essex was released in August 1600, after ten months' confinement, the Queen humiliated him further by forbidding him to approach the Court, and depriving him of one of his main sources of income, a monopoly on the importation of sweet wines.

With such repeated rejections, with Elizabeth still implacably refusing to countenance discussion of her successor, and with Secretary Cecil following his father's footsteps in using every ploy to block an open approach to political issues, it was perhaps inevitable that proud spirits such as Essex and Southampton's should be pushed beyond breaking point (however unwisely) and into outright rebellion. On Christmas Day 1600, at about the time that Shakespeare and his fellows were busy preparing for their Boxing Day performance for the Queen (thought by some scholars to have been *As You Like It*),[2] Essex and Southampton wrote to King James VI of Scotland, Elizabeth's most logical successor, complaining how Cecil and his faction suppressed 'all noble, virtuous and heroical spirits'. Essex warned James that the Cecils were plotting to make the Spanish Infanta successor to the English throne, and said he wanted James to be the first to know that he, Essex, having been 'summoned of all sides' now intended to be active 'to relieve my poor country that groans under her burden'. In plain terms, he intended a coup, and 'by God's favour' he anticipated 'the fairest and likeliest hopes ... of good success'.[3]

Meanwhile so intense was the hatred between the Essex and Cecil factions that on 9 January 1601, three days after Shakespeare and his men had put on their second Christmas–Shrovetide performance for the Court, Southampton suddenly found himself viciously ambushed by the still malevolent Lord Grey of Wilton and a band of his followers, while riding accompanied only by his page, who lost a hand in the fighting. Otherwise Southampton managed successfully to fend off the attack, but it was quite obvious from Grey's short subsequent imprisonment in the Fleet that another attempt on Southampton's life would surely follow. Accordingly, when Grey was released on 2 February, Essex and Southampton called meetings at Southampton's friend Sir Charles Danvers' London mansion, Drury House, with others whom they believed to be of like mind.

From the lists subsequently drawn up, their supporters appear to have included Southampton's play-going companion the Earl of Rutland; the Earls of Bedford and Sussex; the Catholic William Parker; Lord Monteagle with whom Essex had served in Ireland; the Earl of Essex's stepfather Sir Christopher Blount; Essex's sister Lady Rich; his secretary Henry Cuffe; his steward Sir Gelly Meyrick (who had arranged the evening of plays after Southampton's departure for France); Sir Charles Percy, brother of the Catholic Earl of Northumberland, Sir Joscelyn Percy; the future Gunpowder plotter Robert Catesby; Sir Henry Carey, one of the brothers of Shakespeare's company's patron George Carey, and the shadowy Edward Bushell, earlier mentioned as associated with Shakespeare and the Quiney letter (see page 236).[4] Broadly, they were free-thinking people from Essex and Southampton's military and literary circles, with both Catholic and Protestant affiliations suiting the religious tolerance that Essex would seem to have intended to pursue, given any opportunity of real power. Their aim was to settle matters once and for all by capturing members of the current governing party such as Cecil and Raleigh, and simultaneously seizing control of the Court.

At about this time – and we have no way of knowing how much they knew about the meetings at Drury House – 'some of the players' of Shakespeare's company found themselves suddenly approached by Lord Monteagle, Sir Joscelyn and Sir Charles Percy and others who requested them 'to have the play of the deposing and killing of King Richard the second to be played the Saturday next'.[5] Notable here is that the play was specifically to include the central deposition scene, the one regarded as too politically sensitive to be printed at this time. Equally notable is that the performance was to be at the Globe, clearly then intended not to be for any private purpose, but aimed squarely at the general populace.

Arguably this was the most politically sensitive task Shakespeare's company had ever been asked to perform, and frustratingly we have no way of knowing the behind-the-scenes discussions that went on – although the subsequent inquiry was told that those who called upon Shakespeare's company promised them forty shillings over and above their normal takings in order to make it worth their while. Events moved, however, with remarkable swiftness. As more people became aware of the secret plans afoot, it was inevitable that informers would have been at work. Also notices must have been posted of this hitherto unscheduled revival of a play now four years old.

The day booked for the performance was Saturday 7 February, and from subsequent court evidence we know that after having lunched 'at one Gunter's house over against Temple Gate' Sir Christopher Blount, Essex's steward Sir Gelly Meyrick, William Parker, Lord Monteagle, Sir Charles Percy, and Edward Bushell all crossed the Thames and took what must have been privileged and conspicuous positions in galleries around the Globe.

Inevitably someone in Essex's faction must have been playing the double-agent, and it was therefore arguably no coincidence that this same day Essex found himself served with a formal summons to attend the Privy Council forthwith. Fearing renewed imprisonment, and stalling for time by pleading ill-health, that evening he dined with Southampton, Danvers, Sir Christopher Blount, his sister Lady Rich, and others in order to plan the next move. All followers who could be gathered were summoned to assemble in the courtyard of Essex House the next morning, where as they were being mustered by Essex and Southampton there arrived a yet higher deputation from the Court – among these Essex's former gaoler, Sir Thomas Egerton – intent on finding out what was going on. These were seized and held under armed guard, whereupon there was now no going back for Essex, Southampton and their still ill-prepared army of only three hundred.

The original plan seems to have been for them to have gone to St Paul's Churchyard in order for Essex to address the large and potentially supportive gathering of citizens who normally assembled for the morning sermon. But time had been lost dealing with the Court delegation: the now forewarned civic authorities managed to block the City's entrance with a chain, Essex failed in an attempt to get extra weapons from London's Sheriff, and yet worse, Garter King-of-Arms and an accompanying posse managed to ride up to the would-be rebels and read them a royal proclamation declaring Essex a traitor.

Imperceptibly the first of Essex's followers began to melt away, and those who remained found their way repeatedly blocked, most notably by Sir John Leveson, brother of the very Leveson who had been one of Shakespeare and his colleagues' trustees over the Globe. Although a loyal fifty or so fought their way back to Essex House they soon found themselves under siege within it. With casualties increasing, Essex House's womenfolk hysterical, and the government forces bringing up heavy artillery capable of reducing the house and all within it to rubble, Essex and Southampton soon saw little option but to surrender. Within twenty-four hours of the opening hostilities they found themselves in London's ultimate gaol, the Tower, from which, ever thoughtful of his wife, Southampton seems to have contrived to send out this letter:

> Sweetheart, I doubt not but you shall hear ere my letter come to you of the misfortune of your friends. Be not too apprehensive of it, for God's will must be done, and what is allotted to us by destiny cannot be avoided. Believe that in this time there is nothing can so much comfort me as to think you are well and take patiently what hath happened. Contrariwise I shall live in torment if I find you vexed for my cause. Doubt not but I shall do well, and please yourself with the assurance that I shall ever remain
>
> your affectionate husband
H. Southampton[6]

Sadly, the fact that the letter is preserved among Cecil's papers strongly indicates that someone of that faction intercepted it so that Elizabeth Vernon never received it – and this despite whatever bribe Southampton would have paid its would-be carrier.

But even with Southampton, Essex and their most prominent supporters firmly under lock and key Elizabeth's government was by no means confident that they had the rebellion completely contained. During the succeeding days hundreds of troops were brought into the capital from the Home Counties, the justification proven as early as the following Friday when Essex's Captain Thomas Lee, who had attended the Globe performance of *Richard II*, was caught plotting to capture the Queen and force her to sign a warrant for Essex's release. On the Sunday five hundred armed troops stood by during the delivery of the sermon at St Paul's Cross, just in case the preacher incited the congregation to demonstrate on Essex's behalf.

There can be little doubt then that Shakespeare's company must have been quaking in their buskins at this time. On 18 February, the day that Captain Lee was publicly hanged, veteran Shakespeare colleague Augustine Phillips was hauled before government inquisitors, abjectly pleading that he 'and his fellows' had been most reluctant to perform *Richard II* at the conspirators' request. He told his questioners that the Lord Chamberlain's Men considered the play 'to be so old and so long out of use that they should have small or no company at it' (not necessarily true given the decade or more of revivals of *The Spanish Tragedy*). It had only been the 'forty shillings more than their ordinary' that had persuaded them to comply with the request.[7]

Whatever the truth, it was the very next day that Essex and Southampton were brought out to stand trial in historic Westminster Hall, the setting for Richard II's deposition, and precisely as featured in Shakespeare's play. Ironically *Gorboduc* co-author Thomas, Lord Buckhurst, the man to whom the dying Ferdinando had bestowed his trust, and who had succeeded Burghley as Lord Treasurer, presided as Lord High Steward. While there is no reason to doubt Buckhurst's fairness, reportedly when Essex and Southampton heard the name of Southampton's mortal enemy Lord Grey read out as among their jurors they could hardly resist a shared, albeit sardonic laugh. Equally wryly, they would have been more than a little reminded of *Hamlet* when, during a legal argument over Cecil's alleged espousal of the Spanish Infanta, little Secretary Cecil, hitherto apparently absent from the proceedings, agitatedly revealed himself Polonius-like from his place of concealment. He had been listening to everything behind a curtain – or could it have been an arras?

Inexorably, and despite Essex and Southampton both conducting their defence with considerable dignity (the seventeenth-century historian John Speed remarked that Southampton's 'sweet temper did breed most compassionate affections in all men'),[8] the one-day trial proceeded to an all too predictable guilty verdict. Whether or not Southampton had Portia's *Merchant of Venice* sentiments on his mind we have no way of knowing, but his closing words were carefully recorded:

> I do submit myself to death, yet not despairing of her Majesty's mercy; for I know she is merciful, and if she please to extend her mercy to me, I shall with all humility receive it.[9]

Lord High Steward Buckhurst's private inclinations are likewise unknowable, but under law he had only one sentence open to him. Thus upon Essex and upon the man with good reason identifiable as Shakespeare's one-time 'lovely boy' he solemnly pronounced:

> You both shall be led from hence to the place from whence you came, and there remain during her Majesty's pleasure; from thence to be drawn upon a hurdle through the midst of the City, and so to the place of execution, there to be hanged by the neck and taken down alive – your bodies to be opened, and your bowels taken out and burned before your face; your bodies to be quartered – your heads and quarters to be disposed of at her Majesty's pleasure, and so God have mercy on your souls.[10]

For a still edgy government speed was of the essence, because the longer Essex remained alive the greater was the opportunity either for a sympathetic popular uprising or for some ruse to spring him from the Tower. Preparations were therefore swift; Essex's Garter was physically stripped from him (ironically, the vacancy thus created among the Garter Knights was filled within three months by 'nidicock' William, sixth Earl of Derby), and what was purportedly his personal request for a private beheading rather than a public hanging was equally quickly agreed to.

Of particular interest to us is the timing. Someone very highly placed set 25 February, Ash Wednesday,[11] as the date for his execution, and it seems strikingly more than coincidence that the Chamber Accounts show Shakespeare's company as giving their Shrovetide performance before the Queen at Whitehall the preceding night. As usual history does not record the particular play they staged, but American theatre historian Professor Robert Sharpe has cogently suggested there can have been only one logical choice. In Sharpe's words:

> Elizabeth was perfectly capable of both bravado to conceal her real feelings and a very grim sort of humour. It may be that as a gesture of contempt, triumph and warning, she called Shakespeare and his fellows before her that evening in the presence of her uneasy Court and commanded them to perform the play in which she believed they had pointed out her weakness and foretold her deposition by Essex, the play of which they had given a special performance by

request of the Essex conspirators on the eve of the rebellion –
Richard the Second.[12]

For Shakespeare, whatever his part in the play (and some have
suggested this might even have been King Richard), to be obliged to
perform *Richard II* just for the sardonic satisfaction of this
increasingly hideous old woman surrounded by her pretty ladies and
grim bodyguards must have seemed a particularly Topcliffean
torture. For Essex the retribution was altogether swifter if more final.
Between seven and eight the next morning he was led out to a
prepared scaffold within the Tower precincts where, upon the third
attempt, his thirty-five-year-old head was severed from its body, thus
almost exactly fulfilling dying Lord Burghley's prophecy of him
'Bloody and deceitful men shall not live out half their days'. During
the ensuing month – some by the headsman's axe, others by gruesome
hanging, drawing and quartering – Essex was followed by his
stepfather Sir Christopher Blount, his steward Sir Gelly Meyrick, his
secretary Henry Cuffe, and Southampton's friend Sir Charles
Danvers, the latter reportedly preparing himself for the axe 'in most
cheerful manner, rather like a bridegroom, than a prisoner appointed
for death'. This particular piece of imagery, used in the 1631 edition
of Stow's *Annales* but almost certainly derived from an immediately
contemporary newsletter, seems to have haunted Shakespeare for he
would shortly use it for *Measure for Measure*[13] and later for *Antony
and Cleopatra.*[14] In the May deliberately crippling fines were levied
upon the Earl of Rutland (£30,000), the Earl of Bedford (£20,000),
Lord Sandys (£10,000), Lord Monteagle (£8,000), Lord Cromwell
(£6,000), Robert Catesby of Lapworth (4,000 marks), Sir Charles
Percy and Sir Joscelyn Percy (£500 each), Francis Manners (£500)
and Edward Bushell (100 marks).[15]

Meanwhile as execution swiftly followed execution, Southampton,
already sentenced to death, dallied in the Tower, ironically where he
had been conceived during his father's incarceration there twenty-
eight years before.[16] Both his wife and his mother directed
impassioned pleas for his life to Secretary Cecil, his mother
pertinently pointing out that he might never have turned to treason if
the Queen had not so consistently refused him over appointments
and freedom to travel. These pleas seem to have met their mark, for
his sentence was commuted to life imprisonment. A portrait survives
of him from these days that now hangs in Boughton House,

Northamptonshire [see pl. 37]. This portrays him by a glazed window, his hair shorter, his face older and more care-worn, dressed in black, accompanied by a black and white cat said to have climbed down the chimney to join him. At his elbow rests a finely bound book embossed with the Wriothesley coat of arms, azure, a gold cross between four silver falcons, topped with the earl's coronet that had been stripped from him. Although he protected his lands by transferring them to trustees, the government seized all his goods, a remnant of the inventory for these surviving in the Public Record Office.[17]

In fact the Essex affair left its mark on the Queen as well as on Southampton. Her keeper of records at the Tower, William Lambard, carefully noted how when in the August of 1601 he was at Greenwich Palace showing her his digest of the Tower's ancient 'rolls, bundles, membranes', etc, she suddenly 'fell upon the reign of King Richard II, saying, "I am Richard II, know ye not that?"' Lambard, realising she had the Essex affair on her mind, commented 'Such a wicked imagination was determined and attempted by most unkind Gent, the most adorned creature that ever your Majesty made', to which the Queen responded: 'He that will forget God will also forget his benefactors. This tragedy was played forty times in open streets and houses.'[18] It is ironic that this particular remark, from none other than the Queen herself, is our only piece of hard evidence for just how frequently Shakespeare's company performed *Richard II*.

Now while there is no overt record of Shakespeare's attitude to those involved in the Essex affair, there is no reason necessarily to suppose he was wholly on Essex's side, despite his friend Southampton being one of Essex's staunchest supporters. Dr A. L. Rowse has suggested that the sentiments expressed in *Much Ado about Nothing*:

> . . . like favourites,
> Made proud by princes, that advance their pride
> Against that power that bred it[19]

were an allusion to Essex, and since *Much Ado* was entered on the Stationers' Register in August of 1599, these would have to have been Shakespeare's feelings even before Essex's coup.

Much Ado was probably written as a light comedy to offset the heavyweight *Henry v*, *Julius Caesar* and *Hamlet* written for the Globe at around this same time. But even so it is of interest not only for its Essex allusion, but also for being the second instance of Shakespeare introducing Catholic friars into his plays (the first having been in *Romeo and Juliet*), Friar Francis again being a favourable portrayal. Indeed this is rather markedly more so than in *Romeo and Juliet* since, although Friar Francis counts only as a minor character, it is he who correctly perceives heroine Hero's innocence of the infidelity she has been accused of, and whose stratagem (equally desperate to that in *Romeo and Juliet*), succeeds in bringing the story to a happy ending, earning himself the appellation 'this holy friar' in the process.

It is also in *Much Ado* that, thanks to odd instances in the Quarto of 1600 in which actors' names replace those of the characters, we again know which of Shakespeare's company played particular parts. The malapropistic Constable Dogberry, for instance, was played by Will Kemp, and Dogberry's colleague Verges by Richard Cowley. The play may well, however, have been one of the last, if not *the* last, in which the veteran Kemp performed for the Lord Chamberlain's Men, for in February 1600 we find him setting off from the Lord Mayor's House in London, accompanied by his 'taborer' or drummer Thomas Sly, and William Bee his servant, apparently having accepted a bet to morris dance all the way to Norwich. This feat took him nine days and at the end of it he was rewarded by Norwich's Mayor. He later wrote about it in *Kemps Nine Daies Wonder, Performed in a Daunce from London to Norwich*, which was published in 1600, complete with an illustrative woodcut [see fig 8, opposite]. But as Kemp told Anne Fitton, sister of the Queen's maid of honour Mary, he had danced himself 'out of the world'[20] almost certainly meaning, out of the Globe. Indeed that there was some sort of falling out with his Lord Chamberlain's Men's fellows may well be indicated in *Hamlet* in which Hamlet pointedly urges his actors:

> And let those that play your clowns speak no more than is set down for them—[21]

Was this an allusion to Kemp having outworn his extempore style of comic acting? Certainly after his famous dance Kemp seems to have dropped out of any regular performing with the Lord Chamberlain's Men, and is thought to have died around 1603.

Fig 8
Will Kemp, one of the 'principal actors' who worked with
Shakespeare, depicted dancing his way to Norwich, accompanied
by his taborer. Note the morris dancer's bells on his legs.

Meantime such had been the raising of Shakespeare's public profile
by the spectacular Globe productions that the period immediately
preceding the Essex coup was unprecedentedly full of publication
activity. For 4 August 1600 a note on a spare page of the Stationers'
Register lists *As You Like It*, *Henry v* and *Much Ado about Nothing*
as 'to be staied', an apparent attempt to block unauthorised
publication, but even so a bad Quarto of *Henry v* and a good Quarto
of *Much Ado* appeared this same year. There was also a good
Midsummer Night's Dream, a good *Merchant of Venice*, and the
second part of *Henry iv*, together with reprints of *Henry vi*, *Parts ii*
and iii and *Titus Andronicus*. The newly printed works now almost
invariably carried Shakespeare's name as author. Indeed such was
the cachet of his name that the printer William Jaggard brought out
The Passionate Pilgrime. By W. Shakespeare... Sonnets To sundry
notes of Musicke in which only two sonnets (numbers 138 and 144)
actually belonged to Shakespeare. The rest were works by much
lesser writers and Jaggard was quite unauthorised to put it out in
Shakespeare's name.

Meanwhile Marston's newly founded Children of Paul's seems to have continued to give Shakespeare's company trouble, having the edge over the Globe in being able to attract a select, high-spending, sophisticated clientele as was gleefully trumpeted by Marston in his *Jack Drum's Entertainment* repartee:

> *Sir Edward Fortune*: I saw the Children of Paul's last night
>   And troth they pleas'd me pretty, pretty well
>   The apes in time will do it handsomely
> *Planet*: I faith, I like the audience that frequenteth there
>   With much applause: A man shall not be choked
>   With the stench of garlic; nor be pasted
>   To the balmy [?] jacket of a beer-brewer[22]

As pointed out by Sir Edmund Chambers the name 'Sir Edward Fortune' suggests Edward Alleyn of the Henslowe–Alleyn Fortune theatre, indicating a possible alliance between the latter and the Children of Paul's versus their common rival the Lord Chamberlain's Men.

Certainly the Lord Chamberlain's Men, despite all their apparent success with the Globe, seem to have been stung into facilitating the formation of a boys' company to compete with Marston and Derby's Children of Paul's, and in the light of the earlier mentioned Felix Pryor's findings, it would seem to have been in these circumstances that on 2 September 1600 the Burbages leased their still otherwise unused Blackfriars theatre to allow it to be used by the company previously thought to have been Shakespeare's 'little eyases', the Children of the Chapel, under Nathaniel Giles. Such boys' company private entertainments seem to have been perfectly acceptable to the Blackfriars residents because the theatre premises had been earlier used in this way. Although unthinkable of a common theatre production, the select few who came to these private theatre performances were allowed to sit on the stage.

The Children of the Chapel quickly became part of the entertainment circuit, for the Chamber accounts show them performing 'a show with music and special songs' before the Queen, on 6 January, shortly before the Essex rebellion, followed by 'a play' on 22 February, two days before Shakespeare's company's so uncomfortable royal command performance on the eve of Essex's execution. For Shakespeare's company's patron Lord Chamberlain

George Carey, who as we earlier noted, lived in the Blackfriars, the theatre may have been regarded as almost his own private theatre, for it would seem to have provided the entertainment upon the Queen's visit to his home on 29 December 1601. As reported by John Chamberlain:

> The Queen dined this day privately at my Lord Chamberlain's; I came even now from the Blackfriars, where I saw her at the play with all her *candidae auditrices*.[23]

A rare image of both Carey and the Queen at just this time is provided by a painting in Sherborne Castle, Dorset, showing Elizabeth in procession with her gentlemen pensioners and her maids of honour, and surrounded by recognisable members of her Court [see pl. 39]. George Carey is readily identifiable striding protectively ahead of her, his Garter just below his left knee and clasping his sword hilt and his wand of office as Lord Chamberlain. From the absence of the Earl of Essex in the painting, and the prominent presence in the foreground immediately below the Queen of Edward Somerset, fourth Earl of Worcester – Essex's successor as Master of the Horse – Sir Roy Strong has argued for the painting to post-date Essex's execution, being created specifically to commemorate Worcester's appointment in his stead.[24]

If this thinking is correct, then it was almost certainly in the same year as the procession picture was painted that Shakespeare wrote *Twelfth Night*. That the play was created no later than the end of 1601 is attested by a notebook jotting by student lawyer John Manningham, which shows it to have been performed at London's Middle Temple Hall on 2 February 1602:

> At our feast we had a play called *Twelve Night* or *What You Will*, much like the *Comedy of Errors* or *Menaechmi* in Plautus, but most like and near to that in Italian called *Inganni* [Gl'Ingannati].[25]

The fine hall where *Twelfth Night* would have been staged is still extant, thus providing a rare, if not unique, instance of a surviving location in which a Shakespeare play was performed in the author's lifetime, probably with Shakespeare himself among the cast. Although as recognised by Manningham, *Twelfth Night* is not particularly original, being based on the popular Italian comedy *Gl'Ingannati* as retold by Barnabe Tiche in *Riche his farewell to Militarie Profession*, it was in *Twelfth Night* that Shakespeare created, as immortally as Falstaff, the sycophantic steward Malvolio. The character, as played in Middle Temple Hall by a Lord Chamberlain's Men principal actor, was clearly as memorable for Manningham back in 1602 as it continues to be for audiences today. Manningham recalled what he had seen in one of the earliest surviving synopses of any Shakespeare play:

> A good practice in it to make the steward believe his Lady widow was in love with him by counterfeiting a letter as from his Lady in general terms, telling him what she liked best in him, and prescribing his gesture in smiling, his apparel, & c. And then when he came to practise making him believe they took him to be mad.[26]

But *Twelfth Night* was to prove a farewell to comedy, and whether or not it was a reflection of Shakespeare's feelings on the Essex affair and Southampton's imprisonment, literary commentators have noted a new mood of disenchantment in it. As remarked by the editor of the New Cambridge edition, we seem to be dealing 'with a man who (however we speculate on the cause of it) had somehow acquired, or was acquiring, a distrust of men's loyalty, and a suspicion alive to smell the fitch in woman's purity'.[27] Likewise Caroline Spurgeon, in her study of Shakespeare's imagery, noted *Twelfth Night* as the first of a succession of plays in which he begins to use plague images with a different tone. In her words, 'after 1600 every one of them is serious and used in a way that the gravity and horror of the disease are emphasised'.[28]

Likewise in *Troilus and Cressida*, which seems to have been written for private performance at this time, and in which A. L. Rowse has noted 'something of the relationship between Essex and Southampton reflected in that of Achilles and Patroclus', Shakespeare has Ulysses speak of Achilles as

> so plaguy proud that the death-tokens of it
> Cry 'No recovery'.[29]

Part of this new mood may lie in the fact that it was on 8 September of 1601 that Shakespeare's father John is recorded to have been buried at Holy Trinity. In the register he appears as 'Mr. Johannes

Shakspeare', thus dying with the recognised status of a gentleman. He left no formal will so under English common law his Henley Street house automatically passed to elder son William with Mary retaining right of residence and right to a third of his goods. Although he must have been in his early seventies, a good age by Elizabethan standards, John's was the first death of a close member of the family since that of young Hamnet, and it now firmly made Shakespeare the most senior member of the Shakespeare clan.

Another notable feature of this time is the occasional indication of Shakespeare's continued connection with the Stanley family. Curiously, in April of 1600 a so-called 'politique' group, Lord Treasurer Buckhurst among them, were reported favouring Ferdinando's eldest daughter Anne, now twenty, as Elizabeth's successor. But the particular involvement by Shakespeare occurs in his seemingly intended contribution of a poem, the first since his *Lucrece* for the Earl of Southampton, to a work entitled *Love's Martyr: Or Rosalin's Complaint. Allegorically shadowing the truth of Love, in the constant Fate of the Phoenix and the Turtle.* The Stanley connection here is that *Love's Martyr* was produced in honour of the long marital happiness of Sir John Salusbury of Lleweni, north Wales, with Ursula Stanley, Ferdinando's half-sister, a daughter of Ferdinando's father Henry through his long-standing extra-marital relationship with Jane Halsall.

By 1601 Salusbury and his wife Ursula had produced some ten children and were celebrating their silver wedding anniversary, the 'phoenix and turtle' poems of most of the other contributors to *Love's Martyr*, among these Ben Jonson, clearly reflecting this. Perplexingly, however, Shakespeare's haunting poem, very recognisably by him, and sixty-seven lines long, is quite different, presenting the phoenix and turtle as having died, and without leaving children:

> Death is now the phoenix' nest;
> And the turtle's loyal breast
> To eternity doth rest,
> Leaving no posterity—
> 'Twas not their infirmity,
> It was married chastity.

Scholarly explanations of this are almost as varied in number as those providing them. For one, the true Salusbury to whom *Love's Martyr* was dedicated was not Sir John, but his kinsman Captain Owen Salusbury, who had been one of the martyrs of the Essex rebellion, killed in the defence of Essex House.[30] For another, the phoenix and turtle represented Elizabeth and Essex[31] – an appealing theory though rather difficult to sustain given that Elizabeth was still alive. Another theorist has interpreted the turtle-dove as Shakespeare, and his phoenix as Anne Whateley, the mystery woman named on his original marriage licence, and purportedly 'the one and only woman he ever loved'. [32] According to yet another the lyric describes 'the failure of Shakespeare's poetical aspirations' because of his unfortunate over-indulgence in wine'.[33] Perhaps more convincing than most is Professor Ernst Honigmann's suggestion that, unlike the other poems in *Love's Martyr*, Shakespeare's may actually have been written back in 1586, when Sir John Salusbury's brother Thomas was executed as a traitor for his part in the Babington plot, an event that immediately preceded the Salusbury–Stanley marriage and must have overshadowed it.[34] Was the publication of Shakespeare's poem twenty-five years later by way of a *memento mori*?

Whatever the explanation, 'The Phoenix and the Turtle' quite definitely represents an indication of Shakespeare's continuing link with the Stanley family. This same period of 1601–03 seemed to furnish another, for writing in 1664 the antiquarian Sir William Dugdale, noted:

On the north side of the chancel of Tong Church, in the county of Salop, stands a very stately tomb, supported with Corinthian columns. It hath two figures of men in armour thereon lying . . . and this epitaph upon it: 'Thomas Stanley, Knight, second son of Edward, Earl of Derby,' etc.

Dugdale then went on:

These following verses were made by William Shakespeare, the late famous tragedian:

(Written upon the east end of the tomb)
Ask who lies here, but do not weep;
He is not dead, he doth but sleep.
This stony register is for his bones,
His fame is more perpetual than these stones;

And his own goodness, with himself being gone,
Shall live when earthly monument is none.

(Written upon the west end thereof)
Not monumental stone preserves our fame,
Nor sky-aspiring pyramids our name;
The memory of him for whom this stands
Shall outlive marble and defacers' hands;
When all to Time's consumption shall be given,
Stanley, for whom this stands, shall stand in heaven.[35]

'Sky-aspiring pyramids'? Strikingly, the tomb still extant at Tong features four St Peter's piazza style obelisks unmistakeably in the image of those created for the Southampton tomb at Titchfield back in 1594 [see pl. 41]. Although some doubt has been expressed regarding Shakespeare's authorship of the verses, they have persuasive echoes of the *Sonnets*, particularly *Sonnet* 55. As for the date of the monument and who might have commissioned Shakespeare to write the verses, the crucial clue lies in the man whose effigy reposes in the monument's lower tier: Edward Stanley, son of the Thomas and Margaret represented on the upper tier. The cousin of Ferdinando Stanley, who was a confidant at the time of the Hesketh letter back in 1593, Edward was a staunch Catholic whose London home in suburban Battersea was repeatedly under surveillance by Elizabeth's spy master Richard Topcliffe for its harbouring of priests.[36]

Edward Stanley did not die until 1632, long after Shakespeare, which is the prime reason why doubt has been expressed on the Tong epitaph being of Shakespeare's authorship. But clues on the monument's accompanying inscription, not least that this carries no mention of Sir Edward's knighthood bestowed upon him in 1603, show that it can be securely dated to around 1601–02. It is therefore perfectly possible that the epitaph was written by Shakespeare, just as stated by Dugdale. Edward Stanley's prime motive would seem to have been to honour his mother's wishes to be buried along with his father (she had remarried after being widowed), as expressed in her will[37] upon her death in 1596. As for Edward Stanley's incorporated effigy, Shakespeare in none other than *Much Ado*, continuing his already noted penchant for funerary monuments, specifically urged:

If a man do not erect in this age his own tomb ere he dies, he shall live no longer in monument than the bell rings and the widow weeps.[38]

Notably, everything about Edward Stanley and his family, as commemorated in the Tong monument, argues for their strong Catholicism, which yet again raises some key questions concerning Shakespeare's religious leanings.

If Shakespeare had death much on his mind during these early years of the seventeenth century, this was only because, as was becoming increasingly obvious, the Queen's death could not be long away. And there was no one more keenly conscious of this than Elizabeth herself.

CHAPTER 18

One of the King's Men

Such was the darker mood that had infected Shakespeare by 1602 that few would regard the play he most likely wrote at this time, *All's Well that Ends Well*, as one of his greatest. Nevertheless a feature particularly remarked upon by Arden editor G. K. Hunter is that it indicates 'Shakespeare had some knowledge of French ... the atmosphere is decidedly French; the names Parolles, Lavache and Lafeu seem to indicate a mind at work strongly imbued with a consciousness of French meanings'.[1] Not only does this reinforce the surprising acquaintance with French we noted Shakespeare had begun exhibiting with *Henry v*, we now discover what may have been the reason for this.

Thanks yet again to Professor Charles Wallace of the University of Nebraska, for the first time in Shakespeare's working life in London we actually know where he was lodging around the year 1602. In 1909, beavering away in the Public Record Office among great bundles of uncatalogued, unindexed documents preserved from the Elizabethan and Jacobean Court of Requests, Wallace came across testimony given in 1612 by 'William Shakespeare of Stratford upon Avon in the County of Warwick, gentleman'. Not only was this our Shakespeare, even complete with a dreadful signature, it described him as living 'ten years or thereabouts' previously (i.e. at least as early as 1602), in the house of Frenchborn 'tire maker' Christopher Mountjoie and his wife Marie, located at the junction of Silver Street and Mugwell, later Monkwell, Street, in London's parish of St Olave.[2]

Historians, among them Dr A. L. Rowse, have often somewhat loosely translated Mountjoie's tire maker profession as a wig maker, a logical enough associate for the landlord of an actor. But in fact it hardly does justice to the masterpieces of ornamental headdresses that 'tires' actually were. They were far closer to the work of a jeweller than a wig maker. Marie Mountjoie sent in an account for £59 – about £29,500 at today's values – for one of the tires she supplied in 1605.[3] In this light, set in the heart of the city's silver and goldsmiths' quarter, as the name Silver Street implies, Shakespeare's accommodation is hardly likely to have been spartan. Thomas Savage, the Lancashireborn goldsmith who we earlier noted as a trustee for Ferdinando's estates and for the Globe, had a house in the same street, while Lord Chamberlain's Men fellows Heminges and Condell lived a mere stone's throw away in the neighbouring St Mary Aldermanbury parish. And residing in a French-speaking household Shakespeare would have had every advantage to acquire a good working knowledge of French, and to ensure accuracy in the way he deployed it.

But *All's Well that End's Well*'s French background by no means exhausts the play's features of interest. It is above all a story of rings, one given by the King of France to physician's daughter Helena as a token of his protection after she has cured him of an incurable disease, the other a family heirloom owned by the socially superior Bertram, whose hand in marriage to Helena has been granted by the king against Bertram's own inclinations. After being thus obliged to marry Helena, Bertram rushes off to Florence, telling her that until she can get the ring from his finger 'which shall never come off', and until she begets a child by him, she may not consider herself his wife. Following Bertram to Florence Helena resourcefully substitutes herself in darkness in the bed of the Florentine woman whom she finds Bertram seducing, contrives an exchange of the rings, then, back in France makes it appear that she is dead. When Bertram, thinking he is now a widower, returns to Paris to make what he regards as a socially acceptable match, the ring he hands over is the one which the king had given Helena for her protection, whereupon he, recognising this, and suspecting villainy, orders Bertram's arrest. All only ends well when Helena reveals herself as alive, pregnant by Bertram and wearing his ring, whereupon he at last agrees that he will 'love her dearly, ever, ever dearly' – his last words in the play.

Now although, as usual, the name of the play is not stated, the Chamber accounts show that 'John Hemynges and the rest of his companie, servauntes to the Lorde Chamberleyne's Men' gave their last ever performance before the Queen at the royal palace of Richmond [see pl. 40] on 2 February 1603, just six weeks before her death. If it was *All's Well* they performed its theme of the rings would have had an extraordinary appositeness considering the events that followed. For at just about this time George Carey's sister

Katherine, wife of the Lord Admiral and one of Elizabeth's Ladies of the Privy Chamber died, reportedly confessing to the Queen on her deathbed that two years earlier, while the Earl of Essex had been under sentence of death, he had sent via a messenger the ring that the Queen had apparently given him when he was her favourite, as a token of her protection. Although the messenger should have handed this symbolic plea for the Queen's mercy to Lady Scrope, Katherine Carey's sister, thence to be handed to the Queen, on being given it in error Katherine had kept it back so that the Queen never received it.[4]

When Elizabeth heard this, she is said to have responded: 'God may forgive you, but I never can', thereupon falling into the state of deepest melancholy that marked the last weeks of her life. Complaining that her coronation ring, the symbol of her marriage to England, was too tight, she ordered this to be filed from her finger, and refused to go to bed, apparently 'because she had a persuasion that if she once lay down she would never rise'.[5] Her final moments came in the early hours of the morning of 24 March 1603, and when those of her Council who dared tried once again to get her to name her successor, only at the last, and with extreme reluctance, did she reportedly whisper to Cecil (and we have only his word for it), 'I will that a king succeed me, and who but my kinsman the King of Scots'.[6]

All's Well that Ends Well's ring theme is also oddly evocative of the events that immediately followed, for there had been yet another arrangement with a ring between Scotland's King James VI and the same Lady Scrope who should have received the Essex ring. Via an intermediary James had given Lady Scrope a sapphire ring that was only to be returned to him in the event of Elizabeth's death. In a manner typical of the verve of that era, upon the Queen's death Lady Scrope smuggled the ring out of the Palace window to her younger brother Robert Carey (brother also, of course, of Shakespeare's George), who thereupon decided to make an impetuous hell-for-leather dash with it to Scotland to bring the news to James, without even waiting for any formal government approval. In his diary, preserved for us through its publication in 1759 (the original now being lost), Robert recorded how he left London shortly after Elizabeth's death on the Thursday morning, and by that same night had reached Doncaster, a ride of 164 miles. After covering a further 136 miles the next day, by the Saturday night, and a further 97 miles, bloodied by a fall from his horse, he clattered into Holyrood Palace,

Edinburgh, and being immediately ushered into James' private chamber became the first to acclaim him as King of England, at one and the same time presenting the sapphire ring as proof of his news.[7]

In London, meanwhile, Secretary Cecil who, in anticipation of Elizabeth's demise, and in order to secure his own political future, had made his own secret overtures to James, met with the Privy Council to draw up the wording of the formal proclamation 'the high and mighty Prince, James the Sixth, King of Scotland, is now become our only lawful, lineal and rightful liege Lord, James the First, King of England'.[8] Read out publicly first at the Court gates, then by the Whitehall tiltyard, then in the City, before St Paul's, at the cross in Cheapside, and at Cornhill, and finally at the Tower, as noted by diarist Sir Roger Wilbraham it provoked 'no tumult, no contradiction, no disorder in the City; every man went about his business as readily, as peaceably, as securely as though there had been no change . . . the people . . . finding the fear of forty years for want of a known successor dissolved in a minute, do so rejoice as few wished the gracious queen alive again'.[9]

Although where Shakespeare heard the news is unknown, there is no evidence that suggests he was among those who, in Thomas Dekker's words 'rained showers of tears' for the old Queen.[10] Elizabeth's body was brought by barge from Richmond, and for a month lay in state at Whitehall, blazing with the jewels of England before being solemnly lowered into a vault in Westminster Abbey, atop that of her Catholic sister Queen Mary, buried on Elizabeth's orders and left monumentless except for the broken stones of Mary's Catholic altars torn down three years after Elizabeth's succession. Dark Lady Emilia's husband Alphonse Lanier was among the fifty-nine musicians who provided the funereal musical accompaniment.[11] Most of London's literati clamoured to compose appropriate farewell eulogies, and that Shakespeare was certainly expected to do so is suggested by an anonymous versifier's call:

> You poets all, brave Shakespeare, Jonson, Greene
> Bestow your time to write for England's Queen . . .
> Return your songs and Sonnets and your says
> To set forth sweet Elizabeth's praise[12]

The versifier was clearly ignorant of Robert Greene's death. Yet no tribute to Elizabeth has survived accredited to Shakespeare, a silence noted even at the time, particularly on the part of Henry Chettle, the publisher–dramatist who ten years before had been so supportive of Shakespeare in the wake of Greene's *Groats-worth*. Chettle wrote:

> Nor doth the silver-tonguèd Melicert,
> Drop from his honeyed Muse one sable tear
> To mourn her death who gracèd his desert,
> And to his lays opened her royal ear.
> Shepherd, remember our Elizabeth,
> And sing her rape, done by that Tarquin, Death.[13]

As most scholars are agreed, Chettle's 'honey' imagery and clear allusion to *Lucrece* strongly indicate Shakespeare to have been the subject of this rebuke, in which case Shakespeare's silence speaks eloquently enough of his feelings. Those who assume Shakespeare's Protestant orthodoxy often assume likewise his unquestioning admiration of Elizabeth, yet while they are almost certainly right to believe he did not condone the Essex rebellion against her, this is not the same as his approving of her responsibility for the deaths of so many worthy young people, from Mary Queen of Scots to Robert, Earl of Essex, nor of her life imprisonment of the Earl of Southampton. As we have already seen, not only does the very timbre of Shakespeare's work in the wake of Essex's execution and Southampton's imprisonment attest to a deep emotional gloom, he would appear more than anything to have detested the sort of hypocrisy and sycophancy that an insincere eulogy would have demanded.

In the event, even before leaving Edinburgh for a journey to London that would take him five weeks (quite a contrast to Robert Carey's three days), James sent ahead orders for Southampton's immediate release from the Tower – a mark of how closely he identified Essex and Southampton with espousing his claim as Elizabeth's successor. By the time James arrived at Cecil's grand house, Theobalds, just to the north of London, Southampton was able to meet him there and shortly after, as part of a major new honours list, James restored Southampton to his earldom, made him a Knight of the Garter and, to help his ruined fortunes, granted him the same sweet wine monopoly that Elizabeth had taken away from Essex.

For Shakespeare and his company, meanwhile, one effect of the

Queen's death had been an immediate government ban on all stage plays, another was a loss of status through George Carey automatically losing his Lord Chamberlain's post, the company thereupon again becoming simply Lord Hunsdon's Men. More serious, however, was that Carey, now fifty-six, was in markedly declining health. When his younger brother Robert left on his dash to Scotland, he noted the toll taken upon George by many sleepless nights watching the Queen's life slowly ebb away, but George's main trouble seems to have been syphilis, as evident from a contemporary lampoon:

> Chamberlain, Chamberlain,
> He's of Her Grace's kin,
> Fool hath he ever bin
> With his Joan silverpin
> She makes his cockscomb thin
> And quake in every limb
> Quicksilver is in his head
> But his wit's dull as lead
> Lord for thy pity . . .[14]

Though history does not record the name of George's 'Joan silverpin' the nature of his illness is evident from the lampoon's reference to quicksilver, or mercury, always a standard Elizabethan treatment for syphilis. By 6 April, just as James was beginning his progress southwards, Carey was relieved of his duties. Once again, Shakespeare's company faced an uncertain future.

As it happens, James had hardly been in London for more than a few days before he made some crucial decisions concerning the whole acting profession. Although to satisfy something of the City authorities' long-standing hostility towards actors he abolished all troupes of players, he then adroitly reserved to himself the right to maintain one company for his own household, a second for that of his wife, Anne of Denmark, and a third for his nine-year-old son Prince Henry. Accordingly the Alleyn–Henslowe company that had been the Admiral's Men became Prince Henry's Men; the old Earl of Worcester's Men (performing at the Curtain), became the Queen's Men; and the Children of the Chapel at Blackfriars became the Children of the Queen's Revels.

The plum appointment was, however, reserved for Shakespeare's

company. Through what can only have been a special recommendation by someone of influence, on 17 May James instructed his Keeper
of the Privy Seal to draw up for Shakespeare's company Letters Patent
under the Great Seal of England appointing them the King's Men,
that is his own company of players, a title they would carry
throughout the rest of James' reign and beyond that into the reign of
Charles I. Still extant in London's Public Record Office are James'
two original warrants and, as a splendid piece of calligraphy, the
formal Letters Patent drawn up on 19 May, licensing:

> these our servants Lawrence Fletcher, William Shakespeare,
> Richard Burbage, Augustine Phillips, John Heminges, Henry
> Condell, William Sly, Robert Armin, Richard Cowley and the rest
> of their associates freely to use and exercise the art and faculty of
> playing comedies, tragedies, histories, . . . and such others . . . as
> well for the recreation of our loving subjects as for our solace and
> pleasure when we shall think good to see them during our pleasure.
> And the said comedies, tragedies . . . and suchlike to show . . . to
> their best commodity . . . as well within their now usual house
> called the Globe within our county of Surrey, as also within any
> town halls or moot halls or other convenient places within the
> liberties and freedom of any other city, university, town (& c).[15]

At a stroke James had done more for the acting profession and in
particular for Shakespeare's company in the first ten days of his
taking the reins than Elizabeth had done in all her forty-five years.
The new name heading the list of players, that of Lawrence Fletcher,
comes initially as a surprise, but in fact he was an English 'comediane
serviteur' who as early as 1594 had entertained James in Scotland,
and whom James had supported when Edinburgh's city authorities,
like London's, had tried to prevent his settling and performing plays
there.[16] His sudden inclusion in Shakespeare's company may well
have been mostly nominal, for there are few indications that he ever
had an active role.

The fact that Shakespeare's name now preceded all the rest of his
fellows is interesting, suggesting that whoever made the crucial
recommendation for the company to become the King's Men had
Shakespeare particularly in mind, Professor Akrigg, for one,
detecting in this the hand of the newly released Southampton.
Burbage, whose name follows Shakespeare's, had an additional

cause for self-congratulation, having in the January become a father of his first-born daughter whom he named Juliet. For the first time in any official list we can find Robert Armin, successor to Kemp as clown, although he had probably been with the company for some while. Shakespeare most likely wrote the 'wise fool' parts of Feste in *Twelfth Night* and Lavache in *All's Well* specially for him. A notable omission is Thomas Pope, seemingly due to ill health, for his still extant will[17] was made out on 2 July, leaving all his rights in the Globe to 'Marie Clark, alias Wood, and to . . . Thomas Bromley'. Unusual among the wills of the players, Pope's contains no kindly remembrances to those with whom he worked. Since the will was proved on 13 February of the following year he must have died in the interim.

The Letters Patent's full text also includes the words 'when the infection of the plague shall decrease' signalling the ever-dreaded news that hard upon the heels of the government's 'period of mourning' ban on stage plays, plague had again made its return, resulting in further curtailment of the players' activities. So severe was this particular outbreak that by mid-July more than a thousand Londoners were dying per week, causing such an exodus that when on 25 July James was formally crowned as England's first king in fifty years the ceremony was closed to ordinary commoners, and the traditional procession postponed until a time when the city could give him a better welcome.

Sometime during this year Shakespeare's company must have put on some performances at the Globe because Ben Jonson's Folio of 1616 shows his *Sejanus* as performed in 1603 with Richard Burbage and Shakespeare heading such familiar names as Augustine Phillips, John Heminges, Will Sly, Henry Condell and Alexander Cooke. But despite such a distinguished cast *Sejanus* is unlikely to have improved the company's fortunes for, although being written with all Jonson's cherished concern for classical purity and historical accuracy, it proved a box-office flop.

Far more successful for Jonson was the devising of one of the entertainments staged for King James' wife Anne of Denmark's progress southward in the wake of her husband. Jonson's contribution was at the Spencer family seat Althorp (the family home of Ferdinando Stanley and George Carey's wives Alice and Elizabeth), where he devised a suitably amusing playlet with an actor or servant dressed as a satyr springing from a tree to indulge in banter with the Queen of the Fairies. This seems to have started a vogue for similar masque-type court entertainment which Jonson would go on to make his particular forte.

Meanwhile one of the plague's victims was Jonson's seven-year-old son, whose death Jonson psychically 'saw' while staying in Huntingdon, only to have this confirmed by a distraught message from his wife in London.[18] Provincial account books show Shakespeare's company having done their usual touring during the epidemic, performing in Bath, Shrewsbury, Coventry and Ipswich on unspecified dates. James I's Court for its part kept out of London likewise, dallying particularly long at Wilton, seat of Philip Sidney's sister Mary, Countess of Pembroke, and her son, the twenty-three-year-old William Herbert, third Earl of Pembroke, whom James made a Garter Knight at the same time as Southampton, and who was later to be one of the dedicatees of the Shakespeare First Folio. Although the present-day Wilton House is much altered since Countess Mary's time, when its fine collection of books was said to have made it 'like a College', in its Front Hall stands a splendid mid-eighteenth century statue of Shakespeare by Peter Scheemakers, commemorating the undoubted historic fact that Shakespeare's company visited James' Court while it stayed at Wilton between 24 October and 12 December, for the Chamber Accounts record for December 2:

> John Heminges, one of his Majesty's players ... for the pains and expenses of himself and the rest of the company in coming from Mortlake in the county of Surrey unto the Court aforesaid and there presenting before his Majesty one play. £30.[19]

The fact that the company was at Mortlake when they received their summons tallies with the independently known fact that Shakespeare's fellow actor Augustine Phillips, who had received a grilling over the pre-Essex Rebellion performance of *Richard II*, had recently leased a country house there, possibly having the whole company staying with him, rehearsing for new productions and keeping their memories fresh of old ones while they awaited an abatement of the plague.

We may even glimpse at least the ghost of a record of the play they performed for the King on making the eighty-mile journey to Wilton. In August 1865 historian William Cory wrote of a visit to Wilton House when he was told by the then Lady Herbert that 'we have a letter, never printed, from Lady Pembroke [i.e. Countess Mary] to her son, telling him to bring James I from Salisbury to see *As You Like It*.'[20] Apparently the letter, never subsequently found, included the words 'we have the man Shakespeare with us'.

Whatever the truth of the story, that Shakespeare's company, almost inevitably with Shakespeare with them, performed at Wilton on 2 December is a matter of firm historical record. *As You Like It* quite plausibly was the play they presented, as it demanded the minimum of props. We also know that Southampton was with the King at Wilton at this time, and since this represents the first recorded occasion from which we may gauge Shakespeare to have seen his new royal master at close hand, it is of interest to try to recapture something of the chemistry of the encounter. Here we can only note that the first impression James created for those who met him was often less than favourable [see pl. 42]. The sharp-eyed diarist Lady Anne Clifford, only thirteen when she and her mother were introduced to James on his journey south from Scotland, noted:

> we all saw a great change between the fashion of the Court as it is now and of that in the Queen's time, for we were all lousy by sitting in the chamber of Sir Thomas Erskine.[21]

From other sources we learn that although James was two years younger than Shakespeare, he wholly lacked the regal dignity Elizabeth had maintained to the last. Ever fearful of an assassination attempt, he wore heavily padded doublets to protect him against any attack with a stiletto. From a description by Sir Anthony Weldon his tongue was 'too large for his mouth, which ever made him drink very uncomely, as if eating his drink.... His skin was as soft as taffeta sarsenet, which felt so because he never washed his hands, only washed his fingers' ends slightly with the wet end of a napkin'.[22] Apparently due to a drunken wet-nurse 'his legs were very weak ... he was not able to stand at seven years of age; that weakness made him ever leaning on other men's shoulders.' When he did walk, his gait was at best a circuitous shamble 'his fingers ever in that walk fiddling about his cod-piece'. His Scots accent was of the broadest.

Nonetheless this was a passably tolerant, pedantically scholarly, over-demonstrably affectionate man with already twenty years in full charge of the Scottish throne, who would go on to give his English one a further twenty-two of unbroken peace and prosperity. And whatever Shakespeare may privately have thought of James' appearance, James certainly liked what he saw of Shakespeare's company. Upon the Court's moving back to Hampton Court for the Christmas, the Chamber Accounts show the King's Men performing no less than six plays between 26 December and 1 January, followed by a further two at Whitehall the nights of Candlemas and Shrove Tuesday. Not only was this a larger number than Elizabeth had ever called for, James also paid them more handsomely, granting them, besides £53 for the performances themselves, a further £30 'free gift' for their maintenance and relief' till it should 'please God to settle the City in a more perfect health'.[23] As usual we have no information on how many of the productions were Shakespeare's (though there are indications that one was *A Midsummer Night's Dream*)[24] but with the new King and Queen imposing such unprecedented demand upon the 'stock' repertoire, the pressure had to be on for Shakespeare to write anew. There must be considerable interest concerning the first play he wrote for this new regime.

The play that seems most likely is *Measure for Measure*, which has some clear internal pointers to its composition with James in mind, around late 1603 to early 1604. In the early brothel scene Shakespeare has the madame, Mistress Overdone, complain:

Thus, what with the war, what with the sweat, what with the gallows, and what with poverty, I am custom-shrunk.[25]

followed by her servant Pompey's remark a few lines later:

You have not heard of the proclamation, have you?
. . .
All houses in the suburbs of Vienna must be pluck'd down.[26]

Despite the setting being Vienna, this is in fact quite clearly a reference to the London of the 1603 plague (the 'sweat') for on 16 September 1603 there was a specific proclamation calling for the pulling down of houses and rooms in London's suburbs, aimed particularly at the 'dissolute and idle persons' of the brothels and gaming houses surrounding the Globe, while Mistress Overdone's reference to 'the war' demands a time before August 1604 when the long-running feud with Spain was finally settled with a peace treaty.

Another indication of *Measure for Measure*'s date derives from the second act in which the Duke's deputy Angelo remarks how the subjects of:

> ... a well-wish'd king
> ... in obsequious fondness
> Crowd to his presence, where their untaught love
> Must needs appear offence.[27]

In fact James had had little opportunity to feel the pressure of crowds, even during his postponed coronation procession (for which Shakespeare and his fellows were each issued with four and a half yards of 'skarlet red cloth' for their liveries),[28] the populace having been orderly. But at about this same time, having a mind to watch the activities of the dealers at London's Royal Exchange, James went along disguised as a merchant, whereupon, his presence being 'leaked', he suddenly found himself very much the centre of crowd attention, agitatedly warning them, according to a tract, *Time Triumphant*, subsequently co-authored by Shakespeare's Robert Armin, that if they 'in love press upon your sovereign thereby to offend him, your sovereign perchance mistake your love and punish it as an offence'.[29] The closeness of these words to Angelo's in *Measure for Measure* suggests that Shakespeare specifically had Armin's tract in mind when he wrote the play.

A further aspect, as noted by Dr A. L. Rowse, is that Shakespeare appeared to have modelled *Measure for Measure*'s Duke Vincentio upon King James, the fascinating feature of the play thereby being that Shakespeare had the Duke go in disguise, just as James had done at the Royal Exchange, but in the guise of a Franciscan friar. As the story runs, the Duke, claiming the need to go away, temporarily passes his kingdom over to the legalistic and Puritanical Lord Angelo, thereupon taking up the guise of a friar to observe how Angelo conducts state affairs. In the event Angelo, while applying excessively harshly Vienna's death penalty for extra-marital sex, commits the same offence himself. The disguised Duke meanwhile, aided by two real Catholic friars, so manipulates events behind the scenes that Angelo is ultimately brought face to face with the criminality of his hypocrisy, and order is then restored.

From a story loosely based on one from Italian Giraldi Cinthio's *Hecatommithi*, written back in 1565, Shakespeare made *Measure for Measure* a very great Christian play – indeed his most Christian play, founded, as evident from the story line, upon Jesus's central teaching.

> Judge not and you shall not be judged. For with what judgement you judge you shall be judged, and with what measure you mete, it shall be measured to you again.[30]

But the further feature, as has been pointed out by Catholic scholars Father Christopher Devlin and Father Peter Milward, is that, set in Catholic Vienna, and with the Duke disguising himself as a friar, and seriously and movingly hearing confession (besides being Duke, Vincentio notably symbolises God in the play), it is a very Catholic play, in Devlin's words:

> worked out in terms of explicitly *Roman* Catholic, Papist symbols: the proscribed habits of St Francis and St Clare, and the proscribed Sacrament of Confession and Absolution.[31]

In this, his third play to feature Franciscan friars, Shakespeare presents them in the most overtly favourable light yet. And this from what we have construed to be very probably his first play under King James' patronage.

The clue to what was happening here would appear to lie in the real hopes entertained by England's Catholics, in the wake of their forty-five years of repression under Elizabeth, that James, although brought up as a Protestant in a country that had expelled his Catholic mother, Mary Queen of Scots, would bring in a whole new era of toleration for them. These hopes were clearly entertained by the redoubtable Father Persons, writing from Rome within four months of James' accession, to his Jesuit opposite number in England, Father Henry Garnet, that:

> such applause was here generated at this new King's entrance as if he had been the greatest Catholic in the world .... His Holiness here is so far embarked to try what may be done by fair means with him as, until the contrary do appear by manifest proofs and that it be confirmed also by sufficient time, he will hearken to nothing against him.[32]

Encouragingly, such was the state of religious ambivalence that even

James' wife, Anne of Denmark, was secretly of Catholic sympathies. But if in *Measure for Measure* Shakespeare aimed to appeal to James' religious persuasions at a fundamental level, any such aims were subverted by the rather less worthy efforts of others in the theatrical fraternity.

When, in the wake of the plague the theatres were allowed to open again in April 1604, within three months James was being ridiculed on the stage, seemingly with his wife Anne's active encouragement. French ambassador de Beaumont wrote on 14 June 1604: 'For pity's sake consider what must be the state and condition of a Prince whom the preachers openly attack in the pulpit, whom the comedians of the metropolis bring upon the stage, and whose wife attends these representations in order to enjoy the laugh against her husband.'[33]

While there is no clear record of what Shakespeare's company performed at the Globe during the summer season of 1604, in the August James had further plans for them. After Elizabeth's long years of wars with Philip II, who had died in 1598, James now sought peace with a resumption of diplomatic relations, inviting to Somerset House for this purpose a delegation headed by the newly appointed Spanish ambassador Juan Fernandez de Felasco, Constable of Castile, and his train of Spanish and Flemish commissioners. The formal side of their business is commemorated by a magnificent painting in the National Portrait Gallery in London [see pl. 43], showing the negotiators face-to-face, prominent among them Secretary Cecil, created Viscount Cranborne during the proceedings. For the informal side there survives in the Public Record Office an account of the Treasurer of the King's Chamber[34] showing that James paid Augustine Phillips, John Heminges and ten of their 'fellows' to attend the Spanish at Somerset House as 'grooms of the Chamber and Players'. One of these fellows will almost inevitably have been Shakespeare, no doubt wearing his scarlet livery for the occasion[35], but frustratingly there survives no record of what entertainment they performed for the overseas visitors.

What there are signs of is that under the pressure of James and his Queen's unprecedented appetite for theatrical entertainments, the King's Men's repertoire was beginning to run out. This is quite evident from an undated letter from Sir Walter Cope to Cecil, regarding entertainments suitable for the Queen's welcoming her brother from Denmark:

I have sent and been all this morning hunting for players, jugglers and such kind of creatures, but find them hard to find. Wherefore leaving notes for them to seek me, Burbage is come and says there is no new play that the Queen has not seen. But they have revived one called *Love's Labour's Lost*, which for wit and mirth, he says, will please her exceedingly. And this is appointed to be played tomorrow night at my lord of Southampton's, unless you send a writ to remove the *corpus cum causa* to your house in the Strand. Burbage is my messenger, ready attending your pleasure.[36]

The fact that this of all plays was being performed at 'my lord of Southampton's' reinforces our earlier argument that Shakespeare originally wrote it for Southampton, and equally hints, for all the lack of hard evidence, at a continuing close reciprocity between Shakespeare and Southampton's courtly circle.

During the next few years Shakespeare's company would perform an annual average of thirteen Court appearances, compared to the three they had been used to during Elizabeth's last ten years. Their average rate of pay per appearance also doubled. The pressure was therefore on for Shakespeare to write more, and again it is reasonably easy to identify the play he wrote after *Measure for Measure*.

Here, the most crucial document for dating purposes is an account prepared under the supervision of Edmund Tilney, the longstanding Master of the Revels who had dealt with Lord Cobham over the Oldcastle affair, detailing his expenses supplying plays for the year 1 November 1604 to 31 October 1605. Of those performed by 'the King's Majesty's players' Tilney records:

Hallowmas Day, being the first of November a play in the Banqueting House at Whitehall called *The Moor of Venice*

The Sunday following [4 November] a play of *The Merry Wives of Windsor*

On St Steven's Night [26 December] in the Hall, a play called *Measure for Measure*

On Innocent's Night [28 December] the play *Comedy of Errors*

Between New Year's Day and Twelfth Day [5 January] a play of *Love's Labour's Lost*

On the 7 of January was played the play of *Henry the fifth*

The 8 of January a play called *Every One [Man] out of his Humour*

On Candlemas Night [2 February] a play *Every One [Man] in his Humour* . . .

On Shrove Sunday [10 February] a play of *The Merchant of Venice* . . .

On Shrove Tuesday [12 February] a play called *The Merchant of Venice* again commanded by his Majesty.[37]

Under a heading for 'the poets which made the plays' appears the name 'Shaxberd' which seems a more than usually grotesque version of the spelling of Shakespeare's name, and has been suggested as perhaps the rendering of a newly arrived Scottish scribe. Nor have historians been without doubts over the document's authenticity, although thankfully these have been resolved both by chemical tests of the 'ink' and by corroboration of the financial details from indisputably genuine final Declared Accounts.[38] There is now an overwhelming consensus in favour of the document's authenticity.

Given that this is the case, the importance of the Revels Account is that it provides our best record by far of royal and specifically Jacobean appreciation of Shakespeare's plays in his lifetime. For the first time we see an official listing of the plays performed in the royal presence. We are able to see that James liked *The Merchant of Venice* so much – tickled probably by Portia's legalistic niceties in the court scene – that he asked for a repeat performance. We can see that Shakespeare and his fellows were still performing their now hoary old *Comedy of Errors*. We are provided with the first positive record of a performance of *Measure for Measure*. But head of the programme we also see the first record of a performance of Shakespeare's first great tragedy under James' patronage: the play more familiar as *Othello* appearing under its sub-title *The Moor of Venice*.

Now neatly linking *Othello* with its immediate predecessor *Measure for Measure* is the fact that its principal source may again be traced to a story in Giraldi Cinthio's *Hecatommithi*. But why did Shakespeare, so many years after creating Aaron the Moor for *Titus Andronicus*, now choose to devote a whole play to a black man? Here, while the evidence eludes us for exactly what went on behind the scenes, it can hardly have been a coincidence that, as a later piece of entertainment for this Christmas season, Queen Anne of Denmark had asked Ben Jonson to create a masque in which she and her ladies were to appear disguised as 'blackamoors'. Springing directly from

Jonson's virtuous creations for the Queen's arrival at Althorp, followed by even more sumptuous spectacles that he had arranged during the coronation procession, *The Masque of Blackness* set entirely new precedents for female aristocratic behaviour. Before startled ambassadors, amid scenery designed by Inigo Jones for which no expense was spared, a scantily clad and highly pregnant Queen Anne appeared 'strangely mounted ... in a great concave shell, like mother of pearl, curiously made to move on [the] waters and rise with the billow'.

Accompanying her were 'the Ladies Suffolk, Derby, Rich, Effingham, Anne Herbert, Susan Herbert, Elizabeth Howard, Walsingham and Bevil' equally lightly clad, and like the Queen 'their faces and arms up to their elbows ... painted black'.[39] Intriguingly the reference to Lady Derby may well describe Ferdinando's widow the Dowager Countess Alice, blackened, who reportedly like the others 'danced with their men several measures' – slow, stately dances – 'and corantoes' – very lively, literally 'running' dances.

Whatever common origin *The Masque of Blackness* and *Othello* might have shared in a royal whim, what Shakespeare created in *Othello* was something with a power, an emotional charge, and a quality far more enduring than Jonson's production. With little doubt it would have been staged for a small fraction of Jonson's £3,000 budget, out of which Jonson did not even have to pay the performers. Unlike most other of Shakespeare's creations in which he offset tragic themes with comic sub-plots, including *Measure for Measure*, in *Othello* he allowed nothing to interfere with the central story of the innocent young wife Desdemona being murdered by her intensely passionate and doting black husband Othello due to a misunderstanding deliberately engendered by the evil Iago. Both tradition and logic have it that it was Burbage who blacked up to play Othello, and although we have no exact contemporary description, from as early as 1610 there survives an Oxford don's 'review' in Latin of an *Othello* performance that Shakespeare's company gave at Oxford. This conveys that equally as moving as the performances by veterans such as Burbage were those of the young men playing the women's parts, as in the case of the one playing Desdemona, who at the end of the play had to lie motionless and speechless on the great bed that is one of *Othello*'s obligatory pieces of stage furniture. As remarked by the don:

Not only by their speaking but by their acting they drew tears. Indeed Desdemona, killed by her husband, although she always acted the matter very well, in her death moved us even more greatly when lying in bed she implored the pity of the spectators with her face alone.[40]

Notable here is how by sheer acting ability the members of Shakespeare's company, youngsters as well as veterans, 'became' their parts with acting that would seem, at Shakespeare's specific urging, to have been utterly realistic.[41]

Equally notable is that Desdemona is the only name in the play that Shakespeare derived from his source. Each of the others are of his own conjuration – including Othello and, of particular remark, Emilia for Iago's wife. If A. L. Rowse is right that Emilia Lanier was Shakespeare's Dark Lady the use of her name at this time for the wife of one of the blackest of Shakespeare's villains, a woman whom that same villain claims to have had an adulterous affair with Othello, can hardly have been without its own emotional undercurrent. Curiously, the Emilia of *Othello* is no Dark Lady; although worldly, she is basically good-hearted. But overall it is clear that, like an adrenalin surge, the patronage of James I had suddenly released a whole flood of new creativity into Shakespeare. And *Othello* was merely its opening shot.

CHAPTER 19

Under the Tragic Muse

In late May of 1605 there was published a quaint booklet called *Ratseis Ghost, or the Second Parte of his Madde Pranks and Robberies*, principally relevant to us for its recommendation to an actor to get to London, to live frugally there, and then

> when thou feelest thy purse well lined, buy thee some place or Lordship in the Country, that growing weary of playing, thy money may there bring thee to dignity and reputation.

To this, the actor gratefully replies that he will use this good advice:

> for I have heard indeed, of some that have gone to London very meanly, and have come in time to be exceedingly wealthy.[1]

While we cannot be sure that this specifically alluded to Shakespeare, it was apposite enough for him and his fellow sharers in the Globe venture. One indication of the scale of money that Shakespeare certainly made from his holding of shares is that within three years of the Globe opening its doors he was able to invest £320 cash – five times the amount he had paid for New Place – in one hundred and seven acres of prime arable land that he purchased from his wealthy Stratford neighbours the Combes. The indenture for this transaction, signed in Shakespeare's absence by his brother Gilbert in a well-educated hand, is preserved in the Records Office of the Shakespeare Birthplace Trust at Stratford-upon-Avon.[2] It is followed by an even more impressive indenture made out in July 1605 whereby he invested another £440 in a half-interest in a lease of 'tithes of corn, grain, blade and hay' in the Stratford hamlets of Old Stratford, Welcombe and Bishopton.[3] A retirement income was clearly the intention in both instances, but such land-owning also carried with it certain privileges, among these the honour of being buried in the chancel of the local church, thus precisely corresponding to Ratsei's words 'that growing weary of playing, thy money there may bring thee to dignity and reputation'.

That Shakespeare was not alone among his fellows in such status-building is evident from one of his fellow shareholders in the Globe, company veteran Augustine Phillips. 'Sick and weak in body' Phillips made out his will on 4 May 1605,[4] and this shows him, just like Shakespeare, to be a family man with a well-lined purse. Like Shakespeare he clearly had a penchant for a coat of arms, for in a curious note of around 1604 the Rouge Dragon herald at the College of Arms complained to the Earl of Northampton that 'Phillips the player had graven in a gold ring the arms of Sir William Phillip. Lord Bardolph, with the said Lord Bardolph's coat quartered which I showed to Mr York at a small [en]graver's shop in Foster Lane'.[5] This may have been a mere piece of fun on Phillips' part, perhaps from having played one of the red-nosed Bardolphs in Shakespeare's plays. But, like Shakespeare, Phillips definitely raised his status to country gentry. From originating as a mere householder in the parish of St Saviour's, Southwark, where the baptisms of two of his daughters are recorded in 1594 and 1596, and that of a non-surviving son in 1601, he acquired his country property in Mortlake. This, as we suggested earlier, may well have been substantial enough tem-porarily to accommodate members of the company during the 1603 plague. As his will indicates, it certainly gave him the gentlemanly privilege of being buried in the chancel of Mortlake church. For one of Shakespeare's time, this was what 'dignity and reputation' were all about.

For us, however, unquestionably the chief feature of interest of Phillips' will is its tone of affection, as extended both to his family and to his fellow players. The bulk of his estate Phillips shared out between his wife Anne, whom he made executrix, and their four daughters. But in the most kindly manner he also left thoughtful remembrances to his fellow players, thereby providing a virtual company roll-call of these:

I give and bequeath ... amongst the hired men of the company which I am of the sum of five pounds to be equally distributed amongst them. I give and bequeath to my fellow William Shakespeare a thirty shilling piece in gold, to my fellow Henry Condell, one other thirty shilling piece in gold; to my servant Christopher Beeston, thirty shillings in gold; to my fellow

Lawrence Fletcher twenty shillings in gold; to my fellow Robert Armin . . . [ditto]; to my fellow Richard Cowley . . . [ditto]; to my fellow Alexander Cooke [ditto]; to my fellow Nicholas Tooley [ditto] . . . I give to Samuel Gilbourne, my late apprentice, the sum of forty shillings, and my mouse coloured velvet hose, and a white taffeta doublet, a black taffeta suit, my purple cloak, sword and dagger, and my bass viol. I give to James Sands, my apprentice, the sum of forty shillings and a cittern, a bandore and a lute, to be . . . delivered unto him at the expiration of his term of years in his indenture of apprenticehood . . . And [in the event of his wife Anne remarrying] . . . I ordain and make . . . John Heminges, Richard Burbage, William Sly and Timothy Whithorn overseers of this my present testament and last will, and I bequeath . . . for their pains herein to be taken a bowl of silver to the value of five pounds apiece.[6]

Besides more than a hint of the ethos of 'all for one and one for all' so necessary in a company whose success depended on its members' mutual support, readily discernible from Phillips' will, and arguably more so than from any of the earlier documents we have come across, is what a carefully ordered 'family business' of hired men, apprentices, servants and fellows proper that Shakespeare's company of the early 1600s comprised. It provides, indeed, one of the best justifications for our earlier arguments that Shakespeare served a long, thorough, formal apprenticeship as an actor.

There is something reassuringly solid about the way valuable items such as musical instruments, weaponry and fine clothing can be seen thoughtfully passed on to their next most deserving recipient. Equally notable is how Phillips nominates as his legal overseer trusty book keeper Heminges, responsible during the previous eight years for collecting the company's fees from their royal performances, significantly not choosing for this an arguably dreamy writer like Shakespeare. Yet here Shakespeare is being remembered in this modest and domestic document with obvious affection, and here also are those men who were the first to perform *Hamlet*, *Othello* and other timeless plays on the stage. Instead of mere names on a cast list, from Phillips' will Shakespeare and his fellows suddenly emerge as a real 'family'.

With the quest for ideas for what to write next for this family as one of his chief responsibilities, Shakespeare seems, magpie-like, to have looked everywhere. In the case of *Othello*'s successor his inspiration seems to have derived from Court gossip surrounding a death that occurred around the time of Phillips', but in a much less affectionate atmosphere. This was the death of one of Elizabeth I's Gentleman Pensioners, Sir Brian Annesley, whose mind had begun to fail in his last years. Just like Phillips (and indeed Shakespeare), old Annesley had only daughters to succeed him, in his case three, two of whom had married well: Christian, who had become Lady Sandys, wife of the Lord Sandys involved in the Essex rebellion, and Grace, who had become Lady Wildgoose. But while old Annesley was still alive, these two daughters wanted to have their father declared 'altogether unfit to govern himself or his estate', and it was only his third and youngest daughter Cordell who held out against this, petitioning Cecil in October 1603 that her father's services to the late Queen surely deserved better 'than at his last gasp to be recorded and registered a lunatic'. It was ultimately only with the aid of her father's executor Sir William Harvey, who had become the Earl of Southampton's mother's third husband, that Cordell managed to get Annesley's will upheld, thus winning against Lady Wildgoose.[7]

Clearly here was an emotion-jerking real-life tale of inheritance ungratefully received; of a victim of mental weakness cruelly rejected by those of the sufferer's own blood. With his experience of *Hamlet* Shakespeare would have known well how powerfully an audience could be spellbound by the spectacle of insanity on stage, particularly when conveyed by an actor of Burbage's quality. But as it was part of Shakespeare's policy never to represent events happening in his own time and place, some suitable vehicle for setting it in the past was needed, and here there appears to have come to Shakespeare's notice, just about the time of Phillips' death, an old but just re-published play called *King Leir* (*King Leir* was entered on the Stationers' Register on 8 May 1605; Phillips' will proved on 13 May). This was all about a king of Britain with three daughters, two of whom, 'Gonorill' and 'Ragan' ill-treat him, only for him to be saved by the third 'Cordella', at whose intercession Leir is able to live happily ever after.

Important here is that while it is generally recognised that Shakespeare must have read the old *Leir* play before writing his own version,[8] neither in this nor in any of the many other possible sources, such as Holinshed, is the king represented as quite as old as Shakespeare's Lear, nor does he go mad. Similarly the earlier versions lack *King Lear*'s dramatic episode of the old king going out into the howling storm, and its so perverse yet artistically brilliant finale of Lear's and Cordelia's deaths, when the ending could so easily have been made a happy one. We are thus provided with a tantalising glimpse of how a true event and an old play, curiously linked by the name Cordell, became fused in Shakespeare's imagination, and were transmuted into one of the greatest of tragedies.

We can be confident that it was Richard Burbage who took the part of Lear, attested not least by a poetical epitaph published after his death. Likewise, given that Robert Armin was the company clown, it is reasonable to deduce that he played the Fool. But in *King Lear*, Shakespeare also, perhaps more than in any of his previous plays, demanded a great deal of his company's backstage staff in the form of effects for the dramatic storm scene. While in Shakespeare's plays a storm is always indicative of a break-down of the existing order, the *King Lear* storm is the longest and most theatrically obtrusive of all his works. It is almost a character in itself, 'storm still' recurring repeatedly in the stage directions as if to cue the points at which those backstage were artistically free to do their worst with their bass drums, and their stone-filled barrels in competition with Burbage fulminating:

> Rumble thy bellyful! Spit, fire! spout, rain!
> Nor rain, wind, thunder, fire, are my daughters![9]

This would have required the most careful orchestration with the backstage crew.

Notably, just as in *Hamlet* we discovered Hamlet's words of 'madness' to have rather more profundity than might at first appear, so it is in *King Lear*, as when, pretending to his blinded father that he is a madman, Gloucester's unfairly disgraced son Edgar quotes the names of fiends:

> Obidicut; Hobbididence, prince of dumbness; Mahu, of stealing; Modo, of murder; Flibbertigibbet, of mopping and mowing, who since possesses chambermaids and waiting-women.[10]

In fact, these devilish names can be traced to Samuel Harsnett's *Declaration of Egregious Popish Impostures*, a compilation of cases against Catholic priests published in 1603. Among these is the description of a Mass held in a house near Uxbridge, Middlesex, during which there were exorcised from a 'possessed' chambermaid called Sara William devils named Freteretto, Flibberdigibett, Hoberdidance, Modoz and Mohu. The chief interest here is that one of the priests involved in this particular exorcism was the martyred Robert Debdale from Anne Hathaway's Shottery, the same priest, of Shakespeare's own age, who had been released from prison about the time of the Shakespeares' marriage.[11] Shakespeare's undoubted use of Harsnett's book, even if he did not agree with it, strongly argues his interest in this particular case.

With regard to when *King Lear* was performed, the latest this can have been is 26 December 1606, the Stationers' Register for 26 November 1607 recording the entry of the Quarto edition of the play, noting that:

> it was played before the King's majesty at Whitehall upon Saint Stephens night at Christmas last, by his Majesty's servants playing usually at the Globe on the Bankside.

Other clues to *King Lear*'s dates derive from Act I scene II in which Gloucester rages about eclipses of the sun and moon that portend evil, generally reckoned to refer to the eclipse of the moon in September 1605 and the eclipse of the sun in the October.

Extraordinarily, for anyone looking for the outcome of such portents, they need have looked no further than the beginning of the November, when there occurred that best-known of events in James I's reign, the Gunpowder plot: the apparently dastardly Catholic plan to blow up James I and his Parliament on 5 November.

The particular relevance of this to Shakespeare is that those principally involved in the plot came from the same part of the country. The chief of the plotters, Robert Catesby, nine years Shakespeare's junior, had been born at Lapworth, Warwickshire, just a little to the north of Stratford-upon-Avon. His staunchly religious father Sir William Catesby was obliged to sell Lapworth because of the crippling financial penalties that Elizabeth imposed on Catholics. Robert, who had been involved in the Essex rebellion, was married to a niece of Ferdinando Stanley. Fellow conspirators Robert, Thomas and John Winter were from Huddington Hall just to the west of Stratford-upon-Avon. Their sister Dorothea married another plotter, John Grant, grandson of the Edward Grant with whom John Shakespeare did business. Catesby and the Winters, together with their co-conspirator Francis Tresham, were all in fact distant relatives of Shakespeare through his mother Mary Arden.[12] Also involved was the shadowy Edward Bushell mentioned in the Quiney letter to Shakespeare. One of the houses that the plotters used to assemble in was Stratford-upon-Avon's Clopton House, leased as a base from which to seize James I's children, Henry, Charles and Elizabeth who were then staying at Warwick Castle.

The official view of the plot is that it was hatched by these Catholics in protest at James I's failure to do anything for them but reinforce the burdens and restrictions that had been imposed upon Catholics in Elizabeth's time. Catholic historians have seen it rather differently, as a plot invented by the Machiavellian Cecil in order to cause such a wave of anti-Catholic feeling that any possibility of England returning to Catholicism, or even tolerating it, would be buried forever.[13] That Cecil was still up to such tricks is indicated by a lightning arrest of the Earl of Southampton and several of his circle the previous June. This was all over in a day, but with such skulduggery that all official documents on the affair mysteriously disappeared.

Of what really happened in the case of the Gunpowder plot, those familiar with the available evidence generally agree on just two points, that 'the true history of the Gunpowder plot is now known to no man', and that the history commonly received was certainly untrue.[14] The one certainty is that if it shocked English Protestants, it shocked loyal English Catholics even more, since they knew well the backlash it would bring upon them. And if we look to which play Shakespeare wrote in the Gunpowder plot's wake, as generally agreed, there is only one candidate: *Macbeth*.

Notable first of all is Shakespeare's sudden and hitherto unprecedented choice of a play with a Scottish theme. Earlier in 1605 Ben Jonson and his fellow playwrights had incurred James I's anger and a spell in prison for their *Eastward Ho!* as performed by the boys of Blackfriars, which poked fun at James' Scottish accent and at the excessive honours accorded to the Scots he had brought south with him. One especially notorious piece of comedy was delivered by a boy impersonating a familiar-sounding Scottish accent: 'I ken the man weel, he's one of my thirty pound Knights'.

With *Macbeth* Shakespeare tackled a Scottish theme head-on, but with all the seriousness of great tragedy, stemming not least from the fact that James was the direct ancestor of the Banquo whose murder Macbeth arranges in the course of the play.

What may in this instance have given Shakespeare his inspiration was a special playlet performed for James during his visit to Oxford (accompanied by the Earl of Southampton) in the late August of 1605. This re-enacted Banquo's greeting by three 'weird sisters or fairies' as 'no king but to be the father of many kings', as recounted in Holinshed's 'Chronicles', one of Shakespeare's favourite sources. Certainly it was this scene that Shakespeare used for *Macbeth's* dramatic opening, followed by further dramatisations clearly as memorable for those who saw them performed by Shakespeare's fellows as they continue to be for audiences today. There survives a rare description of the play from one who watched it at the Globe on 20 April 1610 and particularly moving for the spectator was the hand-washing scene:

> When Macbeth had murdered the king the blood on his hands could not be washed off by any means, nor from his wife's hands, which handled the bloody daggers in hiding them. By which means they became both much amazed and affronted....

Likewise the Banquo's ghost scene:

> being at supper with his noblemen...[Macbeth] began to speak of noble Banquo and to wish that he were there. As he thus did, standing up to drink a carouse to him, the ghost of Banquo came and sat down in his chair behind him. He, turning about to sit down again, saw the ghost of Banquo, which affronted him so, that he fell into a great passion of fear and fury....

Likewise Lady Macbeth's famous sleepwalking scene:

> Observe also how Macbeth's queen did rise in the night in her sleep, and walked and talked and confessed all. And the doctor noted her words.[15]

In fact, why the minor part of the doctor in this scene specially interested this particular Globe spectator is because he was none other than our old friend the astrologer, plague curer and confidant of Emilia Lanier, Simon Forman.

King James, however, undoubtedly saw *Macbeth* well before

Forman, most probably at Hampton Court in the company of his brother-in-law King Christian of Denmark on 7 August 1606. As remarked by Dr A. L. Rowse, it was putting it 'a little crudely'[16] for a previous commentator, Greg, to suggest that *Macbeth* was 'obviously designed to flatter King James', for Shakespeare repeatedly conveyed his aversion to any such methods. Nonetheless, in a manner quite different to any play written in the time of his previous sovereign, Shakespeare can be seen to have carefully tailored the play to James' interests. For instance, quite aside from the play's obvious Scottishness, as Shakespeare knew, James had written a book on witchcraft, and believed that witches had caused the storms at sea that had beset his wife Anne's bridal journey to Scotland. Shakespeare duly made *Macbeth*'s witches real forces to be reckoned with, their cauldron potion in Act IV scene I being said to be derived from an authentic black magic formula, hence the famous 'curse'.[17] James took an interest in the old superstition that the very touch of a king of England could work cures. Shakespeare accordingly has Malcolm, on fleeing to England, tell Macduff:

> A most miraculous work in this good king,
> Which often since my here-remain in England
> I have seen him do
> ... strangely-visited people,
> All swollen and ulcerous, pitiful to the eye,
> The mere despair of surgery, he cures ...[18]

James was fascinated by his ancestry. Accordingly, into *Macbeth* Shakespeare wrote the masque-like necromantic scene of the line of kings descending from Banquo, featuring the eighth, James himself, bearing

> a glass
> Which shows me many more ...[19]

In passing, it should be observed that it was not a bad piece of prophecy given that the present Queen of England is the twelfth generation directly descended from James. An equal pandering to James may be indicated by the fact that the play is Shakespeare's shortest, and shows signs of cuts. Shakespeare may well have cut it himself to suit the king's notoriously low boredom threshold.

But in what way does the play reflect the aftermath of the Gunpowder plot? A key scene here is the porter scene which comes immediately after Macbeth has killed Duncan. Shakespeare deploys it as a technically necessary device to give the actor playing Macbeth time to wash his hands and change his clothes (a notable instance of Shakespeare always having acting practicalities in mind), and while it explicitly recalls the Hell's-mouth from the old Miracle plays, its chief point of interest is the porter's soliloquy, upon being roused by knocking at the gate:

Faith, here's an equivocator that could swear in both the scales against either scale; who committed treason enough for God's sake, yet could not equivocate to heaven. O come in, equivocator.[20]

As generally recognised, here is a clear reference to the Gunpowder plot, in the wake of which the head of the Jesuits in England, Father Henry Garnet, who had hitherto been living in quiet obscurity, was put on trial. He was accused of knowing what was planned, but declined to warn of it due to the inviolability of information given to him in the confessional. Reportedly, Garnet evoked the Jesuit doctrine of equivocation – that when under pressure one might, to put it in modern political parlance, be economical with the truth. Towards the very end of the play Macbeth himself alludes to equivocation when, told that Birnam Wood is moving, he exclaims:

> I pull in resolution, and begin
> To doubt th'equivocation of the fiend
> That lies like truth.[21]

As pointed out by Catholic scholars, when Macbeth becomes obliged to equivocate, he actually tells the truth. Putting about lies and inventing plots was never the method of the Jesuits, only of their enemies such as Cecil, who had been doing this ever since the Campion–Persons mission of 1580. So was Shakespeare here ever so subtly making a point about the recent Catholic equivocations officially being put about as lies? Emphasising the importance of this for Shakespeare, the point is further made in Act IV's scene with Lady Macduff and her son, in which young Macduff who has been falsely told his father is dead, asks what is a traitor:

Lady Macduff: Why, one that swears and lies.

Son: And be all traitors that do so?

Lady Macduff: Every one that does so is a traitor and must be hang'd.

Son: And must they all be hang'd that swear and lie?

Lady Macduff: Every one.

Son: Who must hang them?

Lady Macduff: Why, the honest men.

Son: Then the liars and swearers are fools; for there are liars and swearers enow to beat the honest men and hang up them.[22]

Out of the mouths of babes and sucklings...? Back in the porter's scene Shakespeare has the porter allude to equivocation in a quite different context with regard to how drink, which provokes a man's desire, but takes away the performance

may be said to be an equivocator with lechery: it makes him, and it mars him; it sets him on, and it takes him off; it persuades him, and disheartens him; makes him stand to, and not stand to; in conclusion, equivocates him in a sleep, and, giving him the lie, leaves him.[23]

As earlier remarked, *Macbeth* is thought to have been performed for the first time at Hampton Court on 7 August 1606, in the presence of James and King Christian of Denmark, and one can only wonder how much Shakespeare's porter's words may have reminded them of how the previous month, on being entertained at Cecil's country house, Theobalds, drink had most certainly impaired the performance. When it came to the masque on the subject of the Queen of Sheba's visit to King Solomon, one previously carefully rehearsed by the Court ladies, the one who was supposed to be the Queen of Sheba tripped ascending the steps to present refreshments to King Christian, depositing her tray of 'wine, cream, jelly, beverage, cakes and spices' straight into his lap. Although this might not have mattered, the King already being drunk himself, when after being cleaned up he led the same lady onto the dance floor, they both fell over and had to be taken off to bed. They were then followed by ladies representing Faith, Hope, Charity, and other virtues whose act similarly hopelessly fell apart as Hope forgot her lines, Charity lost her sisters subsequently finding them 'spewing in the lower hall';

Victory, after one feeble wave of her golden sword, fell sound asleep on-stage, and Peace, reacting to inebriation like a soccer hooligan, battered all about her with her olive branch. As remarked by Court diarist Sir John Harington, who was no Puritan:

> The Gunpowder fright is got out of all our heads, and we are going on as if the Devil was contriving every man should blow up himself by riot, excess, and devastation of time and temperance.[24]

If Shakespeare and his fellow professionals, with their likely strict drink code, observed these antics, how they must have been both amused and appalled by these over-indulged amateurs.

On a more serious note, however, if the Gunpowder plot had been intended as a means of once and for all flushing out Catholics and making them unacceptable, it was certainly successful. Carried on the tide of anti-Catholic feelings, swingeing new legislation was brought in, to catch 'persons popishly affected' who had sometimes attended church 'to escape the laws in that behalf provided', but avoided Anglican communion. Now, unless they received Anglican communion at least once a year they faced fines on an ascending scale starting at £20 a year.

And here of absolute fascination is the way we find – a little over a decade after old John Shakespeare's beliefs had been shown up in a recusancy list – the appearance of Shakespeare's elder daughter Susanna, now nearly twenty-eight, as just such a miscreant in a list drawn up by the churchwarden and sidesmen of Holy Trinity Church, Stratford-upon-Avon, of those who had failed to receive the sacrament at the Easter of 20 April 1606. The list of twenty-two persons, today in Kent County Archives Office, derives from an ecclesiastical court act book formerly among the family papers of the Sackville family at Knole.[25]

That Susanna's offence was not simply an oversight is evident from the fact that the document shows she certainly ignored one summons to attend the vicar's court to explain herself. Yet since the entry also carries the notation 'dismissa', or 'dismissed', the matter was clearly resolved. So did her father quietly pay a bribe to Stratford's vicar? As in so much else of this kind, we simply do not know. Among Stratford's undoubted recusants were the godparents of Shakespeare's other daughter Judith, Hamnet and Judith Sadler. Again curiosity is aroused – had Shakespeare in 1585 knowingly chosen crypto-Catholics for his twins' godparents, or did this pair convert later? In London, Ben Jonson and his wife, undoubtedly converts, were also caught up in the same crack-down.

One other piece of legislation directly affecting Shakespeare in 1606 was an Act in restraint of 'abuses of players', setting a fine of £10 for any actor who should 'jestingly or profanely speak, or use the name of, God, or of Jesus Christ, or of the Holy Ghost, or of the Trinity'. Since many of Shakespeare's old plays carried such expletives they had to be changed to absurd but acceptable alternatives such as 'By Jove', in which regard it may well be no accident that for his next play Shakespeare turned from darkest Christian Scotland to brilliant pagan Egypt and Rome to create *Antony and Cleopatra*.

If *Antony and Cleopatra* may be accounted as another of Shakespeare's finest plays, undoubtedly the prime reason for this is the character of Cleopatra, capping even Desdemona and Lady Macbeth as the most exciting yet rewarding part Shakespeare wrote for a female role. Whoever of the King's Men took this on, almost certainly along with the other roles just mentioned, Shakespeare must have had a lot of confidence in his ability to play a part demanding femininity at its most feline. When actresses became permissible on the English stage, they baulked at Cleopatra. The great tragedienne Mrs Sarah Siddons, for instance, having received huge acclaim for her Lady Macbeth, refused Cleopatra on the grounds that she would hate herself if she played the part 'as it ought to be played'. As remarked by a *Times* reviewer in 1907:

> She [Cleopatra] must have beauty of course, and what is even more important, she must have glamour. She must be able to run at a rapid sweep through the whole gamut of emotion – from dove-like cooings to the rage of a tigress, from voluptuous languor to passion all aflame, from the frenzy of a virago to the calm and statuesque majesty of one of the noblest death-scenes in all Shakespeare.[26]

Part of Shakespeare's authority for this was of course his source Plutarch whose *Lives of the Noble Grecians and Romans*, translated into English by Lord North and printed in the Vautrollier printing shop in 1579, had already been used by him for *Julius Caesar*. Intriguingly a copy of this from Ferdinando Stanley's library, loaned to one Wilhelmi (i.e. William) by Ferdinando's wife Alice, and returned to Sir Edward Stanley in 1611, recently came up for auction and was acquired by the Shakespeare Birthplace Trust. Could this have been the copy that Shakespeare used for *Julius Caesar* and *Antony and Cleopatra*? Just how closely he used but improved upon North's Plutarch is quite apparent from a small extract from the famous description of Cleopatra that occurs in both works:

North's Plutarch	*Shakespeare*
Her barge the poop whereof was of gold, the sails of purple, and the oars of silver which kept stroke in rowing after the sound of flutes, howboys, citherns, viols.	The barge she sat in like a burnished throne, burn'd on the water; the poop was beaten gold; purple the sails and so perfumed that the winds were lovesick with them; the oars were silver which to the tune of floats kept stroke, and made the water which they beat to flow faster as amorous of their strokes.[27]

But did Shakespeare have another authority – a sixteenth-century married man's real-life remembrance of a highly temperamental woman he had actually known to exhibit the very same cocktail of imperiousness, capriciousness, amorality, vulgarity, allure and all else that he wrote into his Cleopatra? As remarked by the Shakespearean scholar John Dover Wilson apropos *Antony and Cleopatra*:

> many believe that Plutarch's tale of a fickle swarthy mistress and infatuated lover who finds it impossible to fling free had a perennial interest for the poet who was confessing sometime about 1594 apparently that a woman 'as black as hell, as dark as night' had left him 'past cure and frantic mad with ever more unrest'.[28]

No Quarto edition of *Antony and Cleopatra* ever appeared, though an entry for one was made in the Stationers' Register 20 May 1608. That the play had been written and performed little later than the end of 1606 is evident from the fact that in 1607 the author Samuel Daniel is recognised to have amended the new edition of his *Cleopatra* having watched Shakespeare's version.

Sadly, 1606 was another plague year, the attributed deaths in London being thirty to fifty per week in the July, rising to a maximum of a hundred and forty-one the week of 2 October. Quite possibly as a result of this same epidemic Shakespeare's London landlady, Madame Mountjoie, died in late October. Probably for the same reason Shakespeare's company can be traced on tour in Leicester, Oxford, Marlborough, Maidstone and Dover around the autumn, presumably following on from their performances for King Christian. Of the Dover performance the town accounts record: 'Item, given to his Majesty's players being here on Saturday last, £2'.[29]

After *Antony and Cleopatra*, possibly the next year, Shakespeare wrote another Roman play, *Coriolanus*, again using North's *Plutarch*. It is set in a period of unrest among Rome's populace against the patricians, the Roman equivalent of aristocracy, because of usury and high corn prices. In May 1607 there was an outright revolt in Northamptonshire spreading into Shakespeare's own Warwickshire, specifically due to high corn prices, and *Coriolanus* may well have been written in reflection of this.

However, in the June of 1607 Shakespeare had an altogether happier event on his mind for, on 5 June the Holy Trinity Church register of weddings shows his elder daughter Susanna, now twenty-four, making a surprisingly late but nonetheless good marriage to thirty-two-year-old doctor John Hall. Unlike most other individuals at Stratford, Dr John Hall emerges as a personality to whom we can add more than a little detail. The son of a Middlesex physician, he was a Queen's College, Cambridge, BA and MA, and therefore – in formal terms at least – considerably better educated than his father-in-law. Although he was not qualified in medicine as such (regulations of these matters were poor in Shakespeare's time), by the time of his marriage to Susanna Shakespeare he had already been practising at Stratford for some seven years. He clearly had a good reputation, as evident from his widespread practice and socially highly placed patients, among them the Earl and Countess of Northampton at Ludlow Castle.

Much is known about Hall's patients, their complaints, and his treatments of them from his published book of case-studies *Select Observations on English Bodies*, and notably these included both Catholics and Protestants – for example Mistress Mary Talbot, 'a Catholic Fair: such as hated him for his religion', Lady Smith 'Roman Catholic, cruelly afflicted with wind', and one Browne, 'a Romish priest, labouring of an ungarick fever in danger of death', comments indicating that Hall was a tolerant Protestant. But frustratingly, although in the book he related his cure of his wife 'miserably tormented by the colic', with the aid of an enema, he included no mention of any treatment of his father-in-law.

Equally disappointing, although one of the officially recommended 'Shakespeare tour' highlights for visitors to Stratford-upon-Avon, is a call at an attractive Tudor house in Old Town billed as Hall's Croft, and purportedly where John and his new bride Susanna lived during the first years of their marriage. There is no serious evidence of the couple ever having occupied the house, despite all the Tudor and Jacobean furniture and even a sixteenth-century dispensary which has been fitted out by the Shakespeare Birthplace Trust.

Having a father with as well-lined a purse as Shakespeare's, we can anticipate that daughter Susanna would have been given a suitably splendid send-off for her wedding. At Hatfield House there hangs a striking Hoefnagel painting of a wedding of about 1600 being celebrated with musicians, dancing, food roasting on a spit, and a long table set out for the feast, which may give us some idea of the style of Susanna's wedding festivities in Stratford. But before the end of 1607 all the joy would have turned to sadness. For the death of a member of the family only three years older than Susanna lay waiting in the wings.

CHAPTER 20

A New Mood

On the morning of 31 December 1607, with the Thames frozen from Westminster to London Bridge, a lone bell-ringer ascended the tower of St Saviour's, Southwark, and from the spacious ringers' room began solemnly to toll the forty-six hundredweight great bell suspended above.[1] For the prostitutes and bear-keepers in the surrounding streets, the barbers and refreshment vendors who had set up stalls on the Thames ice, and the small boys playing ice football,[2] it was a familiar enough sound: the signal of a funeral.

It is a funeral we know about because of an entry that is the last on the page of St Saviour's burial register for December of 1607 as preserved in the Greater London Record Office,[3] against the date number 31, reading simply: 'Edmond Shakespeare, a player, in the Church'. The bell-ringer's involvement is traceable from a corresponding entry for exactly the same date in the St Saviour's fee-book of the period, also preserved in the Greater London Record Office: 'Edmund Shakespeare, a player, buried in the church, with a forenoon knell of the great bell, 20 s[hillings].'

We know Edmund to have been William's youngest brother, his christening recorded in the Stratford-upon-Avon register book for 3 May 1580, but of the rest of his twenty-seven-year life the documentary record is essentially silent. The only exception is an entry for 12 August 1607 in the register of the church of St Giles without Cripplegate (just the other side of the City Wall to where Shakespeare lived in Silver Street), recording the burial of: 'Edward, son of Edward Shackspeere Player, base born'.[4] Despite 'Edward' appearing instead of 'Edmund' in the case of the father, an apparent clerical slip,[5] this seems to suggest that young Edmund fathered an illegitimate child a few months before his death.

The surprise, however – due to the absence of a proper record of Shakespeare's company – is the realisation, derived only from the register of his death, that Edmund must have joined his elder brother's clearly lucrative profession. Although there is no documentary evidence of which company Edmund joined, it is reasonable to infer that this was the King's Men, and that when St Saviour's great bell tolled that icy December morning probably Shakespeare's entire company of actors gathered below in their funeral black. The Chamber Accounts show that only three days earlier they had given the third of three Christmastime performances before the King at Whitehall, and it is perhaps not too much to reconjure them in the mind's eye: Burbage, at the height of his career, his lines as Othello, Macbeth and Lear still mint-sharp in his memory; clown Armin; business manager Heminges and, of course, Shakespeare himself. Undoubtedly an emotional man, did he perhaps while listening to the formal rites think back to those hauntingly epitaphic lines he had so recently written for Macbeth?:

> Life's but a walking shadow, a poor player,
> That struts and frets his hour upon the stage,
> And then is heard no more . . .[6]

Sadly, exactly where they laid poor Edmund is no longer traceable in St Saviour's present-day guise as Southwark Cathedral, but the payment of the handsome sum of twenty shillings (two shillings would have bought a churchyard burial, and a shilling a ringing of the lesser bell) betokens someone sending him to his rest in style and it is difficult to regard this as anyone other than his brother William.

It is also noteworthy that one of the most conspicuous monuments for Shakespeare as his gaze strayed around St Saviour's would have been the tomb of the fourteenth-century English poet John Gower [see pl. 45], a direct contemporary and friend of Geoffrey Chaucer. Today, although moved to a lesser position on the north side of the nave, the Gower tomb is still remarkable for its lifesize polychrome effigy of the poet laid out in death, his head resting on his three main works: *Vox Clamantis*, composed in Latin, *Speculum Meditantis*, in French, and *Confessio Amantis*, in English. The latter contains many translations of tales from Ovid which would inevitably have endeared him to Shakespeare, in which regard it is of no little fascination that the play which Shakespeare is most likely to have written shortly after his brother Edmund's funeral is *Pericles*. This is not only based on the familiar enough tale of Apollonius of Tyre, which Gower culled from antiquity, it also, uniquely for Shakespeare, features Gower himself specially resurrected to speak as Chorus, in deliberately archaic-sounding phrases and primitive tetrameter couplets, at the commencement of each act.

For his writing of Pericles Shakespeare can be proven to have consulted Gower's *Confessio* in one of the sixteenth-century's two printed editions, probably the one published in 1554, and to a lesser extent he also used a story from a collection of old tales known as the *Gesta Romanorum*. But characteristically he radically altered various elements, including completely changing the hero's name from Apollinus, or Apollonius to the altogether more heroic-sounding Pericles, rooted in the Latin *periculum* for peril, and thereby suggestive of the perils he would have to confront.

We can therefore be confident that mentions of performances of *Pericles* refer specifically to Shakespeare's play, subject to one major qualification: that in the recognised canon of Shakespeare's plays, the First Folio of 1623, *Pericles* is the only one not to have been included. This may have been because of a mislaying or loss of his original manuscript at the time the First Folio was put together, but whatever the reason, present-day texts of it rely chiefly on a seriously defective Quarto version, published in 1609 by the minor publisher Henry Gosson, a newcomer to the publication of plays. Curiously, the Stationers' Register shows that on 20 May 1608 the more established publisher Edward Blount had been intending to publish *Pericles*, but seemingly this did not happen, probably because renewed plague caused the theatres to close from the July of 1608 to the December of 1609.

A further complication is that there did appear in 1608, seemingly cashing in on Shakespeare's play, a prose version, *The Painfull Adventures of Pericles Prince of Tyre*, written by the minor dramatist George Wilkins, describing itself on the title page as 'The true history *of the play* [italics mine] of *Pericles*, as it was lately presented by the worthy and ancient Poet John Gower'. The title page of this has a depiction of Gower [see fig 9, overleaf], arguably much as he appeared in the play, and it has been reasonably suggested that since the part of Gower would have been a logical one for Shakespeare to play (just as he very likely took the part of Chorus in *Henry v*, we may even have a picture of Shakespeare in possibly his last acting role. That the play was popular, and had been performed before the closing of the theatres (and therefore within months of Edmund Shakespeare's funeral), seems further attested by the Gosson edition's title page, describing it

Being

The true Hiſtory of the Play of *Pericles*, as it was lately preſented by the worthy and ancient Poet *John Gower*.

John   Gower.

AT LONDON.
Printed by T.P. *for* Nat:Butter
1608.

Fig 9
Shakespeare playing John Gower? This woodcut, from the title page of George Wilkins' *The Painfull Adventures of Pericles Prince of Tyre*, may just possibly depict Shakespeare playing the part of the poet John Gower in *Pericles*.

as 'the late and much admired play, called Pericles Prince of Tyre' and 'As it hath been divers and sundry times acted by His Majesty's Servants at the Globe on the Bankside'.

Of further interest is that mention of a performance of *Pericles* occurs in evidence given during a trial held at Venice in 1617, from which we learn that the Venetian ambassador Giorgio Giustiniani took an illustrious party of his fellow diplomats to see it during his tenure in England:

> All the ambassadors, who have come to England have gone to the play more or less. Giustiniani went with the French ambassador and his wife to a play called *Pericles*, which cost Giustiniani more than 20 crowns. He also took the Secretary of Florence.[7]

Since Giustiniani's tenure in England was only until 23 November 1608, and since the theatres were closed from the July of that year, it is reasonable to infer that the performance attended by Giustiniani was most likely before July 1608, and therefore again within months of Edmund Shakespeare's funeral. But from the fact that such a distinguished party attended, and at such great expense to Giustiniani, it is most unlikely that the venue was anywhere so common as the Globe.

And here of considerable interest is that, defective though the text of *Pericles* might be, it can be clearly discerned as representing a major creative shift in Shakespeare's work away from the uncompromisingly tragic endings that link *Macbeth*, *King Lear*, *Othello*, *Anthony and Cleopatra* and *Coriolanus*.

The play begins murkily enough with severed heads hanging in front of the Palace of Antioch, just as kinsman Robert Catesby's head decorated Parliament House at the time the play was written. We learn also of incest between King Antiochus and his lovely daughter, whose hand Pericles ill-advisedly tries to win by solving Antiochus's riddle, and making his escape in the nick of time. Then after a shipwreck, and exhibiting his prowess in a tournament, Pericles earns the altogether truer love of the King of Pentapolis's daughter, Thaisa, who appears to die during a storm at sea while giving birth to their daughter Marina. Thaisa's body is even cast overboard in a coffin. Furthermore, when daughter Marina grows up she too is supposed dead upon being captured by pirates who then sell her to a Mitylene brothel, where her piety wins her the compassion of Mitylene's governor.

There then follow two very moving recognition scenes. The first is when on a call to Mitylene the deeply despondent Pericles realises that the girl the town's governor rescued from the brothel is his 'dead' Marina; the second is when, upon visiting the Temple of Diana at Ephesus to give thanks, Pericles and Marina find the high priestess there to be none other than long-lost Thaisa, nursed back to health by a kindly physician who had noticed her to be still alive when her coffin had been washed ashore. Assuming that Pericles and her daughter must have died at sea, she had thereupon taken up the nun-like life of a priestess of Diana. What might have been a sad tale is in fact one of the 'happily ever after' variety – all the more refreshing after the tragedies that had gone before.

Over a decade after Shakespeare's death Ben Jonson [see pl. 44], in his *Ode to Himself*, would call *Pericles* 'some mouldy tale'.[8] The play is rarely performed today, and for most critics it is way below Shakespeare at his best, not least on the grounds of some untypical trite language in its first two acts. Yet it has considerable emotional grip as a story, and it is important to see it in the context of what Shakespeare would seem to have been trying to do, and the competition he was then up against. So dazzled have we tended to be by Shakespeare's reputation that it is all too easy to forget that those whose opinions and money mattered in his own time certainly did not see him in anything like the commanding position he has subsequently assumed.

Despite the offence that Ben Jonson had caused with some of his earlier works, in 1608 his reputation was great and arguably considerably greater than Shakespeare's. Capitalising on the success of *The Masque of Blackness*, one new production was *The Masque of Beauty*. Again Queen Anne, the Countess of Bedford and fourteen other ladies were star performers, supported by an ancillary cast of light-bearing cupids, and with the musicians dressed as spirits of the ancient poets. For the marriage of the King's favourite the young Viscount Haddington to the beautiful daughter of the Earl of Sussex, whose family name was Radcliffe, Jonson and his production manager Inigo Jones devised a red cliff (pun, of course, upon 'Radcliffe') to part with a 'loud and full music' to disclose twelve superbly attired gentlemen masquers, followed, for comic relief, by a dance of twelve little boys with a 'variety of ridiculous gesture'.

In terms of costs alone such scenic productions, running up bills of several thousand pounds, make the amounts that King James paid for performances by Shakespeare's company – though highly generous by Elizabeth's standards – seem mere small change. Unlike Shakespeare, Jonson always paid scrupulous attention to scholarship and classical conventions, important not only from the point of view of the King's pedantry, but also to save unfavourable criticism from the ever-pernickity foreign ambassadors at Court. It was precisely because of them, and the prestige value of their reports back to their foreign masters, that the frequent overspending on these productions was accepted with few qualms. Each masque was an international event, with each ambassador vying for the seat of honour. As the Venetian ambassador wrote back home on the subject of *The Masque of Beauty* 'The apparatus and the cunning of the stage machinery was a miracle, the abundance and beauty of the lights immense, the music and the dance most sumptuous'.[9] Nor were the accolades only from the foreigners. As remarked by one modern scholar, G. E. Bentley:

> The poems to Jonson and the long prose passages about him in this time are far more frequent than to Shakespeare; quotations from his work occur oftener, and I find three times as many literary and social references to performances of his plays and masques as to Shakespeare's. Poems about him or references to his work are written in these years by John Donne, Sir John Roe, Sir Dudley Carleton ... John Chamberlain, Sir Thomas Lake, Sir George Buc, Sir Thomas Salusbury.[10]

However rarefied the tastes and extravagances of the Court might seem, something of these was bound to filter through to those lower down the social scale, and it is against this background that it is possible to see Shakespeare in *Pericles* going some way towards pandering to this vogue. The play's opening scenes of Antiochus' court lent themselves to oriental magnificence; the later brothel scenes to decadence, and the Temple of Diana scene to classical perfection. In none of *Pericles*' well-recognised sources is there any tournament scene, but mindful of the continued popularity of the annual Accession Day Tilts, Shakespeare clearly devised this for maximum spectacle, its rapid imitation by another dramatist confirming that it impressed. The scenes of storms at sea, as crucial to *Pericles* as *King Lear*'s land storm, offered the opportunity for more sophisticated special effects than Shakespeare had ever called for in the past. Several opportunities were also offered for music: from the entry of Antiochus' daughter, to the physician's call for music during the revival of the 'dead' Thaisa, and 'heavenly music' heralding Pericles' visionary dream of the goddess Diana.[11]

Whatever modern attitudes towards it, that *Pericles* had a long-lived appeal in its own time, and succeeded in competing with lavish Court productions, is evident from a reference to its performance for the entertainment of the visiting French ambassador at Whitehall in May 1619:

> In the King's great chamber they went to see the play of Pericles, Prince of Tyre, which lasted till two o'clock. After two acts the players ceased till the French all refreshed them with sweetmeats brought on china voiders [trays], and wine and ale in bottles. After, the players began anew[12]

The 'King's great chamber', the Banqueting House at Whitehall which James had had rebuilt in stone and brick in 1606, was where Jonson's masques were staged. That *Pericles* was also 'sundry times acted' at the Globe is evident enough from the title page of the Quarto. But the necessary magnificence of a play like *Pericles* created the need for housing more readily available than the Banqueting House and more sophisticated and weather-proof than the Globe – something very like what old James Burbage had had in mind upon acquiring the Blackfriars Parliament Chamber to refurbish it as a private theatre all those years before.

And here, whether contrived or otherwise, events of 1608 were to play into Shakespeare's company's hands. As described earlier, the Blackfriars had been leased to the Children of the Chapel, later renamed Children of the Queen's Revels, and the enterprise went through mixed fortunes with some indications of the premises having fallen into disrepair.[13] In March 1608, however, matters came to a head due to the performance at the Blackfriars of two plays, the first of which scandalised French ambassador la Boderie; the second of which made ill-judged fun of King James himself. According to a letter sent to Robert Cecil, James 'vowed they [the Children] should never play more, but should first beg their bread'.[14]

The effect of this was that suddenly Shakespeare's company, from whom the Children had been leasing the Blackfriars, had on their hands precisely the private theatre they had been blocked from using for their own performances ten years before. And now times were different. Most notably through their own efforts attitudes towards adult theatrical performances in general had assumed far greater social acceptability. The King's Men had acquired considerably enhanced status, wearing the royal livery, and enjoying a level of royal patronage easily double their very best under Elizabeth, so that whereas the Privy Council had previously frowned upon them, now they looked upon them with indulgence. Audiences wanted more year-round entertainment than could be provided by a Globe that, because of its openness to the elements, was impracticably chilly and uninviting in winter. Accordingly, if the inhabitants of the Blackfriars had not been inconvenienced by the performances put on by the Children, surely there was no reason why productions by the King's Men should cause any greater local nuisance?

There is evidence that by the August of 1608 Shakespeare's company was sufficiently advanced in plans to take over the Blackfriars that its members had formed a syndicate for the purpose. Sadly the original documents for this have not survived, but they are known about from the same lawsuit between business manager John Heminges and his daughter Thomasine from which we earlier learned details of the Globe partnership. With regard to the Blackfriars we discover that Cuthbert Burbage, William Shakespeare, John Heminges, Henry Condell, William Sly and Thomas Evans each received a seventh-part share of the Blackfriars theatre in return for payment of one seventh part of the annual rent of £40. Here again, with the exception of Evans (almost certainly, despite the 'Thomas', actually Henry Evans, former manager of the Children's company), we recognise the now familiar names of the principals involved, though sadly William Sly, a fellow since at least as early as the Lord Strange's Men days was to die within a matter of days. The Blackfriars leases were drawn up on 9 August and Sly's burial appears in the register of the 'players church' of St Leonard's in Shoreditch, on 16 August, with plague inevitably suspected, given a serious new outbreak that had begun only the previous month.[15]

Almost certainly due to this same plague, which caused the London theatres to be closed for a year, Shakespeare's company were not immediately able to utilise their new premises, and as usual in such circumstances they went on tour, being recorded as performing at Coventry on 29 October. Shakespeare will almost certainly have been back to his native Warwickshire some weeks earlier, for another death at this time, though one probably rather due to old age than plague. This was the death of Shakespeare's mother Mary Arden, recorded in the Stratford burial register for 9 September simply as 'Mayry Shaxpere wydowe'.

As the inevitable consequence of the death of a parent, this would have marked the end of an era for Shakespeare, it being generally supposed that after husband John's death Mary remained at the Henley Street house, looked after there by her daughter Joan, who occupied it with her hatter husband Will Hart and their family. For Shakespeare it was a busy time for funerals, for on a date only three days after the burial of his mother, the St Saviour's fee book records 'Lawrence Fletcher, a player, the king's servant, buried in the church, with an afternoon knell of the great bell'.[16] Fletcher was the actor the company had acquired with their aggrandisement as the King's Men, although how much he integrated with the company is unknown. It is notable that his funeral was in the afternoon, a sign in itself of his fellow players' unemployment on account of the plague; also that with twenty shillings again being paid for the great bell, he was buried with exactly the same style as Shakespeare's late brother.

Even with the theatres closed, James' Court determinedly kept up their entertainment during their now traditional Christmas stay at Whitehall, and for Shakespeare's company that meant the preparation of new plays even without the immediate facility to show them in public. In specific recognition of this the Chamber Accounts for the Christmas of 1608/09 show Shakespeare's company as being paid £120 for performing twelve plays on unspecified dates, followed by a supplementary 'reward' of £40

> for their private practice in the time of infection that thereby they might be enabled to perform their service before his Majesty in Christmas holidays.[17]

Once again, frustratingly, we do not know which of Shakespeare's plays were first performed then, but rubbing shoulders with them during that Christmas programme was yet another new Ben Jonson masque, *The Masque of Queens*, performed with the French ambassador as honoured guest 2 February 1609. The first scene must inevitably have reminded its audience of *Macbeth*, for the curtain rose to an Inigo Jones designed Hell-like cavern 'flaming beneath' from which there emerged 'with a kind of hollow and infernal music' a coven of witches who proceeded to perform whirling dances. This was intended to show off as all the more magnificent the second scene, which presented the Queen and her ladies in a re-creation of Chaucer's House of Fame with the Queen as Queen of Fame; a pink-clad Countess of Bedford as Queen of the Amazons and Lady Guildford as Queen of Caria, all descending in triumphal chariots to which the witches were bound, symbolising the triumph of virtue over ignorance and malice.

As Shakespeare seems to have recognised, something along these lines was what audiences would expect for the new Blackfriars theatre, although productions would need to be adaptable for the Globe also. Certainly the theatre's grandiose weather-proof interior provided Shakespeare's company with altogether new opportunities for costuming, lighting and special effects. Although the original building was demolished within forty years of Shakespeare's death, surviving documents, among them James Burbage's indenture of 1596, convey reasonable details of its facilities. From an outside yard (still locatable today from the Blackfriars alleyway known as Playhouse Yard [see fig 10, overleaf]), patrons ascended a 'great pair of winding stairs' leading to the Great Chamber that was the theatre proper [see pl. 47], a sixty-six foot long by forty-six foot wide auditorium[18] capable of seating seven hundred compared to the Globe's accommodation for three thousand. The stage itself, with a platform half the size of the Globe's, seems to have comprised two entry doors, a central 'discovery space', an upper balcony, a curtained music room together with flanking boxes for up to fifteen of the audience entitled by rank or suitably inflated payment to sit on-stage, level with the players. Inclusive of the backstage tiring room, the stage area seems to have comprised a further forty feet by forty-six feet.

Clearly in order to provide a good variety of entertainment for the new customers at the Blackfriars, while keeping happy the old ones at the Globe, more plays were needed than could possibly be provided by Shakespeare alone, and for this purpose Ben Jonson's services were procured, along with those of two up-and-coming dramatists: Francis Beaumont and John Fletcher, university-educated young men still in their twenties and from impeccable backgrounds. There was also a need for more actors, particularly younger ones, not only because of the recent deaths of William Sly and Lawrence Fletcher, but also because of the steadily ageing principals. This was certainly

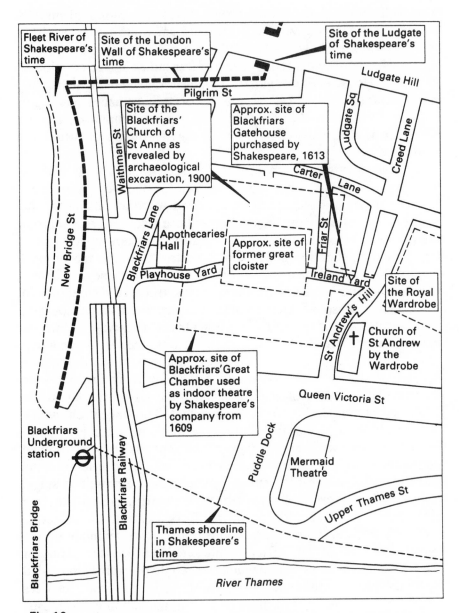

Fig 10

BLACKFRIARS THEATRE

Location in relation to present-day London. The original Blackfriars ecclesiastical buildings occupied roughly the site of the central square dotted rule, with the surrounding lands confined by Puddle Dock, St Andrew's Hill and Creed Lane to the east, Pilgrim Street to the north and the old London Wall to the west.

how, years later in 1635, the Burbage family would recruit the veteran 'youngsters' John Underwood and William Ostler from the old Children's company.

For this period of reorganisation the plague that had begun mid-1608 lingered uncomfortably long. As described by Dekker in 1609:

> Play-houses stand like taverns that have cast out their masters, the doors locked up, the flags ... taken down ... like houses lately infected, from whence the affrighted dwellers are fled, in hope to live better in the country.[19]

With no income other than from the King's Christmas shows, and from perhaps the odd private performance, earnings must have been much lower than usual for Shakespeare's company, and some measure of this is their going on tour early, performances being recorded at Ipswich, Hythe and New Romney in the May of 1609. Yet Shakespeare would seem to have put the time to good use for it is to this period that may be ascribed those plays often described as of his final period, ones written arguably with the Blackfriars very much in mind.

Probably the first of this new mode was *Cymbeline*, rarely performed today, and as generally agreed, far from Shakespeare's best. Set in the first century AD, the main background is that of the Court of the British King Cymbeline, better known historically as Cunobelin, at about the time of the Roman invasion of Britain. A. L. Rowse calls Shakespeare's version of the story 'a tired man's play', exemplified by numerous examples of somewhat unnecessary use of parenthesis, a possible sign of Shakespeare's nervousness writing for a new, choosier and better educated audience than the one he was used to at the Globe. It is also unusual for the number of instances in which he repeats elements from his earlier work – an absent husband's wager on his wife's chastity from *The Rape of Lucrece*; a severed head from *Titus Andronicus*; the resuscitation of a heroine from his recently successful *Pericles*.

Against this, as pointed out by Arden editor J. M. Nosworthy, it needs to be understood that Shakespeare was feeling his way in pioneering a new kind of play – neither comedy nor tragedy; neither straight history nor fantasy-dominated masque – for which he simply had no ready model to act as guide. As far as characterisation goes, the evil Queen, with her flowers and her poisons, is a fairy-tale witch rather than a character as convincing as Goneril or Lady Macbeth. When order breaks down, as it does with more surprises and twists of plot than in any previous play, Shakespeare again invokes fairy tale with a masque-like parade of apparitions. This is followed by a more technically ambitious piece of stage effect than he had ever previously asked for in his plays, when the king of the gods Jupiter descends from the heavens in thunder and lightning. Unquestionably Shakespeare's biggest piece of pandering to (or conceivably, sending up of?), what Jonson, Inigo Jones and their crew of Whitehall ladies had been creating with their masques, this demanded a crane, windlass and counterweight concealed high in the 'heavens' backstage wherever *Cymbeline* was staged. An expensive investment in equipment, this was surely introduced into the script only with the consensus of his fellows that such a contrivance was what the increasingly sophisticated theatrical audience now expected.

Cymbeline is another play of which we are fortunate to have a first-hand account from one who saw it produced within Shakespeare's lifetime. As in the case of *Macbeth* our informant is Simon Forman, and although of *Cymbeline* he omitted to record either when or where he saw it, it can only have been within two years of Shakespeare writing it, since Forman died during the September of 1611. Here particularly noteworthy is that what most powerfully caught his attention, and which he remembered best, was not Jupiter's spectacular descent, but the scene in Cymbeline's daughter Imogen's bedroom in which:

> the Italian [Iachimo] that came from her love [Posthumus] conveyed himself in a chest; and said it was a chest of plate sent, from her love and others, to be presented to the King. In the deepest of the night, she being asleep, he opened the chest and came forth of it. And viewed her in her bed and the marks of her body; took away her bracelet, and after accused her of adultery to her love.[20]

Iachimo's intention at this point in the play is to observe Imogen sufficiently intimately to persuade Posthumus, Imogen's true love, that she is not the paragon of virtue he believes, the setting demanded being a beautifully decorated bedchamber lit by a single taper by which Iachimo can see (and inform the audience in a suitable stage-whisper) that Imogen has

> On her left breast
> A mole cinque-spotted, like the crimson drops
> I' th' bottom of a cowslip.[21]

Here clearly is a scene far better suited to the enclosed, sophisticated intimacy of the Blackfriars than to the open-air Globe, with its daylight and the ever-present danger of a groundling's popping of a beer bottle ruining the whole effect. Also noteworthy is that whereas before Shakespeare would have introduced the palace scenes with flourishes of trumpets, in *Cymbeline* the accent is on music of an altogether richer variety. Another individual brought into the team for this final period of Shakespeare's plays seems to have been Court lutanist Robert Johnson (son of John Johnson, a Court musician who had flourished between 1579 and 1594), who was probably related to the Margaret Johnson who was mother of Shakespeare's Dark Lady Emilia. In his mid-twenties in 1609, Robert Johnson is certainly known to have worked on *Cymbeline* and its successors, and what may well be his musical setting for *Cymbeline*'s song 'Hark, hark, the lark' survives in a manuscript preserved in the Bodleian Library, Oxford.[22] Another notable musical element in *Cymbeline* is its beautiful dirge 'Fear no more the heat o' th' sun'.[23]

Whatever the merits of *Cymbeline*, however, Shakespeare almost certainly regarded it as but a stepping stone for his next work, one of altogether more universally recognised greatness, *The Winter's Tale*. The date of this will almost certainly have been 1610, and quite definitely not later than early 1611, since Simon Forman reported seeing it at the Globe on 15 May of that year.

Fascinatingly, for this quite definitely final period play Shakespeare turned for his main source of inspiration to the romantic story *Pandosto* written in the Armada year of 1588 by none other than the man who had been his bitterest critic, Robert Greene. The book's republication in 1607 may have jogged Shakespeare's memory of it (though the indications are that he used the original edition), but it is hard not to see something deliberate about his use of Greene, not least in the way he effectively shouted out whose work he was using. As pointed out by the great authority on Shakespeare's sources, Kenneth Muir, 'there are more verbal echoes from *Pandosto* than from any other novel used by Shakespeare as a source'.[24] He also, for no apparent plot reason, turned the story inside out so that what in

Pandosto was Bohemia became Sicily in *The Winter's Tale*, and vice-versa. Above all, he transformed what had been an uninspiring work of Greene's into a tragi-comedy of the purest genius – the literary equivalent of Michelangelo's translation of the block of marble another artist had abandoned into his matchless 'David'. In a writer normally lacking any kind of vindictiveness it is hard not to detect at least a glimmer of Shakespeare working off an old score.

Again we can thank Simon Forman for a close eyewitness account of the play, less than four months before his death. In his typical aide-memoire style he wrote:

Observe there how Leontes the King of Sicily was overcome with jealousy of his wife [Hermione] with the King of Bohemia [Polixenes], his friend, that came to see him. How he contrived his death, and would have had his cupbearer to have poisoned [him]: who gave the King of Bohemia warning thereof and fled with him to Bohemia.

Remember also how he sent to the oracle of Apollo, and the answer of Apollo – that she [Hermione] was guiltless and that the king was jealous ... and how, except the child [Perdita the daughter of Leontes, with whom Hermione had been pregnant] was found again that was lost, the king should die without issue. For the child was carried into Bohemia and there laid in a forest and brought up by a shepherd. The King of Bohemia's son married that wench [Perdita]. And how they fled into Sicily to Leontes. The shepherd, having shown the letter of the nobleman by whom Leontes sent away that child, and the jewels found about her, she was known to be Leontes daughter, and was then sixteen years old.

Remember also the rogue [Autolycus] that came in all tattered like Coll Pixie; how he feigned him sick and to have been robbed of all that he had. How he cozened [cheated] the poor man of all his money. And after, came to the sheep-shearing with a pedlar's pack and there cozened them again of all their money. How he changed apparel with the King of Bohemia's son, and then how he turned courtier, etc.[25]

In a sense *The Winter's Tale* again reworks elements previously tried out in *Pericles* and *Cymbeline*, but now by more radical separation of the tragic and the romantic Shakespeare achieved maximum effect. The tragic events, Leontes' jealousy, the intended death by exposure of his infant daughter, the apparent death of Hermione, and the subsequent fate of Antigonus, the man charged with Perdita's exposure (immortalised by that most famous of all stage directions 'Exit, pursued by a bear'), all are dealt with in the first three acts.

Then at the beginning of Act IV Time enters as Chorus to declare the passing of sixteen years, and two scenes later suddenly we step into an idyllic Cotswolds-style pastoral world with songs, sheep-shearing, dancing shepherds, shepherdesses and satyrs, offering everything of the spectacle and enchantment of a Jonson/Inigo masque but with real story. Once again Shakespeare's gift of comic characterisation is found at its most magical in the rogue Autolycus, 'all tattered like Coll Pixie' as Forman describes seeing him on the Globe stage in his pedlar guise; then, garbed as a courtier, insisting to those disbelieving of his rank:

> Whether it like me or no, I am a courtier. Seest thou not the air of the court in these enfoldings? Hath not my gait in it the measure of the court? Receives not thy nose court-odour from me? Reflect I not on thy baseness court-contempt?[26]

From the love of the prince for the shepherdess who is really a princess, events move, as in *Pericles*, to another climactic 'resurrection', when the grieving Leontes believing Hermione, the wife he had wronged, to be dead, is shown what he supposes to be merely a life-like statue of her only to find that it is the still-living Hermione herself.

Notable is that all these 'new mood' plays conformed to the Abuses of Players Act, sticking to pagan themes, even though every now and again, when Shakespeare describes a pagan rite, as in *The Winter's Tale*'s account of the sacrifice to Apollo at Delphi, there are hints, from the words 'reverence of the priests and ceremonies', 'solemn and unearthly manner of the sacrifices', that he may have been thinking of the Catholic Mass. Far more evident, however, is that when Shakespeare's company got back to business, as it certainly did from the end of 1609, *The Winter's Tale* and its companions brought them to new heights of commercial success.

In February 1610 London goldsmith Robert Keysar, one of the former directors of the Children's Company at the Blackfriars, brought to the Court of Requests a case against Richard Burbage and his fellows,[27] claiming that the Burbages, Heminges, Condell 'and others' had promised him a one-sixth interest in the theatre and its profits, and that they had made £1,500 from the Blackfriars between August 1609 and February 1610. Keysar's estimate was strongly denied by the defendants, and is also somewhat difficult to reconcile with the theatres seeming to have been closed until the end of the year, but it is a sure indication that once the enterprise began it brought in such plentiful and lucrative custom that it attracted vultures wanting their pickings. This is further supported by a sworn statement made in 1612 by Edward Kirkham, another individual associated with the Children of the Revels, that the King's Men took £1,000 a winter more at the Blackfriars than they had formerly taken at the Globe.[28]

All too often forgotten in books about Shakespeare and his art is that behind all the high-flown literary ideas and the disciplines of presenting them on the stage there lay a hard-headed clique of businessmen, Shakespeare among them, making commerical decisions every bit as entrepreneurial as today's manufacturers and retail chains. They had come a very long way since their days as Lord Strange's Men. They now carried respect and even clout in high places, one measure of which is the fact that from this time and throughout the next thirteen years there would appear no pirate edition of any new Shakespeare play. Arguably the company, with the Lord Chamberlain's help, now managed successfully to influence the keepers of the Stationers' Register to block any venture of this kind. Even so, before the end of 1609 there was to emerge onto the bookstalls one publication, undoubtedly capitalising on Shakespeare's success, that would bring out some arguably less than welcome skeletons from the past.

CHAPTER 21

'To the Onlie Begetter'

Not long before the death of Shakespeare's actor brother Edmund there had died the Dowager Countess of Southampton, Mary, mother of Shakespeare's early patron the third earl.[1] A letter of 17 November 1607 from her son-in-law Thomas Howard, Earl of Arundel, remarks of her passing:

> Old Southampton, I am sure you hear, is dead, and hath left the best of her stuff to her son, and the greatest part to her husband, the most of which I think will be sold, and dispersed into the hands of many men, of which number I would be one.[2]

The old countess's will, as made out in the April, survives in the Public Record Office,[3] and shows that she indeed left choice items to her son. Besides the dozen manors that had been hers from her marriage settlement with the second earl, she bequeathed him ten pictorial wall-hangings with the story of Cyrus of Persia, 'the pictures in the little Gallery at Copthall' (her home with Heneage), her two grandest beds with all their equipment, four Turkey carpets, and much else. She also left a variety of items to her daughter-in-law and daughter, all her clothes to her two waiting gentlewomen, and made Shakespeare's neighbour, her 'good and loving friend George, Lord Carew, Baron of Clopton' the will's overseer. 'All the rest of my goods and chattels, household stuff and estate' she left 'to my dear and well-beloved husband Sir William Harvey, whom I make sole executor of this my last will and testament'.

It is what possibly lay among those 'goods and chattels' that just *may* be of the greatest Shakespearean interest. It may be recalled that Harvey, besides having served on Essex's expeditions and being of the same generation as the Countess's son, had acted on behalf of Cordell Annesley over the matter of her dementia-suffering father Brian's will. Clearly something of a bond must have developed between him – with his much older wife – and the unmarried Cordell, for in 1609 he and Cordell married, her name notably being given specifically as Cordelia at the time of her marriage.[4] It is against this background that in the same year of this marriage we confront arguably the most enigmatic book-dedication in history:

TO.THE.ONLIE.BEGETTER.OF.

THESE.INSUING.SONNETS.

MR.W.H. ALL.HAPPINESSE.

AND.THAT.ETERNITIE.

PROMISED.

BY.

OUR.EVER-LIVING.POET.

WISHETH.

THE.WELL-WISHING.

ADVENTURER.IN.

SETTING.

FORTH.

T.T.

The 'Insuing Sonnets' are none other than Shakespeare's, the dedication being that to the first published edition, which appeared the year of Sir William Harvey's marriage to Cordell/Cordelia. As baldly declared on the title page:

SHAKE-SPEARES

SONNETS

Never before Imprinted

AT LONDON

By G.Eld for T.T. and are

to be solde by John Wright, dwelling

at Christ Church gate

1609

Consultation with the Stationers' Register reveals the exact date of registration of 'a Booke called Shakespeares sonnettes' to have been

20 May 1609, and we know that it was on the bookstalls by 19 June because Edward Alleyn, who had retired from acting back in 1604, recorded purchasing a copy on that date. The Stationers' Register also identifies the 'T.T.' of the title page and dedication as Thomas Thorpe, a forty-year-old London publisher who during the previous four years had published several of Ben Jonson's works, among them *Sejanus* in which Shakespeare had acted back in 1603, also his masques *of Blackness* and *of Beauty*.

This leaves just 'Mr. W.H.' to be identified, and for Dr A. L. Rowse the logical candidate has to be Sir William Harvey. According to Rowse's scenario the original manuscript of Shakespeare's *Sonnets*, as given to the Earl of Southampton years before, had simply been kept by the Earl's mother. Upon her death Harvey had inherited the manuscript among her 'goods and chattels', and recognising its publication value, had passed it to Thorpe, whereupon the latter dedicated it to Harvey as 'Mr. W.H.'. The good wishes to the 'adventurer ... setting forth' refers to Harvey's marriage, the 'eternitie promised by our ever-living poet' to Harvey's prospects for a family, just as Shakespeare had promised Southampton in the *Sonnets*.

Despite the deceptive straightforwardness of Rowse's solution, an incredible amount of energy has been devoted to arguing for alternative candidates to 'Mr. W.H.' on the assumption that he must have been one and the same as the 'lovely boy' to whom the majority of the *Sonnets* were addressed. Many have mooted William Herbert, Earl of Pembroke, later Lord Chamberlain and one of the pair to whom Heminges and Condell dedicated the First Folio. To complicate matters further, Herbert was the undoubted dedicatee of the two works that Thorpe published immediately after Shakespeare's *Sonnets*.[5]

Not least of the problems here is that while 'Mr' (short for 'Master') was common enough Elizabethan usage for a knight (for example Sir Francis Bacon was frequently 'Master Bacon', and the Countess Southampton often wrote of her second husband, Sir Thomas Heneage as 'Master Heneage') it was far too diminutive a form of address for a Lord, let alone an Earl.[6] Furthermore at the time the *Sonnets* seem to have been written (as distinct from when they were published), Pembroke was a boy far too young to suit Shakespeare's exhortations to marry.

According to another theory, that of the late Leslie Hotson,

'Mr. W.H.' was a Lancashireman named William Hatcliffe, Prince of Purpoole for the Gray's Inn Revels of 1587 (when Shakespeare purportedly wrote his *Sonnets* to him), and who, having fallen on hard times, journeyed to London in 1609 to peddle the *Sonnets* to Thorpe.[7] But Hotson's theory has had few takers.

If, as we argued earlier, Henry Wriothesley Earl of Southampton is the only logical individual to whom Shakespeare addressed the main body of the *Sonnets*, then much of the heat over Mr W.H.'s identity is dissipated. In my view the logical candidate has to be Harvey, but whoever he was, arguably he was publisher Thomas Thorpe's dedicatee, not Shakespeare's. This is further suggested by Thorpe's signing-off initials T.T., and by the different style of the *Sonnets* dedication page compared to those of *Venus and Adonis* and *Lucrece*. The *Sonnets* dedication's Thorpean character is quite evident from the strikingly similar one Thorpe had used for Ben Jonson's *Volpone*, which he published just two years earlier:

TO THE MOST NOBLE

AND MOST AEQUALL

SISTERS

THE TWO FAMOUS UNIVERSITIES

FOR THEIR LOVE

AND

ACCEPTANCE

SHEWN IN HIS POEME

IN THE PRESENTATION:

BEN: JONSON

THE GRATEFULL ACKNOWLEDGER

DEDICATES

BOTH IT, AND HIMSELFE[8]

Whatever the identity of 'Mr. W.H.', and whoever might have made the *Sonnets* manuscript available for publication in 1609, Thorpe had before him quite a coup. Here was a collection of intensely emotional poems from the hand of a now well-established dramatist: one set addressed to a nobleman; the other to an adulteress, both unnamed, yet both surely identifiable to many within the turn-of-the-century Jacobean Court. Also included in the collection was a longish early poem of Shakespeare's, 'A Lover's Complaint', in which the lamenting shepherdess is thought to represent Southampton's wife Elizabeth Vernon, and the young man with 'browny locks' who seduces her, Southampton.

It is important, therefore, to try to ascertain just who Thorpe was; how he had been able to acquire from anyone such a personal manuscript of Shakespeare's; also to determine whether he may or may not have had at least a degree of sanction from the writer. Because of a misleading entry written by Sir Sidney Lee in the 1905 *Dictionary of National Biography*, many have assumed Thorpe to have been a pirate publisher who acted totally without Shakespeare's authority. Such piracy undoubtedly did occur, as in the case of Sir Philip Sidney's equally intimate sonnet series *Astrophel and Stella*. The first publisher, Thomas Newman, congratulated himself upon his 'fortune' to 'light upon' the manuscript, and justified his 'bold' decision to publish it despite Sidney's 'Stella' being still alive, on the grounds of the undesirability that 'anything proceeding from so rare a man should be obscured'.[9] Equally prevalent was the ruse of a publisher to put out as the work of a well-known author writings of an altogether inferior quality. In 1599 printer William Jaggard's publication of *The Passionate Pilgrim* appeared under Shakespeare's name even though this contained only two sonnets that were actually Shakespeare's, and these were used without his authority.

But was Thorpe this sort of operator? As pointed out by Katherine Duncan-Jones, in a career spanning twenty-five years Thorpe put out an impressive list of dramatic, theological and poetic texts and translations, among them Marlowe's translation of Lucan, and works by Ben Jonson and by Chapman. They were often striking for the augustness of the persons to whom they were dedicated.[10]

There also survive two contemporary remarks at least mildly suggestive that Shakespeare may have authorised Thorpe's publication. In the works of the young Scottish literary enthusiast William Drummond of Hawthornden, there occurs an undated mention that:

Sir William Alexander and Shakespeare . . . have lately published their works.[11]

But although Drummond was well acquainted with Alexander whose *Aurora* sonnets were published in 1604, he was too far removed from

Shakespeare for his remark to carry weight. More authoritative is a second remark, made by the contemporary poet Thomas Heywood while complaining of publisher Jaggard's inclusion of works by him under Shakespeare's name in the third edition of *The Passionate Pilgrim*. Condemning Jaggard in his *Apology for Actors* Heywood wrote that Shakespeare 'to do himself right, hath since published them [his sonnets] in his own name'.

Against this it has been noted that had Shakespeare supplied his manuscript to Thorpe he would surely have edited out some of the sonnets of lesser literary merit. Also, unlike *Venus and Adonis* and *Lucrece*, the *Sonnets* contain numerous misprints, as if the author had not been invited to proof-read them, although this may simply reflect *Venus and Adonis* printer Richard Field's greater conscientiousness rather than Shakespeare's. On the whole, particularly given the curtness of the title – *Shake-speare's Sonnets* – and the lack of an author's dedication page along the lines of *Venus and Adonis*'s, the likelihood has to be that Shakespeare did not authorise publication, and that the manuscript came from someone like Harvey. We must also recognise that although, as earlier learned from Francis Meres, Shakespeare had shared some of his 'sugared sonnets' with 'private friends', this does not mean that he was so free with his whole collection. In the case of Sir Philip Sidney's sonnets for instance, these had circulated in two versions: one for Sidney's friends who knew Stella's identity, and another for those who did not, and who would read the poems without discovering any secret passion by which Stella might be compromised.[12]

Whatever the truth, a collection of highly charged and intensely personal poems indicative of Shakespeare's close relationships with two real-life individuals was suddenly in the public domain, and although if we have been correct in dating these sonnets, the events described were long past, if we have correctly identified the individuals to whom they were addressed, both were still very much alive. Southampton was now highly placed in James' Court, while Emilia Lanier, still joylessly married to her royal musician had, as events would show, still much of her old fire.

In this regard it may well be no coincidence that although thirteen known copies survive of Thorpe's 1609 *Shake-speare's Sonnets* – a surprisingly high number compared with the single copy from the first edition of *Venus and Adonis* – no second edition was to appear in Shakespeare's lifetime, or indeed for another thirty years. By contrast the altogether lesser sonnets of Shakespeare's exact contemporary Michael Drayton, already six times printed by 1609, went into three further editions. Although hard evidence is lacking, some form of suppression has to be suspected. Southampton was the one individual best placed to effect this, though it is equally possible that the initiative may have come from the King's Men, given that it was from this time that they appear to have been effective in blocking all further unauthorised publication of new plays by Shakespeare.

Now if Emilia Lanier was the Dark Lady, it can hardly be a coincidence that it was precisely in the wake of the *Sonnets'* publication that she suddenly turned her hand to publishing her own work of this genre. The very next year there was entered for publication a collection of her poetry *Salve Deus Rex Judaeorum*, described on the title page as 'Written by Mistris Aemilia Lanyer, Wife to Captain Alfonso Lanyer, Servant to the King's Majestie', which appeared in 1611. The title page also shows the book to have been printed by Valentine Simmes, a printer who had closely followed Shakespeare's work, having previously produced Quarto editions of *Richard II*, *Richard III*, *Henry IV*, *Part II*, *Much Ado about Nothing*, and a bad Quarto of *Hamlet*.

Lanier's work is notable for its many dedicatory poems to the highest women in the land: James' Queen; the Princess Elizabeth; the Lady Arabella Stuart, and the various Countesses of Kent, Pembroke, Cumberland, Suffolk, Bedford and Dorset. An interesting feature is the surprising quality of her poetry; as remarked by A. L. Rowse 'she is a fair poet. . . . In fact, except for Sidney's sister, the Countess of Pembroke, . . . the best woman poet of the age . . . [with] an easy natural command of iambic pentameter [the metre of Shakespeare's blank verse] and . . . no less easy a command of rhymes. Her defect indeed is that she was too facile and fluent. . . .'[13] From this it is all too easy to see the attraction she would have posed for Shakespeare, by contrast to his almost certainly illiterate wife Anne back in Stratford.

Perhaps the most notable feature of Emilia's book *vis-à-vis* the publication of Shakespeare's *Sonnets* is that mid-way through a rampantly feminist prose address, 'To the Virtuous Reader', she suddenly lashes at:

evil disposed men who, forgetting they were born of women, nourished of women, and that if it were not by the means of women, they would be quite extinguished out of the world . . . do like vipers deface the wombs wherein they were bred, only to give way and utterance to their want of discretion and goodness. . . .[14]

Whether or not this was Emilia's response to what she perceived as an attack on her in the *Sonnets*, only four complete copies of her book survive, and it was not reprinted until the present century.

Curiously, one notable omission from the list of female aristocrats to whom Emilia dedicates her poems was Ferdinando's widow Alice Spencer, dowager Countess of Derby, now married (none too harmoniously) to Lord Egerton, but still very much involved in the literary and dramatic scene, both through her probable participation in Jonson's masques, and as a continuing literary patron. In the same year as the publication of Shakespeare's *Sonnets*, writing-master John Davies of Hereford dedicated his *Holy Rood* to Alice and her three daughters by Ferdinando with the words:

> To the right honourable, well-accomplished Lady Alice, Countess of Derby, my good Lady and Mistress, and to her three right noble daughters ... the Lady Elizabeth Countess of Huntingdon, the Lady Frances Egerton and the Lady Anne, wife to the truly noble Lord Grey Chandos that now is.

In the following year, in *The Scourge of Folly* (entered on the Stationers' Register 8 October 1610), John Davies wrote an epigram to Alice, ending with the atrocious pun: 'Look World, 'tis she whose ALL is Exquisite'.[15] The notable feature for us is that for this same work Davies wrote a particularly interesting eulogy to Shakespeare:

> To our English Terence, Mr. Will Shake-speare
> Some say (good Will) which I, in sport, do sing
> Had'st thou not played some kingly parts in sport,
> Thou hadst been a companion for a King;
> And been a king among the meaner sort.
> Some others rail, but rail as they think fit,
> Thou hast no railing, but a reigning wit
> And honesty thou sow'st, which they do reap
> So, increase their stock which they do keep.[16]

Besides Davies's likening of Shakespeare to the Roman comedy author Terence, particularly notable is the reference to him as 'good

Will', reminding us of Quince's Prologue in *A Midsummer Night's Dream*: 'If we offend, it is with our good will.'[17] Equally notable is the past tense used for Shakespeare as an actor. This suggests that it is no coincidence that Shakespeare's name does not appear with those of Burbage, Heminges, Condell and the other King's Men sharers in the necessarily large cast list for their performance of Ben Jonson's *Catiline* as performed and published in 1611. We may reasonably infer that about this time Shakespeare, now in his mid-forties, decided to give up working as an actor.

But what exactly did Davies mean by Shakespeare having played 'some kingly parts'? The Ghost in *Hamlet*, which there is good reason to believe Shakespeare played, was also a king, but is this a hint of his having performed other kingly roles, perhaps Henry VI and/or Richard II, or is it merely an allusion to the fact that he belonged to the King's Men? Yet more cryptic is his line that if Shakespeare had not 'played some kingly parts', i.e. been an actor, 'Thou hadst been a companion for a King'. Was Davies conceivably referring to the one man who more than any other was a would-be king of Shakespeare's life – Alice Spencer's ill-fated husband, Ferdinando? Davies, with his service to Ferdinando's widow, was well-placed to know all about Shakespeare's background in this regard, making his high opinion of Shakespeare all the more pertinent. But given his emphatic attestation of Shakespeare's 'honesty', frustratingly he does not tell us what exactly he meant by others 'railing', or scoffing. Was this a reference to plays against Shakespeare, such as the Munday-Drayton-Hathway *Sir John Oldcastle*?

We will probably never know, but within weeks of fresh-printed copies of *Shake-speare's Sonnets* coming on sale in London, far out in the Atlantic there was occurring a drama in which Shakespeare was certainly to take a particularly close interest. Back in 1605 the Earl of Southampton and his brother-in-law the Earl of Arundel had despatched a sea-captain to found a colony in Virginia, followed two years later by the formation of the Virginia Company to take charge of this. Then on 24 July 1609 a fleet of nine English vessels was nearing the end of a supply voyage to the new colony when it ran into what the subsequent reports specifically described as 'a cruel tempest', almost certainly a hurricane. Buffeted by the high winds and huge waves the vessels were unable to keep together. One of the two that fared particularly badly was the fleet's flagship, the *Sea Venture*, commanded by Captain Newport and carrying the Admiral,

Sir George Somers; Sir Thomas Gates, the new colony's deputy governor; William Strachey, Secretary to the Virginia Company, and male and female would-be colonists. Leaking too fast for the pumps to cope, *Sea Venture* came to grief just off one of the islands of the Bermudas, grounding 'in between two rocks, where she was fast lodged and locked for further budging'. By great good fortune, however, everyone on board was able to scramble safely ashore, finding themselves on an island so fertile and well provided with hogs, fish and fowl that they were able to live on it for ten months. Using salvaged materials they built two small boats on which they then successfully rejoined the rest of the fleet in Virginia. There they found that they had fared rather better than those already in the colony, several hundred having died from starvation over the wintertime, and an air of mutinous idleness hanging over those who had survived.

The initial reports that reached England were that the *Sea Venture* and all on board were feared lost without trace, so Londoners' joy was all the greater when, in the early autumn of 1610, Captain Newport, Sir Thomas Gates and others returned to tell what had really happened. Both to set this in writing and to allay public concern about the viability of the Virginia enterprise, the Council of Virginia issued *A True Declaration of the state of the Colonie in Virginia* that gave not only a vivid account of the 'tempest' but even the very idea for a play:

> What is there in all this tragical Comedy that should discourage us with impossibility of the enterprise? When of all the Fleet, one only ship, by a secret leak was endangered and yet in the gulf of despair was so graciously preserved.

Whether or not Shakespeare saw this particular pamphlet, in *The Tempest* he certainly conveyed the prevailing mood of marvel at the preservation of all who had been shipwrecked, as when following the dramatic storm at sea with which the play opens, Ariel reports to Prospero: 'Not a hair perish'd'.[18]

One description of the Bermuda story that Shakespeare certainly seems to have read and used was the pamphlet *A Discovery of the Bermudas* which *Sea Venture* voyager Sylvester Jourdan put out smartly upon his return with Newton and Gates in 1610. Here is one description exclusive to Jourdan:

all our men, being utterly spent, tired and disabled for longer labour, were even resolved, without any hope of their lives, to shut up hatches and to have committed themselves to the mercy of the sea ... they were so over-wearied, and their spirits so spent with long fasting, and continuance of their labour, that for the most part they were fallen asleep in corners, and wheresoever they chanced first to sit or lie.

Shakespeare seems to have distilled this into the spirit Ariel's report to Prospero:

> The mariners all under hatches stow'd;
> Who, with a charm join'd to their suffer'd labour,
> I have left asleep ...[19]

Shakespeare also definitely read a report written on 10 July 1610 by the Virginia Company secretary William Strachey (who stayed on in Virginia), which was very shortly after brought back to England by the returning Captain Newport and Thomas Gates.[20] Among details of the 'tempest' exclusive to Strachey is a particularly graphic mention of Sir George Somers seeing 'sea-fire':

> an apparition of a little round light, like a faint star, trembling and streaming along with a sparkling blaze, half the height upon the mainmast, and shooting sometimes from shroud to shroud, tempting to settle as it were upon any of the four shrouds: and after three or four hours together, or rather more, half the night it kept with us, running sometimes along the mainyard to the very end, and then returning.[21]

This can be readily enough identified as the electrical phenomenon known as St Elmo's fire, but for us the particular fascination is that Shakespeare's reading of this passage may well have given him the inspiration to dream up the character of Ariel, who otherwise, along with the rest of the play, derives from no known source. In the second scene of The Tempest, Ariel reports to his master Prospero:

> I boarded the king's ship; now on the beak,
> Now in the waist, the deck, in every cabin,

> I flam'd amazement: sometime I'd divide,
> And burn in many places; on the topmast,
> The yards and bowsprit, would I flame distinctly,
> Then meet and join.[22]

Among other indications that Shakespeare used Strachey's report as his source, Strachey refers to the *Sea Venture*'s crew catching on the rocks birds he called 'sea-mews' – almost certainly the origin of what appears mis-transcribed in *The Tempest*'s First Folio text as Caliban's promise: 'I'll get thee/Young scamels from the rock.'[23] Also in one of his notes Strachey refers to the early description of the Bermuda islands by Gonzalo Ferdinando Oviedo, arguably suggesting names for *The Tempest* characters Gonzalo and Ferdinand.

There are then some powerful indications that Shakespeare took considerable interest in everything written down about the Bermuda shipwreck, and his early transforming of it into *The Tempest* is even more definite. The Revels Account for Hallowmas Night (1 November) 1611 is unusually informative telling us that the King's Players 'presented at Whitehall before the King's Majesty a play called The Tempest'.[24] Here of considerable interest is that while the Council of Virginia's *True Declaration* and Jourdan's pamphlet would both have been readily available to Shakespeare in the public domain, Strachey's account was not. The Virginia Company seem deliberately to have suppressed it because of its candour on the shortcomings of the Virginia venture. As a result it was not published until 1625, nine years after Shakespeare's death, when it became part of *Purchas His Pilgrimes*.

This accordingly raises the interesting question of who, within the closed circle of those 'in the know' about the Virginia enterprise, was Shakespeare on sufficiently friendly terms with to be allowed to read such privileged information? Conceivably this could have been the Earl of Southampton, certainly a major figure in the company, the difficulty being the lack of hard evidence on Shakespeare's continued association with him.

Another yet more plausible alternative has been argued by the late Dr Leslie Hotson.[25] In the parish of St Mary Aldermanbury, close to Shakespeare's fellows John Heminges and Henry Condell, and not far from Shakespeare's Silver Street lodgings, lived the Digges family, owners of a particularly fine house in Philip Lane, immediately off Addle Street where the Hemingeses lived. After the death of the notable Elizabethan engineer and astronomer Thomas Digges in 1595, the family comprised his widow Mrs Anne Digges and their two sons Dudley and Leonard. Some measure of Shakespeare's involvement with the family is indicated by the fact that he would appoint Anne Digges' second husband Thomas Russell to be overseer of his will, while young Leonard Digges would write one of the poetic tributes to him in the First Folio. But the Digges who was particularly involved with the Virginia enterprise was Sir Dudley (knighted by James in 1607), whose enthusiasm for American colonisation had been inherited from his late father's interest in searching for the North West Passage. That Sir Dudley was a friend of Virginia Company secretary William Strachey is evident from the fact that both wrote tributes for Jonson plays, Dudley for *Volpone* and Strachey for *Sejanus*, in the latter of which Shakespeare, Heminges and Condell acted. Independently, Heminges is known to have attended Digges' wedding and signed as a witness.[26] It is easy then to understand that Sir Dudley could well have made Shakespeare party to at least non-classified parts of Strachey's letter, thereby giving Shakespeare the extra background inspiration for writing *The Tempest*.

But Shakespeare took ideas from other sources as well. Quite definitely he read Montaigne's essay 'Of Cannibals' in the translation made by Southampton's Italian tutor John Florio. In the edition published in 1603, Florio had written:

It is a nation ... that hath no kind of traffic, no knowledge of letters, no intelligence of numbers, no name of magistrate, nor of politic superiority; no use of service, of riches or of poverty; no contracts, no successions, no partitions, no occupation but idle; no respect of kindred ... no use of wine, corn, or metal.[27]

Transmuted into the mouth of *The Tempest*'s 'honest old Councellor' Gonzalo this became:

I' th' commonwealth
... no kind of traffic
Would I admit; no name of magistrate;
Letters should not be known; riches, poverty,

And use of service, none; contract, succession,
Bourn, bound of land, tilth, vineyard, none;
No use of metal, corn, or wine, or oil;
No occupation; all men idle, all . . .[28]

As ever with Shakespeare, despite his borrowings, what he produced in *The Tempest* was yet another *tour de force*. Once again we have the sort of storm used for *Pericles*, but now deployed all the more effectively as the opening scene, to make the audience really *feel* they are witnessing a storm at sea. With thunder from the backstage crew; the Ship-Master on the upper level; sea-drenched mariners lurching onto the main stage; the grandee passengers dressed as for a wedding trying to come up via the trap-door from below stage – it is a fascinating exercise to try to reconstruct how the scene would have been managed in Shakespeare's time. The design, presentation and extensive use of music are such that throughout the play he seems to have been thinking particularly of performances in enclosed theatres such as Whitehall's Banqueting Hall and the Blackfriars.

One indication of this is the way Shakespeare's script calls for Prospero and Ariel to leave the stage at the end of Act IV only to re-enter at the beginning of Act V. This is the first known instance in Shakespeare's work of him positively writing in a break between two acts, as would be necessary when a sophisticated audience expected their entertainment to be broken up in this way, but quite unnecessary for the no-interval, no-break productions normal at the Globe. Confirming *The Tempest*'s production at the Blackfriars John Dryden, albeit belatedly, wrote in 1674 that 'The Play . . . had formerly been acted with success in the Blackfriars'.[29]

Equally indicative of Shakespeare writing *The Tempest* for the Blackfriars are two later scenes particularly pandering to the vogue for masques. The first of these is Act III scene iii with its extensive instructions:

Solemn and strange music; . . . Enter several strange Shapes, bringing in a banquet. . . .
Thunder and lightning. Enter Ariel, like a Harpy; claps his wings upon the table; and with a quaint device, the banquet vanishes.

J.C. Adams, author of an authoritative book *The Globe Playhouse*, gave particularly careful thought to how this would have been contrived in Shakespeare's time: Ariel probably descended using the same sort of crane used in *Cymbeline*, momentarily spreading his wings, and thus concealing the mechanism for the banquet's vanishing, probably through the swivelling of a false table top. Even more exotic and masque-like is the first scene of Act IV, in which Juno descends in the same manner as her husband Jupiter had done in *Cymbeline*, followed by dances of nymphs, etc. The extensive nature of the stage directions is probably due to the new complexities demanded by productions of this kind, though as an alternative Dr A. L. Rowse has suggested that Shakespeare was now increasingly writing back home in Stratford.

With such winding-down towards retirement in mind, certainly for many scholars the other great feature of *The Tempest* is that from many of the words Shakespeare put into the mouth of Prospero, he would seem to have written the play – easily ranking among his finest – as a form of swan-song. At the end of the masque Prospero intones:

> Our revels now are ended. These our actors,
> As I foretold you, were all spirits, and
> Are melted into air, into thin air:
> And, like the baseless fabric of this vision,
> The cloud-capp'd towers, the gorgeous palaces
> The solemn temples, the great globe itself,
> Yea, all which it inherit, shall dissolve,
> And, like this insubstantial pageant faded,
> Leave not a rack behind.[30]

Later, in words that might easily be the author's describing his creations, Prospero declares 'I have bedimm'd/The noontide sun',[31] and indeed Shakespeare had done this, with scenes performed early afternoon in the open air, making his audiences believe they were seeing scenes set in blackest night. Prospero goes on to say that he had:

> call'd forth the mutinous winds,
> And 'twixt the green sea and the azur'd vault
> Set roaring war . . .

Yes, Shakespeare had done that too, in the opening scene of *The Tempest*. Prospero even goes to the lengths of declaring, quite inappositely for himself, but most appositely for Shakespeare:

> graves at my command
> Have wak'd their sleepers, op'd, and let 'em forth
> By my so potent Art.

By his indeed so potent art Shakespeare had brought forth from the grave great figures from history, such as Talbot, Gower, Henry v, Cleopatra, Julius Caesar, and so many more, making his audiences believe they were alive again – standing, not on the Globe or Blackfriars stage, but once again on the field of battle, or back in ancient Egypt or Rome.

Nonetheless, it is important not to take such thinking too far. Even in this, one of his most memorable passages, Shakespeare was revamping lines from his favourite Ovid's *Metamorphoses*, both as he knew them from the original Latin, and as translated by Golding in an edition that would have been readily available during his schooldays:

> By charms I make the calm seas rough, and make the rough seas plain
> And cover all the sky with clouds, and chase them thence again.
> By charms I raise and lay the winds, and burst the viper's jaw. . . .
> I call up dead men from their graves: and thee O lightsome moon
> I darken oft, though beaten brass abate thy peril soon.
> Our sorcery dims the morning fair, and darks the sun at noon.[32]

Despite so much of Shakespeare's life being obscure, the fact that he merely rented lodgings in London, that he purchased New Place, and not least that he invested in income-producing land around Stratford, all seem evidence enough that he intended to retire to Stratford. There are signs that he was actively thinking of this around 1609–10 when New Place was temporarily occupied by his cousin Thomas Greene, who was suffering some delay gaining occupancy to the place he wanted to live in. Among Greene's preserved memoranda is a note of around September 1609 stating that he 'perceived I might stay another year at New Place', suggesting that the time was coming when his dramatist cousin would want permanently to return to

Stratford to take up proper residence in the style for which he had worked so long.[33]

But as always with Shakespeare we find the element of the unexpected. Just when it most looks as if he is finally to shake off the dust of London, after, to the best of anyone's knowledge, he had been a tenant throughout his entire working life in the city, we find him buying a London property. Why?

CHAPTER 22

A Curious Purchase

On 11 May 1612, just over six months after the first recorded performance of *The Tempest*, Shakespeare gave evidence at the Court of Requests in Westminster in respect of a minor court case. One of the very few days in Shakespeare's life when we can be sure exactly where he was, we know about this court appearance from the same cache of twenty-six documents discovered by American professor Charles Wallace from which we learned of Shakespeare's lodging in the Silver Street house of tire maker Christopher Mountjoie and his wife Marie.

In 1604 a fellow lodger of Shakespeare's, King's trumpeter's son Stephen Belott, who was one of Mountjoie's three apprentices, had married his employer's only daughter Mary in the local parish church of St Olave. But after the death of Marie Mountjoie two years later, bitterness appears to have developed between Belott and his father-in-law. Mountjoie appears to have been incensed by his daughter and son-in-law setting up a tire-making establishment of their own. The Belotts, for their part, resented Mountjoie having given them a marriage 'portion', that is, a dowry-like allowance of money and household goods, much less than he had originally led them to expect. This latter dispute caused them to bring the action against him in the Court of Requests during which Shakespeare was called upon as witness.

In the evidence he gave, Shakespeare proved unable to be particularly helpful. He stated that he had known both Belott and Mountjoie for some ten years, and that Belott did 'well and honestly behave himself' while in Mountjoie's service, likewise Mountjoie did 'bear and show great goodwill and affection' towards Belott. Although he knew that Mountjoie had promised to give Belott a marriage portion, he could not remember how much this was, nor when it was to be paid. While he and Belott had been lodgers in Mountjoie's house 'they had amongst themselves many conferences about the marriage', and Marie Mountjoie had apparently urged Shakespeare to encourage Belott over this in a manner strikingly reminiscent of that which we earlier surmised the Dowager Countess of Southampton had urged him in respect of her son. But in the face of claims that old Mountjoie had given his daughter and son-in-law no more than £10 and some old furniture, worn blankets, coarse napkins and two pairs of scissors for their marriage portion, Shakespeare pleaded inability to remember exactly 'what implements and necessaries of household stuff' had been given. Nor did he know what sum had been promised to the couple in the event of Mountjoie's death.

Shakespeare thereupon signed his name to this declaration, and however many times he had done so before, this particular specimen [see below], preserved in the Public Record Office with the rest of the Belott-Mountjoie documents, is the earliest of the only six known to survive.

Fig 11
The earliest known Shakespeare signature, 1612. From Shakespeare's deposition in the Belott–Mountjoie dispute, 11 May 1612. (Public Record Office, Court of Requests, Documents of Shakespearean Interest Req. 4/1)

As remarked by Norman Evans of the Public Record Office:

> the dramatist's signature appears in the contracted form 'Wllm Shkp'. The 'p' is usually regarded as a form of the common abbreviation 'p' for 'per', which would make the signature 'Shakper'. Some students maintain that the letter is a long 's' or a mark of abbreviation and read the name as 'Shaks' or 'Shak'. All six of the known signatures differ from each other in some particular and this example is the most awkward of them all.[1]

The signature certainly is awkward, and includes a large blot, possibly attributable, as suggested by Edgar Fripp, to the rough paper on which it is written.[2] Although it is the earliest piece of uncontestedly original handwriting we have for Shakespeare, the signature on its own is too isolated for any easy judgments to be made from it, and we will shortly encounter the other specimens from which better and properly comparative evaluation can be made.

Meanwhile, a little earlier in 1612, there had occurred the death of Shakespeare's forty-five-year-old brother Gilbert, the one to whom he had entrusted the purchase of the land from the Combes in 1602, and who seems to have continued living at the Birthplace house along with his slightly younger sister Joan and her hatter husband Will Hart. Gilbert may possibly have continued his father's trade as glover,[3] although there is no direct evidence of this. The entry for 3 February in the Stratford burial register simply reads 'Gilbert Shakespeare, adolescens', this latter term seeming to have carried the meaning bachelor just as 'adolescentula' was used for spinster.

Whatever Shakespeare's feelings over the death of this second of the four Shakespeare brothers they went unrecorded, as also over the death, later this same year, of his royal patron's son Henry, Prince of Wales, the young man hitherto confidently expected to be James' successor. A vigorous and handsome eighteen-year-old in 1612, Prince Henry had been very much the champion of the Puritans, who were so confident of his support of them when King they had circulated verses about him:

> Henry the 8. pulld down abbeys and cells
> But Henry the 9. shall pull down Bishops and bells.[4]

The Prince's first symptoms of illness – persistent headache and bouts of fever – had begun a little before Shakespeare gave his evidence in the Belott–Mountjoie suit, and his condition steadily worsened until his death early in the November. From the several surviving contemporary accounts, among these a certain Master W.H.'s *Relation of the Sickness and Death of the most Illustrious Henry, Prince of Wales* (curiously no one seems to have suggested this Master W.H. as dedicatee of the *Sonnets*), the cause can be diagnosed as typhoid fever, most likely contracted from the unwashed hands of a carrier of, or sufferer from, the disease who had prepared his food or drink.[5]

Henry's funeral was held on 4 December with a scale of pomp and ceremony hitherto paralleled only by that of Elizabeth, whereupon from London's presses there poured more than thirty literary and poetic expressions of grief, yet as at the death of Elizabeth,

Shakespeare's voice was again strangely silent. Indeed, Henry's death may perhaps not have been quite as much a source of grief as might be expected, even for Henry's mother the secretly Catholic Queen Anne, for she had always preferred her younger son Charles, upon whom there now descended his particularly fateful mantle as heir to the throne.

Meanwhile at no point in James' reign could Hamlet's words 'The funeral bak'd meats/Did coldly furnish forth the marriage tables'[6] have been more appropriate. Coming when it did, Henry's death cut right across the wedding plans for James and Anne's only surviving daughter, the sixteen-year-old Princess Elizabeth. Although there had been both Catholic and Protestant princes among Elizabeth's prospective suitors, her own preference was apparently for the latter, and when there arrived seeking her hand the German Protestant Frederick, Elector Palatine of the Rhine, who was of the same age as her, she received him most warmly. Despite her mother, who still nurtured hopes for a Catholic match, apparently taunting her with the title of 'Goodwife Palsgrave', intimating that she might be marrying beneath her, Elizabeth's response was that she 'would rather be the Palsgrave's wife, than the greatest papist Queen in Christendom'.[7] In the event, much to Anne of Denmark's quiet chagrin, Frederick won general approval, and the couple announced their engagement before James in the Banqueting House at Whitehall on 27 December.

Whatever gloom might have been cast by Henry's death, the Chamber Accounts show the King's Men putting on their biggest programme of plays ever for this winter season,[8] preparations for which must have been hugely exacting. Frustratingly the accounts do not show the individual dates of these performances, but they do record no less than fourteen play titles specifically described as presented 'before the Princess Highness the Lady Elizabeth and the Prince Palatine Elector'. Among those definitely by Shakespeare can be recognised *Much Ado about Nothing* (apparently so well received that it was repeated), also *Othello*, *The Winter's Tale* and *The Tempest*. In addition what the accounts record as *Caesar's Tragedy* is almost certainly *Julius Caesar*, and *Sir John Falstaffe* either the first or second part of *Henry IV*, showing that even after fifteen years Falstaff's ebullience was still drawing fans.

The list's inclusion of *The Tempest* is logical enough in view of the fact that it was Shakespeare's latest play, and there is also a respectable case for his having either introduced into the play, or more likely adapted in Elizabeth and Frederick's honour, the scene in Act IV of the wedding masque which Prospero arranges for his daughter Miranda and her betrothed.[9] According to the general run of this argument, *The Tempest* would have been performed the night of Elizabeth and Frederick's betrothal, 27 December 1612, Shakespeare arranging for the actors playing Juno and Ceres to turn from the play's young lovers to the real-life ones in their audience, offering them their blessings upon their marriage:

Juno: Honour, riches, marriage blessing
          Long continuance, and increasing,
          Hourly joys be still upon you!
          Juno sings her blessings on you.
Ceres:

          . . .
          Spring come to you at the farthest
          In the very end of harvest!
          Scarcity and want shall shun you;
          Ceres' blessing so is on you.[10]

But it is also evident that, regardless of whether Shakespeare had intended *The Tempest* as his last play, someone now persuaded him to write a new work specially for the festivities to accompany Frederick and Elizabeth's marriage, the date of which had been romantically chosen as St Valentine's day, 1613. And it is important to see this new project of Shakespeare's in the context of the festivities as a whole. In the week preceding the marriage, a fireworks display was staged from barges moored opposite Whitehall on the theme of St George's rescue of the Queen of the Amazons, which was only a moderate success due to technical difficulties with some of the set-pieces. This was followed on the wedding eve by a grandiosely staged mock sea battle, in which, using longboats and pinnaces disguised to resemble huge galleons and galleases, a cast of a thousand musketeers and five hundred Thames watermen attempted to re-enact the Venetians defeating the Turks at Algiers, this latter being represented by a huge backdrop set up on the Lambeth shore opposite Whitehall. Due to ineffectual stage-management the royal spectators became bored, and worse, unacceptably large numbers of the amateur 'cast' lost hands and eyes due to mishaps in the firing of hundreds of cannons.

The cost of these ventures (or rather misadventures) was £6,000;[11] that of two masques commissioned by the Inns of Court, for the same festivities £4,000.[12] When seen against these extravagances the £153.6s.8d. paid to the King's Men for their twenty command performances up to the May of 1613, once again appears as small change. Even so a new play put on by the company for the Court was always an event. John Chamberlain wrote of the anticipated performance of 16 February, just two days after Elizabeth and Frederick's wedding:

> Much expectation was made of a stage play to be acted in the Great Hall by the King's players, where many hundred of people stood attending the same.[13]

There can be little doubt this was Shakespeare's *Henry VIII*, a play definitely new at around this time as evident from a highly informative letter written in the June from Sir Henry Wotton to his nephew Sir Edmund Bacon. Referring to the play under its alternative title *All is True*, Wotton marvelled at its spectacular costuming and props:

> set forth with many extraordinary circumstances of pomp and majesty, even to the matting of the stage: the Knights of the Order with their Georges and garters, the guards with their embroidered coats, and the like.[14]

Although Arden editor R. A. Foakes has expressed himself puzzled by this description, on the grounds that *Henry VIII* 'provides no evidence' for such a scene,[15] if he had acquainted himself with the earlier discussed Sherborne Castle procession painting of Queen Elizabeth [see pl. 39] then read Shakespeare's stage directions for the coronation of Anne Boleyn, Elizabeth I's mother, as set out in Act IV scene i of *Henry VIII* he might have thought differently:

> DUKE OF SUFFOLK, *in his robe of estate, his coronet on his head, bearing a long white wand, as High Steward.*
> *A canopy borne by four of the* CINQUE-PORTS; *under it the* QUEEN *in her robe; in her hair richly adorned with pearl, crowned.*
> *Certain* LADIES or COUNTESSES . . . .

It so happens that Southampton's grandfather, Sir Thomas Wriothes-ley, had been Garter King at Arms at Anne Boleyn's coronation and in the stage directions Shakespeare specified his wearing a tabard of the royal arms and, as correctly for Garter King, a gilt crown of oakleaves with an inscribed rim *Miserere mei Deus secundum magnam misericordiam tuam*. Although Shakespeare gave no indication of being aware of Southampton's relation to this particular Garter King, and gave the character only a single short set of lines, they are highly important ones:

> Heaven, from thy endless goodness, send prosperous life, long and ever-happy, to the high and mighty Princess of England, Elizabeth![16]

Exactly the same formula was used after the wedding of the Princess Elizabeth with Prince Frederick, as recorded by Henry Peacham:

> Mr. Garter Principall King of Armes, published the stile of the Prince and Princesse to this effect. All Health, Happinesse and Honour be to the High and Mighty Princes, Frederick ... and Elizabeth.[17]

Both timing and certain elements of content therefore suggest that Shakespeare wrote *Henry VIII* for the wedding of Elizabeth and Frederick, yet it does not appear among those listed in the Chamber Accounts, and if it was the play so eagerly anticipated for 16 February, something definitely went awry, for according to one contemporary account: 'it lapsed contrarie, for greater pleasures were preparing.'[18] Were preparations for the play not yet complete? Or did someone who had seen the script or watched it in rehearsal feel there was something about it that made the play hardly the best entertainment for royal wedding celebrations? The mood Shakespeare set is quite apparent from the Prologue:

> I come no more to make you laugh; things now
> That bear a weighty and a serious brow,
> Sad, high and working, full of state and woe;
> Such noble scenes as draw the eye to flow,
> We now present.

ending, after an exhortation to 'Think ye see/ The very persons of our noble story' with the doom-laden:

> then in a moment, see
> How soon this mightiness meets misery.
> And if you can be merry then, I'll say
> A man may weep upon his wedding day.

Whatever the circumstances, with *Henry VIII* Shakespeare made his first assay on an English history play since *Henry V* fourteen years previously, and came the closest in his historical *oeuvre* to his own time. Regardless of any presentation before the Court at Whitehall, he seems to have devised it – as in the case of *The Tempest* – pre-eminently for presentation at the Blackfriars. This is not only because of its already mentioned splendour, but also because the play's scene of the deliberations over Henry VIII's divorcing of Queen Katherine of Aragon[19] had actually taken place eighty-four years before in the same Blackfriars Great Chamber that was now his company's indoor theatre. Shakespeare knew this from his source, Holinshed,'[20] and he duly set as the scene location: 'London. A hall in Blackfriars', from which one cannot help but feel it must greatly have appealed to him to re-create history in this way – like literally raising the ghosts of the past.

Henry VIII was quite definitely Shakespeare's final play, and it has been suggested that he wrote it in partnership with John Fletcher, the rising young playwright who was son of the Bishop of London and who would go on to succeed Shakespeare as one of the King's Men's leading dramatists. The fact that Heminges and Condell would later include *Henry VIII* in their First Folio of Shakespeare's works argues strongly for it being substantially his, but there are signs of another, and now distinctly Protestant, hand. Important, and arguably Shakespeare's responsibility, is the fact that the play's unequivocal central theme is the tragedy of Henry VIII's divorcing of Katherine of Aragon. As a Catholic Cardinal who becomes agent of the divorce, Wolsey is portrayed as hopelessly compromised by his pandering to a prince as mortal as Henry VIII, hence his 'immortal' last words adapted from ones reported to have been said to Sir William Kingston, Constable of the Tower of London, and a subsequent owner of the Blackfriars:[21]

> Had I but serv'd my God with half the zeal
> I serv'd my King, he would not in mine age
> Have left me naked to mine enemies.[22]

As Henry VIII is portrayed he looks and sounds kingly and authoritative, yet he is a creature of whim and caprice, all too easily swayed by flatterers, his loyalty to them extending no further than the next whisper to reach his ear. Despite the play's ultimate title, Henry is not the play's central character, either as hero or villain.

By contrast, Queen Katherine of Aragon is portrayed as the genuinely heroic victim, in the mould of Cordelia, Desdemona and Hermione before her, full of charity on hearing the news of the downfall and repentance of her chief enemy, Wolsey, and in her dying blessed with that vision of life everlasting reserved for those who, according to traditional belief, 'died well'. Up until this moment Shakespeare's masques had been pagan. Now in this, his final masque, he presents as through the inward eyes of the dignified Spanish Catholic Queen whom Henry VIII so cruelly spurned, that most sacred glimpse of the world beyond that mortals can ever aspire to:

> THE VISION: *Enter solemnly tripping one after another, six Personages clad in white robes, wearing on their heads garlands of bays, and golden vizards on their faces. . . . They . . . dance; and at certain changes, the first two hold a spare garland over her head, at which, as it were by inspiration, she* [Katherine] *makes in her sleep signs of rejoicing, and holdeth up her hands to heaven. And so in their dancing vanish, carrying the garland with them.*[23]

In what is an extended deathbed scene Katherine even goes on to pronounce a blessing upon that future scourge of Protestants, her daughter Mary:

> The dews of heaven fall thick in blessings on her![24]

All this provides a fascinating contrast to the final Act in which the atmosphere of tragedy rolls away, and we suddenly find the Protestant Cranmer the subject of the King's favour, pronouncing *his* blessing upon the infant just born to Anne Boleyn, the future Queen Elizabeth, and prophesying of her:

> Truth shall nurse her,
> Holy and heavenly thoughts still counsel her;
> She shall be lov'd and fear'd.
>
> . . .
>
> God shall be truly known; and those about her
> From her shall read the perfect ways of honour,
> And by those claim their greatness, not by blood.[25]

When Shakespeare has his characters prophesy, they almost invariably utter all-time truths. So if these are Shakespeare's lines they appear thereby as his first clear statement, not only of his approval of Elizabeth herself as an individual, but also of 'those about her' and their 'perfect ways of honour', even of her religion, for in her time 'God shall truly be known'. Cranmer later goes on:

> She shall be, to the happiness of England,
> An aged princess; many days shall see her,
> And yet no day without a deed to crown it. . . .
> But she must die—
> She must, the saints must have her—yet a virgin;
> A most unspotted lily shall she pass
> To th'ground, and all the world shall mourn her.[26]

Nor does the writer of Cranmer's words reserve this unprecedented adulation just for Elizabeth. He declares of James:

> but as when
> The bird of wonder dies, the maiden phoenix,
> Her ashes new create another heir
> As great in admiration as herself,
> So shall she leave her blessedness to one—
>
> . . .
>
> Who from the sacred ashes of her honour
> Shall star-like rise, as great in fame as she was,
> And so stand fix'd.
>
> . . .

> Wherever the bright sun of heaven shall shine,
> His honour and the greatness of his name
> Shall be, and make new nations. . . . our children's children
> Shall see this and bless heaven.[27]

So was Shakespeare up to his old politico-religious subtlety, or had another hand taken over? Dr Rowse, for one, has accepted the 'unspotted lily' passage as a genuine Shakespearean tribute to Elizabeth, and after all back in *Henry v* Shakespeare had referred to Elizabeth as 'our gracious empress'. Yet Cranmer's eulogistic words sound too 'over the top' to be Shakespeare's, and on literary and stylistic grounds the whole fifth act has been doubted as of his authorship. So could it be that Shakespeare's true *valete* not only to *Henry viii* but to his whole career as a dramatist was with Queen Katherine's deathbed scene? And that – in whatever circumstances – it was to Fletcher that he passed the task of giving the play its final Protestant twist, taking it out of the genre of tragedy and thus making it a work written in the same ecumenical spirit which his Protestant son-in-law John Hall displayed in his medical practice? If Shakespeare was Catholic-tinged there is a certain fittingness in his bowing out in this way, England's history for him ending when Henry viii broke with the Universal Church (however flawed this may have been in his time), and taking responsibility for England's Church into his own distinctly spotted hands.

Fletcher would succeed Shakespeare as the King's Men's leading dramatist, and whether Shakespeare did write a couple of works in some sort of partnership with him – a lost ghost story *Cardenio*, and *Two Noble Kinsmen* – is a matter of too involved a literary nature to be tackled here. The one quite definite last work of a creative kind that we know Shakespeare to have been working on is of a different character to anything recorded hitherto.

One of the Earl of Southampton's closest friends, it may be remembered, had been Roger Manners, fifth Earl of Rutland, a fellow playgoer and participant in the Essex rebellion who had died only the previous June. His monument in Bottesford had been made by the same Gerard Johnson workshop in Southwark that had constructed the Titchfield one for the second Earl of Southampton back in 1594. The earldom thereupon fell to Roger's brother Francis who elected to perform as one of the tilters at James i's Accession Day the following March, his chosen *impresa* device, as it would appear, being designed for him by Shakespeare and painted by Burbage. The evidence for this, alluded to much earlier in connection with the Rutland theory of Shakespeare authorship (see page 15), consists of an entry in the Rutland steward's accounts for 31 March 1613 recording a payment of forty-four shillings 'to Mr Shakespeare in gold about my Lord's *impresa*', and another forty-four shillings to 'Richard Burbadge for painting and making it'.[28] The fact that the amount was 'in gold' and totalled forty-four shillings indicates it was paid in new coins called 'Jacobuses', worth twenty-two shillings each.

But now that the Rutland authorship theory can be set firmly aside, the entry is fascinating from a variety of respects. First, given the considerable financial stature and success that Shakespeare and Burbage had by now achieved, it seems absurd to suppose that at this point in their careers, and for such a paltry sum, the pair suddenly chose to take up *impresa*-making as a new service to the aristocracy. That those who could do this sort of thing were much sought-after is quite apparent from Henry Peacham (to whom is attributed the *Titus Andronicus* costume drawing), writing both in 1606 and again in 1612:

> I am sorry that our . . . great personages must seek far and near for some . . . Italian to . . . invent their devices, our Englishmen being held for *Vaunients* [good-for-nothings].[29]

As rightly stressed by Leslie Hotson, Shakespeare and Burbage seem to have been rare experts in the art, Shakespeare having displayed his familiarity with the world of the Accession Day tilts at least as far back as his writing of *Love's Labour's Lost*, also arguably with Burbage producing *impresa* devices for Ferdinando Stanley on his tilt appearances between 1589 and 1592. So is it not likely that he and Burbage were simply reviving an old skill of theirs as a favour to Rutland? Just how, apart from the accounts book entry, Shakespeare and Burbage's contribution to the Tilts could go unnoticed is quite evident from the fact that in the only surviving contemporary description of the 1613 Tilts, Sir Henry Wotton records that none of the emblems was a success except the two carried by the Earl of Pembroke and his brother, some of the rest being so confused 'that their meaning is not yet understood'.[30] Albeit from such a dull-seeming source the delightful feature of the Rutland account book entry is its indication of the continuing strong bond between

Shakespeare and Burbage so that even in the autumn of their lives they continued to pool their skills, Shakespeare creatively dreaming up the original motif, and Burbage using all his painterly gift to translate it into a work of heraldic art.

From exactly the same month in which Shakespeare and Burbage were working on Manners' tournament device, there survives evidence of an altogether different and certainly even more puzzling piece of activity on Shakespeare's part. In the Guildhall Library, and the British Museum, London, there can be found respectively the original title-deed and mortgage of Shakespeare's only acquisition of property in London: part of one of the gatehouses to the Blackfriars precinct in which his company operated their Blackfriars theatre. The original documents were first discovered in the late eighteenth century among the papers of the Fetherstonhaugh family, to whom properties in the area had descended, and the two Shakespeare signatures they carry [see fig 12, below], both universally deemed authentic, follow on from the earliest-known signature, that on the Belott–Mountjoie suit, in exhibiting a lawyer's style abbreviation to the last letters of Shakespeare's name, also some ugly-looking blots.

Fig 12
Shakespeare signatures of 1613. Left, from the original manuscript of the Blackfriars Gatehouse conveyance, 10 March 1613 (preserved in the Guildhall Library, London); right, from the original manuscript of the Blackfriars Gatehouse mortgage, 11 March 1613 (British Library Egerton MS. 1787).

The documents' content shows that Shakespeare, having to the best of anyone's knowledge rented accommodation throughout his working career in London, and now being poised to retire gracefully in his native Stratford, purchased a piece of London property. Although it can certainly be argued that the gatehouse was convenient for the Blackfriars theatre, with a ferry for crossing to the Globe just down the road, even so it is difficult to regard the purchase as anything other than curious. Admittedly the academics have regarded it relatively straightforwardly. For Schoenbaum 'It was, apparently, an investment pure and simple'.[31] For Rowse likewise 'the gatehouse was no more than an investment'.[32] But a man usually likes to have his investments where he can keep an eye on them, and as Schoenbaum insisted in the very same paragraph 'the playwright was now living in retirement at New Place'. So was there something more?

Although the Gatehouse has been long destroyed, its location can be pinpointed with reasonable accuracy. In the words of the deed it was:

All that dwelling-house or tenement, with the appurtenances, situate and being within the precinct, circuit and compass of the late Black Fryers, London . . . abutting upon a street leading down to Puddle Wharf on the east part, right against the King's Majesty's Wardrobe, part of which said tenement is erected over a great gate leading to a capital messuage . . . in the tenure of the right Honorable Henry now Earl of Northumberland . . . and also that plot of ground on the west side of the same tenement . . . which said plot of ground was sometime parcel and taken out of a great piece of void ground lately used for a garden.[33]

From this and related descriptions it can be identified as the upper floor of a long-destroyed building that seems to have straddled the Blackfriars precinct's eastern entrance, at or near where a way called Ireland Yard met St Andrew's Hill, leading down to the river [see fig 10, page 336]. Ireland Yard and St Andrew's Hill still exist in a nondescript set of streets south-west of St Paul's Cathedral. The building closest to the site of Shakespeare's only London purchase today seems to be the quaintly shaped Cockpit public house.

But who did Shakespeare purchase the property from? We are told that the previous owner had been Henry Walker 'citizen and minstrel of London', and its 'now or late' tenant one William Ireland, who gave his name to Ireland Yard. Henry Walker was presumably another of Shakespeare's musical acquaintances along with the already mentioned Robert Johnson. But, rather more significantly, the document also records that previously the Gatehouse had been 'in the tenure of John Fortescue gent'. This was John Fortescue of Lordington, Sussex, whose uncle was Sir John Fortescue, Elizabeth's Master of the Royal Wardrobe (the repository of royal costumery), just over the way from the Gatehouse, and for whom John the nephew seems to have worked in a minor capacity.

Possibly relevantly, around this particular time, 1613, Sir John married Frances Stanley, daughter of the fiercely Catholic Sir Edward Stanley, cousin of Ferdinando and known shelterer of Catholic priests, and for whom, as we have seen, Shakespeare seems to have created the epitaphs for his and his father's monuments at Tong. Lucy Percy, Frances' mother, was the second daughter of Thomas, the very Catholic Earl of Northumberland. John Fortescue the nephew was a near overt Catholic, as was his wife Ellen, daughter of the recusant Ralph Henslowe of Boarhunt, Hampshire, a relative of the Earls of Southampton.[34]

Here the further curiosity of the Gatehouse is that it was one of the most notoriously Catholic places Shakespeare could have chosen in all of London. Back in 1586 Blackfriars resident Richard Frith had reported it as having:

'sundry back-doors and byways, and many secret vaults and corners. It hath been in time past suspected, and searched for papists but no good done for want of good knowledge of the back-doors and byways and of the dark corners.[35]

During the 1590s, the height of the Topcliffe era, the Gatehouse was repeatedly reported for the comings and goings of priests. In 1591, for instance: 'Fennell the priest doth use to come very much to Mr John Fortescue his house'. Richard Topcliffe, to his credit, warned John Fortescue and his uncle that they were courting trouble, culminating in a major raid one day in 1598, when John Fortescue was away, apparently due to a tip-off from an informer, one William Udall. He described it as having 'many places of secret conveyance in it', communicating with 'secret passages across the water'. Once again these 'secret passages' seem to have baffled the searchers, for no priests were found, and although under interrogation Ellen Fortescue and her two very attractive daughters (said to be 'the fairest in London'), admitted they were Catholics they vehemently denied harbouring any priests. This was a clear piece of equivocation if ever there was one since in a later autobiography Jesuit Oswald Greenway recorded how he visited the house the next day, only to be told there had indeed been two priests there, but these had used the hiding places to make their escape.[36]

Seven years later the Gatehouse surfaced again in the annals of the Catholic underground, this time in connection with the notorious

Gunpowder plot. According to a copy of a memorandum of the leading Jesuit Father, John Gerard, preserved to this day at St Cuthbert's College, Ushaw, Durham, shortly before the fateful 5 November 1605 Gerard asked Ellen Fortescue for the use of a private room in the Gatehouse:

> where some persons who did not wish to be seen in his company could meet him unobserved. She, being a prudent woman, did not relish this mention of persons likely to come there who did not wish their visits to be known. He [Gerard] replied that they were excellent men of noble birth, and Catholics; and at last, upon her pressing him to say who they were, named Catesby, Percy, Winter, Digby, and several more, all without exception implicated in the Gunpowder Plot.[37]

To her credit Ellen Fortescue, stout Catholic that she was, declined to admit the plotters, remarking of Catesby, whom she acknowledged she knew slightly 'I never approved, nor his habits and loose way of life'. And when after the plotters' arrest Gerard, now the country's most wanted man, turned up at the Gatehouse 'disguised by a false beard and hair' (one can only wonder from whom these appurtenances of the acting profession might have been obtained), John Fortescue could only groan 'Have you no one to ruin but me and my family?' Arguably weary of all this cloak and dagger business the Fortescues eventually retired to St Omer in France, where Father Persons had founded a school for English Catholics, while one of their two attractive daughters, Elizabeth, married the brother of dramatist Francis Beaumont.[38]

Now in all this the major source of interest is why, with all London to choose from, Shakespeare should have selected, as a purportedly casual investment, this notoriously Catholic Gatehouse, with all its secret hiding places still apparently retaining their secrets. It is not even as though he bought it as a bargain: he paid £140 for it, more than twice the amount he had paid for New Place. So was it really just an 'investment pure and simple'?

Unfortunately the documents of 1613 throw little further light on exactly why Shakespeare chose to buy this particular property. They show that although it was Shakespeare who put up the purchase money, he had three co-purchasers acting as trustees in his interest: William Johnson, John Jackson and John Heminges. Heminges of course we are already familiar with as Shakespeare's business manager, and in fact, he must have been otherwise engaged on the day of the transaction, 10 March, since there is a blank on the tab prepared by the lawyers for his signature. William Johnson, described as 'citizen and vintner of London', seems to have been reasonably convincingly identified by Leslie Hotson as the William Johnson who was landlord of the Mermaid in Bread Street, which was due south of Heminges' house in Addle Street, and where apparently several of those involved in the Gunpowder plot regularly dined together. And thanks again to Hotson researches, Jackson seems identifiable as a Hull shipping magnate who was another habitué of the Mermaid, and who married the sister-in-law of Elias James, a brewer of Puddle Dock Hill who died in 1610, who is another for whom Shakespeare is accredited with having written a poetic epitaph.[39]

Leslie Hotson made elaborate researches into the backgrounds of Jackson and Johnson and into why they might have been associated with Shakespeare, but quite definite intrigue pertains to the very fact of the trusteeship itself. For whereas all Shakespeare's investments in land around Stratford had been for the benefit of his wife and family, creating an estate to which his wife would have an automatic one-third right in the event of his death, the trusteeship arrangement relating to the Blackfriars property had the effect of excluding Anne from any rights to it, except in the unlikely event of her husband, and ultimately herself, outliving all the other trustees.

As we will shortly discover, some further light will be shed on the Blackfriars purchase when Shakespeare makes his will, but meanwhile, still in 1613 and just over three months after the Gatehouse deeds had been signed, the King's Men suffered the biggest single setback in their history. On the sunny[40] afternoon of St Peter's Day, Tuesday 29 June, they were performing *Henry VIII* at the Globe, and had reached the point in the script[41] where the stage directions call for 'Chambers discharg'd' – a backstage volley of small cannon to herald the disguised King Henry's arrival to meet Anne Boleyn – when a stray spark from one of the cannon fell upon the thatch covering the Globe's roof. As related by Sir Edmund Bacon:

Now, King Henry making a masque at Cardinal Wolsey's House, and certain cannons[42] being shot off at his entry, some of the paper, or other stuff wherewith one of them was stopped, did light on the thatch, where being thought at first but an idle smoke, and their eyes more attentive to the show, it kindled inwardly, and ran round like a train, consuming within less than an hour the whole House to the very grounds.[43]

There could well have been two thousand people in the all-wood Globe that afternoon, and as a separate account by John Chamberlain explains, they had 'but two narrow doors to get out'.[44] Almost certainly they owed their lives that day to the fact that well-seasoned oak burns very slowly, for in Wotton's words:

nothing did perish but wood and straw, and a few forsaken cloaks. Only one man had his breeches set on fire, that would perhaps have broiled him, if he had not by the benefit of a provident wit put it out with bottle ale.[45]

In a manner typical of the way news spread, two ballads on the fire were entered on the Stationers' Register the very next day.[46] No surviving printed copies of either are known, but the manuscript for one, *A Sonnett upon the pittiful burneing of the Globe playhouse in London* was in the library of Eshton Hall, Yorkshire up until the present century, and although its present whereabouts are unknown, thankfully its text was published in the *Gentleman's Magazine* in 1816.[47] It is particularly valuable for its vignettes of the activities of Shakespeare's fellows that day:

Out run the Knights, out run the Lords,
And there was great ado;
Some lost their hats, and some their swords –
Then out ran Burbage too;
The reprobates, though drunk on Monday [the previous day]
Prayed for the Fool and Henry Condye . . .
Oh sorrow, pitiful sorrow, and yet all this is true.

The periwigs and drumheads fried
Like to a butter firkin
A woeful burning did betide
To many a good buff jerkin
Then with swollen eyes, like drunken Fleming's

Distressed stood old stuttering Heminges
Oh sorrow, & c.[48]

The above mentioned Fool, almost certainly playing the porter in *Henry viii* was very likely Robert Armin, and the fact that he and "Henry Condye" (quite definitely Henry Condell) needed the prayers of the audience's 'reprobates' suggests that this pair risked their lives during the evacuation of the burning building, probably in an effort to save what they could of properties and costumes. Similarly, for Heminges to have been mentioned last, stuttering from shock, and his 'swollen eyes' apparently badly affected by the smoke, suggests that he likewise had behaved heroically, probably saving the company's more vital papers, and in particular its play books, since those of Shakespeare certainly survived to be used for the First Folio.

Notably, despite the sonnet author's naming of almost all other of the King's Men's principals,[49] Shakespeare is not mentioned, an indication perhaps that (despite his Blackfriars Gatehouse acquisition) he was already spending most of his time back in Stratford.

There is no evidence that Shakespeare continued as a Globe shareholder in the wake of the fire, and it is therefore of great credit to the resolve and resourcefulness of his London-based fellows that within a year the playhouse was rebuilt and back in business, much to the chagrin of the Puritans who contrasted this alacrity with the low priority given to repairs to St Paul's.[50] Such a swift rebuilding is indicated by a letter from John Chamberlain of 30 June 1614, remarking how, on visiting his sister, he found her 'gone to the new Globe, to a play'. Chamberlain also went on:

I hear much speech of this new playhouse, which is said to be the fairest that ever was in England, so that if I live but even years longer, I may chance to take a journey to see it'.[51]

It is this building that we see so photographically in the sketch [see pl. 5] by Wenceslaus Hollar with which we began this book. We know that in order to avoid any recurrence of the St Peter's Day fire the King's Men elected this time for a tiled roof, but according to a survey in 1634 the rest of the building was again 'built of timber'[52] specifically 'for the most part fir timber' according to a carpenter testifying in a lawsuit of the same year. Almost certainly imported from the Baltic, this would have been cheaper than native oak. Although the same carpenter gave the scrap value of the materials as £200 the total cost of the rebuilding has been reliably estimated as more like £1,400.[53] Despite a report in the 1631 edition of Stow's *Annales* that it had been 'at the great charge of King James and many Noble men and others', the entire cost would seem to have been borne by the shareholders. Also, whatever the disposition of the stage in the first Globe, it is quite definite from Hollar's sketch that in this second building it faced north, and was at all performance times completely shaded from direct sunlight. The Globe was now set fair to earn money for the King's Men throughout the rest of the time that a king was allowed to stay on the throne.

On an equally positive note, during this same year of 1614, Penelope Wriothesley, the now sixteen-year-old daughter of the Earl of Southampton, who had been conceived out of wedlock in 1598, married William Spencer, nephew of Ferdinando's widow Countess Alice. Thus within Shakespeare's lifetime a historic union was created between the two great families to whom, as we have argued, he owed his earliest patronage.

But whatever pride the King's Men may have felt in their new premises, their principals were now a substantially older crew than the predominance of young bloods they had been as the Lord Chamberlain's Men of the 1590s, and 1614 would take its toll both on them and among those Shakespeare knew in Stratford. Of the former there died Alexander Cooke, probably the 'Saunder' of Lord Strange's Men's *Seven Deadly Sins* production, and as evident from the cast lists of Jonson's plays, quite definitely performing with the King's Men between 1603 and 1613. Cooke's surviving will[54] is unusual for being written in Cooke's own hand. The preamble is worded 'I, Alexander Cooke, sick of body but in perfect mind, do with mine own hand write my last will and testament'. It also speaks of 'my Master Hemings' suggesting that he had originally been apprenticed to John Heminges. Also, the fact that Cooke's eldest daughter was named Rebecca was almost certainly in honour of Heminges' wife. We learn that Cooke left at least three children, one still in his wife's womb at the time of his writing his will, and the St Saviour's, Southwark, parish records show him being buried there on 25 February 1614, in the same church as Shakespeare's brother Edmund. In the March there died Ellen Burbage, old James' widow, laid to rest along with her husband in St Leonard's, Shoreditch. The company Fool, Robert Armin, is thought to have followed in the November[55] followed in turn on 16 December by another still young 'principal actor' William Ostler, who only three years before had married John Heminges' daughter Thomasine.

Of those Shakespeare knew at Stratford there had died early in 1613 Shakespeare's only remaining brother Richard, of whom even less is known than of Gilbert, followed in March 1614 by Judith Sadler, godmother to his twins, but most prominent of all was bachelor John Combe, the wealthiest man in Stratford. Noted for his money-lending at interest, Combe was quite definitely a friend of Shakespeare's, Shakespeare having purchased land from him more than ten years before, and being remembered in his will with a gift of £5. Besides other Shakespeare connections with the Combe family – his religious education reportedly received from old Benedictine monk Dom Thomas Combe and his 'gentleman's' sword being bequeathed to John Combe's Catholic nephew, another Thomas – the relationship between Shakespeare and Combe seems to have been particularly jocular. According to a repeatedly attested early yarn, during Combe's lifetime, Shakespeare 'merrily fan[ned] up some witty and facetious verses' for him by way of an epitaph:

> Ten in the hundred lies here engraved,
> 'Tis a hundred to ten, his soul is not saved,
> If any man ask who lies in this tomb
> 'O, ho!' quoth the devil, ' 'Tis my John-a-Combe'.[56]

Likewise a manuscript in the Bodleian Library in Oxford from the hand of Nicholas Burgh, a Poor Knight of Windsor, not only attests to this story as early as around 1650, it also provides the more serious and more charitable version Shakespeare reputedly wrote upon Combe's actual demise:

> How ere he lived judge not
> John Combe shall never be forgot
> While poor hath memory, for he did gather
> To make the poor his issue; he their father
> As record of his tilth and seed
> Did crown him in this latter deed.
> Finis W:Shak[57]

Not only is it notable that Combe's monument, set in the same chancel of Holy Trinity in which Shakespeare would be buried, was made in Shakespeare's Southwark by the same Gerard Johnson workshop that had made the monuments for the Earls of Southampton and Rutland, Nicholas Burgh also happens to record a similarly irreverent and equally credible piece of epitaph-making that took place between Shakespeare and Ben Jonson:

> Mr. Ben Jonson and Mr. Wm. Shakespeare being merry at a tavern, Mr. Jonson having begun this for his epitaph: 'Here lies Ben Jonson that was once one', he gives it to Mr. Shakespeare to make up who presently writes:
>
> > 'Who while he liv'd was a slow thing
> > And now being dead is no thing.'

Tenuous though it might seem, there is something all of a piece to Shakespeare's repeated association with all these monuments and epitaphs – as if he really did take a semi-playful, semi-serious interest in such periphera, despite the incredulity and scorn with which they have frequently been treated by professional academics.

But amid all the light-hearted irreverence, as he must have been acutely aware, there loomed the increasing frailty of his own mortality.

CHAPTER 23

'And England Keep my Bones!'

In the Abbot Hall Art Gallery, Kendal, Cumbria, hangs a haunting painting of a very sick-looking man in his night-shirt, sitting propped up in bed, weakly signing his will, while next to him a much healthier looking individual in ordinary day-wear, clearly his lawyer, watches attentively [see pl. 48]. The man depicted writing the will was one Thomas Braithwaite who died in 1607, but for us the painting's importance is that it provides our chronologically closest glimpse of something of the scene in March 1616 at New Place, Stratford-upon-Avon, as the fifty-two-year-old Shakespeare steadily approached meeting his Maker.

'Dying well', a positive preparatory attitude to the onset of death rooted in mediaeval Catholic tradition, remained a matter of very considerable importance to Elizabethans and early Jacobeans of all shades of religious opinion, the Braithwaite deathbed portrait being but one of a fashionable genre. Time and again individuals of substance from the period can be traced making out thoughtfully prepared wills, then within a matter of a few days or weeks their funerals are recorded in the appropriate parish register, and in this regard Shakespeare's end seems no exception. Not for him an untimely assassin's knife, like Marlowe, or dying in penury and squalor, like Robert Greene. Dated 25 March 1616, the will that he made out in clear anticipation of his imminent end survives today in the London Public Record Office [see pls. 49 and 50], no longer on continuous show, but available readily on special application. As concisely described by the pioneering Shakespearean scholar Edmond Malone, who examined it back in September 1776, just after the American Declaration of Independence, it is:

written in the clerical hand of that [i.e. Shakespeare's] age, on three small sheets, fastened like a lawyer's brief. Shakespeare's name is signed at the bottom of the first and second sheets, and his final signature, 'By me William Shakspeare', is in the middle of the third sheet. The name, however, at the bottom of the first sheet is not in the usual place, but in the margin at the left-hand, and so different from the others that we doubted whether it was in his handwriting. He appears to have been very ill and weak when he signed his will, for the hand is very irregular and tremulous. I suspect he signed his name at the end of the will first, and so went backwards, which will account for that on the first page being worse written than the rest, the hand growing gradually weaker.

Today, the strip of parchment Malone mentioned as fastening the sheets 'like a lawyer's brief' has been removed; this was in order for it to go on display. But apart from frayed edges, lost corners, and wear at fold lines the will remains fully legible and in reasonable condition, for which we have much to be thankful, since not only is it our one historical link with Shakespeare's deathbed, its three specimens of his signature represent half the entire total of those deemed authentic. In the absence of an autographed letter the will is arguably the most personal physical relic we have of him, yet even so, as we study it and its content [for the full text, see Appendix C, pp. 476–9], it seems to add to, rather than diminish, the mystery that was Shakespeare.

The appearance of the will is itself not without curiosity. For instance, all the pages are of different sizes, suggesting that whoever the writer, the task was not necessarily performed on one single occasion, the paper being from slightly different batches.

Of the writing, the three signatures, together with the earlier mentioned specimens from the Belott–Mountjoie legal suit and the Blackfriars Gatehouse purchase represent the sum-total of hand-writing that is uncontestedly agreed as Shakespeare's own [see fig 13, overleaf]. The overall evident crudity and clumsiness of the hand, accompanied by no less than four blots in fourteen words, has fuelled many of the doubts that the plays known as Shakespeare's could not possibly have been written by the man responsible for these six signatures. Can this really have been the same man of whom Heminges and Condell would write, in their preface to the First Folio of 1623, that 'his mind and hand went together, and what he thought, he uttered with that easiness that we have scarce received from him a blot in his papers'? Likewise of whom Ben Jonson would note: 'I remember, the players have often mentioned it as an honour to

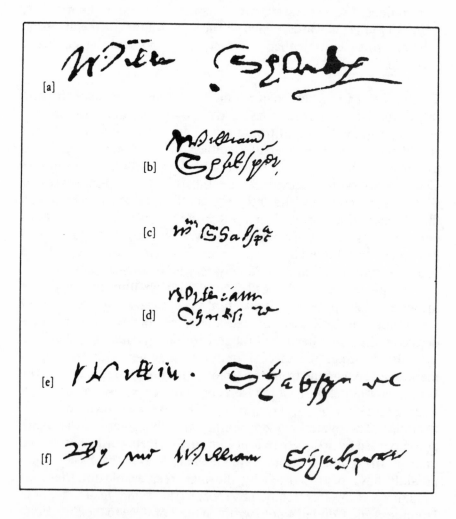

Fig 13
All six surviving Shakespeare signatures: [a] from the Belott–Mountjoie deposition, 11 May 1612; [b] from the Blackfriars Gatehouse conveyance, 10 March 1613; [c] from the Blackfriars Gatehouse mortgage, 11 March 1613; [d] from page one of Shakespeare's will, 25 March 1616 (as preserved in the Public Record Office); [e] from page two of the will; [f] 'By me William Shakspeare', from the third and final page of the will.

Shakespeare, that in his writing, (whatsoever he penn'd), he never blotted out line'?[1]

If the only signatures to have survived had been those from his will, one might, like Edmond Malone, have passed them off as the enfeebled scrawlings of a dying man. But as earlier noted, the Belott–Mountjoie signature, written four years before, is if anything the most awkward. Nor can the writing be easily explained away as the sort of awful scrawl that busy people of all centuries have often developed as a quick way of writing their name. Nor is there any evidence either of alcoholism or any other form of mental impairment.

Rather, upon careful scrutiny, the positive feature of the signatures is that they may be of the greatest help in explaining why, when only forty-eight and still apparently at the height of his powers (when he wrote *The Tempest*), Shakespeare chose to abandon his playwriting. And why, when being called back to write an entertainment for the 1613 royal wedding, he wrote *Henry VIII* in collaboration with another dramatist.

The crucial clue seems to lie in observations made upon the signatures back in 1919 by medical practitioner Dr Ralph W. Leftwich in a little-known lecture to the Royal Society of Medicine. According to Leftwich, the fact that, as exemplified by the Belott–Mountjoie signature, his handwriting was so crude as early as 1612 indicates a condition virtually extinct in today's age of the typewriter and word-processor, but familiar enough to nineteenth-century physicians as scrivener's palsy, or writer's cramp. This came in four main varieties – spastic, tremulous, neuralgic and paralytic – among which Shakespeare, in Leftwich's opinion, suffered:

> essentially from the spastic form. In this the pen is not completely under the control of the writer. Against his will it makes little jerks, unduly long strokes, or unintended marks; and though a good beginning may perhaps be made, the hand very soon tires and refuses to write at all. Sir William Gowers [a specialist in the condition] says that the general effect is that of a letter written in a jolting carriage, and this ... is precisely what Shakespeare's writing suggests.[2]

At the present day Leftwich's opinion has been authoritatively endorsed by handwriting specialist Dr Vernon Harrison, who is frequently consulted on such matters in legal cases, and to whom I am indebted for bringing Leftwich's article to my attention. As observed by Dr Harrison, 'The words "By me William Shak..." on the last page of the will are as good a specimen of the Secretary Script as one could wish; but the hand seems to seize up and the last few letters of the signature are illegible.'[3] Scrivener's palsy was predictably most common among those who wrote voluminously, as Shakespeare undoubtedly did, particularly given that we have no idea how many times he drafted each of his thirty-seven plays, nor how many copies he subsequently made from them.

Now if the scrivener's palsy diagnosis is accepted, this effectively rules out arguments recently advanced by American handwriting specialist Charles Hamilton that the entire will was written by Shakespeare himself.[4] It was specifically to check upon Hamilton's arguments that I made my original approach to Dr Harrison, and after prolonged and characteristically scrupulous consideration his opinion was overwhelmingly opposed to the theory:

> Take the W in William. In all six of the known signatures, this letter ends with a curved down stroke, concave to the left. In the body of the will, the letter W occurs in several places – in William, Warwick and Wardrobe. In none of these places does this letter finish with a downward curve, and the start of the letters is a strongly shaded downward curve, concave to the left, unlike anything we see in the known signatures.[5]

But even if it is accepted that the will's main text was definitely not by Shakespeare, but instead by someone writing on his behalf, it is still very unusual among legal documents for its large number of alterations, substitutions and interpolations. What seems to have begun as a *Januarii* (Latin for January) date at the head of the first page has been crossed out and *Martii* (March), written above. As a composition by the most vivid of writers, it is more stereotyped and lacking in personal warmth than the wills of most of Shakespeare's fellow actors. The opening preamble, for instance, commencing 'In the name of God amen I William Shakespeare ... in perfect health and memory, God be praised', etc, had been used almost word for word in John Combe's will three years before, and seems to derive from the fact that common to both wills was officiating lawyer Francis

Collins of Warwick who appears to have used a standard form as set out by Middle Temple lawyer William West.[6] Collins also seems to have been from a school of lawyers who elected to have their testators declare themselves 'in perfect health' even though the wills' timing vis-à-vis the testators' deaths would indicate otherwise. Other lawyers preferred the more honest 'sick in body but of good and perfect memory'.

But where the physical appearance of the will again becomes interesting is in the writing three quarters of the way down the first page. Suddenly it becomes cramped and close-spaced. This is followed on the second sheet by a crossing-out of the original opening lines, which are still sufficiently legible to make it apparent they do not follow on from the present page one, while two quite different lines are then written in above them, clearly to make a proper sequence. The general deduction, essentially agreed by all serious scholars, is that the will was probably first drafted in the January, then in the March some unexpected circumstances prompted Shakespeare sufficiently to change its provisions for a redraft to be necessary. To save wasting the second and third pages that were still substantially correct, a new first page was substituted, the *Januarii* mistake occurring through the will writer's inadvertent copying from the old and now discarded first original. This also explains the differences in paper sizes between the three sheets.

The likelihood that the will had originally been drafted back in the January suggests that quite aside from his scrivener's palsy, which would not have affected the rest of his physical health, Shakespeare may already have been suffering from some progressive chronic ailment. But even if so, what unexpected circumstances between the January and the March of 1616 could have caused him to change the will during this time? Holy Trinity, Stratford's, register provides the first clue with its entry for the marriage on 10 February of 'Tho Queeny tow Judith Shakspere' – Thomas Quiney to Judith Shakespeare.[7] From this we learn for the first time that after thirty-one years of spinsterhood, Shakespeare's younger daughter Judith had married, her chosen husband being twenty-seven-year-old Stratford tavern keeper Thomas Quiney, younger son of the now deceased Richard Quiney who back in 1598 had written the only surviving letter addressed to Shakespeare.

Now by seventeenth-century standards Judith was of very mature age, and her nuptials might have seemed a source of great joy to her father, but two indications suggest otherwise. First, to get married during the prohibited Lenten season the couple should have procured a special licence from the Bishop of Worcester, just as had been obtained for William and Anne thirty-four years before. Yet for some unexplained reason Thomas and Judith omitted to do so and ignored a consequent summons from the Worcester consistory court, causing Thomas to be excommunicated (usually only temporarily upheld) on 12 March.[8]

Far more serious, however, was that at the same time as Thomas stood with Judith Shakespeare at Holy Trinity's altar one Margaret Wheeler was highly pregnant by him, and on or about the day that Thomas was excommunicated Margaret died giving birth to his child, her burial and that of the child both being entered in the Stratford register on 15 March. On 25 March, when we find Shakespeare changing his will, his new son-in-law was due to appear at Holy Trinity Church's ecclesiastical court the very next day to confess to 'carnal copulation'. The proceedings of Thomas' trial survive in the act book for Holy Trinity Church preserved in the Kent County Archives Office,[9] and from this we know that vicar Rogers sentenced Thomas to perform public penance at Holy Trinity Church on three successive Sundays, dressed only in a white sheet.[10] Although for reasons best known to Rogers the sentence was later transmuted to a five-shilling fine and a privately heard statement of contrition, inevitably the news of Shakespeare's new son-in-law's shameful conduct would have been all over town.

Here the bald official records leave all too much room for huge leaps of speculation about Shakespeare's state of mind over the issue. For instance, it has been suggested that the reason for Judith and Thomas having rushed into marriage without a licence was deliberately to flout Shakespeare's opposition once he knew of Thomas' fornication with Margaret Wheeler. Charles Hamilton, on the basis of his arguments that the will is in Shakespeare's own hand, has interpreted the suddenly cramped handwriting on the first page as from Shakespeare suffering a debilitating stroke, brought on either by his anger at his new son-in-law's dishonourable conduct, or even by Quiney's direct administration of poison.

Nonetheless, it would certainly have taken a considerably less emotional man than Shakespeare not to have been seriously disturbed by his younger daughter entering into such a seemingly ill-advised marriage, and the evidence for this is all there in

Shakespeare's will. The chief benefactor was to be elder daughter Susanna, the one who, it must be remembered, had earlier been listed as a Catholic at the time of the Gunpowder plot, shortly before her marriage to Dr Hall. To Susanna and her heirs Shakespeare left New Place, the houses in Henley Street, the lands in Old Stratford, Bishopton and Welcombe, also the house in Blackfriars. Susanna and her husband also became beneficiaries of all 'goods, chattels, leases, plate, jewels & household stuff' not otherwise disposed of in the will, and were appointed his executors. By contrast Judith was bequeathed just £150, with the promise of another £150:

> if she, or any issue of her body be living at the end of three years.... Provided that if such husband as she shall at the end of the said three years be married unto or attain after do sufficiently assure unto her ... lands answerable to the portion by this my will given ... then my will is that the said £150 shall be paid to such husband as shall make such assurance to his own use.

Now even amid the tedious legalisms the cold words 'such husband' speak volumes of Shakespeare's feelings towards Quiney. Whereas in the will he freely names Susanna's husband Dr John Hall and refers to him as son-in-law (and we need to remember that for all our inferences of Shakespeare's Catholic sympathies, Dr Hall was avowedly Protestant), he cannot bring himself to acknowledge even Quiney's existence. After all the years of lack of truly personal documentation of Shakespeare, suddenly here, from his deathbed, there flash some tantalising glimpses of him as a very human human being.

The same may possibly be true of what the will imparts of Shakespeare's attitude towards his wife. It was common for Elizabethan and Jacobean testators to refer affectionately to their spouses in their wills, old Augustine Phillips, for instance, having been one of many to speak of his 'loving wife' (and even of his 'loving' mother-in-law), yet Shakespeare uses no terms of endearment to anyone throughout his will, and since this is a characteristic notable also of the will of his lawyer Francis Collins, it must be allowed that this may simply be another instance of Collins' stamp upon the document.

Nevertheless, acres of print have been devoted to the fact that

Shakespeare's only reference to his wife throughout the will is his famous interpolation on page three: 'Item I give unto my wife my second-best bed with the furniture'. In fact the bequest of the second bed was not particularly unusual, Thomas Combe in 1608, for instance having left all bedsteads to his wife 'except the best' which 'with the best bed and best furniture thereunto belonging' was left to his son William.[11] And although to the twentieth-century mind such an apparent afterthought might seem an obvious snub, it is quite possible that Anne Shakespeare's continuance at New Place (as was her right), was so completely understood between Shakespeare and the Halls as to need no legal provision for it.

Even so, other slight hints suggest between Shakespeare and Anne a lack of the warmth of affection that existed, for instance, between John and Rebecca Heminges. In a manner hardly to be found in any other will, even in the 'second-best bed' interpolation Shakespeare omits to refer to Anne by her name, neither (with the possible exception of the bed), does he leave her any affectionate keepsake or memento. Also notable is how into the wording on page two of the will: 'Item, I give . . . unto my daughter Susanna Hall all that capital messuage . . . called New Place' there occurs a cryptic interpolation: 'for better enabling of her [Susanna] to perform this my will and towards the performance thereof'.

As pointed out by Professor Ernst Honigmann,[12] here Shakespeare, who after all had already given New Place and the rest to Susanna, seems to be heavily underlining his wish that it should be Susanna *and no one else* who should be in charge upon his demise. Particularly telling is that whereas most testators who left widows made them executors or co-executors of their wills – as in the case of Shakespeare's fellows Phillips, Burbage and even his lawyer Francis Collins – Shakespeare pointedly gave this key responsibility to Susanna. One possibility has to be allowed for that Anne, now sixty and an old lady by seventeenth-century standards, had become senile.

But against all imputations of marital friction between Shakespeare and his wife it also needs emphasising that his plays from *The Comedy of Errors* to *Henry VIII* consistently uphold the joy and sanctity of marriage. In *A Midsummer Night's Dream* it is an 'everlasting bond of fellowship'; in *As You Like It* a 'blessed bond of board and bed'; in *Henry V* a sacrament of 'faith and constant loyalty'; in *Twelfth Night* a 'contract of eternal bond of love'. His very Catholic attitude towards divorce is abundantly clear from his already noted sympathy towards Katherine of Aragon in *Henry VIII*. However tempting might have been the lure of the Dark Lady, and any other of London's witty and literary female sophisticates, it was to provincial homespun Anne that Shakespeare came back to rest and to die, and for her and their daughters that he invested his earnings in New Place and farmlands around Stratford.

Aside from his wife and daughters, Shakespeare might be expected to make due provision for his other relatives, particularly the less fortunate, and thus we see him leaving a life tenancy of the Henley Street 'Birthplace' house to his sister Joan, married to lowly hatter William Hart who would die just a few days before Shakespeare himself. From the words 'wherein she dwelleth' of Henley Street, the will makes clear that Joan and her family were already living in the property. The will's provisions ensured that she would be allowed to live there for the rest of her life, since her rent was set at the peppercorn rate of just one shilling per annum. Joan was also left £20, 'all my wearing apparel' and £5 for each of her three sons, only two of whose names Shakespeare could remember, a blank being left for the third. Interviewed at the end of the eighteenth century, butcher Hart, directly descended from Joan, and still living at the Birthplace house, 'well remembered having, with other boys, dressed themselves as Scaramouches (such was his phrase) in the wearing apparel of our Shakespeare.'[13]

We would not expect Shakespeare to forget his private friends, and it is the will that more than any other document shows us who they were. Thus we find him leaving his sword, the mark of his hard-won status of gentleman, to Thomas Combe, younger son of old Thomas Combe from whom he had purchased his Old Stratford lands, and nephew of the John Combe for whom he had composed the epitaph. Born in 1589, Thomas was a little younger than Shakespeare's son Hamnet would have been had he lived, and it is tempting to see Shakespeare favouring him as a Hamnet substitute. Equally notable is that both Thomas and his elder brother William appear on a recusancy list of 1640–41.[14]

Other beneficiaries quite definitely Catholic and on friendly terms with the Combes were William Reynolds, his late father of the same name having been in his time jailed for recusancy; also Hamnet Sadler, who with his wife had appeared on the recusancy list of 1606. Shakespeare left them both money to buy memorial rings. To squire Thomas Russell of Alderminster, just four miles down the road from Clopton Bridge, who after a long courtship had married Heminges' and Condell's Aldermanbury neighbour Anne Digges, he left £5. And of course he could hardly forget his fellows John Heminges, Richard Burbage and Henry Condell, his acting company's last surviving originals. In what was clearly now a tradition between the actors, he left them – and interestingly, only them among the London theatre crowd – money to buy memorial rings.

Yet refreshing as the will is for what it tells us it is in almost equal measure frustrating for what it does not. Neither it, nor any other surviving document, tells us anything of how and to whom Shakespeare disposed of his shares in the Globe. It is possible that in the wake of the fire he simply surrendered them to the common pool, forfeiting any further returns from them, but also absolving himself of having to pay anything towards the rebuilding. But that is merely a personal guess.

There is also the matter of what he did with whatever books he owned. While early on we envisaged him making use of his patrons' libraries, in later life he was certainly rich enough to buy his own, yet no copy of any book incontrovertibly once owned by him has ever come to light. It could be that those he left, whatever their subsequent fate, were deemed to be among the 'goods and chattels' bequeathed to Susanna and John Hall. But for a man who must have been a great reader it is surprising for him not to have made some special mention of them, as did many others of his time. For instance, Stratford vicar John Bretchgirdle bequeathed his Latin-English dictionary to the scholars of Stratford school; his Horace and Virgil to a godson, and works by Aesop, Cicero, Sallust, Erasmus and others to the five sons of Alderman William Smith. John Florio, who although he died in poorer estate than Shakespeare, left to William Earl of Pembroke: 'all my Italian, French and Spanish books, as well printed as unprinted, being in number about three hundred and forty, namely my new and perfect dictionary, as also my ten dialogues in Italian and English, and my unbound volume of divers written collections and rhapsodies...'.[15] Likewise the scrivener Humphrey Dyson, who wrote the wills for Shakespeare's fellow actors Henry Condell and Nicholas Tooley, in his will[16] required his executor to 'have a care to put off and sell my books to the most profit that he can'.[17]

Although the will also might be expected to provide us with that positive clue to Shakespeare's religious affiliations that has all along eluded us, it does not. Dr A. L. Rowse has argued that the preamble formula indicates that he 'died as he lived, a member of the Church of England',[18] on the grounds that Protestants and Catholics used different formulae, and that Shakespeare's choice was of the former variety. But Professor Schoenbaum, never one of Dr Rowse's greatest fans, has disagreed, arguing that it was not uncommon for both Catholics and Protestants to use the same terms, and certainly other indications in the will make it hard to cast Shakespeare among the staunchest pillars of the Church of England.

For instance, while it was standard at the time for one dying as a gentleman to make a donation to the poor of the parish, Shakespeare's £10 being in this respect more generous than any of his fellows, unlike most of the others Shakespeare left no instruction for churchwardens to distribute the money. Nor, unlike Phillips who willed twenty shillings to the 'preacher who shall preach at my funeral', did he leave any donation or remembrance to any church vicar, either at Stratford or back in London. Nor, despite his considerable interest in epitaphs and funeral monuments that we have repeatedly noted, does Shakespeare set out in the will any direction concerning either how or where he wished to be buried. Thus, back in 1603 Thomas Pope had left £20 'towards the setting up of some monument on me in the said church and my funeral'. In 1605 Augustine Phillips specified his desire 'to be buried in the chancel of the parish church of Mortlake', and later, in 1630 John Heminges would ask 'to be buried in Christian manner in the parish church of St Mary Aldermanbury in London as near unto my loving wife Rebecca Heminges, who lieth interred, and under the same stone which lieth in part over her there ... in decent and comely manner ... in the evening, without any vain pomp or cost'.[19] Shakespeare by contrast simply commends his 'body to the earth whereof it is made'.

Although according to John Ward,[20] vicar of Stratford in the early 1660s, Shakespeare 'died of a fever' following a drinking bout with literary chums Ben Jonson and Michael Drayton little credence need be attached to this late tradition, the exact cause of his death being simply unknown. Shakespeare's memorial on the wall of Holy Trinity Church (of which more later), is the sole record that he died on 23 April, St George's Day, his funeral, listed as that of 'Will.

Shakespere gent', being logged in Holy Trinity's register two days later. Clearly, then, he had lingered on nearly a month after signing his will.

Quite evident, however, is that despite the already noted omissions in his will someone put in hand certain very particular arrangements for his interment, in particular privileged burial in the chancel of Holy Trinity Church, near the north wall, almost certainly because of the status he had acquired by his purchase of an interest in Stratford tithes. But it was what was set over his grave that is fascinating: a plain slab of ordinary stone [see pl. 53] with the words:

GOOD FREND FOR JESUS SAKE FORBEARE
TO DIGG THE DUST ENCLOASED HEARE
BLESTE BE YE MAN T[HAT]Y SPARES THES STONES,
AND CURST BE HE T[HAT]Y MOVES MY BONES

Astonishingly, those who have written biographies of Shakespeare and reproduced the gravestone, Schoenbaum and Rowse among them, have all too rarely commented on one of its most remarkable features: that it bears no name. That it is Shakespeare's grave is strongly enough indicated both from early tradition and from the conventionally identified graves of family in immediate proximity: his wife Anne to his right (spectator's left facing the altar), and his grandson-in-law Thomas Nash, son-in-law Dr John Hall and daughter Susanna to his left. Such a lack of a name, and the surprising individuality of the wording make it almost inconceivable that anyone other than Shakespeare should have composed it, and that he did so is indeed attested by a late seventeenth-century visitor to Stratford, a Mr Dowdall, who in 1697 described being told by the then eighty-year-old clerk that it was 'made by himself [i.e. Shakespeare] a little before his death'.[21]

Not only does this reinforce our argument for Shakespeare's sustained interest in epitaphs, stretching right back to that of old Talbot in *Henry VI, Part I*, at once we see, faithfully sustained even to the grave, those sentiments he had composed back in the halcyon days of sonneteering:

O, lest the world should task you to recite
What merit liv'd in me, that you should love
After my death, dear love, forget me quite,

For you in me can nothing worthy prove

. . .

My name be buried where my body is . . .[22]

> Sonnet 81 illustrates the distinction he made between his noble patron and himself:

Your name from hence immortal life shall have,
Though I, once gone, to all the world must die;
The earth can yield me but a common grave . . .

In all honesty, and despite having attained the status of a gentleman, Shakespeare seems to have regarded himself as too lowly to be considered 'of name'.

But with its so forthright combined blessing and curse what an inscription to compose! The sentiment regarding non-disturbance is not unique. A 1520 monumental brass of John Sedley and his wife, recently stolen from the church at Southfleet, Kent, bore the instruction 'Dyg not wtyn too fote of this tombe' ('Dig not within two feet of this tomb').[23] Nonetheless it is very unusual. As long ago as 1694 Middlesex rector William Hall felt bound to offer the following explanation both of its curse and the seemingly un-Shakespearean doggerel in which it is couched:

There is in this church a place which they call the bone-house, a repository for all bones they dig up; which are so many that they would load a great number of waggons. The poet being willing to preserve his bones unmoved, lays a curse upon him that moves them; and having to do with clerks and sextons, for the most part a very ignorant sort of people, he descends to the meanest of their capacity; and disrobes himself of that art, which none of his contemporaries wore in greater perfection.[24]

Effectively we seem to be seeing Shakespeare taking his stance particularly stridently against the sacrileges he had seen Protestant clerics committing throughout his lifetime, during which it had been all too common for them unceremoniously to turn out old bones of those laid to rest in the Catholic past in order to make way for the monuments and other vanities of the Protestant present. In this same regard it is important to be aware that when Shakespeare was laid in Holy Trinity that April day of 1616 the church was not in the well-maintained state it appears today. Like almost every church in the land it was in disrepair through under-funding, the very chancel in which he was buried being boarded up in order for the congregation to better concentrate on the sermon. It is almost as if Shakespeare's curse was a form of battening-down of the hatches in the hope that one day the church might be returned to the old Catholic rite.

But a more fundamental question is that if Shakespeare did not set down in his will his instructions regarding an interment he clearly cared deeply about, to whom did he entrust them? Here it may be worthwhile to return momentarily to the most over-looked name in Shakespeare's will, and one all the more surprising for its appearing twice, that of John Robinson. This occurs first in reference to the Blackfriars Gatehouse ('all that messuage or tenement with the appurtenances ... situated ... in the Blackfriars in London near the Wardrobe'), which, in his bequeathing of this to Susanna, Shakespeare specifically describes as 'wherein one John Robinson dwelleth'. The name then recurs among the signatures of the will's witnesses, the third to be so featured.

Now Schoenbaum, who omits to note the repetition, in his earlier account of Shakespeare's purchase of the Blackfriars Gatehouse simply mentions that 'Shakespeare *let* [italics mine] it to a John Robinson' – this apparently purely on the strength of Robinson's mention in Shakespeare's will. Then, when writing of the will's witnesses, he equally blandly informs us that 'Robinson was a labourer'. Of course, in the seventeenth century as now, the name John Robinson was sufficiently common that the Shakespeare milieu may have included two John Robinsons, one a tenant in London, the other a labourer in Stratford. But the signature 'John Robinson' suggests someone surprisingly literate for a labourer. Furthermore why, when only two witnesses were necessary, should some hitherto unknown local labourer have been hauled in to witness the dying Shakespeare's will?

The alternative scenario, and a not unreasonable one, is that the will witness and the Blackfriars John Robinson were one and the same, in which case Robinson is immediately raised to the highly interesting status of being the only individual from Shakespeare's London world to have attended him on his deathbed. Furthermore, again only if he was one and the same as the London John Robinson, we may know at last a little more about him.

It is quite definite that back in the reign of Elizabeth I a John Robinson was working as steward to Sir John Fortescue – Master of the Royal Wardrobe directly opposite Shakespeare's Gatehouse, and the uncle of the Catholic John Fortescue who was associated with the Gatehouse itself. He was described as living 'over against Sir John's door', and thereby in the immediate vicinity of, if not actually in, Shakespeare's Gatehouse.[25] And he was probably the John Robinson listed among those Blackfriars' residents who petitioned against the Blackfriars theatre back in 1596. Like John Fortescue and his family, John Robinson was a very active Catholic. In May 1599, the year in which his wife died, he was reported for sheltering Catholic priest Richard Dudley. Furthermore in 1605, that is at the time of the Gunpowder plot, he sent his thirteen-year-old son, Edward, to the training college for English Catholics at St Omer. This Edward in 1613, at the age of twenty-one, presented himself at the English College in Rome for training to become a priest, upon which he told those receiving him that he had 'an only brother, but no sister.'[26] So could this only brother have been named John after his father, and have been not so much Shakespeare's tenant in the Gatehouse, as his appointed guardian of one of London's best places of refuge for Catholic priests? Might he even have been in holy orders like his brother, and have been one and the same as the mysterious Benedictine from whom, according to one Catholic tradition, Shakespeare received the last rites of the Catholic Church?[27]

Such speculation aside, equally as enigmatic as the gravestone is the commissioning of Holy Trinity's other memorial to Shakespeare, the fine polychrome sculptured monument [see pl. 51] set on the chancel's north wall, within a few feet of his grave. Set against a background of white marble, with black marble Corinthian columns, and black touchstone panels, surmounted by the earliest surviving example of usage of the Shakespeare arms, appears a painted bust of Shakespeare, made of Cotswold limestone, and one of the only two surviving likenesses of Shakespeare regarded as authentic. As 'thy Stratford monument' it is mentioned as early as 1623 in a First Folio tribute contributed by none other than Leonard Digges, followed eleven years later by Lieutenant Hammond reporting of his visit to Stratford upon Avon:

in the church in that town there are some monuments . . . [among] those worth observing and of which we took notice . . . a neat monument of that famous English poet, Mr William Shakespeare, who was born here.[28]

Most writers on the memorial, including Schoenbaum, have assumed that it must have been ordered by members of Shakespeare's family, yet against this is the memorial's inscription:

> Stay passenger, why goest thou by so fast?
> Read if thou canst, whom envious death hath placed
> Within this monument Shakespeare: with whom
> Quick nature died. Whose name doth deck his tomb,
> Far more than cost. Since all that he hath writ
> Leaves living art, but page, to serve his wit.

The point is rarely made that among all the contemporary Stratford materials relating to Shakespeare – his family records in the church register, his land deals – this funerary inscription represents the first surviving local acknowledgment of his occupation as a writer. Yet whoever wrote the inscription for the monument, presumably in concert with, if not one and the same as, the individual who commissioned it, appears to have been unaware that Shakespeare was not buried 'within', also, that Shakespeare had deliberately chosen not to 'deck his tomb' with his name. The strong inference therefore has to be that it was commissioned from someone outside Stratford. But who? Shakespeare's fellows were good to each other, but commissioning memorials was outside their league, and in any case, as we will see shortly, they were preoccupied with an altogether more worthy and useful memorial than anything made in paint and stone.

A most important clue comes from mid-seventeenth-century antiquary William Dugdale who in an almanac of 1653 imparts that the maker was 'one Gerard Johnson'.[29] Accordingly, although largely unremarked upon by anyone except specialists in monumental masonry, the Shakespeare memorial in Stratford was created by the very same workshop which we first came across making the Southampton tomb at Titchfield back in 1594, the very tomb that, as we earlier suggested, may well have prompted Shakespeare's *Sonnet* 123, with its reference to 'thy pyramids built up with newer might'.

Throughout Shakespeare's heyday years the Johnson workshop in Southwark received orders for memorials commissioned by other members of the Earl of Southampton's circle, the Earls of Rutland, and the Catholic Gages of Sussex, and only three years before had made a memorial for Shakespeare's friend John Combe. But if the late John Combe's order had been prompted by his friendship with Shakespeare, who might have placed the order for Shakespeare's own? Conceivably could it have been he to whom two decades before Shakespeare had written:

> No longer mourn for me when I am dead
> Than you shall hear the surly sullen bell
> Give warning to the world that I am fled
> From this vile world, with vilest worms to dwell.
> Nay, if you read this line, remember not
> The hand that writ it; for I love you so,
> That I in your sweet thoughts would be forgot,
> If thinking on me then should make you woe.[30]

Is it conceivable that Southampton, as recipient of lines like that, could have dared not provide for the poet who had promised him immortality, that which was within his gift: one of those 'gilded monuments' that, as he had been heavily reminded, were no match for Shakespeare's verse? The memorial inscription in Latin that precedes the English one just below Shakespeare's bust is of an erudition suggestive of Southampton, and perhaps one day some long-buried account may show that the Earl did indeed order from the Johnsons such a memorial in Stratford sometime between 1616 and his own death in 1624.

Meanwhile, in the wake of Shakespeare's death, the acting company of which he had been a part for so many years carried on performing his works, even for the most illustrious of occasions. Worth repeating is an earlier quoted letter from Sir Gerald Herbert to Sir Dudley Carleton at the Hague, dated 24 May 1619, reporting how just four days earlier *Pericles* had been a star attraction among the entertainments staged at Whitehall for the visiting French ambassador:

In the King's great chamber they went to see the play of *Pericles, Prince of Tyre*, which lasted till two o'clock. After two acts the players ceased till the French all refreshed themselves with sweetmeats brought on china voiders [china trays or platters], and wine and ale in bottles. After, the players began anew.[31]

From the reporting of this same occasion we learn of the death of another towering and original figure of the King's Men, one whose loss the Court noticed rather more than Shakespeare's. That same evening, 20 May, William, Earl of Pembroke, wrote to Lord Doncaster in Germany to say how 'being tenderhearted' he had not joined the rest in attending the play because he 'could not endure' to see it 'so soon after the loss of my old friend Burbage'.[32] From the register of St Leonard's Church, Shoreditch, we are able to glean that 'so soon' in Pembroke's case meant two months, for the burial of 'Richard Burbadge, player' is recorded for 16 March, there also surviving several contemporary epitaphs and elegies to Burbage both in written and manuscript form. Although in the longest of the latter the ever-inventive hand of nineteenth-century scholar-trickster Collier has been detected, nonetheless the following lines are generally accepted as authentic:

> He's gone and with him what a world are dead,
> Which he revived, to be revived so.
> No more young Hamlet, old Hieronymo
> Kind Lear, the grieved Moor, and more beside,
> That lived in him, have now forever died.
> Oft have I seen him leap into the grave
> Suiting the person which he seem'd to have
> Of a sad lover with so true an eye,
> That there I would have sworn, he meant to die.
> Oft have I seen him play this part in jest,
> So lively, that spectators and the rest
> Of his sad crew, whilst he but seem'd to bleed,
> Amazed, thought even then he died in deed.[33]

Yet again we see that art of suspending disbelief that had been so cunningly contrived between Shakespeare's lines and Burbage and his colleagues' acting.

With the death of Burbage there remained just two of the great originals of Shakespeare's company, John Heminges and Henry Condell, and to them fell a task that is now so much a part of English heritage that the fact that anyone put it together has been all too easily forgotten: the editing of what would become the First Folio, for Heminges a task made all the harder by the death of his beloved wife Rebecca in 1619.

At least the precedent had been set by Ben Jonson. The very year of Shakespeare's death Jonson published his collected works – all his best plays, his masques, his entertainments and his verse gathered together in a magnificent Folio volume of more than a thousand pages, with the handsomest of title pages, crowded with symbolic figures, Tragedy to one side, Comedy the other. Hitherto such prestigious Folio publication had been for works of medicine and theology, with plays relegated to the realms of cheap quartos, and although Shakespeare almost certainly did not live to see a printed copy, he would very likely have heard, perhaps not without a little envy, that a work of such magnitude was in progress. Certainly it can have been hardly other than the sight of Jonson's volume that prompted Heminges and Condell to decide that while they still had the life and energy they should do the same for the works of Shakespeare.

Read the works of those who argue that the Earl of Oxford was the true author of Shakespeare's works, and of necessity the veteran player editors of the First Folio are presented as liars and cheats for misrepresenting the plays' true authorship. As for those who accept Shakespeare's authorship, the part played by Heminges and Condell has been all too easily minimised and forgotten, for it is too rarely appreciated what a difficult venture they contemplated. Although Jonson had included some plays in his First Folio, even so the rest of his volume consisted of more socially acceptable masques and poems. Moreover, Jonson was socially recognised as a national poet. By contrast, the idea of putting together for purchase by gentlemen – for only they could afford it – a Folio work consisting solely of plays by a common playhouse author was completely without precedent. When in 1622 Henry Peacham included in his *Complete Gentleman* – a guide to what every well-bred gentleman should know – a list of socially acceptable contemporary poets, Shakespeare's name was not among these. Small wonder therefore that Heminges and Condell adroitly dedicated the book to William, Earl of Pembroke, and Philip, Earl of Montgomery, the former at least known to be on their side. In their opening address to the Earls, and speaking of the plays as Shakespeare's orphans and themselves as their 'guardians', Heminges and Condell pleaded:

We have but collected them, and done an office to the dead . . . without ambition either of self-profit, or fame: only to keep the memory of so worthy a friend and fellow alive, as was our Shakespeare.

Then, turning their attention to 'the great variety of readers' they went on:

It had been a thing, we confess, worthy to have been wished that the author himself had lived to have set forth and overseen his own writings; but since it has been ordained otherwise, and he by death departed from that right, we pray you do not envy his friends the office of their care, and pain, to have collected and published them.

Something of the scale of the debt posterity owes to Heminges and Condell may be gauged from the fact that it is arguably only through their First Folio edition that there have survived the eighteen of Shakespeare's plays for which there had appeared no Quarto: *The Tempest, The Two Gentlemen of Verona, Measure for Measure, The Comedy of Errors, As You Like It, The Taming of the Shrew, All's Well that Ends Well, Twelfth Night, The Winter's Tale, King John, Henry vi, Part i, Henry viii, Coriolanus, Timon of Athens, Julius Caesar, Macbeth, Antony and Cleopatra* and *Cymbeline*. Of those plays published in earlier pirated editions, Heminges and Condell declared on the First Folio's title page that theirs were: 'Published according to the true originall copies' and pointed out:

where (before) you were abused with divers stolen and surreptitious copies, maimed and deformed by the frauds and stealths of injurious imposters . . . those are now offered to your view cured and perfect of their limbs, and all the rest, absolute in their numbers, as he conceived them.

The Merry Wives of Windsor, Henry v, and *Part ii* and *Part iii* of *Henry vi* are among the earlier pirated plays for which the First Folio provides the first 'good' texts. Generation after generation of literary scholars have studied the First Folio texts in the finest detail, both by themselves and in conjunction with Quarto editions where available, and what is clear is that Heminges and Condell had before them a collection of original prompt books from the company's own library,

45a

Inspiration for a Shakespeare play?

45.   John Gower's monument in the church that Shakespeare knew as St Saviour's, Southwark, today Southwark Cathedral (right). Shortly after Shakespeare's brother Edmund was buried in this church. Shakespeare wrote *Pericles*, with John Gower brought back to life as Chorus.

45b

Labels visible on map: Gruge · Flete hyll · Olde ba · 14 · Lud gat · Ave Mari · Black Fryers · Creake · drop · The wa · London · S. Andrewes hyll · Bride Well · Black Fryer · Baynardes Castel

The new, exclusive Blackfriars

46.   The precinct of the former Dominican priory of Blackfriars, as depicted on the so-called 'Agas' map. From as early as 1596, Shakespeare's company had acquired here the great Parliament Chamber (possibly the building circled), where Henry VIII's divorce of Katherine of Aragon had been debated. Although Shakespeare's company converted this to an indoor theatre, local residents blocked their use of it for this purpose until 1608. The vertical gap to the left of the map indicates how it was originally made in separate sections, the engravings for which were not in perfect register. (*Guildhall Museum, Aldermanbury, London*)

47. Theatre historian Irwin Smith's conjectural reconstruction of the interior of the Blackfriars theatre. Here Shakespeare's company provided new, lavish productions designed specifically for an exclusive clientele prepared to pay extra for the privilege of being seated indoors, fully protected from any inclement weather. (*Irwin Smith*)

In the hour of our death

48. A dying man signs his will in the presence of his lawyer, from a painting of 1607. No surviving contemporary image brings us closer to the scene at New Place, Stratford-upon-Avon, when the fifty-one-year-old Shakespeare signed his will, witnessed by his lawyer, Francis Collins, on 25 March 1616. (*Abbot Hall Art Gallery & Museum, Kendal, Cumbria*)

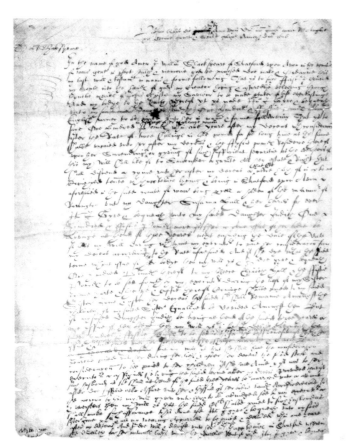

49. The first page of Shakespeare's will. Some have contended that it is in his own hand, and that the suddenly cramped writing towards the bottom of the page are signs that he suffered a stroke. (*Public Record Office, London*)

By me, William Shakespeare

50. The third and last page of Shakespeare's will. Between the eighth and ninth lines can be seen the notorious interpolation 'Item I gyve unto my wief my second best bed with the furniture.' Second among the witnesses to the signature appears the name of the enigmatic 'John Robinson', described in the body of the will as living in the Gatehouse Shakespeare had purchased at Blackfriars. (*Public Record Office, London*)

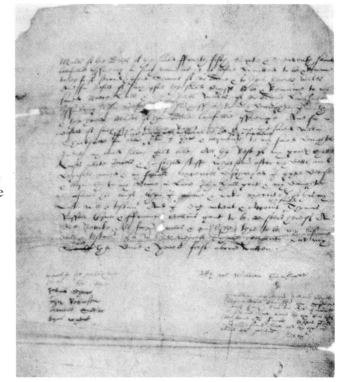

51

True likenesses?

51. Shakespeare's controversial memorial in Holy Trinity Church, Stratford-upon-Avon. The inscription suggests it was commissioned by an outsider to Stratford, and since it was made by the same workshop that, thirty years before, had created the memorial for the Earl of Southampton, could the Earl himself have commissioned it? (*Holy Trinity Church, Stratford-upon-Avon*)

52. The famous Droeshout engraving, from the title page of the First Folio of 1623. Note the line that Shakespeare's plays were here published 'according to the True Originall Copies', indicative that these manuscript copies were still extant at the time of publication. (*British Library*)

Mr. WILLIAM
SHAKESPEARES

COMEDIES,
HISTORIES, &
TRAGEDIES.

Publifhed according to the True Originall Copies.

Martin Droeshout sculpsit London.

LONDON
Printed by Iſaac Iaggard, and Ed. Blount. 1623

GOOD FREND FOR IESVS SAKE FORBEARE,
TO DIGG THE DVST ENCLOASED HEARE.
BLESE BE Y MAN Y SPARES HES STONES
AND CVRST BE HE Y MOVES MY BONES.

53

Death and resurrection

53.   Shakespeare's so enigmatically anonymous gravestone in the chancel of Holy Trinity Church, with its famous curse. (*Holy Trinity Church, Stratford-upon-Avon*)

54.   The timbers of the first bay of Sam Wanamaker's reconstruction of Shakespeare's Globe rising on Bankside, June 1992.

54

direct transcripts from Shakespeare's own manuscripts, and manuscripts in Shakespeare's own hand that collectors would give more than their eye-teeth for should they ever surface today, and that wherever possible they used these as their first point of reference. There can be absolutely no doubt that the scripts had survived the Globe fire of 1613. Heminges, for unexplained reasons, had a house built next to the Globe shortly after Shakespeare's death, and this may well have been to act as a proper office for his work on the First Folio and on the King's Men's accounts, as well as to save him the journey across river back to Aldermanbury. This is almost certainly the house immediately adjacent to the Globe clearly delineated in the Hollar 'photograph' of the early 1640s [see pl. 5].

Whereas previously none of Shakespeare's published plays had been given divisions into acts and scenes, as was classically expected, now for the First Folio someone tried to do this, though whoever he was he grew tired of the task, frequently abandoning the divisions, sometimes even in the middle of a play, as if his heart was not really in it. Thus eighteen plays were given full divisions, eleven divided into acts but not scenes, while six have neither. For the printing of such a necessarily large and expensive volume a consortium of stationers became involved, though oddly, not including Shakespeare's Stratford contemporary Richard Field, who was Master of the Stationers' Company both in 1619 and 1624.

In the event it was the altogether more second-rate house of William Jaggard, earlier notable for some particularly flagrant sharp practice and piracy, that was entrusted with the printing. From minute signs of damage to the lettering and other devices in the surviving copies, studied alongside similar lettering flaws to other works Jaggard was typesetting at this time, a fascinating reconstruction can be made of how the work proceeded through the Jaggard shop. For instance, it can be construed that typesetting began near the end of the summer of 1621, soon after Jaggard had completed Sir Walter Raleigh's *History of the World*, and that the first play to be set was *The Tempest*, probably given this priority because of its relative newness.

Work was interrupted twice in the course of putting together the Folio, one problem seeming to have been the non-availability of a manuscript copy of *The Winter's Tale*, a break in typesetting occurring at this point. This was possibly because the only available copy was needed for prompt purposes, the manuscript that was eventually used seeming to have been specially made by a professional scrivener, Ralph Crane. During another interruption the fault was probably Jaggard's, since the King's Men seem uncharacteristically to have permitted an independent printing of a Quarto edition of *Othello* (ever since 1611 such printings had been successfully blocked), allowed possibly as a warning shot to Jaggard to get on with it.

By rare good fortune one specimen of proof-reading corrections has survived: a page from *Antony and Cleopatra* discovered in the nineteenth century in a parcel of fragments of a First Folio, and this is now in the Folger Shakespeare Library, Washington.[34] In the event all known plays of the Shakespeare canon were included in the First Folio with the exception of *Pericles*.

On 8 November 1623 the First Folio was entered on the Stationers' Register simply as 'Mr. William Shakespeare's Comedies Histories & Tragedies . . . not formerly entered to other men', followed by a listing of those of the plays about to be newly published. But at last, just over three months later on 17 February 1624, the Bodleian Library, Oxford, noted their binding of a copy (copies could be purchased bound or unbound) – the first record that the First Folio was available to the reader. Some thousand copies changed hands, of which two hundred and thirty-eight still survive. At this point, and only at this point, did the immortality of Shakespeare's plays become effectively secured. Even though posterity has never given them due credit, Heminges and Condell had earned more laurels for themselves than they could ever have dreamed of.

CHAPTER 24

'He was . . . for all time!'

When the pioneering purchasers of the Shakespeare First Folio had paid their twenty shillings – three weeks' wages for an ordinary man – and turned to the volume's introductory pages, on the fifth of these they found a glowing poetical tribute from Ben Jonson:

> To the memory of my beloved, the author Mr William Shakespeare: and what he hath left us.

After opening flourishes on the possible abuses of praise, Jonson grandiloquently launched forth on Shakespeare:

> Soul of the Age!
> The applause! delight! the wonder of our Stage!
> My Shakespeare, rise; I will not lodge thee by
> Chaucer, or Spenser, or bid Beaumont lie
> A little further, to make thee a room:
> Thou art a Monument, without a tomb,
> And art alive still, while thy book doth live . . .

In equally extravagant fashion, Jonson went on:

> Triumph, my Britain, thou hast one to show
> To whom all scenes of Europe homage owe.
> He was not of an age, but for all time!

There can be no doubt why Heminges and Condell invited Jonson to contribute such verses of tribute. Although of even humbler origin than Shakespeare, he had achieved true social respectability. On 19 July 1619 he had been awarded an honorary M.A. by the convocation of the University of Oxford, and since he was arguably what today would be called Poet Laureate, his imprimatur was possibly more valuable than that of the Earls of Pembroke and Montgomery. Furthermore, Heminges and Condell had known him for nearly a quarter of a century, acting in his first classical comedy *Every Man in his Humour*, followed by *Every Man out of his Humour*, *Sejanus*, *Volpone*, *The Alchemist* and *Catiline*. In his *Masque of Christmas* performed at Court in 1616 Jonson had referred to 'old Master Heminges'. Heminges' son William had been educated at Jonson's Westminster School, and was hoping to follow in his literary footsteps. Jonson also owed more than a little debt to Shakespeare, thanks to whom, as we noted earlier, he probably received his first real break into the theatrical world's upper echelons.

Even so, due to notes taken by the highly educated and earnest Scottish poet William Drummond, whom four years earlier Jonson had travelled north to visit at his beautiful estate of Hawthornden near Edinburgh, we know something of what Jonson really thought of Shakespeare, at least in 1619 and lulled by Drummond's liberal liquid hospitality. It must be emphasised that it was not only Shakespeare whom Jonson chose to disparage. He professed to be displeased by Spenser, thought Samuel Daniel not a true poet, regarded the late Francis Beaumont as over fond of himself, and criticised Michael Drayton for not having used the possessive correctly in the title of a poem some twenty years back. As for Shakespeare, even though Drummond, already an admirer, was looking for some meaningful insights, all that Jonson could impart was that Shakespeare 'wanted art' and (in *The Winter's Tale*), had ludicrously 'brought in a number of men saying they had suffered shipwreck in Bohemia, where there is no sea near by some one hundred miles.'[1] Aside from this interview with Drummond, in 1631 Jonson would call *Pericles* a 'mouldy tale', complaining that people were still flocking to it, while neglecting his own more serious work.[2]

In this light Jonson's ostensibly glowing tribute to Shakespeare, the most important of any in the First Folio, has to be accorded only a low sincerity rating, Dryden describing it as 'insolent' in 1693, and one modern scholar, T. J. B. Spencer, detecting more than an undercurrent of sneer beneath the oily surface praise.[3] Vain, self-centred and full of contradictions – at one time insulting the Court, at another pandering to it; at one time adopting Catholicism, at another rejecting it – Jonson had every reason to regard Shakespeare as representing everything he most fought against as a dramatist: abandonment of the old classical rules; mixing comedy and tragedy; and being careless about his sources.[4] Yet to whatever extent

Jonson's tongue was in his cheek when writing his tribute to Shakespeare, he proved in it a truer prophet than in perhaps anything else in his writing career, an irony that Shakespeare would have hugely appreciated.

Jonson made one other contribution to the First Folio. In lines printed on its very first page, opposite the engraved portrait of Shakespeare used on the title page [see pl. 52], he assured of the engraver's fidelity to truth:

> O could he [the engraver] but have drawn his wit
> As well in brass, as he hath hit
> His face . . .

Again how one wishes that assurance might be trusted a little more, for it is only from that engraving, and from the Gerard Johnson funerary bust in Holy Trinity, Stratford, that we have some glimpse of what Shakespeare looked like in life. Since few have shown much enthusiasm for the Holy Trinity bust – John Dover Wilson, for one, likened it to 'a self-satisfied pork butcher' – the engraving is all the more important. Below it the tiny inscription 'Martin Droeshout sculpsit London' identifies it as engraved by one of a Flemish dynasty of painters and engravers, founded by John Droeshout, who had come to London about 1566. Like the Johnsons, the Droeshouts worshipped at the Dutch church at Austin Friars (scene of the 'Marlowian' fly-posting back in 1593), Martin being traceable from the church's records as John's grandson, born only in 1601, and therefore still a relatively untried youngster of twenty-two when the First Folio appeared. He may well therefore never have seen Shakespeare in the flesh.

From four very rare specimens of the First Folio, which have the engraving in its proof state, can be traced some of Martin's minor reworking of his plate, yet even so it can be seen that Shakespeare's right-hand sleeve appears not to fit the arm-hole, the shoulders are not drawn in perspective, and the doublet collar fails to show the correct loop and button fastening. Although Baconians, Oxfordians and others have imparted all sorts of cryptic meanings to such infelicities, the likeliest and most straightforward explanation is that Droeshout was a young and relatively inexpert technician whose services Heminges and Condell obtained relatively cheaply, recognising that they could not afford the title page extravaganza that had graced Jonson's First Folio. Probably Droeshout was loaned a painting of Shakespeare to copy from (possibly an oval-shaped miniature), and on making the initial mistake of setting Shakespeare's face too high, was forced to improvise costume details for which he had no guide in the original. If he was trying to reproduce his original exactly, then the stiffly wired collar Shakespeare is wearing firmly dates this as painted not earlier than 1610, that is, some time during the last six years of Shakespeare's life. But another alternative is that the original may have depicted Shakespeare with a large ruff of the kind that had become very old-fashioned by the 1620s, Droeshout thereby making his errors attempting to modernise Shakespeare's appearance.[5]

Modern reactions to Droeshout's engraved likeness vary greatly. Oxford Regius Professor of History Lord Dacre has described it as by 'an unskilful artist' who 'has presented the blank face of a country oaf'.[6] Dr A. L. Rowse, for his part, has enthused 'Have you ever seen a nobler dome of a cranium than on that head? Very large luminous eyes that take in everything, a big sexy nose, voluptuous lips'.[7] The single undeniably positive feature to the Droeshout engraving is that at least it must have met the approval of Heminges and Condell, who had known Shakespeare, whereas all other contenders as 'Shakespeare' portraits are extremely doubtful.

Although the so-called 'Chandos' portrait in London's National Portrait Gallery, notable for the gold earring in the subject's left ear, has been said to be by the hand either of Burbage or by an unknown player called John Taylor, it has no truly firm provenance. The Folger Shakespeare Library 'Felton' portrait with its exaggerated forehead was almost certainly doctored in the late eighteenth century to be passed off as of Shakespeare, and is more likely to be of some unknown Dutch worthy of his time. Bearing the greatest resemblance to Droeshout's likeness is the 'Flower' portrait in the Royal Shakespeare Company collection. But x-rays reveal this to be painted over a late fifteenth-century Italian painting of the Madonna and Child, and the prevailing expert opinion is that it was done not earlier than the eighteen century – almost certainly deliberately to make it appear the original from which Droeshout made his engraving.

All this has made, for a very long time, the urge all the more great to obtain a really true likeness of Shakespeare, an urge perhaps second only in strength to that relating to Jesus Christ. As long ago as 1876 the American J. Parker Norris proposed nothing less than a daring flouting of the curse protecting Shakespeare's grave:

> If we could even get a photograph of Shakespeare's skull it would be a great thing, and would help us make a better portrait of him than we now possess. . . . Open the grave reverently, have the photographers ready, and the moment the coffin lid is removed (if there be any) expose the plates, and see what will be the result.[8]

From before Norris's proposal there can be quoted all sorts of stories of supposed clandestine openings of the tomb. Nineteenth-century vicar Reverend C. L. Langston claimed that ruffians broke into it in 1794, stole Shakespeare's skull, failed in their attempt to sell it, then reburied it in Langston's own church at Beoly, Worcestershire. Did Langston perhaps need funds for his church roof? 'Rip van Winkle' author Washington Irving reported being told by the Stratford church sexton that when a workman was digging a vault close to Shakespeare's grave, the earth caved in, enabling him to peer into where Shakespeare's remains should have been, only to find an empty space.[9] To my astonishment, during my researching this present book a hitherto unknown namesake of mine published a novel, *Black Jenny*, with a gruesomely realistic account of a fictional opening of Shakespeare's grave in which, clearly in keeping with our times, the apparent chief point of interest was Shakespeare's corpse's signs of syphilis.

Today if Shakespeare's remains were exhumed there are the technological means to make a truly accurate likeness, far beyond the dreams of J. Parker Norris back in 1876. One of the chief exponents of the process is Manchester University's Dr Richard Neave who has already made brilliant reconstructions from the skulls of Philip of Macedon and King Midas of Lydia, to name just two better-known examples. Yet having seen in Cairo Museum what exhumation has done for Tutankhamun, my personal hope is that if Shakespeare's curse really has held so far, then it will continue to deter all-comers for a very long time.

Arguably the indistinctness with which we glimpse Shakespeare's earthly likeness is part and parcel of the man, of whom it may well be no accident that no one has left a record of meeting him close to.

Quite possibly one of the most revealing passages about Shakespeare as a man comes from one of the roughest of the jottings made by gossip John Aubrey from his interview with William Beeston, son of the Christopher Beeston who had acted with Shakespeare's company. The partly cancelled note reads: 'the more to be admired, he was not a company keeper. [He] . . . wouldn't be debauched, and if invited to, writ [i.e. wrote] he was in pain.[10]

Although elsewhere, among his more formal material, Aubrey wrote that Shakespeare was 'a handsome, well shaped man, very good company, and of a very ready and pleasant smooth wit',[11] there is no reason to regard these two ostensibly contradictory statements as necessarily incompatible with each other. Quite aside from his writings, Shakespeare must have had considerable personal magnetism to command common stage and sophisticated audiences alike, and to have ingratiated himself so intimately with such a high-born individual as the recipient of the *Sonnets* – the correctness of the Southampton identification notwithstanding. Equally, he would hardly have been trusted by individuals of stature, particularly Catholic ones, if he had been well known for sharing the latest gossip with his chums in the nearest watering hole. Almost certainly his sentiments were as his contemporary, William Camden's, that: 'Wise men do keep their thoughts locked up in the closets of their breasts'.[12]

All through this book we have hinted, and it must be stressed, against the expert opinion of the redoubtable Dr A. L. Rowse and others, at Shakespeare's closet Roman Catholic sympathies, if not outright affiliations. The evidence, it has to be acknowledged, certainly does not leap out at us, the most direct attestation deriving from a late-seventeenth-century vicar, Richard Davies, a one-time chaplain of Corpus Christi College, Oxford, who in the course of adding to materials collected by former scholar William Fulman, set down the following note about Shakespeare, which is still preserved at Corpus Christi:

> He died April 23, 1616, probably at Stratford for there he is buried and hath a monument on which he lays a heavy curse upon anyone who shall remove his bones. He died a papist.[13]

Davies left no explanation of why he made such a positive statement, yet the heavy air of Catholicism surrounding Shakespeare's two earliest patrons, his sentimental *Sonnet* harking to the Catholic past

He dyed a papist.

Fig 14
Evidence of Shakespeare's Catholicism? A cryptic and unexplained remark 'He dyed a papist', made by Richard Davies, Archdeacon of Lichfield (preserved in the Library of Corpus Christi College, Oxford).

of 'bare ruin'd choirs', his sending-up of Protestants such as Sir John Oldcastle, his sympathetic portrayals of Catholic priests such as those in *Romeo and Juliet* and *Measure for Measure*, his father and elder daughter's featuring on recusancy rolls, not least, his careful avoidance of confronting a religious theme head on his plays, all seem of a piece.

As remarked by Graham Greene, arguably with rather more significance than he himself appreciated 'Isn't there one whole area of the Elizabethan scene that we miss even in Shakespeare's huge world of comedy and despair? The kings speak, the adventurers speak ... the madmen and the lover, the soldiers and the poets, but the martyrs are quite silent'.[14] For was this because as a King's Man Shakespeare felt it was simply impossible for him to be more overt in his Catholic sympathies, and that, rather than playing any martyr's role personally, where he could most help was by subtly pleading for the universal Christian values of tolerance, forgiveness and reconciliation via the public stage?

Now we cannot claim any overwhelming assurance of the correctness of this thinking. Nor is any Catholicism Shakespeare possessed likely to have carried with it anything unpatriotic, or endorsing the atrocities that had been committed in Catholicism's as well as Protestantism's name. However, if it is even near the mark it is not peripheral to him, it is central. Arguably, it was what gave him both his compassion towards all vagaries of the human condition, and also his guardedness – discreetly balancing everything, avoiding disclosing his own political and religious affiliations, above all, unlike Jonson, setting his plays in anything but the here and now of his England. Equally arguably, it was what gave him his edge, honed on the ever bitter-sweet stresses of the perilous times in which he moved; like Rembrandt, probing like a searchlight into the very depths of his characters, yet always leaving sufficient shadow to allow an infinity of outside interpretations.

If, as we have hinted, something of Shakespeare's secret Catholicism was locked in his motives for purchasing the Blackfriars Gatehouse, then at no moment was the world to which the Gatehouse *may* have given access more revealed, albeit both fleetingly and tragically, than at the time when the First Folio was within weeks of publication. At three o'clock in the afternoon of Sunday 26 October 1623 a clandestine congregation of some three hundred Catholics assembled for what we can only construe to have been their regular Sunday Mass, held in a secret upper garret 'over the Gatehouse' (though we cannot be sure it was Shakespeare's),[15] somewhere within the great Blackfriars edifice that also incorporated the King's Men's theatre and what had been George Carey's apartments, now occupied by the French ambassador. A greater number than normal seem to have been gathered because of the presence of renowned Jesuit preacher Master Drury, and it was apparently during his homily that disaster suddenly struck. With a horrifying crack a main beam of the floor collapsed under the assembly's weight, plunging them down one floor, then partly through another, which appears to have been the French ambassador's drawing-room. Over ninety people, including the two officiating priests, were killed either from their falls or crushed under the rubble and weight of other bodies. Until this disaster, the very existence of this secret 'church' was quite unknown, and one can hardly believe other than that the Shakespeare Gatehouse, with its mysterious secret passages, and reported comings and goings of priests, somehow held a key to the clandestine Catholic gathering place. Was the enigmatic John Robinson, earlier described as dwelling there, perhaps its clerical guardian?

But if religion meant a great deal to Shakespeare – and it must not be forgotten that for all the ostensible secularity of his plays they are chockful of religious allusions – so also did family. Whatever the friability of his relations with his wife Anne, the money he earned in London he brought back to be translated into Stratford property for her and their daughters' benefit, and late-seventeenth-century tradition has it that Anne (along with her daughters) 'did earnestly desire to be laid in the same grave with him'.[16] Certainly upon her death in 1623 she was laid to rest as near to him as the curse would allow, properly identified on a brass inscribed:

> Here lyeth interred the body of Anne, wife of William Shakespeare, who departed this life the 6th day of August 1623, being of the age of 67 years.

Likewise, and again despite the long years in London, such was the patriarchal status Shakespeare had earned that when in 1635 it fell to his son-in-law Dr John Hall to be the next main member of the family to go to his rest, Hall was laid next to his father-in-law, and his gravestone, bearing Hall's own arms of three talbots heads erased, impaling Shakespeare, in its turn inscribed:

> Here lyeth the body of John Hall
> Gent. He marr[ied] Susanna, the daughter & co-heir
> Of Will Shakespeare, gent. He
> Deceased November 25, a[nn]o 1635, aged 60.

Likewise, upon Susanna's death in 1649 she was laid next to her husband, but again with her relation to Shakespeare the subject of special stress:

> Here lyeth the body of Susanna
> Wife to John Hall, gent, the daughter
>   of William Shakespeare, gent
> She deceased the 11th of July a[nn]o
>   1649, aged 66.

Furthermore, whereas Anne's and John's gravestones had sported accompanying Latin poems, Susanna's was in English, and again with special mention of her father, beginning:

> Witty above her sex, but that's not all
> Wise to salvation was good Mistress Hall
> Something of Shakespeare was in that, but this
> Wholly of him with whom she's now in bliss. . . .

'Wise to salvation': the phrase reminds us that Susanna was the one member of the family, apart from grandfather John, to have featured on a recusancy list, making all the more intriguing the line 'Something of Shakespeare was in that'; if only such messages could have been less cryptic. The Halls' only daughter Elizabeth, just eight when Shakespeare died, in 1626 married the comfortably off Thomas Nash, the couple living for a while in the house next to New Place now called, for Stratford tourism purposes, Nash's house. Nash died in 1647, to be buried immediately next to Shakespeare, almost certainly in a plot that had been also reserved for Elizabeth. However, Elizabeth then remarried, joining her new husband, widower John Bernard, at his Abington Manor home in Northamptonshire, and although her burial is recorded at Abington on 17 February 1670, no surviving gravestone or monument marks the location. She had no children by either marriage.

For all its stormy beginnings, Judith's marriage to Thomas, by contrast, even though Thomas achieved little, showed considerably more promise from the point of view of perpetuating Shakespeare's line. The couple had three sons, the first pointedly named Shakespeare Quiney, who, at least from the date of his christening, 23 November 1616, would seem to have been conceived extremely close to the day Shakespeare breathed his last. Although the infant Shakespeare lived little over a year, he was closely followed by two more sons, Richard and Thomas. They in their turn, however, having survived the danger years of early infancy, succumbed within a few months of each other in 1639, aged twenty-one and nineteen respectively. No graves of any of this Quiney line are known, nor even the date of Thomas' death, Judith's being recorded in the Stratford register on 9 February 1661, a few days after her seventy-seventh birthday. Accordingly, with granddaughter Elizabeth Nash/Bernard's death in 1670 there died Shakespeare's entire direct line, male and female, present-day Shakespeare 'descendants' actually being those descended from Shakespeare's sister Joan.

Back in London, presumably with Shakespeare's memorial rings on their fingers, First Folio pioneers John Heminges and Henry Condell lived on exhibiting every sign of equivalent prosperity to Shakespeare's. Condell's popularity seems evident enough from the will of 'principal actor' Nicholas Tooley in 1623, appointing him a residuary legatee and executor, and leaving £5 to Condell's wife Elizabeth 'as a remembrance of my love'. This was followed a year later by that of fellow 'principal actor' John Underwood appointing his 'loving friend Henry Condell' as one of his executors.

In 1625, a year marked by virulent plague and by the death of James I, the King's Men received a new patron in the person of Charles I, and a new patent, in which John Heminges and Henry Condell come first and second in the list of the company's principals. In the manner of Augustine Phillips and Shakespeare before him, Condell retired about this year to his country house, in his case to rural Fulham. Although he would seem to have been younger than Heminges, it was he who died first, in 1627, his will in the Public Record Office[17] revealing him to have owned a considerable amount of property in the Strand, in Fleet Street and in Middlesex, and showing that he retained his interest in the theatre to his last. The register of St Mary Aldermanbury simply records 'Buried. Mr Condall. December 29, 1627'.

Heminges would seem to have remained active to the end. The Court Minutes of the Grocers' Company show that in November 1621 he paid well over £20 to become a liveried member of the Company, and four years later they record: 'John Heminges and Thomas Tickner, two of the Clothing of this Company appointed to make a Dinner on the 27th March next, as has been accustomed, for the right worshipful the Knights, Aldermen, Wardens and Assistants of this Company'. In 1629 Heminges followed Shakespeare's course in applying for, and being granted, a coat of arms, the College of Arms citation describing him as 'Son and heir of George Hemings of Droitwich in the County of Worcester, Gent', our only indication that Heminges' roots lay not far from Shakespeare's. In 1630, when another very serious plague outbreak caused the theatres to be closed for six months, Heminges, business manager to the last, petitioned King Charles for an aid payment to the King's Men, and although £100 was quickly granted,[18] on 9 October Heminges made out his will, and must have died almost immediately after, since it was proved on the 11th and he was buried on the 12th. The burial register entry reads simply 'John Heminge, player', and it became him, as did the way he chose, although now living by the Globe, to be buried, along with his wife, and with Henry Condell, in the church of St Mary Aldermanbury that he had served, and clearly loved, for so many years.

Of those others whose life Shakespeare had touched, the Earl of Southampton continued to attract literary eulogies, but only just lived to see the First Folio. He was certainly in London at around the time of publication, for he was active on Irish and other matters in the

Parliament of February to May 1624. Shortly after, however, he set off with his eldest son James at the head of an expedition to the Netherlands, only for both to be severely stricken with fever, neither returning to England alive. On 28 December 1624 he and his son were buried in the chancel of St Peter's Titchfield, just a few yards from the now familiar Gerard Johnson monument that we have associated with Shakespeare's *Sonnet* 123.

Alice, Ferdinando's widow, widowed a second time on Thomas Egerton's death in 1617, lived on until 1636, patronising literature to the very end. About 1633, when the then twenty-five-year-old John Milton wrote his masque *Arcades*, he dedicated this to her, describing her as:

> sitting like a goddess bright
> In the centre of her light.

She was buried beneath a recumbent coloured effigy of herself with flaming waist-length hair, guarded by Stanley eagles, in a magnificent four-poster tomb which survives today in Harefield Church, Middlesex.

Whether or not Emilia Lanier has been correctly identified as Shakespeare's Dark Lady, with characteristic perversity she was probably the longest lived of any of Shakespeare's generation. From a case she brought against Middle Temple lawyer Edward Smith, we learn that the year after Shakespeare's death (by which time she had become widowed), she rented a house in pricey St Giles in the Fields, London, with the aim of setting up a school for what she described as 'the education of noblemen and gentlemen's children of great worth'.[19] Clearly this establishment did not prosper, for she fell behind with the rent, was sued, and eventually left the house 'in great decay, and in a nasty and filthy state'. In 1627 she became a grandmother by her son Henry whom she had borne by old Lord Chamberlain Hunsdon, then a grandmother a second time in 1629. But when Henry died in 1633, she found herself responsible for both grandchildren, and fought some strenuous legal battles to improve her income. In her mid-seventies, she survived the first part of the Civil War to be buried in the notorious district of Clerkenwell on 3 April 1645.

Of the places that Shakespeare knew, although these might be expected to survive significantly better than the people, this was rarely the case. Earliest to disappear was the Whitehall Banqueting Hall in which he and his company had entertained King James and his Court to some of his finest plays. This was burned down in 1619, to be rebuilt by Inigo Jones in the form of the present edifice. Upon the outbreak of the Civil War, in September 1642, the Puritanically minded Parliamentarians closed down the Globe and the Blackfriars along with all similar sites of London's 'spectacles of pleasure', whereupon, without prospect of their reopening, their landowners understandably sought alternative means of income. A handwritten note in a 1631 edition of Stow's *Annales* (now in the possession of the Folger Shakespeare Library, Washington), records that the Globe was 'pulled down to the ground by Sir Matthew Brend on Monday the 15 of April, 1644 to make tenements in the room of it'. After these tenements the site became a brewery. The Blackfriars theatre, despite having become the more profitable of the two theatres during Charles I's reign, fared little better. In 1653 Richard Flecknoe wrote poignantly:

From thence passing on to the Blackfriars, and seeing never a playbill on the Gate, nor coaches in the place, nor doorkeeper at the Playhouse door, with his box like a churchwarden, desiring you to remember the poor players, I cannot but say for Epilogue to all the plays that were ever acted there:

> Poor house that in the days of our grand-sires,
> Belonged unto the mendicant friars:
> And where so oft in our fathers' days
> We have seen so many of Shakespeare's plays,
> So many of Jonson's, Beaumont's and Fletcher's.[20]

Within two years of Flecknoe writing these words the Blackfriars was pulled down and used for tenements, the site subsequently for many years being occupied by *The Times* offices, then by the *Observer* newspaper, and today under review for redevelopment. Even so, the Blackfriars survived longer than Ferdinando Stanley's magnificent Lancashire seat of Lathom. A prime Parliamentarian target during the Civil War, and valiantly and successfully defended by Countess Charlotte de la Trémouille, French-born wife of the seventh Earl ('nidicock' William's son), when the Royalist cause was lost nationally, its defenders had no recourse but to surrender. In December 1645

Parliamentarian troops proceeded to destroy it utterly, inevitably including the great hall where Shakespeare's company would have staged their entertainment for the fourth and fifth earls, and if the house at that time contained letters and other records of Shakespeare's early associations with Ferdinando, this was when they met their end.

Hardly had the Restoration time to catch its breath before there followed London's Great Fire of 1666, sweeping away with it Shakespeare's Silver Street lodging house, the Aldermanbury houses of Heminges and Condell, the old College of Arms where Shakespeare had called to apply for his father's coat of arms, and not least old St Paul's where, for all its disrepair and misuse, had stood the bookstalls that had sold the first copies of so many of Shakespeare's plays and poems.

Although ostensibly Stratford's Shakespeare-associated places missed such depredations, in fact New Place, the one house that more than any other would have evoked Shakespeare in his home roots, fell victim to anger on the part of mid-eighteenth-century owner vicar Reverend Francis Gastrell against the Stratford corporation. Detesting the visitors who came to gaze at where Shakespeare lived and died, Gastrell first cut down the mulberry tree that Shakespeare was supposed to have planted, prompting enterprising Stratfordian Thomas Sharpe to purchase the timber and set up a thriving souvenir business from this. Then in 1759 Gastrell had the whole house razed to the ground. Next to go was Shakespeare's Blackfriars Gatehouse. In 1787 George Coleman, speaking of Shakespeare in his *Prose on Several Occasions*, mentions the 'house formerly situated at Blackfriars, but lately taken down on account of the new bridge, which belonged to that poet.' This 'new bridge' can only have been the stone Blackfriars bridge completed in 1769.

It was about this same time that the Earl of Southampton's Titchfield House was allowed to fall into disrepair, much of its stonework being taken away for use in the construction of Cams Hall, near Fareham, so that today all that survives is little more than a ruined facade. As for Shakespeare's so-called 'Birthplace' house, put up for auction in 1847, advertised as 'The Truly Heart-Stirring Relic . . . of England's Immortal Bard' and 'The Most Honoured Monument of the Greatest Genius that ever Lived', it came within a whisker of being bought by the great American showman Phineas T. Barnum for shipping lock, stock and barrel to America. To the eternal credit of the rapidly formed Shakespeare Birthplace

Committee, ancestors of the present Trust, they saved the house for the nation, but sadly then gutted it, flattened John Shakespeare's neighbours' cottages to make a firebreak and room for a suitably picturesque garden, and filled it with indiscriminately acquired furniture that continues to mislead visitors to the present day.

And if these may seem like sins of the ignorant past, the sins of the present century are every bit as dire. The 1920s and '30s saw item after item of Shakespeareana disappear from these shores to form the Folger Shakespeare Library in Washington, so that this now possesses a far superior collection of Shakespearean remains than any single collection to be found in this country. Not least, it has seventy-nine copies of the First Folio, compared to no more than five to be found in any one other place in the world. To none other than Winston Churchill do we owe in 1946 the shipping of Heminges and Condell's beloved St Mary Aldermanbury church, stone by stone, to Fulton, Missouri, where it is today part of Westminster College, leaving the most inadequate of memorials in its place. Incredibly, despite the uncovering as recently as 1989 of the remains of the Rose theatre, whose boards Shakespeare undoubtedly trod, government minister Virginia Bottomley was prepared to sanction the driving of eleven new piles through this site and it took the frantic publicity efforts of actors Dame Judi Dench, James Fox, Sir Ian McKellen and the late Dame Peggy Ashcroft to have the plan stopped – and then by no means satisfactorily.

It is through seeing the many thousands of overseas tourists who daily, like pilgrims, throng Stratford, that the reality sinks in of the sheer diversity of cultures whose hearts and minds Shakespeare has touched, even when translated into languages of which he could have no inkling. Yet with due respect to Stratford's tourist industry, and particularly to its rightly thriving Memorial Theatre, there are many more places and items in Britain that have legitimate associations with Shakespeare but which remain as yet all too little known.

Earlier we mentioned Nicholas Hilliard's exquisite miniature of the young Earl of Southampton, unimaginatively kept with several others in a basement room of Cambridge's Fitzwilliam Museum, with absolutely nothing to indicate that it has any Shakespeare connection. Upon visiting Titchfield House on a summer weekend afternoon the dingy portakabin presumably serving as a visitor information kiosk was boarded up and shut, accompanied by a general air of neglect. Although the Dulwich Picture Gallery to the south of

London houses unique contemporary portraits of Richard Burbage and other actors of Shakespeare's company, during the writing of this book it has come under serious threat of closure, while nearby, at Dulwich College, Henslowe's Diary, containing unique first records of performances of Shakespeare plays upon the London stage, is not even on display to the general public. Likewise Shakespeare's will, arguably his most intimate surviving relic, has been removed from display at the London Public Record Office, apparently due to government cut-backs, while in government educational circles there has even been talk of removing Shakespeare from the national curriculum and replacing his work with the study of current television soap operas.

As we have seen, by far the greater part of Shakespeare's working life was spent in London, chiefly on the Bankside. Yet throughout most of this century the sum-total of recognition of Shakespeare's Globe's one-time presence in this locality has been a bronze plaque erected in 1908 by the Shakespeare Reading Society on a dingy backstreet wall. Whereas during recent decades life-size working reconstructions of Shakespeare's Globe have been built in San Diego; in Ashland, Oregon; in Cedar City, Utah; in Odessa, Texas; in Perth, Australia; in Neuss and Berlin in Germany; and even in Tokyo, in England government thinking has remained indifferent to any such project in London – and this despite the dereliction of so much of post-war Bankside.

It has, therefore, to be a matter of the utmost shame to English establishment circles that it has taken an American, the late Sam Wanamaker, to recognise the utter inadequacy of this, and to have the vision to set in motion the building of a working reconstruction of the Globe in the locality in which it once stood; also to have the sheer tenacity, despite continuing British apathy, to see the project through to a point at which, at the time of his death from cancer in December 1993, it was well under way.

In the wake of Sam Wanamaker's death, how much his enterprise will be realised, and be authentic and able to recapture the atmosphere of the Globe of Shakespeare's day – the no-interval performances, the sellers of oranges, nuts and beer continually moving among the audiences mid-show – remains to be seen. The idea has a peculiar appropriateness to Shakespeare who so repeatedly had his characters envisaging their own dramas repeated on stages centuries into the future, as in Casca's lines in *Julius Caesar*:

How many ages hence
Shall this our lofty scene be acted over
In states unborn and accents yet unknown![21]

The idea of projecting the theatre of Shakespeare's time forward into our present, of giving people today the sights, sounds and flavours of the drama of his past, is a time-busting paradox the man himself would have hugely appreciated. It is also to be infinitely more applauded than any attempt to resurrect his bones.

The magic of Shakespeare is that the words he penned four hundred years ago still send tingles and shivers through the spine, so that even in translation they thrill people in countries that were unheard of in the England of his time. Though any more searching literary appraisal than this would be beyond the essentially historical approach of this book, the biggest disservice anyone can do to Shakespeare is to be so dazzled by his works as to argue that they could not have been written by anyone so ordinary as a Stratford-upon-Avon-born actor. The very essence of Shakespeare was his humanity: that he was neither a blue-blooded nobleman nor a university trained academic, but a humbly born player who wanted to give his calling the sort of material that could really make it soar, to reach every level of society. Where he was different from his contemporaries is that he felt with and for others in all their faults and frailties. In *Julius Caesar* Shakespeare has Julius say of Cassius 'He is a great observer, and he looks quite through the deeds of men', and he could hardly have coined a more appropriate description of himself.

Let literary critic Bernard Levin, from a life-time's appreciation of having seen every Shakespeare play in performance, have the final word:

No other writer, and with the exception of Mozart, no other artist, has brought us so close to the heart of the ultimate mystery of the universe and of man's place in it; no other has felt and presented the numinous with such certainty and power, no other penetrated so deeply into the source from which he derived his genius and from which we all, including him, derive our humanity. The ultimate wonder of Shakespeare is the deep, sustaining realisation that his work, in addition to all its other qualities – poetical, dramatic, philosophical, psychological – is above all *true*. It is hardly surprising that he, alone among mortals, has conquered mortality, and still speaks directly to us from lips that have been dust for hundreds of years, and a heart that stopped beating to mortal rhythms on St George's Day 1616. He alone has defeated the last enemy, that pitiless foe which he called 'cormorant devouring time'; no wonder that he knew it, and thought it no shame – 'Not marble, nor the gilded monuments of princes shall outlive this powerful rhyme' – to proclaim it.[22]

Notes and References

CHAPTER 1 – *Through a Glass Darkly*

1 Hollar's drawing had formerly been in the collection of the late Patrick Allan Fraser of Hospitalfield, Arbroath. See 'Hollar: A Discovery of Iolo A. Williams', *The Connoisseur*, xcii, 1933, pp. 318–21.
2 See in particular John Orrell, *The Quest for Shakespeare's Globe*, Cambridge University Press, 1983.
3 This copy of Stow's *Annales* is now in the collection of the Folger Shakespeare Library, Washington DC, USA.
4 This information derives from another manuscript note in the Folger Shakespeare Library's copy of the 1631 edition of Stow's *Annales*.
5 Leslie Hotson, *The Commonwealth & Restoration Stage*, Harvard University Press, Cambridge, Mass, 1928, p. 6.
6 Public Record Office, Prob 10/484, quoted J. Payne Collier, *Memoirs of the Principal Actors in the Plays of Shakespeare*, Shakespeare Society, 1846, p. 76.
7 For the most up-to-date edition of the full text, see R. A. Foakes & R. T. Rickert, *Henslowe's Diary*, Cambridge, 1961.
8 For the full text, see Foakes & Rickert, op. cit., pp. 276–7.
9 Mark Eccles, 'Jonson's Marriage', *Review of English Studies*, XII, pp. 257ff.
10 Charles Nicholl, *A Cup of News. The Life of Thomas Nashe*, Routledge & Kegan Paul, 1984, p. 183.
11 Blair Worden, 'Shakespeare and Politics', *Shakespeare Survey* 44, 1992, p. 2.
12 Roger Thompson, Series Producer Bookmark, 2 April 1992, personal communication to the author.

CHAPTER 2 – *Was 'Shakespeare' Really Shakespeare?*

1 Nicholas Rowe, *Works of Shakespeare*, 1709, I, as quoted E. K. Chambers *William Shakespeare, A Study of Facts and Problems*, 1930, vol. II, p. 269.
2 Edmond Malone, *Supplement to the Edition of Shakespeare's Plays Published in 1778 by Samuel Johnson and George Steevens*, 1780, i, 654.
3 Quoted in James Corton Cowell, 'Some Reflections on the Life of William Shakespeare: A Paper read before the Ipswich Philosophic Society', MS 294 in the University of London Library, pp. 67–8.
4 Peter Berresford Ellis, 'An Author's Cares', *The Author*, vol. CIII, no. 4, winter 1992, p. 164.
5 For an English language account of M Demblon and other alternative Shakespeares not included in Schoenbaum's *Shakespeare's Lives* (from which much of this chapter is drawn), see Georges Connes, *The Shakespeare Mystery*, Palmer, 1927.

6 Public Record Office, SP 12/271/35.

7 James Greenstreet 'A Hitherto Unknown Noble Writer of Elizabethan Comedies', *The Genealogist* April 1891, pt. 4, p. 205ff; see also vol. VIII, pt. I and vol. VIII, pt. 3.

8 J. Thomas Looney, *'Shakespeare' identified in Edward De Vere the Seventeenth Earl of Oxford*, London, 1920.

9 Charlton Ogburn, *The Mysterious William Shakespeare: The Myth and the Reality*, Dodd, Mead, New York, 1984.

10 The great Washington Shakespeare debate was published in *The American University Law Review*, 37, 1988, pp. 609–826.

11 Aubrey's *Brief Lives*, ed. O. L. Dick, p. 305.

12 Calvin Hoffman, *The Murder of the Man Who Was 'Shakespeare'*, London, 1955.

13 Percy Allen, *Talks with Elizabethans Revealing the Mystery of 'William Shakespeare'*, London, c.1942 (no date given).

14 Nick Nuttall, 'Shall I compare thee to Good Queen Bess', *The Times*, 31 March 1992.

15 Edmond Malone, *An Inquiry into the Authenticity of Certain Miscellaneous Papers and Legal Instruments, Published Dec.24, MDCCXCV and Attributed to Shakespeare, Queen Elizabeth, and Henry, Earl of Southampton: Illustrated by Fac-similes of the Genuine Hand-writing of That Nobleman, and of Her Majesty; A New Fac-simile of the Hand-writing of Shakespeare, Never before Exhibited; and other Authentick Documents*, London, 1796.

16 J. Payne Collier, article in the *Athenaeum*, 31 January 1852.

17 J. Payne Collier, *Diary*, xxvi.40–41, Folger Shakespeare Library, MS.M.a.40.

18 Oscar Wilde, 'The Portrait of Mr. W.H.' in *Blackwood's Edinburgh Magazine*, 146, July 1889. There was also a revised edition published London 1921.

19 Frank Harris, *The Man Shakespeare and his Tragic Life-Story*, London, 1909.

20 Lytton Strachey, 'Shakespeare's Final Period', *Books and Characters French & English*, London, 1922.

21 Leslie Hotson, *Shakespeare's Sonnets Dated*, Rupert-Hart Davis, London, 1949, p. 21.

22 See G. P. V. Akrigg, *Shakespeare and the Earl of Southampton*, London, Hamish Hamilton, 1968, p. 254; also Garrett Mattingley, 'The Date of Shakespeare's Sonnet CVII', *Publications of the Modern Language Association of America*, xlviii, 1933, pp. 705–21.

23 A. L. Rowse, *Discovering Shakespeare*, Weidenfeld & Nicolson, 1989, p. 21.

CHAPTER 3 – *Stratford-upon-Avon – 'One of the Biggest Frauds in England'?*

1 See in particular J. O. Halliwell[-Phillipps], *The Working Life of William Shakespeare. Including Many Particulars Respecting the Poet and His Family Never before Published*, London, 1848. As remarked by Schoenbaum, Halliwell 'is the first biographer of Shakespeare to appreciate fully the significance of the Stratford documents, and to use them systematically.' [*Shakespeare's Lives*, p. 291].

2 Edgar I. Fripp, *Shakespeare's Stratford*, Oxford University Press, London, 1928;

also *Shakespeare's Haunts Near Stratford*, Oxford University Press, London, 1929.

3 Doubt is expressed by Sir Sidney Lee, *A Life of William Shakespeare*, London, 1898, pp. 284–5. But the connection with the Park Hall Ardens is well argued by J. S. Smart in *Shakespeare Truth and Tradition*, Longmans Green & Co., New York, 1928, pp. 69–71.

4 Quoted in Edgar I. Fripp, *Shakespeare: Man and Artist*, Oxford University Press, London, 1938, vol. I, p. 31 after J. O. Halliwell-Phillipps, *Outlines of the Life of Shakespeare*, vol. ii, p. 53.

5 Mark Eccles, *Shakespeare in Warwickshire*, University of Wisconsin Press, Madison, 1963, p. 1.

6 J. O. Halliwell-Phillipps, *Outlines*, op. cit., ii, 53f.

7 See Jane Ashelford, *Dress in the Age of Elizabeth*, Batsford, London, 1988, p. 81.

8 *The Merry Wives of Windsor*, I.iv.20f. See also Fripp, *Shakespeare Man and Artist*, op. cit., p. 79ff.

9 Bretchgirdle's library as detailed in his will shows evidence of Protestant leanings. See Fripp, *Shakespeare Man and Artist*, p. 41; also the same author's *Shakespeare Studies*, pp. 23–31.

10 William Shakespeare, *Plays and Poems*, ed. Edmond Malone, 1790, vol. I, pt. i., p. 124n.

11 A. L. Rowse, *William Shakespeare: A Biography*, Harper & Row, New York, 1963, p. 32.

12 ibid., p. 36.

13 Mark Eccles, *Shakespeare in Warwickshire*, op. cit., p. 56.

14 Shakespeare Birthplace Trust Records Office, Corp Rec. Council Book A. p. 259.

15 Mark Eccles, *Shakespeare in Warwickshire*, op. cit., p. 31.

CHAPTER 4 – *A Curious Testament*

1 For the full text of this intriguing document, see Appendix C, Miscellaneous Documents, p. 468.

2 For detailed background to the document's discovery, see James G. McManaway, 'John Shakespeare's "Spiritual Testament"', *Shakespeare Quarterly*, xviii, 1967, pp. 197–205; also S. Schoenbaum's chapter 'John Shakespeare's Spiritual Testament' in his *William Shakespeare: A Documentary Life*, Oxford, 1975, pp. 41–6.

3 Edmond Malone, *Inquiry into the Authenticity of Certain Miscellaneous Papers and Legal Instruments*, op. cit., pp. 198–9.

4 Sidney Lee, *A Life of William Shakespeare*, (4th ed. of revised version, 1925), p. 647.

5 Herbert Thurston, S. J., 'A Controverted Shakespeare Document', *The Dublin Review*, clxxiii, 1923, p. 165.

6 For a superb facsimile reproduction of this *Testament* in the Folger Shakespeare Library, see S. Schoenbaum, *William Shakespeare: A Documentary Life*, op. cit., pp. 44–5.

7 Quoted in J. H. de Groot, *The Shakespeares and 'The Old Faith'*, New York, 1946, p. 88.
8 Christopher Devlin, S. J., *Hamlet's Divinity*, Rupert Hart-Davis, London, 1963, p. 14.
9 ibid.
10 Peter Milward, S. J., *Shakespeare's Religious Background*, Sidgwick & Jackson, London, 1973, p. 19.
11 Quoted in Patrick McGrath, *Papists and Puritans under Elizabeth I*, Blandford, London, 1967, p. 173.
12 Augustus Jessopp, *One Generation of a Norfolk House*, 1878, p. 96.
13 D. L. Thomas and N. E. Evans, 'John Shakespeare in the Exchequer', *Shakespeare Quarterly*, 35, 1984, pp. 315–8.
14 Nicholas Rowe's *Life* as reprinted in E. K. Chambers, *William Shakespeare*, p. 264.
15 S. Schoenbaum, *William Shakespeare: A Documentary Life*, op. cit., p. 27.
16 Sir Richard Phillips in *The Monthly Magazine; or British Register*, xlv, 1818, p. 2.
17 Leslie Hotson, 'Three Shakespeares', *Shakespeare's Sonnets Dated, and other Essays*, op. cit., pp. 231–3.
18 Mark Eccles, *Shakespeare in Warwickshire*, op. cit., p. 79.
19 State Papers Domestic, Elizabeth, clxiii, 54.55.
20 Quoted in F. X. Walker 'The Implementation of the Elizabethan Statutes against Recusants, 1581–1600', unpublished London University Ph.D. thesis, 1961, p. 222.
21 For detailed background on Hunt, Debdale, etc, and their Catholic connections, see Edgar I. Fripp, *Shakespeare: Man and Artist*, op. cit., p. 181.
22 For detailed background on John and Thomas Cottom and their Catholic connections, see E. A. J. Honigmann, *Shakespeare: the 'Lost Years'*, Manchester University Press, 1985, especially chapter IV.
23 'A survei of the state of the ministerie in Warwickshier', *Dugdale Society* X, 5.

CHAPTER 5 – '*As an Unperfect Actor on the Stage*' [*Sonnet* 23]

1 Bodleian Library, MS. Arch.f.c.37. This page has been removed from the main manuscript of Aubrey's *Brief Lives*, and mounted separately. For an excellent reproduction, see Schoenbaum, *William Shakespeare: A Documentary Life*, p. 58.
2 Frances Yates, *A Study of 'Love's Labour's Lost'*, Cambridge University Press, 1936.
3 John Dover Wilson, *The Essential Shakespeare*, 1932.
4 Edmond Malone, *Plays and Poems*, op. cit., vol. i, pt. I, p. 307.
5 Alfred Duff Cooper, *Sergeant Shakespeare*, Rupert Hart-Davis, London, 1949.
6 See William J. Thomas 'Was Shakespeare ever a soldier?', *Three Notelets on Shakespeare*, 1865.
7 William Bliss, *The Real Shakespeare: A Counterblast to Commentators*, London, 1947.
8 E. K. Chambers, *William Shakespeare*, op. cit., vol. I, p. 17, n. 4.

9 *Hamlet*, III.ii.95ff.

10 Glynne Wickham, *Shakespeare's Dramatic Heritage*, Routledge and Kegan Paul, London, 1969, pp. 4–5.

11 See C. Walter Hodges, *The Globe Restored, A Study of the Elizabethan Theatre*, Oxford University Press, 1968, pp. 32ff. for fascinating and useful discussion of this and its companion Brueghel painting.

12 Ben Jonson, *Poetaster*, III.i.

13 Mark Eccles, *Shakespeare in Warwickshire*, op. cit., p. 13.

14 E. A. J. Honigmann, *Shakespeare : the 'Lost Years'*, op. cit., p. 135.

15 John Stow, *The Annales or Generall Chronicle of England*, edition of 1615, p. 697.

16 Harleian MS. 3885, reproduced in Edgar I. Fripp, *William Shakespeare: Man and Artist*, op. cit., p. 207.

17 See for instance Schoenbaum, *William Shakespeare: A Documentary Life*, op. cit., p. 90.

18 Letter to Walsingham, Harleian MS. 287, f.I, quoted in E .K. Chambers, *The Elizabethan Stage*, vol. II, p. 90. For further details of this tour, see Sally-Beth Maclean 'Leicester and the Evelyns: New Evidence for the Continental Tour of Leicester's Men', *Review of English Studies*, New series, vol. XXXIX, no. 156, 1988, pp. 487–93.

19 Quoted E. K. Chambers, *The Elizabethan Stage*, op. cit., vol. IV, p. 195.

20 ibid., p. 218.

21 ibid., pp. 269–70, after 'An Acte for the punishement of Vagabondes and for Releif of the Poore & Impotent' (14 Eliz. c. 5), printed in *Statutes*, iv, 590.

22 ibid., vol. II, p. 380, after B. Marsh, *Records of the Worshipful Company of Carpenters*, iii, 95.

23 Janet S. Loengard, 'An Elizabethan Law Suit, John Brayne his Carpenter, and the Building of the Red Lion Theatre', *Shakespeare Quarterly* 34, 1983, pp. 298–310.

24 Herbert Berry, *Shakespeare's Playhouses*, AMS Press, New York, 1987.

25 'The view of the Cittye of London from the North towards the Sowth', University Library of Utrecht; MS. 1198 f.83.

26 London County Council *Survey of London*, ed. Sir James Bird and Philip Norman, vol. VIII, *The Parish of St Leonard, Shoreditch*, B. T. Batsford, London, 1922, p. 177.

27 T. W. Baldwin, *The Organisation and Personnel of the Shakespearean Company*, Princeton, 1927.

28 Public Record Office, PROB 10/232, published J. Payne Collier, *Memoirs of the Principal Actors in the Plays of Shakespeare*, op. cit., p. 87.

29 Abbreviated, and spelling and punctuation modernised, after Andrew Gurr, *The Shakespearean Stage 1574–1642*, Cambridge University Press, 1980, pp. 67–8.

30 G. L. Hosking, *The Life and Times of Edward Alleyn*, London, Cape, 1952, p. 29.

CHAPTER 6 – *Trials of a Writer*

1 Bodleian Library, Aubrey MS. 8, f. 45 quoted E. K. Chambers, *William*

Shakespeare, op. cit., II, p. 252; illustrated S. Schoenbaum, *William Shakespeare*, op. cit., p. 205.

2 John Stow, *A Survay of London*, II, 75, 369.

3 E. K. Chambers, *Elizabethan Stage*, op. cit., vol. II, p. 306.

4 Mark Eccles, *Christopher Marlowe in London*, Cambridge, Mass, 1934, pp. 122–6.

5 John Stow, *Survay of London*, II, 74, I, 165; also APC XXV 230 (Privy Council directive to the Middlesex magistrates, 1596), quoted Charles Nicholl, *A Cup of News*, op. cit., p. 39.

6 For an excellent section-by-section publication of this map in book form, with accompanying notes, see Adrian Prockter and Robert Taylor, *The A to Z of Elizabethan London*, Harry Margary, Lympne Castle, Kent in association with Guildhall Library, London, 1979.

7 Francis Osborn, *Traditional Memoryes of the Reign of King James*, Oxford, 1658, p. 47.

8 Visitation Report of Bishop Bancroft, 1598, fol. 59v., quoted Reavley Gair, *The Children of Paul's: The story of a theatre company, 1553–1608*, Cambridge University Press, 1982, p. 26.

9 ibid., f. 60.

10 ibid., f. 6.

11 John Eliot, *The Parlement of Pratlers*, abridged reprint of *Ortho-epia Gallica*, (1593), ed. Jack Lindsay, London 1928, pp. 55–6, from the dialogue headed 'The Booke-seller'.

12 Quoted J. C. Jourdan, *Robert Greene*, New York, 1915, pp. 2 & 6.

13 *Works of Gabriel Harvey*, I, 168, quoted Charles Nicholl, *Cup of News*, op. cit., p. 49.

14 Letter of William Cornwallis, 15 March 1593, quoted *The Athenaeum*, 23 August 1890.

15 Quoted Antonia Fraser, *Mary Queen of Scots*, Weidenfeld & Nicholson, London, 1969, pp. 634–5.

16 Edward Ravenscroft, *Address* to *Titus Andronicus, or the Rape of Lavinia*, 1687, quoted Chambers, *William Shakespeare*, II, p. 254.

17 A. L. Rowse, *Discovering Shakespeare*, op. cit., p. 81.

18 'Moor' from the Greek word *mauros*, 'dark', in Shakespeare's time denoted anyone of dark or black skin.

19 Emrys Jones, *Scenic Form in Shakespeare*, Clarendon Press, Oxford, 1971.

20 Longleat House, Harley Papers, vol. 1, f. 159v.

21 *Titus Andronicus*, II.iii.

22 ibid., II.iii.34.

23 For these arguments, see in particular E. A. J. Honigmann, *Shakespeare: The 'Lost Years'*, op. cit., pp. 61–2.

24 The other example is *The Tempest* (see Arden edition, p. lxxi), kindly drawn to my attention by my copy-editor, Janet Ravenscroft. Notably Shakespeare is widely thought to have intended *The Tempest* as his last play.

25 *The Comedy of Errors*, III.ii.114ff.

26 ibid., II.i. and II.ii, after Psalm 8 and St Paul's letter to the Ephesians 5, respectively.

27 *The Comedy of Errors*, I.ii.97–101.
28 For this suggestion, see Peter Milward, *Shakespeare's Religious Background*, op. cit., pp. 52–3.
29 T. W. Baldwin, *William Shakespeare Adapts a Hanging*, Princeton University Press, 1931.
30 *The Comedy of Errors*, V.i.120.
31 For example, *Titus Andronicus*, II.i., and III.i.89–90.
32 Caroline Spurgeon, *Shakespeare's Imagery and What it Tells us*, Cambridge, 1935, p. 101.

CHAPTER 7 – *Found – The Mystery Patron?*

1 *King John*, I.i.40.
2 ibid., III.i.152–7.
3 ibid., II.i.192–4.
4 ibid., IV.iii.143–5.
5 John Leslie, *Defence of the Right High, Mighty and Noble Princess Mary Queen of Scotland*, 1569.
6 See *King John*, Arden ed. E. A. J. Honigmann, p. lxxiv.
7 Maurice Morgann, *An Essay on the Dramatic Character of Sir John Falstaff*, p. 177.
8 *Henry VI, Part I*, I.i.78–81.
9 ibid., IV.i.15.
10 *Henry VI, Part II*, V.i.203–08.
11 *Henry VI, Part I*, I.iv.
12 ibid., III.ii.25.
13 ibid., V.iii.144.
14 *Henry VI, Part II*, I.iv.12.
15 ibid., IV.ix.
16 *Henry VI, Part III*, V.i.
17 ibid., V.vi.
18 *Henry VI, Part II*, I.iv.18–19.
19 See Maurice Pope, 'Shakespeare's Falconry', *Shakespeare Survey*, 44, 1992.
20 *Henry VI, Part III*, III.i.
21 A. L. Rowse, *William Shakespeare*, op. cit., p. 90.
22 Emrys Jones, *The Origins of Shakespeare*, Clarendon, Oxford, 1977.
23 *Richard III*, IV.iv.39ff.
24 *Henry VI, Part II*, IV.vii.30ff.
25 *Henry VI, Part II*, V.i.122–216; V.ii.1–65; *Part III*, II.vi.1–86.
26 Edward Halle, *The Union of the two noble and illustre famelies of Lancastre and Yorke*, 1548, p. 25.
27 *Henry VI, Part III*, IV.v.23.
28 *Richard III*, IV.iv.497.
29 ibid., V.v.4ff.
30 ibid., V.v.9.
31 See the excellent map of the Manor of Lathom, 'compiled from surviving

documentary, topographical and traditional evidence', produced and published in a limited edition by Gerard Swarbrick, Damwood House, Scarisbrick, Lancs.

32 F. R. Raines, ed., *The Derby Household Books: comprising an Account of the Household Regulations and Expenses of Edward and Henry, Third and Fourth Earls of Derby (by W. Farington)*, Chetham Society, New Series LXXVII, 1917, p. 45.

33 ibid., p. 67.

34 ibid., p. 76.

35 Richard Robinson, *A Golden Mirrour ... whereto be adjoined certaine pretie poemes written on the names of sundrie both noble and worshipfull*, reprinted from the only known copy of the original edition of 1589, intro. Reverend Thomas Corser, Chetham Society, vol. XXIII, 1851, p. 18.

36 Mainy's 'Confession', as published in Samuel Harsnett, *Declaration of Egregious Popish Impostures*, 1603, p. 258ff.

37 British Library, Harley MS. 787, fol. 16b; *Calendar of State Papers, Spain, 1569–79*, pp. 692–3.

38 Thomas Heywood, *The Earls of Derby and the Verse Writers and Poets of the Sixteenth and Seventeenth Centuries*, Chetham Society, vol. XXIX, 1853, pp. 22–4.

39 Steven May, 'Spenser's "Amyntas", Three Poems by Ferdinando Stanley, Lord Strange, fifth Earl of Derby', *Current Philology*, August 1972, pp. 49ff.

40 Historical Manuscripts Commission, *Calendar of the MSS of the Marquis of Salisbury at Hatfield House, Herts*, 1880–1930, vol. IV, p. 104.

41 Public Record Office SP12/239, no. 78, quoted Charles Nicholl, *The Reckoning, The Murder of Christopher Marlowe*, Cape, London, 1992, p. 229.

42 George Peele, *Polyhymnia*, from D. H. Horne (ed.), *Life and Minor Works of George Peele*, Newhaven, 1952, p. 233.

43 See Roy Strong, *The Cult of Elizabeth*, Thames & Hudson, 1977, p. 138. Sir Roy's whole chapter on the Accession Day Tilts, pp. 129–62, is highly recommended for the general background to these occasions.

44 E. K. Chambers, *The Elizabethan Stage*, op. cit., vol. IV, p. 164.

45 See Mary E. Finch, *The Wealth of Five Northamptonshire Families, 1540–1640*, Northamptonshire Record Society, vol. XIX, 1956; also, at a more popular level, the opening chapter of Georgina Battiscombe's *The Spencers of Althorpe*, Constable, London, 1984.

CHAPTER 8 – *Entry into History*

1 For the full text, see Foakes and Rickert, *Henslowe's Diary*, op. cit., p. 16.

2 ibid., pp. 304–06.

3 ibid., p. 9.

4 London County Council, *Survey of London*, ed. Sir Howard Roberts and Walter H. Godfrey, *Bankside (the parishes of St Saviour's and Christchurch, Southwark)*, London County Council, 1950, pp. 71–2, pl. 59.

5 For background to the protests, and the inept government handling, see Martin Biddle, 'The Rose reviewed: a comedy (?) of errors', *Antiquity* 63, 1989, pp. 753–60.

6 For archaeological evaluations, see R. A. Foakes, 'The Discovery of the Rose Theatre: Some Implications', *Antiquity* 63, 1989, pp. 421–9; Andrew Gurr, 'The Shakespearean Stages, 40 Years On', *Shakespeare Survey* 41, 1989, pp. 1–12; Hedley Swain with Simon Blatherwick, Julian Bowsher and Simon McCudden, 'Shakespeare's Theatres', *Current Archaeology*, no. 124, May 1991, pp. 185–9.

7 John Orrell and Andrew Gurr, 'What the Rose Can Tell Us', *Times Literary Supplement*, 9–15 June 1989, pp. 636 & 649; *Antiquity* 63, 1989, pp. 421–9.

8 John T. Murray, *English Dramatic Companies, 1558–1642*, London, 1910, 2 vols, pp. 82–3.

9 E. K. Chambers, *The Elizabethan Stage*, op. cit., II, p. 392.

10 E. A. J. Honigmann, *Shakespeare's Impact on his Contemporaries*, Macmillan, London, 1982, p. 77.

11 *Henry IV, Part II*, Arden ed. A. R. Humphreys, p. xvi.

12 E. K. Chambers, *The Elizabethan Stage*, op. cit., IV, p. 307.

13 ibid., p. 308.

14 ibid., p. 310.

15 E. K. Chambers, *William Shakespeare*, op. cit., II, p. 310.

16 Thomas Nashe, *Pierce Penilesse his supplication to the Divell*, quoted E. K. Chambers, *The Elizabethan Stage*, op. cit., vol. IV, pp. 238–9.

17 ibid., p. 239.

18 See Charles Nicholl, *A Cup of News*, op. cit., p. 87.

19 See family tree in Christopher Devlin, S. J., *The Life of Robert Southwell, Poet and Martyr*, Longmans, Green, London, 1956, p. 264.

20 Public Record Office, State Papers Domestic Elizabeth I, S.P. 12/243, no. 76. See excellent reproduction of the original in Schoenbaum, *William Shakespeare: A Documentary Life*, op. cit., p. 39.

21 Robert Greene, *Groats-worth of witte, bought with a million of Repentance*, 1592, sig. A3ᵛ.

22 *Henry VI, Part III*, I.iv.137.

23 E. K. Chambers, *The Elizabethan Stage*, op. cit., vol. IV, p. 241.

24 A. L. Rowse, *Discovering Shakespeare*, op. cit., pp. 69–70.

25 ibid.

26 S. Schoenbaum, *William Shakespeare: A Documentary Life*, op. cit., p. 115.

27 Quoted E. K. Chambers, *William Shakespeare*, op. cit., vol. II, p. 189.

28 ibid., p. 253.

29 Charles Nicholl, *A Cup of News*, op. cit., pp. 89–90.

30 The first edition has been lost, but according to Nicholl, May 1592 is the likeliest date. See *A Cup of News*, op. cit., p. 94, also Nicholl's note 44, p. 294.

CHAPTER 9 – *'Unto Southampton do we Shift our Scene'* [*Henry v*, II.i.42]

1 For original text, see Foakes & Rickert, *Henslowe's Diary*, op. cit., p. 283.

2 ibid., p. 284.

3 ibid., p. 285.

4 E. K. Chambers, *The Elizabethan Stage*, op. cit., vol. IV, pp. 311–2.

5 ibid., p. 313.
6 E. K. Chambers, *William Shakespeare*, vol. II, pp. 212–3.
7 ibid., p. 313.
8 The confirmation of Heminges' arms, granted in 1628, describes him as 'John, son and heir of George Hemings of Droitwich, in the county of Worcester, Gent.' See Collier, *Memoirs of the Principal Actors in the Plays of Shakespeare*, op. cit., p. 72.
9 See reproduction of the entry in Schoenbaum, *William Shakespeare: A Documentary Life*, op. cit., p. 131.
10 Marchette Chute, *Ben Jonson of Westminster*, Souvenir, London, 1978, pp. 18–19.
11 *Henry IV, Part I*, V.i.129–40.
12 Edwin Miller, *The Professional Writer in Elizabethan England*, Harvard University Press, 1959, pp. 125–6.
13 *Apollinis et Musarum Euktika idyllia*, Oxford, 1592, reprinted Charles Plummer, *Elizabethan Oxford*, Publications of the Oxford Historical Society, VIII, 294.
14 *A Midsummer Night's Dream*, V.i.93.
15 *Calendar of State Papers Domestic, 1591–4*, pp. 463, 503.
16 *Calendar of State Papers Domestic 1581–90*, p. 448.
17 *Calendar of State Papers Domestic 1591–4*, p.151–2; John Stow, *Annales*, op. cit., 1615, p. 764.
18 *The Works of Thomas Nashe*, ed. Ronald B. McKerrow, vol. III, p. 87, quoted Charles Nicholl, *A Cup of News*, p. 305, n. 29.
19 Hampshire Record Office, Ref. 5M 53/1556–8.
20 Peter Levi, *The Life and Times of William Shakespeare*, Macmillan, London, 1988, pp. 96–7.
21 Quoted Paul H. Kocher, *Christopher Marlowe: A Study in his Thought, Learning and Character*, Chapel Hill, 1946, pp. 34–6.
22 *Venus and Adonis*, lines 231–4.
23 Bodleian Library, Ashmole MS. 1729, ff. 189r–190r.

CHAPTER 10 – *'My Mistress' Brows are Raven Black'* [*Sonnet* 127]

1 *Sonnet*, 34.
2 *Sonnet* 131.
3 *Sonnet* 129.
4 *Sonnet* 152.
5 *Sonnet* 131.
6 *Sonnet* 138.
7 *Sonnet* 142.
8 *Sonnet* 141.
9 *Sonnet* 150.
10 *Sonnet* 133.
11 *Sonnet* 134.
12 *Sonnet* 144.
13 *Sonnet* 147.

14 For Dr A. L. Rowse's discussion of his Dark Lady findings, see particularly his *Simon Forman: Sex and Society in Shakespeare's Age*, Weidenfeld, London, 1974, chapter VI; his introduction to *The Poems of Shakespeare's Dark Lady*, Cape, London, 1978; and his *Discovering Shakespeare*.

15 A. L. Rowse, *Discovering Shakespeare*, op. cit., p. 45.

16 Professor Stanley Wells, Letter to *Times Literary Supplement*, 11 May 1973, p. 528.

17 *Sonnet* 80.

18 The full text of this poem was only discovered in 1971. See Arthur Freeman, 'Marlowe, Kyd and the Dutch Church Libel', *English Literary Renaissance* 3, 1973.

19 On subsequent publication in its unfinished state, it was dedicated to Walsingham by the printer, Edward Blount – see Charles Nicholl, *The Reckoning*, op. cit., p. 24.

20 *Calendar of State Papers Domestic, 1591–4*, pp. 335–6.

21 Law sessions had been moved here on account of the plague.

22 Henslowe Papers, quoted E. K. Chambers, *William Shakespeare*, op. cit., vol. II, p. 314.

23 A. L. Rowse, *Discovering Shakespeare*, op. cit., pp. 68–9.

24 *Love's Labour's Lost*, I.i.161–6.

25 ibid., I.ii.8.

26 ibid., III.i.60.

27 John Florio, *First Fruites*, sig.S3.

28 *Love's Labour's Lost*, IV.ii.92–3.

29 ibid., IV.iii.249.

CHAPTER 11 – *'Murder Most Foul' [Hamlet*, I.v.27]

1 *Henry VI, Part I*, IV.vii.61ff.

2 See G. Lambin 'Here Lyeth John Talbot', *Études Anglaises* 24, Oct–Dec. 1971, pp. 361–76.

3 Edward Webbe, *Travels*, ed. Arber, p. 32.

4 Hampshire Record Office, ref. no. 5M53/262.

5 For discussion of the problems relating to the Earl of Pembroke's Men, see Chambers, *The Elizabethan Stage*, op. cit., vol. II, pp. 128–9.

6 Barry Coward, *The Stanleys: Lords Stanley and Earls of Derby 1385–1672*, Chetham Society, Manchester, 1983, pp. 31–2.

7 *The Taming of the Shrew*, Induction ii.110–12.

8 The fact of this miscarriage appears to have been missed by all previous historians, including Dr A. L. Rowse. Yet it is explicitly stated in the 'trewe reporte' detailed in note 11 of this chapter.

9 Although Buckhurst was far too highly placed to be overtly a Catholic, his religious sympathies nonetheless provoked this comment from Catholic writer Father Christopher Devlin: 'He was frequently to the fore as a persecutor [of Catholics], but nearly always in response to some stimulus from higher quarters. He had been a good friend to Robert Persons when Persons was planning his

flight overseas for conscience's sake, and for some reason the English Catholics continued perseveringly to repose a certain trust in him. He is said on good authority to have been reconciled on his death-bed by Father Richard Blount.' Christopher Devlin, S. J., *The Life of Southwell*, op. cit., p. 231.

10 Public Record Office, PROB 11/84.

11 'A trewe reporte and observaunce of the sicknes and death of F. late Erle of Derby . . .', compiled by Ferdinando's secretary John Golborne, and preserved until comparatively recently among the Muniments at Berkeley Castle, Gloucestershire. This is now in the Gloucestershire County Record Office, ref. MF 1161 Letter Book no. 2, no. 79. Another copy is at Knowsley, and a closely related account appears in Stow's *Annales*, pp. 767–8, also in Camden.

12 Personal correspondence, Dr Michael Clift, Gloucestershire physician, who consulted a colleague, both arriving independently at the same diagnosis.

13 *Les Reportes del Cases in Camera Stellata*, ed. Baildon, 1894, pp. 13–19.

14 Gloucestershire County Record Office. From the Berkeley Castle Muniments, ref. MF 1161. Letter Book no. 2, Letter of Sir George Carey to his wife on the death of the Earl of Derby. For the full text, see Appendix C Miscellaneous Documents, p. 474.

15 For discussion and sources, see Schoenbaum, *Shakespeare's Lives*, op. cit., pp. 173–4. Schoenbaum remarks 'The attempt to identify Aetion in *Colin Clout* with Shakespeare is a failure, as must be any effort to pin down with certainty so ambiguous a reference.'

16 S.P. 12/249/92, as quoted in Leslie Hotson, *I, William Shakespeare*, Cape, London, 1937, p. 154.

17 Historical Manuscripts Commission, *Calendar of the MSS. of the Marquis of Salisbury at Hatfield House, Herts*, op. cit., vol. IV, p. 527.

18 Quoted in Charlotte Stopes, *Life of Henry, Third Earl of Southampton, Shakespeare's Patron*, 1922, p. 86.

19 A. L. Rowse, *William Shakespeare*, op. cit., p. 205.

20 Rutland MSS.1.321, quoted in A. L. Rowse, *Shakespeare's Southampton*, Macmillan, London, 1965, p. 98.

21 *A Midsummer Night's Dream*, V.i.2ff.

22 ibid., I.ii.40.

23 ibid., IV.ii.31ff.

24 ibid., V.i.32ff.

25 ibid., V.i.108.

26 John Davies of Hereford, *The Scourge of Folly*, 1610, as quoted in E. K. Chambers, *William Shakespeare*, op. cit., vol. II, p. 214.

27 *A Midsummer Night's Dream*, V.i.412.

28 ibid., V.i.390.

29 J. Crehan, 'Shakespeare and the Sarum Ritual', *The Month*, Jul–Aug 1964, p. 47–50.

30 Charlotte Stopes, *Life of Henry, Third Earl of Southampton*, op. cit., p. 63.

31 See E. K. Chambers, *William Shakespeare*, op. cit., vol. II, p. 318.

32 E. K. Chambers, *The Elizabethan Stage*, op. cit., vol. IV, p. 316.

33 ibid., pp. 164–5, after Exchequer, Pipe Office, Declared Accounts E. 351/542 f. 107b.

CHAPTER 12 – *Lord Chamberlain's Man*

1 G. B. Harrison and R. A. Jones (eds.), *A Journal of all that was accomplished by Monsieur de Maisse, 1597*, London, 1931, p. 93.

2 T. W. Baldwin, *The Organisation and Personnel of the Shakespearean Company*, op. cit., p. 304.

3 Samuel Rowlands, *The Letting of Humour's Blood in the Head-Vein*, quoted in E. K. Chambers, *The Elizabethan Stage*, op. cit., vol. II, p. 334.

4 'To them Arbactus, Mr Pope, to him Will Foole . . .' From the 'Platt' of the *Seven Deadly Sins*, in Dulwich College. See text in Appendix C, Miscellaneous Documents, p. 472.

5 William Ingram, *The Business of Playing*, Cornell University Press, 1992, pp. 100–102.

6 Quoted E. K. Chambers, *William Shakespeare*, op. cit., vol. II, p. 213.

7 Public Record Office, PROB 10/484, quoted in J. Payne Collier, *Memoirs of the Principal Actors . . .* , op. cit., p. 63.

8 E. A. J. Honigmann, *Shakespeare : the 'Lost Years'*, p. 143.

9 Dulwich College, Muniment no. 16, quoted Foakes & Rickert, *Henslowe's Diary*, p. 306.

10 See Andrew Gurr and John Orrell, *Rebuilding Shakespeare's Globe*, Weidenfeld, London, 1989, p. 64–5.

11 John B. Heath, *Some Account of the Worshipful Company of Grocers*, London, 1854, p. 96.

12 From the *Gesta Grayorum: or, The History of the High and Mighty Prince, Henry Prince of Purpoole. . .* , 1688, p. 22, reproduced Chambers, *William Shakespeare*, op. cit., vol. II, pp. 319–20.

13 For detailed accounts of the Danvers feud, see A. L. Rowse, *Shakespeare's Southampton*, op. cit., p. 98ff., and G. P. V. Akrigg, *Shakespeare and the Earl of Southampton*, op. cit., p. 41ff.

14 Masuccio Salernitano, *Il Novellino*.

15 A. L. Rowse, *Shakespeare's Southampton*, op. cit., p. 104; Akrigg, *Shakespeare and the Earl of Southampton*, op. cit., p. 48.

16 *Romeo and Juliet*, I.v.5–8.

17 ibid., III.ii.21–5.

18 ibid., I.ii.8–9.

19 ibid., I.iii.13–22.

20 Quotations vary slightly. Father Christopher Devlin, in his already cited *The Life of Robert Southwell*, has 'I cannot answer for his religion, but I wish to God that my soul may be with his' (p. 324).

21 H. S. Bowden, *The Religion of Shakespeare*, London, 1899, p. 266.

22 *Romeo and Juliet*, V.ii.5ff.

23 ibid., IV.i.111.

24 *The Diary of Samuel Pepys*, ed. R. Latham and W. Matthews, vol. III, 1970, p. 39.

25 Quoted in Lily B. Campbell, *Shakespeare's 'Histories', Mirrors of Elizabethan Policy*, Huntington Library, California, 1947, p. 179.

26 ibid., p. 173.

27 ibid., p. 177.

28 ibid., p. 179.
29 *Richard II*, II.i.40–50.
30 ibid., II.i.17–23.
31 *Richard II*, Arden ed. Peter Ure, p. xxxiv.
32 *Richard II*, II.i.210.
33 ibid., V.ii.12–20.
34 ibid., IV.i.321.
35 ibid., IV.i.222–6.
36 Quoted E. K. Chambers, *William Shakespeare*, op. cit., vol. II, pp. 320–1, after Historical Manuscripts Commission, *Calendar of the MSS. of the Marquis of Salisbury at Hatfield House, Herts*, XXXVI.60.

CHAPTER 13 – *'To Show the World I am a Gentleman'* [*Richard II, III.i.27*]

1 Nicholas Rowe, from *Life*, in *Works of Shakespeare*, op. cit., i, p. x.
2 For the going rates, see Edwin H. Miller, *The Professional Writer in Elizabethan England*, op. cit., pp. 125–8.
3 Loseley MS. No. 348. For full transcription of the text, see Irwin Smith, *Shakespeare's Blackfriars Playhouse*, New York University Press, 1964, pp. 471–5.
4 Irwin Smith, *Shakespeare's Blackfriars Playhouse*, op. cit., p. 162.
5 E. K. Chambers, *The Elizabethan Stage*, op. cit., vol. IV, p. 319.
6 Quoted A. L . Rowse, *Shakespeare's Sonnets: The Problems Solved*, Harper & Row, New York, 1964, p. xli & xlii.
7 Source mislaid.
8 This portrait is often wrongly attributed to Nicholas Hilliard, due to Oliver's use, in this instance, of a Hilliard-style inscription for the date and Carey's age. I am grateful to Eiler Hansen of Berkeley Castle for correcting me on this.
9 Quoted Charles Nicholl, *A Cup of News*, op. cit., p. 182.
10 ibid.
11 *King John*, III.iv.93. For A. L. Rowse's comments, see his *Discovering Shakespeare*, op. cit., p. 91.
12 *Richard II*, III.i.24–7.
13 College of Arms MS. Vincent 157, art 23 & 24, reproduced Schoenbaum, *William Shakespeare*, op. cit., pp. 168–9.
14 E. K. Chambers, *William Shakespeare*, op. cit., vol. II, p. 19.
15 ibid., pp. 19–20.
16 Nicholas Roscarrock, poem, preface to John Bossewell, *Works of Armorie*, 1572.
17 E. K. Chambers, *William Shakespeare*, op. cit., vol. II, p. 23.
18 Charles Hamilton, *In Search of Shakespeare*, Hale, London, 1985.
19 Cotton MS. Jul C III, f. 280.
20 E. K. Chambers, *The Elizabethan Stage*, op. cit., vol. IV, p. 319.
21 *The Merchant of Venice*, I.i.25–8.
22 ibid., III.ii.32.
23 Court of King's Bench, Controlment Roll, Michaelmas Term 1596, K.B.29/234.

24 Translation from J. Q. Adams, *Shakespearean Playhouses*, Boston, 1917, pp. 167–8.
25 Quoted in E. K. Chambers, *The Elizabethan Stage*, op. cit., vol. IV, pp. 319–20.

CHAPTER 14 – *Hand of the Censor*

1 Edmond Malone, *An Inquiry into the Authenticity of Certain Miscellaneous Papers and Legal Instruments*, op. cit., pp. 215–6.
2 Exchequer, King's Remembrancer, Subsidy Roll E.179/146/354, quoted N. E. Evans, *Shakespeare in the Public Records*, HMSO, London, 1964, p. 9.
3 Public Record Office, Exchequer, Lord Treasurer's Remembrancer, Pipe Rolls, E.372/444, m. This is dated 6 October 1600.
4 S. Schoenbaum, *William Shakespeare*, op. cit., p. 63, from information supplied by Professor William Ingram.
5 From G. B. Harrison, *The Life and Death of Robert Devereux, Earl of Essex*, London, 1937, after *A Journal of all that Was Accomplished by Monsieur de Maisse*, 1597, tr. & ed. G. B. Harrison & R. A. Jones, London, 1931.
6 John Foxe, *Actes and Monuments of matters happening in the Church*, 1563, p. 266.
7 Nicholas Rowe, from *Life*, in *Works of Shakespeare*, i, pp. viii–ix.
8 John Dennis, *Epistle* to *The Comicall Gallant*, 1702, quoted Chambers, *William Shakespeare*, op. cit., vol. II, p. 263.
9 Charles Gildon, *Remarks on the Plays of Shakespear* in *The Works of Mr William Shakespear. Volume the Seventh*, 1710, quoted E. K. Chambers, *William Shakespeare*, op. cit., p. 262.
10 Due to a mistake in the *Dictionary of National Biography* most authors other than Rowse incorrectly make him the seventh Lord Cobham. For the correct numeration of the Cobham lineage see G. E. Cokayne *The Complete Peerage of England, Scotland and Ireland*, revised Vicary Gibbs, London, St Catherine's Press, 1913, III, 348–50, 8.
11 Quoted E. K. Chambers, *William Shakespeare*, op. cit., vol. II, p. 242.
12 Robert R. Fehrenbach, 'When Lord Cobham and Edmund Tilney "were at odds"', *Shakespeare Studies*, XVIII, 1986, pp. 87–101.
13 Quoted E. K. Chambers, *William Shakespeare*, I, p. 375.
14 Rowland Whyte, letter of 6 March 1600. This and other letters by Whyte are to be found in A. Collins, ed., *Letters and Memorials of State, Written and Collected by Sir Henry Sydney, Sir Philip Sydney, Sir Robert Sydney, etc.*, London, 1746, 2 vols.
15 Quoted A. L. Rowse, *Shakespeare's Southampton*, op. cit., p. 144.
16 Charles Nicholl, *A Cup of News*, op. cit., p. 252.
17 Alan Keen and Roger Lubbock, *The Annotator: The Pursuit of an Elizabethan Reader of Halle's Chronicle*, Putnam, London, 1954, pp. 61–2.
18 E. K. Chambers, *William Shakespeare*, II, p. 213, after N[icholas] D[oleman] (alias for Robert Persons), *The Third Part of a Treatise, Intituled: of three Conversions of England; conteyning An Examen of the Calendar or Catalogue of Protestant Saints . . . by John Fox*, 1604, p. 31.

19 Quoted in E. K. Chambers, *The Elizabethan Stage*, op. cit., vol. II, p. 217, after Speed *History of Great Britaine*, ix.15.
20 *Henry IV, Part I*, II.i.9.
21 ibid., II.i.10.
22 J. E. T. Rogers, *History of Agriculture and Prices in England*, Clarendon Press, Oxford, 1887, vol. V, p. 268.
23 *Henry IV, Part I*, II.i.43.
24 Edgar I. Fripp, *Shakespeare's Haunts*, op. cit., pp. 33–4.
25 *Henry IV, Part I*, III.i.53ff.
26 Robert H. Fehrenbach, 'When Lord Cobham and Edmund Tilney . . .', op. cit., p. 101, n.29, after Historical Manuscripts Commission *Report on the Manuscripts of Lord de L'Isle & Dudley preserved at Penshurst Place*, II (1934), p. 233–46.
27 Samuel Schoenbaum has opted for the occasion having been the Garter Feast at Whitehall on the St George's Day, 23 April, on the grounds that the Queen did not attend the Windsor ceremony.
28 *The Merry Wives of Windsor*, II.iii.78.
29 ibid., III.iii.11–12.
30 ibid., III.i.4ff.
31 ibid., V.v.64–70.
32 ibid., I.i.16ff.
33 ibid., III.i.10ff.
34 E. K. Chambers, *The Elizabethan Stage*, op. cit., vol. IV, pp. 321–2.
35 ibid., pp. 322–3.
36 ibid., p. 323.
37 B. M. Ward, 'The Chamberlain's Men in 1597', *Review of English Studies*, ix, 1933, pp. 55–8.
38 S. Schoenbaum, *William Shakespeare*, op. cit., p. 173.
39 British Library, MS Portland Loan 29/246, p. 18.
40 This verbal description accompanies Vertue's sketch. A curious footnote to the story of Shakespeare's purchase of New Place is that, within two months of the handover, his vendor William Underhill lay dead at Fillongley, near Coventry. This was another house which he used alternately with New Place, Underhill apparently being unable to bear returning to Idlicote after his wife died there in 1590. According to an enquiry he had been poisoned by his eldest son and heir, Fulke Underhill, who although a minor, was two years later executed at Warwick for his crime. Whether there may have been some dispute over the money which Underhill had received from Shakespeare we have no way of knowing.
41 Quoted E. K. Chambers, *William Shakespeare*, op. cit., vol. II, pp. 101–02.
42 Birthplace Trust Records, Office, Stratford-upon-Avon, ref. MS.ER 27/4.

CHAPTER 15 – '*Most Excellent . . . for the Stage*' [*Francis Meres, 1598*]

1 From E. Guilpin, *Skialetheia, or a shadowe of Truth . . .* , 1598 sig. D6, quoted E. K. Chambers, *The Elizabethan Stage*, op. cit., vol. II, p. 398.
2 G. B. Harrison (ed.), *Romeo and Juliet*, Penguin, Harmondsworth, 1953, p. 18.

3 Rowland Whyte, from A. Collins, ed., *Letters and Memorials of State, Written and Collected by Sir Henry Sydney* . . . , op. cit., vol. II, p. 81.

4 ibid., p. 90.

5 ibid., letter of 15 February, quoted R. B. Sharpe, *The Real War of the Theatres*, D. C. Heath, Boston, 1935, p. 156.

6 Francis Meres, *Palladis Tamia: Wit's Treasury*, f. 282. A full text of Meres' references to Shakespeare is given in E. K. Chambers, *William Shakespeare* . . . , op. cit., pp. 193–5.

7 A. L. Rowse, *Discovering Shakespeare*, op. cit., pp. 61–4.

8 T. W. Baldwin, *Shakspere's* Love's Labour's Won; *New Evidence from the Account Books of an Elizabethan Bookseller*, Carbondale, Ill, 1957.

9 S. Schoenbaum, *William Shakespeare*, op. cit., p. 141.

10 Francis Meres, *Palladis Tamia*, op. cit., sig. Oo6.

11 *As You Like It*, III.iii.73.

12 ibid., IV,i.88.

13 ibid., III.v.81–2.

14 ibid., IV.i.95.

15 Charles Nicholl, *The Reckoning*, op. cit., chapter 9.

16 *As You Like It*, III.iii.8.

17 Nicholas Rowe, *Works*, op. cit., i, pp. xii–xiii.

18 Marchette Chute, *Ben Jonson of Westminster*, op. cit., p. 73.

19 E. K. Chambers, *The Elizabethan Stage*, op. cit., vol. II, p. 304.

20 Ben Jonson's own account, quoted Marchette Chute, *Ben Jonson of Westminster*, op. cit., p. 78.

21 Herbert Berry, *Shakespeare's Playhouses*, AMS Press, New York, 1987, p. 39.

22 ibid., p. 85.

23 In his *William Shakespeare: A Documentary Life* Schoenbaum wrongly gives the year as 1597, but this is not in dispute.

24 King's Bench, Coram Rege Roll, Hilary Term, 13 James I, K.B. 27/1454, *rot.* 692. For discussion, see N. E. Evans, *Shakespeare in the Public Records*, op. cit., pp. 14–15.

25 Hedley Swain and others, 'Shakespeare's Theatres', op. cit., p. 187.

CHAPTER 16 – *'This Wooden "O"'* [*Henry v*, Prologue. 13]

1 C. W. Wallace, 'Shakespeare's Money Interest in the Globe Theatre', *The Century Magazine*, lxxx, 1910, 500–12; also 'Shakespeare and his London Associates as Revealed in Recently Discovered Documents', *University Studies* X, University of Nebraska, 1910.

2 Court of Requests, Documents of Shakespearean Interest, Req. 4/1; Court of Requests, Miscellaneous Books, Req. 1. See N. E. Evans, *Shakespeare in the Public Records*, op. cit., pp.16–17.

3 See N. E. Evans, *Shakespeare in the Public Records*, op. cit., p. 13.

4 Quoted E. K. Chambers, *William Shakespeare*, op. cit., vol. II, p. 53.

5 P. C. Carter, *The History of the Church and Parish of St Mary the Virgin, Aldermanbury*, Collingridge, London, 1913.

6 Public Record Office, PCC (78 Wood); see transcript in Honigmann, *Shakespeare: the 'Lost Years'*, p. 143.
7 Barry Coward, *The Stanleys, Lords Stanley and Earls of Derby, 1385–1672*, Chetham Society, Manchester 1983, p. 45.
8 Chancery, Inquisitions Post Mortem, C. 142/257/68.
9 John Orrell, *The Quest for Shakespeare's Globe*, p. 153–5. Orrell's book has been invaluable for much of the preceding discussion on the Globe's original appearance.
10 See 'Sunlight at the Globe', *Theatre Notebook*, 38, 1984, pp. 69–76.
11 *Henry v*, V.Prologue.30–32.
12 Thomas Platter, *Travels in England*, trans. from the German by Clare Wiliams, Cape, London, 1951, pp. 166–7.
13 *Henry v*, V.Prologue.26–8.
14 Dulwich College Henslowe Papers, Muniment no. 22, Foakes & Rickert, *Henslowe's Diary*, op. cit., pp. 306–10.
15 The date of 1599 for *Mirror of Martyrs'* composition, i.e. immediately contemporary with *Julius Caesar*, can be inferred from Weever's remark in his dedication that the work was 'some two years ago . . . made fit for the print'.
16 As reprinted in *The Hystorie of the Moste Noble Knight Plasidas, and Other Rare Pieces . . .* Printed for the Roxburghe Club, 1873, p. 180.
17 Quoted E. A. J. Honigmann, *Shakespeare: the 'Lost Years'*, op. cit., p. 57.
18 Reproduced as E6a after p. 92 in E. A. J. Honigmann's *John Weever*, Manchester University Press, 1987.
19 In the *Sonnets* there is one exception, no. 126, generally regarded as an *envoi*, or signing-off poem, to conclude those addressed to the 'lovely boy'.
20 Historical Manuscripts Commission, Lord de L'Isle and Dudley (Penshurst Place), II, 415.
21 Public Record Office, SP 12/271/35.
22 Reavley Gair, *The Children of Paul's*, op. cit., p. 120.
23 *Hamlet*, I.i.114–5.
24 ibid., III.ii.100.
25 ibid., II.ii.336–42.
26 ibid., II.ii.343–9.
27 ibid., II.ii.358.
28 Felix Pryor, *The Mirror and the Globe: William Shakespeare, John Marston and the Writing of Hamlet*, Handsaw, London, 1992.
29 *Hamlet*, II.ii.375.
30 Not least of the problems is Shakespeare's source vis-à-vis the authorship of the earlier play of the same name, often referred to by scholars as *Ur-Hamlet*. Mentioned by Tom Nashe as early as 1589 [Preface to Greene's *Menaphon* in Nashe, *Works* iii, 315–6], a single *Hamlet* is listed in Henslowe's Diary as performed at Newington Butts in June 1594. On or about 1596 Thomas Lodge in his *Wit's Misery* alluded to a pale-vizarded 'ghost, which cried so miserably at the Theatre, like an oyster-wife, *Hamlet, revenge*' [Lodge, *Wit's Misery*, 1596, p. 56.] The general opinion is that this was a play by Kyd, along the lines of his *Spanish Tragedy*. But remembering that Shakespeare's acting companions Kemp, Bryan and company had all visited Hamlet's Elsinore around 1586 it is equally possible

that the young Shakespeare himself wrote this early, now lost, version, in 1599/ 1600 substantially revising it to give it the maturity expected of his work at this time.

31 *Hamlet*, I.v.9–20.
32 ibid., I.v.76.
33 ibid., I.v.190.
34 ibid., I.v.131–2.
35 ibid., V.ii.351.
36 Quoted in Frederick Boas, *University Drama in the Tudor Age*, Clarendon Press, Oxford, 1914, p. 345, and here rendered into modernised English.

CHAPTER 17 – '*Like Favourites Made Proud*' [*Much Ado about Nothing*, III.i.9–11]

1 Rowland Whyte, from A. Collins, ed., *Letters and Memorials of State, Written and Collected by Sir Henry Sydney* . . . , op. cit., vol. II, p. 132.
2 R. B. Sharpe, *The Real War of the Theatres* . . . , op. cit., p. 181.
3 Quoted in Helen Georgia Stafford, *James VI of Scotland and the Throne of England*, New York, 1940, p. 215, after Add. MSS. 31022.
4 Historical Manuscripts Commission, *Calendar of the MSS. of the Marquis of Salisbury at Hatfield House, Herts*, op. cit., vol. XI, p. 44.
5 Examination of Augustine Phillips, State Papers Domestic Elizabeth, cclxxviii.85, quoted E. K. Chambers, *William Shakespeare*, op. cit., vol. II, p. 325.
6 Historical Manuscripts Commission, *Calendar of the MSS. of the Marquis of Salisbury at Hatfield House, Herts*, op. cit., vol. XI, p. 35.
7 Quoted in E. K. Chambers, *William Shakespeare*, op. cit., vol. II, p. 325.
8 John Speed, *The History of Great Britaine*, London, 1623, p. 1213.
9 David Jardine, *Criminal Trials*, London, 1847, I, 361, quoted G. P. V. Akrigg, *Shakespeare and the Earl of Southampton*, p. 126.
10 David Jardine, *Criminal Trials*, op. cit., I, p. 363–5.
11 Edgar I. Fripp, *Shakespeare, Man and Artist*, op. cit., p. 541.
12 R. B. Sharpe, *The Real War of the Theatres*, op. cit., p. 183.
13 *Measure for Measure*, III.i.83–5.
14 *Antony and Cleopatra*, IV.xiv.99–100.
15 Edgar I. Fripp, *Shakespeare, Man and Artist*, p. 541.
16 Charles Nicholl, *A Cup of News*, p. 160.
17 Public Record Office, E154/6/50.
18 Quoted in E. K. Chambers, *William Shakespeare*, op. cit., vol. II, p. 326, after *Memorandum*, printed in J. Nichols, *The Progresses and Public Processions of Queen Elizabeth*, 1788–1807, vol. III, p. 552, from Lambard family MS.
19 *Much Ado About Nothing*, III.i.9–11.
20 Quoted E. K. Chambers, *The Elizabethan Stage*, op. cit., vol. II, p. 326.
21 *Hamlet*, III.ii.36.
22 *Jack Drum's Entertainment*, V.i.102, quoted E. K. Chambers, *The Elizabethan Stage*, op. cit., vol. II, p. 20.
23 State Papers Domestic, Elizabeth, cclxxxii, 48.
24 Roy Strong, *The Cult of Elizabeth*, op. cit., p. 17ff.

25 British Museum MS. Harley 5353.

26 ibid.

27 Introduction to *Twelfth Night*, The New Cambridge Shakespeare, X, XV–XVI.

28 Caroline Spurgeon, *Shakespeare's Imagery*, op. cit., p. 131.

29 *Troilus and Cressida*, II.iii.172.

30 William H. Matchett, *The Phoenix and the Turtle*, P. & T. Marton & Co., London, 1965.

31 A. B. Grosart (ed.), *Robert Chester's 'Love's Martyr'*, New Shakspere Society, 1878.

32 W. J. Fraser Hutcheson, *Shakespeare's Other Anne*, Glasgow, 1959, p. 68.

33 John F. Forbis, *The Shakespearean Enigma and the Elizabethan Mania*, New York, 1924, 200–01.

34 E. A. J. Honigmann, *Shakespeare: the 'Lost Years'*, op. cit., chapter IX.

35 Sir William Dugdale, *Visitation of Shropshire*, 1664, College of Arms MS.C.35.f.20. For most helpful discussion on these epitaphs, see E. A. J. Honigmann, *Shakespeare: the 'Lost Years'*, op. cit., chapter VII.

36 Public Record Office, State Papers 12, ccxxx viii. n. 62.

37 Public Record Office, PCC (92 Drake).

38 *Much Ado about Nothing*, V.ii.67–9.

CHAPTER 18 – *One of the King's Men*

1 *All's Well that Ends Well*, Arden ed. G. K. Hunter, p. xxv. The names 'Lavatch' and 'Lafew' have been changed to the more usual spellings.

2 Court of Requests, Documents of Shakespearean Interest, Req. 4/1; Court of Requests, Miscellaneous Books, Req. 1. For discussion see N. E. Evans, *Shakespeare in the Public Records*, op. cit., pp. 28–30.

3 Leslie Hotson, *Shakespeare's Sonnets Dated*, op. cit., p. 182.

4 Thomas Birch, *The Court and Times of James the First; illustrated by authentic and confidential letters from various public and private collections*, 2 vols, 1848, pp. 206–07.

5 Quoted in J. B. Black, *The Reign of Elizabeth, 1558–1603*, Clarendon Press, Oxford, 2nd edition, 1959, p. 495.

6 ibid., p. 496.

7 *The Memoirs of Robert Carey*, ed. F. H. Mares, Clarendon Press, Oxford, 1972, p. 63.

8 John Manningham, *Diary of John Manningham, of the Middle Temple, 1602–03*, Camden Society, Old Series, XCIX, 1868, p. 147.

9 *The Journal of Sir Roger Wilbraham, Solicitor-General in Ireland and Master of Requests, for the years 1593–1616*, ed. H. S. Scott, 1902, Camden Society, Third Series, 4, *The Camden Miscellany*, vol. X, p. 54.

10 *Wonderful Year 1603 – The Non-Dramatic Works of Thomas Dekker*, ed. A. B. Grosart, London, 1884, p. 88.

11 A. L. Rowse, *The Poems of Shakespeare's Dark Lady*, op. cit., p. 18.

12 *A Mourneful Dittie, entituled Elizabeths Losse*, undated, quoted E. K. Chambers, *William Shakespeare*, op. cit., vol. II, pp. 212–3.

13 Quoted A. L. Rowse, *William Shakespeare*, op. cit., p. 357.
14 Quoted R. B. Sharpe, *The Real War of the Theatres*, op. cit., p. 186.
15 Public Record Office, Chancery Patent Rolls C 66/1608 m. 4.
16 Marchette Chute, *Shakespeare of London*, E. O. Dutton, New York, 1949, p. 255.
17 Public Record Office, PROB 10/224.
18 *Ben Jonson*, ed. C. H. Herford, Percy and Evelyn Simpson, 11 vols, Oxford, 1925–52, vol. I, pp. 139–40.
19 E. K. Chambers. *The Elizabethan Stage*, op. cit., vol. IV, p. 168.
20 F. W. Conish, *Extracts from the Letters and Journals of William Cory*, 1897, p. 168.
21 Quoted V. Sackville-West, *Knole and the Sackvilles*, Heinemann, London, p. 51.
22 Sir Anthony Weldon, *The Court and Character of King James*, ed. 1817, p. 55.
23 E. K. Chambers, *The Elizabethan Stage*, op. cit., vol. II, p. 210.
24 ibid., vol. IV, p. 118.
25 *Measure for Measure*, I.ii.76.
26 ibid., I.ii.85–90.
27 ibid., II.iv.27–30.
28 Lord Chamberlain's Department, Special Events L.C.2/4 (5).
29 *Time Triumphant* Sig B2, quoted *Measure for Measure* Arden ed. J. W. Lever, p. xxxiv.
30 Gospel according to Matthew, 7, vv. 1–2.
31 Christopher Devlin, *Hamlet's Divinity*, Rupert Hart-Davis, London, 1963, p. 27.
32 Father Persons to Father Antony Rivers, i.e. to Father Garnet, his companion, 6 July 1603; printed in *Miscellanea*, II, Catholic Record Society, p. 213.
33 F. Von Raumer, *History of the Sixteenth and Seventeenth Centuries*, J. Murray, 1835, vol. II, p. 206.
34 Audit Office, Declared Accounts, Treasurer of the Chamber, A.O.1/388/41.
35 Ernest Law, *Shakespeare as a Groom of the Chamber*, London, 1910.
36 Historical Manuscripts Commission, *Calendar of the MSS. of the Marquis of Salisbury . . .*, op. cit., xvi, 415.
37 Public Record Office, Audit Office, Accounts Various, A.O.3/908/13.
38 Audit Office, Declared Accounts A.O.1/2046/11 – see A. E. Stamp, *The Disputed Revels Accounts*, Shakespeare Association, 1931.
39 Dudley Carleton, quoted G. P. V. Akrigg. *Jacobean Pageant, or The Court of James I*, Hamish Hamilton, London, 1962, p. 150.
40 From a Latin letter quoted in Geoffrey Tillotson, '*Othello* and *The Alchemist* at Oxford', *Times Literary Supplement*, 20 July 1933, p. 494.
41 For example, *Hamlet* III.ii.1–34.

CHAPTER 19 – *Under the Tragic Muse*

1 Quoted Chambers, *William Shakespeare*, op. cit., vol. II, p. 215.
2 Shakespeare Birthplace Trust Records Office, ref. MS. ER 27/1.
3 ibid., ref. MS. ER 27/2.
4 Public Record Office, PROB/232.
5 From a manuscript, *A brief discourse of the causes of discord amongst the officers*

of arms..., present whereabouts unknown – see E. K. Chambers *The Elizabethan Stage*, op. cit., vol. II, p. 333, n. 4.

6 Full text given in J. Payne Collier, *Memoirs of the Principal Actors in the Plays of Shakespeare*, op. cit., pp. 85–7.

7 See G. M. Young, *Today and Yesterday*, 1948, pp. 300–01.

8 *King Lear*, Arden ed. Kenneth Muir, p. xxxii.

9 *King Lear*, III.ii.14–15.

10 ibid., IV.1.60ff.

11 See Alan Keen & Roger Lubbock, *The Annotator*, op. cit., pp. 101–02.

12 See Leslie Hotson, *I, William Shakespeare*, op. cit., p. 197. Bushell was to be connected by Shakespeare's daughter Judith's marriage to Thomas Quiney, whose older brother Adrian married Edward Bushell's sister Eleanor. See family tree, Appendix A, p. 454–5.

13 Hugh Ross Williamson, *The Gunpowder Plot*, Faber, London, 1951, p. 195.

14 John Gerard, S. J., *What was the Gunpowder Plot?*, London, 1897, p. 234.

15 Bodleian Library, Oxford, Ashmole MS 208, f. 207 ff. Spelling and punctuation as modernised by A. L. Rowse in *Simon Forman*, op. cit., p. 303ff.

16 A. L. Rowse, *William Shakespeare*, op. cit., p. 379.

17 For a suitable spine-chilling account of this, see actor Richard Huggett's *The Curse of Macbeth and other Theatrical Superstitions*, Picton Publishing, Chippenham, 1981.

18 *Macbeth*, IV.iii.147–51.

19 ibid., IV.i.119–20.

20 ibid., II.iii.8ff.

21 ibid., V.v.42–4.

22 ibid., IV.ii.47–57.

23 ibid., II.iii.29–34.

24 Sir John Harington, *The Court of King James*, p. 113, quoted Edgar I. Fripp, *Shakespeare: Man and Artist*, op. cit., p. 654.

25 Kent County Archives Office, Maidstone, Sackville MSS, ref. U269 Q22, pp. 37 & 39. See also H. A. Hanley, 'Shakespeare's Family in Stratford Records', *Times Literary Supplement*, 21 May 1964, p. 441. An excellent reproduction of the entry appears in Schoenbaum, *William Shakespeare: A Documentary Life*, op. cit., p. 235.

26 *The Times*, 4 January 1907, quoted in *Antony and Cleopatra*, New Cambridge Shakespeare, p. 59.

27 *Antony and Cleopatra*, II.ii.195–201.

28 *Sonnet* 147.

29 E. K. Chambers, *William Shakespeare*, op. cit., vol. II, p. 333.

CHAPTER 20 – *A New Mood*

1 For information on the weight of the great bell in Shakespeare's time, I am grateful to Michael Uphill, Master of the Southwark Cathedral Society of Bellringers. The present tenor bell was recast from the metal of the Shakespearean great bell in 1735 by Samuel Knight of Holborn in a special

foundry set up for the purpose in Winchester Yard, adjacent to what is today Southwark Cathedral.

2 We know about these from a contemporary pamphlet *The Great Frost: cold doings in London, except it be at the Lottery*, Jan 1608, quoted Edgar I. Fripp, *Shakespeare, Man and Artist*, op. cit., p. 687.

3 Greater London Record Office, Shelfmark P92/SAV/3001.

4 Guildhall Library, shelfmark MS. 6419/2.

5 See G. E. Bentley, *Shakespeare: A Biographical Handbook*, New Haven, 1961, p. 81.

6 *Macbeth*, V.iv.24–6.

7 Quoted E. K. Chambers, *William Shakespeare*, op. cit., vol. ii, p. 335.

8 ibid., p. 210.

9 Quoted Marchette Chute, *Ben Jonson of Westminster*, op. cit., p. 170.

10 G. E. Bentley, 'Shakespeare and the Blackfriars Theatre', *Shakespeare Survey*, I, p. 44.

11 The success of those modern productions which have given due weight to these scenic opportunities is attested by the following account of a Birmingham Repertory Theatre production of 1954: 'For many who saw it, both the scholarly and the unscholarly in the audience, this production was a profound experience. The sea seemed to provide a unity to the play, linking the first part to the second. The chorus Gower delivered his lines slowly in sing-song fashion . . . The brothel scenes were oriental. Lysimachus's conversion by Marina was fully serious and moving. The climax in the recognition scene moved many to tears. The whole effect was fairytale-like, to which the colour of the costumes and the lights contributed skilfully.' Quoted *Pericles*, Arden ed. F. D. Hoeniger, p. lxix.

12 Letter of Sir Gerald Herbert to Sir Dudley Carleton at the Hague, 24 May 1619, quoted J. O. Halliwell, *A Copy of a Letter of News . . .* , 1865, p. 11.

13 Irwin Smith, *Shakespeare's Blackfriars Playhouse*, op. cit., p. 247.

14 State Papers Domestic, James I, xxxi, 73, quoted E. K. Chambers, *The Elizabethan Stage*, op. cit., vol. II, pp. 53–4.

15 Fifty plague deaths were recorded for the week ending 28 July 1608, and more than forty each week for the rest of the year, with a maximum of 147 at the end of September.

16 E. K. Chambers, *The Elizabethan Stage*, op. cit., vol. II, p. 318.

17 Chamber Accounts, D.A.543 m. 214, quoted Chambers, *The Elizabethan Stage*, op. cit., vol. IV, pp. 174–5.

18 For the dimensions, see 'Rastall and Kirkham vs. Hawkins', King's Bench, Easter Term, 1609, Coram Rege Rolls, Easter 7 James I, membrane 456, transcript in Irwin Smith, *Shakespeare's Blackfriars Playhouse*, op. cit., p. 517.

19 Thomas Dekker, *Work for Armourours*, (*Works*, 1609, vol. IV, p. 96).

20 Transcript from A. L. Rowse, *Simon Forman*, op. cit., pp. 304–05. For an excellent reproduction of the original text, see Schoenbaum, *William Shakespeare: A Documentary Life*, op. cit., p. 215.

21 *Cymbeline*, II.ii.37–9.

22 Bodleian Library, ref. MS. Don. c. 57.

23 *Cymbeline*, IV.ii.258–81.

24 Kenneth Muir, *Shakespeare's Sources*, Methuen, 1957, vol. I, p. 247.

25 After A. L. Rowse, *Simon Forman*, op. cit., pp. 306–07, but with modifications.
26 *The Winter's Tale*, IV.iv.719ff.
27 Court of Requests, Documents of Shakespearean Interest, Req. 4/1.
28 G. E. Bentley, 'Shakespeare and the Blackfriars Theatre', op. cit., p. 47.

CHAPTER 21 – *'To the Onlie Begetter'*

 1 A. L. Rowse, *Shakespeare's Southampton*, p. 194 says she died in April, but the letter of Thomas Howard (see note 2) would suggest it was nearer to November.
 2 Edmund Lodge, *Illustrations*, III, 209.
 3 Public Record Office, ref. P. C. C. Huddleston, 86.
 4 Sir Gyles Isham, 'The Prototypes of King Lear and His Daughters', *Notes and Queries*, CXCIX, 1954, pp. 150–51.
 5 Katherine Duncan-Jones, 'Was the 1609 Shakespeare's *Sonnets* really unauthorised?', *Review of English Studies*, 1983, p. 163.
 6 A. L. Rowse, *Shakespeare's Sonnets*, op. cit., p. xliv.
 7 Leslie Hotson, *Mr. W. H.*, Rupert Hart-Davis, London, 1964.
 8 Reproduced Katherine Duncan-Jones, 'Was the 1609 . . . ?', op. cit., p. 159.
 9 For further discussion and sources, see Charles Nicholl, *A Cup of News*, op. cit., p. 83.
10 Katherine Duncan-Jones, 'Was the 1609 . . . ?', op. cit., p. 155.
11 *Works of William Drummond of Hawthornden*, Edinburgh, 1711, p. 226.
12 John Buxton, *Sir Philip Sidney and the English Renaissance*, p. 184.
13 A. L. Rowse, *The Poems of Shakespeare's Dark Lady*, op. cit., p. 17.
14 ibid., p. 77.
15 Quoted Thomas Heywood, *The Earls of Derby and the Verse Writers of the Sixteenth and Seventeenth Centuries*, Stanley Papers I, pp. 40–41.
16 Quoted in E. K. Chambers, *William Shakespeare*, op. cit., p. 214.
17 *A Midsummer Night's Dream*, V.i.108.
18 *The Tempest*, I.ii.218.
19 ibid., I.ii.230.
20 This was addressed to an unidentified 'Noble Lady', that is, the wife of a nobleman. A. L. Rowse has suggested Elizabeth, Countess of Southampton being 'as likely as any'. *William Shakespeare*, op. cit., p. 431.
21 William Strachey, 'True Repertory of the Wracke', from *Purchas His Pilgrimes*, 1625, vol. XIX, 5ff.
22 *The Tempest*, I.ii.196–201.
23 ibid., II.ii.161–2.
24 Quoted in E. K. Chambers, *William Shakespeare*, op. cit., vol. II, p. 342.
25 Leslie Hotson, *I, William Shakespeare*, op. cit., ch. IX.
26 *The Tempest*, Arden ed. Frank Kermode, p. xxviii.
27 *The Essayes or Morall, Politike and Militarie Discourses of Lo. Michaell de Montaigne*, trans. John Florio, 1603, vol. I, p. 210.
28 *The Tempest*, II.i.142–8.
29 John Dryden, Preface to his adaptation *The Tempest, or, The Enchanted Island*, 1674.

30 *The Tempest*, IV.i.148–56.
31 ibid., V.i.41.
32 *The XV Bookes of P. Ovidius Naso, entytuled Metamorphosis . . .*, translated 'into English meeter' by Arthur Golding, 1567.
33 Edgar I. Fripp, *Shakespeare, Man and Artist*, op. cit., p. 725.

CHAPTER 22 – *A Curious Purchase*

1 N. E. Evans, *Shakespeare in the Public Records*, op. cit., p. 29.
2 Edgar I. Fripp, *Shakespeare, Man and Artist*, op. cit., p. 761.
3 ibid., p. 762.
4 Sir John Harington, *Nugae Antiquae*, 2 vols, London, 1804, II, 3.
5 *The Illness and Death of Henry Prince of Wales in 1612: A Historical Case of Typhoid Fever*, London, 1882.
6 *Hamlet*, I.ii.180–81.
7 Robert Coke, *A Detection of the Court and State of England during the Four Last Reigns and the Inter-Regnum*, London, 1694, I: 64.
8 Quoted in E. K. Chambers, *The Elizabethan Stage*, vol. IV, pp. 180–81.
9 The list of scholars to have suggested something along these lines includes Fleay, Dover Wilson, Greg and Akrigg.
10 *The Tempest*, IV.i.106–17.
11 *The Letters of John Chamberlain*, ed. Norman Egbert McClure, 2 vols, Philadelphia, 1939, vol. I, p. 418.
12 ibid.
13 *The Magnificent Marriage of the Two Great Princes Frederick Count Palatine and the Lady Elizabeth*, 1613.
14 Quoted E. K. Chambers, *William Shakespeare*, vol. II, p. 343, after L. Pearsall Smith, *The Life and Letters of Sir Henry Wotton*, 2 vols, 1907, vol. II, p. 32.
15 *Henry VIII*, Arden ed. R. A. Foakes, p. xxviii.
16 *Henry VIII*, V.v.1–3.
17 Henry Peacham *The Period of Mourning . . . together with Nuptiall Hymnes*, 1613, H2.
18 *The Magnificent Marriage of the Two Great Princes . . .*, op. cit.
19 *Henry VIII*, II.iv.
20 'The place where the cardinals should sit to hear the cause of matrimony betwixt the King and the Queen was ordained to be at the Blackfriars in London; where in the great hall was preparation made . . .' Raphael Holinshed *The Chronicles of England, Scotland and Ireland*, Vol. III, p. 907; Everyman edition p. 192.
21 Quoted in Irwin Smith, *Shakespeare's Blackfriars Playhouse*, p. 23 – 'if I had served God as diligently as I have done the King he would not have given me over in my grey hairs.'
22 *Henry VIII*, III.ii.455–7.
23 ibid., IV.ii.
24 ibid., IV.ii.133.
25 ibid., V.v.28ff.

26 ibid., V.v.56–61.

27 ibid., V.v.39–54.

28 Rutland MSS.iv.494 (Accounts of the Steward of the Earl of Rutland) in Belvoir Castle, Leicestershire. For an account of the discovery, see Sidney Lee, 'A Discovery about Shakespeare', *The Times*, 27 December 1905. A reproduction of the entry appears in S. Schoenbaum, *William Shakespeare: A Documentary Life*, p. 220.

29 Quoted Leslie Hotson, *Shakespeare by Hilliard: A Portrait Deciphered*, Chatto & Windus, London, 1977, p. 25. I do not support Hotson's claim that the Hilliard portrait represents Shakespeare, but his book is nonetheless very valuable for its many insights on the making of *impresa* devices.

30 *Reliquiae Wottoniae*, see Edgar I. Fripp, *Shakespeare: Man and Artist*, op. cit., p. 406.

31 S. Schoenbaum, *William Shakespeare: a Documentary Life*, op. cit., p. 223.

32 A. L. Rowse, *William Shakespeare*, op. cit., p. 445.

33 Quoted in full in E. K. Chambers, *William Shakespeare*, op. cit., vol. II, pp. 154–7.

34 ibid., p. 166.

35 T. Wright (ed.), *Queen Elizabeth and her Times. A Series of Original Letters*, 2 vols, 1838, vol. II, p. 249.

36 J. Morris, *Troubles of our Catholic Forefathers related by Themselves* (3 vols), Burns & Oates, London, 1872, vol. I, p. 141.

37 Quoted in the original Latin in E. K. Chambers, *William Shakespeare*, op. cit., vol. II, p. 168; translation based on Leslie Hotson, *I, William Shakespeare*, op. cit., p. 180.

38 E. K. Chambers, *William Shakespeare*, op. cit., vol. II, p. 167.

39 Bodleian Library, ref. Rawlinson, Poet MS. 160 f. 41. Leslie Hotson devoted a complete essay to Elias James 'Shakespeare Mourns a Godly Brewer', in his *Shakespeare's Sonnets Dated*, op. cit., pp. 111–24.

40 'In all that sunshine weather' – according to the *Sonnet upon the Pittiful burneing*, see note 47, below.

41 *Henry viii*, I.iv.49.

42 Chambers has chambers!

43 L. Pearsall Smith, *The Life and Letters of Sir Henry Wotton*, op. cit., vol. II, pp. 32–3.

44 Sir Ralph Winwood, *Memorials of Affairs of State in the Reigns of Queen Elizabeth and James i collected (chiefly) from the original papers of the Right Honourable Sir Ralph Winwood, Kt*, 3 vols, London, 1725, vol. III, p. 469.

45 L. Pearsall Smith, *The Life and Letters of Sir Henry Wotton*, vol. II, p. 32–3.

46 E. Arber, *Transcript of the Registers of the Company of Stationers, 1554–1640*, 5 vols, 1875–94, vol. III, p. 528.

47 John Haslewood, *The Gentleman's Magazine*, 1816, lxxxvi, p. 114.

48 Quoted in full in E. K. Chambers, *The Elizabethan Stage*, vol. II, pp. 420–21.

49 John Lowin, to whom tradition attributes the part of Henry viii, is another notable omission.

50 For example Henry Farley: 'And I have seen the Globe burnt, and quickly made a Phoenix', Henry Farley, *The Complaint of Paules*, 1616.

51 Quoted Thomas Birch, *The Court and Times of James the First*, 2 vols, London, 1849, vol. I, p. 329.
52 E. K. Chambers, *The Elizabethan Stage*, op. cit., vol. II, p. 426.
53 ibid., p. 423, n. 6.
54 Public Record Office, PROB 10/311.
55 Emma Marshall Denkinger, 'Actors Names in Registers of St Botolph, Aldgate', *Publications of the Modern Language Association of America*, vol. XLI, p. 95.
56 Nicholas Rowe, *Life*, in *Works of Shakespeare*, 1709, quoted in E. K. Chambers, *William Shakespeare*, op. cit., vol. II, p. 269.
57 Bodleian Library, ref. Ashm. MS. 38.

CHAPTER 23 – '*And England Keep my Bones!*' [*King John*, IV.iii.10]

1 From *Timber: or Discoveries; Made upon Men and Matter*, 1642, quoted E. K. Chambers, *William Shakespeare*, op. cit., vol. II, p. 210.
2 Ralph W. Leftwich, 'The Evidence of Disease in Shakespeare's Handwriting'. *Proceedings of the Royal Society of Medicine. Section of the History of Medicine*, 1919, 12, pp. 28–42.
3 Letter of Dr Vernon Harrison to the author, 12 January 1993.
4 Charles Hamilton, *In Search of Shakespeare*, Robert Hale, London, 1986.
5 Letter of Dr Harrison, op. cit.
6 William West, *Simbelography, which may be termed the Art, or Description, of Instruments and Presidents* (i.e. Precedents), Stationers' Company, 1612.
7 Stratford Birthplace Trust Records Office, ref. DR243/1, Stratford parish register marriages, f. 13v.
8 Worcestershire Record Office, MS 802/BA 2760, Visitation Act Book, 1613–7, f. 27v, quoted in E. K. Chambers, *William Shakespeare*, op. cit., vol. II, p. 8.
9 Kent County Archives Office, Maidstone, Sackville MSS, shelfmark U269 Q22.
10 E. R. C. Brinkworth, *Shakespeare and the Bawdy Court of Stratford*, Phillimore, London, 1972.
11 Likewise William Palmer of Leamington, Gloucestershire, left 'unto Elizabeth my wife all her waring apparel and my second-best fetherbed'. Quoted Mark Eccles, *Shakespeare in Warwickshire*, op. cit., pp. 164–5.
12 E. A. J. Honigmann, 'The Second-Best Bed', *New York Review*, 7 November 1991, p. 27ff.
13 Samuel Ireland, *Picturesque Views in the Upper, or Warwickshire Avon*, London, 1795, p. 189.
14 J. P. Yeatman, *The Gentle Shakespeare*, 4th ed., 1906, p. 192.
15 John Florio, will of 20 July 1625, Public Record Office, P.C.C.97 Hele, quoted Arthur Acheson, *Shakespeare's Lost Years in London*, 1920, pp. 252–6.
16 Public Record Office, P.C.C.17, Russell.
17 E. A. B. Barnard & H. A. Shield, *New Links with Shakespeare*, Cambridge University Press, 1930.
18 A. L. Rowse, *William Shakespeare*, op. cit., p. 451.
19 Public Record Office, PROB 10/484, quoted in full in Collier, *Memoirs of the Principal Actors in the Plays of Shakespeare*, op. cit., pp. 73–7.

20 Diary of John Ward, quoted E. K. Chambers, *William Shakespeare*, op. cit., vol. II, p. 249.

21 Letter of 'Mr Dowdall', quoted E. K. Chambers, *William Shakespeare*, op. cit., vol. II, p. 259.

22 *Sonnet* 72.

23 Letter of Leslie Smith of the Monumental Brass Society to the *Sunday Times*.

24 Bodl. Rawl. MS D. 377 f. 90, quoted E. K. Chambers, *William Shakespeare*, op. cit., vol. II, p. 260.

25 Historical Manuscripts Commission, *Calendar of the MSS., of the Marquis of Salisbury at Hatfield House, Herts*, op. cit., vol. IX, p. 186. See also E. K. Chambers, *William Shakespeare*, op. cit., vol. II, pp. 168–9.

26 H. Foley, 'The Diary of the English College, Rome, for 1579–1773' in *Records of the English Province of the Society of Jesus*, Burns & Oates, London, 1880, vol. VI.

27 J. Gillow, *Bibliographical Dictionary of English Catholics*, 1885–1902, entry under 'Shakespeare', p. 496.

28 British Library, Lansdown MS. 213, f. 315, quoted E. K. Chambers, *William Shakespeare*, op. cit., vol. II, pp. 242–3. Encouraging advocates of the theory that the Earl of Oxford wrote the works of Shakespeare, the first known reproduction of this memorial, by antiquary William Dugdale in his *Antiquities of Warwickshire*, 1656, shows Shakespeare without his pen. The 'Oxfordians' usually ignore a much more faithful 'with pen' sketch by George Vertue (British Library, MS Portland Loan 29/246, p. 17), reproduced Schoenbaum, *William Shakespeare: A Documentary Life*, p. 152. This dates from 1737, still eleven years earlier than the bust's earliest known refurbishment in 1748. In concert with the references by Digges and Hammond, this enables us to be confident that the memorial we see today is essentially the same as that created within seven years of Shakespeare's lifetime.

29 See William Hamper (ed.), *The Life, Diary and Correspondence of Sir William Dugdale*, 1827, p. 99.

30 *Sonnet* 71.

31 Quoted in J. O. Halliwell ed., *A Copy of a Letter of News . . .* , 1865, p. 11.

32 Quoted E. J. L. Scott, article in *Athenaeum*, 1882, i.103.

33 C. M. Ingleby, *Shakespeare, The Man and the Book*, 1877, 1881, vol. II, p. 169.

34 Edwin E. Willoughby, *The Printing of the First Folio of Shakespeare*, Bibliographical Society, Oxford, 1932, p. 63.

CHAPTER 24 – 'He Was . . . for All Time!'

1 Quoted E. K. Chambers, *William Shakespeare*, op. cit., vol. II, pp. 206–07.

2 *Pericles*, Arden ed. F. D. Hoeniger, p. lxvi.

3 T. J. B. Spencer, 'Ben Jonson on his beloved. The author Mr William Shakespeare', *The Elizabethan Theatre*, IV, ed. G. R. Hibbard, Macmillan, London, 1974.

4 See Marchette Chute, *Ben Jonson of Westminster*, op. cit., p. 273.

5 J. L. Nevinson, 'Shakespeare's Dress in his Portraits', *Shakespeare Quarterly*, Spring 1967, p. 104.

6 Quoted, without source, in Charlton Ogburn, *The Mysterious William Shakespeare*, op. cit., p. 60.

7 A. L. Rowse, *Discovering Shakespeare*, op. cit., p. 160.

8 J. Parker Norris in *American Bibliopolist*, April 1876, quoted Schoenbaum, *Shakespeare's Lives*, op. cit., p. 339.

9 Washington Irving, *The Sketchbook of Geffrey Crayon, Gent.*, New York, 1819–20, no. vii.65.

10 Bodleian Library, ref. Aubrey MS. 8, f. 45.

11 Bodleian Library, ref. MS Arch F.c. 37.

12 Quoted, without source, in Peter Levi, *The Life and Times of William Shakespeare*, Macmillan, London, 1988, p. xx.

13 Quoted E. K. Chambers, *William Shakespeare*, op. cit., vol. II, p. 257.

14 Graham Greene, Introduction to *John Gerard, the Autobiography of an Elizabethan*, trans. Philip Caraman, Longmans, Green, London, 1951.

15 For a full account, see Henry Foley, S. J., *Records of the English Province of the Society of Jesus*, 7 vols, Burns & Oates, London, 1877, vol. I, pp. 77–98. Our knowledge of the geography of the Blackfriars in Shakespeare's time is frustratingly imprecise, and although Irwin Smith has attempted to reconstruct it in *Shakespeare's Blackfriars Playhouse*, the accuracy of his groundplan is far from certain.

16 'Mr Dowdall', quoted E. K. Chambers, *William Shakespeare*, op. cit., vol. II, p. 259.

17 Public Record Office, P.C.C. 18 Barrington, quoted in full in J. Payne Collier, *Memoirs of the Principal Actors in the Plays of Shakespeare*, op. cit., pp. 145–9.

18 J. Payne Collier, op. cit., pp. 70–71.

19 Public Record Office, Chancery records C2/L11/64 James I.

20 Quoted E. K. Chambers, *The Elizabethan Stage*, op. cit., vol. II, p. 514, n. 4.

21 *Julius Caesar*, III.i.112–4.

22 Bernard Levin, *Enthusiasms*, Cape, London, 1983.

Family Trees

I. Family tree of William Shakespeare, showing how his direct line died out with his grandchildren. Reproduced after A. L. Rowse & John Hedgecoe, *Shakespeare's Land. A Journey through the Landscape of Elizabethan England*, Chronicle Books, San Francisco, p. 14.

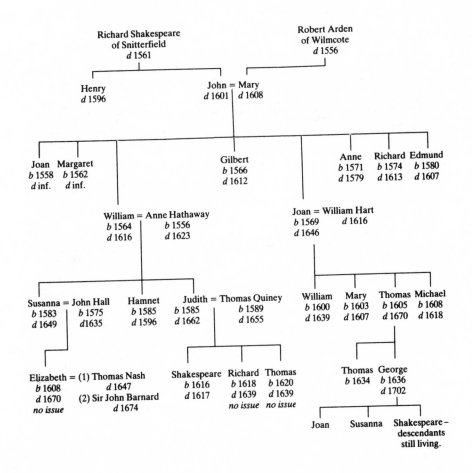

II. Family tree showing William Shakespeare's connections with the Quineys, Bushells, Grevilles, Winters, Ardens, Sheldons, Russells, Catesbys and Treshams, several of these involved in the Gunpowder and related plots. Reproduced after Peter Levi, *The Life and Times of William Shakespeare*, Macmillan, London, pp. xiv–xv.

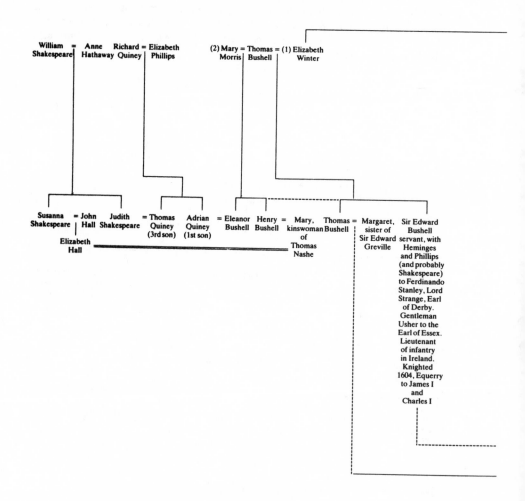

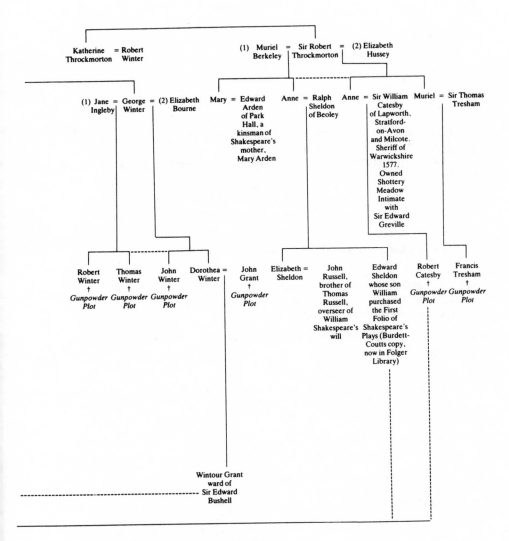

Greville, Sheldon and Catesby were also second cousins,
through their grandmothers, the three sisters Willington

APPENDIX B
Chronology

1552   John Shakespeare fined for having an unauthorised dunghill outside his house in Henley Street, Stratford-upon-Avon.

1553   Stratford Grammer School founded.

1554   Thomas Brend buys the site upon which the future Globe Theatre will be built.

1556   John Shakespeare appointed Taster of bread and ale.
2 Oct. John Shakespeare buys Henley Street house.
24 Nov. Robert Arden bequeaths to his youngest daughter Mary his land in Wilmcote.

1557   John Shakespeare and Mary Arden marry, probably at Aston Cantlow, though no record has survived of exactly where and when.

1558   *15 Sept.* Mary and John's first-born daughter Joan is christened at Holy Trinity Church, Stratford. She dies less than two years later.
17 Nov. Elizabeth I succeeds to the throne.

1561   *Jan.* John Bretchgirdle appointed vicar at Holy Trinity, Stratford.
John Shakespeare serves as one of the two chamberlains administering borough property and revenues.

1562   *2 Dec.* Christening of second Shakespeare daughter, Margaret, who also dies in infancy.

1564   Birth of Christopher Marlowe.
26 Apr. William Shakespeare, first of four sons of John and Mary, christened at Holy Trinity, Stratford.
Summer. Two hundred people killed by the plague in Stratford.

1565   *4 July.* John Shakespeare elected as alderman, and on 12 September installed in this office, qualifying him for the title 'Master Shakespeare'.

1567   James Burbage and John Brayne create London's earliest purpose-built playhouse at the Red Lion, Whitechapel.
13 Oct. Gilbert Shakespeare, a brother for William, christened.

1568   John Shakespeare elected as Stratford's bailiff, the local equivalent of mayor.
Mary Queen of Scots takes refuge in England.
7 July. Christening of Richard Burbage.

1569   *27 Jan.* At St Botolph's, Bishopgate, London, christening of Emilia Bassano (later, Lanier), thought by Dr A. L. Rowse to have been Shakespeare's 'Dark Lady'.

15 Apr. Christening of a second Joan Shakespeare, the only sister of William to survive, and indeed outlive him.
Nov. Rebellion of Catholic northern earls.

1570 John Shakespeare accused of usury, and fined 40 shillings.
Feb. Henry Carey, Lord Hunsdon, future patron of Shakespeare's acting company, crushes the rebellion of the northern earls.
25 Feb. Elizabeth I excommunicated by the Pope.

1571 John Shakespeare becomes deputy to the new bailiff of Stratford, Adrian Quiney.
Simon Hunt commences as master at Stratford Grammar School.

1572 *Jan*. John Shakespeare and Quiney ride to London on borough business.
Petition for patent submitted by the acting company to become known as Leicester's Men.
28 Sept. Christening of Anne Shakespeare, another sister for William.

1574 *11 Mar*. Christening of third Shakespeare son, Richard.
10 May. First known patent to players granted to Leicester's Men, with James Burbage among those named as patentees.

1575 Stratford schoolmaster Simon Hunt goes to Douai, revealing his Catholic leanings. He is succeeded by Thomas Jenkins.
Player Jerome Savage secures patronage of Earl of Warwick, and initiates building of a theatre at Newington Butts.
In Stratford, John Shakespeare buys next door house to his Henley Street property.

1576 James Burbage and John Brayne construct 'The Theatre', Shoreditch.
John Shakespeare applies for coat of arms, though this is not progressed at this stage.

1577 Beginning of declining fortunes for John Shakespeare. He stops attending council meetings.

1578 John Shakespeare mortgages his wife's house and land at Wilmcote to Edmund Lambert to raise £40. Excused payment of levy for poor relief.

1579 *4 Apr*. Anne Shakespeare buried.
London entrepreneur Philip Henslowe acquires a substantial estate as a result of marrying his employer's widow.
Stratford schoolmaster Jenkins succeeded by John Cottom, brother of a Catholic priest, Thomas.
Marriage of Ferdinando, Lord Strange to Alice Spencer.
John and Mary Shakespeare sell a ninth of their Snitterfield property.

1580 Last performance of Coventry Cycle of Mystery Plays.
3 May. Christening of last Shakespeare child, Edmund.
June. Arrest and imprisonment of John Cottom's Catholic priest brother, Thomas. Also of Robert Debdale, son of the Hathaways' neighbours.

John Shakespeare fined £40 by the Queen's Bench.
10 Dec. Christopher Marlowe starts at Corpus Christi College, Cambridge.

1581   Arrest and torture of Thomas Cottom, along with Edmund Campion.
4 Oct. Death of second Earl of Southampton.
Death of Anne Hathaway's father, Richard.

1582   John Cottom replaced at Stratford Grammar School, probably because of his brother's Catholicism.
John Shakespeare petitions Queen's Bench against four creditors.
30 May. Execution of Thomas Cottom.
20 Sept. Debdale released from prison.
27 Nov. Special licence issued for the marriage of William Shakespeare to 'Anne Whateley' of Temple Grafton.
Bond issued for Shakespeare's marriage to 'Anne Hathaway' (already three months pregnant by Shakespeare), of Hewlands Farm, Shottery.
Michaelmas/Nov. Puritan Alexander Aspinall becomes Stratford's schoolmaster.

1583   *26 May.* Christening of Susanna Shakespeare, first-born daughter of William and Anne.
Execution of Mary Arden's Catholic cousin, Edward, for treason.
Queen's Company formed by Master of the Revels.

1585   *2 Feb.* Christening of Shakespeare twins, Hamnet and Judith.
Philip Henslowe buys his first property, possibly a brothel.
Philip II of Spain plans his Armada.
Robert Debdale re-arrested as part of the Babington plot implicating Mary Queen of Scots.
11 Oct. Trial of Mary Queen of Scots.
12 Oct. Earl of Southampton enters St John's College, Cambridge at the age of twelve.
Dec. Death sentence pronounced on Mary by Elizabeth.
21 Dec. Robert Debdale executed.
Earl of Leicester's Men appear at Court.

1587   Publication of new edition Holinshed's *Chronicles of England, Scotland and Ireland*, to become an important historical reference for Shakespeare.
London entrepreneur Philip Henslowe builds the Rose, the first theatre on Bankside.
8 Feb. Execution of Mary Queen of Scots. An elaborate State funeral of Sir Philip Sidney held at the same time to distract public attention.
The Armada delayed for a year, thanks to Drake.
John Shakespeare replaced as alderman.
The Queen's Men perform at Thame and Stratford; the Earl of Leicester's Men at Lathom House.

1588   *29 Feb.* Young Earl of Southampton admitted as a member of Gray's Inn.
Marriage of John Heminges, future fellow actor of Shakespeare's, to Rebecca Knell, widow of actor killed in fight at Thame the previous year.
Armada reaches the Channel, and is defeated.

Sept. The Earl of Leicester dies, and his company of actors passes to Ferdinando, Lord Strange.

Sept. Death of celebrated clown Richard Tarlton.

Oct. Catholic priest William Hartley publicly executed at Shoreditch, close to the Burbage 'Theatre'.

1589 *6 June.* The Earl of Southampton receives his M.A.

Henri of Navarre tries to gain rightful succession to the French throne following the assassination of Henri III.

1591 The Earl of Southampton takes part in Accession Day Tilts, along with Lord Strange.

1592 Philip Henslowe commissions changes at the Rose, and begins his Diary, recording performances of Lord Strange's Men at the Rose. His entry for 3 March of a play entitled 'Harey the vj' is almost certainly one of the Shakespeare trilogy of that name.

Mar. John Shakespeare named as a recusant.

Lord Strange becomes patron to Thomas Nashe.

Privy Council orders closure of theatres following a riot by apprentices.

Possible commencement of the *Sonnets*.

Satirist Thomas Nashe praises Shakespeare in print in his *Pierce Penilesse*.

3 Sept. Death of university-educated dramatist Robert Greene, leaving behind posthumous condemnation of Shakespeare as 'an upstart crow', his heart 'wrapped in a Player's hide' who fancies himself as creator of blank verse. This is published shortly after as *Greene's Groats-worth of Witte*.

18 Oct. Emilia Bassano, already pregnant by Lord Chamberlain Henry Hunsdon, marries Alphonse Lanier. If she was one and the same as the 'Dark Lady' of the *Sonnets*, it is probably around the same time that she has an affair with William Shakespeare.

Dec. Lord Strange's Men, probably including Shakespeare, appear at Court, then at the Rose again.

1593 Performances in London theatres stopped by a particularly bad outbreak of plague.

18 Apr. Venus and Adonis, with Stratford-born Richard Field as printer, entered in the Stationers' Register.

Severe anti-Catholic measures passed by Parliament.

30 May. Death of Christopher Marlowe, his killer pardoned with suspicious ease and swiftness.

12 June. First recorded purchase of a published copy of *Venus and Adonis*. This is dedicated to the Earl of Southampton.

25 Sept. Ferdinando, Lord Strange succeeds his father as fifth Earl of Derby. Ferdinando hands suspected 'plotter' Richard Hesketh over to the government. Hesketh is executed shortly after.

Possible writing of *Love's Labour's Lost* for the Earl of Southampton at about this time.

1594 *1 Jan.* Henslowe's Diary records the performance of '*Buckingham*', possibly Shakespeare's *Richard III*.

24 Jan. Henslowe's Diary records performance of *Titus Andronicus.*

6 Feb. Titus Andronicus entered in the Stationers' Register.

12 Mar. Pirate edition of Shakespeare play to become known as *Henry vi, Part ii* entered in the Stationers' Register. This and *Titus Andronicus* will appear with no mention of Shakespeare's authorship.

16 Apr. Ferdinando, fifth earl of Derby, dies at Lathom, his symptoms strongly suggestive of arsenic poisoning.

Southampton's mother marries again; *A Midsummer Night's Dream* may have been written to celebrate the wedding.

2 May. Performance of *The Taming of a Shrew* recorded by Henslowe.

9 May. The Rape of Lucrece entered in the Stationers' Register. This is again dedicated to the Earl of Southampton, and in more familiar terms than before.

May. Ferdinando's acting company plays at Winchester under the name of his widow, Alice Spencer.

Reorganisation of Shakespeare's company as the Lord Chamberlain's Men, under patronage of Henry Carey, Lord Hunsdon.

4 Oct. Henry Danvers, a friend of the Earl of Southampton, kills Henry Long, with whom there has been a long-standing feud. Aided by the Earl of Southampton, Danvers and his brother escape to France. This event possibly inspires Shakespeare's writing of *Romeo and Juliet.*

Winter. Probable time when the last of the *Sonnets* written.

Dec. Shakespeare and the Lord Chamberlain's Men perform before the Queen.

28 Dec. The Comedy of Errors performed at Gray's Inn.

1595   Shakespeare mentioned among members of the Lord Chamberlain's Men paid £20 for plays performed before the Queen while the Court was at Greenwich during the Christmas.

Richard II written, performed later that autumn.

23 Sept. Rumours of a romance between Southampton and Elizabeth Vernon.

Death of Sir Thomas Heneage, the Countess of Southampton's second husband.

1596   Likely year of writing of *Merchant of Venice.*

22 July. Death of Shakespeare's company's patron Lord Chamberlain Henry Carey, to be succeeded as Chamberlain by Lord Cobham. Carey's company is re-named Lord Hunsdon's Men, after their new patron George Carey, second Lord Hunsdon.

11 Aug. Shakespeare's son Hamnet is buried; his death may be alluded to in *King John.*

Sept. James Burbage buys and converts part of the former Dominican priory of Blackfriars into an indoor theatre.

20 Oct. Renewed application for a coat of arms is made in the name of John Shakespeare.

Likely year of Hunsdon's Men performing *Henry iv* plays at the Theatre, Shoreditch.

29 Nov. Shakespeare and three others issued with Writ of Attachment to keep the peace.

Although conversion of the Blackfriars theatre is complete, residents prevent its use by petitioning the Privy Council.

Dec. Henry IV performed at Court for the first time; Lord Cobham forces a name-change from Oldcastle to Falstaff.

1597 *Jan.* Death of James Burbage.

17 Mar. Following the death of Lord Cobham, Shakespeare's company's patron George Carey, second Lord Hunsdon, is appointed Lord Chamberlain. Shakespeare's company accordingly resumes title 'Lord Chamberlain's Men'.

Apr/May. Probable first performance of *The Merry Wives of Windsor* at the Garter ceremonies at Windsor.

4 May. Shakespeare buys New Place, Stratford.

28 July. Privy Council orders closure of all London theatres.

29 Aug. Richard II entered in the Stationers' Register.

Ban on theatres lifted.

20 Oct. Richard III entered in the Stationers' Register.

15 Nov. Romeo and Juliet entered in the Stationers' Register.

Richard II and *Richard III* published.

Shakespeare reported for non-payment of five shillings tax.

1598 *24 Jan.* Stratfordian Richard Quiney is asked to contact Shakespeare about investment in Stratford land.

4 Feb. Stratford records show Shakespeare as owner of corn and malt, and living at New Place.

15 Feb. Earl of Southampton sails for France, having first made Elizabeth Vernon pregnant.

25 Feb. Henry IV, Part I entered in the Stationers' Register.

10 Mar. Love's Labour's Lost published, the first of Shakespeare's plays to carry his name on the title page.

22 July. The Merchant of Venice entered in the Stationers' Register.

Aug. Southampton, having been informed of Elizabeth Vernon's pregnancy, secretly returns to England to marry her, then returns to France. Upon the news reaching the Queen, Elizabeth Vernon is imprisoned, and Southampton recalled.

Sept. Ben Jonson imprisoned for murder, converts to Catholicism while in prison.

7 Sept. Francis Meres' *Palladis Tamia* entered in the Stationers' Register, providing a list of at least some of the plays Shakespeare had written thus far.

1 Oct. Shakespeare listed as defaulter for non-payment of taxes in the parish of St Helen's church, Bishopsgate.

25 Oct. Richard Quiney, on business in London, writes to Shakespeare asking for a loan.

Nov. Southampton returns to England and is imprisoned.

Dec. Richard III (Q2) published. Likewise *Richard II* (Q2 and Q3) and *The Rape of Lucrece*.

28 Dec. With no little stealth, the fabric of the Shoreditch Theatre is dismantled and taken across the Thames to be rebuilt as the Globe.

1599   *21 Feb*. Shakespeare and others become lessee/shareholders in the Globe. Globe completed some time before May.
Mid-year. Likely staging of *Henry v* at the Globe.
1 June. Government bans satires.
June. John Weever publishes an Epigramme with the first allusion to Shakespeare's *Sonnets*.
Sept. Julius Caesar performed at the Globe.
28 Sept. Earl of Essex imprisoned, after impetuous return from expedition to Ireland.
6 Oct. Shakespeare again recorded as owing taxes at St Helen's parish, Bishopsgate.
Oct. Romeo and Juliet (Q2) and *Henry iv, Part i* (Q2) published. Also *Venus and Adonis* (Q3).

1600   Philip Henslowe and his son-in-law Edward Alleyn commission the building of the Fortune theatre to be in competition with the Globe.
Mar. Will Kemp leaves the Lord Chamberlain's Men after dancing from London to Norwich.
Hamlet written in this year?
22 July. The Merchant of Venice entered in the Stationers' Register.
4 Aug. Henry v, As You Like It, Much Ado about Nothing entered in the Stationers' Register.
23 Aug. Much Ado about Nothing and *Henry iv, Part ii* entered in the Stationers' Register as 'by Shakespeare'.
Christening of Shakespeare's nephew, son of his sister Joan Hart.
26 Aug. Essex freed.
Autumn. Fortune theatre built.
2 Sept. Blackfriars theatre leased to Henry Evans for use by the Children of the Chapel.
8 Oct. A Midsummer Night's Dream entered in the Stationers' Register.
28 Oct. The Merchant of Venice entered in the Stationers' Register.

1601   *9 Jan*. Southampton is attacked by Lord Grey, who is given lenient term of imprisonment.
7 Feb. By special request of members of the Earl of Essex's circle, Shakespeare's Lord Chamberlain's Men give special performance of *Richard ii* at the Globe.
8 Feb. Abortive rebellion by Essex, Southampton and others. Essex and Southampton arrested.
13 Feb. Plot by Captain Lea to have Essex released fails.
18 Feb. Captain Lea hanged.
19 Feb. Essex and Southampton are tried in Westminster Hall and sentenced to death.
24 Feb. Lord Chamberlain's Men perform before the Queen, possibly presenting *Richard ii*.

25 Feb. Essex beheaded.

Mar. Other plotters sentenced and executed.

Forty shillings owed by Shakespeare's wife to Thomas Whittington bequeathed to Stratford poor.

8 Sept. John Shakespeare buried at Holy Trinity, Stratford.

12 Oct. Death of Nicholas Brend, owner of Globe site.

1602 *18 Jan. The Merry Wives of Windsor* entered in the Stationers' Register.

2 Feb. Twelfth Night performed at Middle Temple.

1 May. Shakespeare pays £320 to the Combe family for land in Old Stratford. Death of Richard Quiney.

26 July. Hamlet entered in the Stationers' Register.

28 Sept. Shakespeare buys land and cottage in Chapel Lane, Stratford.

1603 *2 Feb.* At Richmond Palace Shakespeare's company give their last performance before the Queen.

7 Feb. Troilus and Cressida entered in the Stationers' Register.

19 Mar. Theatres closed pending the imminent death of Elizabeth.

24 Mar. At Richmond Palace, death of Elizabeth I. Shakespeare is notably not among those who write obituary tributes to her.

10 Apr. Southampton released from Tower on orders of James I.

19 May. Lord Chamberlain's Men become the King's Men, with Shakespeare's name prominent in the patent, also a new member of the company, Lawrence Fletcher.

May. Hamlet (Q1) published.

2 July. Southampton and Pembroke created Knights of the Garter.

25 July. Because of another severe outbreak of plague, James I crowned in a private ceremony.

9 Sept. Death of George Carey, second Lord Hunsdon.

2 Dec. Shakespeare's company performs before James at Wilton, probably *As You Like It.*

Henslowe Diary ceases.

1604 *Measure for Measure* written this year.

Shakespeare and others issued with red cloth for the formal entry of James I into London.

Shakespeare named as one of King's Men in Privy Council warrant.

July. Shakespeare sues Phillip Rogers for non-payment of malt supplied by him.

Shakespeare's company, as the King's Men, entertain Spanish delegation at Somerset House. As a result of this delegation, a peace treaty is signed with Spain.

1 Nov. Othello performed at Whitehall.

4 Nov. The Merry Wives of Windsor performed at Court.

26 Dec. Measure for Measure performed at Court.

Hamlet (Q2) and *Henry IV, Part I* (Q3) published.

1605 *Jan. Love's Labour's Lost* performed at Court, also Ben Jonson's *The*

Masque of Blackness. This latter, with sets by Inigo Jones, opens new era of spectacle in the theatre.

7 Jan. Henry v performed at Court.

10 and 12 Feb. The Merchant of Venice performed at Court.

Shakespeare is among beneficiaries in the will of his fellow actor Augustine Phillips, receiving thirty shillings.

24 July. Shakespeare invests £440 in tithes on Welcombe property.

Richard iii (Q4) published.

Nov. Gunpowder plot, in which several of the plotters are from the environs of Stratford-upon-Avon.

1606   Profanity laws passed.

Macbeth written this year, with allusions to the Gunpowder plot.

Shakespeare's daughter Susanna named as recusant, also Hamnet and Judith Sadler, and Ben Jonson and his wife.

Marriage of Augustine Phillips' widow Anne to John Witter, who thus acquires a share in the Globe.

30 Oct. Burial of Madame Mountjoie, Shakespeare's Silver Street landlady.

26 Dec. King Lear performed at Whitehall by King's Men.

1607   *5 June*. Marriage of Susanna Shakespeare to Dr John Hall, at Holy Trinity, Stratford.

12 Aug. Edward, illegitimate son of Shakespeare's brother Edmund, buried at St Giles, Cripplegate, London.

5 Sept. Hamlet performed on board 'Dragon' in Sierra Leone.

26 Nov. King Lear entered in the Stationers' Register.

31 Dec. Edmund Shakespeare buried at St Saviour's, Southwark.

1608   *21 Feb*. Christening of Elizabeth, daughter of Susanna and John Hall.

20 May. Antony and Cleopatra entered in the Stationers' Register.

July. Richard Shakespeare summoned by Stratford ecclesiastical court, and fined one shilling.

9 Aug. Blackfriars theatre leased for twenty-one years by Shakespeare and his colleagues.

16 Aug. William Sly buried at St Leonard's, Shoreditch.

9 Sept. Burial of Shakespeare's mother Mary at Holy Trinity, Stratford.

12 Sept. Burial of Lawrence Fletcher.

23 Sept. Christening of Michael Hart, Shakespeare's nephew.

16 Oct. Shakespeare becomes godfather to William Walker.

1609   *20 May. Shakespeare's Sonnets* entered in the Stationers' Register.

Pericles (Q1 and Q2) published, also *Troilus and Cressida*.

Gilbert Shakespeare summoned to appear in the Court of Requests.

8 Oct. The Scourge of Folly entered in the Stationers' Register. This includes a poem to Shakespeare written by John Davies, and seems to indicate that he had given up acting.

1610   Completion of land conveyancing begun by Shakespeare in 1602.

Summer. The King's Men present *The Winter's Tale* at the Globe.

Death of Master of the Revels, Edmund Tilney.

1611 *10 Feb.* Witter releases his rights in the Globe to Heminges.
20 Apr. Simon Forman sees *Macbeth* performed at the Globe.
30 Apr. Simon Forman sees *Richard II* performed at the Globe.
15 May. Simon Forman sees *The Winter's Tale* performed at the Globe.
Publication of Emilia Lanier's poems as *Salve Deus Rex Judaeorum*.
Pericles (Q3), *Hamlet* (Q3) and *Titus Andronicus* (Q3) published.
Sept. Death of Simon Forman.
1 Nov. First known performance of *The Tempest*, at Court.

1612 Burial of Gilbert Shakespeare.
11 May. Shakespeare in court as a witness in Belott–Mountjoie dispute.
Death of fifth Earl of Rutland.
Richard III (Q5) published.

1613 *28 Jan.* John Combe wills five pounds to Shakespeare.
4 Feb. Burial of Shakespeare's last brother, Richard.
Feb. The King's Men perform fourteen plays during the celebrations for the marriage of Princess Elizabeth to Frederick, Elector Palatine.
Susanna Hall accused of adultery by John Lane.
10 Mar. Shakespeare buys Gatehouse at Blackfriars in London.
31 Mar. Shakespeare and Richard Burbage are each paid forty-four shillings for designing and creating an *impresa* shield for the new Earl of Rutland, for his part in the Accession Day Tilts.
29 June. The Globe burnt to the ground, apparently caused by a cannon spark during a performance of *Henry VIII*.
15 July. Susanna Hall wins action for defamation of character against John Lane.
26 Oct. Shakespeare's company sign new lease on the Globe site.

1614 *25 Feb.* Burial of fellow-actor Alexander Cooke.
30 June. Globe theatre reported as already back in business.
July. Death of John Combe, the wealthiest man in Stratford, for whom, according to Stratford tradition, Shakespeare wrote an epitaph.
9 July. Fire sweeps through Stratford, destroying buildings.
5 Sept. Shakespeare documented as owning 127 acres in Stratford.
17 Nov. Shakespeare and his son-in-law, Dr John Hall, in London on business concerning Stratford tithes.

1615 Shakespeare is named concerning possible land enclosures.

1616 Publication in this year of Folio edition of Ben Jonson's works.
Jan. Probable first drafting of Shakespeare's will.
10 Feb. Shakespeare's daughter Judith marries Stratford vintner Thomas Quiney.
12 Mar. Thomas and Judith Quiney excommunicated for having married in Lent without special licence.
25 Mar. Shakespeare signs his will.

26 Mar. Thomas Quiney tried for fornication, having made pregnant one Margaret Wheeler who had died in childbirth.
17 Apr. Burial of Shakespeare's brother-in-law William Hart.
23 Apr. Death of William Shakespeare, according to his monument in Holy Trinity.
25 Apr. Shakespeare buried in Holy Trinity, Stratford.
23 Nov. Christening of Shakespeare Quiney, Shakespeare's first grandson by his daughter Judith.

1617   *8 May.* Infant Shakespeare Quiney buried.
Shakespeare's lawyer, Francis Collins, dies.

1618   Shakespeare's Blackfriars Gatehouse is conveyed to John Greene and Matthew Morris.

1619   *13 Mar.* Death of Richard Burbage.
28 Apr. John Witter, Augustine Phillips' widow's second husband, is involved in Court of Requests case against Heminges and Condell.
3 May. The Lord Chamberlain acts to halt the unauthorised publication of Shakespeare's works in Quarto.

1620   Christening of Thomas Quiney, jnr.

1621   *6 Oct. Othello* entered in the Stationers' Register.

1622   *21 Feb.* Landowner Matthew Brend, having become of age, assumes control of the Globe site.
Apr. Matthew Brend is knighted.
22 Apr. Marriage of Shakespeare's granddaughter Elizabeth Hall to Thomas Nash.

1623   *2 Feb. Twelfth Night* performed at Court.
8 Aug. Burial of Shakespeare's wife Anne near her husband at Holy Trinity, Stratford.
8 Nov. Having been compiled by Shakespeare's fellow actors John Heminges and Henry Condell, the First Folio of Shakespeare's 'Comedies, Histories & Tragedies' is entered in the Stationers' Register.
Marriage of Globe site-owner Sir Matthew Brend to Frances Smith.

1624   *12 Mar.* Sir Matthew Brend gives the Globe site to his wife.

1625   Death of James I and accession of his son Charles I.

1627   Henry Condell makes his will and dies soon after.

1630   *9 Oct.* John Heminges makes his will.
12 Oct. Burial of John Heminges.

1635   Dr John Hall leaves his books and manuscripts to his son-in-law Thomas Nash.

1642 *2 Sept.* The Globe and other London theatres closed down by order of Parliament.

1643 *July.* Charles I's Queen Henrietta Maria sleeps at New Place for two nights while holding court at Stratford during the Civil War.

1644 *15 Apr.* With the Globe still closed, and failing to produce revenue, Sir Matthew Brend pulls it down to make way for tenements.

1645 Burial of Emilia Lanier at Clerkenwell.

1649 *5 June.* Marriage of Shakespeare's granddaughter Elizabeth Nash to John Bernard.
11 July. Death of Susanna Hall.

1662 *9 Feb.* Burial of Judith Quiney.

1670 *17 Feb.* Burial of Elizabeth Bernard, thus extinguishing the direct line of Shakespeare's descendants.

1759 Owner of New Place, Reverend Francis Gastrell, pulls the house down in a fit of pique.

1787 The Gatehouse formerly owned by Shakespeare described as being demolished to make way for the building of Blackfriars bridge.

1847 *16 Sept.* Sale of Shakespeare's 'birthplace' house is announced at the London Auction Mart.

1989 *Spring.* Foundations of the Rose theatre uncovered.

APPENDIX C
Miscellaneous Documents

1580[?] SPIRITUAL WILL OF JOHN SHAKESPEARE

1. Portion of the will missing when discovered in 1757, but reconstructible from a 1638 published edition of the same Testament, described as 'made by S. Charles Borrom. Card. & Arch. of Millan', as follows:

In the name of the Father & of the Son, and of the Holy Ghost, Amen.

I [John Shakspear] a most miserable sinner, knowing myself to be mortal, and born to die without knowing the hour, where, when or how, to the end that I be not surprised upon a sudden, am resolved through the help and aid of my sweet Saviour, to make myself ready for this uncertain hour, seeing he vouchsafeth me now a fit time. Wherefore sincerely, from the bottom of my heart, I give the world to understand of this my last Will and testament, in manner following.

I

First, I here protest and declare in the sight and presence of Almighty God. Father, Son and Holy Ghost, three Persons and one God, and of the B.V. Mary, and of all the holy Court of Heaven, that I will live and die obedient unto the Catholic, Roman & Apostolic Church, firmly believing all the twelve Articles of the Faith taught by the holy Apostles, with the interpretation and declaration made thereon by the same holy church, as taught, defined & declared by her. And finally I protest that I do believe all that which a good and faithful Christian ought to believe: in which faith I purpose to live & die. And if at any time (which God forbid) I should chance by suggestion of the Devil to do, say or think contrary to this my belief, I do now for that time, in virtue of this present act, revoke, infringe and annul the same, & will that it be held for neither spoken, or done by me.

II

Secondly. By this my last Will, I protest, that, at my death I will receive the sacraments of Penance & Confession, the which if by any accident I should not be able to have, or make, I do in virtue of this present, resolve from this instance, for that time, to make it from my heart, accusing myself of all my sins committed in thought, word & work, as well against God as against myself and my neighbour, whereof I do repent me with infinite sorrow, & desire time of penance, bitterly to bewail the same, for that I have offended my Sovereign Lord & God, whom I ought to love and serve above all things. The which I now firmly purpose, with his grace, to do as long as I shall live, without ever more offending him.

III

Item, I [John Shakspear] do protest, that at the end of my life I will receive the most Blessed Sacrament, for my *Viaticum* or last journey, that by means of so divine a pledge, I may perfectly reconcile & unite myself unto my Lord. The which if through any accident, I should not then be able to perform, I do now for that time, declare that I will receive it. . . .

2. Portion of the seemingly geniuine will of John Shakespeare, as discovered in 1757, and transcribed by Edmond Malone:

. . . at least spiritually, in will adoring and most humbly beseeching my Saviour, that he will be pleased to assist me in so dangerous a voyage, to defend me from the snares and deceits of my infernal enemies, and to conduct me to the secure haven of his eternal bliss.

IV

Item, I John Shakspear do protest that I will also pass out of this life, armed with the last sacrament of extreme unction: the which if through any let or hindrance I should not be able to have, I do now also for that time demand and crave the same; beseeching his Divine Majesty that he will be pleased to anoint my senses both internal and external with the sacred oil of his infinite mercy, and to pardon me all my sins committed by seeing, speaking, feeling, smelling, hearing, touching, or by any other way whatsoever.

V

Item, I John Shakspear do by this present protest that I will never through any temptation whatsoever despair of the divine goodness, for the multitude and greatness of my sins, for which although I confess that I have deserved Hell, yet I will steadfastly hope in God's infinite mercy, knowing that he hath heretofore pardoned many as great sinners as myself, whereof I have good warrant sealed with his sacred mouth, in holy writ, whereby he pronounceth that he is not come to call the just, but sinners.

VI

I John Shakspear do protest that I do not know that I have ever done any good work meritorious of life everlasting: and if I have done any, I do acknowledge that I have done it with a great deal of negligence and imperfection; neither should I have been able to do the least without the assistance of his divine grace. Wherefore let the Devil remain confounded; for I do in no wise presume to merit Heaven by such good works alone, but through the merits and blood of my Lord and Saviour, Jesus, shed upon the cross for me most miserable sinner.

VII

Item, I John Shakspear do protest by this present writing, that I will patiently endure and suffer all kind of infirmity, sickness, yea and the pain of death itself: wherein if it should happen, which God forbid, that through violence of pain and agony, or by subtility of the Devil, I should fall into any impatience or temptation of blasphemy, or murmuration against God, or the Catholic faith, or give any sign of bad example, I do henceforth, and for that present, repent me, and am most heartily sorry for the same: and I do renounce all the evil whatsoever, which I might have then done or said; beseeching his divine clemency that he will not forsake me in that grievous and painful agony.

VIII

Item, I John Shakspear, by virtue of this present testament, I do pardon all the injuries and offences that anyone hath ever done unto me, either in my reputation, life, goods, or any other way whatsoever; beseeching sweet Jesus to pardon them for the same: and I do desire, that they will do the like by me, whom I have offended or injured in any sort howsoever.

IX

Item, I John Shakspear do here protest that I do render infinite thanks to his Divine Majesty for all the benefits that I have received as well secret as manifest, and in particular for the benefit of my creation, redemption, sanctification, conservation and vocation to the holy knowledge of him and his true Catholic faith: but above all, for his so great expectation of me to penance, when he might most justly have taken me out of this life, when I least thought of it, yea even then, when I was plunged into the dirty puddle of my sins. Blessed be therefore and praised, for ever, his infinite patience and charity.

X

Item, I John Shakspear do protest that I am willing, yea I do infinitely desire and humbly crave, that of this my last will and testament the glorious and ever Virgin Mary, mother of God, refuge and advocate of sinners (whom I honour specially above all other saints), may be the chief executress, together with these other saints, my patrons (saint Winefrid), all whom I invoke and beseech to be present at the hour of my death, that she and they may comfort me with their desired presence, and crave of sweet Jesus that he will receive my soul into peace.

XI

Item, In virtue of this present writing, I John Shakspear do likewise most willingly and with all humility constitute and ordain my good angel, for defender and protector of my soul in the dreadful day of Judgment, when the final sentence of eternal life or death shall be discussed and given; beseeching him, that, as my soul was appointed to his custody and protection when I lived, even so he will vouchsafe to defend the same at that hour, and conduct it to eternal bliss.

XII

Item, I John Shakspear do in like manner pray and beseech all my dear friends, parents and kinsfolk, by the bowels of our Saviour Jesus Christ, that since it is uncertain what lot shall befall me, for fear notwithstanding least by reason of my sins I be to pass and stay a long while in Purgatory, they will vouchsafe to assist and succour me with their holy prayers and satisfactory works, especially with the holy sacrifice of the Mass, as being the most effectual means to deliver souls from their torments and pains; from the which, if I shall by God's grace, goodness and by their virtuous works be delivered, I do promise that I will not be ungrateful unto them, for so great a benefit.

XIII

Item, I John Shakspear do by this my last will and testament bequeath my soul, as soon as it shall be delivered and loosened from the prison of this my body, to be entombed in the sweet and amorous coffin of the side of Jesus Christ; and that in this life-giving sepulchre it may rest and live, perpetually enclosed in that eternal habitation of repose, there to bless forever and ever that direfull iron of the lance which, like a charge in a censer, forms so sweet and pleasant a monument within the sacred breast of my Lord and Saviour.

XIV

Item, lastly I John Shakspear do protest, that I will willingly accept of death in what manner soever it may befall me, conforming my will unto the will of God; accepting of the same in satisfaction of my sins, and giving thanks unto his Divine Majesty for the life he has bestowed upon me. And if it please him to prolong or shorten the same, blessed be he also a thousand times; into whose most holy hands I commend my soul and body, my life and death: and I beseech him above all things, that he never permit any change to be made by me John Shakspear of this my aforesaid will and testament. Amen.

I John Shakspear have made this present writing of protestation, confession and charter, in presence of the blessed Virgin Mary, my angel guardian, and all the celestial court, as witness hereunto: the which my meaning is, that it be of full value now presently and forever, with the force and virtue of testament, codicil, and donation in cause of death; confirming it anew, being in perfect health of soul and body, and signed with mine own hand; carrying also the same about me; and for the better declaration hereof, my will and intention is that it be finally buried with me after my death.

'Pater noster, Ave Maria, Credo
'Jesu, son of David, have mercy on me.
                              Amen.'

The original of this will, as discovered in 1757, was extant in 1790, since it was transcribed by the notable scholar Edmond Malone in that year. Subsequently, however, it disappeared, not being found among Malone's papers after his death, and for many years its authenticity was doubted. However, the discovery of a published copy of 1638, now in the Folger Shakespeare Library, Washington, strongly argues for its genuineness. Spelling and punctuation have been modernised by the author.

1592 [?] PLOT OF THE SECOND PART OF THE SEVEN DEADLY SINS

Rare example of the running order for a play performed by Lord Strange's Men, as originally hung in the actors' dressing-room, or tiring house.

*The plot of the Second Part of
the Seven Deadly Sins*

A tent being placed on the stage for Henry the Sixth. He in it asleep. To him the Lieutenant, a Pursuivant [attendant], R. Cowley, Jo Duke & 1 Warder, R. Pallant; to them Pride, Gluttony, Wrath and Covetousness at one door; at another door Envy, Sloth and Lechery. The three put back the four and so exeunt.

———

Henry awaking, enter a Keeper J. Sincler. To him a servant T. Belt to him. Lidgate & the Keeper exit, then enter again. Then Envy passeth over the stage. Lidgate speaks

———

A sennet [trumpet fanfare]. Dumb show

———

Enter King Gorboduc with councillors. R. Burbadg. Mr. Brian. Th. Goodale. The Queen with Ferrex and Porrex and some attendants follow. Saunder. W. Sly. Harry. J. Duke. Kitt. R° Pallant. J. Holland. After Gorboduc hath consulted with his lords he brings his 2 sons to several seats. They enving [?] on one other, Ferrex offers to take Porrex his crown. He draws his weapon. The King, Queen and Lords step between them. They thrust them away and menacing each other's exit. The Queen and Lords depart heavily

———

Enter Ferrex crowned with drum and colours and soldiers one way. Harry. Kitt. R. Cowley. John Duke. To them at another door Porrex, drum & colours & soldiers. W. Sly. R. Pallant. John Sincler. J. Holland.

———

Enter Queen with two councillors. Mr. Brian Tho Goodale. To them Ferrex and

Porrex several ways with drums and powers, Gorboduc entering in the midst between. Henry speaks
————————

Alarms with excursions. After, Lidgate speaks
————————

Enter Ferrex and Porrex severally, Gorboduc still following them. Lucius Damasus Mr. Bry T. Good
————————

Enter Ferrex at one door, Porrex at another. The fight. Ferrex is slain. To them Videna the Queen. To her Damasus, to him Lucius.
————————

Enter Porrex sad with Dordan his man. R.P. W. Sly. To them the Queen and a Lady. Nich. and Saunder and Lords R. Cowly Mr. Brian. To them Lucius running
————————

Henry and Lidgate speak. Sloth passeth over.
————————

Enter Giraldus Phronesius Aspatia Pompeia Rodope. R. Cowly. Th. Goodale. Ro Go. Ned. Nick.
————————

Enter Sardanapalus Arbactus Nicanor and Captains marching. Mr. Phillipps, Mr. Pope, R. Pa. Kit. J. Sincler. J. Holland
————————

Enter a Captain with Aspatia and the Ladies. Kitt.
————————

Lidgate speaks.
Enter Nicanor with other Captains. R. Pall. J. Sincler. Kitt. J. Holland. R. Cowly. To them Arbactus, Mr. Pope. To him Rodope Ned. To her Sardanapalus like a woman, with Aspatia, Rodope, Pompeia, Will, Fool. To them Arbactus and 3 musicians Mr. Pope. J. Sincler. Vincent. R. Cowly. To them Nicanor and others. R.P. Kitt.
————————

Enter Sardanapalus with the Ladies. To them a Messenger Tho. Goodale. To him Will, Fool running
————————

Enter Arbactus pursuing Sardanapalus, and the Ladies fly. After enter Sarda. with as many jewels, robes and gold as he can carry. Alarm.
————————

Enter Arbactus Nicanor and the other Captains in triumph. Mr. Pope R.Pa. Kitt. J. Holl. R. Cow. J. Sinc.
————————

Henry speaks and Lidgate, Lechery passeth over the stage
————————

Enter Tereus, Philomela, Julio, R. Burbadge, Ro., R. Pall, J. Sink
————————

Enter Procne, Itys and Lords. Saunder. Will. J. Duke. W. Sly. Harry
————————

Enter Philomela and Tereus, to them Julio

Enter Procne, Panthea, Itys and Lords. Sander. T. Belt. Will. W. Sly. Harry. Th. Goodale. To them Tereus with Lords R. Burbadge, J. Duk., R. Cowley

A dumb show. Lidgate speaks.
Enter Procne with the sampler. To her Tereus from hunting with his Lords. To them Philomela with Itys' head in a dish. Mercury comes and all vanish. To him 3 lords. Th. Goodale. Harey. W. Sly.

Henry speaks to him. Lieutenant, Pursuivant and Warders. R. Cowly, J. Duke, J. Holland, Joh. Sincler. To them Warwick, Mr. Brian.

Lidgate speaks to the audience and so exits

The original is preserved in the Archives Room, Dulwich College, London SE21. Spellings and punctuations have been modernised, except in the case of the actors' names. This is for the reason that while some of these latter can readily be recognised – e.g. 'R. Cowly' as Richard Cowley – other identifications are more conjectural.

1594, 22 April, LETTER OF SIR GEORGE CAREY TO HIS WIFE ELIZABETH SPENCER, REGARDING THE DEATH OF FERDINANDO, FIFTH EARL OF DERBY:

Never previously published, this letter contains important details of how the news of Ferdinando's death reached London, and Carey's attitude towards Ferdinando's theoretical successor, his brother William:

My sweet life, Know how glad by writing to make thee know how often it pleaseth the best content of my thoughts in absence to shew that I forget thee not. Than sorrowful any cause of grief thereby should grow unto thee upon a sudden there, before due consideration had, you shall understand that on Friday night I came to town, where I recontred within an hour after the most unpleasing news that could happen and most contrary to my expectations.

[This was] of the Earl of Derby's late and hateful death, whom I never thought so much to have loved in his life, as I find greatly to have been grieved for after his death, and whom I find much more lamented after his death than to the world known in his life. . . . The good service he did to her Majesty and the realm, and no private ill desert of his own, shortened his days, not by any ordinary vichess [vicissitude?] of nature, but by villainous poisoning, witchcraft and enchantment, whereof the bottom not yet found, but in my hope and the courses I have taken, trust shall be answered.

The poisoning [has been] made manifest by the judgment of Doctor Case and three other physicians all affirming that his disease could be no other but flat poisoning. The witchcraft [has come to light] partly by the confession and manifest demonstration in acts of a witch apprehended and in prison for it. The enchantment [was] evident by the finding of his picture framed in wax with one of his own hairs pricked directly in the heart thereof. By practice of some of them your sister [i.e. Countess Alice Spencer] not aveinte [enceinte? – i.e. pregnant] before without any cause to be imagined why, [was] brought a bed before her time of a boy child.

These unfortunate accidents with patience and wisdom you must digest, as not by sorrow to be recalled, or by grief to be remedied. And now to comfort yourself with the well-doing of your sister who useth her sorrow in measure not to hurt herself, and hath approved her wisdom in her extremity as her love to him in his life. For in the time of his sickness, [Ferdinando] finding himself at the first stricken with death ... hath by good advice in law given Lathom, Knowsley, Colham, the Isle of Man and whatsoever he hath in England (besides what Henry the 7th gave to his ancestors) from the nidicock his brother, to your sister and her daughters, whereby we yet hold that both she and they will be exceeding great marriages.

Upon Saturday in the afternoon I went with my Lord and Lady [i.e. Henry Carey, Lord Hunsdon, his father] to the Court. That night [I] attended the Queen's walking abroad, and after she had kindly demanded for you, and refused to bid me welcome because I had taken no leave of her, we entered into speech of the Earl's death, and your sister's great sorrow. Truly her Majesty had a feeling compassion, and with tears witnessed it to them. ... She professed she thought not that any man in the world loved her better than he did, that he was the most honourable, worthiest and absolutely honest man that she had in her life ever known.

[She affirmed] that contrary to the threatened trouble and ... of your sisters by the young Earl she would protect, defend and do what her friends or self could best devise in her behalf, and that I should rest assured none should have the bringing up or disposing of the young ladies [i.e. Ferdinando and Alice's daughters] but your sister. Yesterday she testified to the Lords of the Council what a loss her self and the realm had sustained by his death, and took order with Mr Vice Chamberlain, the Master of the Rolls and myself to appoint commissioners for the examination and trial of the Earl's death, which this day were to dispute.

Now to leave off out of this tragedy, you shall understanding [sic] that the Vice Chamberlain [Sir Thomas Heneage] is thought shall marry the Lady Southfil [Southampton], and no infection to grow to the one from the other, both being poisoned with the pox alike. The Lady Moyle Finch is happiest to supplant my sister Hobby in the bedchamberlain and Bes[s] Bridges hast forsaken the Earl of Bedford and taken the Earl of Southfil. So in haste, sweet love, as sorry to leave speaking to thee I wish myself in place of my lines. From Blackfriars the 22 April. My law cause is to sustain some delay for want of a solicitor. Yours faithfully, without thought of change

George Carey xx

For many years preserved among the muniments at Berkeley Castle, Gloucestershire, this letter is today in the Gloucestershire Record Office, ref. MF 1161 Letter Book no. 2. Spellings and punctuations have been partially modernised.

1598, 25 October, LETTER OF RICHARD QUINEY TO SHAKESPEARE

(Addressed)

H[aste?] To my loving good friend and countryman, Mr Wm. Shackespere, deliver these.

(Letter proper)

Loving Countryman, I am bold of you, as of a friend, craving your help with £30 upon Mr Bushell's and my security, or Mr Mytton's with me. Mr Rosswell is not come to London as yet, and I have especial cause. You shall friend me much in helping me out of all the debts I owe in London, I thank God, and much quiet my mind, which would not be indebted. I am now towards the Court in hope of answer for the despatch of my business. You shall neither lose credit nor money by me, the Lord willing, and now but persuade yourself so as I hope, and you shall not need to fear, but with all hearty thankfulness I will hold my time and content your friend, and if we bargain further you shall be the paymaster yourself. My time bids me hasten to an end and so I commit this [to] your care and hope of your help. I fear I shall not be back this night from the Court. Haste. The Lord be with you and with us all. Amen. From the Bell in Carter Lane the 25 October 1598. Yours in all kindness,

Ryc. Quyney

Preserved in the Shakespeare Birthplace Trust Records Office as MS. ER 274. Spellings and punctuations have been modernised.

1616, 25 March, SHAKESPEARE'S WILL

Preserved in the Public Record Office, London, as PROB 1/4. Items printed in round brackets appear as deletions in the original text. Spellings and punctuations have been modernised.

Vicesimo Quinto die (Januarij) Martij Anno Regni Domini nostri Jacobi nunc RegisAnglie &c decimo quarto & Scotie xlix.° Annoque domini 1616.

T[estamentum] W[illel]mj Shackspeare.

R[ecognoscatu]r.

In the name of God, Amen. I, William Shackspeare, of Stratford-upon-Avon in the county of Warwick, Gent., in perfect health and memory, God be praised, do make and ordain this my last will and testament, in manner and form following;- that is to say:

First, I commend my soul into the hands of God my Creator, hoping, and assuredly believing, through the only merits of Jesus Christ my Saviour, to be made partaker of life everlasting; and my body to the earth, whereof it is made.

Item, I give and bequeath unto my (sonne in L) daughter Judith one hundred and fifty pounds of lawful English money, to be paid unto her in manner and form following: that is to say, one hundred pounds in discharge of her marriage portion, within one year of my decease, with consideration after the rate of two shillings in the pound for so long time as the same shall be unpaid unto her after my decease; and the fifty pounds residue thereof, upon her surrendering of, or giving of such sufficient security as the overseers of this my will shall like of, to surrender or grant all her estate and right that shall descend or come unto her after my decease, or that she now hath of, in, or to, one copyhold tenement, with the appurtenances, lying and being in Stratford-upon-Avon aforesaid, in the said county of Warwick, being parcel or holden of the manor of Rowington, unto my daughter Susanna Hall, and her heirs forever.

Item, I give and bequeath unto my said daughter Judith one hundred and fifty pounds more, if she, or any issue of her body, be living at the end of three years next ensuing the day of the date of this my will, during which time my executors to pay her consideration from my decease according to the rate aforesaid: and, if she die within the said term, without issue of her body, then my will is, and I do give and bequeath one hundred pounds thereof to my niece, Elizabeth Hall; and the fifty pounds to be set forth by my executors during the life of my sister, Joan Hart, and the use and profit thereof coming, shall be paid to my said sister Joan, and after her decease the said fifty pounds shall remain amongst the children of my said sister, equally to be divided amongst them: but if my said daughter Judith be living at the end of the said three years, or any issue of her body, then my will is, and so I devise and bequeath the said hundred and fifty pounds to be set out by my executors and overseers for the best benefit of her and her issue, and the stock not be paid unto her so long as she shall be married and covert baron (by my executors and overseers); but my will is, that she shall have the consideration yearly paid unto her during her life; and after her decease the said stock and consideration to be paid to her children, if she have any, and if not, to her executors or assigns, she living the said term after my decease; provided that if such husband as she shall at the end of the said three years be married unto, or at any [time] after, do sufficiently assure unto her, and the issue of her body, lands answerable to the portion by this my will given unto her, and to be adjudged so by my executors and overseers, then my will is, that the said hundred and fifty pounds shall be paid to such husband as shall make such assurance, to his own use.

Item, I give and bequeath unto my said sister Joan twenty pounds, and all my wearing apparel, to be paid and delivered within one year after my decease; and I do will and devise unto her the house, with the appurtenances, in Stratford, wherein she dwelleth, for her natural life, under the yearly rent of twelve pence.

Item, I give and bequeath

[In left margin now illegible William Shakspere]

(Sheet 2)

unto her three sons, William Hart, —— Hart, and Michael Hart, five pounds a-piece, to be paid within one year of my decease. (To be set out for her within one year after my decease by my executors with the advice and directions of my overseers for her best profit until her marriage and then the same with the increase thereof to be paid unto her).

Item, I give and bequeath unto (her) the said Elizabeth Hall, all my plate that I now have (except my broad silver and gilt bowl), at the date of this my will.

Item, I give and bequeath unto the poor of Stratford, aforesaid, ten pounds; to Mr Thomas Combe, my sword; to Thomas Russell, Esq., five pounds; and to Francis Collins, of the borough of Warwick, in the county of Warwick, Gent., thirteen pounds six shillings and eightpence, to be paid within one year after my decease.

Item, I give and bequeath to (Mr Richard Tyler the elder) Hamlet [Hamnet] Sadler twenty-six shillings eightpence, to buy him a ring; to William Reynolds, Gent., twenty-six shillings eight pence, to buy him a ring; to my godson William Walker, twenty shillings in gold; to Anthony Nash, Gent., twenty-six shillings eight pence; and to Mr John Nash, twenty-six shillings eight pence (in gold); and to my fellows, John Hemynge, Richard Burbage, and Henry Cundell, twenty-six shillings eight pence a-piece, to buy them rings.

Item, I give, will, bequeath, and devise unto my daughter Susanna Hall, for better enabling her to perform this my will, and towards the performance thereof, all that capital messuage or tenement, with the appurtenances, in Stratford aforesaid, called the New Place, wherein I now dwell, and two messuages or tenements with the appurtenances, situate, lying, and being in Henley Street, within the borough of Stratford aforesaid; and all my barns, stables, orchards, gardens, lands, tenements, and hereditaments whatsoever, situate, lying, and being, or to be had, received, perceived, or taken within the towns, hamlets, villages, fields, and grounds of Stratford-upon-Avon, Old Stratford, Bishopton, and Welcombe, or in any of them, in the said county of Warwick; and also all that messuage or tenement, with the appurtenances, wherein one John Robinson dwelleth, situate, lying, and being in the Blackfriars in London, near the Wardrobe; and all other my lands, tenements, and hereditaments whatsoever; to have and to hold all and singular the said premises, with their appurtenances, unto the said Susanna Hall, for and during the term of her natural life; and after her decease, to the first son of her body lawfully issuing; and to the heirs males of the body of the said first son lawfully issuing; and for default of such issue, to the second son of her body lawfully issuing, and (so) to the heirs males of the body of the said second son lawfully issuing; and for default of such heirs, to the third son of the body of the said Susanna lawfully issuing; and to the heirs males of the body of the said third son lawfully issuing; and for default of such issue, the same so to be and remain to the fourth, (son) fifth, sixth, and seventh sons of her body, lawfully issuing one after another, and to the heirs

·Willm Shakspere

(Sheet 3)

males of the bodies of the said fourth, fifth, sixth, and seventh sons lawfully issuing, in such manner as it is before limited to be, and remain to the first, second, and third sons of her body, and to their heirs males; and for default of such issue, the said premises to be and remain to my said niece Hall, and the heirs males of her body lawfully issuing; and for default of (such) issue, to my daughter Judith, and the heirs males of her body lawfully issuing; and for default of such issue, to the right heirs of me the said William Shackspere for ever.

Item, I give unto my wife my second-best bed, with the furniture.

Item, I give and bequeath to my said daughter Judith, my broad silver-gilt bowl. All the rest of my goods, chattels, leases, plates, jewels, and household stuff whatsoever, after my debts and legacies paid, and my funeral expenses discharged, I give, devise, and bequeath to my son-in-law, John Hall, Gent., and my daughter Susanna, his wife, whom I ordain and make executors of this my last will and testament. And I do entreat and appoint the said Thomas Russell, Esq., and Francis Collins, Gent., to be overseers hereof. And do revoke all former wills, and publish this to be my last will and testament. In witness whereof, I have hereunto put my (seal) hand, the day and year first above written.

By me,

William Shakspeare

Witness to the publishing hereof.
Fra. Collins,
Julius Shaw,
John Robinson,
Hamnet Sadler,
Robert Whattcott.

[Endorsed] Probatum coram magistro Willielmo Byrde legum doctore Comissario &c^do die mensis Junij Anno Domini 1616. Juramento Johannis Hall unius executoris &c &c de bene &c Jurato. Reservata potestate &c Susanne Hall alteri executori &c cum venerit &c petitura

Inventorium exhibitum

Bibliography

Acheson, Arthur, *Shakespeare's Lost Years in London, 1586–1592*, Quaritch, London, 1920

Adams, J. Cranford, *The Globe Playhouse, its design and equipment*, Harvard University Press, Cambridge, Mass, 1942

Akrigg, G. P. V., *Jacobean Pageant, The Court of King James I*, Hamish Hamilton, London, 1962

– *Shakespeare and the Earl of Southampton*, Hamish Hamilton, London, 1968

Alexander, Peter, (ed.), *William Shakespeare; The Complete Works*, Collins, London & Glasgow, 1951, with numerous reprints

Allen, Percy, *Talks with Elizabethans Revealing the Mystery of 'William Shakespeare'*, London, circa 1942 (no date given)

Arber, Edward, (ed.), *A Transcript of the Registers of the Company of Stationers of London; AD 1554–1640*, 5 vols., London, 1875

Arden Edition of the Works of Shakespeare, various editions, London, 1899–

Arts Council of Great Britain, *1564–1964 The Shakespeare Exhibition* (catalogue of the Shakespeare Quater-Centenary Exhibition), Stratford-upon-Avon, Edinburgh, London, 1964

Ashelford, Jane, *A Visual History of the Sixteenth Century*, Batsford, London, 1983

– *Dress in the Age of Elizabeth I*, Batsford, London, 1988

Asimov, Isaac, *Asimov's Guide to Shakespeare*, Avenel, New York, 1978

Aubrey, John, *Brief Lives*, ed. O. L. Dick, London, 1949

Bacon, Delia, *The Philosophy of the Plays of Shakspere Unfolded*, London, 1857

Bagley, J. J., *The Earls of Derby 1485–1985*, Sidgwick & Jackson, London, 1985

Baldwin, T. W., *The Organisation and Personnel of the Shakespearean Company*, Princeton University Press, 1927

– *William Shakespeare Adapts a Hanging*, Princeton University Press, 1931

– *Shakspere's Love's Labour's Won: New Evidence from the Account Books of an Elizabethan Bookseller*, Carbondale, Ill, 1957

Barnard, E. A. B. & H. A. Shield, *New Links with Shakespeare*, Cambridge University Press, 1930

Bentley, G. E., 'Shakespeare and the Blackfriars Theatre', *Shakespeare Survey* I, Cambridge University Press, 1948

Berry, Herbert, *Shakespeare's Playhouses*, AMS Studies in the Renaissance, no. 19, New York, 1987

Black, J. B., *The Reign of Elizabeth, 1558–1603* (2nd edition), Oxford University Press, 1959

Bletherwick, Simon, and Andrew Gurr, 'Shakespeare's factory: archaeological evaluations on the site of the Globe Theatre at 1/15 Anchor Terrace, Southwark Bridge Road, Southwark', *Antiquity* 66, 1992, p. 315–33

Bligh, E. W., *Sir Kenelm Digby and his Venetia*, Sampson Low, London, 1932

Boas, Frederick S., *University Drama in the Tudor Age*, Clarendon Press, Oxford, 1914

Boswell-Stone, W. G., *Shakespeare's Holinshed*, Blom, New York, 1896, re-issued 1966

Bowden, H. S. *The Religion of Shakespeare*, Burns & Oates, London, 1899

Bradbrook, Muriel, *The School of Night: A Study in the Literary Relationships of Sir Walter Raleigh*, Cambridge University Press, 1936

Brinkworth, E. R. C., *Shakespeare and the Bawdy Court of Stratford*, Phillimore, London, 1972

Bullough, Geoffrey, *Narrative and Dramatic Sources of Shakespeare*, 8 vols., London, 1957–75

Burgess, Anthony, *Shakespeare*, Cape, London, 1970

Campbell, Lily B., *Shakespeare's 'Histories', Mirrors of Elizabethan Policy*, The Huntington Library, San Marino, 1947

Carey, Sir Robert, *Memoirs*, ed. F. H. Mares, Oxford University Press, 1972

Carter, Pierson Cathrick, *The History of the Church and Parish of St Mary the Virgin, Aldermanbury*, Collingridge, London, 1913

Chambers, E. K., *Notes on the History of the Revels Office under the Tudors*, A. H. Bullen, London, 1906

- *The Elizabethan Stage*, 4 vols., Clarendon Press, Oxford, 1923

- *William Shakespeare. A Study of Facts & Problems*, 2 vols., Clarendon Press, Oxford, 1930

Chute, Marchette, *Shakespeare of London*, Souvenir, London, 1977 (first published New York, 1949)

- *Ben Jonson of Westminster*, Souvenir, London, 1978 (first published New York, 1953)

Clubb, Louise George, *Italian Drama in Shakespeare's Time*, Yale University Press, New Haven, 1990

Collier, J. Payne, *Memoirs of the Principal Actors in the Plays of Shakespeare*, Shakespeare Society, 1846

Collins, A., (ed.), *Letters and Memorials of State, Written and Collected by Sir Henry Sydney, Sir Philip Sydney, Sir Robert Sydney, etc.*, 2 vols., London, 1746

Colman, E. A., *The Dramatic Use of Bawdy in Shakespeare*, Longman, London, 1974

Connell, Charles, *They Gave us Shakespeare, John Heminge & Henry Condell*, Oriel Press, Stocksfield, 1982

Connes, Professor Georges, *The Shakespeare Mystery*, Palmer, 1927

Cooper, Rt Hon. Alfred Duff, *Sergeant Shakespeare*, Rupert Hart-Davis, London, 1949

Coward, Barry, *The Stanleys – The Stanleys Lords Stanley and Earls of Derby, 1385–1672*, Chetham Society, 3rd Series XXX, Manchester, 1983

Crofts, J., *Shakespeare and the Post Horses*, Bristol, 1937

Dawson, Giles E., & Laetitia Kennedy-Skipton, *Elizabethan Handwriting 1500–1650*, New York, 1966

De Groot, John Henry, *The Shakespeares and 'The Old Faith'*, New York, 1946

Denkinger, Emma Marshall, 'Actors Names in Registers of St Botolph, Aldgate', *Publications of the Modern Language Association of America* XLI, pp. 91–109

Devlin, Christopher, 'The Earl and the Alchemist', 3 pts, *The Month*, 1953

– *The Life of Robert Southwell, Poet and Martyr*, Longmans, Green, London, 1956

– *Hamlet's Divinity*, Rupert Hart-Davis, London, 1963

Donnelly, Ignatius, *The Great Cryptogram: Francis Bacon's Cipher in the So-called Shakespeare Plays*, New York, 1888

Duncan-Jones, Katherine, 'Was the 1609 *Shakespeare's Sonnets*, really unauthorised?', *Review of English Studies*, 1983, pp. 151–71

Durning-Lawrence, Sir Edwin, *Bacon is Shakespeare*, London, 1910

Dutton, R., 'Hamlet, An Apology for Actors and the Sign of the Globe', *Shakespeare Survey* 41, Cambridge University Press, 1989

Eccles, Mark, *Christopher Marlowe in London*, Cambridge, Mass, 1934

– *Shakespeare in Warwickshire*, University of Wisconsin Press, Madison, 1963

– 'Jonson's Marriage', *Review of English Studies* XII, pp. 257ff.

Esdaile, K. A., (Mrs), *English Church Monuments 1510–1840*, Oxford University Press, 1946

– 'Some Fellow-Citizens of Shakespeare in Southwark', *Essays and Studies*, New Series, V, 1952, 26

Farley, Henry, *The Complaint of Paules*, London, 1616

Fehrenbach, Robert J., 'When Lord Cobham and Edmund Tilney "were at odds" . . .', *Shakespeare Studies* XVIII, 1986, pp. 87–101

Fido, Martin, *Shakespeare*, Hamlyn, London, 1978

Finch, Mary E., *The Wealth of Five Northamptonshire Families, 1540–1640*, Northamptonshire Record Society vol. XIX, 1956

Fisher, Sidney, *The Theatre, the Curtain and the Globe*, Montreal, 1964

Flatter, Richard, *Hamlet's Father*, Heinemann, London, 1949

Foakes, R. A., and R. T. Rickert, *Henslowe's Diary*, Cambridge University Press, 1961

Foley, H., *Records of the English Province of the Society of Jesus*, Burns & Oates, London, 7 vols., 1877

Fox, Levi, 'The Heritage of Shakespeare's Birthplace', *Shakespeare Survey* I, Cambridge University Press, 1948, pp. 79–87

Fripp, Edgar I., *Shakespeare's Stratford*, Oxford University Press, Humphrey Milford, London, 1928

– *Shakespeare's Haunts near Stratford*, Oxford University Press, 1929

– *Shakespeare Studies, biographical and literary*, Oxford University Press, London, 1930

– *Shakespeare: Man and Artist*, 2 vols., Oxford University Press, 1938

Gair, Reavley, *The Children of Paul's: The story of a theatre company, 1553–1608*, Cambridge University Press, 1982

Galloway, David, (ed.), *Norwich 1540–1642* 'Records of Early English Drama', Toronto, 1984

Gardiner, H. C., *Mysteries' End: An Investigation of the Last Days of the Medieval Religious Stage*, New Haven, Conn, 1946, reprinted in *Yale Studies in England*, vol. 103, 1967

Gerard, John, *What was the Gunpowder Plot?*, London, 1897

– *John Gerard, An Autobiography of an Elizabethan*, trans. Philip Caraman, with intro. by Graham Greene, Longmans, Green, London, 1951

Gibson, H. N., *The Shakespeare Claimants*, Methuen, London, 1962

Green, H., *Shakespeare and the Emblem Writers*, Trubner and Co., London, 1870

Greene, Robert, *Greene's Groats-worth of witte, bought with a million of Repentance*, W. Wright, London, 1592

Greenstreet, James H., 'A hitherto unknown noble writer of Elizabethan comedies', *The Genealogist*, April 1891, pt. 4, p. 205ff.

Greg, W. W., *Elizabethan Dramatic Documents*, 2 vols., Oxford, 1931

Gurr, Andrew, *The Shakespearean Stage, 1574–1642*, Cambridge University Press, 1970

– *Playgoing in Shakespeare's London*, Cambridge University Press, 1987

– 'The Shakespearean Stages, 40 Years On', *Shakespeare Survey* 41, 1989, 1–12

– with John Orrell, *Rebuilding Shakespeare's Globe*, Weidenfeld, London, 1989

Halle, Edward, *The Union of the two noble and illustre famelies of Lancastre and Yorke*, London, 1548

Halliwell [-Phillipps], J. O., *The Working Life of William Shakespeare, Including Many Particulars Respecting the Poet and His Family Never before Published*, London, 1848

– *Reliques, Some Account of the Reliques Illustrative of Shakespeare in the possession of J. O. Halliwell*, London, 1852

– *Outlines of the Life of Shakespeare*, London, 1881

Hamilton, Charles, *In Search of Shakespeare. A study of the Poet's Life and Handwriting*, Robert Hale, London, 1986

Hare, Michael, 'The Documentary Evidence for the Southampton Monument in Titchfield Church', *Fareham Past and Present*, Titchfield History Society, Book V, vol. 2

Harlowe, C. G., 'Nashe's visit to the Isle of Wight', *Review of English Studies* XIV, 1969, pp. 15ff

Harrison, G. B. (tr. & ed.), with R. A. Jones, *A Journal of all that was accomplished by Monsieur de Maisse, 1597*, London, 1931

Harrison, G. B., *The Life and Death of Robert Devereux, Earl of Essex*, London, 1937

– *A Second Elizabethan Journal, being a record of those things most talked of during the years 1595–1598*, Routledge, London, 1974

Harsnett, Samuel, *A Declaration of Egregious Popish Impostures*, 1603

Heath, J. B., *Some Account of the Worshipful Company of Grocers*, London, 1867

Hentzner, Paul, *Paul Hentzner's Travels in England During the Reign of Queen Elizabeth*, trans. Richard Bentley, 1797

Heywood, Thomas, *The Earls of Derby and the Verse Writers and Poets of the Sixteenth and Seventeenth Centuries*, The Stanley Papers I, Chetham Society, vol. XXIX, 1853

Hilton, Delia, *Who was Kit Marlowe?*, Weidenfeld, London, 1977

Historical Manuscripts Commission, *Calendar of the MSS. of the Marquis of Salisbury at Hatfield House, Herts*, Eyre and Spottiswoode, London, 1880–1930

Historical Manuscripts Commission, *Report on the Manuscripts of Lord de L'Isle and Dudley preserved at Penshurst Place*, vol. II, 1934

Hodges, C. Walter, *The Globe Restored, A Study of the Elizabethan Theatre*, Oxford University Press, 1968
– *Shakespeare's Second Globe*, Oxford University Press, 1973
Hoffman, Calvin, *The Murder of the Man who was 'Shakespeare'*, London, 1925
Honigmann, E. A. J., *Shakespeare's Impact on his Contemporaries*, Macmillan , London, 1982
– *Shakespeare: the 'Lost Years'*, Manchester University Press, 1985
– *John Weever, A Biography of a Literary Associate of Shakespeare and Jonson . . .* , Manchester University Press, 1987
– 'The Second-Best Bed', *New York Review of Books*, 7 Nov 1991, p. 27ff.
Horne, D. H., (ed.), *The Life and Minor Works of George Peele*, Newhaven, 1952
Hosking, G. L., *The Life and Times of Edward Alleyn*, Cape, London, 1952
Hotson, Leslie, *The Death of Christopher Marlowe*, London, 1925
– *The Commonwealth and Restoration Stage*, Harvard University Press, Cambridge, Mass, 1928
– *Shakespeare versus Shallow*, London, 1931
– *I, William Shakespeare do appoint Thomas Russell, Esquire . . .* , Cape, London, 1937
– *Shakespeare's Sonnets Dated and other Essays*, Rupert Hart-Davis, London, 1949
– *Mr. W.H.*, Rupert Hart-Davies, London, 1964
– *Shakespeare by Hilliard: A Portrait Deciphered*, Chatto & Windus, London, 1977
Huggett, Richard, *The Curse of Macbeth and other Theatrical Superstitions*, Picton, Chippenham, 1981
Ingleby, C. M., *A complete view on the Shakespeare controversy concerning the Authenticity and Genuineness of the Manuscript Matter Affecting the Works and Biography of Shakespeare published by Mr J. Payne Collier as the Fruits of his Researches*, London, 1861
Ingram, William, 'The Playhouse at Newington Butts: A New Proposal', *Shakespeare Quarterly* xxi, 1970, pp. 385–98
Jarrett, J. E., 'The Grafton Portrait of Shakespeare', *Bulletin of the John Rylands Library* vol. 29, no. 1, July 1945
Jeayes, I. H., *A Catalogue of the Charters and Muniments in the possession of the Rt Hon. Lord Fitzhardinge, at Berkeley Castle*, C. T. Jefferies, Bristol, 1892
Jones, Emrys, *Scenic Form in Shakespeare*, Clarendon Press, Oxford, 1971
– *The Origins of Shakespeare*, Clarendon Press, Oxford, 1977
Keen, Alan, & Roger Lubbock, *The Annotator: The Pursuit of an Elizabethan Reader of Halle's Chronicle Involving some Surmises about the Early Life of William Shakespeare*, Putnam, London, 1954
Kirkwood, A. E. M., 'Richard Field, Printer, 1589–1624', *The Library*, 4th Ser., xii, 1931, pp. 1–39
Kocher, Paul H., *Christopher Marlowe: A Study in his Thought, Learning and Character*, Chapel Hill, 1946
Kökeritz, Helge, *Mr William Shakespeare's Comedies, Histories and Tragedies*, Facsimile edition, Geoffrey Cumberlege, Oxford University Press, London, 1955
– *Shakespeare's Pronunciation*, Yale University Press, New Haven, 1953
Lambin, G., 'Here Lyeth Iohn Talbot', *Études Anglaises* 24, Oct–Dec 1971, pp. 361–76

Laroque, François, *Shakespeare's Festive World: Elizabethan Seasonal Entertainment and the Professional Stage*, Cambridge University Press, 1991

Law, Ernest, *Shakespeare as a Groom of the Chamber*, London, 1910

Law, R. A., 'The Roman Background of Titus Andronicus', *Studies in Philology*, N. Carolina XL, 1943, pp. 145–53

Lee, Sir Sidney, *A Life of William Shakespeare*, London, 1898

Leftwich, Ralph W., 'The Evidence of Disease in Shakespeare's Handwriting', *Proceedings of the Royal Society of Medicine, Section of the History of Medicine*, 1919, 12, pp. 28–42

Leishman, J. B., (ed.), *The Three Parnassus Plays (1598–1601)*, London, 1949

Lever, J. W., 'Three Notes on Shakespeare's Plants', *Review of English Studies* III, New Series, p. 117–29

Levi, Peter, *The Life and Times of William Shakespeare*, Macmillan, London, 1988

Levin, Bernard, *Enthusiasms*, Cape, London, 1983

Llewellyn, Nigel, *The Art of Death, Visual Culture in the English Death Ritual*, Reaktion, London, 1992

Lodge, Edmund, *Illustrations of British history, Biography and Manners in the Reigns of Henry VIII, Edward VI, Mary, Elizabeth and James I, Exhibited in a Series of Original Papers Selected from the Mss. of the Noble Families of Howard, Talbot and Cecil*, 3 vols., London, 1838

Loengard, Janet, 'An Elizabethan Lawsuit: John Brayne, his carpenter, and the building of the Red Lion Theatre', *Shakespeare Quarterly* 34, 1983, pp. 298–310

London County Council, *Survey of London*, ed. Sir James Bird and Philip Norman, vol. VIII, *The Parish of St Leonard, Shoreditch*, B. T. Batsford, London, 1922

– *Survey of London*, ed. Sir Howard Roberts and Walter H. Godfrey, vol. XXII, *Bankside (The Parishes of St Saviour and Christchurch, Southwark)*, London County Council, 1950

Looney, J. Thomas, *Shakespeare Identified in Edward De Vere the Seventeenth Earl of Oxford*, London, 1920

McGrath, Patrick, *Papists and Puritans under Elizabeth I*, Blandford, London, 1967

McKerrow, Ronald B., *The Works of Thomas Nashe*, revised with supplementary notes by F. P. Wilson, 5 vols., Oxford University Press, 1958

Maclean, Sally-Beth, 'Leicester and the Evelyns: New Evidence for the Continental Tour of Leicester's Men', *Review of English Studies*, New Series vol. XXXIX, no. 156, 1988, pp. 487–93

McLure, N. E., (ed.), *The Letters of John Chamberlain*, American Philosophical Society, Philadelphia, 1939

McManaway, James G., 'John Shakespeare's "Spiritual Testament"', *Shakespeare Quarterly* 18, 1967, pp. 197–205

Malone, Edmond, (ed.), *Supplement to the Edition of Shakespeare's Plays published in 1778 by Samuel Johnson and George Steevens*, London, 1780

– *William Shakespeare, Plays and Poems*, London, 1790

– *An Inquiry into the Authenticity of Certain Miscellaneous Papers and Legal Instruments, Published Dec. 24, MDCCXCV and Attributed to Shakespeare, Queen Elizabeth and Henry, Earl of Southampton: Illustrated by Fac-similes of the Genuine Handwriting of That Nobleman, and of Her Majesty; A New Fac-simile of the Handwriting of Shakespeare, Never before Exhibited; and other Authentick Documents*, London, 1796

Mathew, F. J., *An Image of Shakespeare*, Cape, London, 1922

May, Dr Stephen H., 'Spenser's "Amyntas": Three Poems by Ferdinando Stanley, Lord Strange, Fifth Earl of Derby', *Modern Philology*, 70, 1972, pp. 49–52

Miller, Edwin Haviland, *The Professional Writer in Elizabethan England*, Harvard University Press, Cambridge, Mass, 1959

Milward, Peter, *Shakespeare's Religious Background*, Sidgwick & Jackson, London, 1973

Montaigne, *Essays*, trans. John Florio, Nonsuch edition, 2 vols.

Morris, John, *Troubles of our Catholic Forefathers related by themselves*, 3 vols., Burns & Oates, London, 1872

Muir, Kenneth, *The Sources of Shakespeare's Plays*, Methuen, London, 1977

Murray, J. T., *English Dramatic Companies, 1558–1642*, 2 vols., London, 1910

Nicholl, Charles, *A Cup of News. The Life of Thomas Nashe*, Routledge & Kegan Paul, London, 1984

– *The Reckoning. The Murder of Christopher Marlowe*, Cape, London, 1992

Noble, Richard, *Shakespeare's Biblical Knowledge*, 1935

O'Connor, Gary, *William Shakespeare: A Life*, Hodder & Stoughton, London, 1991

Ogburn, Charlton, *The Mysterious William Shakespeare: The Myth and the Reality*, Dodd, Mead, New York, 1984

Onions, C. T., *A Shakespeare Glossary*, Oxford, 1911

Orgell, Stephen, & Roy Strong, *Inigo Jones: The Theatre of the Stuart Court*, London, 1973

Orrell, John, *The Quest for Shakespeare's Globe*, Cambridge University Press, 1983

– and Andrew Gurr, 'What the Rose can tell us', *Antiquity* 63, 1989, pp. 421–9

Osborn, Francis, *Traditional Memoryes of the Reign of King James*, Oxford, 1658

Platter, Thomas, *Travels in England*, trans. from the German by Clare Williams, Cape, London, 1951

Pope, Maurice, 'Shakespeare's Falconry', *Shakespeare Survey* 44, 1992

Prockter, Adrian, & Robert Taylor, *A to Z of Elizabethan London*, Harry Margary, Lympne, Kent, 1979

Procter, W. G., 'The Manor of Rufford & the Ancient Family of the Heskeths', *Transactions of the Historical Society of Lancashire & Cheshire*, 1908, LIX, p. 93ff.

Pryor, Felix, *The Mirror and the Globe, William Shakespeare, John Marston and the writing of Hamlet*, Handsaw, London, 1992

Puttenham, George, *The Arte of English Poesie, 1589*, ed. Gladys Doidge Willcock & Alice Walker, Cambridge, 1970

Raines, F. R., (ed.), *The Derby Household Books; comprising an Account of the Household Regulations and Expenses of Edward and Henry, Third and Fourth Earls of Derby (by W. Farington)*, The Stanley Papers II, Chetham Society, New Series LXXVII, 1917

Read, Conyers, *Lord Burghley and Queen Elizabeth*, Cape, London, 1960

Robinson, Richard, of Alton, *A Golden Mirrour conteining certaine pithie and figurative visions prognosticating good fortune to England . . .*, 1589, reprinted with intro. by Reverend Thomas Corser, Chetham Society vol. XXIII, 1851

Rogers, J. E. T., *History of Agriculture and Prices in England, 1259–1793*, Clarendon Press, Oxford, 1866–1902

Rosenberg, Martin, *The Mask of Othello*, University of Califonia Press, Berkeley, 1961

Rowse, A. L., *William Shakespeare: A biography*, Harper & Row, New York, 1963
- *Shakespeare's Sonnets, the Problems Solved*, Harper & Row, New York, 1964
- *Shakespeare's Southampton*, Macmillan, London, 1965
- 'Bisham and the Hobys', *Times, Persons, Places*, London, 1965, pp. 188–218
- *The Elizabethan Renaissance. The Life of the Society*, Macmillan, London, 1971
- *Simon Forman: Sex and Society in Shakespeare's Age*, Weidenfeld, London, 1974
- *The Poems of Shakespeare's Dark Lady:* Salve Deus Rex Judaeorum *by Emilia Lanier*, Cape, London, 1978
- *Discovering Shakespeare: A Chapter in Literary History*, Weidenfeld, London, 1989
- with John Hedgecoe, *Shakespeare's Land. A Journey through the Landscape of Elizabethan England*, Chronicle, San Francisco, 1987

Rye, W. B., *England as seen by foreigners in the Days of Elizabeth and James the First*, London, 1865

Sanctuary, Gerald, *Shakespeare's Globe Theatre*, International Shakespeare Globe Centre, 1992

Schanzer, Ernest, 'Thomas Platter's observations on the Elizabethan stage', *Notes and Queries* 201, 1956, pp. 465–7

Schoenbaum, S., *Shakespeare's Lives*, Oxford University Press, 1970; also new edition, Clarendon Press, Oxford, 1991
- *William Shakespeare: A Documentary Life*, Oxford University Press, 1975
- *Shakespeare, The Globe and the World*, Oxford University Press, 1979

Scott-Giles, C. W., *Shakespeare's Heraldry*, Dent, London, 1950

Scoufos, Alice Lyle, 'Nashe, Jonson and the Oldcastle Problem', *Modern Philology* LXV, 307–24

Sharpe, Robert B., *The Real War of the Theatres, Shakespeare's Fellows in rivalry with the Admiral's Men 1594–1603*, D. C. Heath & Oxford University Press, Boston and London, 1935

Simpson, Frank, 'New Place. The only representation of Shakespeare's house, from an unpublished manuscript', *Shakespeare Survey* 5, 1952, pp. 55–7

Smart, J. S., *Shakespeare, Truth and Tradition*, Longmans, Green, New York, 1928

Smith, Irwin, *Shakespeare's Blackfriars Playhouse: Its History and its Design*, New York University Press, 1964

Speed, John, *The History of Great Britaine*, London, 1623

Spencer, T. J. B., 'Ben Jonson on his beloved The Author Mr William Shakespeare', *The Elizabethan Theatre* IV, Macmillan, 1974

Spielmann, M. H., *The Title-Page of the First Folio of Shakespeare's Plays. A Comparative Study of the Droeshout Portrait and Stratford Monument*, Oxford University Press, London, 1924

Spurgeon, Caroline F. E., *Shakespeare's Imagery & what it tells us*, Cambridge University Press, 1935

Stopes, Charlotte C., *The Life of Henry, third Earl of Southampton, Shakespeare's Patron*, Cambridge University Press, 1922

Stow, John, *The Annales, or Generall Chronicle of England, begun by J. Stow . . . continued and augmented . . . unto the end of . . . 1631, by E. Howes*, London, 1631

Streitberger, W. R., 'On Edmund Tyllney's Biography', *Review of English Studies*, New Series 29, 1978, pp. 11–35

Strong, Roy, *Tudor and Jacobean Portraits*, 2 vols., London, 1967

– *The Cult of Elizabeth*, Thames & Hudson, London, 1977

Swain, Hedley, with Simon Blatherwick, Julian Bowsher and Simon McCudden, 'Shakespeare's Theatres', *Current Archaeology* 124, May 1991, pp. 185–9

Thomas, D. L., & N. E. Evans, 'John Shakespeare in the Exchequer', *Shakespeare Quarterly* 35, 1984, pp. 315–8

Thurston, Herbert, 'A Controverted Shakespeare Document', *The Dublin Review* clxxiii, 1923

Titherley, A. W., *Shakespeare's Identity: William Stanley, 6th Earl of Derby*, Warren & Son, Winchester, 1952

Wallace, C. W., 'Shakespeare in London', *The Times*, 2 & 4 Oct 1909; also (on Globe) 1 May 1914

– 'Shakespeare's Money Interest in the Globe Theatre', *The Century Magazine* lxxx, 1910, pp. 500–12

– 'Shakespeare and his London Associates as Revealed in Recently Discovered Documents', *University Studies* X, University of Nebraska, 1910

Walmsley, D. M., 'Shakespeare's Link with Virginia', *History Today*, April 1957, pp. 229–35

Ward, B. M., *The Seventeenth Earl of Oxford, 1550–1604*, London, 1928

– 'The Chamberlain's Men in 1597', *Review of English Studies* IX, 55

Watkins, Ronald, *On Producing Shakespeare*, Michael Joseph, London, 1950

West, V. Sackville, *Knole and the Sackvilles*, Heinemann, London, 1922

West, William, *Simbelography, which may be termed the Art, or Description, of Instruments and Presidents* [i.e. Precedents], Stationers' Company, 1612

Wickham, Glynne, *Shakespeare's Dramatic Heritage*, Routledge and Kegan Paul, London, 1969

Williams, Iolo A., 'Hollar: A Discovery of Iolo A. Williams', *The Connoisseur* xcii, 1933, pp. 318–21

Williamson, Hugh Ross, *The Gunpowder Plot*, Faber & Faber, London, 1951

Willoughby, Edwin Elliott, *The Printing of the First Folio of Shakespeare*, Oxford University Press for the Bibliographical Society 1932, from Supplements to the Transactions of the Bibliographical Society 1932–5, Supps 6–10

Wilson, F. P., *The Plague in Shakespeare's London*, Oxford University Press, 1927

Wilson, J. Dover, *The Essential Shakespeare*, London, 1932

– *The Manuscript of Shakespeare's* Hamlet *and the Problems of its Transmission*, 2 vols., Cambridge University Press, 1963

Worden, Blair, 'Shakespeare and Politics', *Shakespeare Survey* 44, 1992, pp. 1–15

Yates, Frances, *John Florio*, Cambridge University Press, 1934

– *A Study of Love's Labour's Lost*, Cambridge University Press, 1936

– 'Elizabethan Chivalry: The Romance of the Accession Day Tilts', *Journal of the Warburg and Courtauld Institutes* XXI, 1958

Young, G. M., essay 'Shakespeare & the Tenners', *Today & Yesterday*, 1948; also *Notes & Queries* CXCIX, 1954, pp. 150–51

Index

Note: The Chronology and illustrations are not included in the index.
QE is used to stand for Queen Elizabeth I; WS for William Shakespeare.